# Excavations alongside Roman Ermin Gloucestershire and Wiltshire

## The archaeology of the A419 / A417 Swindon to Gloucester Road Scheme

## Volume 1: Prehistoric and Roman activity

*By Andrew Mudd, Robert J. Williams and Alan Lupton*

*With major contributions by*

*T Allen, A Barclay, S Lawrence, S Mortimer, J Muir, A Parkinson and J Timby*

*and contributions by*

*D Allen, L Allen, K Atherton, K Ayres, P Blinkhorn, P Bradley, A Boyle, G Campbell, K M Clark, C Cropper, G B Dannel, J A Davies, B Dickinson, T Durden, H Drake, M Henig, N Jeffries, G McDonnell, D Mackreth, N Mitchell, W R G Moore, A Powell, R Pelling, M Robinson, F Roe, R Scaife, I Scott, K Welsh and D Williams*

*Editor Angela Boyle*

*Illustrations by M Costello, R Goller, M Middleton, L Padilla and R Read*

Oxford Archaeological Unit
1999

Volume 1 ISBN 0–904220–17–6
Series ISBN 0–904220–16–8

Printed in Great Britain by
UNiSKiLL Ltd
Eynsham, Oxfordshire

The publishers wish to acknowledge with gratitude
the funding by RMS Ltd
which made this publication possible.

*Front cover:* *Area excavation at Birdlip Quarry (left), reproduced by permission of RCHME (ref. NMR 15424/03). Preston Enclosure (right), © Neil Thomas, PES ref. 4846/21*
*Back cover:* *The dewpond at Daglingworth quarry.*

# Volume 1: Contents

# Volume 2: Contents

# Volume 1: List of figures

**CHAPTER 1**



**CHAPTER 2**



**CHAPTER 3**

**CHAPTER 4**

**CHAPTER 5**



# Volume 2: List of figures

**CHAPTER 6**



**CHAPTER 7**

**CHAPTER 8**



**CHAPTER 9**

# Volume 1: List of tables

**CHAPTER 1**



**CHAPTER 2**



**CHAPTER 4**



# Volume 2: List of tables

**CHAPTER 7**

**CHAPTER 8**

# Volume 1: List of plates

**CHAPTER 1**



**CHAPTER 2**



**CHAPTER 3**



**CHAPTER 4**

**CHAPTER 5**



# Volume 2: List of plates

**CHAPTER 6**



**CHAPTER 8**

# Acknowledgements

The A419/A417 Design, Build, Finance and Operate (DBFO) contract was awarded to Road Management Services (Gloucester) Ltd (RMS) in January 1996 by the Secretary of State for Transport. The construction project was undertaken by RMS's sister company Road Management Group Construction Joint Venture (RMGJV), both companies are a consortium of four equal partners, AMEC, Alfred McAlpine, Brown and Root and Dragados. The Oxford Archaeological Unit (OAU) were contracted by RMGJV's environmental and landscape consultants, Chris Blandford Associates (CBA) to provide the total archaeological input. The Highways Agency's Department's Agent for the project was WSP Civils (formerly Frank Graham Consulting Engineers).

The successful integration of the civil engineering works with the archaeological excavations and watching briefs resulted from the close-co-operation of many individuals from the different companies involved. The following deserve special mention and thanks for all their help and assistance. Bob Golding (RMGJV – Project Director). John McGinty (RMGJV – Project Manager), Phil Smith (RMS – Agent) Mike Reid (RMS – Assistant Agent), Derek Parody (Parkman/Howard Humphreys – Designers Principal), Peter Bigby (RMGJV – Chief Engineer), Tony Zandona and Dave Willis (WSP Civils Engineers – Department's Agent) and Philip Russell-Vick and Mark Holland (CBA).

Thanks are also due to other RMGJV staff and their sub-contractors for their unstinting help and patience in providing a variety of services, particularly include the following: Rob Ayres, Steve Ayres, Sue Barlow, Peter Bundell, Andy Bowyer, Dave Cox, Jeff Curry, Colin Edwards, Tony Fielden, Duncan Gibson, Ian Gillett, Keith Godson, Dave Ireland, John Kirby, John Nichols, Dave Pickering, Richard Pollard, Keith Titman, Dave Wooldridge, Richard Young, and last, but not least, Packie McGettigan, RMGJV's Plant Manager for never failing to get the right plant to the right place at the right time.

In addition grateful thanks must be expressed to Helen Glass and Dave Maynard of CBA, who acted as Project Archaeologists, for their support and enthusiasm during the setting up, execution and publication of the project. The Department's Agent's archaeological advisors (Jan Wills and Charles Parry of Gloucestershire County Council) monitored the archaeological work, and Jan Wills and Roy Canham (County Archaeologists for Gloucestershire and Wiltshire respectively) gave invaluable advice on the archaeology of the region.

We would like to acknowledge the co-operation of English Heritage who are responsible for the management of the Scheduled Ancient Monuments which were affected by the road scheme. Liaison was maintained throughout the project with the County Archaeologists for Gloucestershire and Wiltshire and with English Heritage.

An archaeological project the size and complexity of the A419/A417 DBFO Road scheme could not have been completed both within time and budget without the unstinting assistance of numerous staff of the Oxford Archaeological Unit. George Lambrick, OAU's Deputy Director, was the Project Director and was instrumental in both setting up the project and ensuring the intellectual coherence and credibility of what at first seemed to be a varied assortment of sites of different periods and types.

The principal Field Directors and Supervisors were Richard Brown, Sean Cook, Rob Early, Alan Lupton, Brian Matthews, Andrew Mudd, Jeff Muir, Paul Murray, Andrew Parkinson, Mick Parsons, Phil Piper, Mark Roberts, Ken Welsh and Duncan Wood, ably and professionally assisted by Assistant Supervisors and Field Technicians too numerous to mention by name. Suffice it to say they know who they are, and all must be congratulated on their enthusiasm and perseverance, especially those who worked at Birdlip Quarry, in deepest winter.

The core watching brief staff consisted of Sean Cook, Mark Gocher, Andy Mayes, James Mumford, Paul Murray and Mike Simms whose endurance must be congratulated given the long hours involved and the often tedious nature of the work. Leigh Allen (Finds Manager), Greg Campbell (Environmental Manager), Paul Hughes (Graphics Manager) and Nicky Scott (Archives Manager) all gave invaluable assistance and support at every stage of the project. Dr Mark Robinson provided the main environmental advice during both the fieldwork and post-excavation phases of the project. Other members of staff including Tim Allen, Alistair Barclay, Paul Booth, Theresa Durden and David Jennings have all given invaluable advice during the post-excavation stage. Dave Wilkinson provided Health and Safety advice. Particular mention must be made of Angela Boyle whose editing skills have ensured the seamless transition of draft texts into the finished publication. Dr Martin Henig and Dr Ann Woodward acted as academic referees. Roger Featherstone (RCHM[E]) provided OAU with some invaluable aerial photographs.

Mention must be given to those who lay behind the scenes, whose contribution to the project is difficult to describe or define precisely, but without whose efforts and assistance the work would have been so much more difficult, namely: Alison Gledhill, Simon Palmer, Kay Procter, David Stevens, Louise Waltham, Graham Walton and Ianto Wain.

We are grateful to Bryn Walters for permission to reproduce his aerial photograph of Latton 'Roman Pond' (Plate 4.7).

Fiona Roe would like to acknowledge the Department of Earth Sciences, University of Oxford, for the use of facilities, and Jeremy Hyde, who made the thin section. Roger Howell assisted with the necessary fieldwork. She would also like to thank Sue Byrne at Gloucester Museum, Robert Clary at Chedworth Roman Villa, Guy Kilminster at Cheltenham Museum and Judy Mills and John Paddock at Corinium Museum.

Adrienne Powell would like to thank Kate M. Clark for examining and reporting on the skeletal pathology within the animal bone assemblages at Duntisbourne Grove and Middle Duntisbourne, Kevin Rielly for sharing unpublished data from Bagendon and Ditches and Dave Webb who provided photographs for the report.

Leigh Allen is grateful to Arthur MacGregor for his identification of the horn vessel from Cowley Underbridge Trench 6.

Angela Boyle would particularly like to thank Paul Hughes, Mike Middleton and Rob Reed for their advice and many long hours working on the final illustrations for the project at short notice.

Bob Williams
Project Manager
July 1999

# Summary

The Oxford Archaeological Unit undertook a series of excavations along the line of the Swindon to Gloucester DBFO road improvement in 1996 and 1997. The road ran between Nettleton in the Gloucestershire Cotswolds and Cricklade on the Thames. The work was undertaken on behalf of the construction consortium Road Management Group (RMG). The work was carried out according to specifications approved and monitored by the Highways Agency, and included a range of mitigation strategies selected as appropriate archaeological responses. In addition a scheme-wide watching brief was undertaken along the 25 km route. The sites examined included both those identified from previous surveys and evaluations, and new discoveries.

The work entailed the excavation of around thirty-five sites, or parts of sites, of differing types and periods. These included two adjoining Bronze Age ring ditches near Preston, middle Iron Age settlements at Highgate House, Preston and Ermin Farm, late Iron Age enclosures at Duntisbourne Grove and Middle Duntisbourne, a Roman settlement at Birdlip Quarry, and a medieval kitchen block at Street Farm, Latton. In addition there were a number of other discoveries relating particularly to Roman Ermin Street. These included a probable roadside funerary monument and trackway at Field's Farm, Roman trackway ditches and quarries at Court Farm, Latton and part of a late Roman midden at Weavers Bridge. Ermin Street itself was examined with seven trenches through the Roman and later roads. Burford Road (Akeman Street) was examined in two sections with less significant results.

Important environmental evidence was obtained from work at Latton 'Roman Pond' (within a Scheduled Ancient Monument) and in the Churn Valley. A programme of radiocarbon dating was also undertaken, both in relation to the environmental sequences and the earlier prehistoric and Iron Age sites.

A consistent theme of fieldwork was the coincidental discovery of small numbers of prehistoric features as a result of stripping large areas (such as at Birdlip Quarry, Duntisbourne Grove and Trinity Farm). Less surprisingly, numbers of Roman, medieval and post-medieval field boundaries were recorded as well as traces of ridge-and-furrow cultivation. The evidence for earlier boundaries and agriculture has been presented along with other miscellaneous features in summary form.

*Plate 1.1 Aerial view of route south-east of Cirencester with Cricklade in the distance. The route runs south of the Scheduled Ancient Monument at Latton. The excavations at Lower Street Furlong and Fosse Farm are in the foreground. Reproduced by permission of RCHME (ref. NMR 15425/36).*

# Chapter 1: Introduction

*by Andrew Mudd, Alan Lupton and Simon Mortimer*

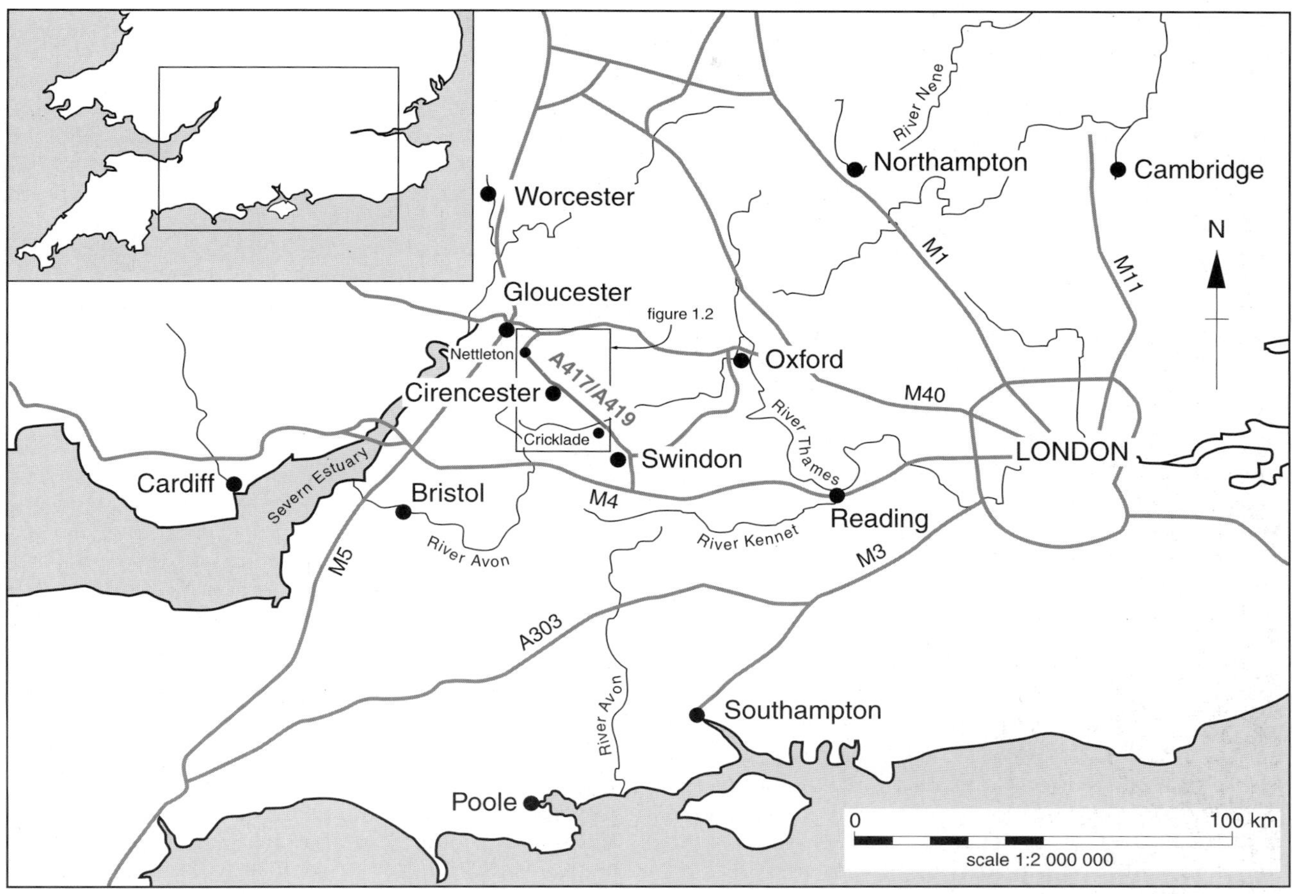


*Figure 1.1 Project location*

## PROJECT LOCATION

The archaeological work, which is the subject of this report, was undertaken in advance of and during the construction of the A419/A417 Trunk Road Improvement between Swindon and Gloucester in south-western England (Fig. 1.1). The stretch of new road ran for approximately 25 km between Nettleton in the Gloucestershire Cotswolds (SO948136) and Cricklade (Wiltshire) on the Thames (SU102944). It closely followed the line of the existing A417 and A419, formerly Ermin Street, with the addition of bypasses around Cirencester and Stratton and the village of Latton (Fig. 1.2).

On the northern section of the route the road joined the existing A417 at a new roundabout just south of Birdlip Quarry (Fig. 1.3). The new road formed a second carriageway, added to the line of the existing road, running south-east as far as Daglingworth Quarry. From here the Cirencester and Stratton Bypass ran across Bagendon Downs south of Peewits Hill, crossing the Churn Valley on a viaduct near Trinity Farm. The Bypass then ran across Baunton Downs, through Hare Bushes plantation and under the Burford Road (A429) before passing east of the village of Preston. It linked with the A419 south of Cirencester at Driffield Crossroads and followed the existing road to a junction with Spine Road south-east of Fosse Farm. From here the Latton section swept behind Latton Creamery and Street Farm, rejoining the A419 south of Latton village. The final section took it to a new junction with the Marston Meysey road near Weavers Bridge where it joined the existing Cricklade Bypass.

## GEOLOGY AND TOPOGRAPHY

In broad terms the area traversed by the road scheme can be divided into two topographic zones; the Cotswolds, forming a zone of upland Jurassic limestone, and the Upper Thames Valley which is a lowland area of river gravels and alluvial pockets. The intermediate zone around Cirencester, roughly between the White Way and Driffield, has a more complex geology of limestones and clays of the Forest Marble and Cornbrash Series (Figs 1.4–5).

The northern section of the route between Birdlip Quarry and the Churn Valley crosses limestone of the Great Oolite series. The route gradually descends from about 270 m (885 ft) above sea level at Birdlip Quarry to about 150 m (490 ft) near Exhibition Barn (Fig. 1.5), although the highest section of the route is along Gloucester Beeches (280 m, 915 ft). The geology is characterised by outcrops of the underlying Fuller's Earth in many of the valleys, an impermeable clay which forms a spring line, and the upper valleys are therefore relatively well-watered.

South of the White Way, about as far as Witpit Lane, the underlying geology is Forest Marble, which consists of weakly structured limestone, bedded with clays, sands and silts. The underlying Great Oolite outcrops near Burford Road have been the object of extensive quarrying. South of Witpit Lane a thin band of hard Cornbrash limestone, overlying the Forest Marble, predominates as far as Fosse Farm. Here there is a small outcrop of Oxford Clay, but in the Latton section the underlying geology is First Terrace river gravels which form a very flat topography, descending from about 84 m OD to 80 m OD. Floodplain alluvium is found closer to the rivers Churn and Thames south of Weavers Bridge.

## PROJECT BACKGROUND

The archaeological work carried out by the Oxford Archaeological Unit was the third stage of a programme of archaeological investigation along the road corridor. The eventual DBFO scheme was developed by linking together three previous road schemes; the North of Stratton to Nettleton Improvement (NOSNI), the Cirencester and Stratton Bypass and the Latton Bypass. The initial desk-based assessments (Stage 1) and field evaluations (Stage 2) for each of these sections were undertaken as separate projects and to slightly different specifications, principally by the Cotswold Archaeological Trust and Gloucestershire County Council Archaeology Service, with some preliminary work also undertaken by Thamesdown Archaeological Unit. From the results of these investigations a scheme-wide Outline Project Design was formulated, constituting the basis of the Stage 3 archaeological mitigation, the results of which form the subject of this report.

### Stage 1 – Desk-top assessment

The initial phase of investigation in the NOSNI section comprised a desk-based survey of the Preferred Route for the new road commissioned by the Historic Buildings and Monuments Commission and undertaken by Gloucestershire County Council Archaeology Service (GCCAS) in 1988. This was prompted by a request from Jan Wills, County Archaeologist for Gloucestershire, for funding to undertake a preliminary study of the new road. The assessment of the Cirencester and Stratton Bypass was carried out by Cotswold Archaeological Trust (CAT) in 1990 for WSP Civils (formerly Frank Graham Consulting Engineers), agents for the Department of Transport. Though undertaken before detailed information on the proposed route was available, these surveys collated published and unpublished documentary material and aerial photographs, together with the results of fieldwalking of arable land and a walkover survey of non-arable land, to identify a number of areas of potential archaeological interest (Russett 1989a and b; CAT 1990a).

Archaeological investigation of the route of the Latton Bypass commenced with a field evaluation conducted by Thamesdown Archaeological Unit for the Department of Transport on the cropmark focus of Scheduled Ancient Monument 899 (Digby 1988), although some evaluation of the area had already been undertaken in advance of the construction of a water pipeline between Latton and Blunsdon (Digby 1977; 1987). A combination of fieldwalking, geophysical survey and limited excavation demonstrated the monument to be principally of Roman date, with a concentration of occupation debris in the north-east quarter of the scheduled area. As a result of this investigation, and following discussion with English Heritage, the route was moved 30 m to the south-west in order to protect this area.

A desk-top assessment of the Latton area was then commissioned from CAT by WSP Civils (formerly Frank Graham Consulting Engineers) on behalf of the Highways Agency (CAT 1990b). The consultation of cartographic sources, sites and monuments records and aerial photographs together with field visits led to the identification of 17 areas of archaeological potential. In the initial proposal the Latton bypass did not extend to the Marston Meysey junction. Once the decision had been made to extend the route, an additional desk-based assessment was undertaken (CAT 1991c).

### Stage 2a - Field evaluation

Following the Stage 1 assessment, an intensive field survey of the preferred route for the NOSNI section was undertaken by GCCAS (GCC 1990). This survey prospected for additional sites of archaeological interest by systematic surface collection, aerial survey and the consultation of aerial photographs taken since the Stage 1 survey. Identified sites were further evaluated by geophysical survey and trial excavation. This process highlighted a number of sites which required more detailed investigation before road construction.

The desk-top assessment of the Cirencester and Stratton section identified 24 areas of archaeological potential along the preferred route (CAT 1990a). Geophysical survey of these areas was followed in 1991 by evaluation trenching and test-pitting (CAT 1991a). During the Public Inquiry into the

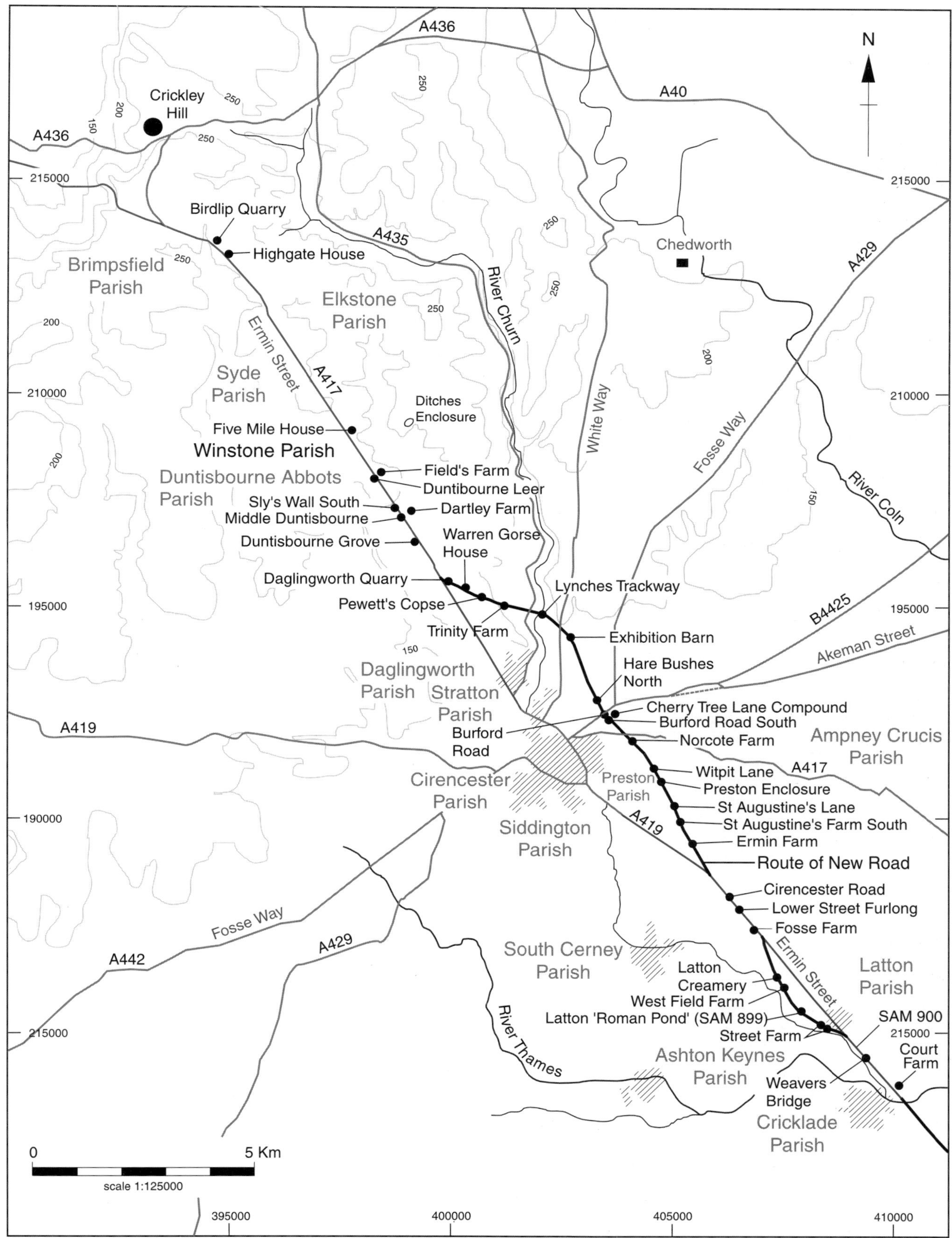


*Figure 1.2 Map of the DBFO route showing the locations of the excavation sites.*

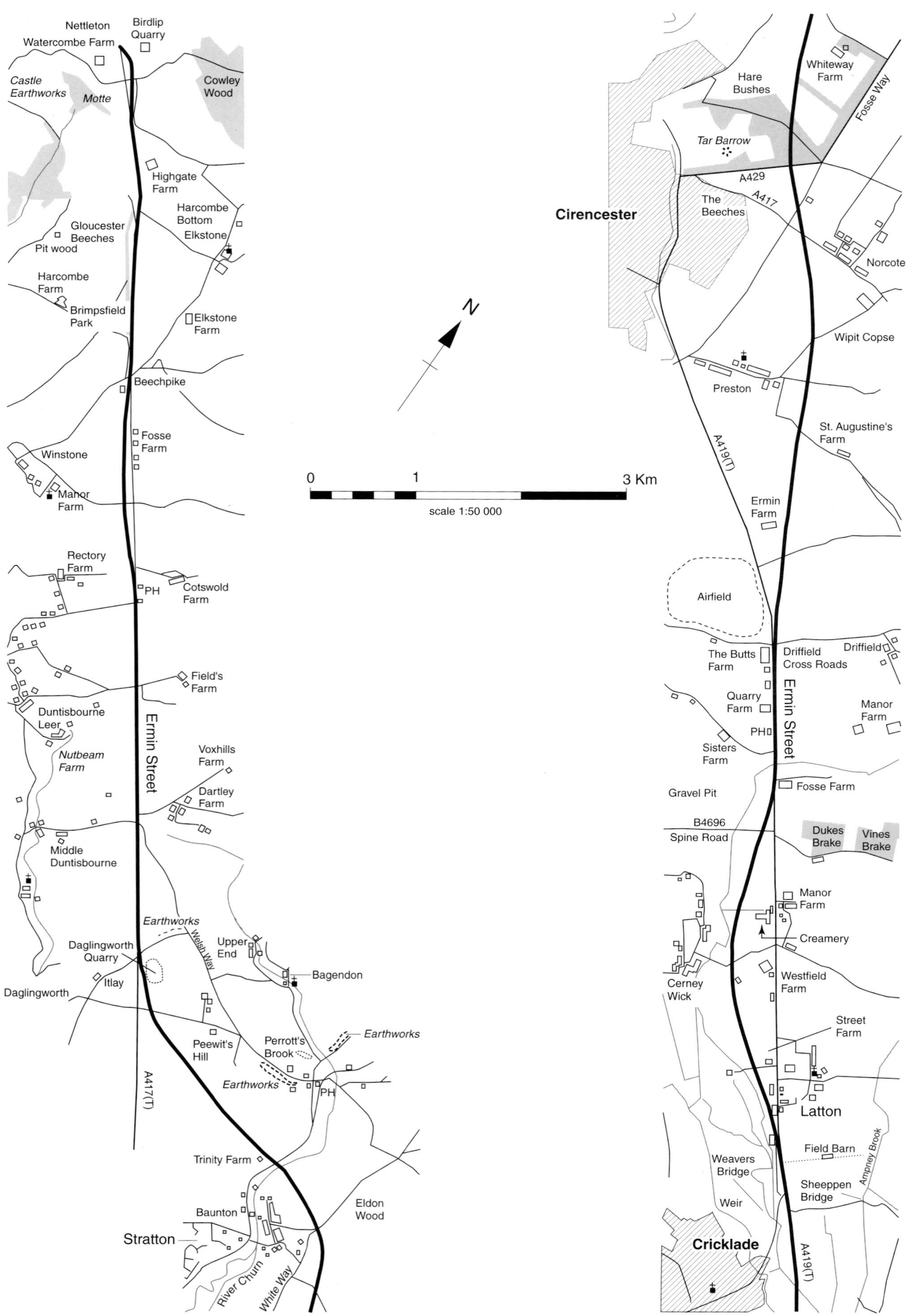


*Figure 1.3 Detailed map of DBFO route.*

Preferred Route, additional geophysical survey was undertaken in two areas of archaeological potential where access had been previously denied. Owing to access restrictions, only one of these areas was subsequently investigated by evaluation trenching (CAT 1993).

Stage 2 in the Latton area comprised 17 evaluation trenches, targeted on the areas of potential identified in the desk-top assessment, together with monitoring 42 ground investigation trial pits (CAT 1991b). An evaluation of the section to the Marston Meysey junction was completed later (CAT 1994a).

**Stage 2b - Project brief**

Following the production of the three separate Stage 2 assessment reports, both GCCAS and CAT were commissioned by WSP Civils (formerly Frank Graham Consulting Engineers) on behalf of the Highways Agency to produce Outline Project Designs for all three schemes. The project design for the NOSNI section was produced by GCCAS (GCC 1994) while CAT produced the project designs for the Cirencester and Stratton and Latton sections (1994b and c). These were combined into one document referred to as DBFO Invitation to Tender - Volume 6 Construction Requirements.

The Outline Project Designs summarised the sites of archaeological interest and defined a programme of archaeological works to mitigate the effects of the road construction, justified where necessary with reference to current archaeological guidelines. In addition to defining the requirements of the Stage 3 mitigation on a site-specific basis, the Outline Project Designs included a more general Archaeological Requirements section defining the non-site specific requirements of the archaeological work.

The Outline Project Designs formed the 'Brief' in response to which tenders were prepared. It was also incumbent upon the successful tenderer to produce a more detailed specification, otherwise known to the Oxford Archaeological Unit as a 'Written Scheme of Investigation' (WSI), explaining how the requirements of each site's project design would be discharged in the field (OAU 1996). This process was subjected to a certification procedure which required the work to be undertaken and completed according to the terms of the contract. The archaeology was therefore integrated into the development not only in terms of its time scale, but also as a contractually bound core construction requirement. The process was monitored by the Archaeological Agent appointed by the Highways Agency.

**Stage 3 - Archaeological mitigation**

The Oxford Archaeological Unit was awarded the third stage of archaeological works, under contract to the Road Management Group (RMG) consortium through Chris Blandford Associates (CBA), their environmental consultants.

Whereas the Stage 1 and Stage 2 assessments had treated the three component sections of the overall scheme as separate entities, the Stage 3 mitigation dealt with the archaeological aspects of the development as a scheme-wide project.

A scheme of works was devised that provided the best correlation between the archaeological and construction requirements of the road. A total of 35 sites were the subject of further archaeological investigation. The mitigation strategies for these sites ranged from preservation *in situ* to full excavation and included several levels of sampling defined by the terms sample excavation, selective sample excavation, strip and record and targeted watching brief. There was also the provision for further evaluation of areas of potential not covered by the Stage 2 assessments. The individual strategies applied to each site are summarised in Table 1.1. In addition, OAU was to carry out a scheme-wide watching brief on all the remaining areas.

Initially, each site was referred to by the paragraph number used in the original brief. It soon became clear, however, that this system was too clumsy for everyday use and an eponymous system of site names and codes was adopted. The complete list of sites is shown in Table 1.1. The name of the parish precedes the name of the site in the overall site code.

A number of significant discoveries were made during the watching brief. Two of the sites, Preston Enclosure and Ermin Farm, were of sufficient importance to merit the designation of a site name and code (PRENC 96 and PREM 96). Off-site works, most notably the construction of the main compound at Cherry Tree Lane, were also monitored and, in this instance, resulted in the discovery of sufficient archaeology to merit a site name and code (CIRCL 96).

Two additional evaluations were undertaken (Dartley Farm and Daglingworth Quarry). Only the latter discovered any significant archaeology in the form of a stone-lined dewpond. Following the submission of a specification for its further investigation, the part within the Compulsory Purchase Order (CPO) boundary was excavated.

In most cases the archaeological mitigation was undertaken to the programme defined in the Brief. However, in some instances, most notably at Birdlip Quarry, the archaeological programme was extended to cover additional work which was not originally anticipated.

Fieldwork on the project started in February 1996 and was almost completed by February 1997 (Fig. 1.6), leaving a number of sections through Ermin Street to be completed later in 1997.

## ARCHAEOLOGICAL BACKGROUND

The archaeological background to the project was researched from primary and secondary sources in the Stage 1 and Stage 2 assessments (Russett 1989a and b; GCC 1990; CAT 1990a, 1990b, 1991a, 1991b). Countywide archaeological syntheses are also

*Table 1.1 Individual site mitigation strategies*

| OAU Site Name | OAU Code | Mitigation Strategy | Date |
|---|---|---|---|
| NOSNI | | | |
| Birdlip Quarry | COWBQ 96 | Preservation *in situ*/Excavation | Early-middle Neolithic, Roman |
| Highgate House | COHH 96 | Preservation *in situ*/Excavation | Middle Iron Age |
| Five Mile House | DAFMH 96 | Excavation | Post-medieval |
| Duntisbourne Leer | DADL 96 | Excavation | Early prehistoric |
| Field's Farm | DAFF 96 | Excavation | Roman |
| Sly's Wall South | DRSWS 96 | Excavation | Roman, post-medieval |
| Middle Duntisbourne | DAMD 96 | Excavation | Early Neolithic, late Iron Age |
| Dartley Farm | DRDFM 96 | Excavation | No archaeological features |
| Duntisbourne Grove | DRDG 96 | Excavation | Early-middle Neolithic, late Iron Age |
| Daglingworth Quarry | DAGQ 96 | Evaluation/Excavation | Post-medieval |
| Ermin Street Sections | ERMIN 96 | Excavation of 15 Transects | Roman, medieval, post-medieval |
| Cirencester and Stratton Bypass | | | |
| Warren Gorse House | DAGWGH 96 | Strip and record | Undated walls |
| Pewet's Copse | BAPC 96 | Strip and record | Putative trackway, undated |
| Trinity Farm | BAGTF 96 | Strip and record | ?Mesolithic, late Neolithic, early Bronze age |
| Lynches Trackway | BAULT 96 | Excavation | Middle Iron Age |
| Exhibition Barn | BAUEXB 96 | Strip and record | Roman |
| Hare Bushes North | BAUHBN 96 | Strip and record | Early-middle Neolithic |
| Burford Road | CIBFRD 96 | Excavation | Later prehistoric |
| Cherry Tree Lane Compound | CIRCL 96 | Off-Site work - Strip and record | Mesolithic, later prehistoric |
| Burford Road South | CIBRS 96 | Strip and record | Later prehistoric |
| Norcote Farm | PRNOF 96 | Excavation | Neolithic, later prehistoric, Roman |
| Witpit Lane | PRWPL 96 | Strip and record | Medieval |
| Preston Enclosure | PRENC 96 | Excavation | Middle Iron Age |
| St. Augustine's Lane | PRSAL 96 | Excavation | Middle Iron Age |
| St. Augustine's Farm South | PRSTAS 96 | Excavation/Strip and record | Neolithic, late Neolithic-early Bronze Age, |
| Ermin Farm | PREM 96 | WB discovery - Strip and record | Middle Iron Age |
| Latton Bypass | | | |
| Cirencester Road | LADRCI 96 | Sample Excavation and WB | Roman ?road surface, medieval plough furrow, post-medieval quarry pit |
| Lower Street Furlong | DRLF 96 | Excavation | Later prehistoric |
| Fosse Farm | LAFOS 96 | Sample Excavation | Plough furrows, undated |
| Latton Creamery | LAC 96 | Sample Excavation | Ditch, undated |
| Westfield Farm | LAWF 96 | Sample Excavation | Roman |
| Latton 'Roman Pond' | LARP 96 | Excavation | Prehistoric, late Bronze Age, medieval |
| Street Farm | LATST 96 | Sample Excavation/ Selective Sample Excavation | Medieval, post-medieval |
| Court Farm | LACFM 96 | Sample Excavation | Roman |
| Weavers Bridge | LAWBR 96 | Excavation | Roman |

available, in particular *Iron Age and Romano-British Monuments in the Gloucestershire Cotswolds* (RCHME 1976) *Archaeology in Gloucestershire* (Saville 1984c), *Prehistoric Gloucestershire* (Darvill 1987) and *Roman Gloucestershire* (McWhirr 1986b). More locally, the archaeology of the environs of Cirencester has been assessed in *Cirencester: Town and Landscape* (Darvill and Gerrard 1994). These published and published sources form the basis of the following brief summary.

## Mesolithic

Over 40 Mesolithic sites are known in Gloucestershire, mostly concentrated in the Cotswolds on the higher ground overlooking the Severn Vale (CAT 1991a, 119–120). These are known exclusively from flint scatters. Mesolithic flint artefacts have been recorded in the parishes of Cowley, Elkstone, Brimpsfield, Syde, Duntisbourne Abbots and Bagendon in the vicinity of the road corridor (GCC 1990, 2). Within the study area, flints of probable late Mesolithic date were the earliest remains discovered, and covered an area of about 100 $m^2$ on land just south of the London Road near Norcote Farm, Preston (SP 041021). Surface collection in this field augmented an earlier assemblage recovered by Mr S F Coombs from the same area (CAT 1990a, 19–20). This site is unusual in its relatively low-lying location on the Cotswold dipslope but plough-zone material generally offers limited potential for understanding the nature of the occupation and the economic exploitation of the landscape. Very little Mesolithic archaeology is known from the southern part of the route. A few, possibly Mesolithic, flints were recovered from evaluation in the Creamery Field, north-east of Cerney Wick, and Beggars Field, east of Cerney Wick (CAT 1991b, 69).

### Neolithic

Neolithic sites and findspots are not uncommon in the Cotswold uplands of Gloucestershire. Causewayed enclosures are known at Crickley Hill and Peak Camp, both on the Cotswold scarp edge, not far from Birdlip. Funerary monuments are more widespread but are confined to the uplands, generally above 120 m (Darvill 1987, fig. on page 41 and 49–62) and include chambered long barrows in Brimpsfield, Duntisbourne Abbots and Duntisbourne Rouse, close to the road corridor (GCC 1990, 2). In this region, as elsewhere, there is a problem identifying non-monumental sites. Evidence of settlement in the form of scatters of flint artefacts is also concentrated in the uplands with only rare finds on the lower ground and in the valleys, at least until the late Neolithic (Darvill 1987, 46). There is, however, some evidence for Neolithic activity on the lower ground within the road corridor. A scatter of Neolithic/Bronze Age flint came from the field north of Hare Bushes, Baunton, (SP 03400325), which appears to be part of a wider spread of flint to the west (CAT 1991a, 55–6). Surface finds of flint also came from land east of the White Way in the same parish (CAT 1991a, 53–4). In the Thames Valley an oval enclosure south-west of Westfield Farm, Latton, (Wilts. SMR SU09NE621) was provisionally dated to the late Neolithic/early Bronze Age (CAT 1991b, 44–5). There is a similar enclosure south-east of Latton (Wilts. SMR SU09NE600) which lies within Scheduled Ancient Monument 900. A Neolithic pit (Wilts. SMR SU09NE100) was found in the same field.

### Bronze Age

As with the preceding period, settlements are rare in Gloucestershire, although the widespread distribution of round barrows and ring ditches suggests that occupation was extensive both in the Cotswolds and in the Thames Valley (Darvill 1987, 95–114). Barrows and ring ditches occur mostly in a dispersed pattern, and more rarely in clusters. A group of ring ditches lies east of the village of Preston, where an adjoining pair (Glos. SMR 3072) fell within the road corridor at St Augustine's Farm South. Two larger ones lie nearby (Glos. SMR 3068 and 3069), possibly aligned on an ill-defined feature which has been interpreted (somewhat dubiously) as a polygonal enclosure (Glos. SMR 3067; RCHME 1976, 95). Further south, two cropmark ring ditches either side of Harnhill Lane (Glos. SMR 2388a and 2390) were evaluated and later taken out of the development corridor. There are many other ring ditches close to the road corridor, but not forming such close groups. A Bronze Age flint scatter was also identified within the road corridor south of Norcote Farm, Preston, but appeared to lack associated features (CAT 1991a, 73–4).

### Iron Age

The Iron Age in Gloucestershire is identified mainly by its hillforts which tend to lie on the high ground of the Cotswolds. Other settlements are known, but except in the east of the county in the Thames Valley, they are relatively scarce compared with other regions of the country such as Wessex and the Upper Thames in Oxfordshire. Excavations have also been on a small scale and the sites are not generally well-defined. At the evaluation stage of the current project only one early to middle Iron Age site (Highgate House, Cowley) was identified in the northern section of the route, and none was found in the Cirencester area (CAT 1991a, 127). In the Thames Valley a sub-rectangular enclosure within the Scheduled Ancient Monument at Latton (Wilts. SMR SU09NE201) was found to be Iron Age and Iron Age pottery came from other evaluation trenches in this area (CAT 1991b, 74–75). The late Iron Age in the region is particularly notable for the high-status dyke complex at Bagendon. This is widely regarded as the centre of the Dobunnic tribal polity, although its precise nature and date are controversial and it appears to have had importance in the Roman period. The evaluation discovered no material associated with this complex north or east of Cirencester, but to the north-west two late Iron Age/early Roman enclosures were identified at Middle Duntisbourne and Duntisbourne Grove. South of Cirencester, the relationship between the Iron Age and Roman cropmark settlements at Latton (Scheduled Ancient Monument 899) is unclear, but in the Upper Thames region settlements (such as Claydon Pike, Fairford and those in the Ashton Keynes area) often show a continuity of location from the late Iron Age through to the early Roman period (CAT 1991b, 76–77).

### Roman

Roman activity in the Cirencester region was intense and widespread. Cirencester was the site of a military fort and later a *civitas* capital, *Corinium Dobunnorum*, and there is some evidence that it became a provincial capital in the 4th century (Holbrook 1994). Settlements of high and low status are known within the immediate environs of the town and further afield. Ermin Street (now largely followed by the A417 to the

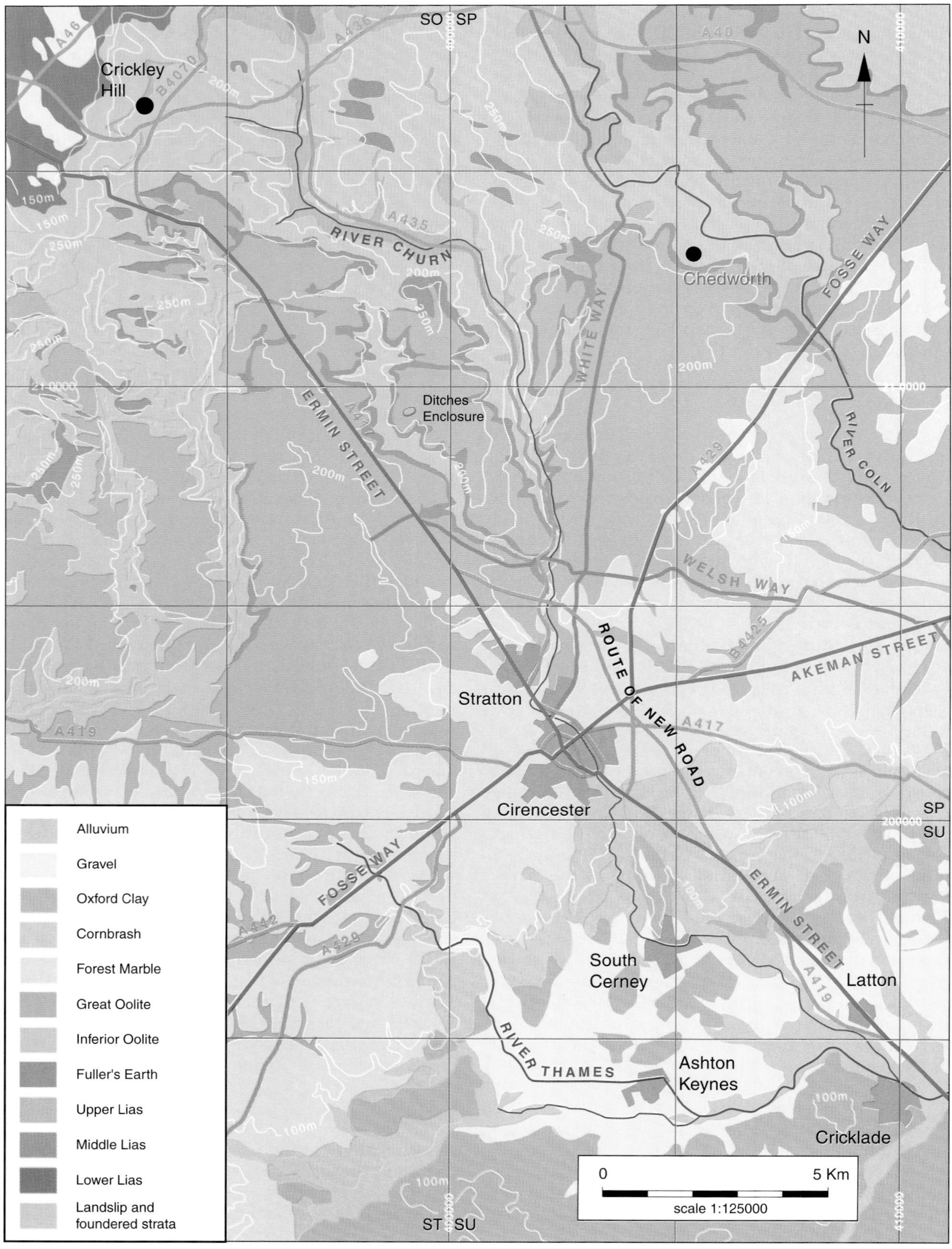


*Figure 1.4 Geology. (Source: Geological Survey of England and Wales sheets 235 and 252).*

north of Cirencester and the A419 to the south) was constructed shortly after the conquest, linking the forts at Kingsholm (Gloucester) and Leaholme (Cirencester) with the conquered territory to the east. The Fosse Way and Akeman Street also converge on the town, and there is a case to be made for the White Way, which runs towards the villa at Chedworth, being of Roman or earlier origin (Darvill and Holbrook 1994, 51–3).

The desk-top assessment and field survey produced surprisingly little evidence for Romano-British activity within the survey area. A settlement was identified at Birdlip Quarry, Cowley, at the northern end of the route, and a site of less certain status was found at Weavers Bridge near Cricklade at the southern end of the route. A roadside funerary monument, several trackways and quarry pits were also recognised at Field's Farm, Duntisbourne Abbots. Settlements in the vicinity of the road scheme, but lying outside the development corridor include those at Birdlip Bypass (Darvill 1984b), Pit Wood, Syde (RCHME 1976, 116), Field's Farm (op. cit., 48), Duntisbourne Leer (ibid.), Stancombe, Duntisbourne Rouse (op. cit., 49), Cave Close, Daglingworth (op. cit., 41), Baunton Downs (op. cit., 13), Witpit Copse, Preston (Glos. SMR 3176), Worms Farm, Siddington (RCHME 1976, 102), and Field Barn, Latton (Wilts SMR SU09NE303). The extensive settlement west of Latton (Scheduled Ancient Monument 899) lay directly on the proposed line of the new road but was largely avoided by design modifications to the route.

### Early medieval

Little is known about the area in the early medieval period. In rural areas a model of continuity from Roman to medieval estates has been longstanding (Gerrard 1994a, 95) and it is possible that the Saxon invasion may have had little impact on rural settlements in Gloucestershire (GCC 1990, 4). The evidence for the status of Cirencester as a royal, ecclesiastical and commercial centre has also been assessed (Gerrard 1994, 90), however, little archaeological evidence can be brought to bear on these questions. The only hint of early Saxon settlement in the road scheme region comes from a few sherds of pottery found north-west of Latton (Wilts. SMR SU09NE400). Elsewhere, the known pattern of pre-Conquest churches and later villages provides a picture of later Saxon settlement in the region. Trinity Mill, Bagendon is known to have had pre-Conquest origins.

### Medieval and post-medieval

The later medieval settlement pattern appears to have been very similar to that today, with villages located in the valleys of the Cotswolds and on the gravel terrace. Deserted and shrunken medieval settlements are, however, known at Stockwell Farm, Birdlip and from the parishes of Brimpsfield, Winstone and Elkstone (GCC 1990, 4). There is some indication that most deserted settlements are subsidiary hamlets rather than main villages with a church (Aston and Viner 1984, 282). Farms deserted as a consequence of enclosure are to be expected in the region although few have been securely identified (Gerrard and Viner 1994, 135).

The possible site of a deserted settlement was found between Preston and Witpit Copse, where spreads of 11th–13th century pottery were found on either side of Witpit Lane (CAT 1991a, 136). At Latton, there is early cartographic evidence of houses lying to the west of Ermin Street and plots running back to the river Churn. Pottery of 12th–15th century date came from this area in the evaluation, although no structures were identified (CAT 1991b, 78–9). Pottery from close to Fosse Farm, Driffield, also suggested medieval/post-medieval occupation, probably under the present farm buildings (ibid.).

One of the chief post-medieval agricultural features within the road corridor is the water-meadow system in the Churn valley at Trinity Mill which, while not unique, has value in that it displays a coherent group of historic landscape features - the drainage channels, leat and the mill itself (CAT 1991a, 138). Traces of ridge-and-furrow cultivation also survive in the region but generally lack value as interpretative units (CAT 1991a, 137). The most common post-medieval/early modern type of monument affected by the new road were the turnpike roads, whose main archaeological interest lies in their method of construction and their importance as an element of the archaeological continuum (CAT 1991a, 142). Parts of the infilled Thames and Severn canal also lay within the road corridor, but this had little value as an archaeological feature.

## PROJECT AIMS

The first part of this section outlines the overall archaeological objectives of the road project. The second part summarises some of the project's principal research themes identified in the Stage 1 and 2 assessments, and restated in the Archaeological Project Design, General Strategy and Methodology Document (OAU 1996). The third part offers an amplification of these academic themes undertaken upon the completion of the fieldwork. These were presented in full in the post-excavation assessment and publication proposal (Lupton and Williams 1997).

### Scheme-wide objectives

The ultimate objective of the project as defined in the Outline Project Design was the preservation, either *in situ*, or by record, of all identified deposits of archaeological significance within the proposed route. For those sites which were to be preserved by record, the purpose was to undertake an appropriate level of archaeological recording and sampling of all significant deposits. An appropriate level of recording for each site was defined in terms of its perceived significance with regard to nationally defined research priorities (English Heritage 1991b). A further stated objective was to ensure the long term curation of the

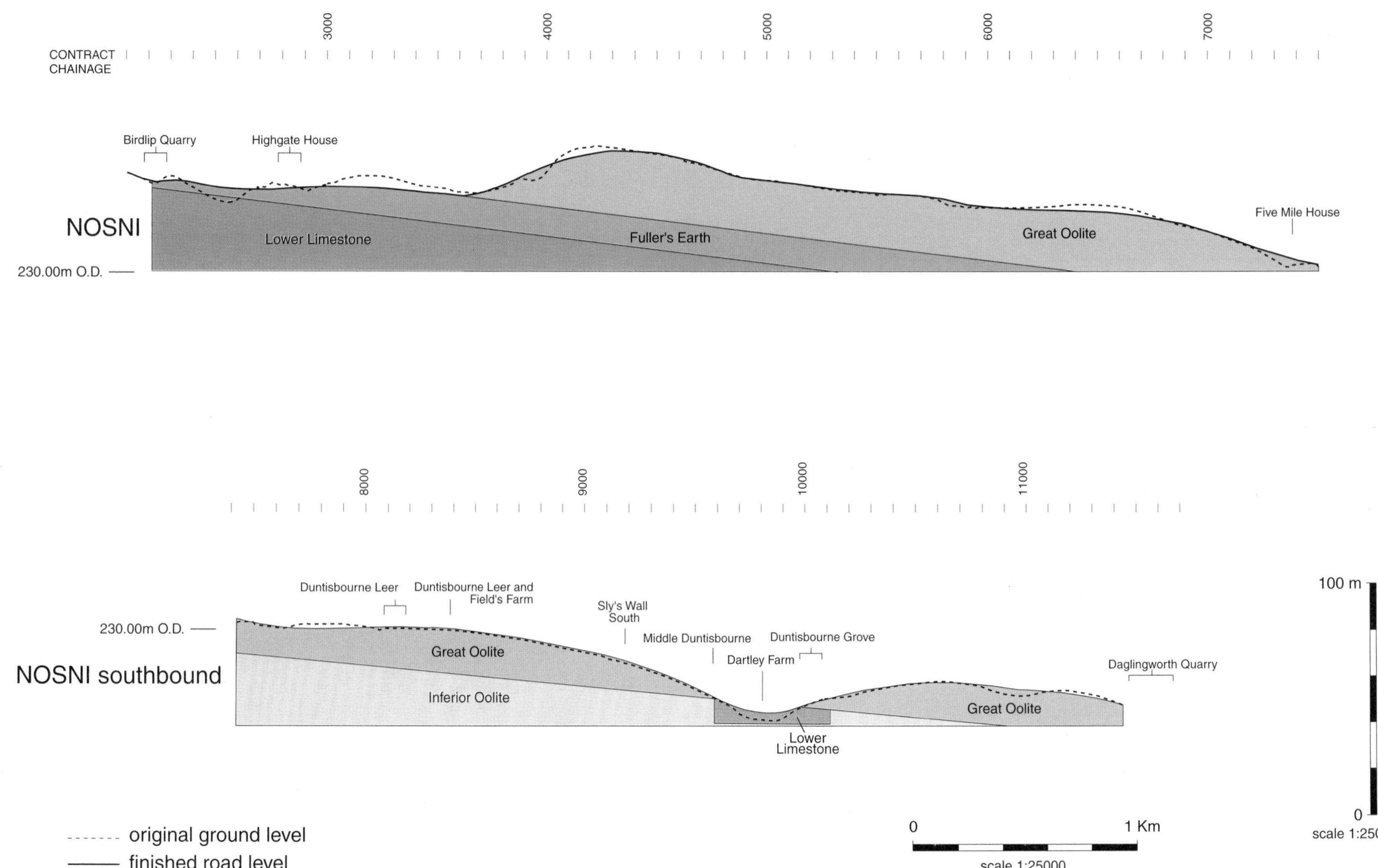
CONTRACT CHAINAGE
3000
4000
5000
6000
7000
Birdlip Quarry
Highgate House
NOSNI
230.00m O.D.
Lower Limestone
Fuller's Earth
Great Oolite
Five Mile House
8000
9000
10000
11000
Duntisbourne Leer
Duntisbourne Leer and Field's Farm
Sly's Wall South
Middle Duntisbourne
Duntisbourne Grove
Dartley Farm
Daglingworth Quarry
230.00m O.D.
NOSNI southbound
Great Oolite
Inferior Oolite
Great Oolite
Lower Limestone
100 m
0
scale 1:2500
0
1 Km
scale 1:25000
original ground level
finished road level

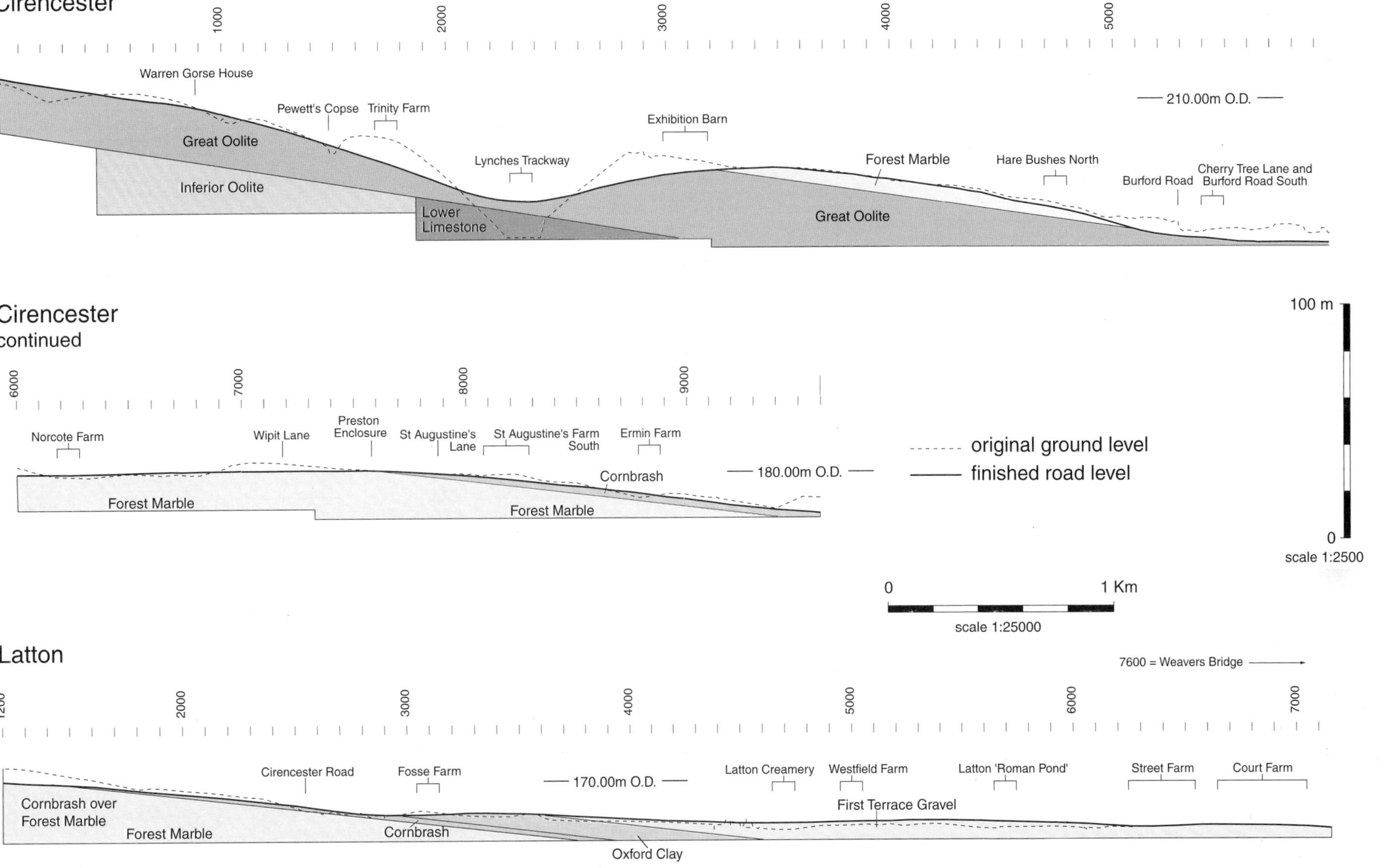


*Figure 1.5 Geological profile. (Based on RMG engineer's drawing).*

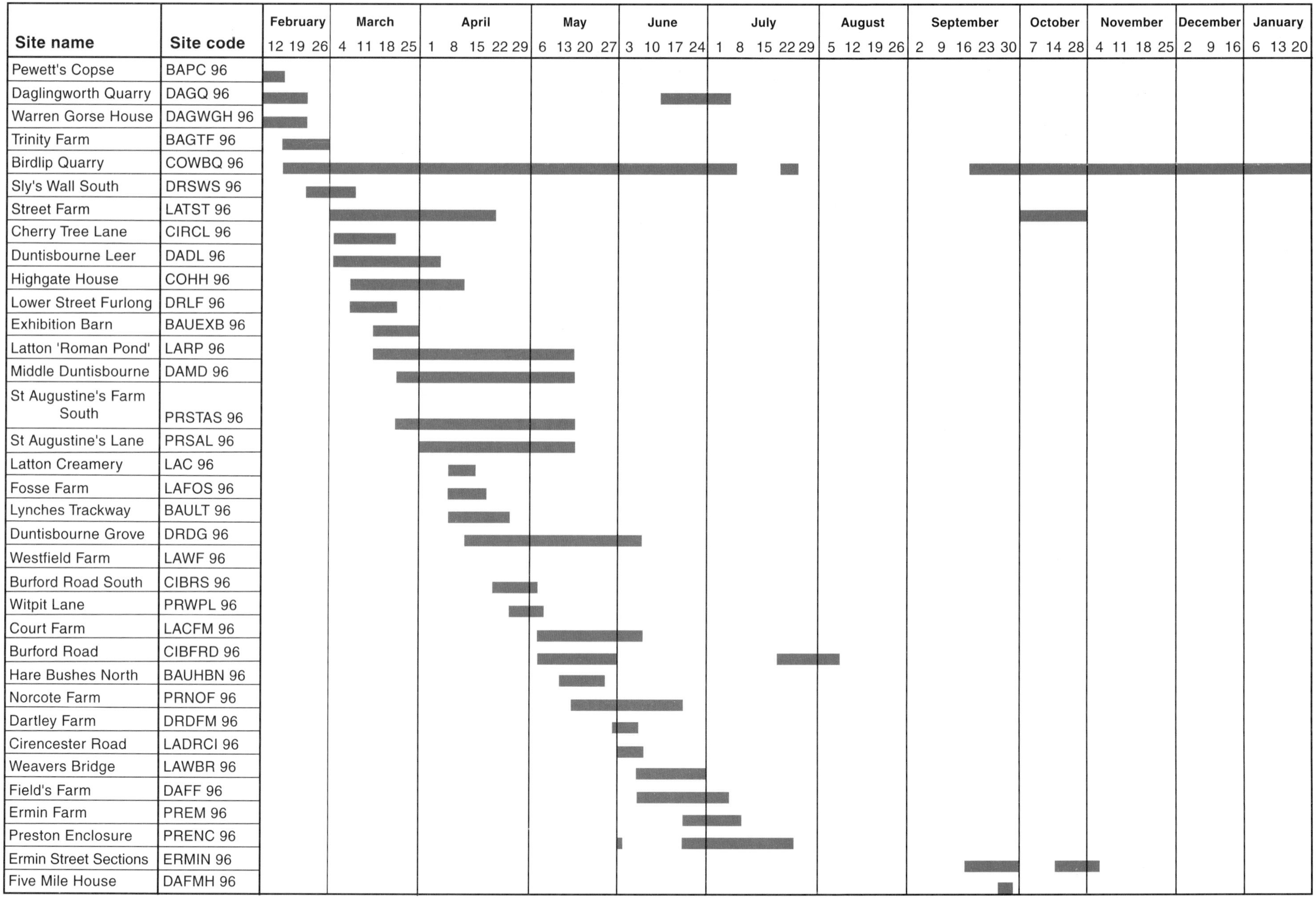

| Site name | Site code | February | March | April | May | June | July | August | September | October | November | December | January |
|---|---|---|---|---|---|---|---|---|---|---|---|---|---|
| | | 12 19 26 | 4 11 18 25 | 1 8 15 22 29 | 6 13 20 27 | 3 10 17 24 | 1 8 15 22 29 | 5 12 19 26 | 2 9 16 23 30 | 7 14 28 | 4 11 18 25 | 2 9 16 | 6 13 20 |
| Pewett's Copse | BAPC 96 | | | | | | | | | | | | |
| Daglingworth Quarry | DAGQ 96 | | | | | | | | | | | | |
| Warren Gorse House | DAGWGH 96 | | | | | | | | | | | | |
| Trinity Farm | BAGTF 96 | | | | | | | | | | | | |
| Birdlip Quarry | COWBQ 96 | | | | | | | | | | | | |
| Sly's Wall South | DRSWS 96 | | | | | | | | | | | | |
| Street Farm | LATST 96 | | | | | | | | | | | | |
| Cherry Tree Lane | CIRCL 96 | | | | | | | | | | | | |
| Duntisbourne Leer | DADL 96 | | | | | | | | | | | | |
| Highgate House | COHH 96 | | | | | | | | | | | | |
| Lower Street Furlong | DRLF 96 | | | | | | | | | | | | |
| Exhibition Barn | BAUEXB 96 | | | | | | | | | | | | |
| Latton 'Roman Pond' | LARP 96 | | | | | | | | | | | | |
| Middle Duntisbourne | DAMD 96 | | | | | | | | | | | | |
| St Augustine's Farm South | PRSTAS 96 | | | | | | | | | | | | |
| St Augustine's Lane | PRSAL 96 | | | | | | | | | | | | |
| Latton Creamery | LAC 96 | | | | | | | | | | | | |
| Fosse Farm | LAFOS 96 | | | | | | | | | | | | |
| Lynches Trackway | BAULT 96 | | | | | | | | | | | | |
| Duntisbourne Grove | DRDG 96 | | | | | | | | | | | | |
| Westfield Farm | LAWF 96 | | | | | | | | | | | | |
| Burford Road South | CIBRS 96 | | | | | | | | | | | | |
| Witpit Lane | PRWPL 96 | | | | | | | | | | | | |
| Court Farm | LACFM 96 | | | | | | | | | | | | |
| Burford Road | CIBFRD 96 | | | | | | | | | | | | |
| Hare Bushes North | BAUHBN 96 | | | | | | | | | | | | |
| Norcote Farm | PRNOF 96 | | | | | | | | | | | | |
| Dartley Farm | DRDFM 96 | | | | | | | | | | | | |
| Cirencester Road | LADRCI 96 | | | | | | | | | | | | |
| Weavers Bridge | LAWBR 96 | | | | | | | | | | | | |
| Field's Farm | DAFF 96 | | | | | | | | | | | | |
| Ermin Farm | PREM 96 | | | | | | | | | | | | |
| Preston Enclosure | PRENC 96 | | | | | | | | | | | | |
| Ermin Street Sections | ERMIN 96 | | | | | | | | | | | | |
| Five Mile House | DAFMH 96 | | | | | | | | | | | | |

*Figure 1.6 Programme of works.*

data recovered, and its dissemination in a form appropriate to its academic value in line with nationally defined guidelines (English Heritage 1991a).

### Research themes

Encompassed within these broad objectives, a number of key overall research themes were recognised and were summarised as follows:

1 The environmental development of the Upper Thames Valley and Cotswold dipslope in relation to past human exploitation.
2 The earlier prehistoric to later prehistoric transition in domestic occupation and land-use.
3 Later prehistoric predecessors to the Roman settlement pattern.
4 Roman settlement and land-use patterns in the vicinity of Cirencester.
5 The origins and development of Ermin Street, its relationship to local road networks, and its later development and use up to the turnpike era.

Other themes were also recognised in the Outline Project Design, but these were either less significant or less likely to be readily addressed than the key themes defined above. However, the fact that the road scheme represented a transect through different geographical zones close to a major Roman city, Cirencester, whose hinterland it traversed, together with the specific unifying factor of Ermin Street, gave the project a strong degree of overall coherence. In this light, it was realised that some discoveries of relatively minor intrinsic interest could take on a greater value when seen within this wider context. It was also recognised that further themes could emerge from unexpected discoveries during fieldwork and in the post-excavation analysis.

### Amplification of research themes

Following the results of the post-excavation assessment it was clear that all five major themes outlined above continued to be broadly relevant and could be addressed more specifically.

A) With regard to theme 1, the road scheme offered the opportunity of examining a transect through the landscape, from the edge of the Cotswold escarpment in the north-west to the Upper Thames Valley in the south-east, and comparing the development of settlement and land-use between these two broad zones. These topics could be addressed through considerations of the character of the sites and their environmental indicators. Palaeo-ecological information is rare in this region and the environmental sequences from waterlogged deposits at Latton 'Roman Pond' (Scheduled Ancient Monument 899) and those from sediments in the Churn Valley at Lynches Trackway, were seen to be of exceptional significance.

B) Theme 2 was explored through the examination of a small number of earlier prehistoric pits at Duntisbourne Grove (Duntisbourne Abbots) and Trinity Farm (Bagendon). These sites added to the limited corpus of material of this period from the region, but the extent and nature of earlier prehistoric settlement remained unclear. The later prehistoric sites provided a great deal more information about settlement and land-use, particularly from the boundaries and settlements near Preston, at St Augustine's Farm South, Preston Enclosure and Ermin Farm. These sites offered some basis for comparing the evidence for earlier and later prehistoric settlement patterns and economic strategies between the Cotswolds and the Thames Valley.

C) The results of the excavations at Middle Duntisbourne and Duntisbourne Grove, were particularly relevant to theme 3; the pre-Roman settlement pattern. In their date and assemblages of material these sites showed affinities with the high-status settlements at Bagendon and Ditches hillfort, but were clearly crossed by Roman Ermin Street. They offered some potential for contributing to the debate about the nature of settlement here around the time of the Roman conquest.

D) The settlement at Birdlip Quarry, Cowley was of direct relevance to research theme 4, providing some insight into the nature of Roman roadside settlement. The settlement formed part of a distinctly Roman pattern, probably determined by the presence of Ermin Street, rather than by any Iron Age predecessor, but its markedly 'native' form offered a contrast to most of the evidence of Roman occupation in the Cotswolds.

E) The excavations through Ermin Street and those at Birdlip Quarry were especially relevant to theme 5. While there was little artefactual dating evidence for the origins and development of Ermin Street, there was information on road construction and use from the Roman period through to the turnpike era. In addition, the relationship between the major Roman roads and adjacent trackways could be addressed at sites such as Field's Farm, Duntisbourne Abbots and Court Farm, Latton.

## STRUCTURE OF THE REPORT

With these revised aims in mind, the approach taken was to produce a thematic, chronologically structured report on the discoveries of the study, rather than a series of individual site reports. It was felt that this most effectively gave due weight to the individual findings within the overall picture, thus neither giving too much weight to minor discoveries nor underplaying their cumulative value, as might occur if they were dealt with separately. Some site elements have, however, been treated out of a strict chronological framework, particularly where the division of a site between periods was unclear and required justification, or where the site elements for a particular period were so minor as to make separate treatment overly fastidious.

Chapter 2 incorporates all the discoveries pertaining to the early prehistoric period. For the purposes of this report the early prehistoric period is defined as everything pre-dating the end of the Bronze Age (*c*. 700 BC). Chapter 3 deals with material relating to the later prehistoric or Iron Age period (*c*. 700 BC – 43 AD), Chapter 4 with the Roman period, Chapter 5 with Roman roads and their later developments, and Chapter 6 with the medieval and post-medieval periods. Chapter 6 appears in volume 2. The second volume of the report also contains the artefactual and environmental reports (Chapters 7 and 8) and a discussion chapter (Chapter 9). The appendices contain technical detail relating to the animal bone and pollen analysis as well as the radiocarbon dates. A running sequence of catalogue numbers has been applied to the artefacts in chapter 7. These are referred to throughout the volume and appear on the relevant illustrations.

## LOCATION OF ARCHIVE

The paper archive of the Stage 3 archaeological works has been security copied and a copy deposited with the National Monuments Record. The finds and archive from the sites in Gloucestershire have been deposited with the Corinium Museum, Cirencester and that from the sites in Wiltshire with Swindon Museum.

# Chapter 2: The Earlier Prehistoric Period

*by Alan Lupton with Jeff Muir*

## INTRODUCTION

A number of early prehistoric sites were investigated along the route of the new road (Fig. 2.1). Though the remains were widely dispersed, in both physical and temporal terms, when considered together they make an important contribution to a greater understanding of this period in Gloucestershire and north Wiltshire.

A single Acheulian handaxe of Palaeolithic age represents the earliest object found during work on the road scheme, although its exact provenance is unknown (Fig. 7.3.24). The earliest traces of activity belong to the Mesolithic period with the discovery of a possible early Mesolithic microlith in a tree-throw hole at Cherry Tree Lane (Fig. 7.3.23), while less diagnostic flintwork was recovered from a number of other sites. An important series of pits containing flints, fired clay and pottery dating to the succeeding Neolithic period was recovered at Duntisbourne Grove. In addition, Neolithic flints were found at the sites of Birdlip Quarry, Hare Bushes North, Middle Duntisbourne, Norcote Farm and St Augustine's Farm South. Pottery and flints from the following late Neolithic/early Bronze Age period were discovered at the sites of Trinity Farm and Preston Enclosure and the ring ditches of two early Bronze Age barrows were investigated at St Augustine's Farm South. Later Bronze Age activity is rare and includes small quantities of residual pottery from St Augustine's Lane and St Augustine's Farm South. Additional material of probable early prehistoric date was recovered from the site of Duntisbourne Leer. In this chapter, each of these discoveries will be examined in detail and an assessment made of their local and/or regional significance.

## PALAEOLITHIC AND MESOLITHIC ACTIVITY

The flint handaxe (Fig. 7.3.24) was discovered during the watching brief in the Latton area in gravel hardcore material brought into the site for construction. The source of the gravel hardcore is not precisely known and, therefore the exact provenance of the handaxe is uncertain. However, following consultation with the engineers it is believed likely that the gravel derived from the adjacent quarry at Latton Lands. Typologically the axe belongs to the Acheulian tradition of the Lower Palaeolithic, which is found widely over northern Europe (Barton 1997). Acheulian axes appear in a variety of sizes and are thought to be multi-purpose tools used for both domestic and hunting purposes. Acheulian industries are usually associated with the remains of *Homo erectus,* although such associations are extremely rare in Britain.

The discovery of an early Mesolithic microlith at Cherry Tree Lane (Fig. 7.3.23) supplements the scarce distribution of material from this period. Such microliths are thought to have been mounted in bone or wooden hafts to form harpoons or spears. Unfortunately, this isolated find adds little to our poor understanding of the early Mesolithic period in the vicinity of the road scheme. Other possible Mesolithic flintwork came from Trinity Farm, while other sites contained flintwork that could also be of this date. eg. Birdlip Quarry and Duntisbourne Grove (see Durden, Chapter 7). The Mesolithic of this region has been discussed by a number of authors (Saville 1984a; Darvill 1987, Holgate 1988). Evidence for the early Mesolithic in the Cotswolds and Upper Thames Valley is quite scarce in contrast to the number of later Mesolithic sites that are known from the same area.

## THE NEOLITHIC AND EARLY BRONZE AGE PERIOD (4000–1750 CAL BC)

A number of sites produced evidence for small-scale activity of this date most of which can be described as being of domestic character. The only funerary monuments were the two contiguous barrow ditches of early Bronze Age date at St Augustine's Farm South. The evidence can be broadly divided into the following two phases: early and middle Neolithic (4000–2900 cal BC) domestic activity characterised by surface scatters and pit deposits; late Neolithic and early Bronze Age (2500–1750 cal BC) domestic and funerary activity characterised again by pit deposits, surface scatters and barrows. The first phase is associated with the recovery of small quantities of Plain Bowl and Peterborough Ware pottery, while the second is characterised by Beaker and early Bronze Age pottery. However, on sites where only flintwork was recovered it was only possible to assign either earlier or later Neolithic dates. Consequently, the Neolithic material from the road scheme is divided into earlier and later Neolithic categories.

Most of the recovered evidence consisted of flintwork and to a lesser extent pottery, while some of this material was also found associated with charred plant remains and animal bone fragments. The dating of sites and features had to rely on relatively small groups of material that often contained few diagnostic elements. Most of the earlier prehistoric pottery consisted of relatively small sherds (see Barclay, Chapter 7). Dates based solely on small groups of flint and small numbers of often poorly preserved pottery will always appear somewhat imprecise. Some

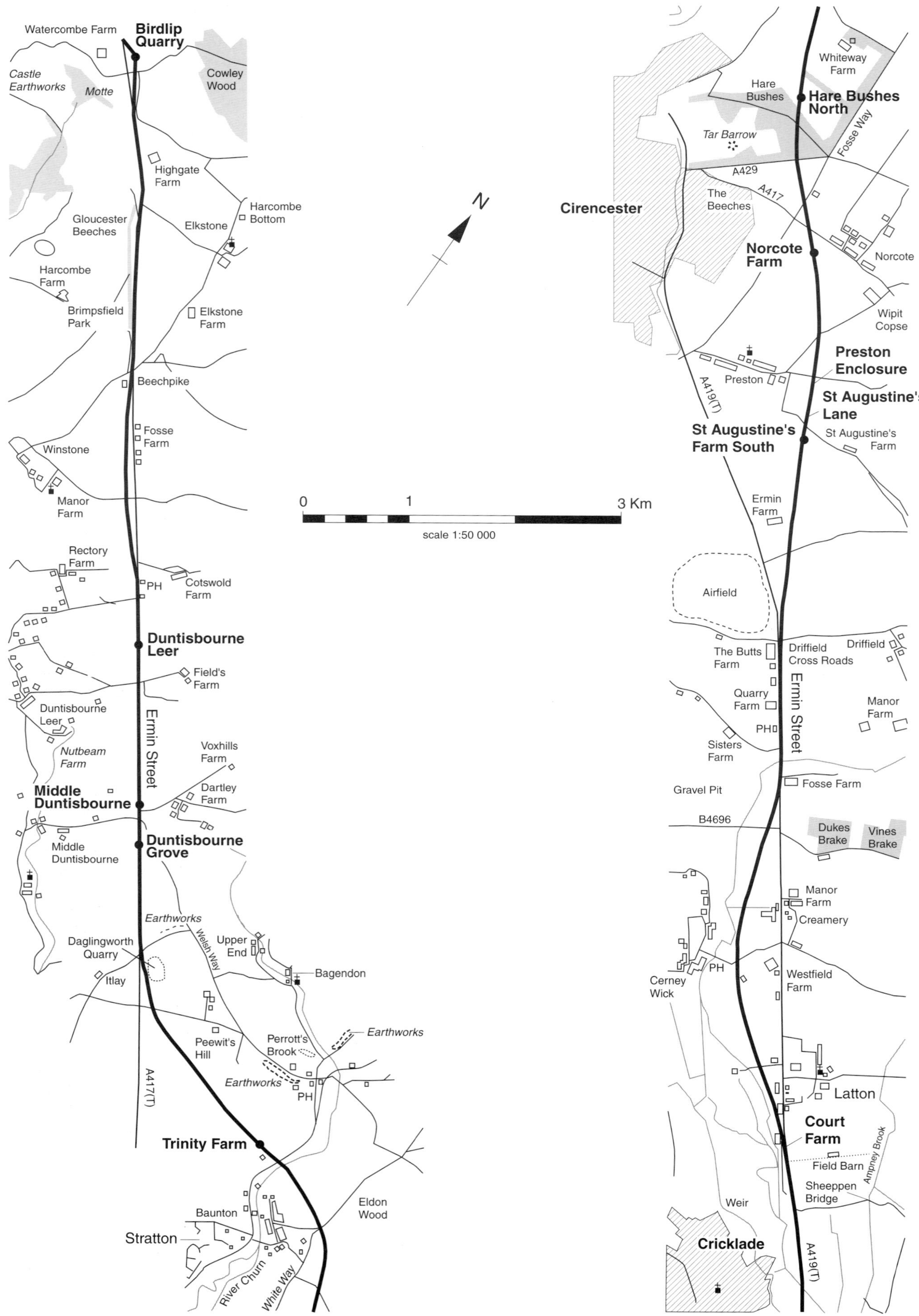


*Figure 2.1 Locations of earlier prehistoric sites.*

features clearly contained material of mixed date raising the possibility of residuality and redeposition. Many of the excavated features consisted of pits that were dug essentially to receive deposits of material culture together with assemblages of ecofacts. The composition of the material buried within these features may best be interpreted as the residue from domestic occupation that has been collected deliberately or even placed within a temporary midden prior to burial. Under these circumstances it would be easy to see how finds of earlier date could have become incorporated into deposits. Where pottery is present in these features it can be used to provide a reliable and refined date within the Neolithic and early Bronze Age. In certain cases radiocarbon determinations were obtained to verify the dates provided by the pottery and flintwork (see Appendix 1).

### The early and middle Neolithic (*c.* 4000–2900 cal BC)

The route connects the Downs to the south with the Cotswolds to the north-west and cuts obliquely across the most western part of the Upper Thames Valley. To the south and just beyond Cricklade are the Marlborough Downs and to the east are the Berkshire Downs. A small number of early Neolithic long barrows are known from the Downs and these include the excavated examples at Wayland's Smithy and Lambourn (Kinnes 1992), while the massive early Bronze Age barrow cemetery at Lambourn is only 20 km to the south-east and the massive Neolithic and early Bronze Age monument complex at Avebury is only 25 km to the south-west. As the path of the road scheme cuts across the Upper Thames Valley it runs within 10 km of the Lechlade area. Lechlade sits at the confluence of the river Leech with the Thames and to the east is one of the major concentrations of early Neolithic causewayed enclosures to be found anywhere in southern England, while west and north of Lechlade are other monuments of this type. One of these enclosures known only as a cropmark is located at Down Ampney just 2 km from the line of the road, while the cropmark of a probable early Neolithic oval barrow and other ring ditches are also known (Leech 1977, map 3). Also at Lechlade are two cursus-dominated monument complexes, one of which, located at Buscot Wick may be a major example of its type (Darvill 1987, 76). Both cursus monuments were probably built in the middle Neolithic, while other monuments known from cropmarks at Buscot Wick could be even earlier in date (Barclay and Hey in press). To the north the road cuts across the Cotswolds and its northern extent runs near to the enclosures at Southmoor Grove, Rendcomb, Crickley Hill and Peak Camp (see Darvill 1987, 41), it also passes through the distribution of Cotswold-Severn long cairns.

Material of this date is scarce on sites excavated on the road scheme, but some of the flints and pottery found at Birdlip Quarry, Middle Duntisbourne, Duntisbourne Grove, Norcote Farm and St Augustine's Farm South may be early to middle Neolithic. Single sherds of early Neolithic pottery were also recovered from St Augustine's Lane and Court Farm.

The pre-Beaker late Neolithic (*c.* 2900–2250 BC) seems to have been a time of considerable social change, as the causewayed enclosures and long cairns which had characterised the latter part of the fourth millennium had largely been abandoned before the end of the 4th millennium BC. This phase of the Neolithic is characterised by the use of a new style of pottery known as Grooved Ware and by new monument forms such as henges, hengiform ring ditches and timber and stone circles. The evidence for activity of this period is very limited in the region generally, and on the sites excavated in the course of the road scheme, the only possible evidence was in the form of lithic artefacts. At Lechlade a number of finds of Grooved Ware have been made, while a hengiform ring ditch near the cursus may also date to this phase (Darvill 1987, 71; Barclay in prep. b).

Settlement sites of Neolithic date as defined by groups of pits and postholes are comparatively rare in the region (Darvill 1987). In general pit digging is perhaps more common in the mid-late Neolithic and early Bronze Age. Consequently, the series of early Neolithic pits found at Duntisbourne Grove and the Beaker pits from Trinity Farm represent significant discoveries.

In the following section each of the sites which produced Neolithic material will be discussed in greater detail, and where possible, will follow the chronological sequence outlined above. In addition, a number of later sites produced residual finds details of which can be found in the specialist reports below (see Chapter 7).

#### *Birdlip Quarry*

A considerable number of small flint flakes were recovered from the sieving of two contexts; 81, one of a number of fills in a Roman period corn dryer (see Chapter 4 below), and 89, the fill of an oval-shaped shallow pit (88), both found in the northern part of the site (Fig. 2.2). Indeterminate prehistoric pottery sherds were recovered from fill 89, and also from a Roman occupation layer, 253. Small numbers of flints were recovered from a large number of other Roman contexts (Fig. 7.4.25–7). A number of other possible pits were found in the vicinity of pit 88, but none contained any artefacts. A summary of Neolithic/early Bronze Age pit contents appears in Table 2.2.

Most of the flint flakes were small and broad, though there were smaller amounts of blade-like material. The material had been produced using a combination of hard and soft hammers; a fragment of a flint hammerstone was recovered from context 81. A small blade core, a blade core fragment, part of a core tablet and a leaf-shaped arrowhead attest to earlier Neolithic activity on the site, however, the presence of broad flakes, multi-platformed flake cores and a steeply flaked scraper would appear to suggest a later Neolithic date for some of the material that was recovered. Though much of the material was derived

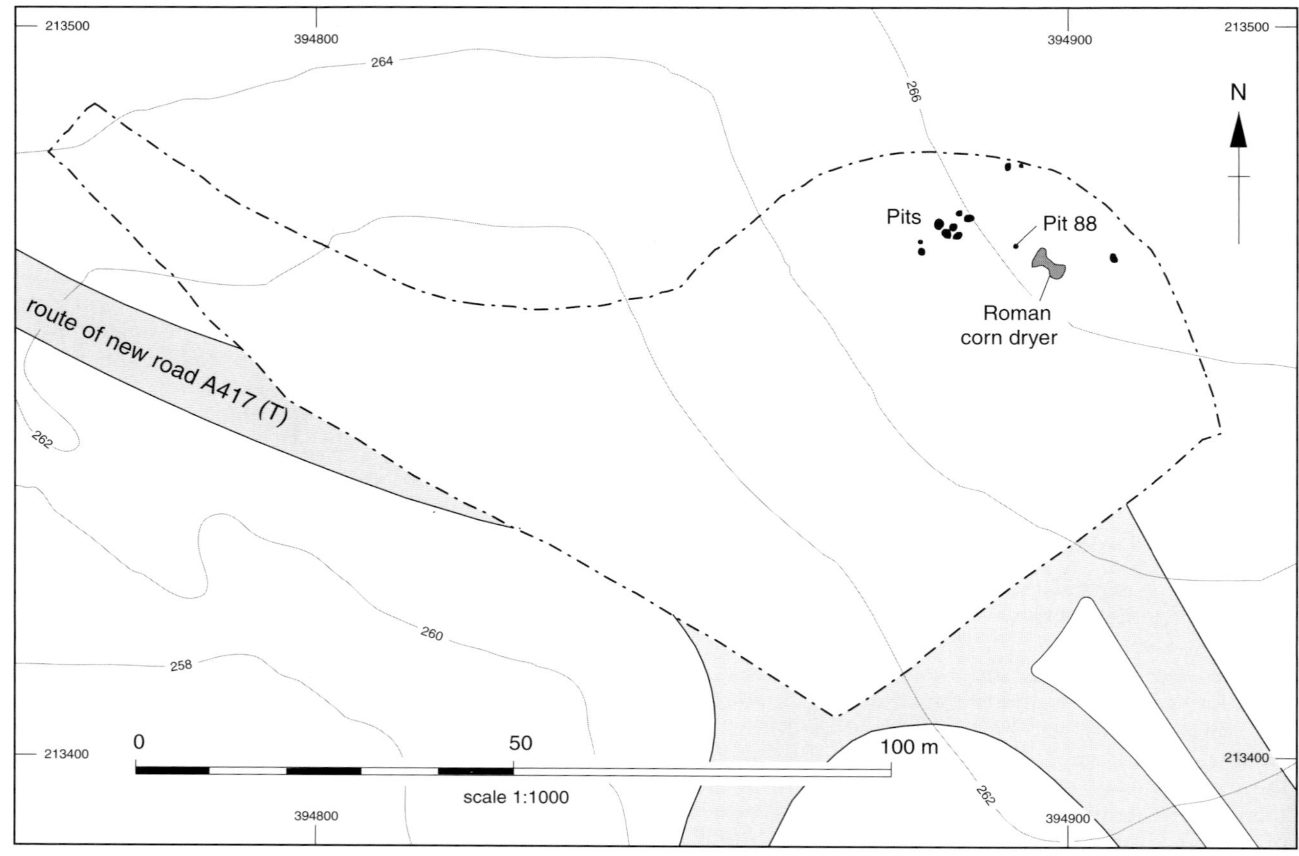


*Figure 2.2 Birdlip Quarry, Neolithic features.*

from disturbed contexts, the northern part of the Birdlip Quarry site had clearly been a focus of human activity for much of the Neolithic period.

### Hare Bushes North

The presence of a Neolithic/early Bronze Age flint scatter previously noted in the topsoil suggested that earlier prehistoric features might be present.

Due to the presence of an overhead cable the site of Hare Bushes North was divided into two areas; Area 1, a trapezoidal area *c.* 38 x 80 m and to the south, Area 2, a lozenge shaped area *c.* 15 x 50 m. Removal of the topsoil revealed a pattern of widely scattered features in both excavation areas (Fig. 2.3). Upon closer investigation the majority proved to be either periglacial in origin or tree-throw holes.

The only feature of interest in Area 1 was a tree-throw hole (1011) (Fig. 2.4) which contained nine worked flints (Fig. 7.4.28–9), including four serrated flakes, and two fragments of a pebble hammer (Fig. 7.41.679). Pebble hammers have been found in assemblages ranging in date from the Mesolithic through to the Bronze Age. The flint assemblage from the whole site consisted of 17 pieces, including flakes, serrated flakes and a flake core. A later Neolithic date is likely though an early Bronze Age date would also be possible. The presence of the pebble hammer fragments and the four serrated flakes may perhaps indicate a structured deposit of some significance. Serrated flakes have a date range from the Mesolithic to the early Bronze Age.

It should be remembered that the position and orientation of the road corridor dictated the location of both Areas 1 and 2 and hence the location of the main density of the surface flint scatter remains unexcavated to the west. The excavated area may be on the periphery of any early prehistoric activity.

Four features located at this site may well be of prehistoric date. Unfortunately, no datable artefacts were recovered from either a roughly circular pit (1005), located towards the southern edge of Area 1 of the excavation, or a possible posthole (1013), located in the south-eastern corner (Fig. 2.4). Similarly, no dating evidence was recovered from 1019, a circular pit with an irregular profile and 1025, a sub-circular pit, both located in the south-western part of Area 2.

### Duntisbourne Grove (Table 2.1)

The excavation at Duntisbourne Grove was designed to investigate a rectilinear cropmark identified on aerial photographs (Fig. 3.41). Evaluation of the feature in 1990 interpreted the cropmark as a middle-late Iron

*Table 2.1 Summary of Neolithic/early Bronze Age pit contents*

| Site | Context | Contents |
|---|---|---|
| Early-middle Neolithic | | |
| Birdlip Quarry | Pit 88 | Worked flint, pottery (indeterminate date) |
| Duntisbourne Grove | Pit 62 | Worked flint, early Neolithic pottery, charcoal |
| | Pit 94 | Worked flint, late Neolithic pottery, charcoal, fired clay, hazelnut shells, saddle quern rubber fragments, burnt animal bone |
| | Pit 142 | Worked flint, charcoal, fired clay, hazelnut shells |
| | Pit 144 | Worked flint |
| | Pit 182 | Worked flint, charcoal |
| Late Neolithic/early Bronze Age | | |
| Trinity Farm | Pit 8 | Worked flint, Beaker pottery, hazelnut shells, burnt limestone |
| | Pit 10 | Worked flint, Beaker pottery, hazelnut shells, burnt limestone |
| | Pit 12 | Worked flint, Beaker pottery |

Age enclosure, which had been cut by later Romano-British quarrying activity. Consequently, most of the archaeology at Duntisbourne Grove is discussed in Chapters 3 and 4. However, south of the enclosure in the south-west corner of the site, lay a small group of shallow prehistoric features (Fig. 2.5–6). At first they were obscured by the density of natural features in this area, but intensive cleaning highlighted a number of areas with a greyer soil which, on investigation, filled various pits and postholes.

The features seemed to be of two main types; pits containing stony fills which produced few or no finds (type 1), and pits which were rich in prehistoric artefacts and contained varying amounts of charcoal or other burnt deposits (type 2) (see Fig. 2.7). The prehistoric artefacts consisted largely of flint, dating predominantly to the Neolithic period, and sherds of contemporary pottery. The type 1 pits are, however, of uncertain date and need not be associated with the Neolithic activity. The largely stony fills could indicate a natural origin.

### *Type 1 pits*

Pit 223 was located over 15 m to the east of 182 (Fig. 2.6), but contained a stony fill similar in character to the primary fill of pit 182 and to that seen in pits 243 and 241 (Fig. 2.7). Though no finds were recovered from the associated fill (224), pit 223 may have originally formed part of the group of prehistoric features found in the south-western portion of the excavated area. The pit was truncated on its eastern side by the large Iron Age enclosure ditch 8.

Pit 241 was located 0.50 m to the south-west of 243 (Fig. 2.6) and, like the former, contained a stony fill which incorporated no dating evidence (Fig. 2.7). Despite the lack of comparable finds, the location of pit 241 strongly suggests that it was associated with the other prehistoric features in the vicinity.

Pit 243 was the easternmost feature in the group (Fig. 2.6). It was roughly circular and contained a single very stony silt clay fill (Fig. 2.7). Though located in the same area as the artefact-rich pits no finds were recovered from this feature. Feature 243 was unusual in that it seemed to be associated with an arc of five postholes (196, 194, 261, 264 and 217) arranged fairly evenly at a distance of 0.15–0.25 m around its west and south-western edge. No dating evidence was recovered from any of the postholes and their original function remains enigmatic.

### *Type 2 pits*

Pit 62, located 0.70 m to the north-east of pit 142 (Fig. 2.6), was the smallest of the prehistoric pits excavated in the south-western part of the site. It was approximately circular in shape and like pit 142 had been cut into an underlying periglacial feature. The primary fill (84) was completely sterile and may even have been part of the periglacial deposit (Fig. 2.7). The upper fill (63), however, contained charcoal flecks, numerous pieces of flint and five sherds from an earlier Neolithic bowl (Fig. 7.6.36).

Pit 94 located approximately 1 m west of pit 241 was another slightly larger circular pit (Fig. 2.6), which contained a sequence of three fills (Fig. 2.7). The primary deposit (113) consisted of a heavily burnt clay silt mixed with large quantities of charcoal and burnt animal bone. It also contained numerous flint flakes, including a crested flake (Fig. 7.5.35), a small number of flint tools including two leaf arrowhead tips (Fig. 7.5.30), two later Neolithic pottery sherds and four fragments of fired clay. The sherds are Peterborough Ware, possibly of the Fengate substyle (Fig. 7.6.37). This material presumably relates to domestic activity in the vicinity of pit 94, as there were no signs of burning on the sides or base of the feature. The hazelnut shells from this fill have provided an earlier Neolithic radiocarbon date of 3654–3370 cal BC (95% confidence) (4761±57 BP; NZA-8671, R24151/15). This is supported by the flintwork, but the pottery would seem to be slightly later in date.

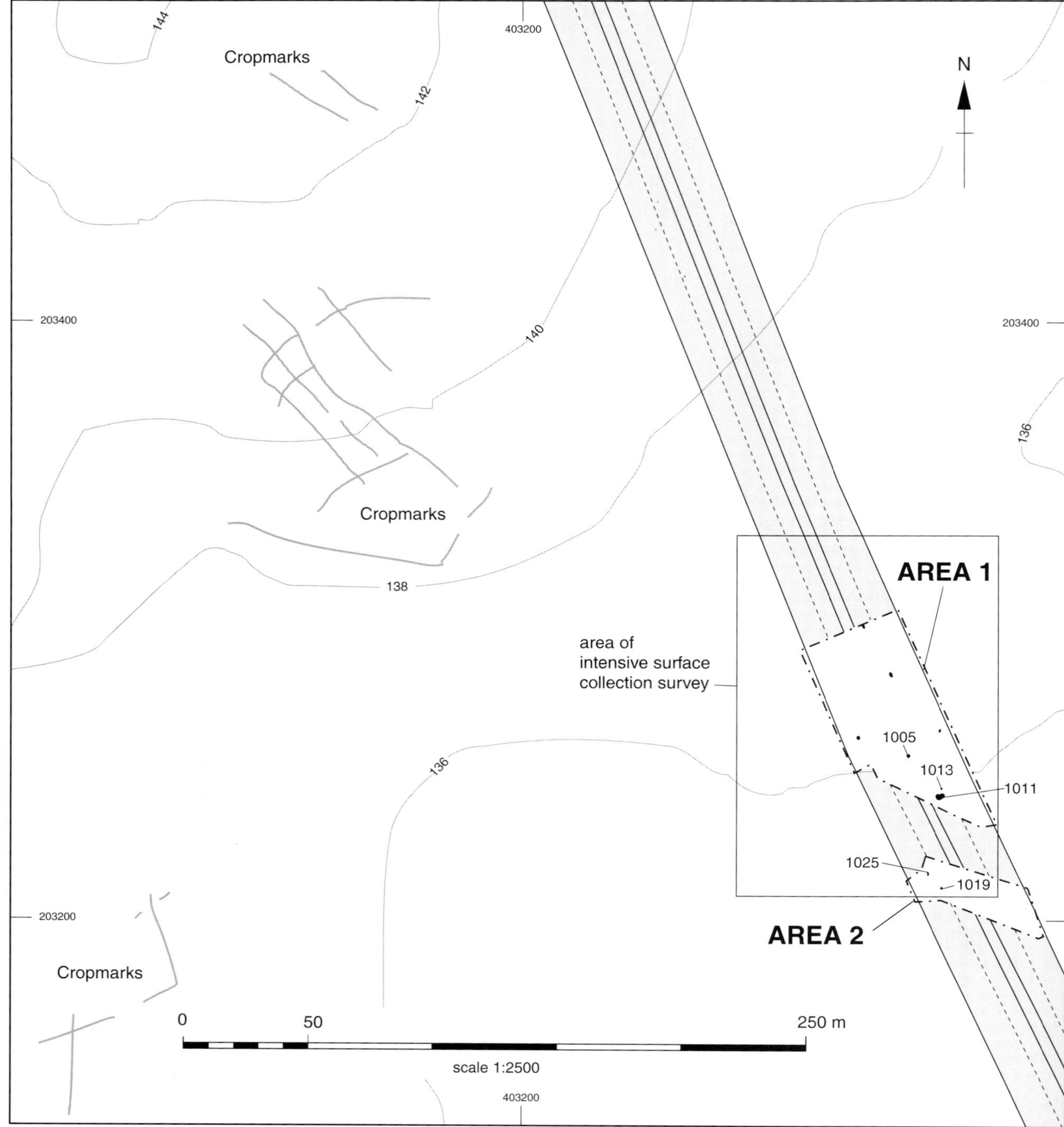


*Figure 2.3 Hare Bushes North, location of trenches.*

The secondary and tertiary fills (111 and 95) were much cleaner and quite different in character. Both deposits contained reasonably large quantities of flint debitage, but had very few natural inclusions. A crude chisel arrowhead (Fig. 7.5.31) of later Neolithic date was recovered from fill 95. Other signs of domestic activity included occasional flecks of charcoal in both deposits and two fragments of saddle quern rubbers made from May Hill sandstone from context 111 (Fig. 7.41.680–681).

Pit 142 was located less than a metre to the north-east of pit 94 (Fig. 2.6). This feature also contained a sequence of three fills (Fig. 2.7) and was cut by linear pit 144 (see below). The primary fill (191) was completely sterile, representing gradual erosion of the periglacial feature into which the pit had been cut. The secondary and tertiary fills (168 and 143) contained relatively large quantities of flint flakes, including four serrated flakes (Fig. 7.5.32–4), two from each fill. Fill 168 also contained charcoal flecks and

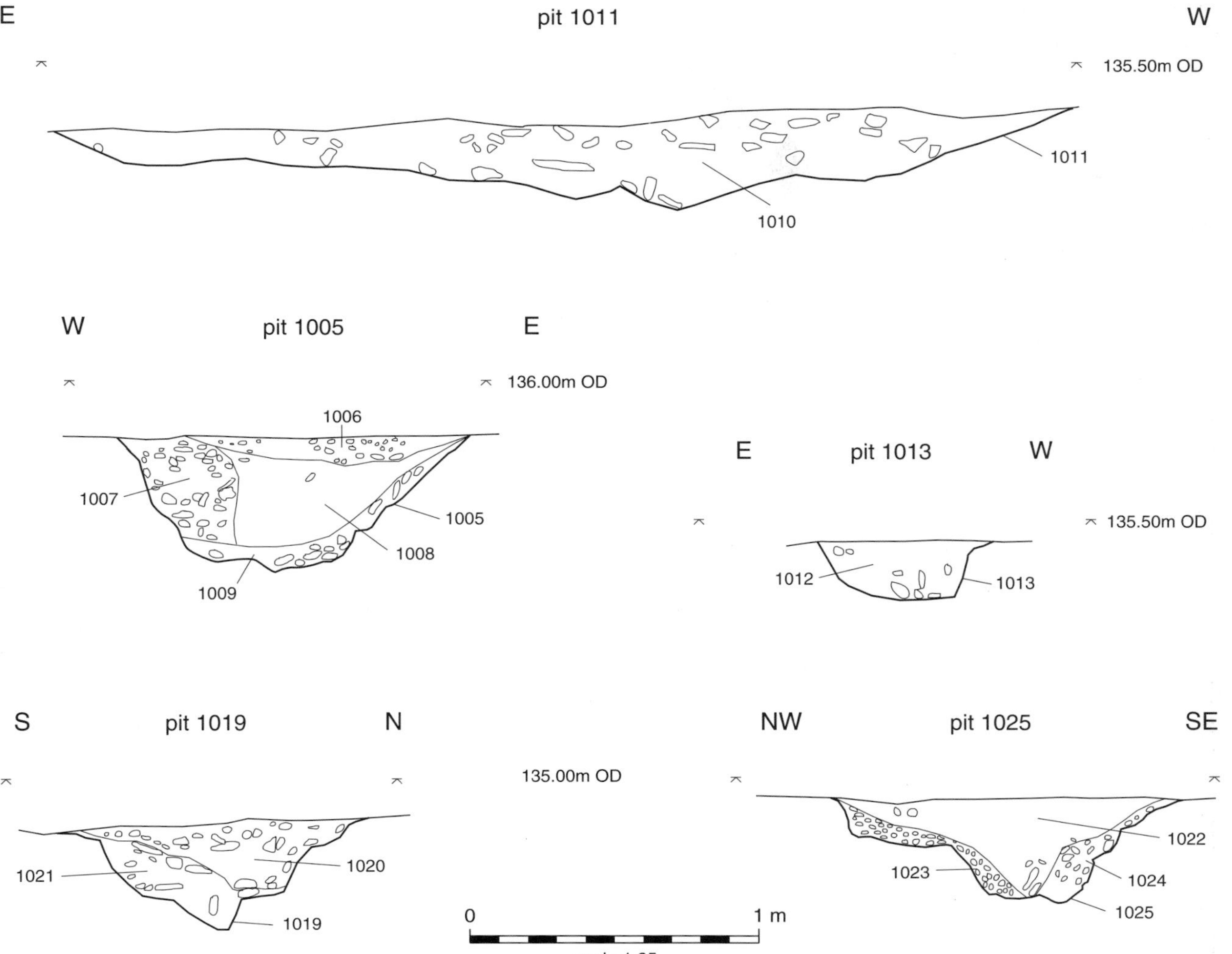


*Figure 2.4 Hare Bushes North, sections.*

156 fragments of burnt clay. Hazelnut shells from 168 have provided an earlier Neolithic radiocarbon date of 3641–3354 cal BC (95% confidence) (4717±60 BP; NZA-8672, R24151/16), a date broadly in accordance with the associated lithics.

Pit 144 was located less than a metre to the north-west of pit 62 and in contrast to the rest of the prehistoric features was elongated in plan rather than circular/oval (Fig. 2.6). This difference in plan does not seem to have corresponded to any major difference in function, as both fills were similar to those in pit 144 (Fig. 2.7). They also contained flintwork of a broadly Neolithic date similar to that seen in pits 94, 142 and 62. The only retouched piece was a burnt and broken serrated flake, however, the feature was obviously later in the chronological sequence of pits, as it truncated both pits 142 and 182 (see below).

Pit 182 was initially though to be part of pit 144 mentioned above. However, subsequent excavation revealed that 182 was a small circular pit which had been truncated by pit 144 (Fig. 2.6). The primary fill (227) was stony and devoid of finds, but a few flints were recovered from a secondary silty clay deposit (183), which also contained flecks of charcoal (Fig. 2.7).

*Discussion*

Flint artefacts from a number of the pits, including leaf arrowheads, blades, a partly discoidal flake core, a possible tortoise core, serrated flakes and an almost complete crude chisel arrowhead, indicate a date range from the earlier to the later Neolithic for these features. Radiocarbon dates indicate an earlier Neolithic date for pits 94 and 142, a date which is generally supported by the character of the lithics from the same fill. The latter pit also contained earlier Neolithic bowl pottery. Pit 94 is of interest, however, as the primary fill also contained sherds of middle

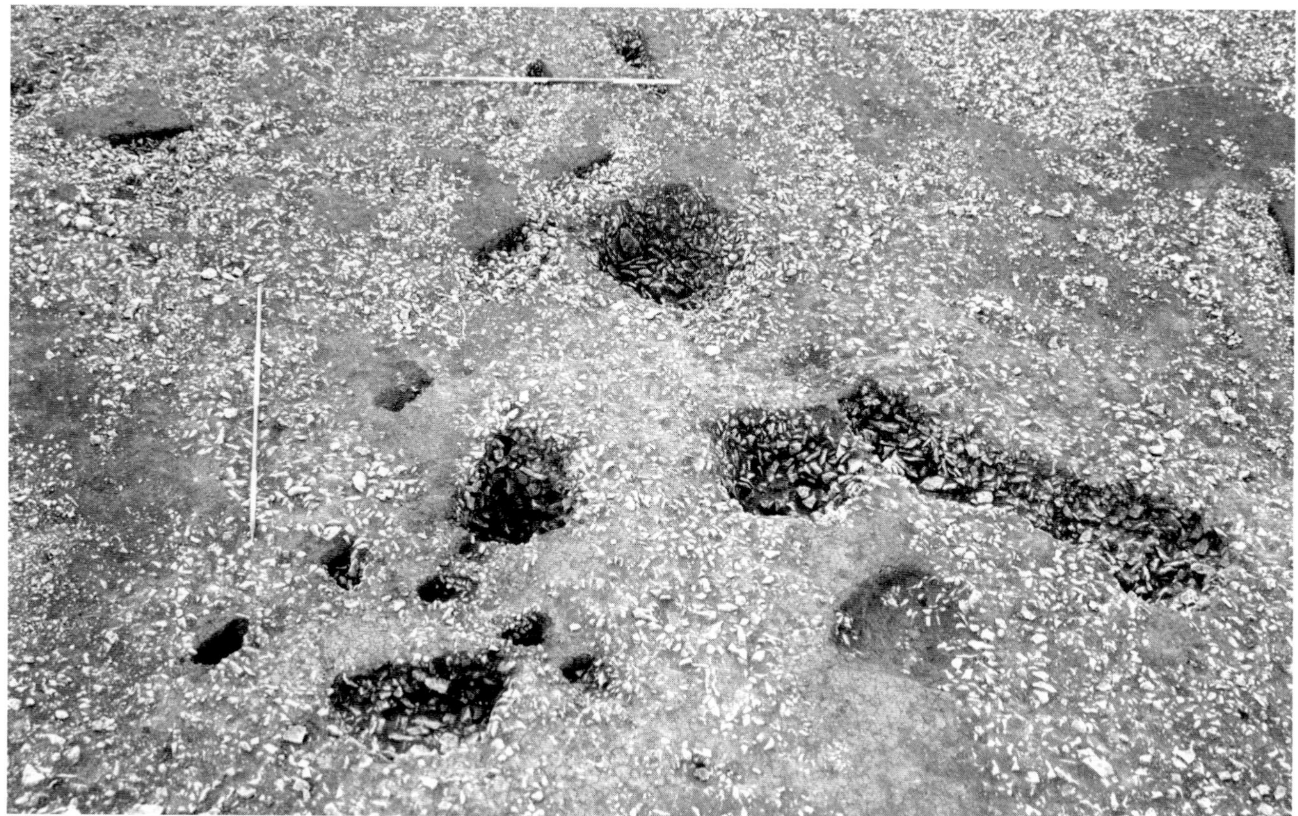

*Plate 2.1 Duntisbourne Grove, group of Neolithic pits. looking south-west.*

Neolithic Peterborough Ware, and the upper fills some lithics which are typical of the later Neolithic, namely the chisel arrowhead and the tortoise core. This would suggest that the pit had been open for a considerable length of time.

Analysis of the soil from the primary fills of pits 94 and 142 indicated the presence of occasional grains of *Triticum* sp. (wheat) and *Hordeum* sp. (barley). A glume base of *T. spelta* found in the uppermost fill of pit 142 (context 143) indicates that this layer contains some later contamination, as *T. spelta* is not known prior to the Bronze Age. A single stone of *Crataegus* sp. (hawthorn) was also identified, together with numerous hazelnut shell fragments. The *Crataegus* sp. stone may have been introduced with firewood, while the latter are likely to represent edible resources collected in the wild. Three samples also contained identifiable charcoal including Pomoideae (hawthorn etc.). Such an assemblage is typical of the Neolithic, where cereal cultivation is represented but plays a minor role in the diet compared to collected wild plant resources (Moffett *et al.* 1989; Thomas 1991, 20).

The original function of these pits remains unclear, but the association of worked flint, pottery, saddle quern rubbers, fired clay and burnt plant remains strongly suggests the presence of domestic activity in the vicinity. Thomas has suggested, however, that many of the isolated pits which have been interpreted as the remnants of Neolithic settlements may in fact have had ritual and emotive, rather than functional, origins (1991, 56–78). In his schema the Neolithic population was relatively mobile and did not continuously inhabit specific locales. By intentional burial of materials redolent of domestic contexts, charcoal, bones, pottery etc., Neolithic peoples were concept-ually 'fixing' the notion of domesticity and social order on the largely untamed landscape. If this were the case, then the earlier Neolithic date for some of the pits combined with the presence of some later Neolithic pottery and flintwork is interesting; it suggests that the concept of exerting a cultural influence over nature (by deliberate deposition of items charged with domestic affinity) may have been of long lasting importance in Neolithic society. It is possible that the arc of postholes around pit 243 may also be connected with this activity.

Though apparently restricted to the south-western part of the excavation area, the possibility remains that other shallow features of a similar date may have been removed from other parts of the site by later activity. Most of the pits were clustered together in apparent isolation just to the south of the large Iron Age enclosure ditch. Perhaps upcast from this ditch formed a protective layer over these features. Significantly, the natural limestone does seem to change at just this point; north of the enclosure ditch it is angular and frost shattered, whereas to the south (i.e. where the pits are located) the natural is much more rounded as if it had been protected from the frost.

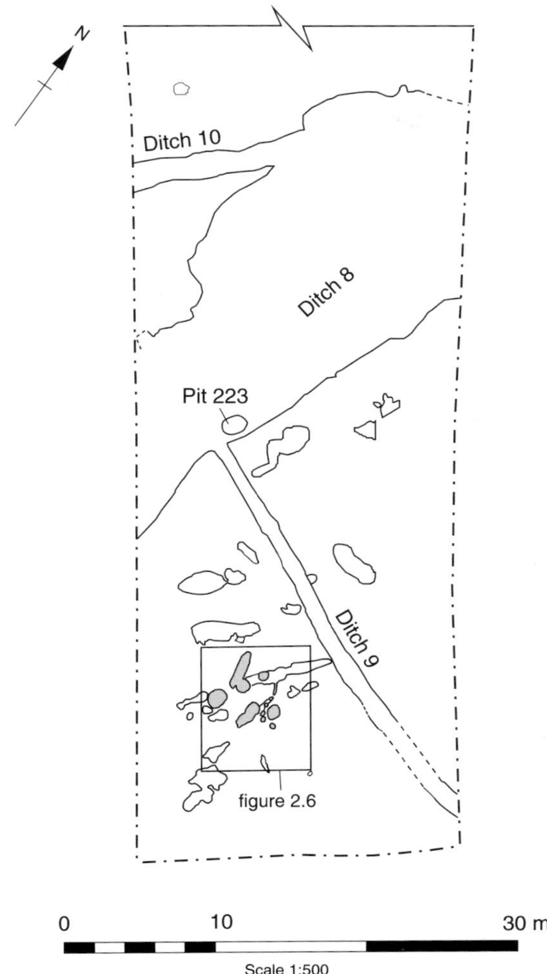


*Figure 2.5 Duntisbourne Grove, Neolithic pits: location in relation to late Iron Age ditches.*

### Middle Duntisbourne

A total of 20 flints was recovered from the excavation at Middle Duntisbourne. All were derived from contexts thought to date to the late Iron Age/early Roman period (see below Chapter 3, Fig. 3.35), but typologically most of the material relates to the Neolithic period. One of the flints, an unfinished leaf arrowhead (Fig. 7.3.22), is typical of the early Neolithic.

### Norcote Farm

The Stage 2 assessment had identified a possible flint scatter in the Norcote Farm area. This scatter contained material ranging in date from the Mesolithic to the Bronze Age. However, only 19 flints were recovered from 40 test pits targeted on this putative scatter, and many of the remaining 20 flints from the site were found in either medieval/post-medieval plough furrows, or were derived from the remnant of an earlier ploughsoil seen at the southern end of the site. This ploughsoil probably dates to the Roman period (Figs 3.31–2). The assemblage comprised a mixture of material of likely Neolithic date, including narrow and broad flakes, a blade core fragment and a serrated flake. A fragment of a small, keeled flake core, made of grey chert, formed part of the assemblage. It is similar in appearance to Portland Chert and may, therefore, have been imported from the south coast. Similar cherts, however, have been found in the Pebble Beds and other Tertiary deposits in central southern England (Holgate 1988, 64). These deposits extend into parts of the Thames catchment, so it is possible the chert had not been brought such a great distance.

A substantial ditch (235/239) was oriented north-south across the site. Although no dating evidence was recovered from its fills, its sinuous nature and division into two segments was reminiscent of the probable Iron Age and indeterminate prehistoric ditches found at St Augustine's Farm South and St Augustine's Lane. There was a single break in the ditch towards its southern end. The section north of the break (235) was up to 2 m wide and 0.8 m deep with a regular profile. The section running south after the break (239) was shallower, at 0.47 m deep, and also narrowed to the south to 0.76 m. The ditch contained two or three silty clay fills, all devoid of finds.

### St Augustine's Farm South

A total of 20 flints was recovered from the excavation at St Augustine's Farm South. The material consisted mostly of broad flakes of probable Neolithic date, but was derived from a variety of features which date to later periods (Figs 3.2–3). The original focus of this

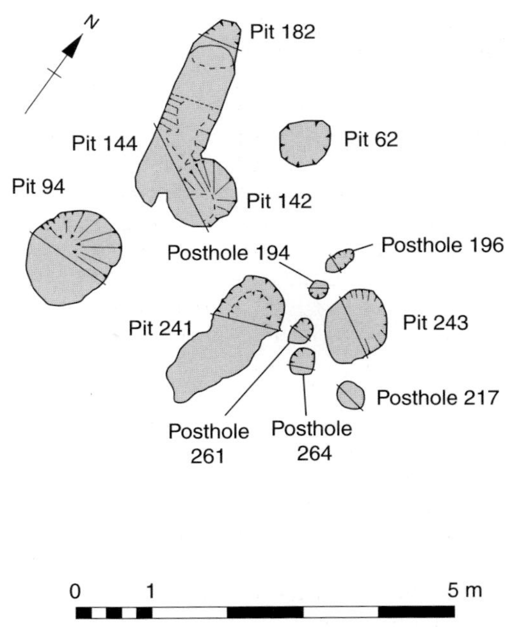


*Figure 2.6 Duntisbourne Grove, plan of Neolithic pits.*

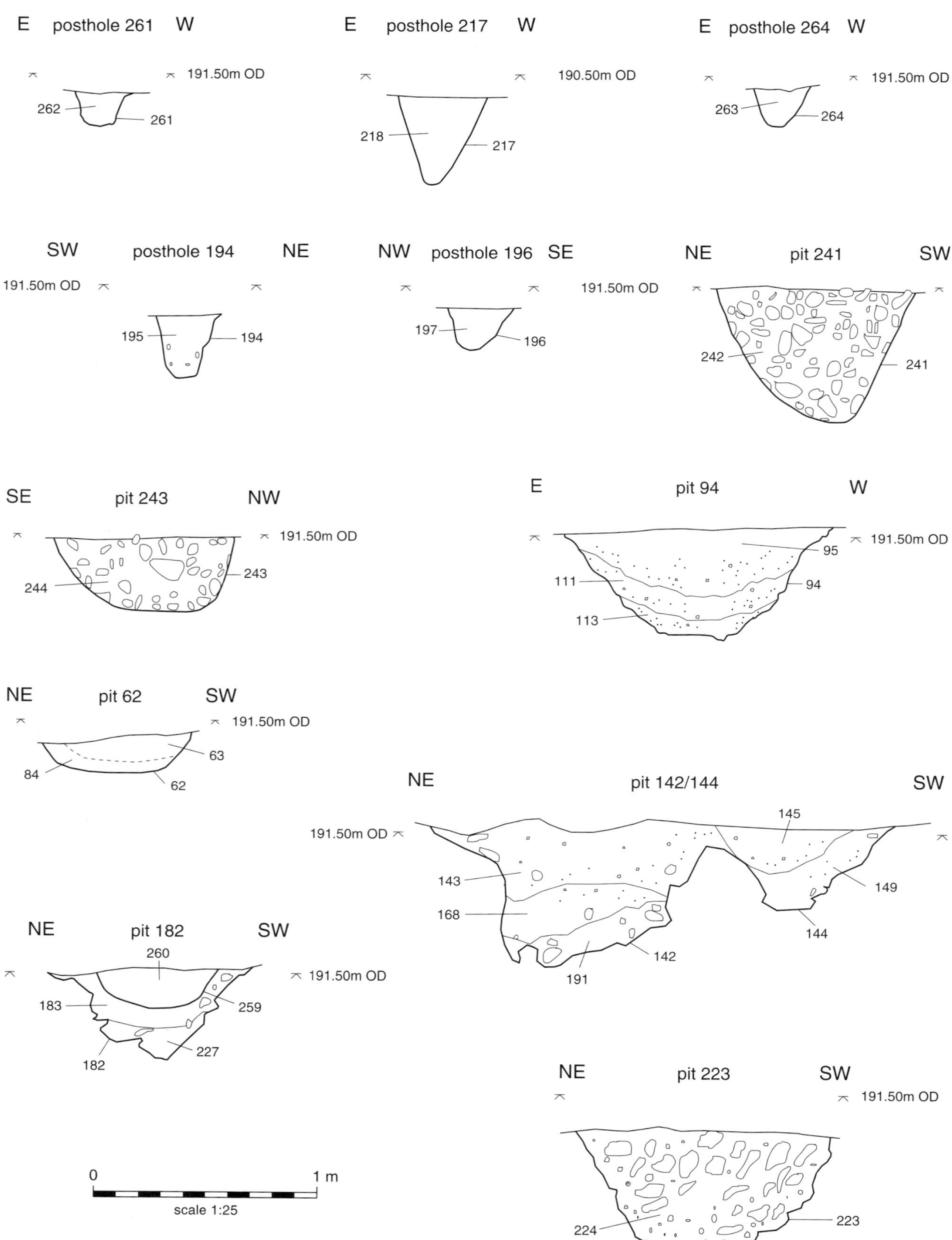


*Figure 2.7 Duntisbourne Grove, sections through pits and postholes.*

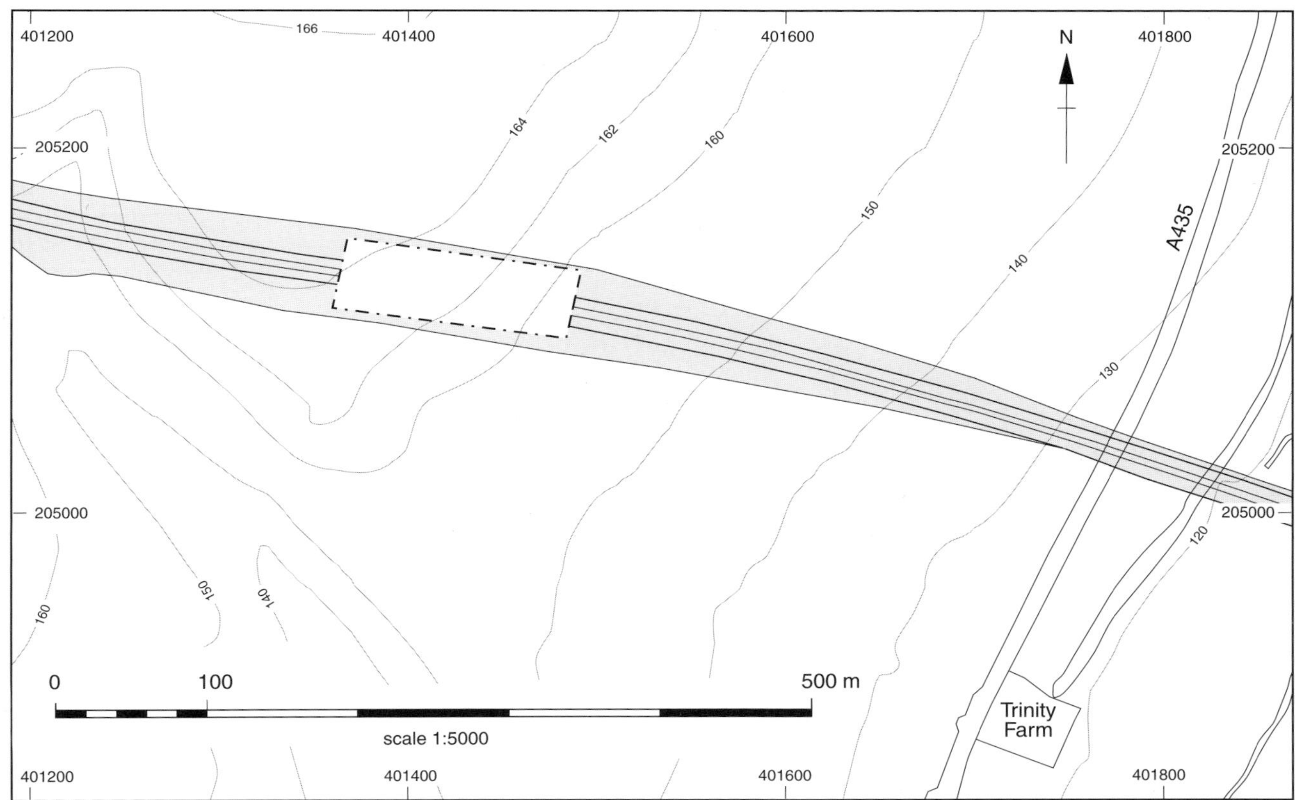


*Figure 2.8 Trinity Farm, location of excavation area.*

Neolithic activity has either been destroyed by later activity or was located outside the excavation boundary. The presence of Neolithic activity in the vicinity is also attested by an early Neolithic sherd found in the fill of one of the Iron Age segmented ditch sections (context 3165, ditch 3123, segment 3114; see Barclay, Chapter 7). A second sherd from this context may also be early Neolithic.

### *Court Farm*

A residual early Neolithic sherd was recovered from Court Farm.

## The late Neolithic/early Bronze Age period

Beaker pottery and associated flintwork dating to the late Neolithic/early Bronze Age (*c.* 2500-1700 BC) was found on four sites on the road scheme: Trinity Farm, Preston Enclosure, St Augustine's Lane and Court Farm. A large number of sherds were recovered from Trinity Farm, while only two sherds were found at Preston Enclosure, with only single sherds from St Augustine's Lane and Court Farm. The series of pits from Trinity Farm, which contained an important group of stylistically 'early' Beaker pottery, was the most significant of these discoveries. The sherds from the other sites appear to be residual. The contiguous ring ditches at St Augustine's Farm South represent the ploughed-out remains of round barrows, and date to the early Bronze Age period (*c.* 2000–1700 BC).

### *Trinity Farm*

Three heavily truncated pits (8, 10 and 12) containing struck flint and 164 Beaker sherds were located in the north-east corner of the Trinity Farm excavation area (Fig. 2.8). The pits were arranged in a linear fashion on a north-north-west – south-south-east alignment (Fig. 2.9). It is possible that some of the sherds from separate pit fills derive from the same vessels. In addition, a tree-throw hole (context 28) found to the south-west of this group also contained a Beaker sherd. No other prehistoric features were encountered within the trench but it remains possible that other related features may have existed beyond the edge of the excavation area.

#### *Pit 8*

Pit 8 was the most southerly of the three pits. Roughly circular in plan, it measured 0.86 m in diameter, had a maximum depth of 0.18 m and contained a single dark brown clay silt fill (7) (Fig. 2.10). The pit was totally excavated, producing 29 sherds of Beaker pottery (Fig. 7.6.38–42), flint scrapers, cores and flakes (Fig. 7.1–2: 12–5), and fragments of burnt limestone. A number of the pottery sherds were decorated with

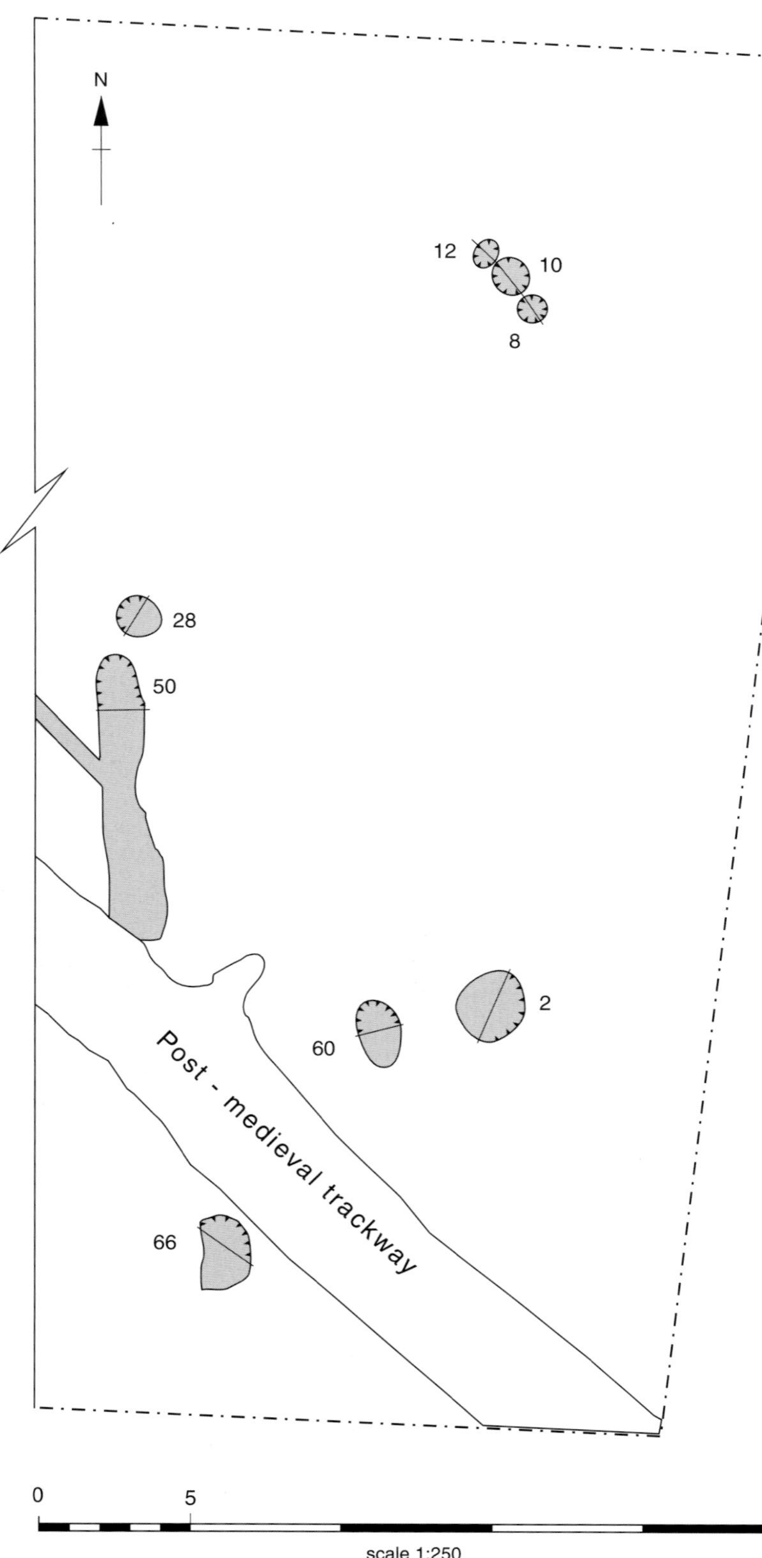


*Figure 2.9 Trinity Farm, plan of Beaker pits and other features.*

comb and finger-nail decoration characteristic of the Wessex/Middle Rhine style dating to the early Beaker period. Hazelnut shells from the fill of this pit were radiocarbon dated to 2476–2142 cal BC (95% confidence) (3876±57 BP; NZA-8673, R24151/17), a date which would support that provided by the pottery.

*Pit 10*

This was the central pit and was slightly larger and a little deeper than the other two, measuring 1.20 m in diameter, with a maximum depth of 0.22 m (Fig. 2.10). The single associated fill (9) was a dark brown clay silt which contained 122 sherds of Beaker pottery (Fig. 7.6.43–9), pieces of burnt limestone and ten flint scrapers (Fig. 7.1.1–5, 7.1.7–11, 7.2.16–17), including a thumbnail scraper, a type characteristic of the Beaker period. Hazelnut shells from the pit fill were radiocarbon dated to 2462–2047 cal BC (95% confidence) (3836±58 BP; NZA-8674, R24151/18), a date which would support that provided by the pottery.

*Pit 12*

The northernmost feature, pit 12, was the smallest of the three; measuring 0.60 m in diameter and 0.06 m in depth (Fig. 2.10). Thirteen sherds of Beaker pottery (Fig. 7.6:50–2) were recovered from the single associated clay silt fill (11), together with a small number of flint flakes and a scraper (Fig. 7.1.6).

*Tree-throw hole 28*

A roughly circular tree-throw hole (28), 1.4 m in diameter and 0.26 m deep, was discovered approximately 15 m to the south-west of pit 8 (Fig. 2.10). A single sherd of Beaker pottery was found on the surface of its single clayey silt fill (27).

*Discussion*

Beaker domestic assemblages are rare in Gloucestershire (Ellison 1984, 115; Darvill 1987, 81–8). The fact that the Trinity Farm pits contain pottery of what can be described as early within the Beaker sequence, which is relatively unusual in southern England compared to the more numerous assemblages of coarser domestic ware, increases the importance of this discovery. Comparable assemblages of fine vessels are recorded from Roughground Farm, Lechlade (Darvill 1993) and the Marlborough Downs area (Cleal 1992). Part of a fine beaker was also found at Crickley Hill (Dixon 1971, fig. 8.15), however, the only vessel with typological affinities with the

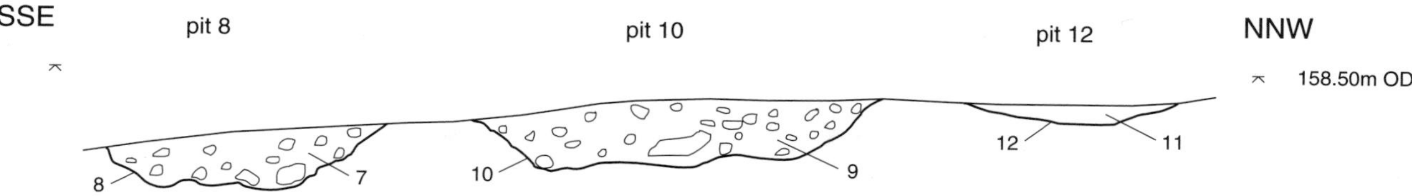


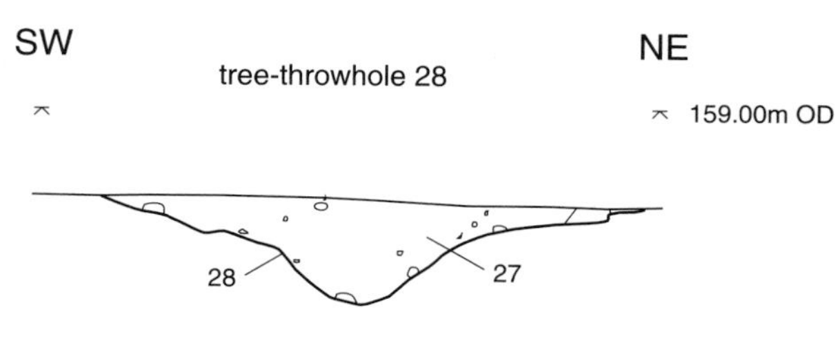


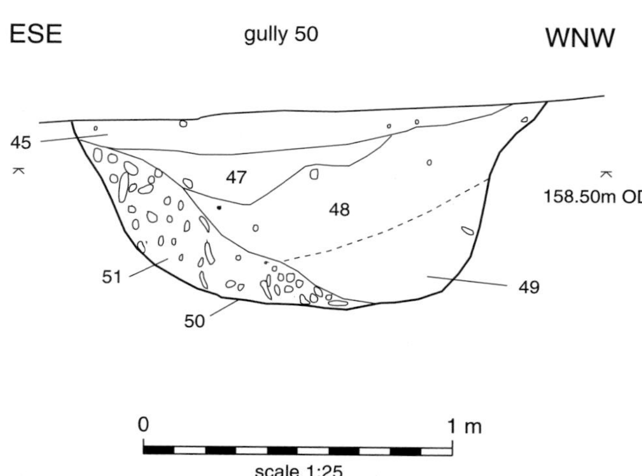


*Figure 2.10 Trinity Farm, sections.*

material from Trinity Farm is a probable Wessex/ Middle Rhine funerary beaker from Sale's Lot, Withington (O'Neil 1966).

As material of this date is scarce in the region extensive samples were taken from all the pits for environmental remains. The samples all contained large numbers of nut shell fragments of *Corylus avellana* (hazel), while pit 10 also contained occasional grains of *Hordeum* sp. (barley) and a spikelet fork of *Triticum* sp. (wheat). Charcoal identified as *Quercus* sp. (oak), *Corylus* (hazel) and Pomoideae (hawthorn etc.) was also recovered from pit 10. Such assemblages are typical for settlement sites of late Neolithic/early Bronze Age date.

Mollusc samples taken from the pits provide additional insight into environmental conditions in the vicinity of the later Neolithic/early Bronze Age features. One pit contained both open-country (*Pupilla muscorum* and *Vallonia excentrica*) and shade-loving species (*Discus rotundatus* and *Oxychilus cellarius*), suggesting a relatively open landscape with some scrub, though the latter could represent a rock-rubble element in the habitat. The other two pits contained little apart from the burrowing species *Cecilioides acicula*.

It is difficult to assess the extent to which the land around Trinity Farm was actively cultivated. No crop processing remains were discovered at the site and the high percentage of hazelnut fragments demonstrates the continued importance of gathered wild food in the late Neolithic/early Bronze Age diet. No bones were recovered from any of the pits, thus precluding any discussion of the role of animals in the economy of this period.

The pits at Trinity Farm are interesting in themselves, however. The overall size of the Beaker sherds from the pits was relatively small, which may indicate that the material was broken and collected in a midden-like deposit prior to deposition in the pit. The character of the lithics from the pits, particularly pit 10, is also worthy of note. Pit 10 contained ten scrapers, which represents a considerable quantity of retouched material for one pit deposit and suggests the deliberate selection of material for deposition. This, alongside the selection of possible midden material (Beaker sherds) for placing in the pits, would indicate some form of structured deposition. Comparable to this is pit 1260 from Roughground Farm, Lechlade, which also contained Beaker sherds and a quantity of retouched flintwork (Darvill 1993, 18). It is, therefore, difficult to speculate how representative of everyday domestic activity the material from these pits might be (cf. Thomas 1991, 56–78).

### St Augustine's Farm South

St Augustine's Farm South comprised three separate excavation areas; Area O, Area N(a) and Area N(b) (Fig. 2.11). Area O was approximately rectangular in shape, measuring 100 x 35 m. It was the southernmost of the three excavation areas and was purposely located to examine two contiguous ring ditches which lay in the path of the proposed road. Stripping of the topsoil revealed parts of two contiguous ring ditches in the north-western portion of the excavated area. Approximately half of both ring ditches lay within the excavation area so that only one junction between the two fell within it. Examination of this junction suggested that the northern ring ditch (3005) had been attached or joined onto the southern ring ditch (3012). The evaluation revealed that no upstanding barrow

*Plate 2.2 Cropmarks in the vicinity of St Augustine's Lane, with Preston Enclosure (middle left). Reproduced by permission of RCHME (ref. NMR 4637/41).*

earthworks had survived and that ploughsoil covered the natural subsoil.

*Southern ring ditch 3012*

This ring ditch had been investigated during the evaluation by excavating a single trench across its interior (Fig. 2.12). A sherd from a Collared Urn was discovered from the subsoil context 6 (see Barclay, Chapter 7 and Fig. 7.6.53) and could originally have come from a cremation deposit. Ring ditch 3012 had an internal diameter of *c.* 18 m (Fig. 2.12). Its excavation had clearly involved the exploitation of natural weaknesses in the bedrock, as it was not quite circular in plan. The ditch varied considerably in both width and depth around its circuit. The northern section was some 1.6 m at its widest point and reached a maximum depth of 0.56 m. The southern section in comparison measured 1.20 m across at its widest extent and was only 0.30 m deep (Fig. 2.13, 3018, section 43).

The ditch fills consisted of a primary eroded natural layer, followed by a stony deposit, which may represent partial collapse/subsidence of the covering mound, since removed by ploughing. The uppermost fills consisted of the largely stone-free silty clay soil seen in many of the features on the site. Unfortunately, no dating evidence was recovered from any of the sections excavated through ring ditch 3012. Only four flint flakes were recovered and these were not diagnostic of any particular period.

*Plate 2.3 Bronze Age ring ditches and sinuous Iron Age boundary ditches at St Augustine's Farm South and St Augustine's Lane. Reproduced by permission of RCHME (ref. NMR 15425/10).*

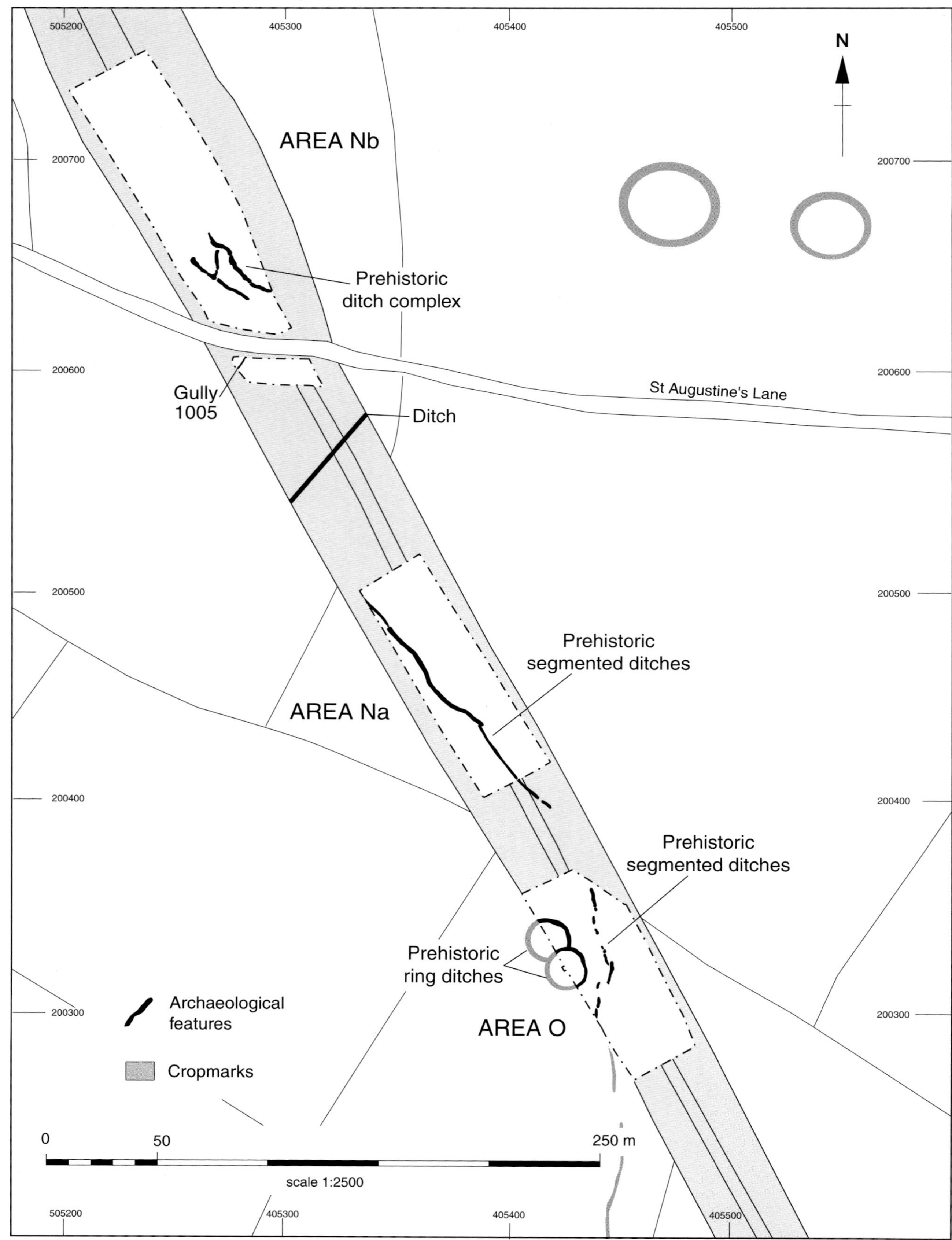


*Figure 2.11 St Augustine's Farm South and St Augustine's Lane, excavated features and cropmarks, all areas.*

*Plate 2.4 St Augustine's Farm South, segment 3097 through the northern ring ditch 3005, looking north-west.*

Stripping of the interior of the ring ditch revealed a single, nearly central cremation deposit (3109) and three small, circular features (3058, 3060 and 3062). The former was irregular and roughly triangular in plan, 0.85 x 0.74 m in extent and contained frequent pieces of oak charcoal and small fragments of burnt bone set within a dark, clay silt matrix (Fig. 2.13, section 64). No grave goods were recovered, and as the cut was very shallow, it is likely that most of the cremation and any associated grave goods could have been ploughed away. Three possible postholes, placed on an east-west alignment, were found in the south-east quadrant on the barrow's interior. All had irregular profiles and were located on the line of natural joints in the bedrock (Fig.2.13). It is uncertain whether they were real or natural features. No finds were recovered from them.

*Northern ring ditch 3005*

With an internal diameter of *c.* 15 m, the northern ring ditch was smaller than its southern counterpart (Fig. 2.12). Conversely, the ditch, which contained four or five fills, proved to be slightly more substantial with a maximum depth of 0.66 m (Fig. 2.13, section 44). The

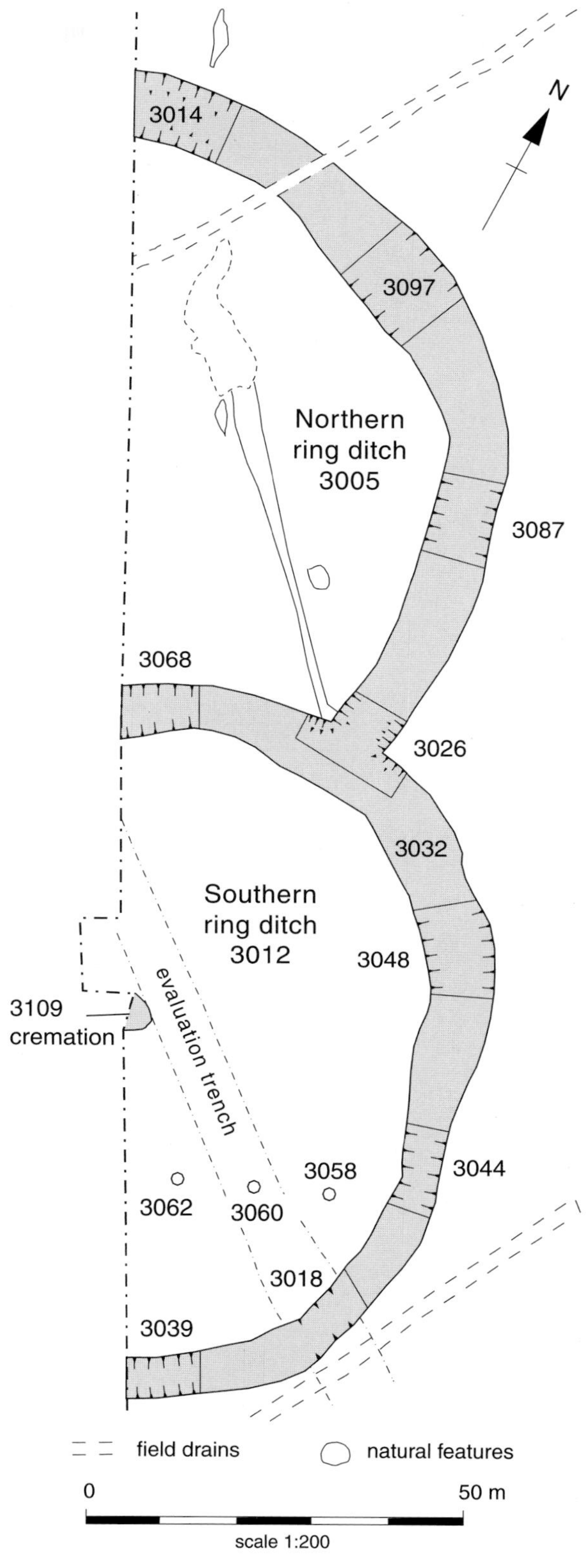


*Figure 2.12 St Augustine's Farm South, Area O, plan of Bronze Age ring ditches and internal features.*

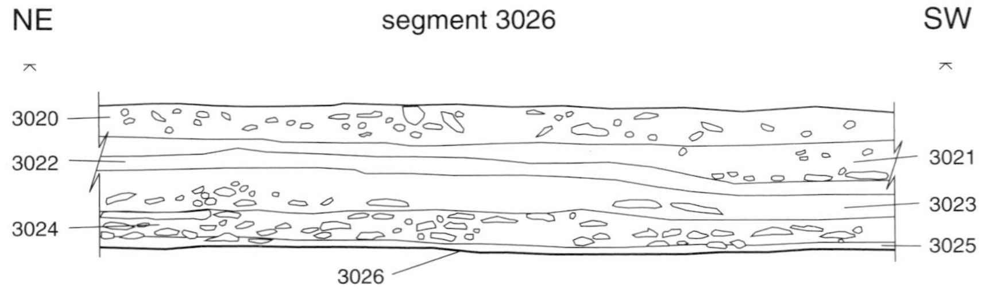


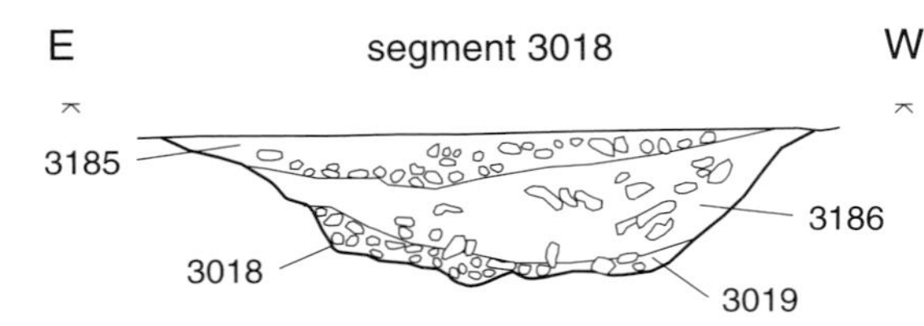


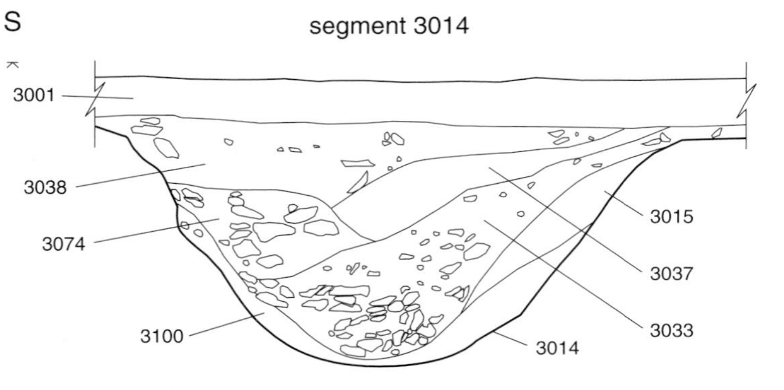

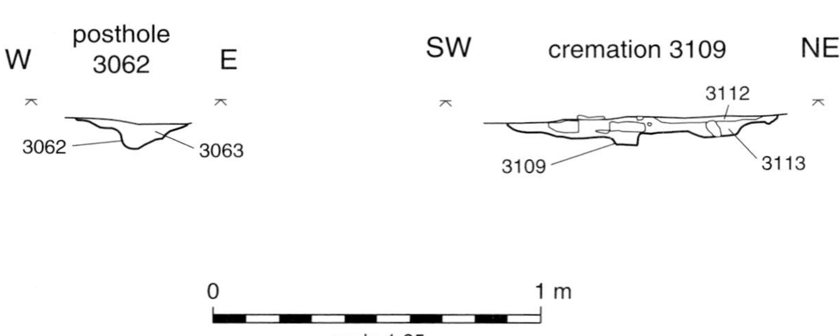


*Figure 2.13 St Augustine's Farm South, sections.*

sequence of ditch deposits was nearly identical to that seen in the southern ring ditch. A single small sherd from an early Bronze Age urn was recovered from the largely stone-free upper fills. Despite this sherd being redeposited, its manufacture is likely to be broadly contemporary with the construction and primary use of the monument. Ten pieces of flint were also recovered from the ditch fills, including a fragmentary flake core from the primary fill. The flint was not particularly diagnostic, though a broad Neolithic/early Bronze Age date would be appropriate. An early Bronze Age radiocarbon date of 1940–1644 cal BC (95% confidence) (3482±60 BP; NZA-8614, R24151/12) was obtained on bone from context 3094, the lowest fill of the ring ditch. This date is in accordance with the early Bronze Age date suggested by the monument form and the pottery sherd. No internal features were located apart from a deep natural feature, interpreted as a frost crack.

### *Discussion*

The two ring ditches appear to form part of a dispersed cemetery with at least two other barrows known from cropmarks (Fig. 2.11, NMR SP0500/6, 11). The ring ditches of many such barrows are known from the area of the road scheme, mostly from aerial photographs (see Leech 1977, maps 1–3; Darvill 1987, 95). The majority of ring ditches are thought to belong to early Bronze Age barrows, though it should be noted that some might be mid or late Neolithic (Kinnes 1979), while others could represent cremation enclosures belonging to the middle Bronze Age (Barclay *et al.* 1995). The area contains few large barrow cemeteries and instead is characterised by relatively small barrow clusters. No large barrow cemeteries like the ones that exist around the Oxford area of the Upper Thames or for that matter Lambourn on the Downs are known. In fact the small group of barrows from St Augustine's Lane is typical of the area. Contiguous barrows are rare within the Upper Thames valley, although a number are known from sites around Oxford. Sometimes they are found to form part of linear barrow groups, although others like the one under discussion

*Plate 2.5 St Augustine's Farm South, segment 3044 through the southern ring ditch 3012, looking south.*

here appear isolated. Their form may be related to so-called twin or multiple barrows, where a single ditch is found to enclose more than one mound or to multiple ditched barrows. As Bronze Age barrows exhibit great variety in shape and size there is no reason to see this barrow as being particularly unusual.

It is unfortunate that so little of the central deposit from the southern ring ditch remained, as this may have allowed further refinement of the date of this monument. It is likely, according to the stratigraphic evidence, that it predates the northern ring ditch, but it is uncertain by how much. Logically the partial ring ditch is attached to the complete one and therefore later, although this is not absolutely certainly the case since it would have been possible to have done it the other way round or to have dug both simultaneously. The fills indicate that both ditches were open and then filled in together. Despite the truncation of the cremation deposit, it is not unusual to find an unaccompanied cremation at the centre of a barrow in the Upper Thames Valley. The row of three postholes found within the interior of the same barrow, could be unrelated or of uncertain origin, but one possibility is that they belong to a pyre structure as similar arrangements have been found at other sites (Harden and Treweeks 1945, fig. 8).

### *Area N(b)*

### Gully 1005

Located immediately to the south of St Augustine's Lane and oriented north-east to south-west, gully 1005 was the only feature of archaeological significance which appeared in area N(b) (Fig. 2.11). The gully was extremely regular in appearance, *c.* 0.60 m wide and

*Plate 2.6 St Augustine's Farm South, segment 3039 through the southern ring ditch 3012, looking west.*

fairly shallow, surviving to a depth of some 0.20 m over most of its length, except in its centre section where it had been heavily truncated by a plough furrow. There was a suggestion that the gully had begun to curve slightly at its southern extent but this may have been an effect produced by later ploughing.

The only find that was recovered from the fill of this gully was a single sherd of indeterminate prehistoric pottery. Consequently, the relationship between this feature and the Iron Age segmented ditch system seen in Areas N(a) and O to the south-east remains unclear. Given that the gully was oriented on a completely different alignment and was not made up of different sections, it would seem safer to assume that they were not related.

A watching brief in the area between Areas N(b) and N(a) revealed a second gully or ditch 1.4 m wide on a similar alignment to 1005 (Fig. 2.11). Whether the features were contemporary and part of the same land division is not clear, but again it seems unlikely that this second gully was related to the Iron Age segmented ditch system uncovered in Areas N(a) and O.

## LATER BRONZE AGE

Pottery identified in both the evaluation and excavation represents the only evidence for later Bronze Age activity along the road scheme. None of this pottery is diagnostic and its date is not certain. Some, as suggested in the pottery report, could be Iron Age (see Barclay, Chapter 7). In addition, a residual sherd of probable late Bronze Age date was recovered from a later feature at Court Farm.

## UNDATED EARLY PREHISTORIC FEATURES

### Duntisbourne Leer

Two small areas, situated 223 m apart, were excavated at the site of Duntisbourne Leer. The excavation areas were positioned to examine two pairs of parallel linear ditches which aerial photographs and the Stage 2 evaluation suggested were Romano-British trackways or minor roads running at right angles to Ermin Street (Fig. 4.2). A group of features of possible prehistoric date, including a gully and four pits, was revealed between the two trackway ditches in Area 1. No earlier prehistoric pottery was recovered. Six pieces of struck flint were found on this site, including a barbed and tanged arrowhead (Fig. 7.3.18) from the ploughsoil. The latter would be of Beaker/early Bronze Age date.

#### *Gully 49*

A shallow linear gully with a terminal at the south-western end was observed running north-east to south-west for a length of 7.5 m before being truncated at its north-eastern end by later ploughing. Three sections were excavated across the gully, but the only find that was recovered was a thick flint flake.

#### *Pits 4, 41 and 43*

Three closely spaced pit features (4, 41 and 43), situated just beyond the gully terminal, were on the same alignment as gully 49. Pits 41 and 43 were oval in shape, shallow and filled with a 'clean' reddish brown subsoil. Neither of the pits contained any finds. In contrast, pit 4 produced a flint scraper, a burnt core fragment and a flake. Analysis of the reddish brown fill of pit 4 (deposit 3) revealed carbonised material and more than 700 fragments of hazelnut shell, *Corylus avellana*. Though cereal remains were absent, the hazelnut shells and the flint scraper suggest a broad Neolithic/early Bronze Age date for the deposit. The discovery of a barbed and tanged arrowhead from the surface adjacent to Area 1 suggests that an early Bronze Age date is perhaps more likely.

#### *'Pit' 46*

Another feature, 'pit' 46, was situated on the southern edge of the excavated area. The full extent of the feature was not exposed, but if it was originally a pit it was much larger than any of the pits seen immediately to the south-west of gully 49. The fill of feature 46 was a reddish brown silt which contained occasional charcoal flecks. No other finds were recovered from the deposit.

# Chapter 3: The Later Prehistoric Period

*by Tim Allen, Alan Lupton and Andrew Mudd with Jeff Muir and Simon Mortimer*

## INTRODUCTION

This chapter deals with the Iron Age (*c.* 700 BC–AD 50). A total of 12 sites dating to this period was investigated along the route of the road scheme (Fig. 3.1). Most of these sites fall within the middle and late Iron Age (400 BC onwards), with very little earlier material identified.

The field evaluations (Stage 2) had suggested that middle-late Iron Age sites existed at Highgate House, Middle Duntisbourne and Duntisbourne Grove. A later prehistoric/Roman settlement was also thought to exist at Lower Street Furlong.

The present excavations led to some revisions of the dating by demonstrating that the material from Highgate House was largely middle Iron Age in date, while the sites at Middle Duntisbourne and Duntisbourne Grove were occupied at the very end of the late Iron Age. In addition, the segmented ditches at St Augustine's Farm South and St Augustine's Lane, which were found in association with the earlier Bronze Age ring ditches (Chapter 2), are considered to be almost certainly Iron Age on the basis of radiocarbon dating. Iron Age pottery was also recovered from a small number of the features identified at Lower Street Furlong and Cherry Tree Lane/Burford Road South and Court Farm. The latter are described with the Roman features in chapter 4. Iron Age pottery sherds were recovered from Lynches Trackway.

In addition to these discoveries, two unexpected sites on the road scheme - Preston Enclosure and Ermin Farm – proved to be of Iron Age date. The polygonal cropmark at Preston Enclosure was identified from aerial photographs in the vicinity of St Augustine's Lane. The Ermin Farm enclosures lay concealed beneath colluvial deposits and were discovered during the course of the scheme-wide watching brief. Another discovery was an isolated inhumation found near Lynches Trackway, Baunton, which was radiocarbon dated to the Iron Age.

The results of these discoveries will be presented in this chapter. The sites are examined, as far as possible, in chronological order, while an assessment of the regional significance of the later prehistoric evidence from the road scheme appears in Chapter 9.

## THE MIDDLE IRON AGE

### St Augustine's Farm South and St Augustine's Lane

*by Andrew Mudd and Jeff Muir*

Excavation and watching brief carried out along a 450 m length of the road north and south of St Augustine's Lane, Preston, revealed a complex of segmented ditches, which formed a linear boundary, with pits and postholes to the south. The complex ran between a pair of excavated Bronze Age ring ditches (see Chapter 2) and a group of cropmark ring ditches to the north (Fig. 2.11). Four excavations were carried out with watching brief areas in between.

The sites spanned four fields on level ground. All had been heavily ploughed with traces of ridge-and-furrow indicating ploughing dated from at least the medieval period (Chapter 6). The modern ploughsoil truncated the earlier furrows and directly overlay the cornbrash.

#### *St Augustine's Farm South*

The site lay to the south of St Augustine's Lane (Fig. 2.11). The main linear ditch alignment was traced for a distance of 210 m through Areas Na (110 m) and O (60 m), and can be identified as a cropmark for a at least a further 50 m south of that (NMR 148/177). Overall, the alignment runs south-east and curves south and then south-west around the ring ditches in Area O.

*Area O (Figs 3.2–3.3)*

Segmented ditch system 3123

Ditch system 3123 consisted of twelve discrete segments: 3182, 3153, 3084, 3114, 3105, 3155, 3134, 3130, 3148, 3139, 3169 and 3122. Although sharing a common orientation, these were not all in one line, but lay on at least two parallel alignments. The ditch segments were 0.20–0.65 m deep and most had been excavated through the limestone bedrock into underlying clay. Segment lengths varied considerably from 1.50 m to over 10 m in length. In almost every case one end of each segment, usually the northern end, was wider and deeper than the other. The segment profiles appear to have been dictated by the local nature of the bedrock, but in general the majority were steep-sided with a rounded or irregular base. The gap between the ditch segments varied considerably from 0.10–3.75 m.

The fills of the ditch segments tended to be mid to dark brown or greyish brown silts with varying quantities of limestone. There was a reddish cast to some of the fills which made them similar to some of the natural features on the site. The basal fills were usually very stony. Infilling probably occurred

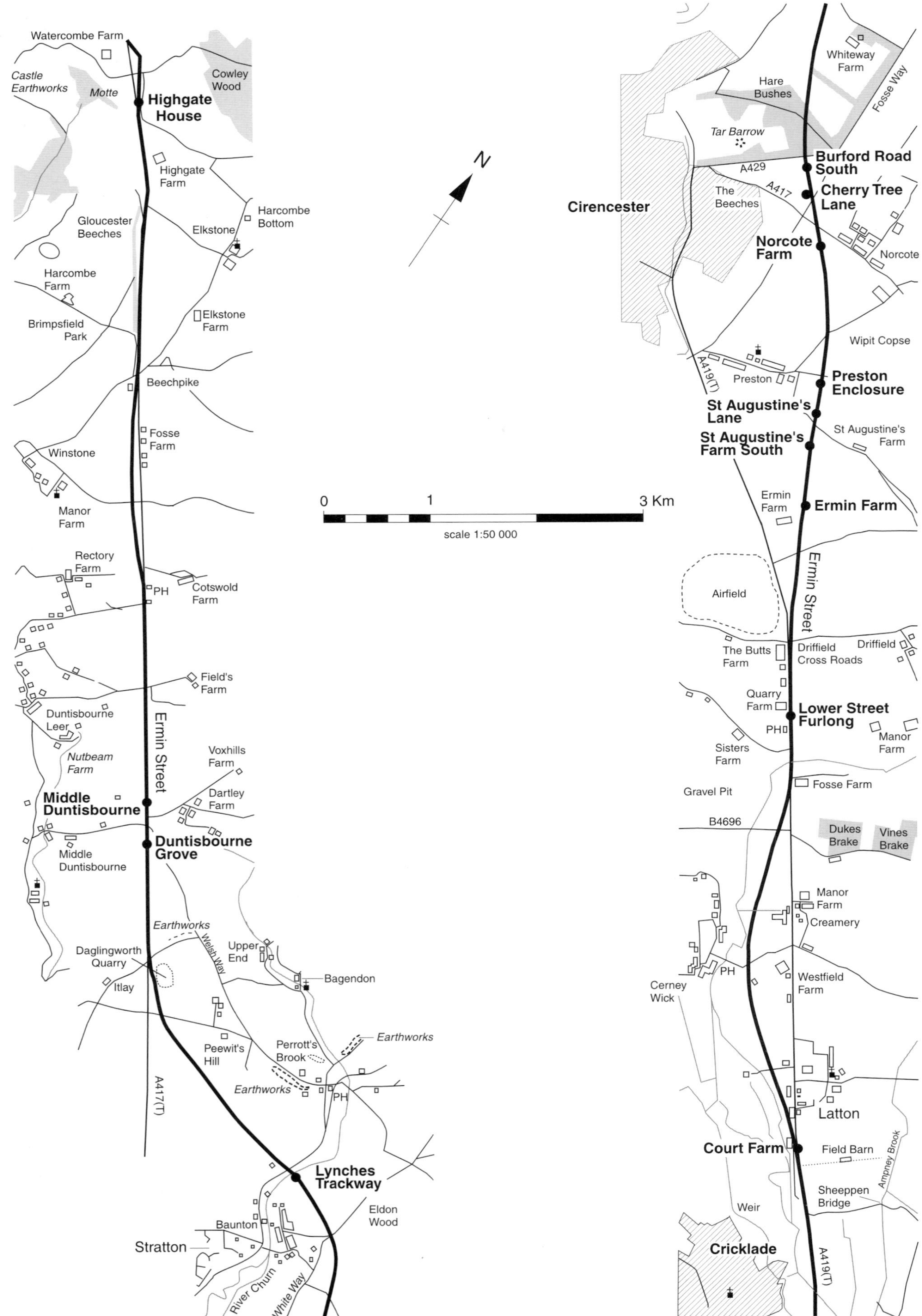


*Figure 3.1 Locations of later prehistoric sites.*

naturally in all the segments. Variations in the fills and profiles of some of the sections suggested that some of the segments may have been recut, but there was no conclusive evidence of this. Finds from the ditches were scarce and comprised a single sherd of probable Iron Age pottery from context 3121 (the middle fill of 3122 – Fig. 3.3), and two flint flakes and three indeterminate prehistoric sherds from 3102, the main fill of 3105.

The pits *(Fig. 3.4)*

Some 20 m south-east of the segmented ditch at the south end of the area two circular pits were found and were half-excavated.

Pit 3011 was 1.1 m in diameter and survived to a depth of 0.75 m. It contained four fills (3007–3010), all of which appeared to represent natural silting. The uppermost fills consisted of the typical reddish brown silt found elsewhere on the site as a natural deposit, gradually giving way to dark more clay-rich deposits towards the bottom of the pit.

Eleven sherds of pottery of probable Iron Age date were recovered from layer (3008). A single, fragmented bone was found in the primary fill of the pit (3010) which provided a radiocarbon date of 403–96 cal BC (95% confidence) (2237±68 BP; NZA-8615, R24151/13) indicating a middle Iron Age date for the feature. A few pieces of burnt limestone were recovered from each of the four fills.

Pit 3083 was located 14 m to the south-west of pit 3011. It was 1.2 m in diameter and nearly 1 m deep, and contained a sequence of seven fills, which, like the deposits in pit 3011, became darker and increased in clay content with depth. Fill 3078 formed a mound in the centre of the pit and appears to represent a deliberate dump. It contained lumps of green clay which appeared to be redeposited natural, and without particular significance, although confirming the deliberate origin of the fill.

No pottery was recovered, but fragments of two animal long bones came from fill 3080, and, from the upper fill 3076, a single fragment of cremated bone together with a flint flake. A radiocarbon date of 396–125 cal BC (95% confidence) (2234±56 BP; NZA-8619, R24151/14) was obtained from one of the long bones.

Postholes *(not illustrated)*

During the watching brief, a cluster of seven postholes were discovered about 150 m south-east of Area O. They fell within an area of about 20 m x 15 m but formed no recognisable pattern. Four of them yielded a total of 58 g of Iron Age pottery.

*Area N(a) (Figs 3.5–6)*

A further 110 m of the segmented ditch system was uncovered to the north of Area O in Area N(a). In this area the segmented ditch system consisted of three ditches (2003, 2004 and 2005) which formed a near continuous boundary running north-west.

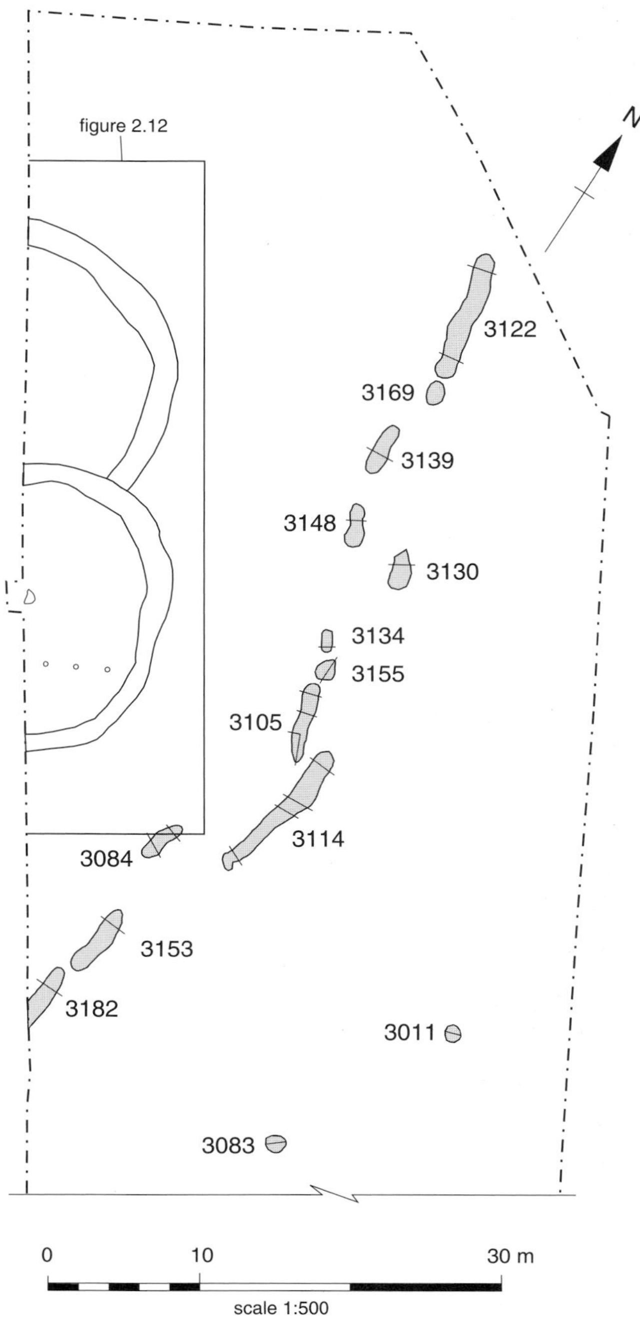


*Figure 3.2 St Augustine's Farm South, Area O, plan of segmented ditch system 3123 and pits 3011 and 3083.*

Ditch 2005

The most southerly segment, ditch 2005, was straight and of fairly constant width (0.8–0.9 m), but varied in depth according to the solidity of the bedrock. The northern terminal overlapped with ditch 2004 and was apparently cut by it. A radiocarbon date of 409–193 cal BC (95% confidence) (2294±59 BP; NZA-8766, R24151/11) was obtained from bone fragments from 2024, the primary fill of the ditch.

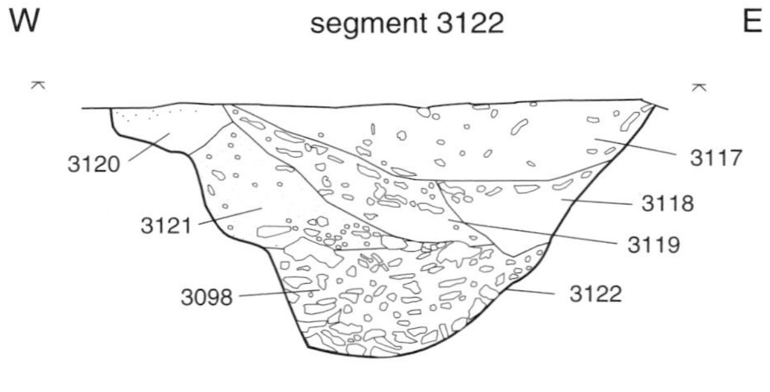


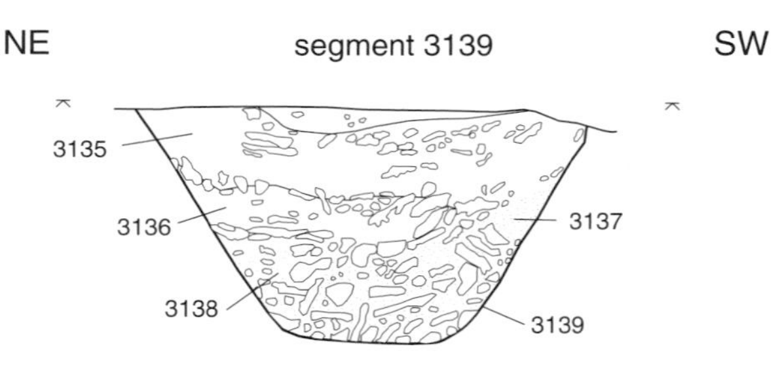


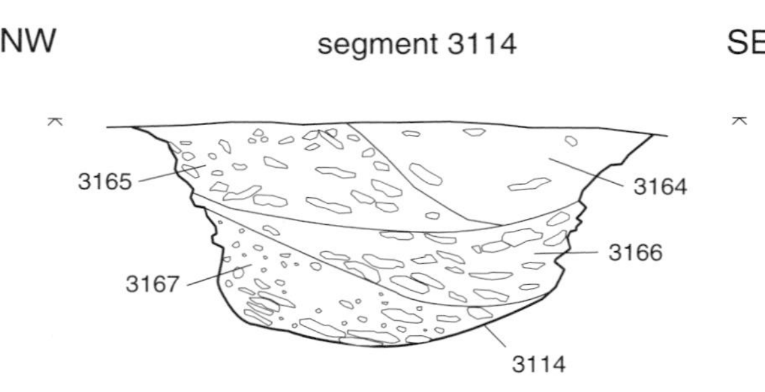


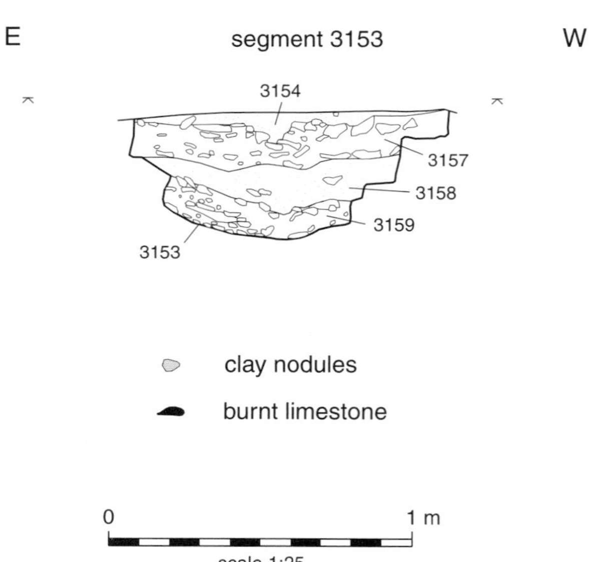


*Figure 3.3 St Augustine's Farm South, Area O, sections.*

Although ditch 2005 terminated just short of the southern baulk, a new segment of ditch continuing the same alignment was revealed in the watching brief. It appears that it would have joined up with the segmented ditch in Area O (Fig. 2.11).

### Ditch 2004

Though forming part of the same land boundary, ditch 2004 was of a slightly different character. Some 63 m long and wider than either 2003 or ditch 2005, the ditch was much more irregular and sinuous in plan, with more variable silt/clay fills. It ranged from 1.5–2.10 m wide and up to 0.4 m deep. Cut through cornbrash into a band of heavily jointed limestone, it appeared that the depth of the ditch depended largely on the local solidity of the bedrock. It was clear that as far as possible, the original excavators had followed the natural jointing in the limestone, making excavation easier and perhaps accounting for a marked kink in the centre of the ditch. The southern terminal of 2004 cut the terminal of 2005, the northern terminal stopped just short of that of ditch 2003.

### Ditch 2003

Ditch 2003, some 18 m in length, was the most northerly of the three linear ditches. The ditch, which contained two main sandy silt fills, was relatively constant in its orientation, width (1.20 m) and depth (*c.* 0.30 m), except at the south end where it narrowed slightly before terminating. At the terminal a possible posthole (2017 – Fig. 3.6, section 38) was found. This was truncated by medieval ploughing and no definite relationship with the ditch could be established, but 2017 may have been contemporary with ditch 2003.

### Watching brief: undated ditch

During groundworks a rectilinear ditch, 1.4 m wide and 0.38 m deep, was recorded running north-east – south-west between Area N(a) and Area N(b) (Fig. 2.11). There were no finds. Its uniform, straight character suggests that it was not connected with the segmented ditch system and it is considered likely to be later, although it appears to be unrelated to the modern topography. It does not appear as a cropmark although there are other linear cropmarks in the neighbourhood, one of which, on approximately this alignment, bisects the larger of the ring ditches to the north-east (Plate 2.2).

### *Area N(b)*

Further north, Area N(b) lay immediately to the south of St Augustine's Lane. Here a linear gully (1005) about 1 m wide and just 0.13 m deep was the only archaeological feature present. There were no finds. This gully was approximately parallel to the ditch just described some 50 m to the south.

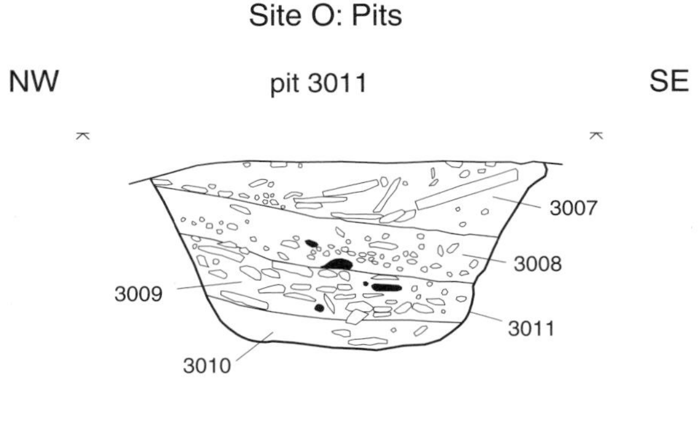


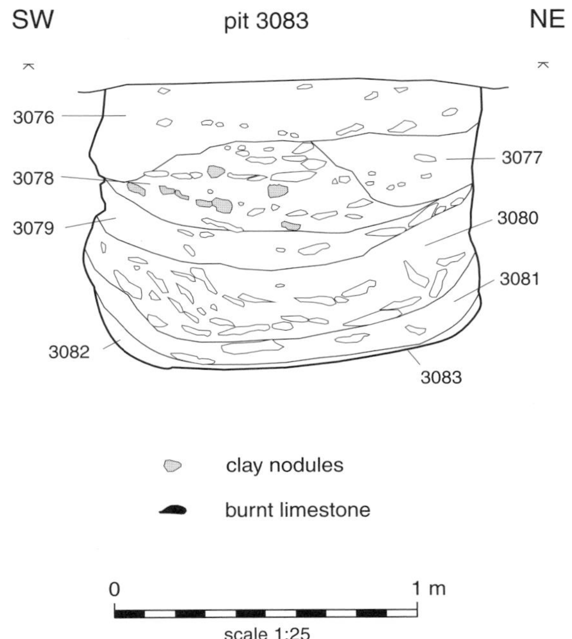


*Figure 3.4 St Augustine's Farm South, Area O, sections.*

***St Augustine's Lane*** *(Figs 3.7–8)*
*by Andrew Mudd and Jeff Muir*

A rectangular area, 135 x 40 m in extent was stripped immediately to the north of St Augustine's Farm South to examine a possible rectangular enclosure interpreted from aerial photographs (RCHME 1976, 95). Instead, a complex of segmented ditches at the southern end of the site in the shape of an irregular H was revealed. The complex was interpreted as an alignment of north-south ditch lengths cut by two approximately parallel groups of ditches running north-west to south-east. There was also a small ditch segment or pit (90) which was not part of either of these alignments. The ditches were separated by narrow causeways, in some cases no wider than 0.1–0.2 m. The segments appeared to follow fissures in the limestone bedrock and in most cases they were only dug as deep as the underlying natural clay 0.3 m below. All the ditch segments contained a similar sequence of fills, which normally comprised a very stony lower/main fill overlain by a largely stone-free light brown silt loam.

*Ditches 19, 24 and 56*

The earliest alignment was that of ditches 19, 24 and possibly 56. Ditch 19 was clearly cut by ditch 35 which formed part of the south-western ditch group 19 (Fig. 3.8, section 9). Ditch 56 may be associated, as it was similarly aligned and appeared to be cut by ditch 149 of the north-eastern group (Fig. 3.8, section 28, segment 58), though the intrusion of a modern land drain made this uncertain. The ditch segments were generally a little over 1 m wide and varied in depth between 0.10 m and 0.28 m.

*South-west ditches 39, 46 and 153*

The south-western ditch group was made up of three segments. The segments varied in width from 1.4–1.7 m. Ditches 39 and 153 were cut to a depth of over 0.4 m through the limestone and into the underlying clay; the northernmost ditch segment, 46, which followed a fissure in the rock for part of its length, did not penetrate through the limestone. The north-western terminals of ditches 46 and 149 (below) ended opposite one another.

*North-east ditches 25, 148 and 149*

The north-eastern ditch was made up of three separate segments similar in character to those of the south-west group. In many places the ditch segments followed natural fissures in the limestone. Though varying in length and width, the three segments were all dug through the limestone to the top of the underlying clay. Twelve sherds of shell-tempered pottery were recovered from the bottom of these ditches, and another 67 sherds from the upper fills. The pottery is probably Iron Age.

***Discussion***

*Dating*

The segmented ditch complexes at St Augustine's Farm South and St Augustine's Lane are similar both in character and alignment, although it appears they would not have joined. The pottery from St Augustine's Farm South was limited and undiagnostic in date. However, the radiocarbon determination from the primary fill of ditch 2005 would suggest that the complex is Iron Age, rather than earlier. Virtually identical radiocarbon dates were obtained from samples in pits 3011 and 3083 in Area O indicating a middle Iron Age date for these features. Although their position does not necessarily mean that they were part of the ditch system, they lie isolated from contemporary settlements and, like the ditches, can be seen as defining boundaries. They did, however, contain more occupation material than the

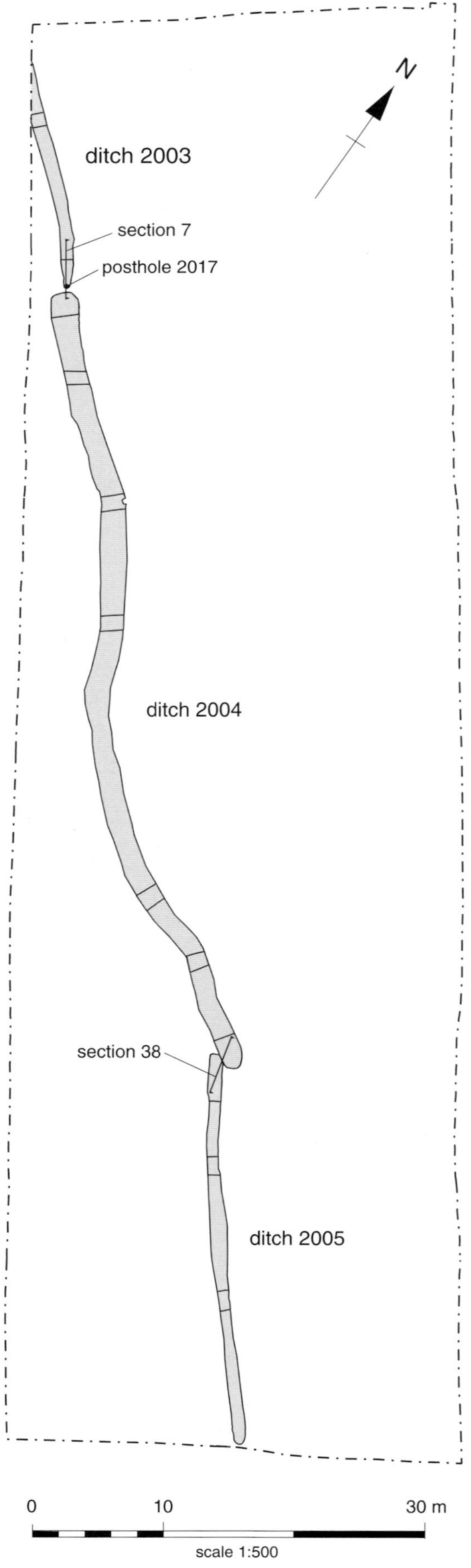


Figure 3.5 St Augustine's Farm South, Area Na, plan of segmented ditches.

ditch segments, and it is possible that the pits were slightly later additions to the complex. The dating evidence for the complex of three intercutting alignments at St Augustine's Lane was sparse. The 79 sherds of shell tempered pottery were not reliable as dating evidence, but most likely to be Iron Age, an interpretation which is compatible with the radiocarbon dating from St Augustine's Farm South.

*The purpose of the segmented ditches*

The segmented linear ditches varied considerably within the area of the excavations. In Area N(a) the segments were long and the boundary virtually continuous, whereas elsewhere the segments were shorter, more irregular and the gaps wider. It is possible that the boundary was originally continuous, and that truncation is responsible for the gaps between segments, though in Area O some of the gaps were considerable. In this case the boundary may simply reflect the way in which the digging was organised, either by large numbers of people each excavating individual or group lengths, or by a smaller number of people working intermittently.

Equally, most of the ditch segments were shallow and few were dug below the limestone. The segments may simply have been quarries for limestone along the line of a pre-existing boundary, or have been dug to construct an upstanding wall alongside, which formed the boundary proper. It was argued that short lengths of similar segmented ditch alignments at Mingies Ditch, Hardwick, Oxon. were dug as gravel pits alongside an existing boundary, and others showed evidence of an adjacent hedge (Allen and Robinson 1993, 91). The sequence of ditches in Area O cannot be determined stratigraphically. In Area N(a), however, it seems that ditch 2004 may have been dug later. If so, a gap some 63 m in length would have existed in the original land boundary which was subsequently plugged by the excavation of 2004.

The intercutting alignments at St Augustine's Lane show a change of alignment from north-south to north-west to south-east. The segments of the earlier alignment had at least partly silted up by the time the parallel north-west - south-east alignments were dug, but the new segmented ditches appear to have been aligned upon the ends of the earlier alignment, and they were presumably still visible. It is therefore possible that all three alignments were in contemporary use, and that adjacent walls or banks surrounded three sides of one or more enclosures.

The linear boundary seemed to respect the southern pair of excavated ring ditches, apparently using them as an axis or marker around which to change direction slightly. This suggests that these were still upstanding at the time. The alignment of the boundary divides these ring ditches from the pair of cropmark ring ditches 300 m further north, which appear to represent

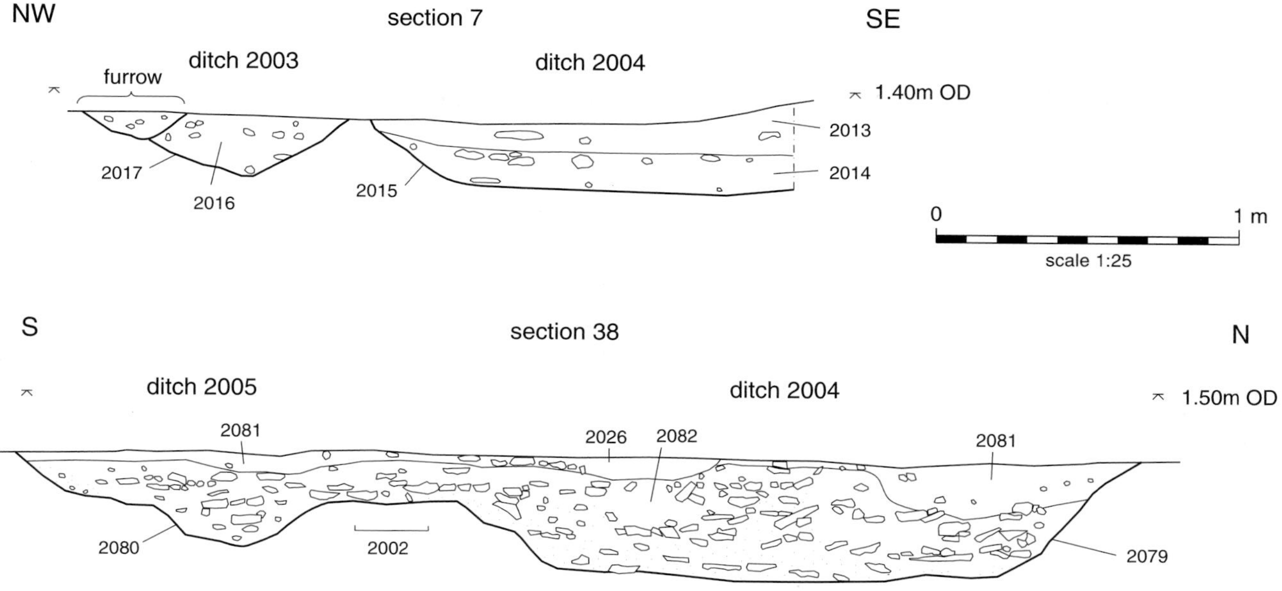


*Figure 3.6 St Augustine's Farm South, area Na, segmented ditch sections.*

a separate cemetery. It is possible that this boundary marks a continuing territorial division between local population groups in this area.

There was little environmental evidence from the site as few plant remains survived in the excavated deposits. Of the 39 soil samples taken from the ditches and pits at St Augustine's Farm South, only three contained charred plant remains other than charcoal and these consisted of very occasional weeds, *Hordeum* sp. (barley) grain or indeterminate cereal grain. Two further deposits produced some charcoal of identifiable size, all of *Quercus* sp. (oak). The identifiable animal bones consisted of two fragments of a horse radius and one cattle bone, though large limb bone fragments were frequent in the remaining 96 bones of the poorly preserved assemblage. The animal bone assemblage from St Augustine's Lane was also small (54 bones from the prehistoric contexts). The charred plant remains provided little information beyond indicating a general background of poorly preserved cereals. The samples cannot be taken as indicators of the immediate environment, though they do reflect the consumption of cereals and meat by the local inhabitants.

The quantity of finds was small, and the excavated areas appear to be peripheral to settlement. The pits at the southern edge of the excavations, together with the posthole group found 150 m to the south, could indicate that a settlement lay in this direction. Pits are known in association with Iron Age linear boundaries on the gravel terraces at Lechlade, Glos. (Allen *et al.* 1993, 36–7; King in Boyle *et al.* 1998, 272–3; Thomas and Holbrook in Boyle *et al.* 1998, 282–3), but not always in close association with settlement foci. In Iron Age domestic contexts, short alignments of segmented ditches have been mentioned (above) at Mingies Ditch in Oxfordshire, and segmented ditches and pits appear to have defined a settlement 'enclosure' at The Park, Guiting Power, in the Gloucestershire Cotswolds (Marshall 1990).

Segmented ditches or pit alignments stretching over long distances are well known as cropmarks in parts of Iron Age Britain, for instance in the Nene and Great Ouse basin, where Knight listed 114 examples (Knight 1984, 259) and in North Yorkshire (eg. Powlesland 1985), but are not particularly common in the Upper Thames region or the Cotswolds. Two long alignments of circular pits are known from cropmarks at Binsey (Benson and Miles 1974, 52-4) and at Northfield Farm, Long Wittenham (Benson and Miles 1974, 36–7), both in Oxfordshire. Excavated examples are much fewer. A late Iron Age alignment of circular pits was excavated near Lechlade at Langford Downs, Oxon. (Williams 1947, 47 fig. 14), and this particular expression of boundary definition appears to have been long-lived. The Lechlade area provides a further comparison with this part of Preston in that the segmented ditches and pit alignments formed part of an early Iron Age system of land division within which earlier Bronze Age barrow groups were incorporated.

The excavations have established that the crop-mark plot of a rectangular enclosure on this site (RCHME 1976, 95) can be dismissed. The possible polygonal enclosure to the north-east (which lies outside the road corridor) is unclear on cropmark evidence and remains unsubstantiated. The Stage 2 evaluation (CAT 1991; Trench 532 and magnetometer survey in this area) yielded inconclusive results although a 0.65 m-deep, undated ditch was en-countered somewhere in this locality. It may belong to a third ring ditch or other feature aligned on the two clear ring ditches in this field (Fig. 2.11).

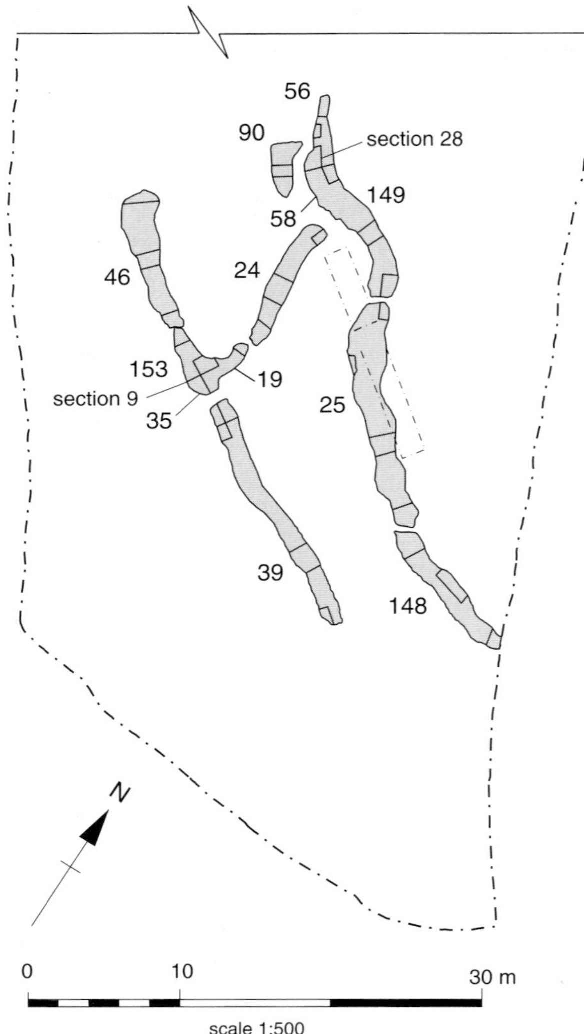


*Figure 3.7 St Augustine's Lane, plan of segmented ditches.*

**Preston Enclosure**
*by Andrew Mudd and Simon Mortimer*

An aerial photograph (Plate 3.1) revealed a polygonal cropmark which had not been identified in the earlier assessments, lying partly concealed by a modern hedgerow, some 400 m north of St Augustine's Lane. The site therefore came to light very late in the project. It lay on a similar level or gently undulating topography to the sites at St Augustine's Lane and St Augustine's Farm South, with an underlying geology of cornbrash. About 25% of the enclosure lay in the path of the new road and was excavated.

An area of 30 x 116 m was stripped of topsoil. A series of east-west aligned medieval/post-medieval plough furrows measuring 2–3 m in width ran across the earlier enclosure, and were removed. Hand-cleaning revealed the enclosure ditch and entrance and a number of internal features (Figs 3.9–10). Two complete arms of the enclosure ditch were revealed, the southern one a little over 40 m long and the northern one terminating after a little over 30 m. The eastern terminal and the angle of the southernmost length of ditch were also revealed. The enclosure measured about 65 m north-south.

The cropmark indicates that the ditches enclosed an area of about 0.38 ha. The hexagon was not geometrically precise, having notably shorter lengths of ditch on the eastern and western sides. However, opposed sides of the hexagon appear to have been parallel and approximately the same length.

***Enclosure ditch 1***
***(segments 3, 59, 86, terminals 41 and 66)***

Three complete sections were excavated through the enclosure ditch and both terminals were also half sectioned (Figs 3.11–13). The ditch had a splayed V-shaped profile, which narrowed from a maximum width of *c.* 4 m to a flattish bottom which was approximately 0.5 m wide. The ditch was from 1.0 m to 1.4 m deep.

*Ditch segment 3 (Fig. 3.11)*

The initial compact silty clay fill of the ditch (135) contained a few fragments of bone and burnt stone. An enhanced precision AMS date on animal bone from this context gave a date of 396–188 cal BC (95% confidence level) (NZA 8573, R24151/5). The secondary fill (134) was a compact mid orange-brown silty clay deposit, similar to the natural material into which the ditch was cut. There were no finds.

The subsequent dark brown compacted clayey silt deposit (4) appears to have been the result of natural silting of the partially filled ditch. A small number of undated pottery sherds, bone fragments and pieces of burnt stone were recovered, and a radiometric sample of horse skull and teeth gave a date of 385–199 cal. BC (95% confidence level) (R24151/7).

Fill 4 was overlain by a loose silty clay deposit mixed with large amounts of small-medium limestone rubble (5). This material was thicker towards the north-western side of the ditch section, suggesting that it may have derived from an internal bank. A single sherd of middle Iron Age pottery weighing 10 g was recovered from this fill. The uppermost layers were 6 and 7, both compacted mid-brown silty clays (which were probably both parts of a single deposit). These appear to have accumulated through natural silting within the weathering cone of the ditch. Four small sherds of Roman pottery (2 sherds of samian and 2 of Severn Valley ware, weighing only 4 g) were found with a single middle Iron Age sherd in layer 6. This shows that a hollow in the top of the enclosure ditch was open into the early Roman period.

*Ditch segment 59 (Fig. 3.11)*

The dimensions and shape of the ditch profile and the stratigraphic sequence seen in the second ditch section *c.* 20 m to the north-west were essentially similar to those in segment 3 outlined above. Two sherds of middle Iron Age pottery (weighing 6 g) were found within the primary silting deposit (60).

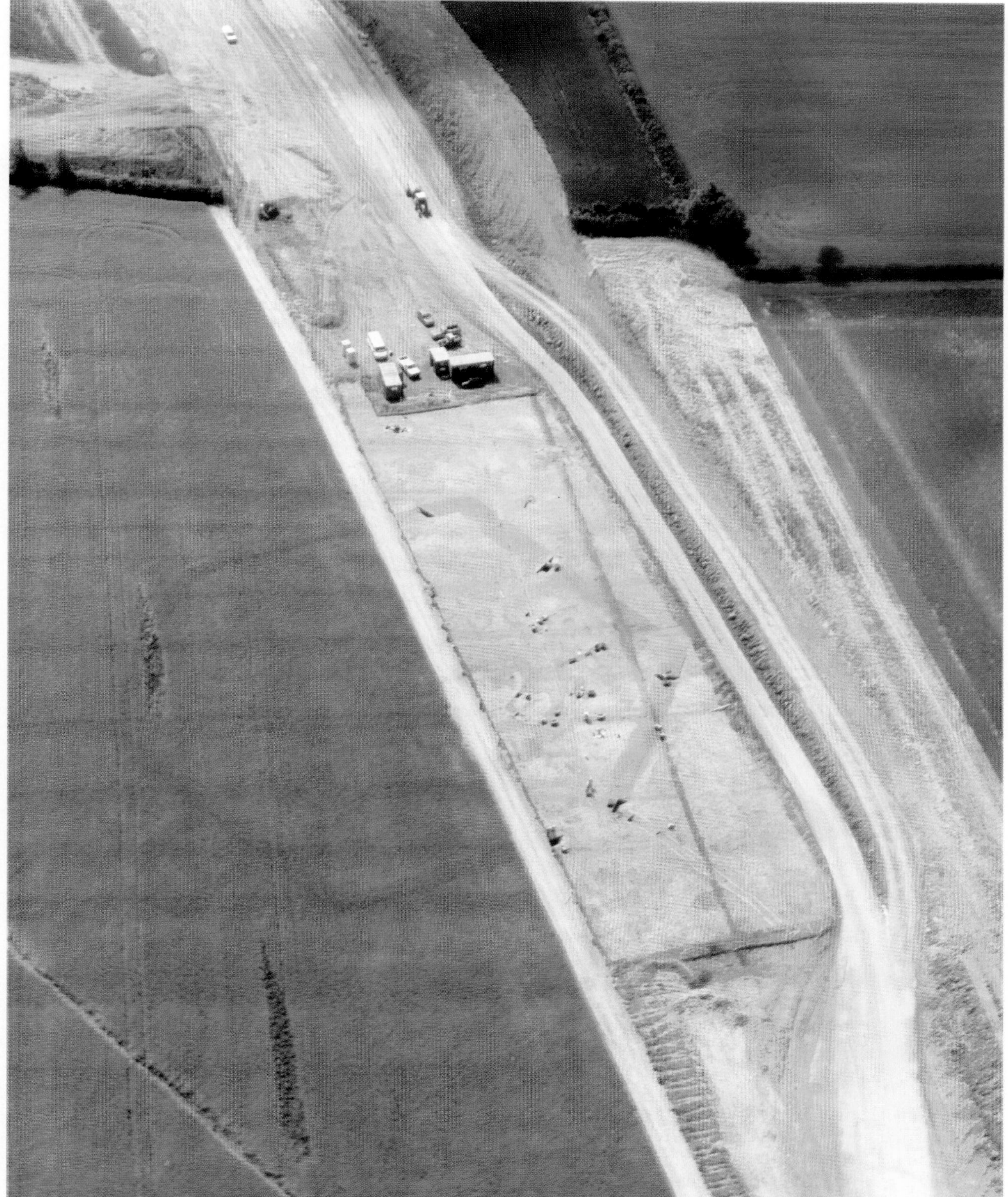

*Plate 3.1 Hexagonal middle Iron Age enclosure at Preston. The entrance faces north-west. Reproduced by permission of Neil Thomas (PES ref. 4846/21).*

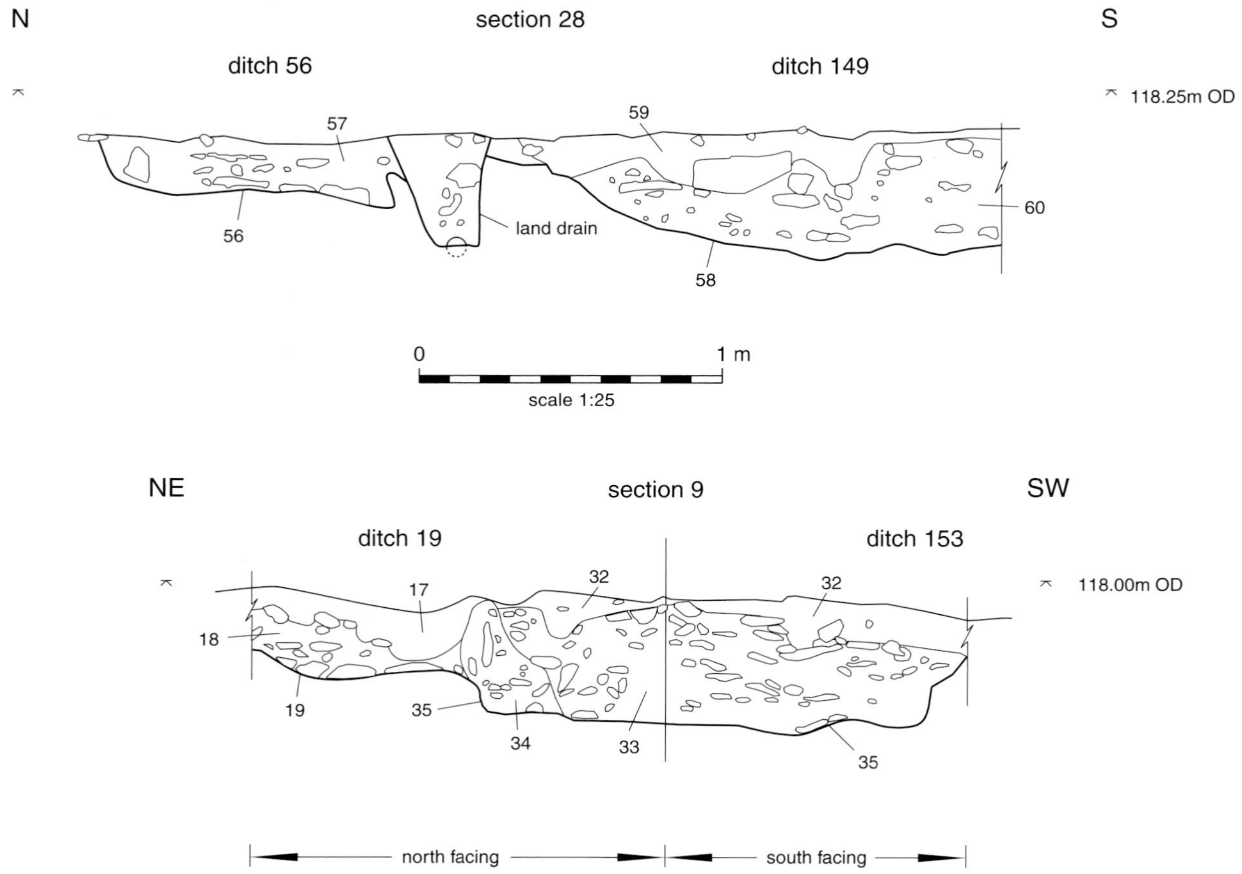


*Figure 3.8 St Augustine's Lane, segmented ditch sections.*

The second and third fills, 61 and 62 respectively were both mid orange-brown silty clay (like fill 134). A large sherd of middle Iron Age pottery (weighing 28 g) was found within fill 61. Layer 62 was overlain by fill 63, a compact mid to dark brown silty clay equivalent to layer 4, and this was followed by similar compacted silty clay deposits (64 and 65). These last deposits incorporated 54 large sherds (785 g) of middle Iron Age pottery in association with animal bones and a saddle quern fragment of May Hill Sandstone (cat. 687).

*Ditch segment 86 (Fig. 3.12)*

Owing to a change in the sub-surface geology to a much stonier natural, enclosure ditch segment 86, located *c.* 28 m to the north-west of segment 59, had a more angular profile than those seen in either the first or the second segments. The primary fill, 122, was a compact yellowish-brown silty clay mixed with small pieces of abraded limestone, which was probably the result of natural silting. This was sealed by a thicker and stonier band of greyish-brown clayey silt, 123 which derived from both sides of the enclosure. The third fill was an equally stony mid brown clayey silt deposit 124 that contained a sherd of limestone-tempered pottery. Fills 123 and 124 appear to have been deliberately dumped into the enclosure ditch, but the final fill, 125, was more likely to have resulted from the natural infilling of the shallow hollow left in the top of the ditch.

*Segment of western terminus 66 (Fig. 3.12)*

Excavation of the western terminus identified a sequence of seven fills. Primary silting (85) was devoid of finds, and was overlain by a much thicker stonier band of reddish-brown silty clay (84), which contained two tiny sherds of pottery and several pieces of bone. Unlike the primary deposit, this secondary fill appears to have been deliberately dumped into the enclosure ditch terminus. The subsequent fill, 83, was a largely stone-free silty clay deposit, probably the result of natural deposition, which did not contain any finds. The fourth and sixth fills (82 and 80) were composed of limestone rubble, while the intervening fifth and final seventh fills (81 and 79) were silty clay deposits. None of these later layers contained any finds. The western terminus was cut by a series of gullies 191, 192, 193 and 194, which also appeared to date to the middle Iron Age.

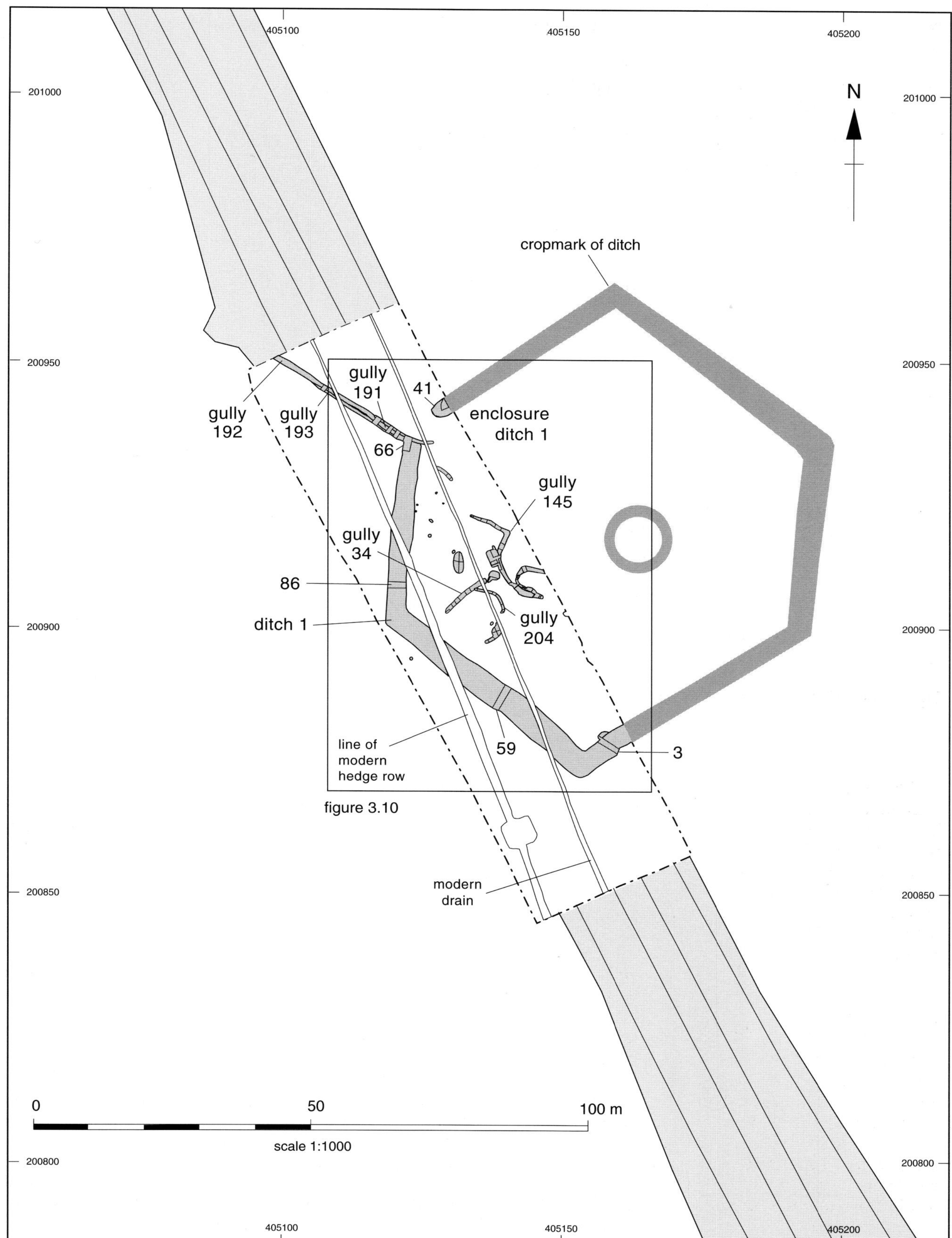


*Figure 3.9 Preston Enclosure, plan and cropmark of site.*

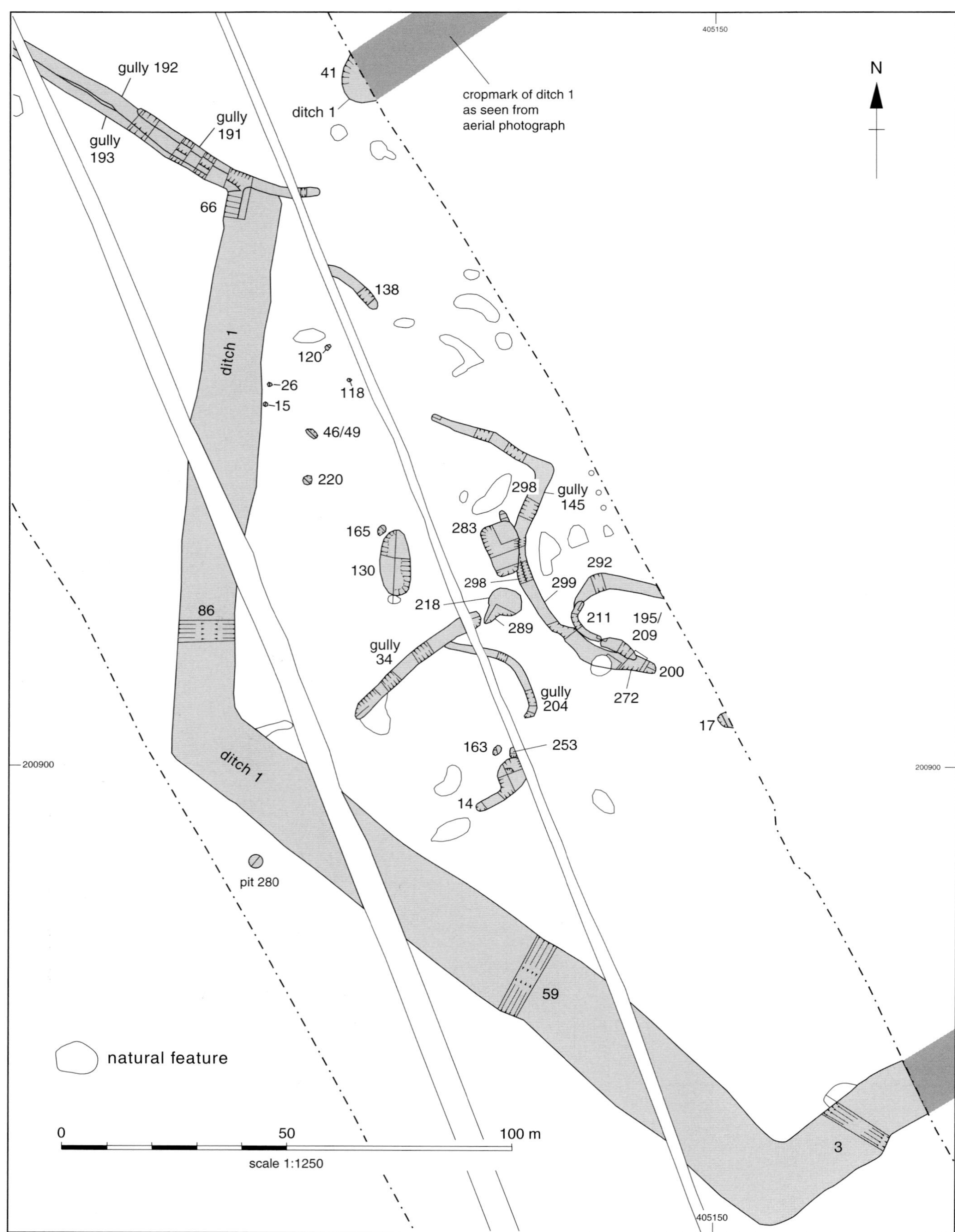


*Figure 3.10 Preston Enclosure, detailed plan of internal features.*

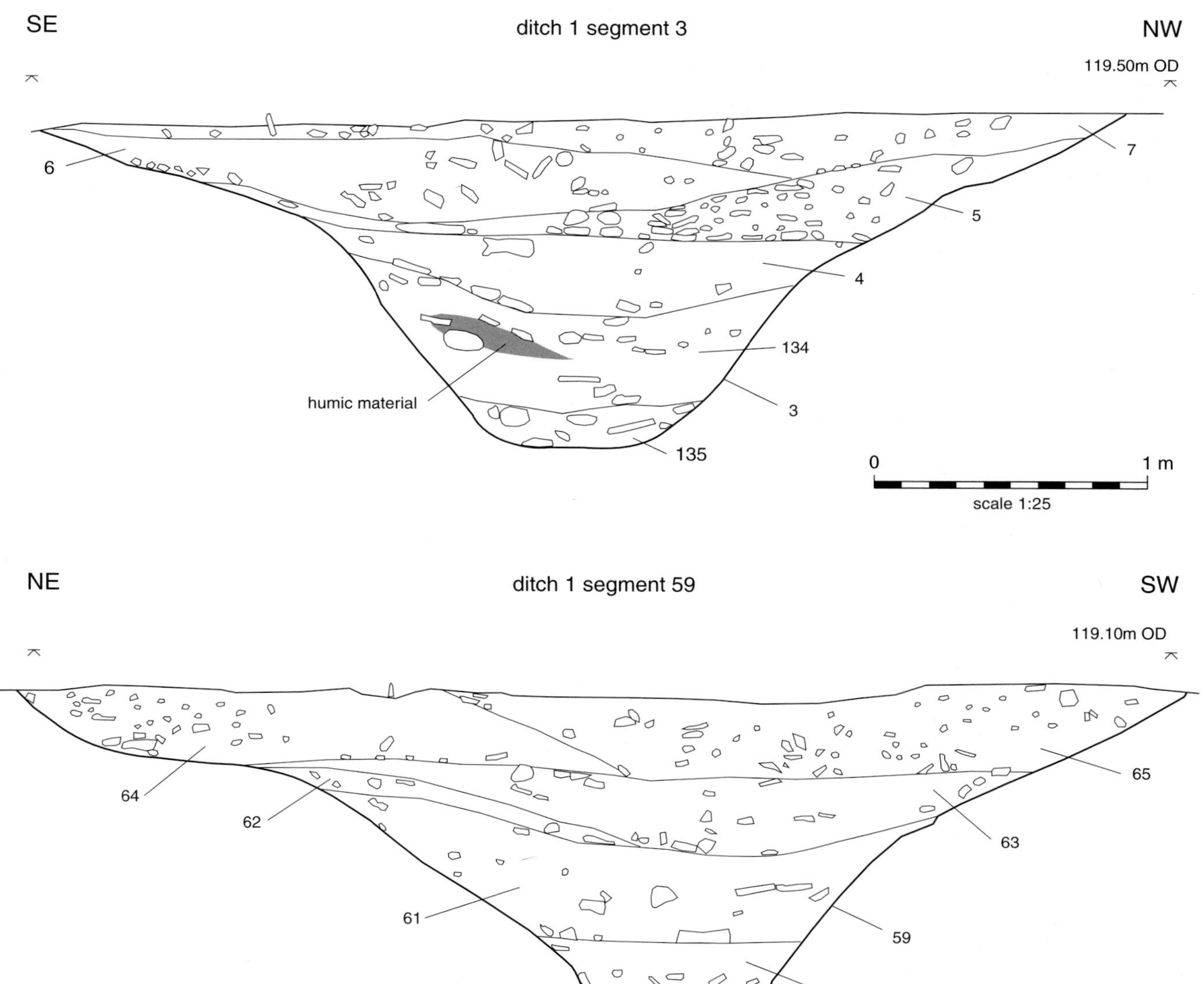


*Figure 3.11 Preston Enclosure, ditch 1 sections.*

*Segment of eastern terminus 41 (Fig. 3.13)*

A short section of the eastern terminus was identified against the eastern baulk, giving an entrance *c.* 7 m wide. Examination of this feature demonstrated that while both termini were equally steep-sided and roughly flat-bottomed, the eastern terminus was significantly deeper; 1.4 m as opposed to 1 m. Though only *c.* 7 m from the western terminus, the sequence of deposits in the eastern terminus was quite different. Four superimposed approximately horizontal bands of compacted clay silt material were revealed, (45–42). The uniformity of these deposits strongly suggests that they were derived from natural silting. All except the uppermost layer (42) produced occasional finds of bone and burnt stone.

No traces of any pits or post settings were found in the immediate vicinity of either terminus. A pair of irregular features due south of the eastern terminus proved on examination to be natural. The enclosure entrance therefore does not seem to have been provided with a gate.

*Features within the interior of enclosure ditch 1 (Fig. 3.10)*

Features within the enclosure comprised a system of gullies (145, 299, 298, 272, 195/209, 211, 34, 204) apparently demarcating different zones within the interior, six pits (130, 283, 165, 218, 289 and 14) and a group of small postholes (15, 26, 120, 118, 46/49, 220). Numerous other features were sample-excavated but proved to be shallow and amorphous, and were most probably natural solution hollows and root disturbances.

With the exception of two small postholes (15 and 26) none of the features lay within 2.5 m of the enclosure

*Plate 3.2 Preston Enclosure, entrance in foreground.*

ditch. This suggests that there may have been an internal bank, perhaps revetted internally over a short length by three postholes (120, 46/49 and 220) in line. Gully 191 may mark the limit of the bank at the entrance. The two small postholes 15 and 26 both lie very close to the edge of the ditch, and may have formed an external revetment for the bank at this point. The presence of an internal bank was also suggested by fill 5 within enclosure ditch segment 3, and perhaps by the limestone layers 82 and 80 within the western ditch terminal 66 (see above).

### Gullies 204, 253, 211 and 195/209

The earliest phase of activity appears to have consisted of a group of slight gullies in a band across the middle of the enclosure. Curving gullies 204 and 253 formed a semicircular enclosure just south of the south-western angle of the enclosure. Gully 204 was 0.2 m deep and filled with a dark yellow-brown silty clay fill. Fragments of bone, flint flakes and burnt stone were recovered but no pottery. Gully 253 was deeper and filled by silty clays 12 and 11 (Fig. 3.14). At the north-west end gully 204 was removed by a later gully 34 (below). Arcs of gully 204 and 253 formed a semicircle of 8–9 m diameter, which, when projected to complete the circle, would have reached the suggested internal bank. There was a smaller gap or entrance 2 m wide on the south-east. On the southern side of the entrance gap was an irregular silt-filled feature (13) of uncertain significance which had been disturbed by a land drain, and a small posthole (163), 0.13 m deep.

It is possible that the gullies were eaves drainage features marking the site of a roundhouse, one of whose doorposts was represented by posthole 163. Later gully 34 follows the projected continuation of the arc of gully 204, and may have recut a continuation of that gully.

North-east of gully 204 was a narrow curving gully 211, which was not fully cleared and was therefore only planned approximately. This formed a U-shaped crook *c.* 3 m wide, which was later extended by a short *c.* 2.5 m long gully, 195/209. No finds were recovered from any of these features, which were subsequently cut by a later set of boundary gullies (see below).

### Gullies 145, 299, 298 and 272

Gullies 145, 299, 298 and 272 formed a straight length of gully oriented approximately towards the north-west entrance, and a curving arc. The straight length, numbered 145, was narrow (*c.* 0.75 m), steep-sided and relatively deep (*c.* 0.5 m), becoming progressively shallower towards its northern terminus. The gradual fall suggests that drainage may have been one of its original functions. It was filled with compact dark yellow-brown silty clay mixed with small abraded stones and flecks of charcoal (fills 29, 33, 93, 284, 137, 288). Finds from these deposits included a residual

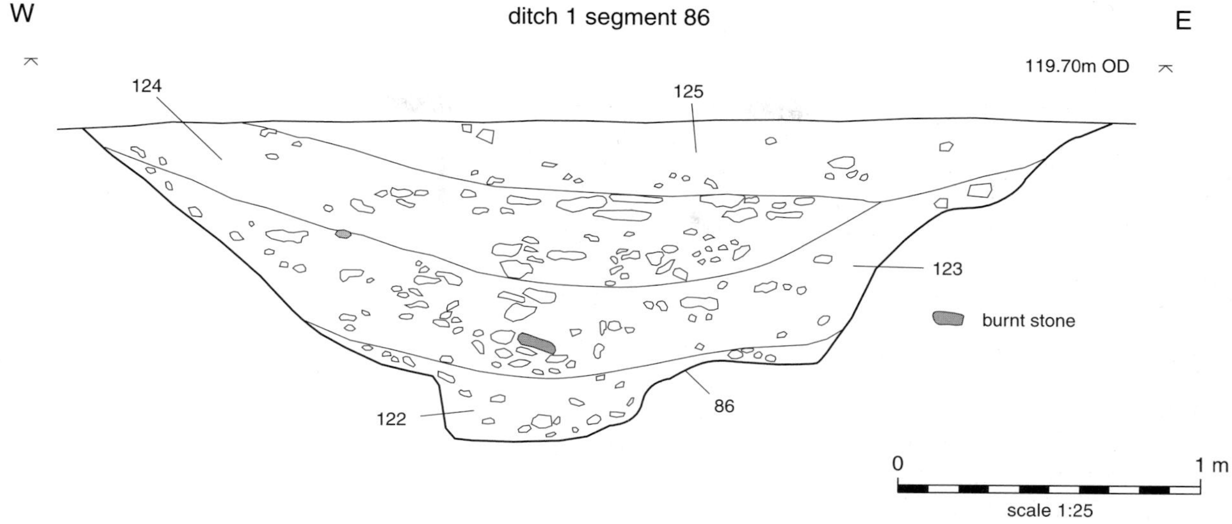


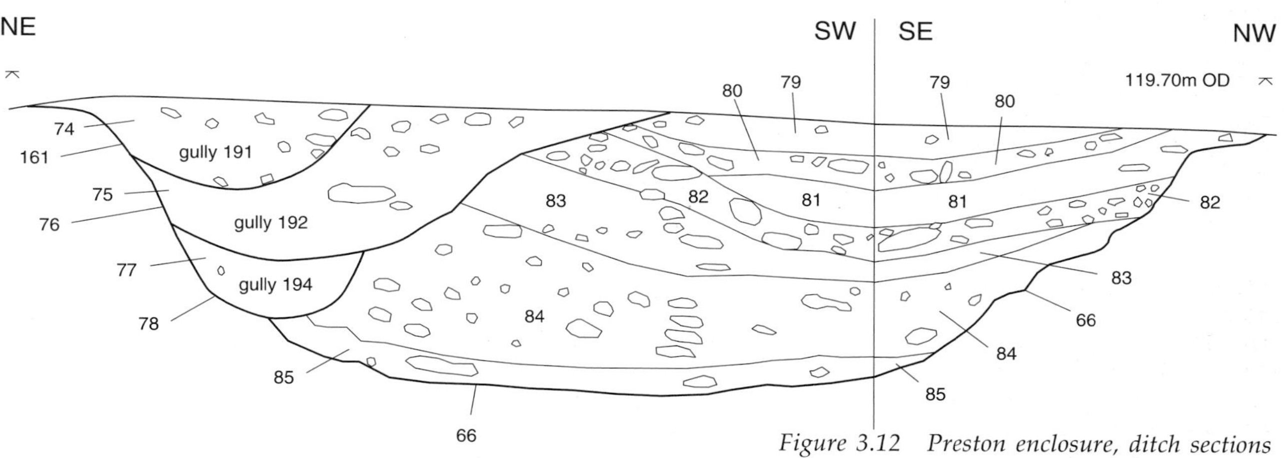


*Figure 3.12 Preston enclosure, ditch sections*

early Bronze Age flint arrowhead (Fig. 7.13.19) together with 15 sherds (80 g) of limestone-tempered pottery and 10 sherds (27 g) of shell-tempered ware .Other finds included bone and burnt stone.

The curving arc continuing from 145 was numbered 299. This had an uncertain relationship with another similar but slightly deeper cut 298 on its west side. Both had shallow U-shaped profiles and contained similar largely stone-free silty fills. Gully 298 was aligned due north and was cut by pit 283, terminating just north of it. At the south end both gullies merged imperceptibly, and the stratigraphic relationship between them could not be ascertained. Continuing south-east the curving gully widened towards the south terminal, and was numbered 272. This cut earlier lengths of gully 195/209.

At both ends the curving gully ended less than 2.5 m from the eastern edge of the excavation. If projected, the arc described by gullies 299 and 272 would form a circle some 14 m in diameter, and the arc may have been part of a circular enclosure with opposing entrances, one towards the main enclosure entrance on the north-west, the other on the south-east. The fact that 272 cut earlier lengths of gully along much the same line suggests that gully 299–272 was redefining an earlier enclosure of some sort in the same location.

## Gully 34

South-west of gully 299–272 was another gully 34. This was of very similar character to 299, and the two gullies may have formed two sides of an enclosure on the west side of the interior, with an entrance some 3 m wide between them on the south-east giving access to the area of enclosure 204/253.

## Pits 130, 283, 165, 218, 289 and 17

All of the pits were oval or sub-rectangular rather than circular, all had sloping sides, and all were much wider and longer than they were deep. Where the pits

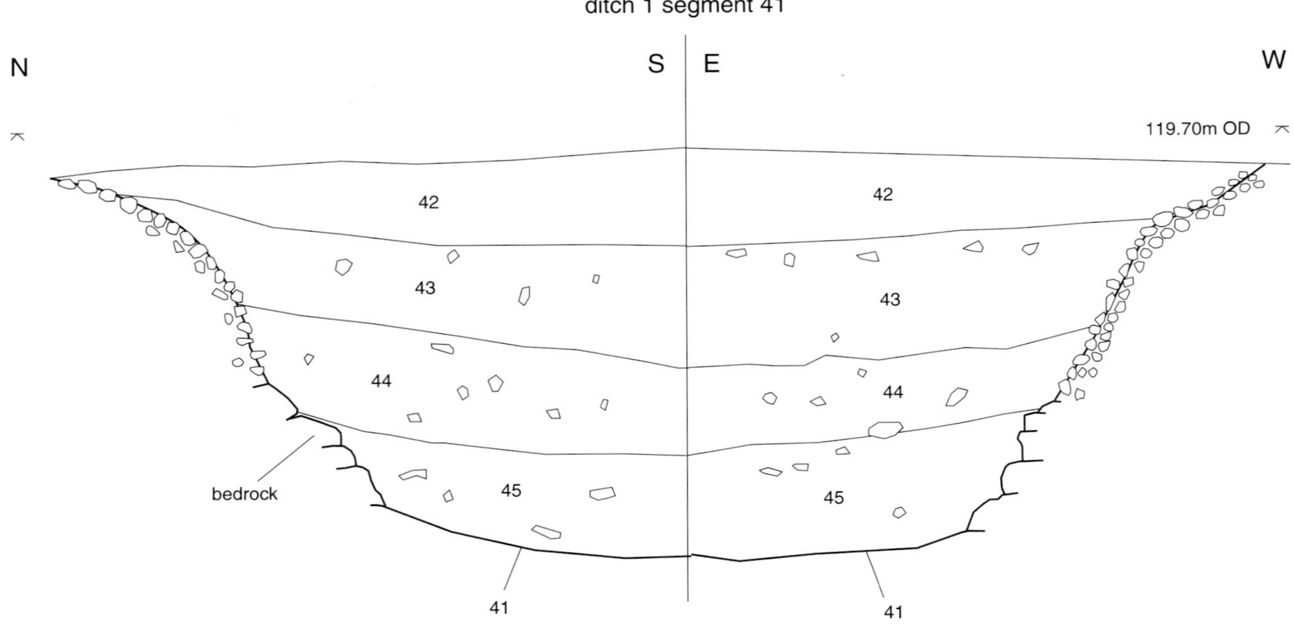


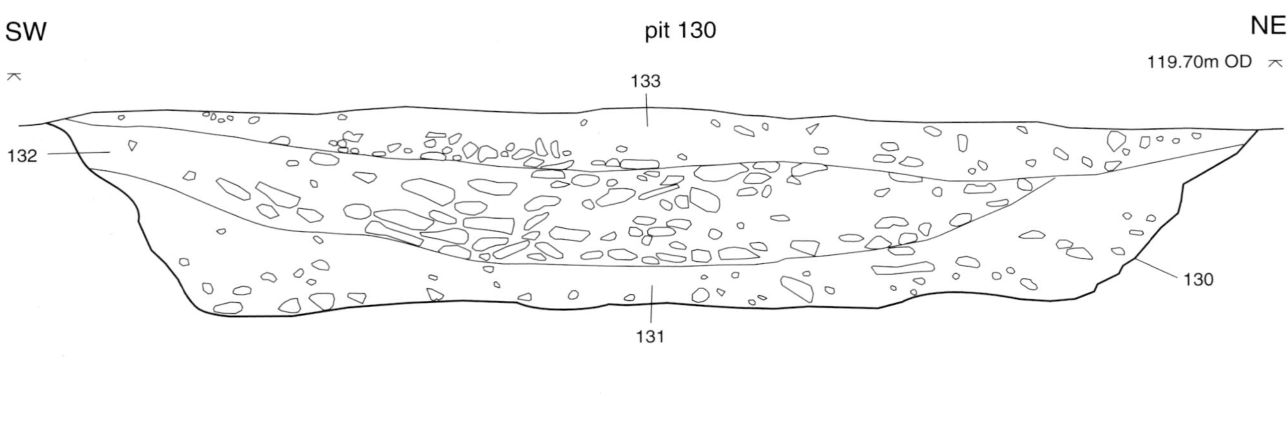


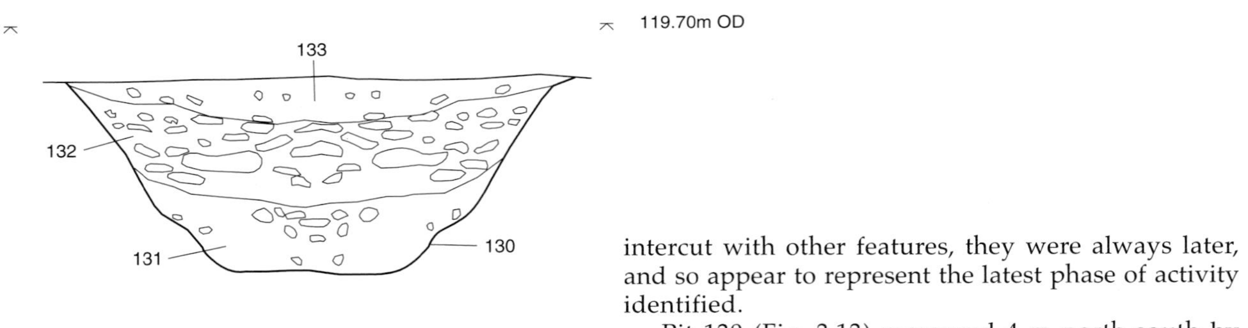


*Figure 3.13 Preston Enclosure, ditch 1 and pit 130, sections.*

intercut with other features, they were always later, and so appear to represent the latest phase of activity identified.

Pit 130 (Fig. 3.13) measured 4 m north-south by 1.7 m east-west. It was located approximately 22 m south of the eastern terminus of the enclosure ditch. Excavation of the north-western and south-eastern quadrants of the feature showed that it was 0.65 m deep, steep-sided and flat-bottomed and contained three fills. The primary deposit, 131 was an orange-brown silty clay. It yielded 6 sherds (45 g) of pottery together with several pieces of animal bone. The next fill (132) was much stonier, and contained a large number of finds, including 8 sherds (11g) of pottery, animal bones, burnt stone and part of a shale bracelet (Fig. 7.40.675). The tertiary fill, a grey brown clayey silt 133, contained 15 sherds (36g) of pottery of a mixture of fabrics. This probably accumulated through natural silting.

A single small oval pit or posthole (165), measuring 0.40 x 0.60 m and 0.18 m deep, was found adjacent to pit 130 on the north-west. The two features did not intercut, and it is not clear if they were associated.

A second sub-rectangular pit, 283 (Fig. 3.14) was found approximately 5 m to the east of pit 130. It was slightly smaller (2 x 3.2 m), and deeper (0.7 m) than pit 130, but equally steep-sided and flat-bottomed. Pit 283 contained two silty clay fills, 285, 286; the upper fill 285 produced 15 sherds (34 g) of pottery, together with bone and pieces of burnt stone. The pit was cut into two narrow gullies, 298 and 299, and an earlier L-shaped gully, 145.

Two shallow intercutting pits, 218 and 289 (Fig. 3.14), were found less than 1 m south of pit 283. Both pits were oval and varied in width between 1.28 m and 1.5 m, but were only 0.2 m deep. Both were filled with mid brown silty clay.

South-east of gully 272, feature 17 was found in the edge of the excavation and only partly revealed. It was probably the edge of another shallow pit.

#### Feature 14 *(Fig. 3.14)*

Feature 14 was located approximately 10 m to the south of pits 218 and 289. It was oval, with a maximum width of 1.95 m and a maximum depth of 0.50 m. The sides and base were irregular and for this reason it was recorded on site as a tree-throw hole. However, it is perhaps more likely to have been a pit cutting across earlier gully 253. The bottom fill of the pit was 10, a yellow-brown silty clay with a thin band of limestone rubble; the upper fills (8 and 9) were both dark grey brown silty clays. This feature appears to have been used for disposing of rubbish, as it contained 224 sherds of Iron Age pottery weighing 639 g, representing the largest assemblage from the site (Fig. 7.7.55–57). Other finds included significant quantities of bone and burnt stone, together with a small number of flint flakes and a saddle quern fragment of Upper Old Red Sandstone (cat. 686).

#### Postholes 15, 26, 120, 118, 46/49 and 220 *(Figs 3.14–15)*

Postholes in the excavated part of the interior were few. A group of six postholes was found clustered south of the western terminal of enclosure ditch 1. The only find from any of these features was a small frit bead from posthole 26. The group did not form any kind of coherent plan, though from their size and relative positions they can be grouped into three pairs, 15 and 26, 220 and 46/49, and 118 and 120, respectively 1.5 m, 3 m and 2.5 m apart. Pairs of postholes such as these have been interpreted, usually without good evidence, as holding posts used for agricultural purposes, for instance as drying racks. In this case, however, five of the six postholes may have held posts supporting revetments for a bank.

#### *Features external to enclosure 1*

External features comprised a series of narrow gullies leading from the western terminus of the enclosure ditch and a small pit.

#### Gullies 194, 193, 192 and 191

A series of recut gullies cut the western terminus of enclosure ditch 1. The earliest gully (194) was up to 0.75 m deep, nearly as deep as the main enclosure ditch, (Fig. 3.12, segment 66) but extended only 7.5 m north-west. It cut at least the lower fills of the ditch terminal. Gully 194 was replaced by a shallower gully 193 (0.55 m deep) which was at least 30 m long, continuing into the northern edge of the excavation. This was recut by a slightly more sinuous gully 192 (Fig. 3.16, section 43, segment 169), which cut through all of the surviving fills of the main enclosure ditch. Finally 192 was replaced by gully 191, which was only 12 m long, extending nearly 10 m outside the enclosure and 2.5 m into the interior. The gullies were filled with reddish and greyish brown silt loams containing varying quantities of limestone.

All but the last of these gullies started within the western terminal of the main enclosure ditch, suggesting that the enclosure was still in active use although the ditch was partially or completely infilled. The latest gully also respected the entrance to the enclosure, and it has been suggested that it may have marked the extent of the internal bank (see above). These features contained only Iron Age pottery, and are therefore likely to have been associated with the main phase of use of the enclosure.

#### Pit 280 *(Fig. 3.16)*

A small, shallow pit, 280, was found south of the westernmost external angle of the enclosure ditch. Sixty-five sherds (113 g) of predominantly early to middle Iron Age pottery was recovered from the fill making it roughly contemporary with enclosure ditch 1. Charred grain from the fabric of a shell-tempered vessel (Fabric H2) from this feature (Appendix 1, sample 8) yielded an AMS date of 2309 +/- 57 BP (471–466 BC plus 416-199 BC at the 95% confidence level; NZA 8670, R24151/8).

### Discussion

#### *Dating and sequence*

The excavation yielded a small assemblage of pottery in fabrics typical of the middle Iron Age, although containing little which could be closely dated (see Timby, Chapter 7). Three radiocarbon dates corroborate this, and centre around the 4th and 3rd centuries cal.

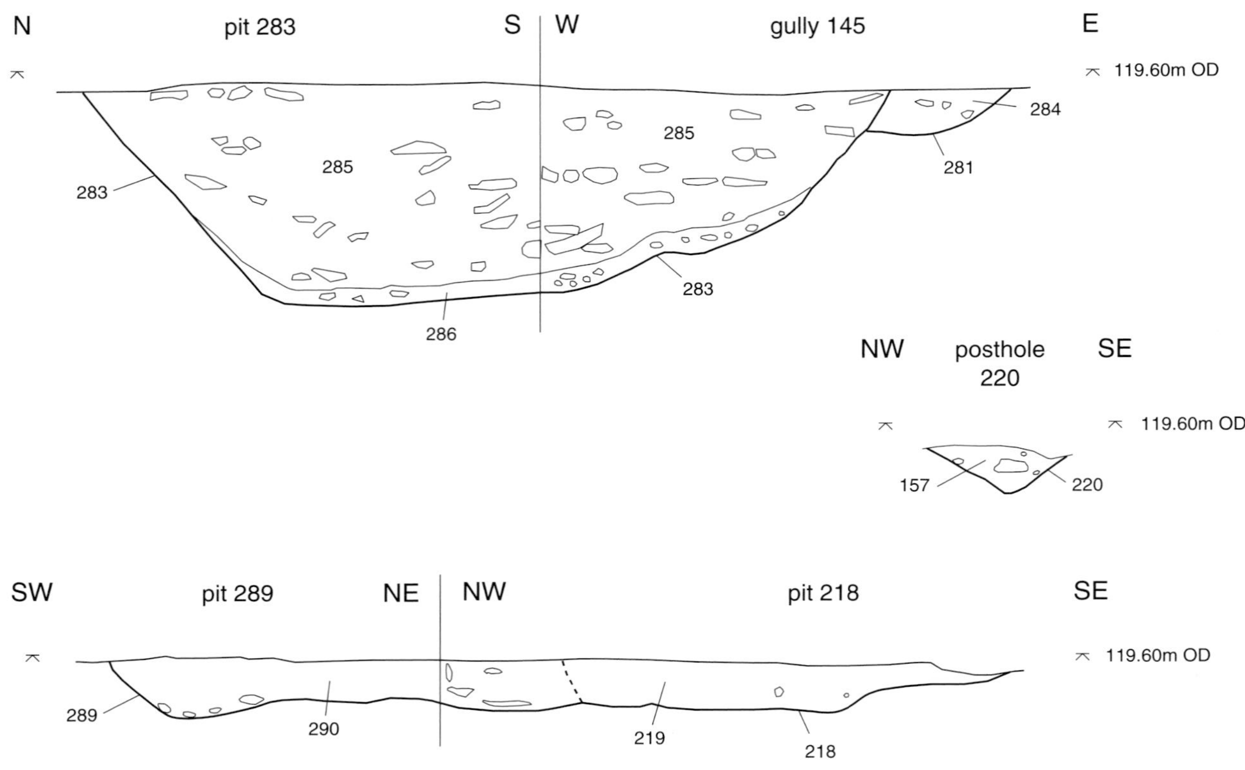


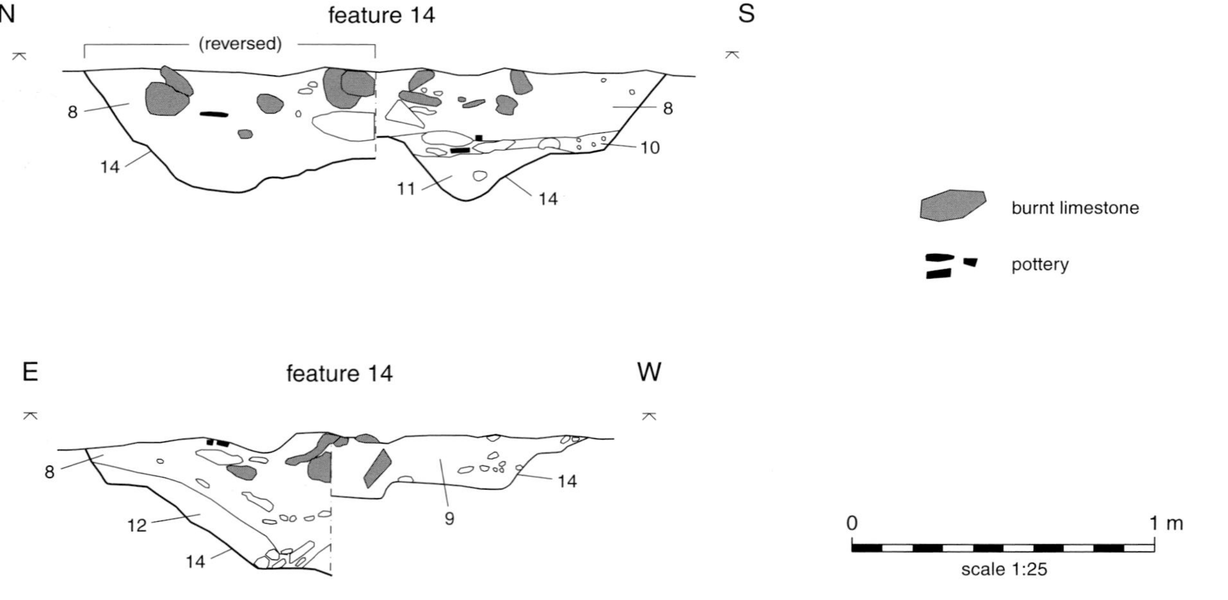


*Figure 3.14 Preston Enclosure, pits and other features, sections.*

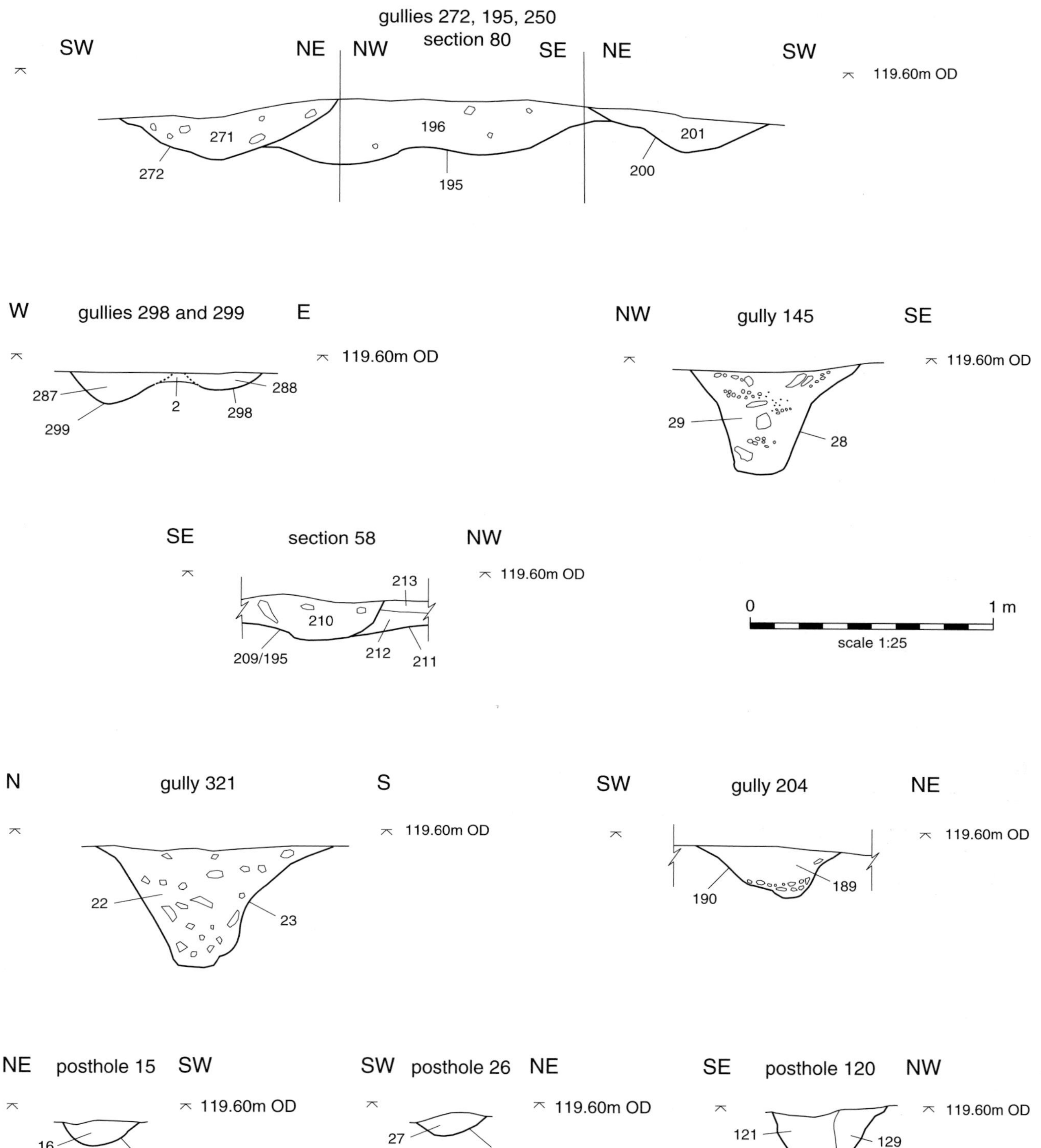


*Figure 3.15 Preston Enclosure, gullies and postholes, sections.*

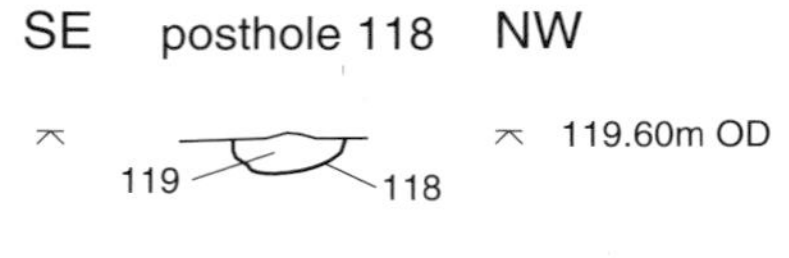


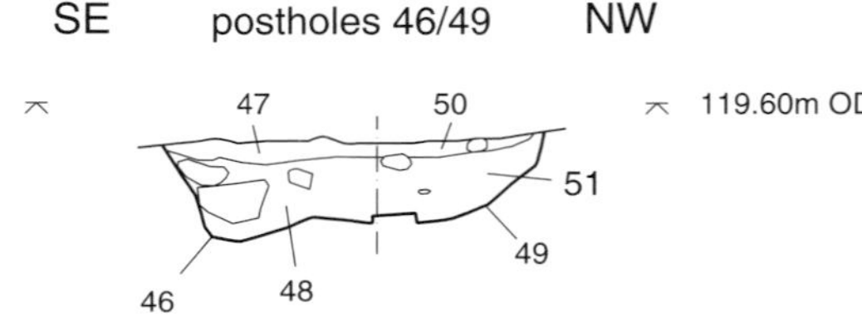


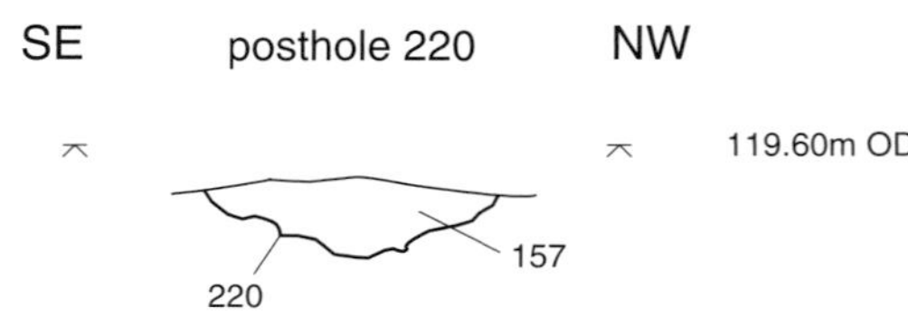


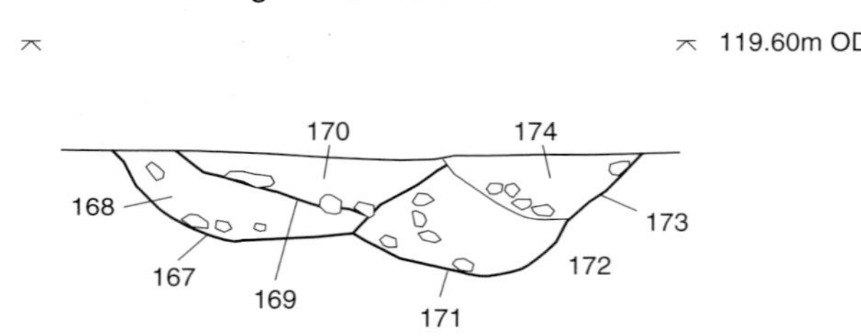


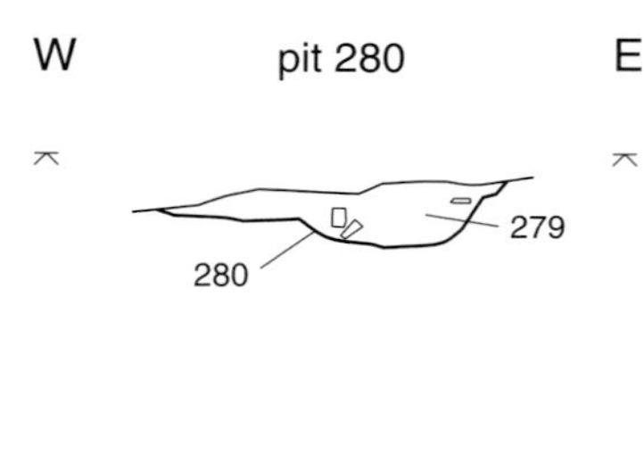


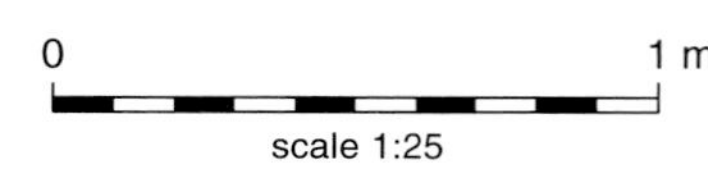


*Figure 3.16 Preston Enclosure, gullies and postholes, sections.*

BC (Appendix 1). The pottery included one or two forms diagnostic of the early Iron Age; these come from one of the stratigraphically latest ditches, and would appear to have been redeposited. The stratigraphic development within the enclosure seems to represent modifications to a layout of a single phase rather than a discrete early Iron Age phase to the settlement. The early Iron Age sherds may therefore derive either from an isolated earlier feature, or may indicate that the origins of the enclosed settlement lay at the transition between the early and middle Iron Age, at the beginning of the 4th century BC. The small number of Roman sherds from upper ditch fills and superficial contexts are insufficient to suggest occupation of the site in the Roman period.

The excavated ditch segments showed no evidence of recutting. The sequence of ditch fills suggests natural silting, represented by primary spills followed by thick deposits of redeposited natural in all the excavated segments. The eastern terminal (41) had very uniform silt fills. Where the ditch cut natural silt (segments 3 and 59) an upper weathering cone was formed, the effect of prolonged erosion, and the wide profile of segment 86 in the stonier northern part of the site may be interpreted in the same way (Fig. 3.12). Most of the upper fills of the enclosure ditch can be attributed to natural silting, with occasional inclusions of domestic refuse, within a more stable ditch profile. This would appear to indicate that the ditch was not maintained during the occupation. An internal bank is suggested by the distribution of features within the enclosure, and the collapse of an internal bank is suggested by stony layer 5 in segment 3 (Fig. 3.11). This may also be the explanation for stony layers 82 and 80 in the western ditch terminal 66 (Fig. 3.12). A similar interpretation may be placed upon the upper part of layer 124 in segment 86 (Fig. 3.12). There is no particular reason to suggest the deliberate slighting of the bank rather than infilling through natural erosion, although this is a possibility.

It is a matter of debate how long such ditches took to silt up, but this may have occurred in less than 100 years. The rubbish dumping in the top of the silted ditch (fills 64 and/or 65, segment 59), and the recut ditches leading out from the north-west entrance, however, suggest that the use of the enclosure continued for some time after the ditch had silted up.

### *Form and function*

The cropmarks indicate that the Preston Enclosure is hexagonal. While not quite a regular hexagon, it can be seen to be more or less symmetrical about the east-west and north-south axes. Polygonal enclosures are common in this period, but these tend to be far more irregular than Preston Enclosure. Other hexagonal enclosures include the large enclosure at Farley Mount (Cunliffe 1991, fig. 12.1), and the 'banjo' enclosure at Preshaw House (ibid., fig. 12.5), both in Hampshire. A number of the excavated examples from the Upper Thames Valley are irregular polygons, including the inner and outer enclosures at Mingies Ditch,

Oxfordshire (Allen and Robinson 1993) and the enclosure at Watkins Farm, Northmoor, Oxfordshire (Allen 1990, 74, fig. 34). In the Cotswolds excavations have been more limited. Allen (1990, 73) argued prosaically that the shape of these enclosures derives from their being dug between marker posts around the perimeter, and recognised a degree of symmetry in their layout. Preston Enclosure may simply represent one extreme within the spectrum of Iron Age polygonal enclosures, although the precision with which it was laid out makes it unusual. It is possible that this was of particular significance, although there is nothing from the associated features and finds that indicate that the settlement was of special character.

The depth of the enclosure ditch (averaging 1.2 m) is similar to that of the excavated enclosures at Rollright (1.5 m) (Lambrick 1988, 82), Watkins Farm (1.1 m) (Allen and Robinson 1993) and Mingies Ditch (just under 1 m) (Allen 1990). It is argued above that Preston Enclosure had an internal bank some 2–3 m wide just inside the enclosure ditch. A bank or wall was identified from a slump of limestones within the ditch at Rollright (Lambrick 1988, 82–3, fig. 57), and suggestions of an upcast mound with a hedge upon it at Mingies Ditch and a probable hedge at Watkins Farm.

Both the enclosure at Watkins Farm and that at Rollright enclose a very similar area to Preston Enclosure (0.42 ha, 0.38 ha and 0.38 ha respectively). The outer enclosure at Mingies Ditch was slightly larger, at 0.48 ha, but this broad similarity perhaps suggests that this order of size was optimal for farmsteads of a certain type. The evidence from the more extensively excavated enclosures suggested that they had been occupied by a relatively small group of people such as a nuclear or extended family, and Preston Enclosure may have been similar.

The recut ditch extending north-west from the enclosure entrance may belong to the class of antennae ditches known from Wessex early Iron Age enclosures such as Little Woodbury, Wilts. and Gussage All Saints, Dorset (Cunliffe 1991, 217–218). More locally, a pair of antennae were found just outside the entrance at Mingies Ditch (Allen and Robinson 1993, 22, figs 8 and 29), and a single ditch attached to the enclosure ditch terminal at Watkins Farm (Allen 1990, 5, figs 3 and 7). Such ditches are believed to have been connected with the funnelling of livestock into their respective enclosures, suggesting that livestock were corralled within the Preston Enclosure on occasions.

As only 25% of the interior was excavated, the conclusions that can be reached about the site as a whole are inevitably tentative. No direct evidence of structures survived, but it is likely that the curvilinear gullies in the central part of the site defined the positions of circular or partly circular buildings. It is possible that a line of such structures ran across the middle of the enclosure, as another annular gully is visible on the cropmark photograph on this alignment (Plate 3.1). One of the excavated gully complexes (145/299/272) had entrances facing both the main enclosure entrance and the area to the south, while gullies 204/253 appear to have faced onto the south area.

There may have been an enclosure on the western side in front of the buildings, in which some of the pits and postholes were dug, but the area to the rear seems to have been devoid of features. The interior therefore seems to show signs of zoning. Such internal organisation of farmsteads is common, being evident in the Upper Thames at Mingies Ditch (Allen and Robinson 1993) and Watkins Farm (Allen 1990), and in Northamptonshire at sites such as Aldwincle and Blackthorn (Knight 1984, 228, figs 49, 60 and 203).

The pits that were found are not typical grain storage pits. The three larger pits all contained sizeable assemblages of domestic rubbish, suggesting that they lay close to domestic foci. None of them impinged significantly upon the areas defined by the curving gullies, and this may indicate that the houses within these gullies remained standing after their surrounding gullies had silted up.

There is insufficient evidence to establish the basis of the economy of the settlement. There was a low density of charred cereal remains which consisted of wheat and barley, with fewer than half the 19 samples assessed containing any charred material at all (see Pelling, Chapter 8). This may be due to taphonomic factors rather than a lack of crop processing on the site. The absence of typical grain storage pits within the excavated area is of uncertain significance. It is possible that the water table was relatively high, making underground grain storage impracticable, as was the case at Mingies Ditch (Allen and Robinson 1993) and Groundwell Farm (Gingell 1992). Alternatively, pits may have been zoned in a different part of the site, although none appear as cropmarks (Plate 3.1) as surely they would if they approached the depth of the enclosure ditch. Raised grain stores may have been used instead. Grain was certainly consumed, as two fragments of saddle quern were recovered (cat. 686–687). Animal bones were relatively plentiful although bone was poorly preserved and only 23% were identifiable (see Powell, Chapter 8). Cattle and sheep/goat predominated, as is usual in the farming settlements in the region.

It has been suggested that the 'banjo' enclosures of Wessex, to which Preston Enclosure is superficially similar, occupied marginal land and may have formed a specialised component of a wider settlement system (Cunliffe 1991, 223). This has also been suggested for Mingies Ditch, occupying a low-lying site in the Upper Thames Valley which would have been suitable for exploiting floodplain pasture (Allen and Robinson 1993, 143). However, it is unclear whether sites of broadly similar form in the Cotswolds can be interpreted in these terms, or whether they are more likely to be relatively independent, mixed farming settlements (Hingley 1984a, 80; Allen and Robinson 1993, 149). There was insufficient evidence to establish whether or not the settlement at Preston Enclosure was based on some kind of specialism and its position in the overall settlement pattern in the Iron Age remains unclear.

## Ermin Farm

*by Andrew Mudd and Simon Mortimer*

The enclosure complex at Ermin Farm was not identified in either the Stage 1 or Stage 2 assessments of the Cirencester and Stratton bypass. A watching brief of the road corridor between the excavation at St Augustine's Farm South and the Harnhill road identified two ditch termini. The area, which had been partially sealed by colluvium, was archaeologically stripped to reveal an approximately square enclosure, part of a parallel enclosure to the west and a number of ancillary linear features (Fig. 3.17). The underlying cornbrash limestone was overlain by a mid brown silty subsoil, averaging around 0.3 m thick but deepening towards a small valley to the north. The stripped area was peppered with tree-throw holes, showing that this had been wooded at one time.

### *Enclosure 49 (segments 6, 10, 28, 29, 43, 54)*

Enclosure 49 was sub-rectangular and measured 24 m north-south by 21 m east-west. A single entrance 2.5 m wide was found west of centre on the southern side. The enclosure ditch, which had a 'V-shaped' profile with fairly steep, unbroken sides, was from 1.7–2.2 m wide and between 0.55 m and 1.06 m deep (Fig. 3.18, segments 6 and 43).

Finds were sparse within all the excavated segments except the eastern terminal (segment 6). Here the lower fills (5 and 4) contained rich assemblages of bone, charcoal and pottery (Fig. 7.8.58–59). Fill 5 also contained two iron strips and a fragment of a bronze-working crucible (see McDonnell, Chapter 8). These two contexts yielded over a third of all the pottery from the site by sherd count and about 60% by weight. The other ditch sections, including the opposite terminal (10) yielded only occasional and usually small fragments of pottery from the middle and upper fills. Three of the excavated sections (including terminal segment 6) had a thick stony fill spilling down the inner side of the enclosure, suggesting that there may have been an internal upcast bank which had slipped (or had been pushed) into the ditch.

#### *Features extending from enclosure 49 (Figs 3.17–3.18)*

Ditch 85 ran south-west from the south-eastern corner of enclosure 49 and continued beyond the southern edge of the excavation. The relationship between this ditch and the main enclosure was not established by excavation, but in plan the uppermost fill of both was the same, and they are assumed to have been contemporary. Where sectioned the ditch measured 0.95 m wide and 0.30 m deep. No finds were recovered from the primary silting (layer 84), but the secondary fill (83) contained fragments of bone, a small piece of daub and pottery (Fig. 7.8.62) contemporary with that found in the enclosure ditch. It is not clear whether this ditch is part of a second enclosure south of 49, or part of an associated field system.

Just outside the south-west corner of the enclosure an east-west ditch (segment 15) was recorded in the drainage ditching. This appears to be a continuation of the southern arm of the enclosure ditch westwards. Five metres to the east of enclosure 49 the terminal of another probable ditch, 42, was visible. It measured 1.1 m wide and 0.55 m deep. The short length of ditch that lay within the excavation ran north-south parallel to enclosure 49. No finds were recovered, but its proximity to the main enclosure and similar alignment suggests that it may be Iron Age.

#### *Pits associated with enclosure 49 (Fig. 3.18)*

The interior of the enclosure contained only three small, shallow probable pits (51, 53 and 61) in the south-east corner. The probable pits produced no finds, but are considered likely to be archaeological features because they were comparatively regular, and because of their proximity to another small and shallow pit 59 (similar to feature 61), which lay just south of the enclosure east of the entrance. This pit contained four sherds of limestone-tempered pottery, probably Iron Age, and some burnt limestone. The three pits inside the enclosure all lay only 2 m from the edge of the ditch, and may therefore have been sealed by the proposed internal bank, part of a group of four pits predating the digging of the enclosure. Alternatively, they may all have been dug up against the inner edge of the bank.

### *Enclosure 48 (segments 19, 39, 63 and 68)*

Five metres to the west of enclosure 49 was an L-shaped ditch 48, one arm of which ran parallel to enclosure 49, the other turned westwards and continued the line of the northern side of 49. This ditch may well have formed the north-eastern corner of a second enclosure parallel to the first. Two sections were excavated through the ditch in the main site, and two others were recorded in the drainage ditching for the new road. The enclosure ditch measured between 1.8 m and 2.5 m wide and varied in depth between 0.7 m and 1 m. One hundred and twelve sherds, (415g) of pottery were recovered from the lowest fill (57) of segment 63 (Fig. 7.8.60–61), and indicated a date broadly contemporaneous with enclosure 49. A replicated AMS radiocarbon date of 363–111 cal BC (95% confidence) was obtained from bone from fill 57 (NZA 8579, R24151/9). As with enclosure 49, stony deposits were seen to overlie the lower fills of the enclosure ditch, but in contrast to the eastern enclosure, these suggested an external, rather than internal, bank. The upper part of the ditch silted up naturally, and contained few finds. A replicated AMS radiocarbon date of 403–357 cal. BC and 287–250 cal BC (95% confidence) was obtained from a bone in fill 71, segment 68 (NZA 8616, R24151/10). Only a small area of this putative enclosure lay within the road corridor, and no features were found within it.

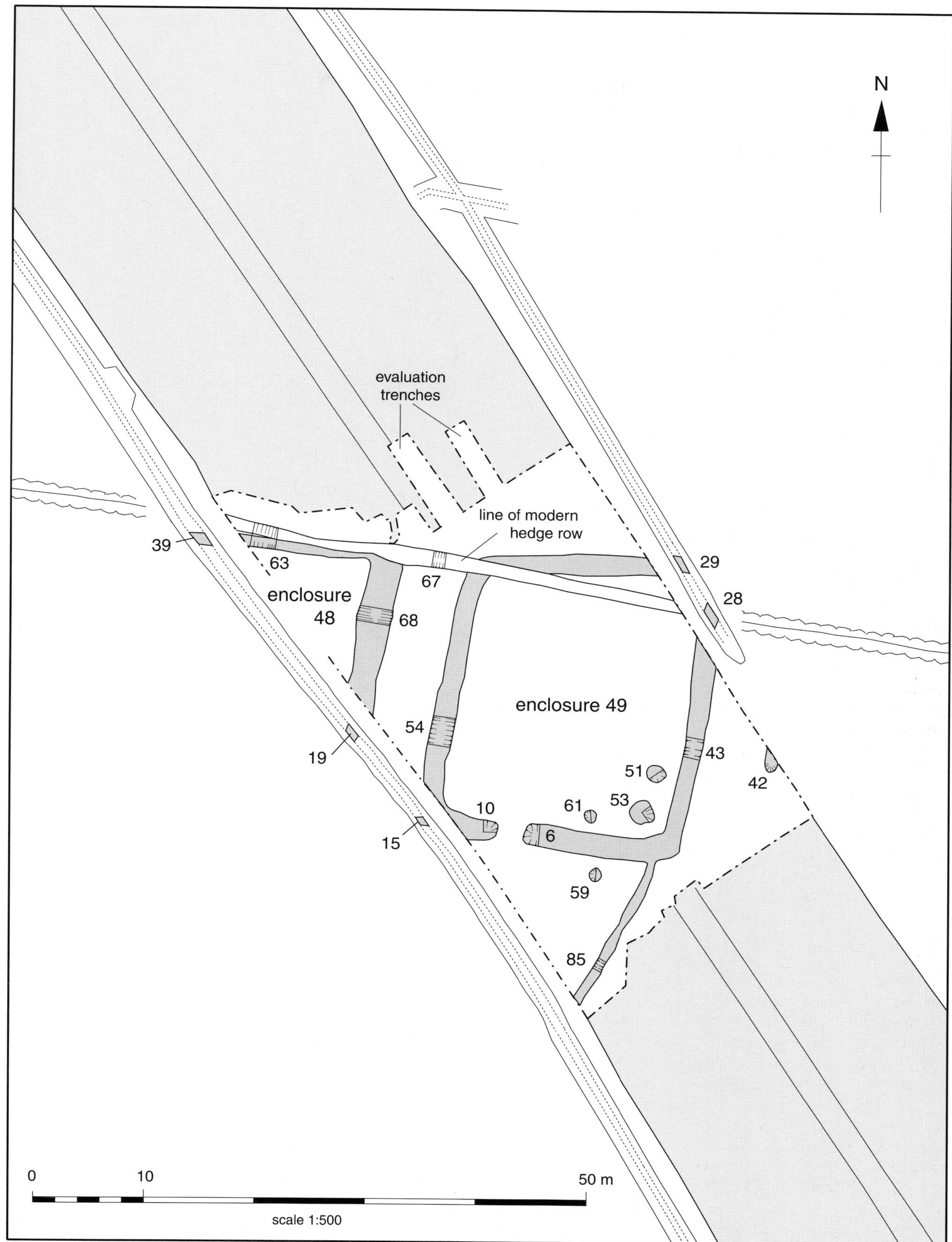


*Figure 3.17 Ermin Farm, plan of excavated features.*

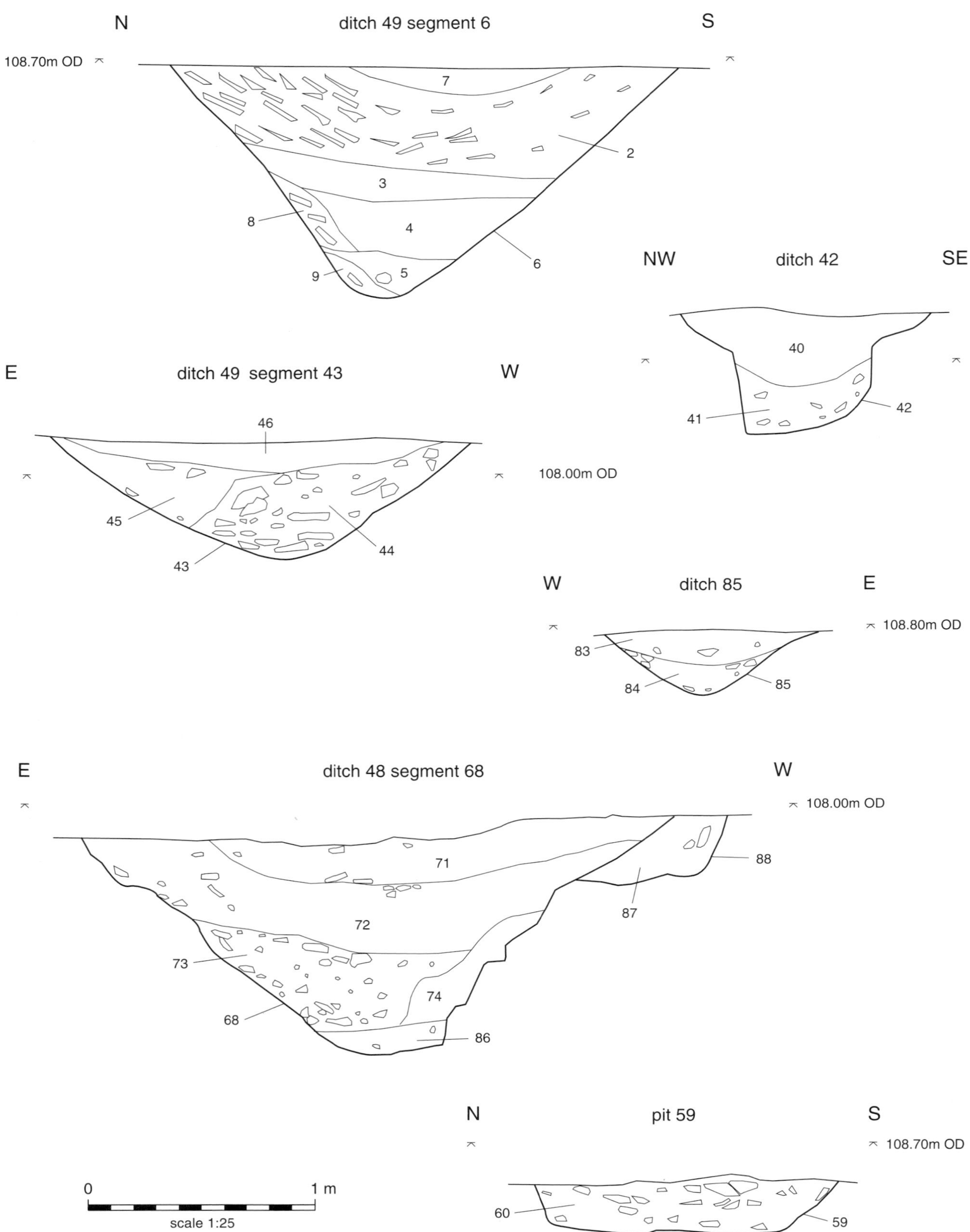


*Figure 3.18 Ermin Farm, enclosure ditches and other features, sections.*

### Discussion

*Date and sequence*

The groups of pottery from the enclosure ditches 48 and 49 and from associated gully 85 are securely middle Iron Age. Two replicated AMS radiocarbon dates were obtained from bone within ditch 48. These came out at 363–111 cal BC (sample 9) and 403–357 plus 287–250 cal BC (sample 10) at the 2-sigma ranges and confirm the middle Iron Age date (*c.* 400–150 BC). The 1-sigma calibrated range for sample 10 (395–371 cal BC) may suggest that the occupation lay within the earlier part of the range. The 1-sigma calibrated range for sample 9, which came from the bottom of enclosure ditch 48, was slightly later (339–309 cal BC plus 210–173 cal BC) but still supports a date in the 3rd or 4th century BC, rather than later. The saucepan pot (Fig. 7.8.61) from this ditch is a form most usually dated to the 3rd century BC or later, and the combined evidence perhaps suggests that a date in the 3rd century BC is to be preferred. Although there are differences in the proportions of pottery fabric types between enclosures 49 and 48, the samples of pottery are too small to place any significance on this, and the enclosures may well have been coeval.

The sequence of enclosure ditch silts suggests that the occupation may have been short-lived. No recutting of the ditch was evident and there was little sign that the ditch sides had been heavily weathered. After the accumulation of the initial deposits, which contained almost all the finds, the ditches appear to have been deliberately filled with material which may have been the original upcast spoil, and later natural silting filled the remaining void. There were few finds from the upper fills and all could have been redeposited from the earlier occupation.

*Form and function*

The excavation suggested that the site was of ordered form with two enclosures – one small sub-rectangular enclosure and another of undetermined though possibly similar form – aligned side by side. The only internal features were three possible pits, which may in fact have been covered by the suggested internal bank. Enclosure 49 would have been of a size suitable for at most two buildings, although there was no trace of any. The site was not cut by plough furrows and the fact that it had been covered by up to 0.3 m of colluvium might suggest that plough truncation had not been severe and that the absence of internal features was genuine. There was, however, no surviving Iron Age ground surface, and it is not certain at what date the colluvium sealed the site, so some truncation may have occurred before that.

Relatively little of the ditches of either enclosure was dug. In enclosure 49 finds were sparse except in the eastern ditch terminal. Finds were in general most prolific at the entrance, and the presence of an internal bank may have discouraged rubbish dumping elsewhere around the enclosure ditch. Most of the pottery from enclosure 48 came from the north arm of the ditch, putatively at the back of the enclosure, and this is consistent with the limited evidence for an external, rather than an internal bank. The environmental evidence was limited. A low presence of cereals was registered from four of the seven samples assessed (see Pelling, Chapter 8), while animal (particularly sheep) bones were present, though the site assemblage is small (see Powell, Chapter 8). Given the small sample excavated, the refuse overall is consistent with domestic occupation either within or close to these enclosures.

Sub-rectangular enclosures of this order of size are listed by Knight (1984) at sites such as Pennyland (enclosures 1, 2, 3 and 4), Milton Keynes (enclosure 3), and occur on a number of sites in the Upper Thames Valley, including Cleveland Farm, Ashton Keynes, near Cirencester (Newman 1994, fig. 24.2). They are found both with and without evidence of an internal roundhouse. The extent of the settlement at Ermin Farm remains unclear and the enclosures may have been components of a larger site, such as at Pennyland (Williams 1993) and probably Cleveland Farm (Newman 1994). However, small and relatively isolated groups of enclosures are known from the Upper Thames Valley in Oxfordshire, for instance at Farmoor (Lambrick and Robinson 1979, 26, fig. 33) and (probably) at Gill Mill, Ducklington (Lambrick 1992b, 96, fig. 33), and from Claydon Pike, Fairford in Gloucestershire (Hingley and Miles 1984, fig. 4.4). The middle Iron Age settlement at the latter site is interpreted as a shifting residence of a relatively small group of people, rather than a larger agglomeration (ibid., 63). A nearby site lies south of Driffield some 2 km away where a pair of small cropmark enclosures, possibly of Iron Age date, back on to a boundary ditch (RCHME SU0798/1). They appear to represent a small, isolated settlement in a well-ordered landscape, and the Ermin Farm enclosures may have been similar.

The back of the Ermin Farm enclosures coincided with the line of the present field boundary, two cuts of which were recorded in the section through segment 63. It is conceivable that this boundary represents continuity from middle Iron Age land division, but far more likely that the common line and alignment is coincidental and related to the local topography, particularly the small stream which runs parallel to the north.

## Highgate House
*by Andrew Mudd and Alan Lupton*

The excavation at Highgate House investigated a clear L-shaped cropmark (Gloucester SMR no. 4698) identified in the Stage 2 evaluation as a partially enclosed Iron Age site (Fig. 3.19). A substantial area of the site was to be preserved *in situ*. Consequently, the excavation comprised two trenches; a 4 x 70 m trench (Trench 1) focused on the enclosure ditch and its northern terminus and a 15–18 x 60 m area excavation (Trench 2) centred partly on the enclosure ditch and on the enclosed settlement area (Fig. 3.19). In addition, a third 5–6 x 19 m trench, Trench 3, was excavated in

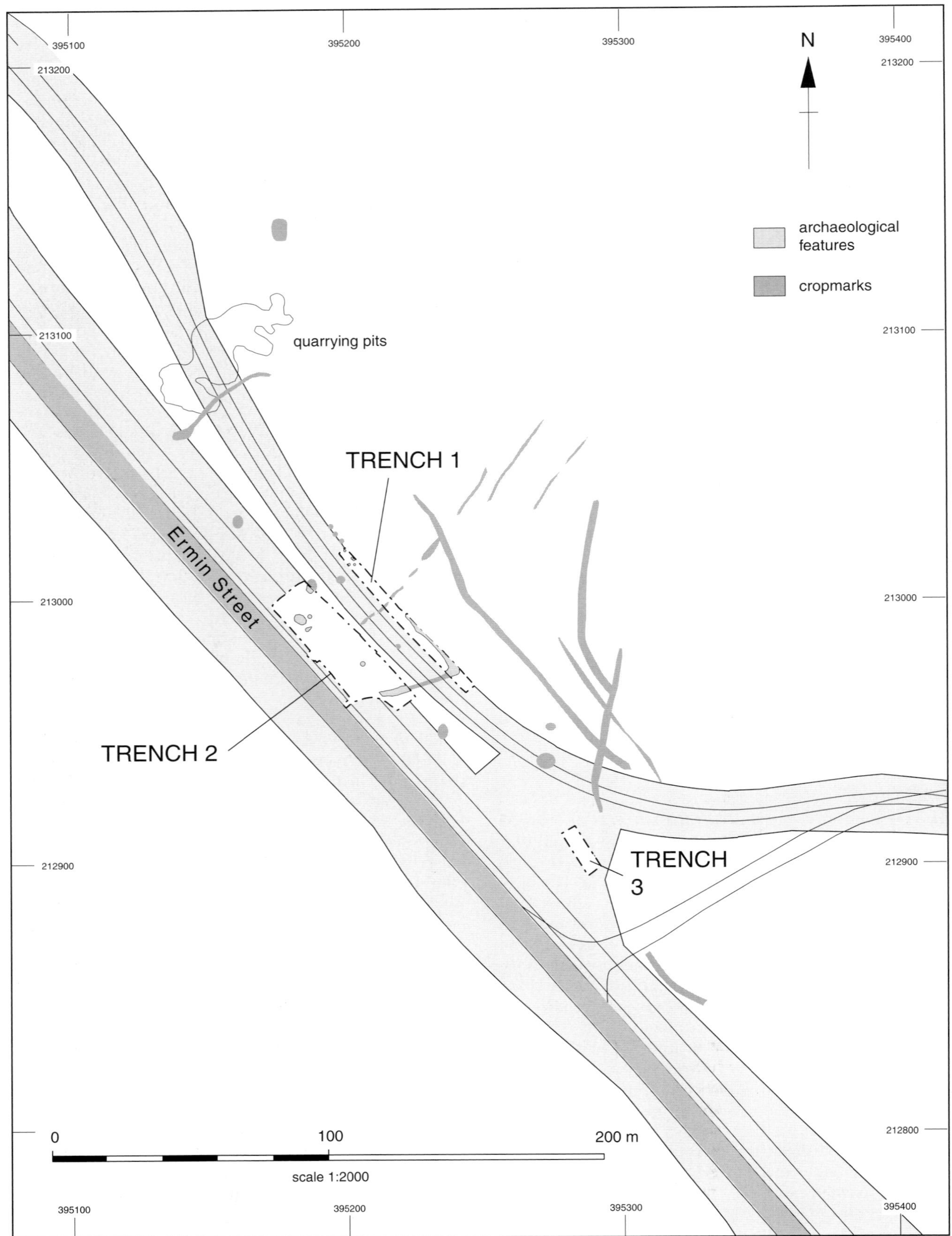


*Figure 3.19 Highgate House, site plan and cropmarks.*

*Plate 3.3 Highgate House, enclosure ditch 144.*

the area of a proposed balancing pond to the south (Fig. 3.19) in order to investigate possible *in situ* Iron Age occupation deposits sealed by a thick layer of colluvium at the head of a dry valley.

### *Enclosure ditch 144 (Fig. 3.20)*

Following stripping of the topsoil and hand-cleaning of Trench 1 some 29 m of enclosure ditch 144 was revealed against the northern baulk, with a square-ended terminal at the north-west end. At the south-east end the ditch returned west-south-west across both Trenches 1 and 2. Within Trench 2 the ditch had been removed on the south by a massive linear quarry (see below, Chapter 5). Three sections, (103/112, 209 and 222) were excavated through the west-south-west arm, and the terminal of the north-western arm (131) was half-sectioned (Figs 3.21–3.22). In all but the terminal the sequence of fills was much the same: fine silt with decayed limestone fragments at the edges of the ditch, and layers of loose limestones infilling the middle right to the bottom. The latter were interpreted on site as sitting within a recut that closely followed the line of the original ditch, and had almost completely cleaned it out. The loose limestones were interpreted as deriving either from slipping or deliberate slighting of an adjacent upcast bank. The section examined in the evaluation had suggested that the bank had been an internal one (GCC 1990, 38), although this was not particularly evident from the sections examined in the current work. Above the limestone layers the upper part of the ditch appeared to have silted up naturally, interspersed with occasional dumps of domestic debris.

Segment 103 (Fig. 3.21) revealed a *c.* 3 m wide and 1.40 m deep V-shaped rock-cut ditch with a compacted mixture of decayed limestone fragments and silty brownish yellow soil (104) at the sides. This was without finds. The lower central part of the ditch was filled with layers 105 and 106, almost exclusively comprised of loose limestone fragments, which may have lain within a recut (112). These fills contained very few finds. Above 106 the subsequent deposits 108, 109, 110 and 111 were relatively stone-free greyish brown silts which appear to represent natural silting in the ditch top. However, 24 sherds (87 g) of Malvernian limestone ware (fabric MALVL1) (Fig. 7.8.63) and a fragment of briquetage (see Barclay, Chapter 7) were recovered from layers 109, 110, 111, suggesting continuing occupation of the site.

The sequence of deposits in segment 209 was similar (Fig. 3.22). The ditch (209) was V-shaped and rock-cut. Like 103, it had a light reddish-brown clayey silt (208) at the sides, and a well compacted mixture of small-medium limestone fragments and greyish-brown clayey silt (220) in the middle, again described as lying within a recut, 212. Layer 220 was sealed by a thick deposit of loose small-large limestone rubble (210), the upper part of which contained nine sherds (23 g) of Malvernian limestone ware and bone. Two radiocarbon dates from cattle bone gave the following results; 395–44 cal BC (sample 2) and 389–49 cal BC

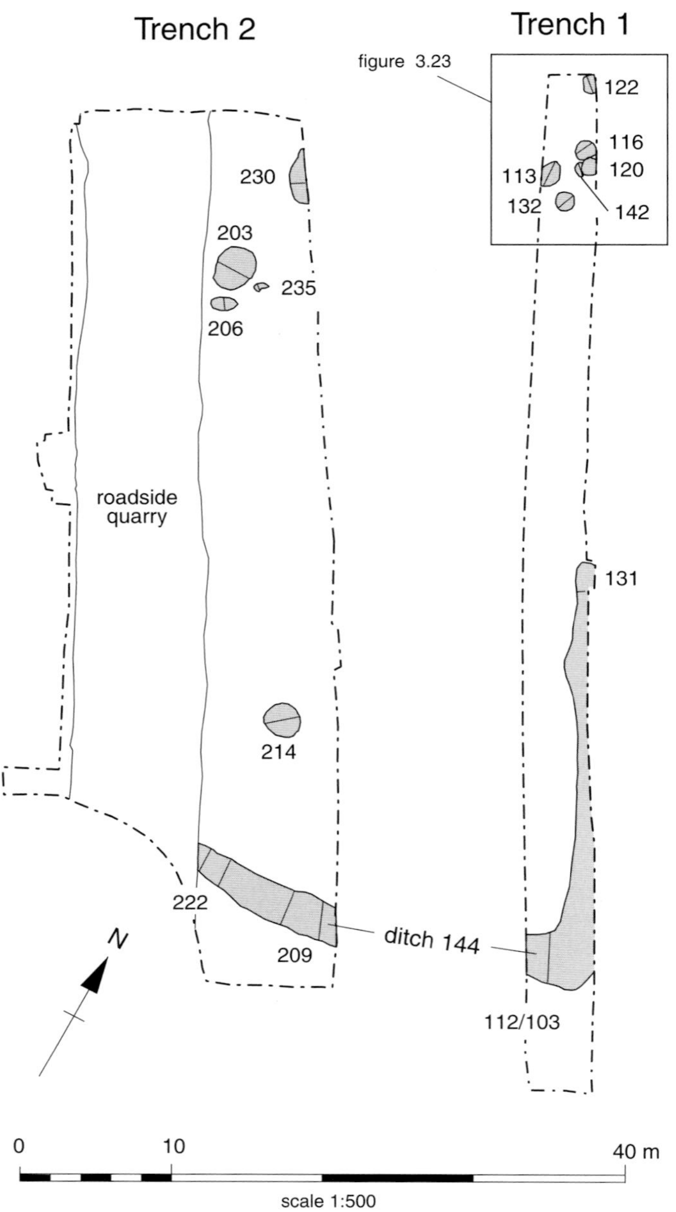


*Figure 3.20 Highgate House, plan of trenches 1 and 2.*

(Appendix 1), indicating a backfilling within the middle Iron Age. Deposit 210 is equivalent to deposits 105 and 106 in Trench 1, and may derive from an upcast bank. This deposit was followed by a compacted pale brown silt 213, which like 211 and 221 resulted from periodic silting in the top of the ditch. Sixty-nine sherds (260 g) of mixed Iron Age pottery, mostly Malvernian limestone wares, were found within layer 211, indicating domestic activity close by (Fig. 7.8.64–67).

Segment 222 had a sequence of fine silts against the sides (Fig. 3.22 and Plate 3.4). Above a 0.60–0.70 m thick band of primary silting material (224) was a layer of compacted yellowish-brown silty clay (225). This was sealed by a similar deposit (226), which in turn lay beneath a thin layer of compacted orange-brown clayey silt (227). In the middle of the ditch was loose limestone rubble (228), described as lying within recut 223. This contained four sherds (3 g) of Malvernian pottery, a fragment of briquetage (see Barclay, Chapter 7), and a few fragments of bone. The bone gave a radiocarbon date very similar to those from 210 (391–57 cal BC (95% confidence) (R24151/4). The overlying compacted silty clay deposit (229) probably represents the subsequent natural infilling of the ditch. A single sherd (29 g) of possible late Iron Age grog-tempered pottery was recovered from fill 229.

Both the profile and the filling sequence revealed in the section across the ditch terminus, 131, were different (Fig. 3.21). Although similarly steep-sided the ditch had a flat bottom and was only 1 m deep. The primary silt (130) included animal bones, from one of which a radiocarbon date was obtained, giving two-sigma ranges of 402–360 cal BC and 281-256 cal BC (Appendix 1, sample 1). Layer 130 was overlain by a predominantly stony deposit incorporating burnt stone and flecks of charcoal (129). Stratified above this was a red-brown silty clay (128), which contained nine sherds (33 g) of Malvernian limestone ware, bone, flint and burnt stone. This was sealed by another stony layer (127) similar to 129; the relationship between the stony fills 129 and 127 and deposits 105 and 106 in ditch segment 131 is uncertain. Stony layer 127 was overlain by 126, a dark grey-brown clayey silt containing large amounts of Iron Age pottery (79 sherds, 501 g including most of the local limestone wares from the site), bone and burnt stone. The quantity of cultural material in the terminal of enclosure ditch 144 suggests that it was used for the deposition of domestic refuse.

#### *Pits located within Trench 1 (113, 116, 120, 122, 132, 142) (Figs 3.20, 3.23–4)*

A group of six pits was discovered: most were shallow (*c.* 0.20–0.40 m) and all (except pit 132 which was circular) were oval-shaped, with vertical sides and flat or flattish bottoms. The cluster was located *c.* 20 m to the north of the excavated terminus of enclosure ditch 144. Most of the pits had a regular form, with their well-cut sides and flat bottoms. They may have been dug as storage pits although most were rather shallow to be typical Iron Age grain stores.

The northernmost pit in this group, 122, had three fills; a reddish-brown primary silting deposit (125), an intermediate stonier, dark grey-brown clayey silt layer (124) and a final deposit made up largely of limestone fragments (123) which may represent the deliberate backfilling of the pit after it had fallen out of use. Fill 125 contained eight tiny sherds (7 g) of middle Iron Age pottery and pieces of burnt stone.

Pit 142 also had a sequence of three fills; a brown silty clay primary deposit, 135 an intermediate stonier

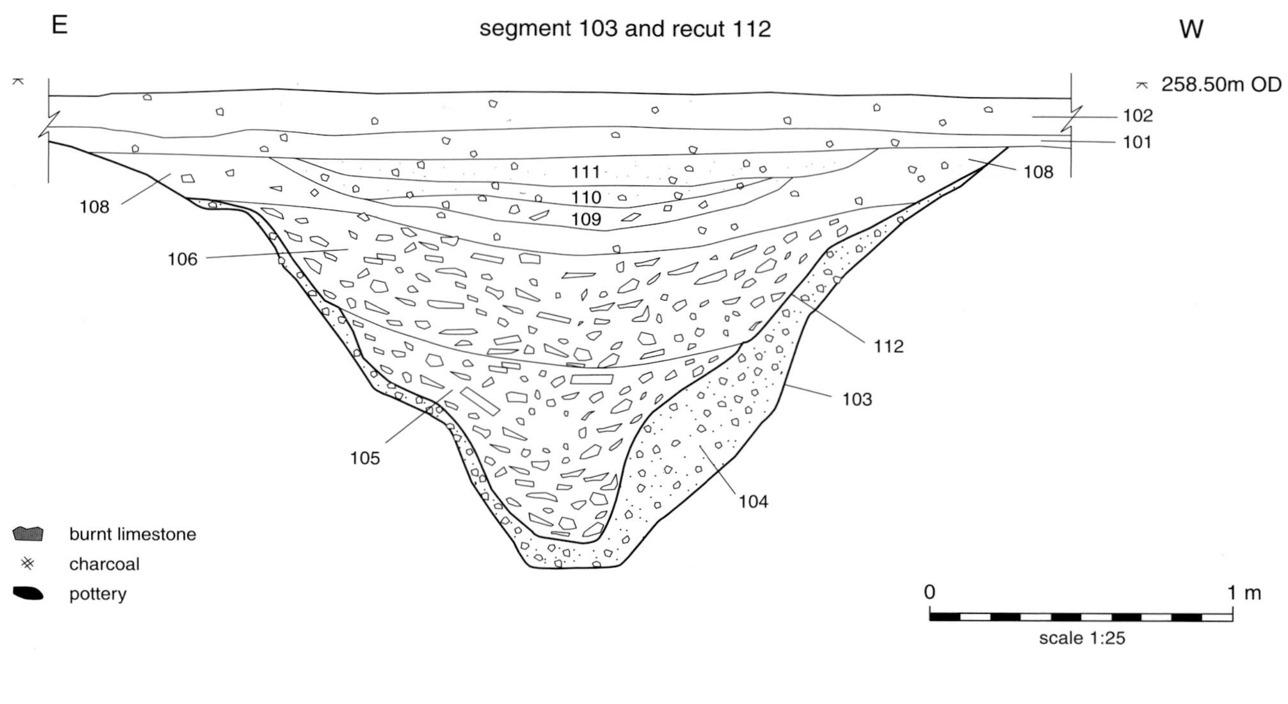


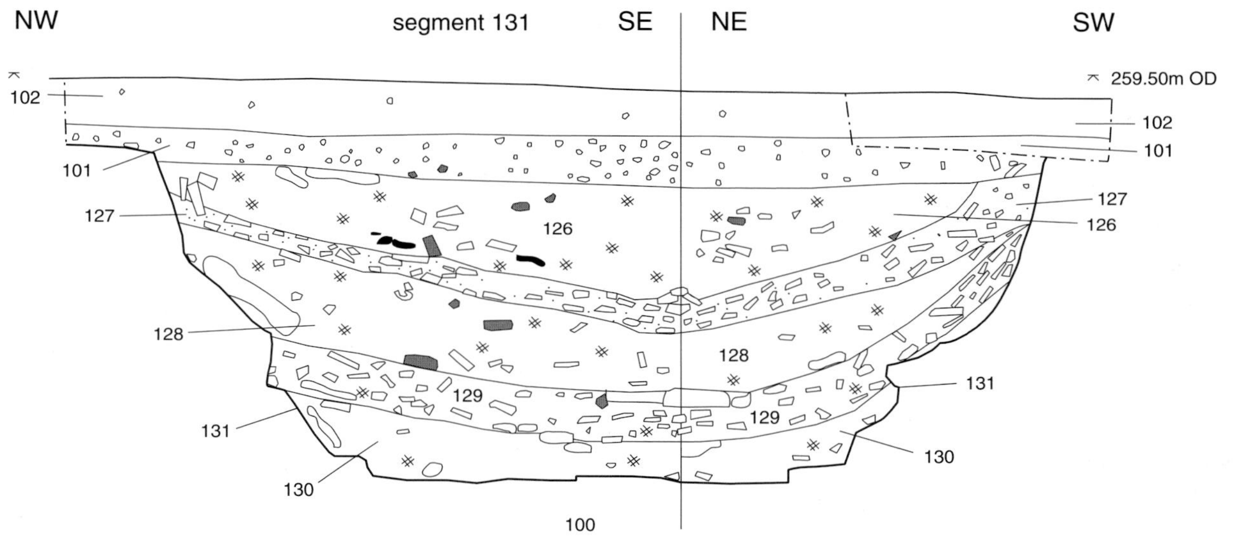


*Figure 3.21 Highgate House, enclosure ditch sections in trench 1.*

layer, 134 and a final reddish brown silty clay deposit, 143, which contained five fragments (3 g) of Malvernian limestone ware and bone. Pit 142 was cut by pit 120.

Pit 116 contained a similar sequence of fills to that seen in pit 142 and likewise was also cut by pit 120. In this case, however, the secondary and tertiary fills, 118 and 117 respectively, contained 3 sherds (18 g) of limestone-tempered pottery and burnt stone.

Pit 120 was 0.90 m deep; considerably deeper than any of the other pits in the group. It had four fills, consisting of a thin primary silting deposit, 141, a 0.45 m-thick band of yellowish-brown silty clay mixed with limestone fragments (140), another thin reddish-brown silty clay layer (139), and a final stony deposit, 138. The basal fill, 141, contained three sherds (20 g) of Iron Age pottery. A further 15 sherds (30 g) of similar pottery were recovered from the upper fills, 138 and 139.

Pit 132 had a single fill comprising a mixture of brown silty clay soil and numerous small-large limestone fragments (133), which contained a scrap (1 g) of Malvernian limestone ware in association with a few pieces of bone and burnt stone.

To the west of these pits lay a possible pit, 113, which was somewhat more irregular in plan than the others. No finds were recovered from either of the feature's two fills, 114 and 115. Although it had a reasonably flat bottom, it did not have the vertical sides

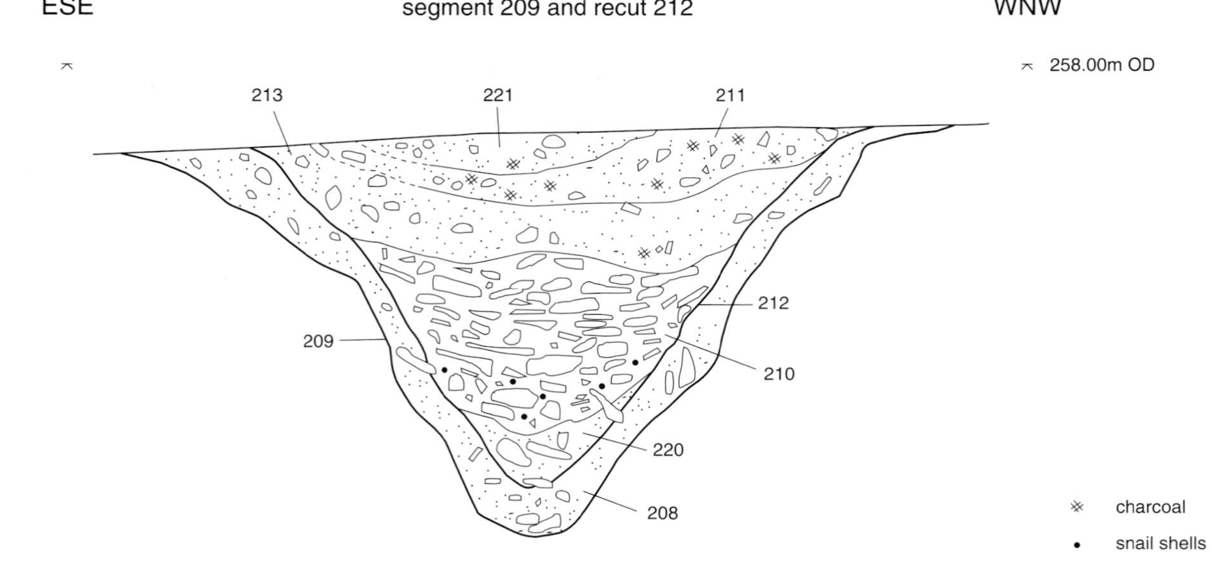


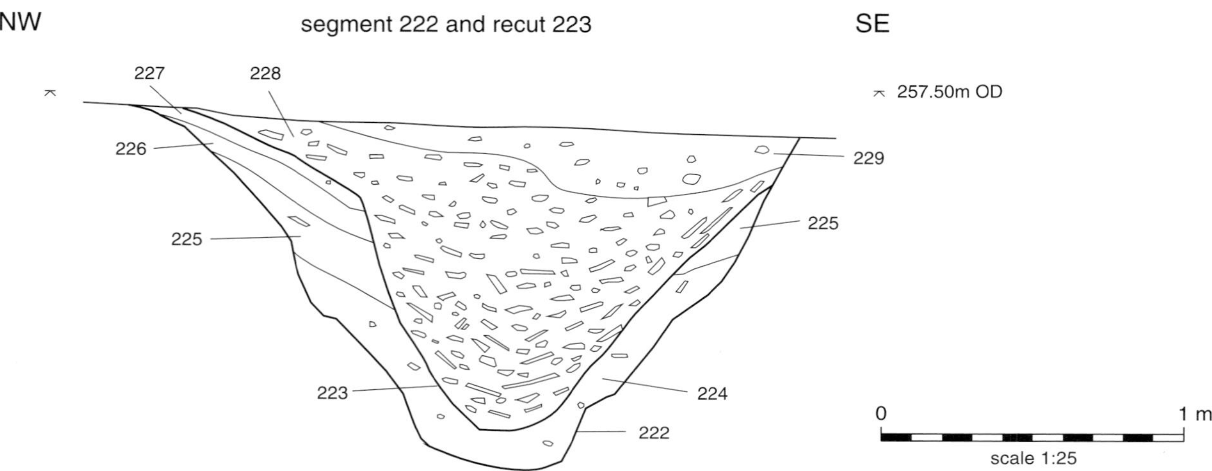


*Figure 3.22 Highgate House, enclosure ditch sections in trench 2.*

seen in all the other pits in this group and may have been a tree-throw hole.

Three further pits, similar in size and profile to those mentioned above, were discovered just to the north of Trench 1 during the watching brief in the sides of the 'V-ditching'. These were not observed in plan, but were approximately 0.6 m, 0.5 m and 0.4 m deep with fills of mid to greyish brown silt. Several sherds of Iron Age limestone-tempered pottery were retrieved from the middle fill of one of them.

### *Pits located within Trench 2 (203, 206, 214, 230, 235) (Fig. 3.25)*

As with Trench 1, a number of pits were found, clustered west of enclosure ditch 144. The northernmost pit, 230, extended beneath the northern baulk (Fig. 3.20). It was a substantial oval-shaped steep-sided feature, cut to a depth of *c.* 1.05 m, which contained a total of five fills (205, 230–232, 234). These were essentially yellowish or reddish brown silts with varying quantities of decayed and platey limestone and all appeared to have been the result of natural infilling of the pit as the sides collapsed. There was a marked lack of cultural material. Only the uppermost layer, 233, contained any finds of archaeological interest; a sherd of possible Roman pottery and three small iron nails (more likely Roman than Iron Age in date).

South of pit 230 lay a group of three pits; 203, 206 and 235. All three were oval-shaped, shallow and contained a single fill. Only the largest pit in this group, 203, produced any finds; a sherd (2 g) of middle Iron Age pottery, an oxidised Roman sherd (5g) and several pieces of bone. The Roman sherd may be intrusive as the site was heavily rutted in this area. Whether the pits were for storage is unclear, but they appear to be part of a zone of pits to the north-west of the enclosure.

In addition to these pits, a 1.20 m-deep circular pit, 214, was discovered within the enclosure in a more isolated position. Its form was more typical of a storage pit. It may have had a thin lining of blue clay (219) on the base. The sides of the pit appear to have collapsed while the feature was open (218) before it was deliberately backfilled with loose limestone rubble (217) to a depth of 0.70 m. The subsequent clayey silt deposits, 216 and 215, appear to have been the result of natural infilling. No finds were recovered from any of these fills.

### *The dry valley and colluvium in Trench 3 (Fig. 3.26)*

Trench 3 was situated over a partially infilled dry valley and was designed to further investigate possible *in situ* Iron Age deposits identified in the evaluation. Beneath the modern topsoil (300) was a sequence of four reddish brown silt loams (up to 1 m thick altogether), all of which were excavated by machine, and were sterile. The latest of these colluvial layers, 301, overlay a fine, stonier deposit (302). Below this layer, 303, which contained very few inclusions, was the most substantial, increasing from 0.10 m thick at the northern end to 0.40 m across most of the trench. The underlying deposit, 304, only appeared in the northern third of the trench, thinning out towards the south-east. Very few molluscs were preserved in the colluvial sequence (see Robinson, Chapter 8). A probable Roman sherd was recovered from layer 306 just below 303, perhaps indicating that the colluvial sequence derived from post-Roman ploughing.

Beneath 304 lay a thin band of stonier colluvium, 305, which contained some charcoal flecks, burnt clay and bone. This overlay 306, which was a very pale reddish brown silt containing water snails (*Anisus leucostoma*). This may suggest local water seepage. The underlying reddish brown silt loams (307, 308 and 312) showed mineral staining. Layers 307 and 308 contained most of the Iron Age pottery from this trench (20 sherds, 42 g) as well as some bone. The assemblage was dominated by Malvernian limestone wares. There was also a single curved bodysherd of possible late Iron Age or early Roman date from 308. The average size of sherds from the colluvium was under 2 g, compared with over 4 g for those from the ditches and pits, and it is therefore unlikely that the Iron Age pottery was *in situ*. It is more likely to have derived from the adjacent settlement, perhaps from a surface midden, through post-Iron Age ploughing.

A single flint associated with a small patch of burnt clay and charcoal was found within the lowest colluvial deposit excavated, 312. This perhaps attests human activity of earlier prehistoric date within the dry valley itself.

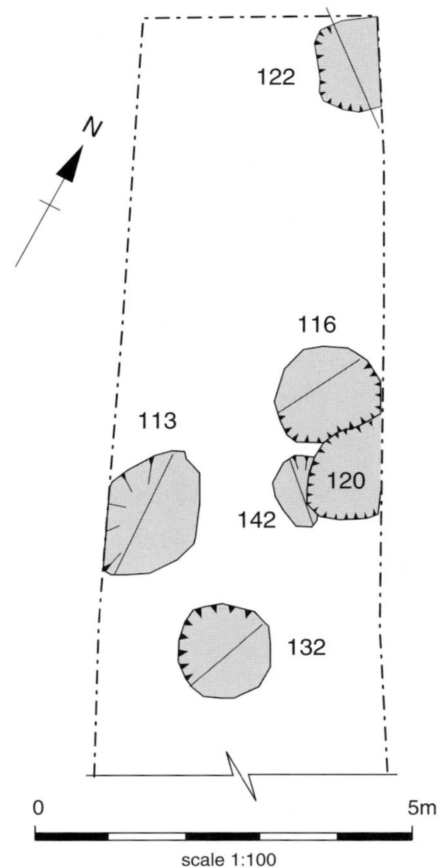


*Figure 3.23 Highgate House, plan of pits in trench 1.*

A 0.10–0.15 m thick band of dark reddish-brown clay was found below 312 in the northern part of the trench. This sterile layer appears to have been deposited naturally. Below this material lay the natural weathered limestone substrate which fell away gradually towards the south-east (i.e. towards the lowest point of the dry valley).

### *Discussion*

#### *Dating and sequence*

The quantity of pottery from the excavations (293 sherds) was meagre and the material fragmentary, although the fabrics indicate a middle Iron Age date. The presence of Malvernian limestone-tempered ware throughout the fills of the enclosure ditch may suggest a date in the later part of the middle Iron Age (see Timby, Chapter 7). Four radiocarbon dates were obtained from the lower fills of the enclosure ditch (Appendix 1, samples 1–4) all of which are middle Iron Age. The dates can tentatively be placed in sequence, that from the primary silting at the terminus being first, the three dates from the limestone fills a little later. This suggests a date as early as the 4th century BC for the start of occupation, with the limestone fills falling between *c.* 350 BC and *c.* 150 BC. Occupation material continued to be deposited in the

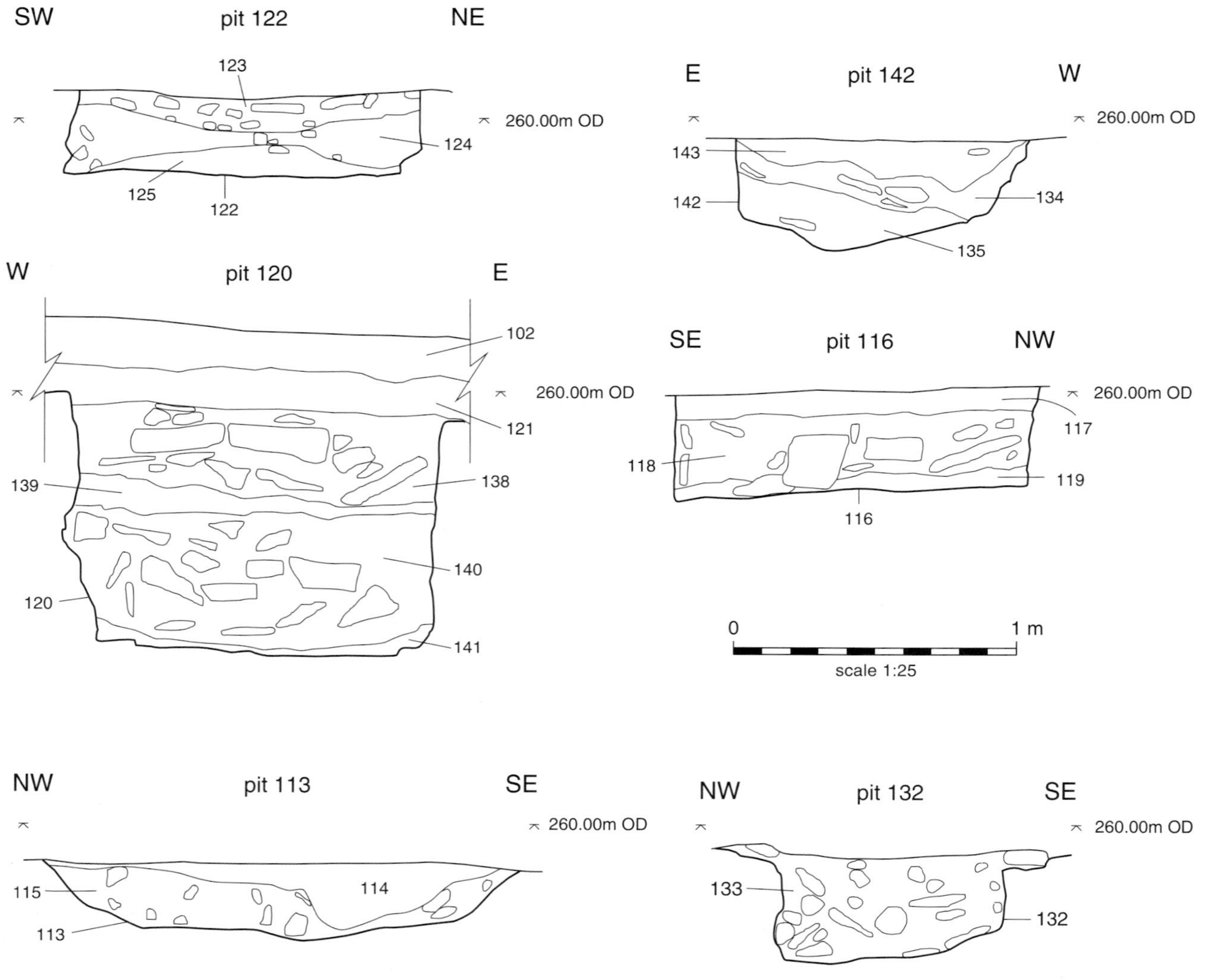


*Figure 3.24 Highgate House, pits in trench 1, sections.*

top of the ditch, and a single grog-tempered sherd from the top of segment 223 (fill 229) may suggest that the site was occupied as late as the 1st century BC.

The sequence of fills within the enclosure ditch is open to alternative interpretations. The excavators believed that the ditch had been recut almost completely on the same alignment, but alternatively the fine silt fills of the 'early' cut, contrasting with the stony fill of the later one, may simply represent the pattern of natural silting within a ditch of a single phase. No finds were retrieved from the primary silts of the ditch, except at the ditch terminal (segment 131), but these were of the same character as the pottery found in the 'later' cuts. The 4th-century BC radiocarbon date (sample 1) from the primary fill of the ditch terminal also argues against a yet earlier phase of ditch, for which no artefactual evidence was obtained. This re-assessment suggests the whole of the fill sequence can be interpreted as belonging to one phase, either through natural silting of the ditch edges and adjacent bank, or by deliberate infilling. The latter interpretation may be favoured (as it was in the initial evaluation – GCC 1990, 38) in view of the depth of the rubble fill, which cannot have entirely derived from the weathered edges of the ditch, and also appears too dense and uniformly distributed to have been the result of the slippage of a bank (Plate 3.4).

The finds from the pits were fewer although the pottery showed the same range of fabrics as that from the ditch. A phasing sequence based on ceramics is not generally possible. The Roman sherd from pit 203 is not considered reliably provenanced, but even if it were it need indicate no more than that the pit was left open and accumulated later material in its top. The stepped profile of pit 230 is unusual on the site, and may in fact indicate that it was a quarry (if so, most probably Roman). Alternatively it may have been stepped for functional reasons (for instance to gain access) or that the profile resulted from the collapse of the pit walls. The sides of pit 214 appear to have

*Plate 3.4 Highgate House, ditch 144, segment 222, looking north-east. Showing rubble infill and fill of possible earlier ditch (left).*

collapsed before the pit was partly backfilled and then left to fill in. In contrast, the pits in Trench 1 and those in the watching brief seem to have been substantially, if not entirely, backfilled when they went out of use, with pit 120 plausibly capped with stone. This may indicate a pattern of functionally distinct pits in different areas of the site, or there may be a chronological factor whereby the location of pits shifted westward and the later pits were left open when the site was abandoned.

This latter interpretation is tenuous on the limited evidence but accords with the sequence interpreted at the middle Iron Age site at Birdlip Bypass, where the majority of pits appear to have been only partially filled at the end of their use before the site was abandoned, and final infilling was only completed in the 1st century AD when the site was re-occupied (Parry 1998). Hints of a similar pattern of occupation and abandonment have been noted from The Bowsings Guiting Power, and The Beeches, Cirencester (op. cit.).

*Form and function*

The excavations were limited in extent and the overall form of the settlement remains undefined. The L-shaped ditch, while shown to be fairly substantial, appears on present evidence to be only one element in a wider spread of settlement features and cannot necessarily be considered as the focus of occupation. The arms of the ditch were shown to be about 27 m and 27–35 m long, since the east-west arm did not appear on the other side of the much later roadside quarry and must have terminated somewhere within it. It is possible that another ditch was obliterated by the roadside quarry turning the L into three sides of a rectangular enclosure. A section through the quarry showed that it had been dug to a depth of 1.7 m and would have removed the enclosure ditch had it existed here. The cropmarks of the site (Fig. 3.19), which are restricted to the field on the eastern side of the A417, appear to indicate at least one other large ditch and several smaller linear features, but these do not form enclosures either. Possibly the ditch was simply a quarry from which the drystone walls of more functional enclosures were built, but its V-shaped profile, and its regular and continuous dimensions around two sides, suggest not. Alternatively the wider landscape was enclosed by walls or hedges, and the ditches demarcated particularly strong boundaries within this, or formed a convenient angle into which to drive livestock for temporary corralling.

No house sites were identified, although this may be due to the relatively small scale of the excavation, or to plough truncation, rather than genuine absence. Pits were located to the north both inside and outside this partial enclosure and the pottery from Trench 3, over 50 m to the south, suggests that occupation originally also extended some way in this direction. The cropmarks to the east also show a number of other ditches, pits and probable quarries, but it is not known how many (if any) belong to the Iron Age settlement. A substantial linear ditch running for over 100 m appears to be of a similar size to enclosure ditch 144 and may mark the eastern boundary of the settlement. If this were to be the case, the area of settlement would have been extensive, but it remains unclear whether this forms part of an enclosure and it is not possible to be sure that the settlement can be classified as an 'enclosed' rather than an 'open' one.

Little light can be thrown on the economy of the Highgate House settlement. The range of artefacts was very limited. Animal bones were fairly common but were poorly preserved, and only a small proportion (17%) were identifiable (see Powell, Chapter 8). Most were of cattle, although this dominance may simply reflect the better preservation of larger bones. Pits of the type usually interpreted as grain stores were present, but only in small numbers within the excavated area. There was a low concentration of charred plant remains (present in only 16 of the 28 samples assessed) but this did include spelt wheat and barley, both typical Iron Age crops (see Pelling, Chapter 8). Overall it is difficult to gauge the significance of arable agriculture in the economy.

Though limited, the evidence from Highgate House is similar to that from other middle Iron Age settlements in the Cotswolds (see Parry 1998 for a discussion of some of the Cotswold sites). Generally, there is little clear indication of the form or nature of these sites, principally because of the limited nature of excavations undertaken. The shortage of evidence for house structures is typical, with domestic foci possibly only identified at The Park, Guiting Power and Guiting Manor Farm (Parry op. cit., 54–55). Pits are often common, although not particularly densely distributed, and sometimes appear to occur in discrete clusters or zones both inside (eg. The Bowsings, The Park, Guiting Manor Farm) and outside (eg. Birdlip Bypass, Rollright, Huntsman's Quarry) ditched enclosures. There is therefore some indication of functionally distinct areas within these settlements, although their overall spatial organisation is still far from clear.

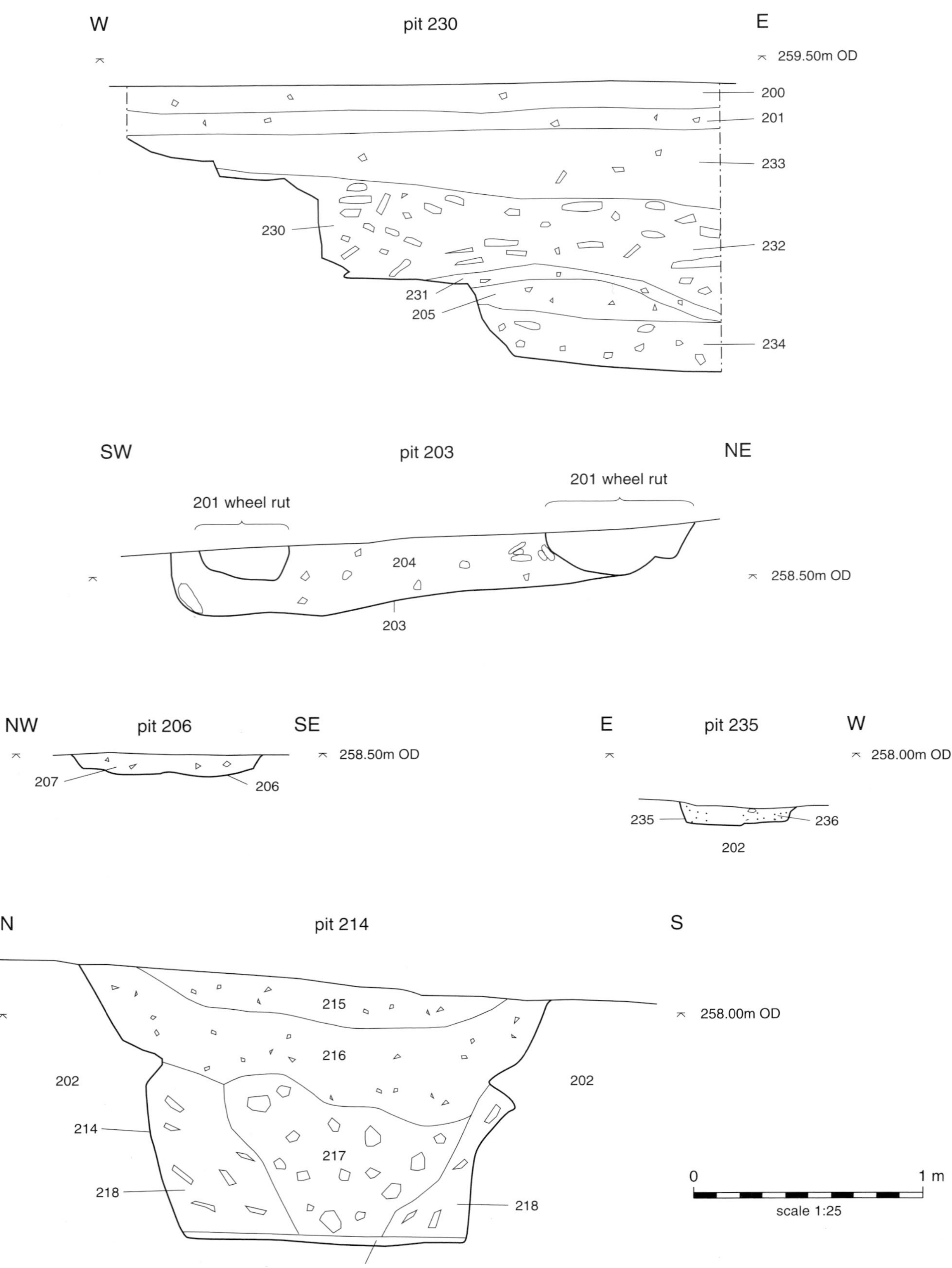


*Figure 3.25 Highgate House, pits in trench 2, sections.*

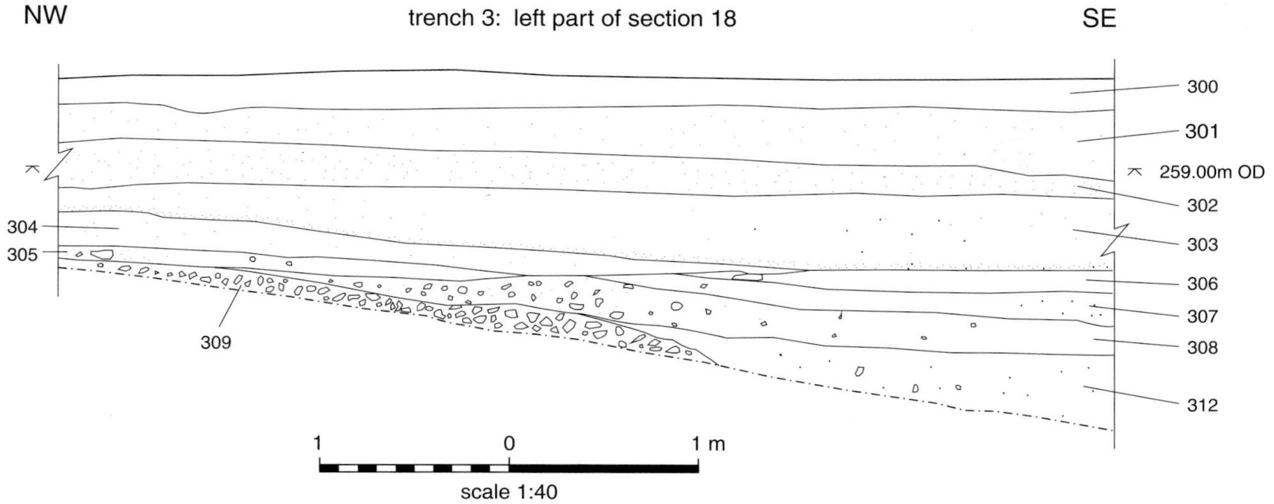


*Figure 3.26 Highgate House, trench 3, section through colluvium (part).*

One aspect of the site which deserves mentioning is the high proportion of Malvernian pottery on the site (see Timby, Chapter 7), amounting to 59% of the entire assemblage (42% by weight). This compares with 10% by weight from the middle Iron Age occupation at Birdlip Bypass, 15% from Guiting Power and 8% from Salmonsbury (Parry 1998). The ware was not present at Preston Enclosure or Ermin Farm. The proportion from Highgate House is similar to that in the handmade assemblages from the 1st-century AD occupations at Birdlip Bypass, Ditches hillfort and West Hill Uley. Guiting Manor Farm produced an assemblage which comprised 40% Malvernian Ware (Parry pers. comm.). A small quantity of briquetage also came from Highgate House (see Barclay, Chapter 8). Unless the radiocarbon dating can be discounted, it is possible that this site was importing Malvernian ware in large quantities significantly earlier than other sites examined in the region. The reason behind this and its implication for the nature of the site here cannot be explored without a bigger sample of excavated sites and better definition of the systems of production and exchange in the middle Iron Age.

## MISCELLANEOUS LATER PREHISTORIC FEATURES

*By Andrew Mudd, Jeff Muir and Andrew Parkinson*

### Lower Street Furlong *(Fig. 3.27)*

The majority of the features found at Lower Street Furlong were the result of medieval or post-medieval activity and are dealt with in Chapter 6. However, a small number, comprising a curvilinear ditch, a narrow gully and a linear ditch, probably all date to the later prehistoric period. A large number of tree-throw holes were also revealed. These were undated.

#### *Tree-throw holes*

A large number of features on this site proved to be tree-throw holes, some of which showed signs of burning. Their distribution is shown on Fig. 3.27. A hearth-like feature (CAT 1991a, 113) found in the Stage 2 evaluation (Trench 546) was probably a similar feature. Although no dating evidence was recovered from any of the excavated examples, the pits may relate to earlier prehistoric land clearance in the area. One was shown to pre-date ditch 27 (below). The light scatter of worked flints identified in the Stage 1 assessment, which may be taken together with the three redeposited pieces from ditches 27 and 55 of the excavation, are not directly associated with any of the excavated features and may derive from unrelated prehistoric activity.

#### *Ditches 27, 45 and 55*

A 32 m length of curving ditch (27) was discovered against the southern baulk in the central part of the excavation. Sections excavated through the feature revealed a shallow U-shaped profile, approximately 0.6 m wide and 0.3 m deep. Finds were rare but included a few crumbs of limestone-tempered Iron Age pottery. A late prehistoric date seems quite likely for the curvilinear ditch, since its course in both directions would intercept Roman Ermin Street lying only 10 m or so to the south-west, and so it is likely to pre-date that road.

A short distance to the north of the curving ditch was a *c.* 1 m section of narrow ditch (45), which also ran into the southern baulk. No finds were recovered from this shallow feature, but the associated single orange-brown silty-clay fill (44) was very similar to that seen in the curvilinear feature.

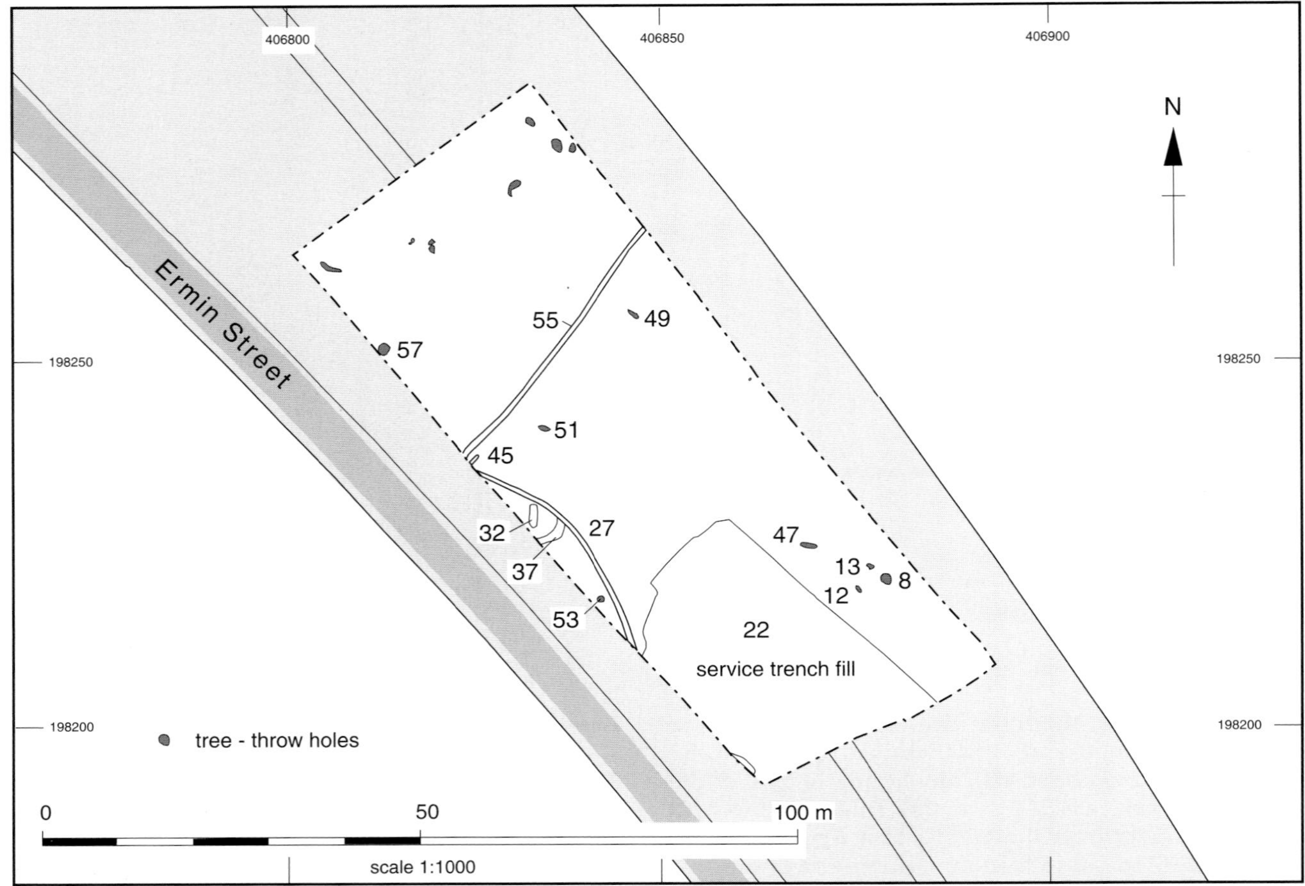


*Figure 3.27 Lower Street Furlong, plan of later prehistoric gullies and earlier tree-throw holes and pits.*

Equally, a shallow linear ditch (55) running approximately north-south across the full width of the site, may have been an Iron Age feature, as its fill was similar in character to that of the curvilinear ditch but was devoid of finds.

These features are all likely to have been field boundaries as there was no indication of nearby settlement.

### Cherry Tree Lane and Burford Road South *(Fig. 3.28)*

Construction of the RMG compound and the associated temporary accommodation area provided the opportunity to examine the area close to the junction of Burford Road and Cherry Tree Lane alongside the road corridor itself. The road trenches are described in chapter 5. The work took place in three stages leading to the investigation of three separate areas.

#### *Cherry Tree Lane Area 1*

The first stage of the work, involved the stripping of topsoil over the main compound area. This area was located over a natural undulation in the landscape which formed a relatively shallow, elongated depression running north-east to south-west across the site. The soil was stripped to formation level and bedrock was exposed only on the ridges at the northern end of the site. The upper slopes of the depression were covered by a layer of relatively modern colluvium containing medieval and post-medieval pottery and tile. The base of the depression was occupied by a more substantial layer of fine orange colluvium containing medieval pottery. These deposits were not removed. Two possible hearths located within this earlier hillwash, and a post-medieval ditch, are described in Chapter 6. Two circular pits (12 and 13) were revealed in the area just above the natural depression and are described below.

#### *Cherry Tree Lane Area 2*

The second stage of the work involved a watching brief during topsoil stripping to the south of the compound, over an area which was to be used for contractors' temporary accommodation. Much of the site proved to be devoid of archaeological features, but a sequence of two intercutting pits (35 and 47) and a later ditch (40) were revealed close to the north-east corner adjacent to Cherry Tree Lane. The extent of the pits and the ditch was never fully defined due to the presence of a heavy layer of plough-disturbed grey clay which sealed most of the features.

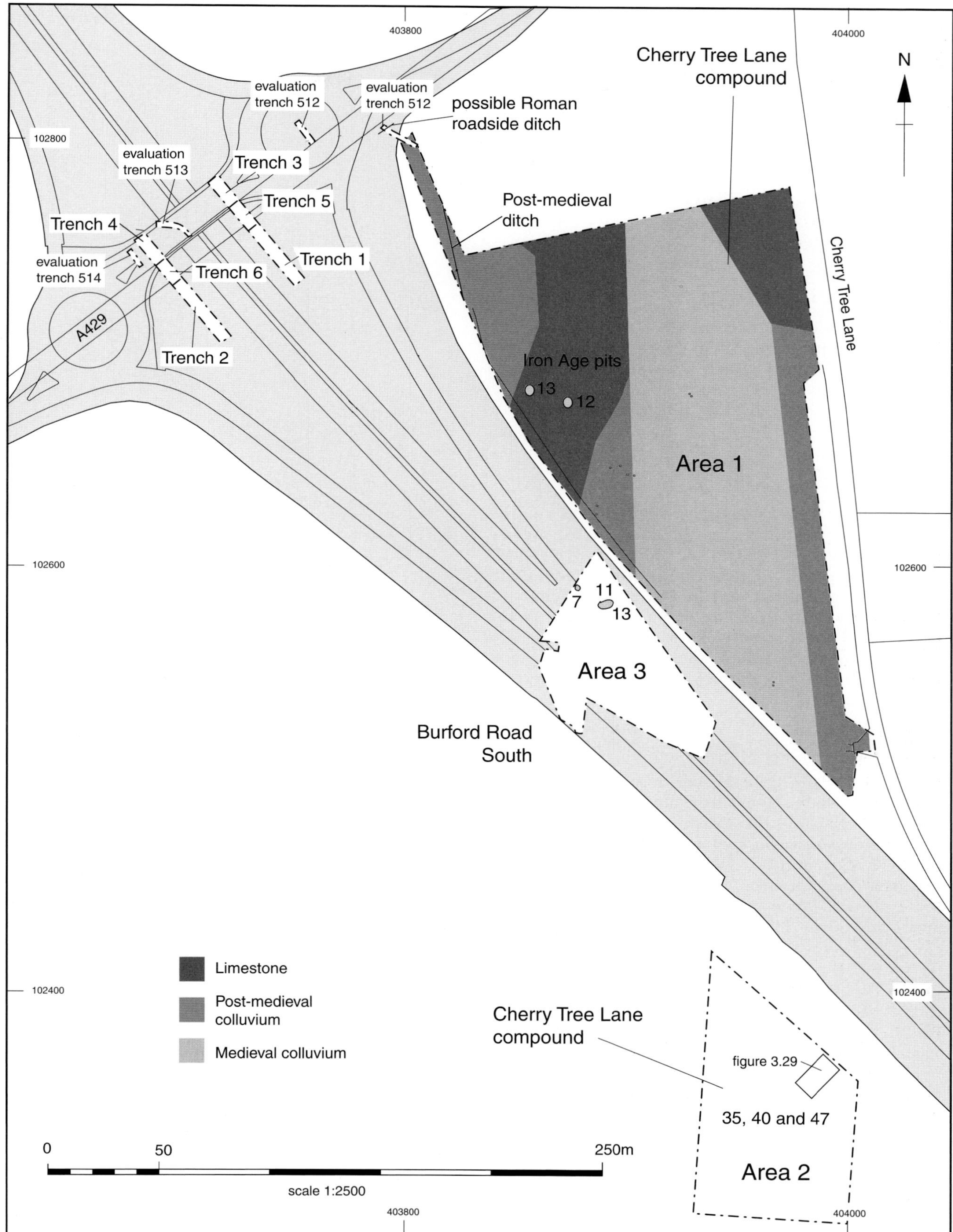


*Figure 3.28 Plan of area south of Burford Road, showing Cherry Tree Lane Sites 1 and 2, Burford Road South and the trenches through Burford Road (chapter 5).*

***Burford Road South Area 3***

This area was located within the road corridor to the south-west of the main compound area. The site was on the crest of a natural rise in the bedrock where a light scatter of flintwork had been identified in the Stage 1 assessment. However, stripping revealed no features of interest apart from a small cluster of three circular/oval pits (7, 11, 13) located in the northern corner of the excavated area. No dating evidence was recovered from any of these pits and their interpretation is uncertain.

*Pit 12 (Figs 3.28 and 3.30)*

Pit 12, 2.80 m in diameter and 0.27 m deep, was cut into the solid limestone bedrock. It contained a single stony fill (17) from which several sherds of Iron Age pottery were recovered. No other finds were discovered and the original function of the feature is unclear.

*Pit 13 (Figs 3.28 and 3.30)*

Located a few metres to the west of pit 12, pit 13 was of a similar character but rather broader (4.4 m). Again, this feature was rock-cut and contained a single sherd of Iron Age pottery. The dating is supported by the discovery of spelt wheat in a sample of charred remains (see Pelling, Chapter 8). A post-medieval sherd found on the surface of the feature was probably derived from the topsoil. As with pit 12, no other finds were recovered and the original function of pit 13 remains unclear.

*Pit 35 (Figs 3.29–30, section 16)*

The earliest feature in the southern area, 35, was a large sub-rectangular pit truncated by a later pit, 47 on the north side. Pit 35 contained heavily burnt deposits of wood charcoal and limestone fragments in a silty clay matrix. These were interleaved with thin, charcoal-rich layers. An area of 6.0 x 5.60 m was hand cleaned over the feature, which exposed its approximate surviving extent. An L-shaped slot was excavated as far as the water table would allow (0.75 m). The upper fills of the feature contained a large number of fragments (about 80 g) of friable shell-tempered pottery, suggesting a later prehistoric date (see Barclay, Chapter 7). The pottery is not closely dateable but may be early Iron Age.

*Pit 47 (Fig. 3.30)*

At the north end, pit 35 was cut by a second large feature, 47. This extended at least 5 m north-south, but was not entirely cleared in plan and its full extent is uncertain. Like pit 35 it extended below the water table. A sequence of six fills were recorded in section consisting of light to dark greyish brown silts. No dating evidence was recovered and the interpretation of the feature remains unclear.

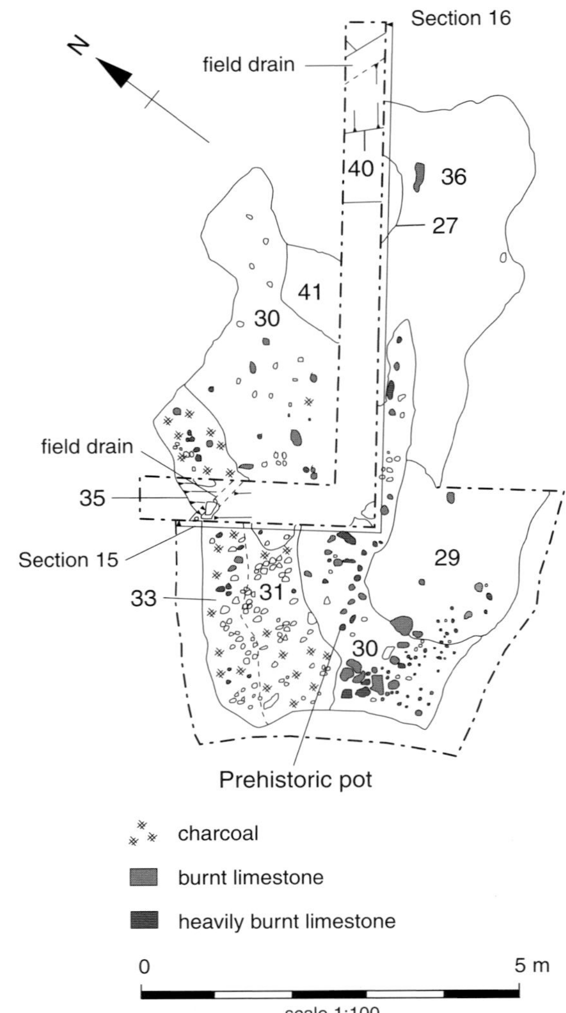


*Figure 3.29 Cherry Tree Lane site 2, plan of pit 35, pit 47, and ditch 40.*

*Ditch 40 (Fig. 3.30)*

Examination of the section revealed a V-shaped feature, possibly a ditch, cut into the top of pit 47. This feature had a width of 1.0 m and a maximum depth of 0.44 m, and contained three very similar fills, all sterile. The feature was overlain by two spreads, 36 and 27, which were not removed, and hence the ditch was not traced in plan. A small quantity of prehistoric pottery, recovered from layers 27 and 36 may have been residual since a post-medieval sherd also came from 27. Conversely, this sherd may have been intrusive from later plough activity or from a modern field drain which was also cut ditch 40. The date of the feature therefore remains unresolved.

***Discussion***

The scattered nature of the features precludes a satisfactory synthesis of the archaeology in the Cherry Tree Lane/Burford Road South area. This problem is

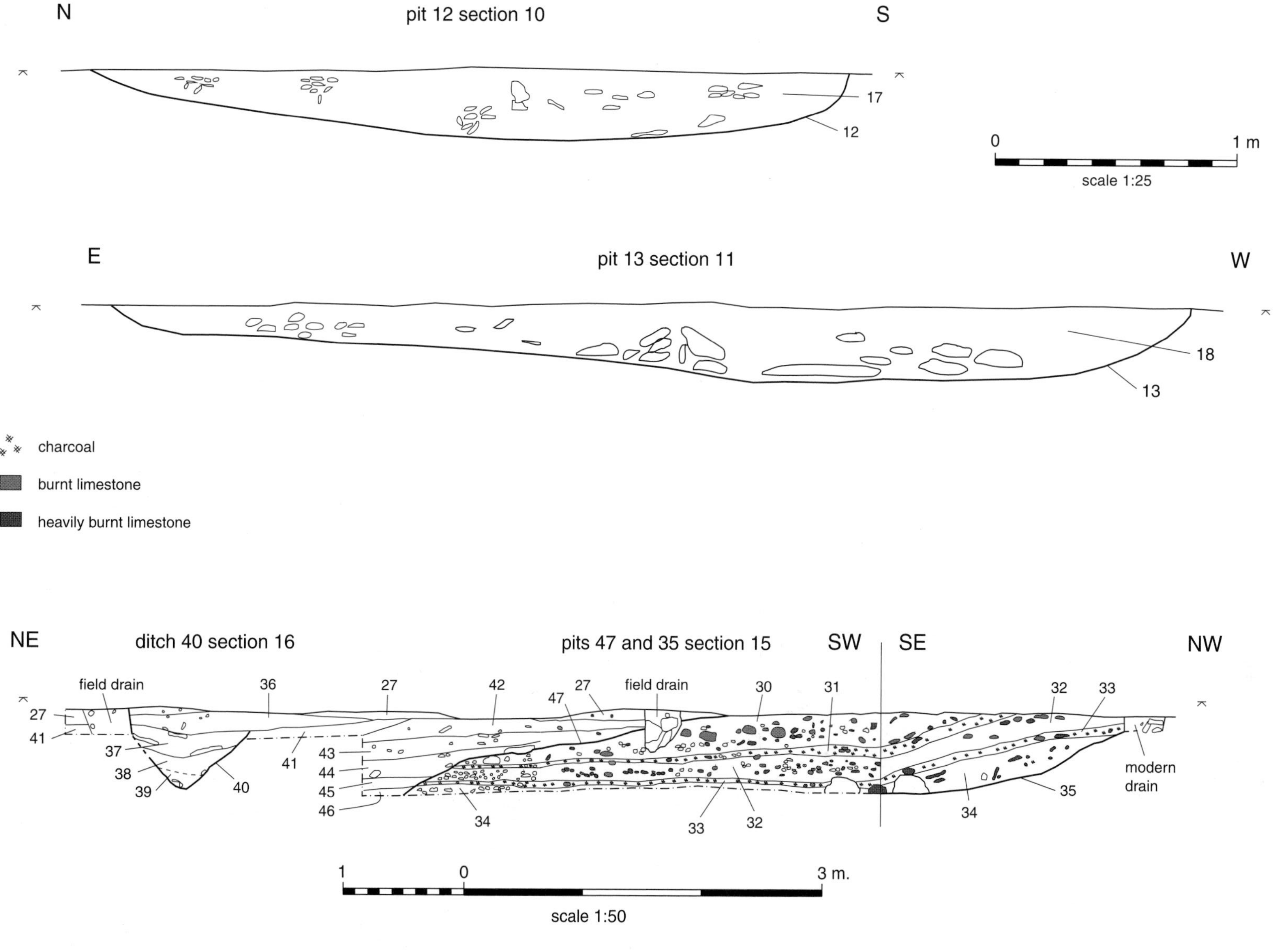


*Figure 3.30 Cherry Tree Lane, pits 12, 13 35 and 47, ditch 40, sections.*

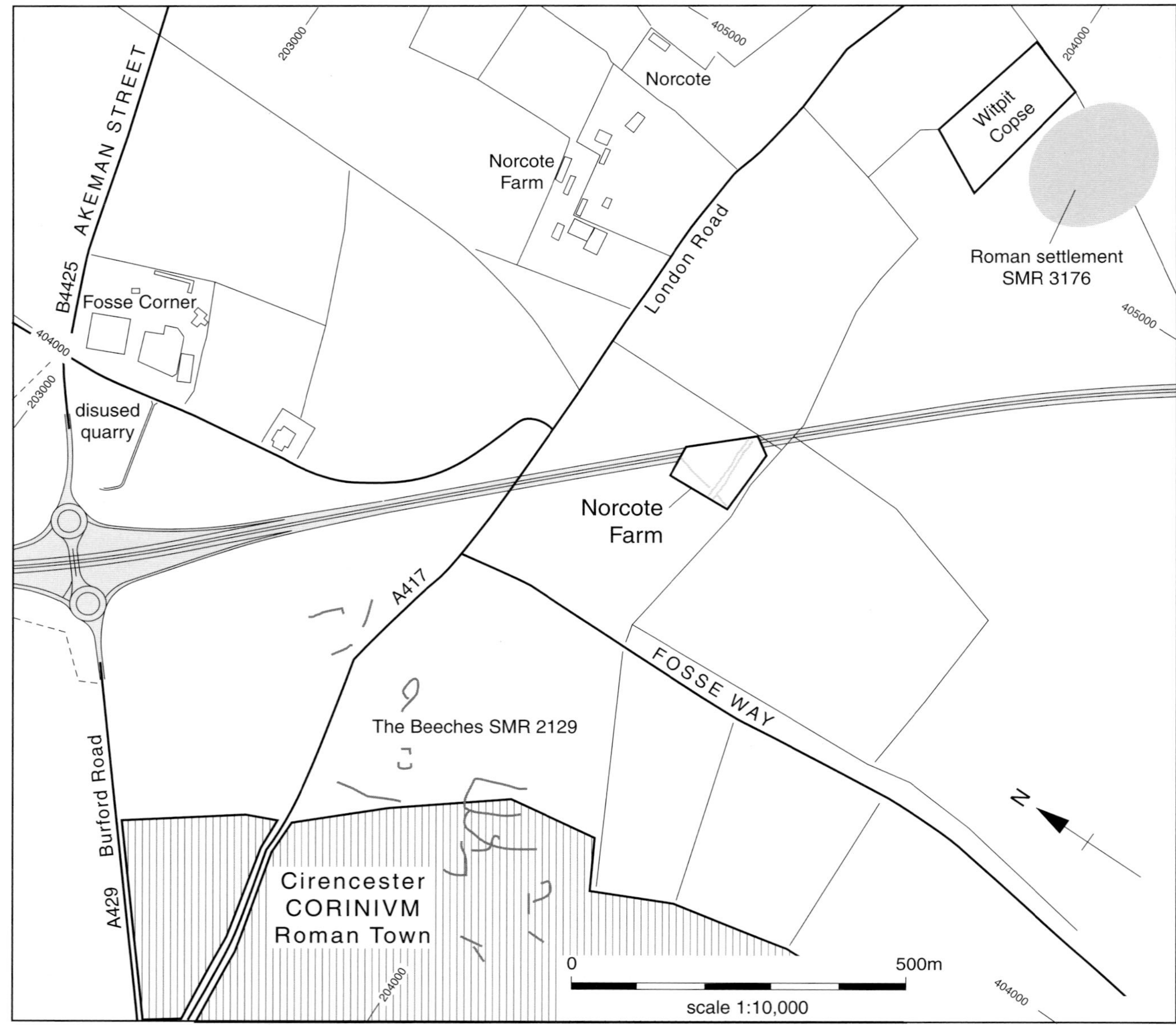


*Figure 3.31 Norcote Farm, trench location and nearby sites.*

compounded by the fact that many of the features are either undated or are associated with small quantities of undiagnostic and possibly residual pottery. Nevertheless, there does appear to be a low level of later prehistoric activity in the area and it is possible that more extensive remains are sealed within the colluvium. Pit 35 contained material of the character of later prehistoric 'burnt mound' deposits. The specific function of this type of site has been much debated (Buckley 1990; Hodder and Barfield 1990) and no conclusions can be drawn from the evidence from this particular feature.

**Norcote Farm** *(Figs 3.31–32)*

An area of about 0.7 ha was stripped primarily to identify any subsoil features associated with a scatter of worked flint (see Chapter 2). No associated features were found although an alignment of two sinuous ditches (235 and 239) were revealed, and four later and slighter cross-ditches (240, 241, 242 and 243). The latter are likely to be Roman in date (Chapter 4) and the former probably later prehistoric.

***Ditches 235, 239 and gully 206***

A sinuous ditch (235) ran south-south-west across the site for 58 m and terminated within the excavation area. The Stage 1 geophysical survey indicated that it extended at least 30 m further north. Six sections were excavated across this ditch which had a broad U-shaped profile throughout its length and was typically 1.80 m wide and 0.70 m deep. The ditch was cut through a substrate of clay and bottomed onto

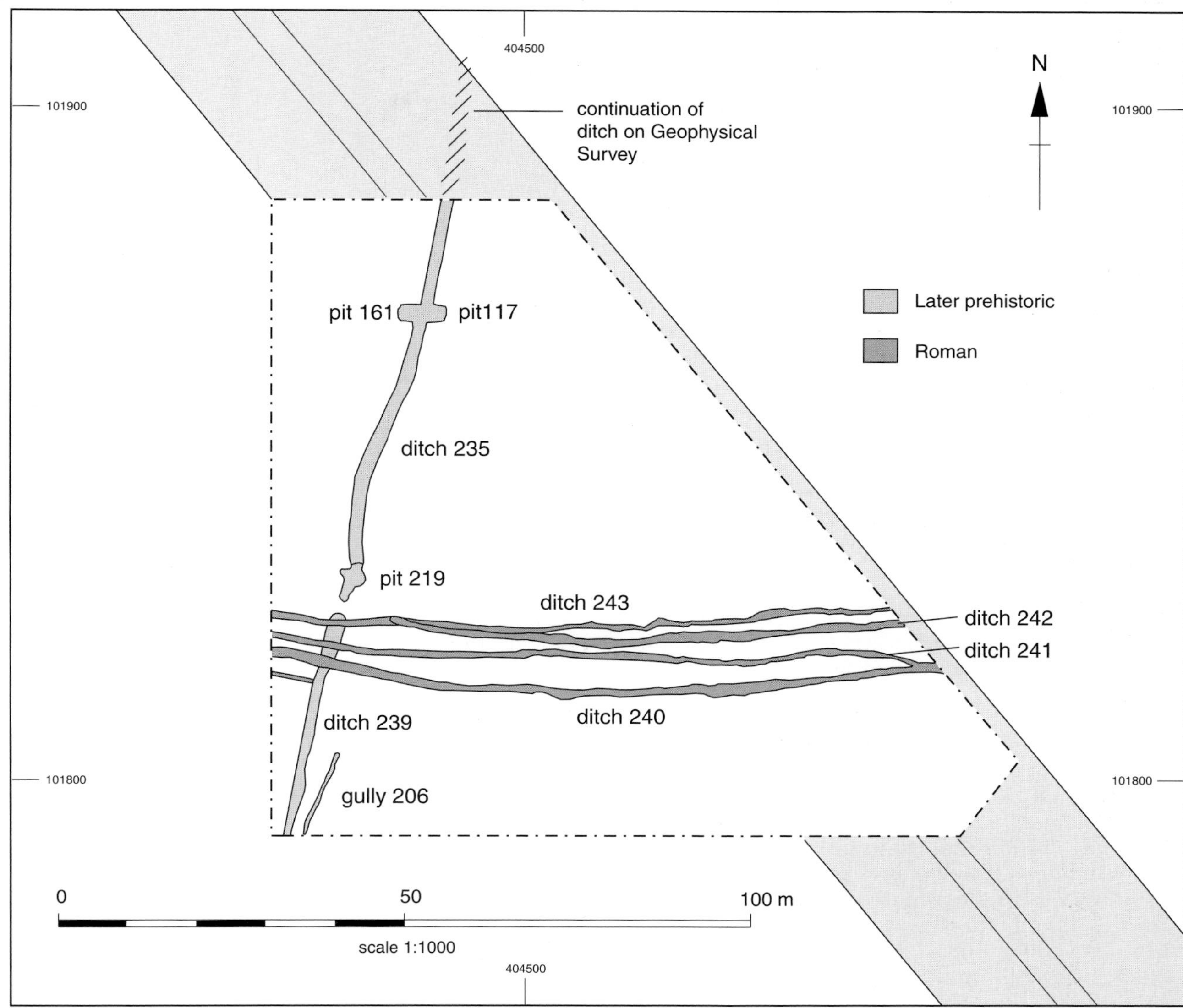


*Figure 3.32 Norcote Farm, plan of excavated features.*

limestone bedrock. It contained three distinct clay fills, which broadly comprised a mottled, partly gleyed orange-brown primary fill, a dark greyish brown middle fill and a mid brown upper fill. Limestone slabs came from the primary fill in the section with pits 117 and 161.

Another substantial ditch (239) continued on the same alignment as ditch 235 after a gap of 1.75 m. Although slightly wider at the northern end (2 m), the ditch decreased in size towards the south where the ground rises. At the south-western end of the site ditch 239 was 0.78 m wide and 0.20 m in depth. The fills generally consisted of a greyish brown clay with some gleying towards the base.

In the south-western corner of the site, gully 206 ran approximately parallel to ditch 239 for a short distance. It was about 0.6 m wide and 0.2 m deep with a similar light greyish brown clayey silt fill.

### *Pits 219, 117 and 161*

At the terminal of ditch 235 a large pit, 219, (about 3.8 m in diameter) had been cut to the same depth as the ditch. Although the ditch had almost completely silted up it probably formed a hollow (or was marked by a bank or hedge alongside) as the pit lay astride the ditch.

Pits 117 and 161 were cut into either side of ditch 235 towards the northern edge of the site. They were both sub-circular, about 2.5 m in diameter and about 0.4 m deep. Pit 117 was partly backfilled with slabs of limestone, but otherwise the fills of these features were very similar to those of ditch 235. These features are undated.

### *Discussion*

Both ditches were undated by artefactual evidence. However, ditch 239 was cut by a series of shallow east-west ditches which probably date to the Roman period (Chapter 4). The earlier ditches are reminiscent of the sinuous ditches at St Augustine's Farm South and St Augustine's Lane and a later prehistoric date appears to be the most likely. They did not follow any topographic features although both the termini ended in a hollow forming the lowest part of the field. The lack of finds in the ditches suggests no occupation in the immediate vicinity. The nearest Iron Age site appears to be that at The Beeches (Glos. SMR 2129), about 0.5 km to the west (Fig. 3.31), and the Norcote Farm ditches may represent land division associated with that settlement. The pits appeared to be later than the ditches although they may have been associated with this boundary.

### The Lynches Trackway Iron Age Burial *(Fig. 3.33)*

This burial was discovered by workmen during the course of construction work on the east scarp of the Churn valley (Fig. 8.23). Subsequent excavation revealed a human skeleton lying in a tightly crouched position on its left side, facing the east, in an oval pit 1.2 x 0.8 m in extent. The area immediately surrounding the burial pit was cleaned but no other burials or traces of associated features were found.

Though slightly disturbed by machine, the bones were in excellent condition and virtually complete. The skeleton was identified as the remains of a young, adult male, approximately 17–25 years old who may have suffered from iron deficiency in childhood (see Boyle, Chapter 8). The tightly crouched position of the body may indicate that it had been bound.

No dating evidence was recovered from the grave fill. However, a series of three AMS dates on a femur strongly indicate that the burial is of middle Iron Age date, with calibration at the 95% confidence level to 355 BC to 289 BC and 235 BC to 33 BC (NZA 8620, R24151/22). The 68% confidence level indicates a preferred date in the early 1st or 2nd century BC. There seems no reason to doubt this date despite its unexpected lateness. The form of the burial in a tightly crouched position within a flat grave is reminiscent of the later Bronze Age tradition. Iron Age burials in purpose-dug graves are uncommon, or not commonly recognised, in Gloucestershire and the Upper Thames region. One of middle to late Iron Age date is known from Roughground Farm, and another from the same site is undated (Allen *et al.* 1993, 45, fig. 32 burials 1275 and 1215). At Yarnton, just north of Oxford, a middle Iron Age cemetery has recently been identified by radiocarbon dating (Hey *et al.*, 1999). Elsewhere, Iron Age burials tend to be found in settlement features, but are not generally common. Three found at West Lane, Kemble, have been reported recently (King *et al.* 1996). In two cases the skeletons were complete and had apparently been inserted into already partially filled pits containing middle Iron Age pottery. Both were crouched; one on its right side facing north-west, and the other prone possibly with the wrists tied to the ankles. The other burial comprised only two bones but may originally have been more complete and

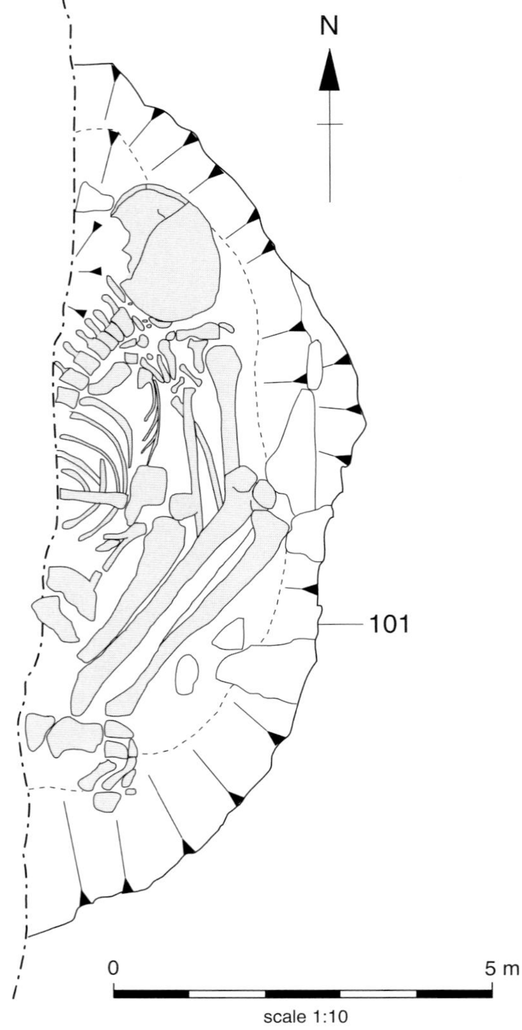


*Figure 3.33 Lynches Trackway, plan of isolated Iron Age inhumation.*

disturbed by the later insertion. There were other pits present but it is unclear whether this was part of a settlement. A number of middle Iron Age pit burials were also found at Salmonsbury (Dunning 1976). Three of these were adults in crouched positions and two were infants. Adult body parts were also found in other pits. To judge by the tiny area of the enclosure examined, it is possible that human burial was relatively common at this site. Other examples from the region include one from Shipton Oliffe, one from Shorncote. There are also late Iron Age inhumations from Barrow Wake, Birdlip, Cowley (RCHME 1976, 39).

The Lynches Trackway burial was not apparently associated with a settlement, although the presence of some Iron Age pottery from the trackway itself suggests that one lay nearby. In her dissertation, Wilson (1981) argued that in the early Iron Age inhumations tended to be located at boundaries away from settlement, but that by the middle Iron Age some burials took place in settlement contexts (Wilson 1981). The burial from The

*Plate 3.5 Middle Duntisbourne, ditch 121.*

Lynches trackway may perhaps be interpreted as showing aspects of both boundary and domestic character.

## THE LATE IRON AGE

### Middle Duntisbourne

*by Andrew Mudd and Alan Lupton*

#### *Cropmark enclosures*

Prior to the 1990 evaluation this site was known as a series of undated superimposed rectilinear cropmarks aligned obliquely to Ermin Street (Fig. 3.34). The Stage 2 field evaluation examined three of these, establishing two of the features as possible settlement boundary ditches dating to the late Iron Age / early Roman period. A third ditch was undated. The pottery assemblage had affinities with those from excavations at Bagendon and Ditches hillfort (GCC 1990, 61).

A rectangular area of *c.* 7300 m$^2$ was stripped to expose the whole area of the ditched enclosure cropmark situated within the road corridor. No features other than the ditches were identified except an irregular linear silty clay spread running along the north-eastern side of the excavation. On investigation this feature proved to be the remains of a medieval/ post-medieval hollow way (see Chapter 6).

The features consisted of an east-west ditch (4), two approximately north-south ditches (310 and 121), both with northern terminals within the excavation area and a fourth ditch (140) just east of ditch 310 (Fig. 3.35). The cropmark shows that ditch 310 runs south for about 70 m to join ditch 4 forming the south-western corner of a large enclosure (Fig. 3.35). The eastern ditch (121) appears from the cropmark to continue beyond the intersection with ditch 4 and then turn west-south-west. Ditch 140 also appears to turn west-south-west some 10 m south of the stripped area.

#### *Ditch 121* (*Figs 3.34–7*)

Nine sections were excavated at regular intervals along this feature and a further segment (320) examined the relationship with ditch 4. The ditch generally had a rounded V-shaped profile and was about 1.3 m deep, shallowing to 0.6 m at the terminal (segment 311). The terminal was also relatively narrow (1.4 m) with the ditch widening towards the south to about 2.2 m. In some sections the ditch was even wider with a shallower upper slope suggesting some recutting or other disturbance (segments 148 and 285) while segment 272 (Fig. 3.37, section 41) had suffered some truncation across the top of the ditch.

The primary silting was a thin reddish brown basal and edge silting which nowhere contained any finds. The main fills of the ditch consisted of one or two limestone rubble deposits with an average depth of 0.6–0.8 m. In segments 182 (Fig. 3.36, section 31) and 205 (not illustrated) deposits of charcoal and burnt

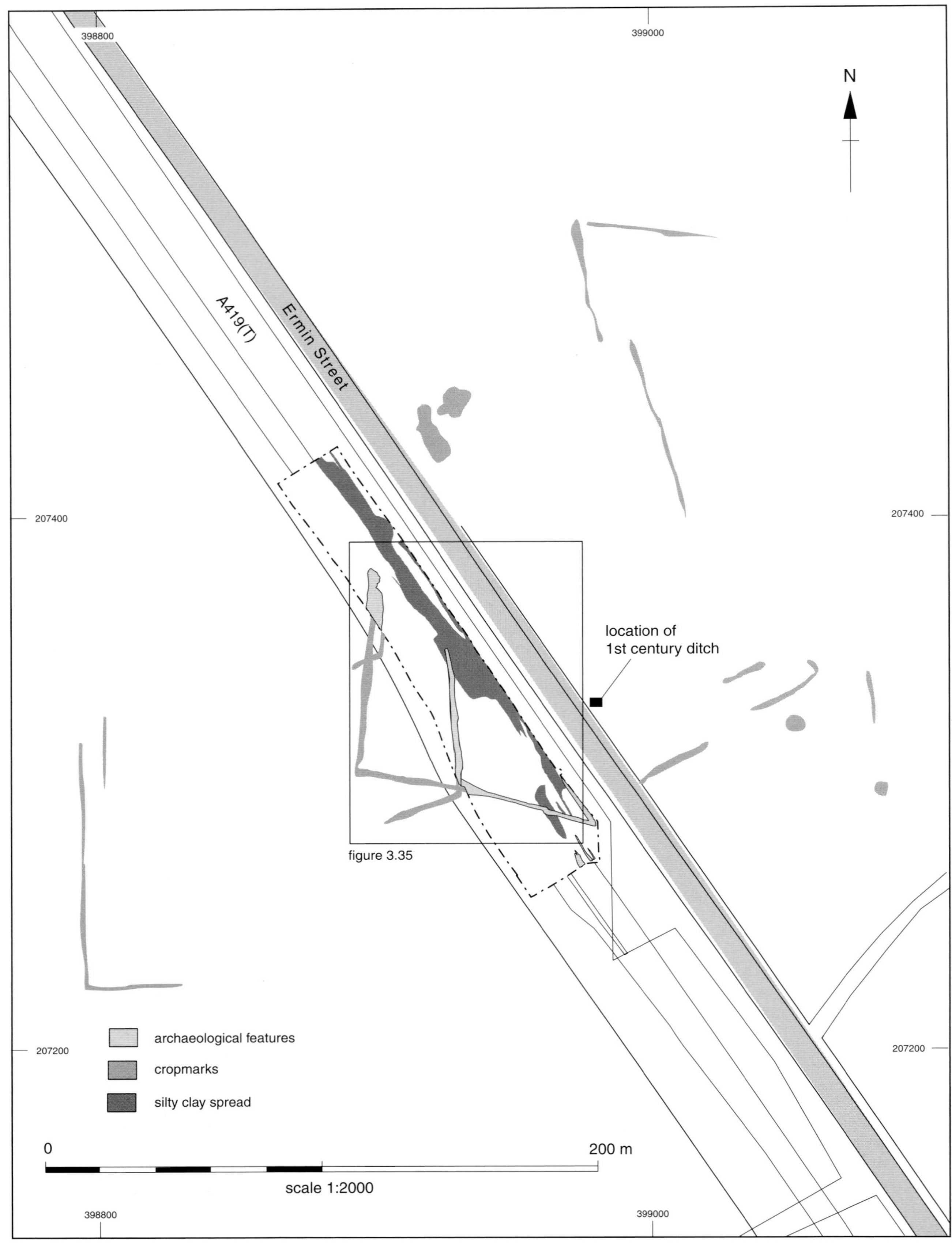


*Figure 3.34 Middle Duntisbourne, site location, adjacent cropmarks and ditch found in watching brief.*

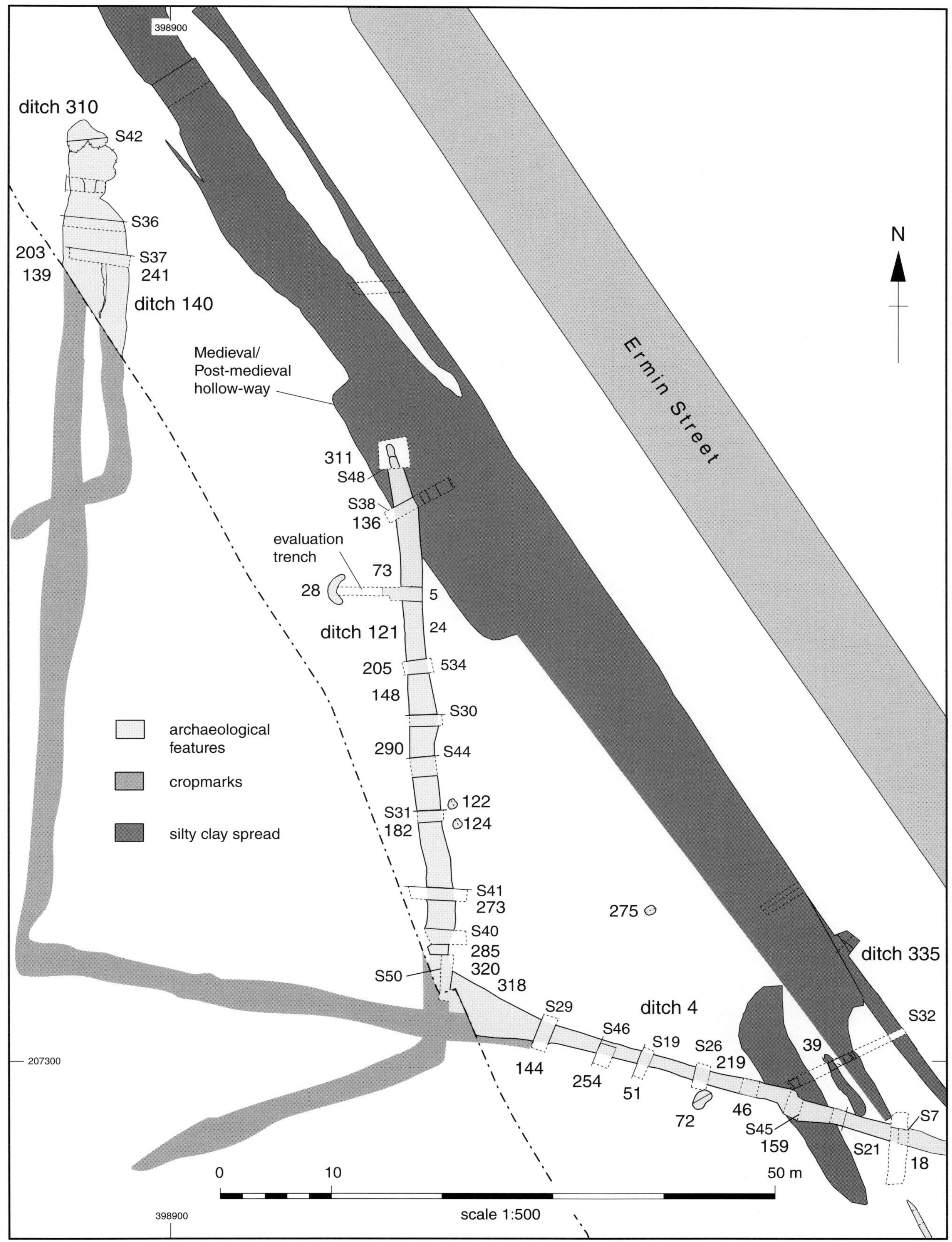


*Figure 3.35 Middle Duntisbourne, plan of excavated features (part) and cropmarks.*

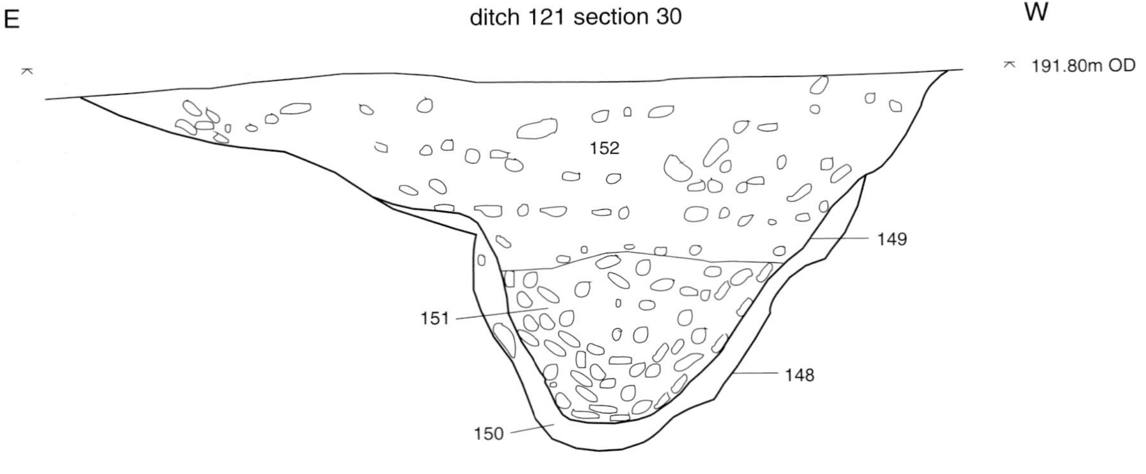


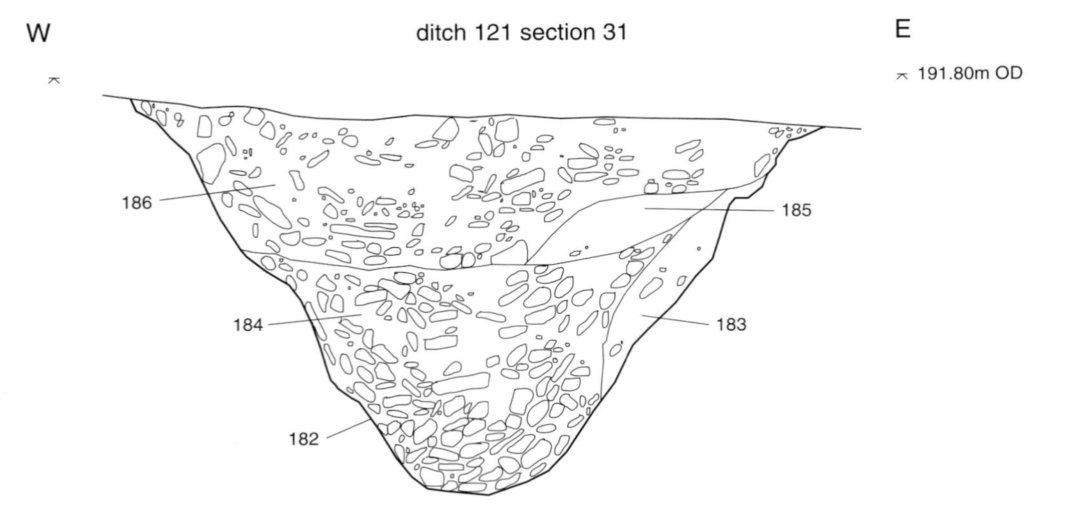


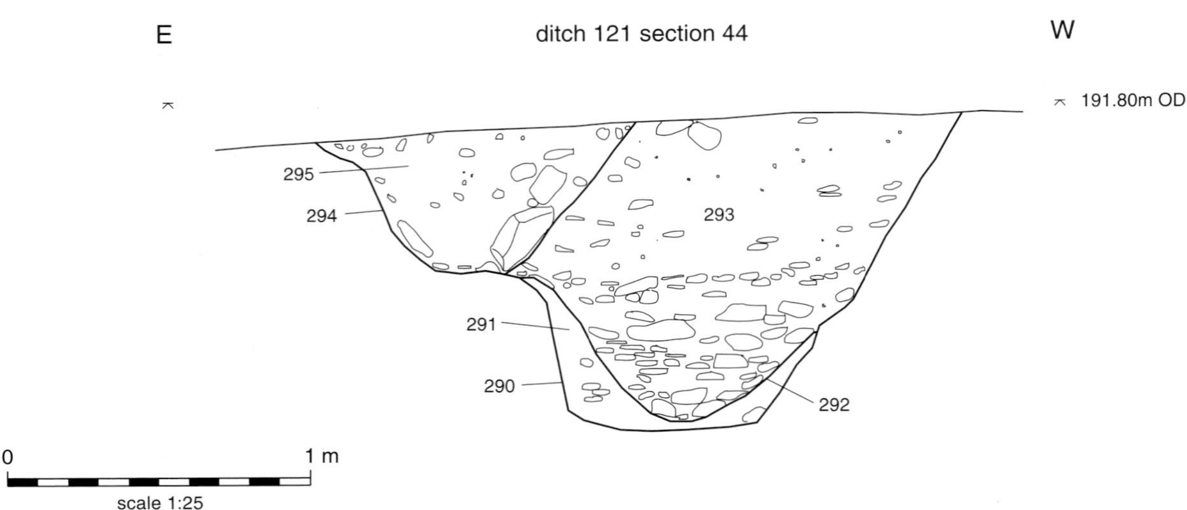


*Figure 3.36 Middle Duntisbourne, ditch 121, sections 30, 31 and 44.*

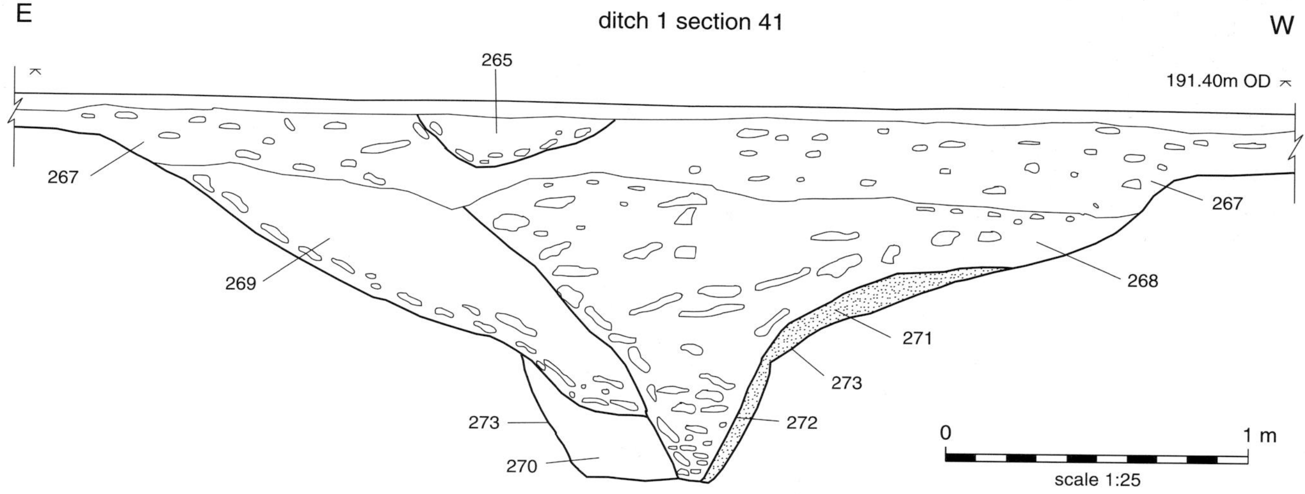


*Figure 3.37 Middle Duntisbourne, ditch 121, section 41.*

stone (185 in section 31) lay sandwiched between rubble deposits, perhaps suggesting two episodes of infilling. However, it is possible that these merely reflect an individual dumping event. At the terminal (not illustrated) limestone rubble 312 was overlain by fill 313, from which a copper alloy pin (SF 34) was recovered. This was overlain by a further rubble layer, 314.

The limestone fills appear to represent a quick backfilling of the feature, probably from the original upcast bank. There was no indication from which side the rubble had derived. The upper rubble deposit in segment 148 (fill 152) was noted to be layered, as if deliberately laid, and the limestone deposits were interpreted on site as representing the deliberate backfilling of the ditch.

The distinction between the basal silts and the later rubble infill was quite marked except at the northern end of the ditch, and it is possible that two distinct cuts were represented for most of the ditch's length. However, the fine silts of the 'early' cut, contrasting with the stony later fills, may simply represent the pattern of natural silting within a ditch of a single phase. Some of the sections showed anomalies which were atypical of the ditch as a whole. In segment 290 (Fig. 3.36, section 44) a later cut (294) on the eastern side of the ditch was quite clear. This was filled with a less stony deposit and was not evident in any of the other ditch segments, so it was most probably a pit. Segments 148 (Fig. 3.36, section 30) and 285 (not illustrated) showed broad, shallow extensions on the eastern side making their profiles asymmetrical. It is possible that these represented recuts, but they were not traceable in the intervening sections. Segment 272 (Fig. 3.37, section 41) was anomalous in its broad composite profile, and the fact that it had a comparatively stone-free silt on the eastern side which appeared to represent the fill of an earlier feature. The difficulty of tracing a recut through the length of the ditch makes the interpretation of these sections problematic, but the evidence seems to point to variations in the original cut and backfill or possible local recutting.

Excavation of the intersection with ditch 4 (segment 320) showed ditch 121 to be the earlier. The dating of ditch 121 is, however, imprecise. There were no finds from the primary fills, and pottery from the rubble infilling was sparse and quite undiagnostic, comprising mostly early Severn Valley Wares and variants thereof. Most of the pottery came from the upper fill (152) of segment 148 (Fig. 3.36, section 30) which represents the final infilling. The pottery included a single sherd of Savernake Ware which is conventionally dated relatively late.

### *Ditch 4* (*Figs 3.38–39*)

Seven cross-sections were excavated through ditch 4 and a further two partial sections at the western and eastern ends to examine its relationship with ditches 121 and 335 respectively. Ditch 4 consisted of a single steep-sided V-shaped cut with an average depth of 1–1.2 m in most of the excavated sections, slightly shallower at the eastern end. Though the exact sequence of fills varied between the excavated sections, most of the profiles exhibited a similar succession of four or five fills. Above a thin, orange-brown primary silting was a deposit of stone with occupation material. (Fig. 3.39, section 46, fill 289; Fig. 3.38, section 19, fill 84; section 20, fill 68). This only infilled the ditch up to halfway. Mollusc samples from segment 144 (section 29) showed a large number of shade-loving species within the rubble fill (57), including true woodland (rather than rock-rubble) species (see Robinson, Chapter 8). This would suggest that the rubble accumulated gradually, probably through natural erosion, rather than being a deliberate infilling. The rubble was succeeded by deposits of greyish silt, often

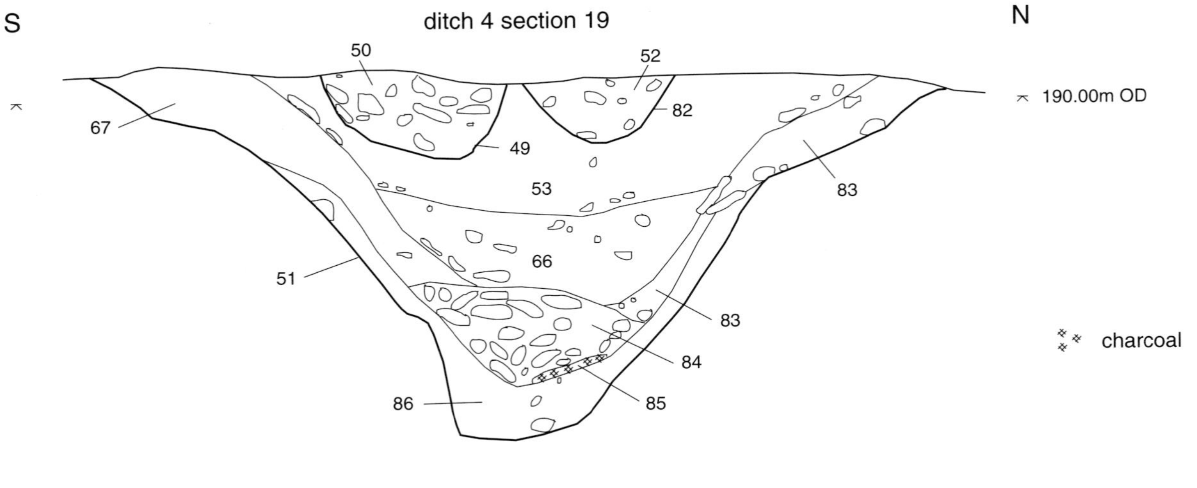


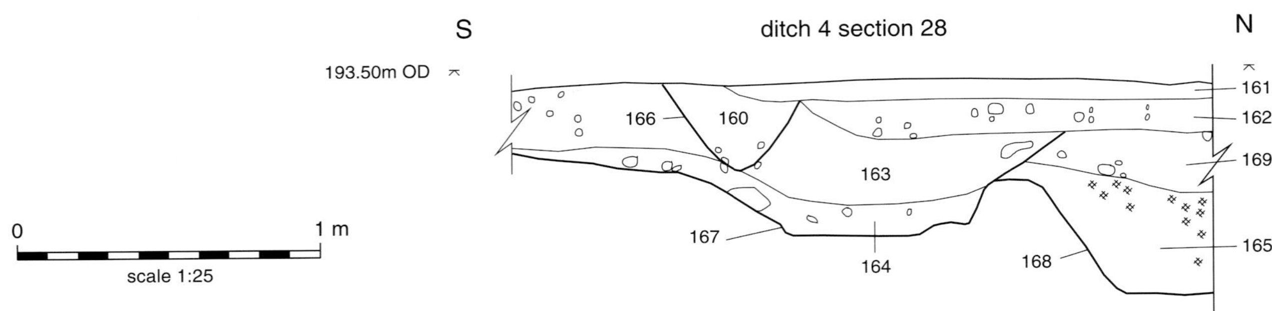


*Figure 3.38 Middle Duntisbourne, ditch 4, sections 19 and 28.*

with abundant charcoal and other occupation-related deposits, representing accumulations within a more stable environment. The later fills tended to be lighter greyish or reddish brown silts with fine limestone which probably mostly accumulated naturally. The mollusc evidence from fills 56 and 153 indicated that woodland was still present, but higher up fills 54 and 55 contained mostly open country species. These upper deposits were up to 0.5 m thick at the western end of the ditch (eg. Fig. 3.39, section 46, fills 287?, 256 and 255) but became very shallow at the eastern end.

The ditch sections yielded a large quantity of finds including about 90% of the pottery from the site (see Timby, Chapter 7). The pottery is of particular interest as it included several continental imports, including a sherd of Arretine ware (unstratified) of possible Tiberian date (Fig. 7.9.69), Gallo-Belgic *terra nigra, terra rubra* wares and whiteware butt beakers (Camulodunum type 113, eg. Fig. 7.9.77). The assemblage was dominated by early Severn Valley wares, with Savernake Ware jars and Malvernian limestone-tempered jars and hammer-rim bowls of the late Iron Age tradition also common. Among the other finds present were six brooches (five of copper alloy and one of iron) of Late La Tène, Colchester, and Penannular types (Figs 7.20.507, 508, 511, Fig. 7.22.521–2). None of these need date later than around AD 60–65 (see Mackreth, Chapter 7), supporting a mid-1st century date for the occupation.

The sequence of finds within the ditch does not help refine the chronology. There were few finds from the primary silts, although these included early Severn Valley ware from 48 (segment 46), Malvernian ware from 157 (segment 159) and fine white-slipped Gallo-Belgic ware (FWWSOX) from both these deposits. The subsequent accumulation of rubble and domestic refuse contained most of the finds, including Savernake ware. There is some suggestion that Savernake Ware became more common later on since 57% of sherds (40 % by weight) came from the upper silting deposits, compared with 32% of all other pottery. By contrast, only 5% (18% by weight) of Savernake Ware came from the lower rubble fill, which contained 50% (44% by weight) of all the other pottery. It is possible that this distribution has chronological significance.

Close to the eastern baulk, ditch 4 was truncated by ditch 335 (Fig. 3.38, section 28 – not shown on plan) which ran parallel to the line of the A417. It could well be a Roman roadside ditch and is discussed below (Chapter 5). Though no clear continuation of ditch 4 to the east beyond Ermin Street is evident from the aerial photographs, a steep-sided ditch was observed during the drainage works along the eastern edge of

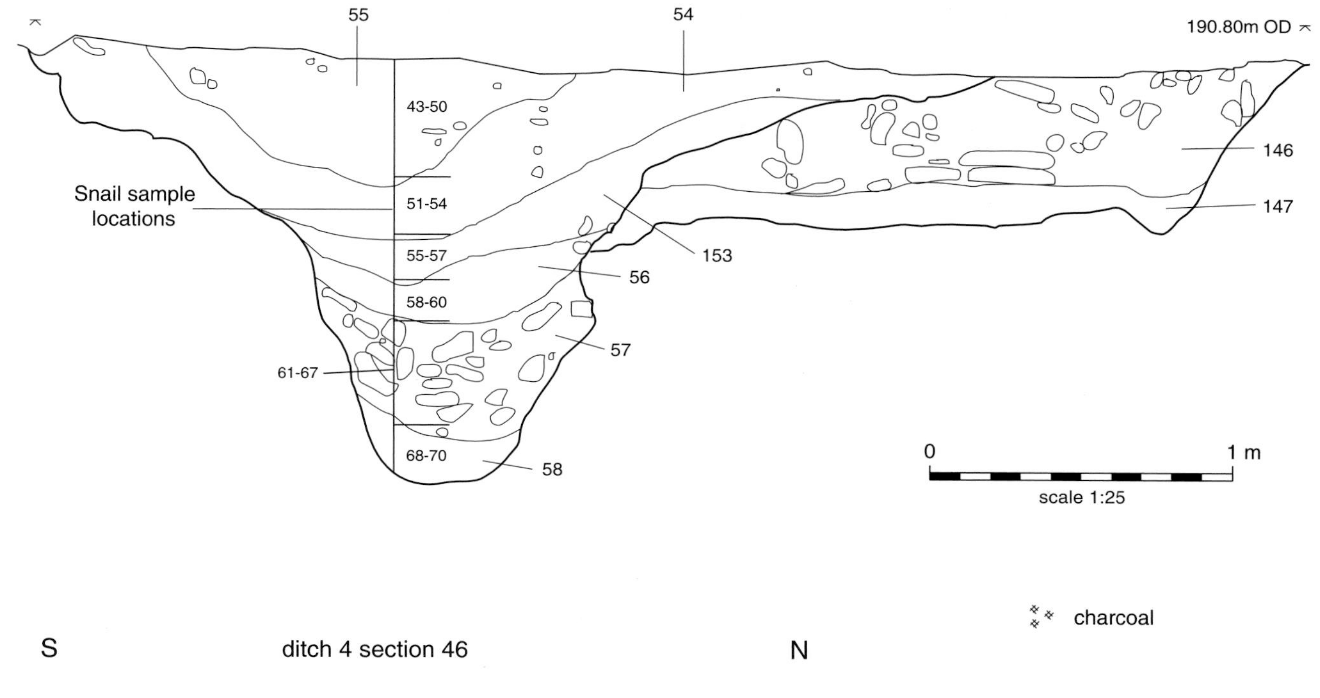


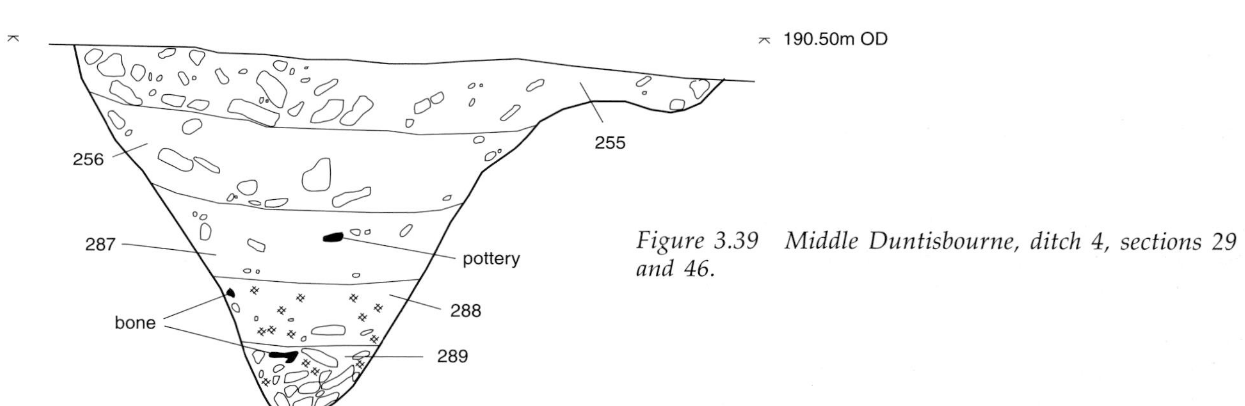


*Figure 3.39 Middle Duntisbourne, ditch 4, sections 29 and 46.*

the road corridor (Fig. 3.34). This feature (chainage 9652, feature 3) was about 1.4 m wide and 0.7 m deep and contained Savernake ware, pre-Flavian South Gaulish samian and Malvernian hand-made limestone ware. The direction in which the ditch ran was not clear, but it could represent a return to ditch 4 forming the third side of an enclosure which would therefore have been about 90 m east to west. Alternatively, the feature may have been unrelated to the enclosure.

### *Ditch 310 (Fig. 3.40)*

Four sections excavated through the westernmost cropmark feature revealed a north-south oriented ditch (310) with another shallower ditch (140) on its eastern side, both ditches truncated by later features. These later features consisted of a complex of ill-defined hollows which appear to have been quarries.

Ditch 310 was about 1.2 m deep with steep sides and a rounded base. Like ditch 4 it had a thin primary silt overlain by limestone rubble layers which largely filled the ditch. The abrupt terminal (Fig. 3.40, section 42, segment 250) probably finally silted up naturally, but elsewhere the upper fills had been truncated. Only a small number of sherds and animal bones were recovered from any of the ditch fills, but the pottery included two fragments of *terra nigra* from fill 210 (Fig. 3.40, segment 139, section 37), suggesting a similar date to the deposits in ditch 4. The form of the two ditches was also similar and may support the conclusion, arrived in the evaluation stage, that ditches 310 and 4 formed two arms of a large enclosure, or partial enclosure open to the north.

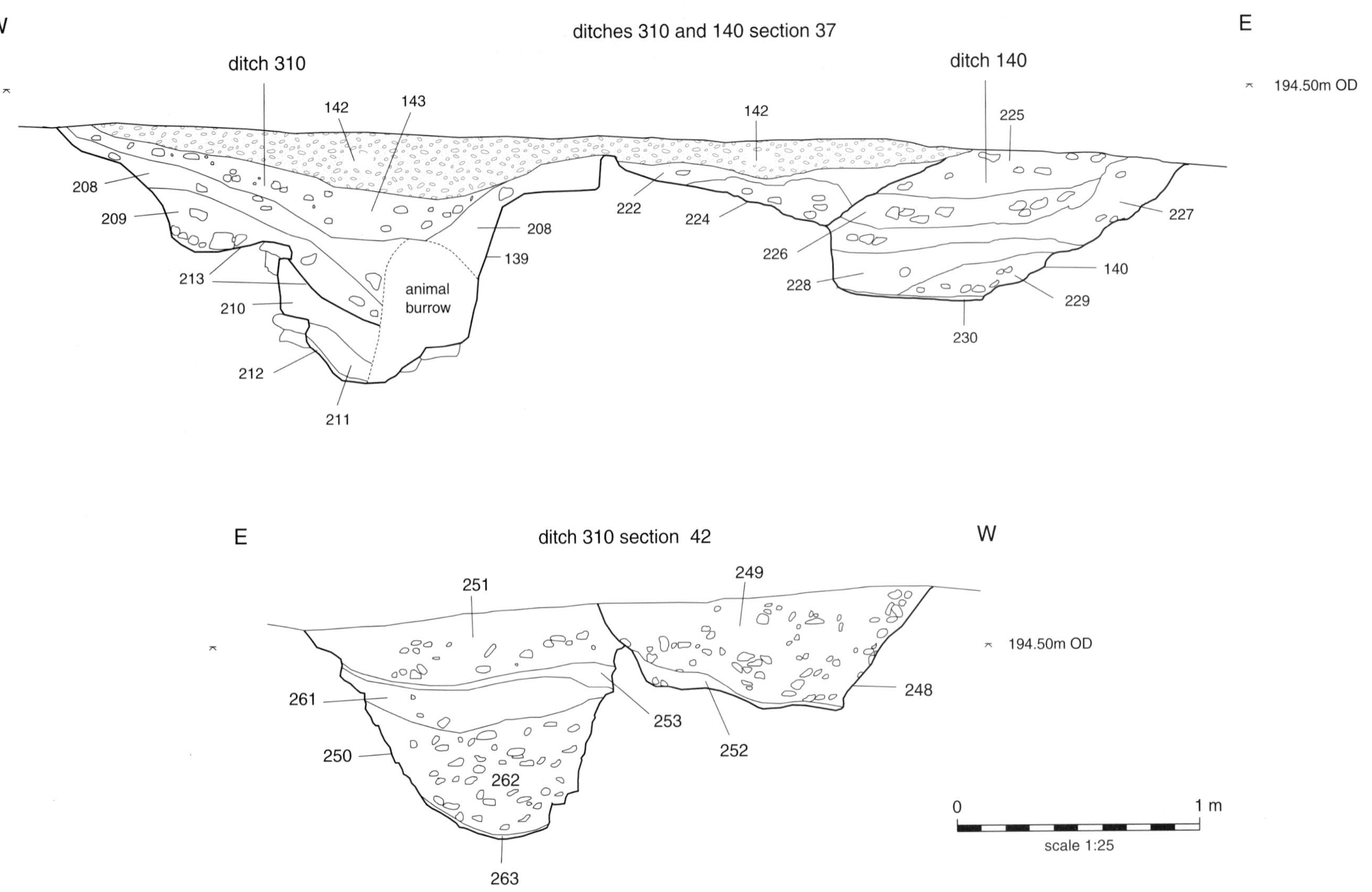


*Figure 3.40 Middle Duntisbourne, ditch 310, sections 37 and 42.*

***Ditch 140** (Fig. 3.40, section 37)*

To the east of 310, and running approximately parallel, a ditch was tentatively identified in section 37. It was about 0.8 m deep with a broad flat base. Its western edge was truncated by quarrying, but it would have been about 2 m wide. There were also signs of this ditch in segment 241 (not illustrated) but the amount of later quarrying made this identification uncertain. It would have terminated approximately 7 m south of the end of ditch 310. The sequence of deposits was broadly similar to that seen in ditch 310, with a thin layer of primary silting sealed beneath a series of superimposed silty clay fills mixed with varying proportions of limestone. There were few finds of any sort. The excavations were unable to demonstrate the relationship between ditches 140 and 310 directly, but the interpretation of section 37 (Fig. 3.40) shows that ditch 140 was completely filled when cut by quarry pit 224, while ditch 310 was still partly open. This would suggest that ditch 140 was the earlier. In the evaluation (Field 40 Trench 1, GCC 1990, 57–61, fig. 20), a large ditch was recorded as cutting the eastern side of the 1st-century enclosure ditch. However, the dimensions of this feature, which was about 5 m wide at the top with a flat, 2.6 m-wide base, suggest that the feature was a quarry pit rather than ditch 140.

The cropmark evidence suggests that, while ditch 310 represents the return of ditch 4, ditch 140 belongs to another L-shaped, or sub-rectangular feature lying to the west. It follows a course approximately parallel to ditch 121 to the east perhaps indicating that, despite some difference in form, the two ditches could be coeval, and the stratigraphic relationships of these ditches, both of which appear to be earlier than the linked ditches 4 and 310, does not contradict this. There were too few finds to date these ditches closely, but the close proximity of the terminals of ditches 310 and 140, their similar alignments, and the evidence for the deliberate infilling of ditch 121, perhaps indicates that ditches 4 and 310 immediately followed the abandonment of the earlier ditches.

***Later quarries***

The uppermost fills of both ditches 310 and 140 were truncated by later pitting which had apparently quarried the ditch sides (Fig. 3.40, section 37, cuts 231 and 224; section 42, cut 224). Most of the deposits associated with this activity produced few finds other than small scraps of bone, though a small number of early Severn Valley ware sherds, most probably redeposited, were recovered from the upper quarry fills. It is possible that the quarrying was related to the construction of nearby Ermin Street.

***Discussion***

*Date and sequence*

The excavations indicated two phases of occupation, the first represented by ditches 121 and (probably) 140, and the second by the partial enclosure formed by ditches 4 and 310. There was very little dating evidence for the first phase. The rubble in ditch 121 suggested that it had been deliberately infilled before the second phase ditches were dug. Ditch 310 was, however, on a similar alignment to the earlier ditches perhaps suggesting continuity of some landscape boundaries within a reorientation of the land parcels at this location.

The second phase of occupation can be dated to the end of the Iron Age or very early Roman period on the basis of the pottery from ditch 4. The sequence of deposits and dating evidence has been described in some detail (above). Most of the finds came from the lower rubble fills and subsequent dark silts. This material includes some large sherds, including four sherds (297 g) of Savernake Ware from rubble deposit 57 (Fig. 3.39, section 29), and 18 joining sherds of a White Ware butt beaker from the equivalent context (fill 69) in segment 40. Indeed, the average sherd weight of Savernake Ware from the lower rubble deposits was 87 g, compared with 30 g overall. It seems clear that material was being deposited while the ditch was infilling, rather than being rubbish which accumulated after abandonment.

Occupation continued throughout the filling of the ditch. Although pottery from the uppermost 0.5 m was generally sparser (with the exception of Savernake Ware), it still contributed about 30% of the pottery from the site. Sherd sizes were not notably smaller (with the exception, again, of Savernake Ware) and twenty-four sherds from a Black Micaceous fineware jar came from the upper fill of segment 40 (Fig. 7.9.81).

The indications that the site was not abandoned until late in the sedimentary sequence has implications for the nature of the occupation. There is clear evidence for a wooded environment from the mollusca in the lower fills – not only in the primary rubble but also in the occupation-rich silts which accumulated immediately above them (Fig. 3.39, section 29, fills 56 and 153). It is evident that there was woodland in very close proximity to the ditch and it is possible that it was regenerating over the ditch during the occupation. The mollusc evidence indicates that site abandonment may have coincided with the clearance of the woodland, and a hiatus in the molluscan sequence, which was evident at the top of fill 153 (Fig. 3.39, section 29), after which open country mollusca predominated (see Robinson, Chapter 8).

*Form and function*

There was little evidence as to the overall nature of the site which comprised solely ditches forming rectilinear partial enclosures. Ditches 4 and 310, together with ditch 3 in the watching brief, may have defined an area of about 0.6 ha. The cropmarks present a wider but still very incomplete picture, suggesting that the pattern of ditches may have extended over a broad area on both sides of the A417, although the picture is very incomplete (Fig. 3.34).

On the basis of the quantity and variety of finds recovered, it appears reasonable to regard this as a

*Plate 3.6 The enclosure at Duntisbourne Grove.*

settlement, although there were no features within the enclosed area and there was no identifiable focus of occupation. The absence of evidence for structures may be attributable to plough erosion, although the lack of pits is probably real. An appraisal of this site is hampered somewhat by the shortage of area excavations on sites of this date in the region to establish what features might be expected to have survived. Ditch 4 contained most of the finds, which were sparse elsewhere, perhaps suggesting that the associated occupation was quite limited in extent.

The character of the settlement is made more enigmatic by the fact that it was sited in woodland or in a woodland clearing. Woodland may also have been allowed to regenerate over the ditches while the site was still occupied. While, from a site-specific viewpoint, it is possible that the woodland molluscs in the ditches may have been related to local overgrown hedges, the same environmental evidence from Duntisbourne Grove and from under Ermin Street at Dartley Bottom, strongly suggests a local background of woodland in the late Iron Age. This may account for the high percentage of pig bones in the domestic faunal assemblage. Pigs were the most numerous species individually (38%) and accounted for 29% of animals present based on a calculation of the minimum number of individuals (MNI) (see Powell, Chapter 8), although they may still be under-represented in the assemblage due to poor preservation. There was a very low level of charred plant remains from the site with some cereal grains present. As far as it goes, the evidence suggests that animal husbandry was a more important component of the economy of the site than cereal production.

## Duntisbourne Grove

*By Andrew Mudd and Steve Lawrence*

### *Enclosure ditches and later quarrying*

The excavation at Duntisbourne Grove was undertaken to investigate a rectilinear cropmark identified on aerial photographs. The cropmark appears to indicate three sides of a substantial sub-rectangular enclosure up to 180 m across (north-south) and at least 110 m east-west, which was truncated on the north-east corner by the A417 (Plate 3.6). Trial-trenching in 1990 suggested that the cropmark was a late Iron Age enclosure with later Romano-British quarrying along the upper profile of each ditch (GCC 1990, 56).

An area of *c.* 25 x 130 m was stripped of topsoil, revealing the two anticipated linear cropmarks (Fig. 3.41): the northern arm of the enclosure ditch (114) oriented approximately east-west and the eastern arm (8) approximately north-south. In addition, a small number of other ditches (9, 10 and 11) and pits were identified. As the evaluation had suggested, there was no surviving evidence of structures or occupation within the enclosure, and only a thin modern ploughsoil directly overlying the limestone bedrock. A group of Neolithic pits and postholes was found in the south-west corner of the site; these have already been discussed in Chapter 2.

The excavation of the enclosure ditches indicated that both had been used as quarries, most probably while they were still open. It proved difficult during the excavation and post-excavation stages to differentiate deposits associated with the enclosure ditches themselves from those redeposited from later quarrying. Feature numbers often relate both to the ditches and the quarry cuts, with fill numbers used to differentiate deposits associated with each phase of activity. The origin of some of these deposits is still equivocal, and the evidence is open to different interpretations. For this reason the ditches and quarries are described together in this report, although the quarrying clearly indicates a radically different form of land use, which may relate to the construction of Ermin Street (see Chapter 9 below).

#### *Northern ditch 114 (segments 68, 117 and 202) (Figs 3.42–43, sections 29, 30 and 49)*

Three sections were excavated across the northern arm of the enclosure ditch, and revealed a ditch 1.4 m deep cut into the tabular limestone. Varying little in profile the broad U-shaped ditch gradually increased in width east to west from 2 m to 3.8 m with a *c.* 0.5 m wide ledge along its southern edge (the interior side of the enclosure). The north (exterior) side of the ditch

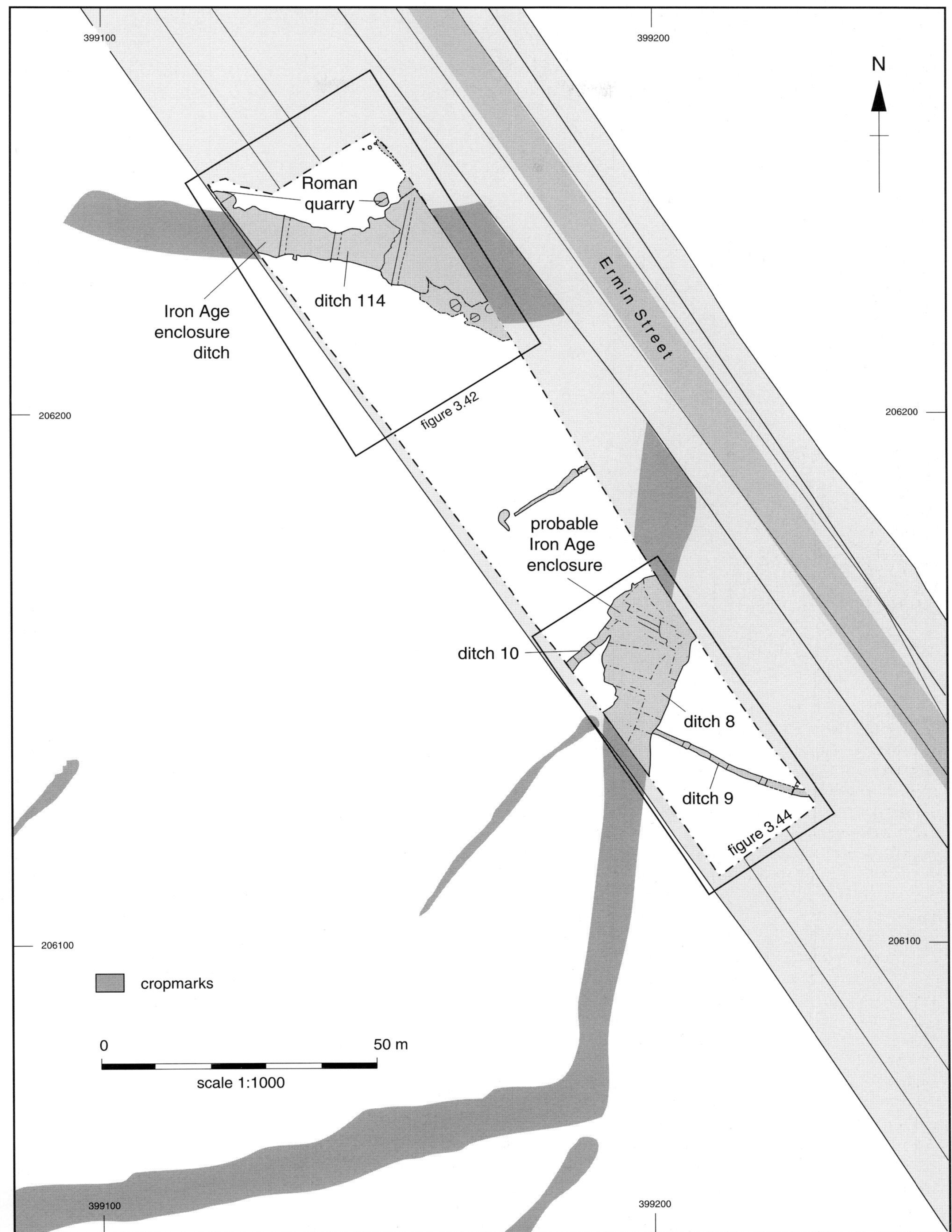


*Figure 3.41 Duntisbourne Grove, general site plan with cropmark plot.*

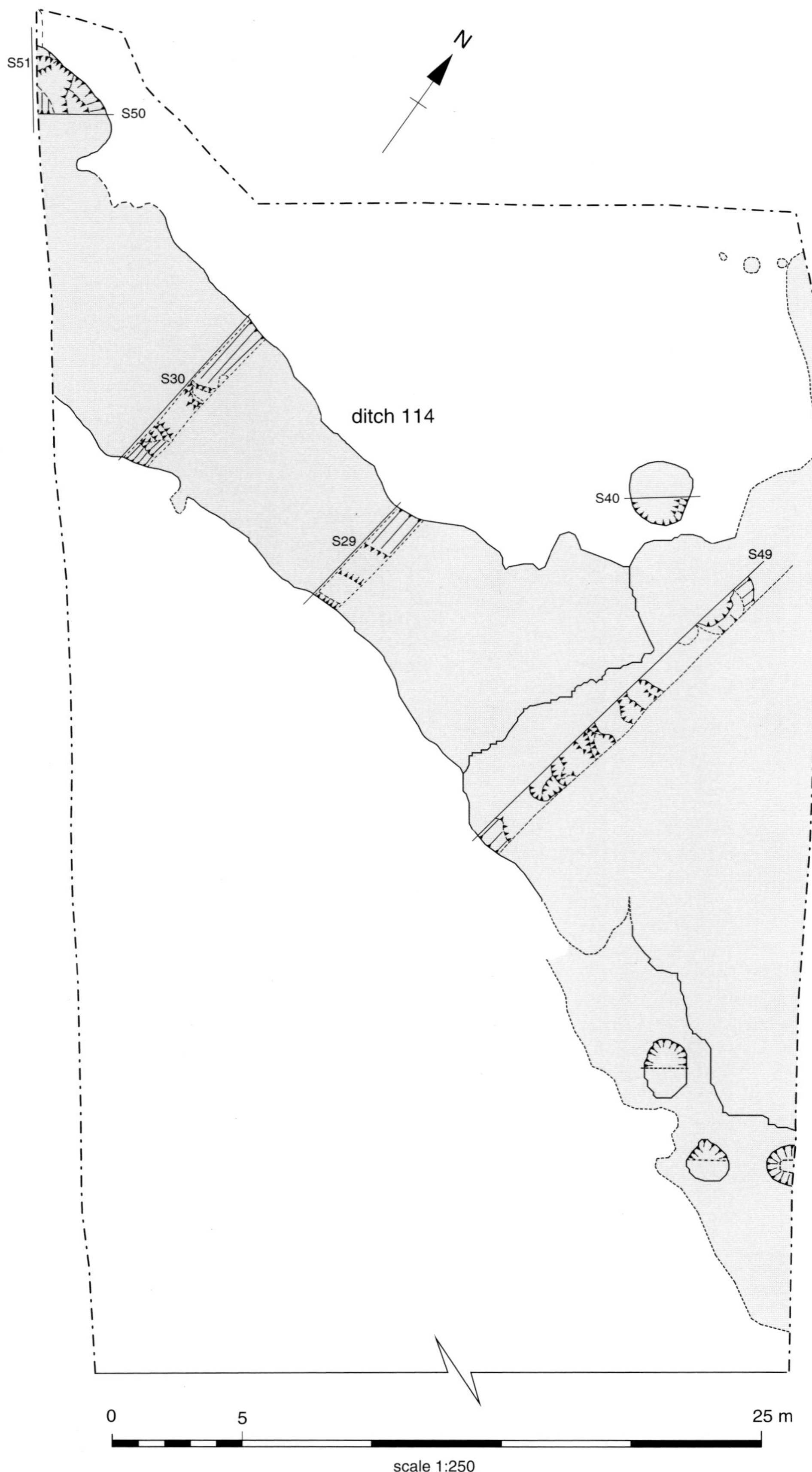


*Figure 3.42 Duntisbourne Grove, site plan north.*

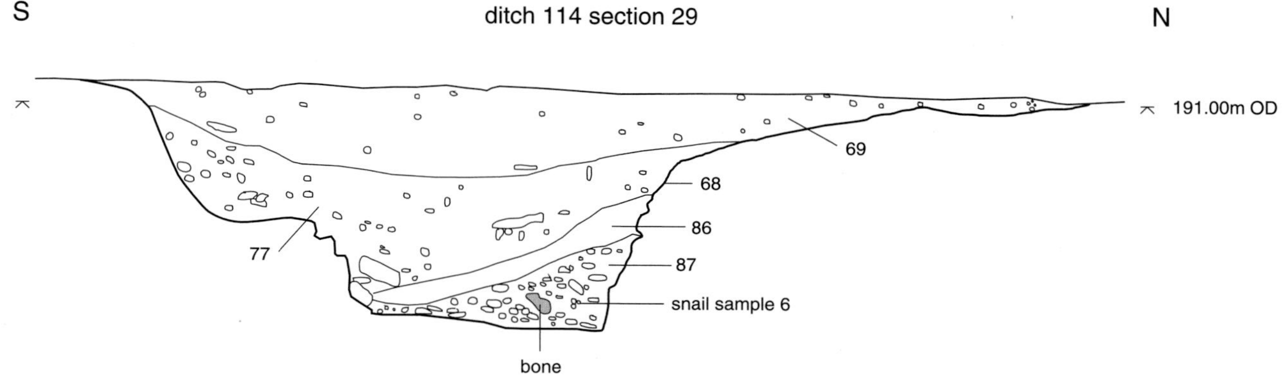


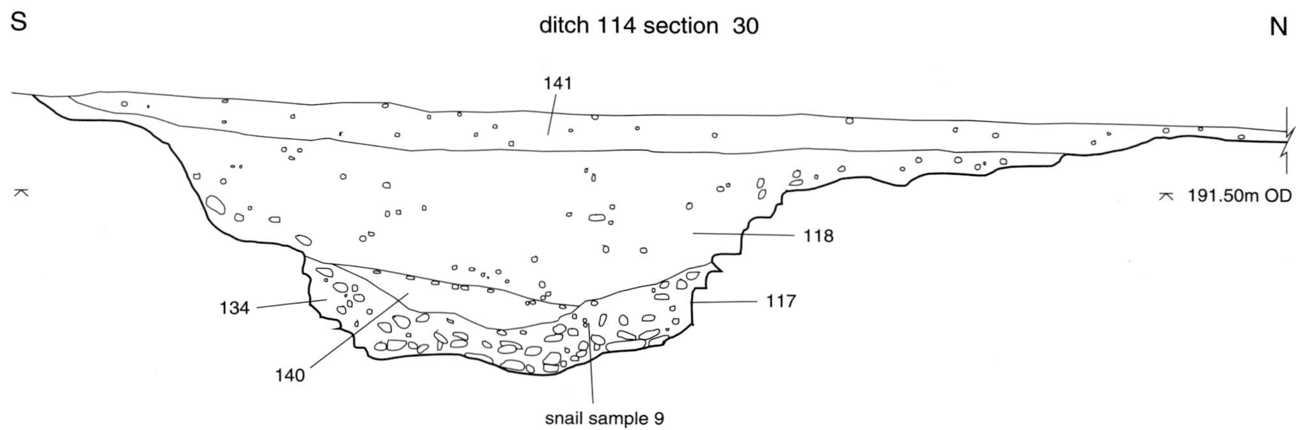


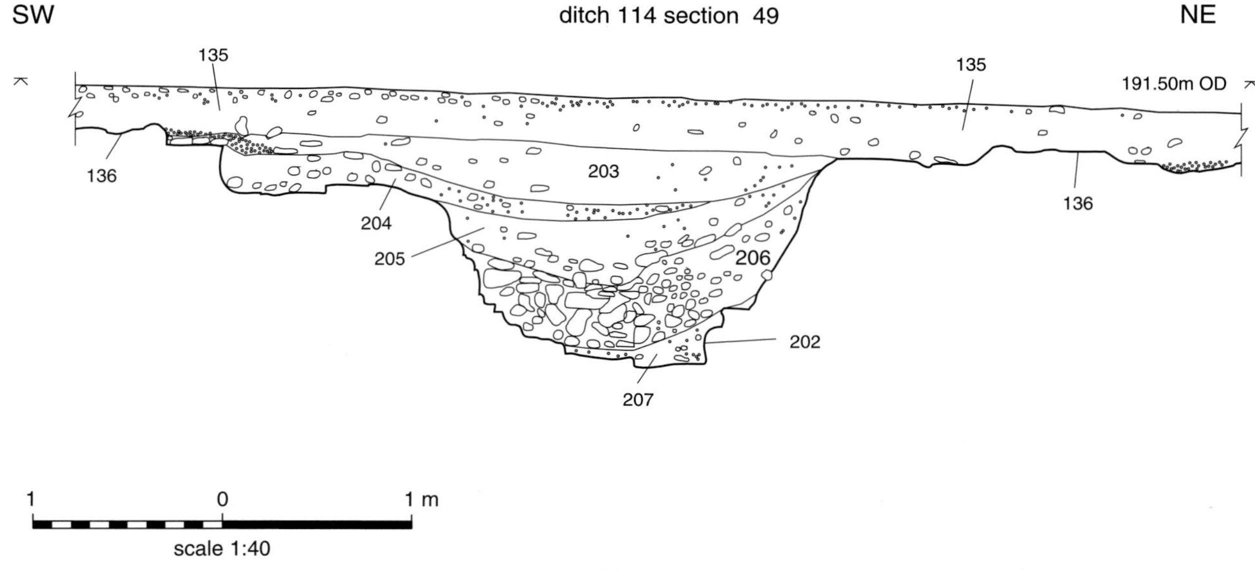


*Figure 3.43 Duntisbourne Grove, ditch 114, sections 29, 30 and 49.*

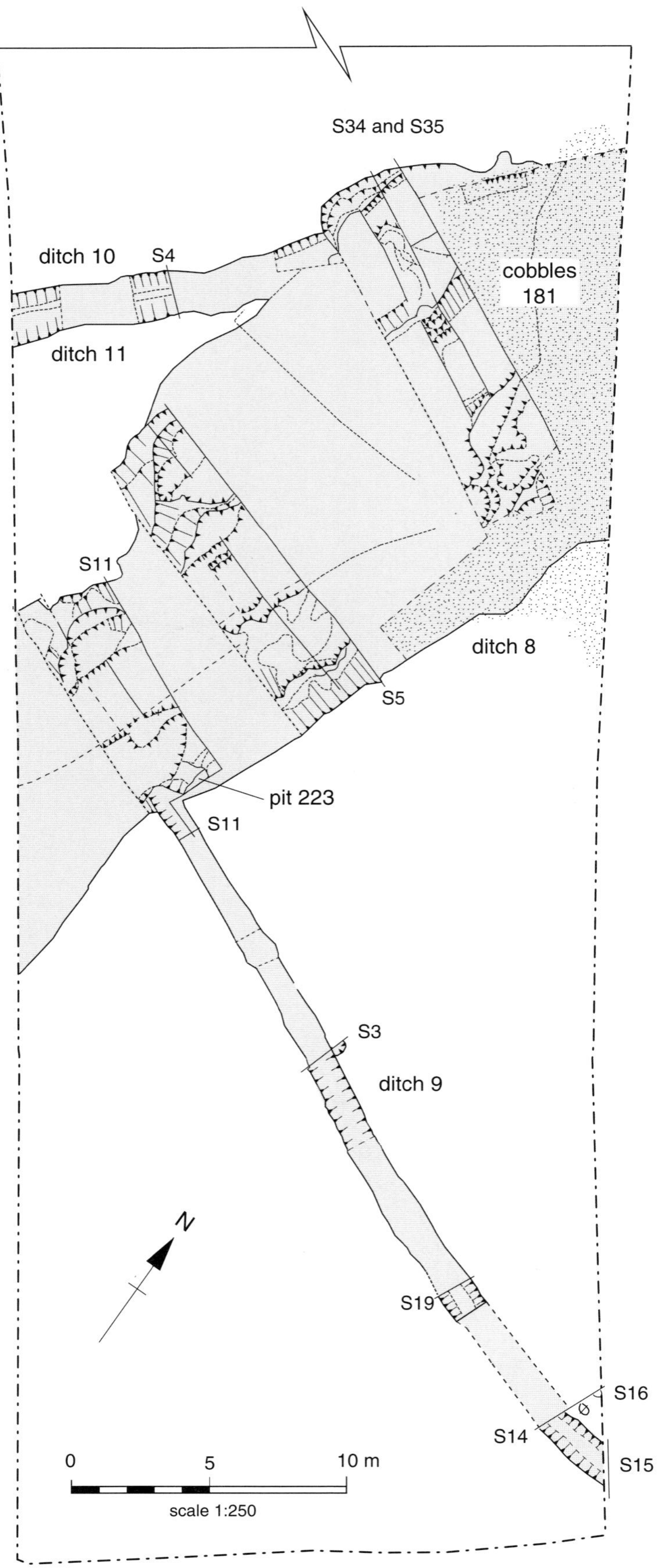


*Figure 3.44 Duntisbourne Grove, site plan south.*

also splayed out at the top, forming a very shallow slope a further 2.2 to 2.8 m wide, making the surviving ditch more than 6 m wide at the top. Quarrying of the surface limestone (Fig. 3.43, section 49, fill 135) had removed this part of the ditch as it approached the line of Ermin Street.

An identical sequence of fills was identified in the two western sections (cuts 68 and 117) with a broadly similar sequence in the eastern section (Fig. 3.43, sections 29 and 30). To the west an unevenly deposited and loosely compacted limestone rubble and silt primary fill (87 and 134) covered the base of the ditch. Two snail samples (samples 6 and 9) from these deposits indicated a woodland environment (see Robinson, Chapter 8). This was followed by natural silting (fills 86 and 140). The next deposit, limestone rubble within a matrix of silty clay (layers 77 and 118), was interpreted on site as deliberate backfill. This left a shallow undulating hollow 0.2 to 0.45 m deep, which silted up gradually (layers 69 and 141).

Virtually the same sequence was represented in the section closest to the line of Ermin Street (cut 202). Here, however, there was a discrete primary fill (207) before the mixed limestone and silt fill (206) equivalent to the primary fill in the other cut sections. Fill 206 was more stony and also contained larger pieces of limestone than the corresponding deposits, possibly because the ditch was narrower, and thus the limestone was more concentrated. As in the other cuts across the ditch, the rubble is likely to have been a natural accumulation, though perhaps derived in part from a collapsed bank or drystone wall. If so, this section would suggest that it derived from the inside, as would be expected. The silting which followed (layer 205), which appears to represent a horizon of stability throughout the length of the ditch, was also more substantial here. The subsequent backfilling was represented by a thin layer of limestone gravel (204) overlain by silts with less limestone (203).

The top of the ditch was filled with silt 135, which also filled the shallow quarry voids (136) either side of the ditch. This was overlain in cut 202 along the north-eastern limit of the site by an intermittent layer of limestone cobbling, similar to layer 181 which was present across the surface of ditch 8.

The lower part of the ditch profile is probably not modified by later quarrying, and the lower rubble fills (134, 87 and 207/206) are interpreted as silting (and perhaps slipping of a bank) during its early use. The subsequent, largely stone-free silts (140, 86

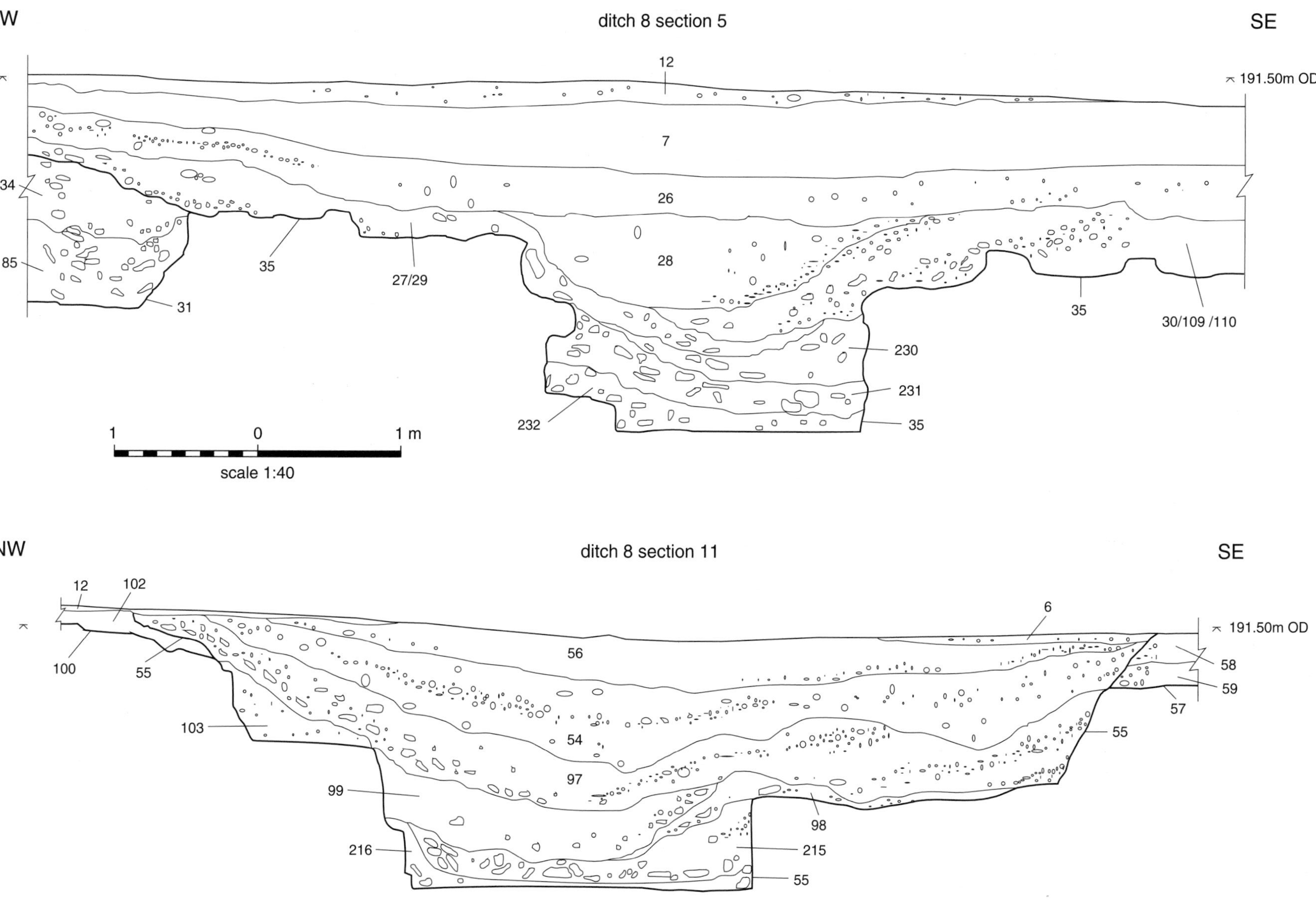


*Figure 3.45 Duntisbourne Grove, ditch 8, sections 5 and 11 (part).*

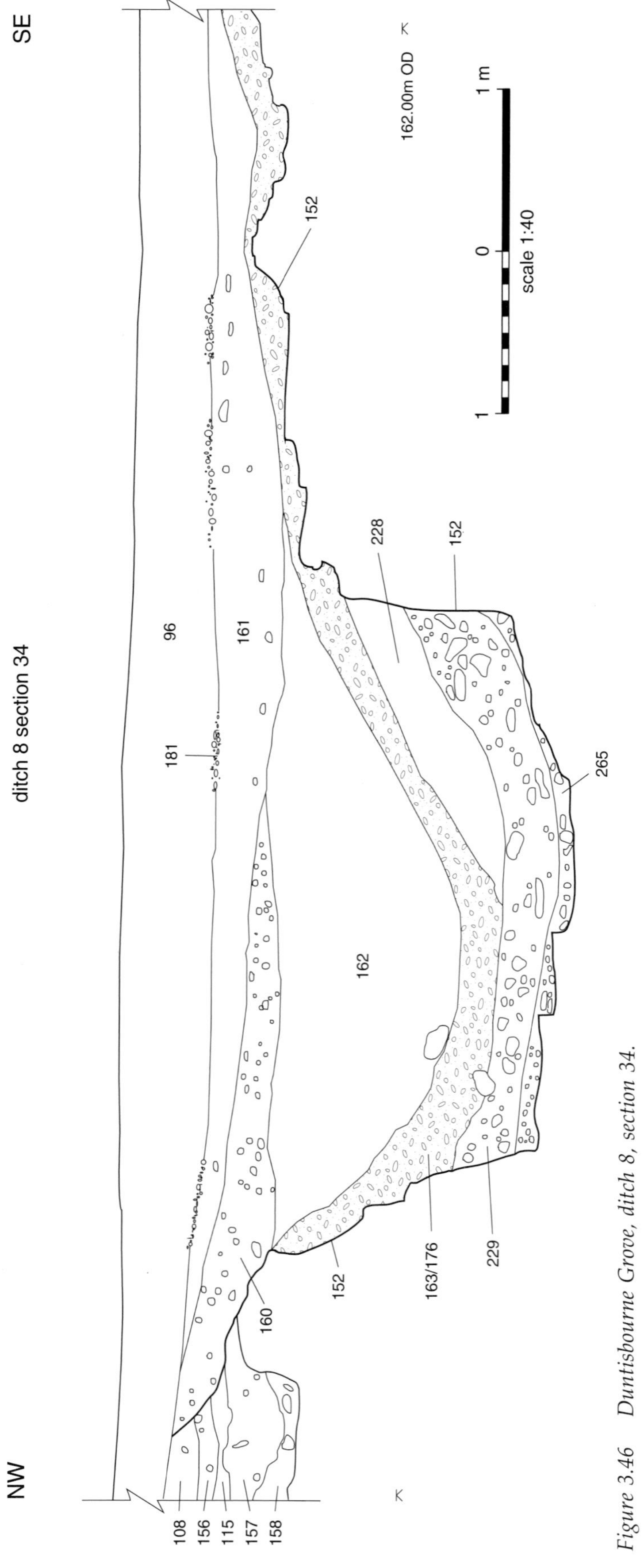


*Figure 3.46 Duntisbourne Grove, ditch 8, section 34.*

and 205) can be seen as an episode of gradual silting once the ditch sides had stabilised, again during the use of the ditch. There were, however, few finds from these deposits.

It is unclear whether the infilling of the ditch (represented by layers 118, 77 and 204/203) occurred before the quarrying into the ditch sides or after it. Much depends on the interpretation of the shallow ledge on the internal side of the ditch. If this was an original feature, there is no particular difficulty in seeing the ditch filled before the quarrying, represented here by feature 136, which would then have been restricted to the upper edges of the largely filled ditch. The ledge might have been for ease of access into the ditch whilst it was being dug; a similar possible step was found on one side of the innermost defensive late Iron Age ditch at Abingdon in Oxfordshire (Allen 1993).

Alternatively, it is possible that the ditch was still largely open when the enclosure was abandoned, and that the internal ledge was the result of post-abandonment quarrying. This interpretation of later quarrying within a largely open feature appears to be supported by the sequence in ditch 8 (see below).

There were relatively few finds from ditch 114. The vessels represented in the assemblage suggest occupation in the 1st century AD, beginning in the very late Iron Age and continuing through the Claudio-Neronian period and into, but not beyond, the Flavian period. The date of the final infilling of ditch (and quarry) is not clear, but there are no diagnostically later sherds and it is possible that it took place in the early post-conquest period.

### *Southern ditch 8 (segments 35, 55 and 152) (Figs 3.44–46)*

The eastern side of the enclosure ditch differed on the surface from the northern ditch, having a very broad soilmark (up to 15 m wide) with slightly irregular edges. Three sections were excavated across this, revealing a ditch with vertical sides and a flat base becoming larger towards the north-east corner. The depth increased from 1.7 m to 2.65 m as the ditch ran north, and the width from 2.2 m to a maximum of 3.5 m (Fig. 3.46, section 34). The upper part of the ditch had been extensively quarried, accounting in part for its enlarged dimensions and irregular appearance.

Unlike the northern arm of the ditch (114) the base of ditch 8 was sealed by a more substantial primary silting deposit up

*Plate 3.7 Duntisbourne Grove, the southern enclosure ditch 8.*

to 0.3 m thick (216/232/265.). This was succeeded by a limestone rubble deposit (215, 231, 229), probably equivalent to the limestone and silt fills (87/134/206) in ditch 114, but which was not so deep here as it spread across a much broader ditch. This contained several small sherds of pottery, including Malvernian Ware, early Severn Valley Wares and Savernake Ware. In sections 34 and 5 the next deposit was a far siltier sediment with fewer stones (228, 230), which may perhaps be equated with the phase of stable silting in ditch 114 represented by layers 86/140/205. It was followed by dumps of stony material (163/176, 27/29, 30/109/110) which may represent quarry waste. The limestone dumps spilling off the quarried ledges into the lower part of the ditch clearly demonstrate that the enclosure existed as a substantially open ditch when the quarrying commenced. This interpretation would therefore see the primary silts, the rubble fill and the overlying silts as fills of the original ditch, and everything above as relating to infilling the quarry hollow. With the extensive quarrying along both edges of the ditch, these stony deposits that follow indicate backfilling using the resultant quarry waste as well as nearby occupation material.

In section 11 the sequence may have been different, with quarry waste fill 98 apparently underlying a thick silty clay deposit 99 (Fig. 3.45). This could indicate a substantial gap between quarrying and backfilling in some places. The upper levels of the ditch and quarry were filled with dumped layers with a higher silt content (162, 54, 28); deposit 162 (Fig. 3.46, section 34) was particularly deep due to the thinner layer of underlying quarry waste (163/176). The variation in the quantity of quarry waste was largely due to the fact that quarrying did not take place all along the edge of the ditch, but was concentrated in larger pit-like quarries adjacent to it. Where more of the ditch profile remained intact less rubble and overburden was deposited or spilled into it, and more deliberate infilling with material like silty soil 162 was required to level this to the same height as the remainder of the ditch. The latest closely datable pottery from the site, a sherd of South Gaulish samian manufactured between AD 60–75, came from this deposit (Fig. 7.10.96).

Further backfill followed, consisting of limestone rubble (160) and another more silty layer (in cut 35) equivalent to layer 26. This left an undulating hollow 0.4–0.6 m deep along the top of the combined ditch and quarry, now 12-15 m wide. Limestone cobbles (181) were placed across the surface of the infilled ditch and quarry in cut 152, and this horizon was overlain by a homogenous relatively rubble-free silting layer (7, 56, 96) which levelled up the remainder of the enclosure ditch and quarry to the surface of the surrounding geology.

The sequence of fills in ditch 8 appears to represent a rapid infilling of the enclosure after abandonment. The interpretation offered would suggest that there was an episode of relative stability between the initial rubble fill of the lower part of the ditch and the later quarrying, represented by deposits of relatively stone-free silts. This correlates with the interpreted sequence in ditch 114. There was far more pottery from ditch 8 than from ditch 114 (including fineware imports), but it does not help refine the chronology, nor aid much in the interpretation of the fills. The lower fills contained Savernake Ware, Malvernian Ware and early Severn Valley Wares, which were present throughout the profile. There were no notable primary deposits of occupation material within the ditch, most sherds being small and potentially redeposited.

*The smaller ditches 9, 10 and 11*

In addition to the large enclosure ditches three smaller ditches were found within the excavation. Ditches 10 and 11 lay west of enclosure ditch 8, ditch 9 lay immediately east of it. Ditches 10 and 11 ran parallel north-east to south-west, while ditch 9 ran east-south-east.

Ditch 9 (cuts 44, 13, 81 and 45)

Ditch 9 ran from the edge of enclosure ditch 8 on an east-south-easterly alignment for 30 m and continued beyond the east edge of the excavation. On the west it did not reappear beyond the enclosure ditch. Subsequent quarrying (55) along the east edge of the enclosure ditch resulted in a ledge 1.2 m deep and cut 2.4 m into the side of the ditch. This quarrying cut through the fills of ditch 9, removing any potential relationship between the enclosure and smaller ditch.

Ditch 9 possessed an uneven profile. The sides varied between near-vertical and sloping, though for most of its length it was 1–1.2 m wide and had a flat base *c.* 0.5 m wide. The ditch widened to 1.6 m towards the south-east due to the greater weathering of the upper ditch sides. Ditch 9 survived up to 0.5 m deep.

The sequence of fills remained relatively consistent throughout the length of the ditch. The lower half of the ditch contained two or three silts (73, 74 and 89) with differing proportions of small limestones, except at the west end where there was only a single such fill (59). A heavily burnt layer (64) 0.2 m thick sealed the lower silts; this had been dumped in two main concentrations, with a thin water-eroded ashy layer between, the whole deposit extending for more than 18 m along the ditch. A variety of artefacts was mixed into the burnt debris including a quern fragment (cat. 683), a brooch (Fig. 7.21.518), a spindlewhorl (SF 5) and the largest assemblage of pottery from the site (Fig. 7.10.110, 113–115). The pottery showed some differences from the assemblage from ditch 8 (see Timby, Chapter 7), perhaps indicating that ditch 9 was infilled slightly earlier. The imported fine wares and fragments of amphorae are consistent with a date very late in the Iron Age or in the mid-1st century AD. Savernake Ware was present, albeit in low proportions (6% by number and 20% by weight), and this should indicate an immediately post-conquest date.

A final layer of silting (47/58) levelled the redundant ditch hollow. This soil was cut by the quarrying that took place in the sides of enclosure ditch 8 while it was still open, supporting the ceramic indications that ditch 9 was earlier.

Although scarce, the charred remains from burnt deposit 64 were consistent with those of similar date from the enclosure ditch fills at Middle Duntisbourne. These primarily consisted of hazelnut shells and charcoal of *Prunus* and Pomoideae (Hawthorn etc.) each suggestive of hedge-like habitats or open woodland with shrub cover. The molluscan assemblage recovered from cut 45 (section 15) was without woodland fauna (see Robinson, Chapter 8), in contrast to the wooded environment indicated by snails from the northern enclosure ditch (114).

Ditch 10 (segments 16, 24 and 48)

An 11 m length of ditch (10) was found running south-west from the edge of enclosure ditch 8, and continued into the western edge of the excavation area. As with ditch 9, the silted and infilled ditch had subsequently been truncated by quarrying activity (150) along the edge of the enclosure ditch, and no relationship with the enclosure ditch survived.

The character of the ditch was regular throughout its length. It was 1.8 m wide, with a more pronounced and angular V-shaped, flat-based profile than that of ditch 9. The ditch reduced in depth from 0.8 m to 0.5 m where it joined the enclosure, but this was a result of the undulating surface of the natural limestone, as the comparative level along the base of ditch 10 varied very little.

The sequence of soils in the ditch was consistent, but the thickness of the fills reflected the varying depth of the ditch. Two episodes of silting (first 22 and later 19, both 0.1 m thick) were separated by a loose limestone and silt deposit 0.2 m thick (21). The upper silt was overlain by a charcoal-rich layer (18), probably deliberately dumped. This may correspond to layer 64 in ditch 9. The top of the ditch was filled by a reddish silt (17).

A variety of sherds was recovered from all but the primary silting fill. These consisted of a mixture of native Malvernian wares and proto/early Severn Valley forms with Savernake wares. The mixture of wares is consistent with the pottery from the other ditches, including those of the enclosure, dating to the mid 1st century AD. As with ditch 9, however, that fact that ditch 10 had completely silted up prior to the quarrying activity, may suggest that it was earlier than ditch 8, which had remained open.

Ditch 11 (segments 172, 221 and 51)

Ditch 11 ran approximately parallel to ditch 10 on a north-east to south-west alignment, some 27 m to the north-west. The orientation of both ditches was also perpendicular to the line of Ermin Street. Ditch 11 was the least substantial of all the ditches on the site, surviving only 0.2 m and 0.8 m wide on the north-east (cut 51), and gradually petering out to the south-west, fading out after *c.* 16 m within the excavated area.

The ditch had only one fill, a homogenous reddish-brown stone free silt (52). This contained only four sherds of abraded pottery. Towards the north-east edge of the excavation the ditch fill was overlain by an intermittent spread of cobbling, possibly a continuation of layer 181 (see below).

*Later cobbled surface 181 (Fig. 3.44)*

Towards the northern end of the exposed length of ditch 8 (in cut 152) a distinctive layer of worn limestone cobbles (181) ran across the surface of both ditch 8 and the quarries either side. The cobbled layer consisted of small, tightly packed rounded limestone pieces and slabs compacted into the surface of upper silty fill (161) of the enclosure ditch and quarries, and was most substantial along the north-eastern baulk of the excavation parallel to the line of Ermin Street. The layer was generally only the thickness of a single stone, but was 0.1 m deep towards either edge of the ditch where it was best preserved. Across the centre of the ditch the surface had settled into the underlying ditch fills, and in the process the cobbles had been loosened and displaced, so preservation was poorer.

The tightly-packed *in situ* cobbles were confined to the limits of cut 152 (ditch 8), those over the south-east side of the quarry being sporadic. Similar patches of sporadic cobbling were found across the surface of ditch 11 and the northern enclosure ditch 114 and its adjacent quarries in cut 202. These suggest the cobbles extended across the site on a north-west to south-east alignment parallel to the line of Ermin Street.

An assemblage of 48 sherds was recovered from the cobbling layer mostly consisting of Malvernian wares. This was a similar assemblage to those from the ditches and quarries and may be entirely re-deposited. The absence of later wares, however, may suggest that the cobbling was also of the 1st-century pre-Flavian period. There was no evidence of wheel ruts, later repairs/re-surfacing or 'road' wash silts upon the cobbling, perhaps suggesting that it had a short period of use. A single thick silting layer (96) containing further 1st-century sherds sealed the surface, levelling the remaining 0.55 m deep hollow across the ditch and quarries. A complete hipposandal was recovered from the lower levels of the later silting although this was to the side of the surface (Fig. 7.33.630).

Although only the south-western edge of the surface was revealed within the limit of the excavation, this lay some 20 m from the edge of the modern Ermin Street. At Dartley Bottom only 150 m to the north-west of the site, excavation showed that the Roman road lay directly underneath the modern road (Ermin Street Trench 8). The cobbled surface at Duntisbourne Grove is therefore unlikely to be a continuation of this, but could represent a second 1st-century carriageway alongside the Roman road. A similar surface of cobbles parallel to Ermin Street was also present at Birdlip Quarry and one may also have existed within the line of the roadside ditch at Field's Farm (both on the opposite side of the road to that at Duntisbourne Grove). These, however, were both dated to the 4th century and not at such a distance from the line of the main road surface.

### *Discussion*

*Date and sequence*

Analysis of the ditch sequences and fills suggests that there were two phases of occupation followed by abandonment. The partly open enclosure ditches were subsequently used as stone quarries which were later filled in. The dating evidence indicates that this sequence of events occupied a relatively brief period within the 1st century AD.

The pottery and stratigraphic evidence suggest that ditches 9 and 10 were filled in earlier than the main enclosure ditches 8 and 114, and may represent a distinct phase of activity on the site. Ditch 11 was parallel to ditch 10, and may also have belonged with this early pair of ditches, though it may have been later. The cropmark evidence suggests that there was another ditch of similar dimensions to ditch 9 just west of enclosure ditch 8, which ran south-west approximately parallel to ditches 10 and 11. Yet another cropmark ditch on the same alignment is visible some 70 m to the south-west (Fig. 3. 41). These ditches may represent a system of late Iron Age land boundaries predating the main enclosure.

Within the enclosure ditches (8 and 114) the lower sequence of fills have been interpreted as the primary accumulation of primary silt and rubble, followed by relatively stone-free silting once the ditch profile had stabilised. This is supported by the woodland molluscan assemblage from rubble layers in the northern enclosure ditch 114, which indicate a gradual accumulation of sediment within a ditch which had become overgrown. An identical picture came from ditch 4 at Middle Duntisbourne. The interpretation of the fills in the eastern enclosure ditch 8 is less clear, but a similar sequence seems likely.

The pottery from the enclosure ditches indicates a very similar date to that from ditches 9 and 10, mostly mid-1st century AD. The size of sherds in the ditches is not very large, and this, together with the lack of chronological change in the pottery throughout the stratigraphic sequence, has raised doubts whether the material might not be redeposited. There are, however, numbers of sherds from single vessels in the lower ditch fills, and there is a clear difference in ditch 8 between the average size of the sherds from the lower fills and those from the clearly redeposited fills of the upper part of the ditch and the quarries; the average weight of Savernake Ware sherds being 17.5 g as opposed to 8.1 g, and the weight of the other wares 4.8 g as opposed to 3.1 g. The size and weight of sherds from ditch 4 at Middle Duntisbourne were heavier still; 30 g for Savernake ware and 5.5 g for the rest, so the pottery from the lower enclosure ditch fills is clearly not freshly deposited rubbish, but is not as comminuted as the material in the backfill of the quarries. The general absence of greywares from the lower deposits may also be chronologically significant. Of the 49 sherds (150 g) from ditch 8, all but one (1 g) came from the upper quarry infills; the single tiny sherd from silt deposit 228 (cut 152) may be intrusive. A similar view may be taken of a small greyware sherd (1 g) from layer 87 in ditch 114. A single sherd of Dorset Black Burnished Ware, which is clearly later than the rest of the pottery, came from quarry fill.

There are three possible interpretations of the pottery evidence. The first proposes that the occupation was contemporary with the small ditches 9 and 10, and that this ended when the large enclosure ditch was dug. The second takes the large and small ditches to be contemporary, despite their odd orientations in relation to one another, though the smaller ditches (which contained a much lower proportion of greywares) were infilled first. The third possibility is that the early ditches predated the occupation, which began when the large enclosure ditch was dug.

Despite their smaller size, ditches 9 and 10 contained about 50% of all the pottery from the site (most coming from ditch 9). Sherds of the same whiteware vessel were found in both ditches 9 and 10, strengthening the suggestion that they were contemporary. There is, however, no trace of any other features associated with the dumped material in the ditches. The lack of finds in the lower fills of ditches 9 and 10, contrasted with the concentration of finds in the upper burnt soil fill, shows that the occupation occurred late in the life of these ditches, indeed the extent of this deposit may indicate that this was deliberate infilling when the ditch was no longer needed. Alternatively, these ditches may have been contemporary with the main enclosure, but were simply filled in before the main enclosure ditches. Further sherds of the whiteware vessel, for instance, came from the eastern enclosure ditch.

On balance, the most plausible interpretation of the evidence is to envisage the smaller ditches as a system of field or enclosure boundaries without domestic occupation, which were then infilled with domestic material shortly after the main enclosure ditch was dug. The lower fills of the main enclosure contain finds from the occupation, but the excavated parts of the ditch were not immediately adjacent to domestic activity, and were not used routinely for rubbish dumping. The date of the occupation was brief, centred in the mid-1st century AD. Some chronological progression is indicated by the increasing proportions of greywares from the lower to upper enclosure fills, suggesting that pottery was still arriving on site during or after the quarrying phase, probably in the later 1st century AD.

The quarrying of the open enclosure ditches may have been for the construction of Ermin Street which overlies the north-east corner of the cropmark enclosure. This hypothesis, while reasonable on circumstantial grounds, is difficult to envisage if the traditional dating of Savernake Ware as post-conquest is accepted, since the ware was present in the primary fills of both enclosure ditches, as well as in the earlier ditch, ditch 9. These must pre-date the quarrying which, according to the accepted dating of Ermin Street, would have taken place within a decade or so of the conquest.

Apart from the consideration of the site's relationship to Ermin Street, the quantity, size and frequency of Savernake Ware throughout the enclosure ditches, alongside the more typical late Iron Age and early Roman transitional industries such as Malvernian and proto-early Severn Valley wares, suggests that the conventional view of this pottery as a post-conquest 'marker' needs reconsideration. However, it should however be borne in mind that the relationship of Ermin Street to the enclosure ditches was not established directly by the excavation, and that there is no direct evidence that the quarrying was related to the construction of the original road. The quarrying may have related to the resurfacing of the road, or indeed to operations unconnected with it. This would allow the occupation to be of early Roman date, as suggested by the received dating of the pottery, although the alignment of the ditches in relation to the existing Roman road would be odd to say the least.

### *Form and function*

The enclosure at Duntisbourne Grove was sited on a gentle north-facing slope within 0.5 km of the contemporaneous site at Middle Duntisbourne and would have overlooked it across the col at Dartley Bottom. Cropmarks of the site are very clear and show what appears to be three sides of a roughly square enclosure, a little over 2 ha in area. The absence of a cropmark on the western side may mean that the enclosure was open here. Another, rectilinear, cropmark approaches the enclosure from the south-west, although it is not entirely clear that this is an archaeological feature. Both the enclosure ditches examined were larger than those at Middle Duntisbourne, although the eastern one (ditch 8), which was 2–4 m wide and up to 2.6 m deep, was consistently larger than the northern one (ditch 114). There was no clear indication of the presence or location of an accompanying bank.

The size of the ditches varied, being only 1.4 m deep on the downhill side, but up to 2.6 m deep on the eastern side. The effort involved in the construction of these ditches suggests that the enclosure was intended to be defensible, though it cannot be classed as a major fortification. There was no surviving indication of a bank; the 'enclosure' occupied an elevated but not eminently defendable position with higher ground to the south and south-east, perhaps making it unlikely that it was constructed primarily for strategic purposes.

The original dimensions of the eastern ditch were similar to those of the outer enclosure at Ditches (Trow 1988), and the enclosure ditch at The Bowsings (Marshall 1991). Ditches has been defined as a 'hillfort' (RCHME 1976, 85) but the recent excavations have questioned this status and a clear distinction between 'hillforts' and 'enclosures' is acknowledged to be difficult to maintain (Trow op. cit., 38). The Bowsings has been interpreted as a defensive stronghold based on the size of the ditch and the siting of the enclosure (Marshall *op. cit.*, 14). The dimensions of the defensive ditches at Salmonsbury and Abingdon are not dissimilar, the latter being no more than 2.7 m deep, though considerably wider, and occurring in series (Allen 1993). It is perhaps more instructive to compare Lower Duntisbourne with enclosures such as Gorhambury, Hertfordshire, where a rectangular enclosure dating to the first half of the 1st century AD was surrounded by ditches which grew in size from only 2–3 m wide and 1.2 m deep to 4 m wide and up to 2.5 m deep (Neal *et al.* 1990, 12–13). The ditches varied in depth around the enclosure, and the excavators interpreted this as being due to the desire to heighten the bank to give the impression of greater strength around some parts of the perimeter.

Like Middle Duntisbourne there was no trace of structures within the enclosure at Duntisbourne Grove and no obvious focus for occupation. It must, however, be remembered that only *c.* 10% of the interior was investigated; at Gorhambury the late Iron Age occupation was not spread evenly throughout the enclosed area, and indeed large areas were blank. The large quantity of finds from ditch 9 may suggest that occupation was focussed outside the enclosure initially; perhaps this part of the interior was largely for stock. The molluscan assemblage from the northern ditch showed that, as with Middle Duntisbourne, the ditch had become overgrown with woodland or scrub while it was silting up. This situation is at variance with the generally open country fauna from ditch 9 to the south, which may be due to chronological differences between these features, but may imply that the site was on the southern margin of the woodland. This appears to be supported by the animal bone assemblage, which shows a greater proportion of cattle (50% MNI) than Middle Duntisbourne, although the percentage of pig (30% MNI) was still high. There were few cereal remains. Hazelnuts were present in the samples from ditch 9. These sample compositions were similar to those from the Neolithic pits in this part of the site, leading to the suggestion that there may have been redeposition in the ditch (see Pelling, Chapter 8). However, there were no redeposited Neolithic artefacts from this ditch and the contextual integrity of the samples themselves appears sound. Accepting this, it is possible to suggest that the charred remains could have come from woodland margins or hedgerows.

An assessment of the function and status of the sites at Duntisbourne Grove and Middle Duntisbourne in the context of the settlement pattern in the 1st century AD is problematic since so few sites have been defined, and even basic forms and classifications are either lacking or controversial (Darvill 1987, 159–169). It therefore remains unclear whether the Duntisbournes can be considered to be 'types' of site on morphological or other grounds. Since these sites were broadly coeval they can perhaps be interpreted as two parts of the same settlement unit, with the ditches at Middle Duntisbourne essentially outliers of the main enclosure at Duntisbourne Grove. On the basis of the range of fine ware imports the sites can be defined as of 'high status'. Enclosures such as Gorhambury were elite residences of the late Iron Age, which would certainly fit the limited evidence from Duntisbourne Grove. Given the proximity of Bagendon and Ditches lying about 2.5 km to the south-east and north-east respectively, it is, however, unclear whether this status would have been relative to surrounding sites, or whether it was purely an indication of proximity to the centre of regional power. Other contemporaneous sites are also poorly understood. The status of Salmonsbury in the late Iron Age is unclear (Darvill 1987, 164) although some imported items were found as well as two Dobunnic silver coins. It may have been a regional centre like Bagendon, but this is by no means certain (*ibid.*). Frocester Court, some 10 miles south of Gloucester, also yielded some *terra nigra* imports and two Dobunnic coins (Price 1983). The Bowsings Enclosure, Guiting Power, interpreted as a local stronghold, was without 'Belgic' wares or other finds indicative of high status (Marshall 1991), although this might be a reflection of an earlier date or distance from Bagendon, rather than its status as such.

The Duntisbourne sites can certainly be seen to be lying within the sphere of influence of Bagendon, and may, like Ditches, be seen as part of the 'Bagendon complex' (Trow 1988, 39), although, unlike Bagendon and Ditches, there was no evidence for coin manufacture from the excavations at the Duntisbourne sites and this may be a significant distinction. Elsewhere contemporaneous sites of presumed lower status have been found at Birdlip Bypass (Parry 1998), although this occupation was poorly defined.

Whether the Duntisbourne sites had a particular role in the regional political economy is impossible to be sure of at present. The pronounced woodland environment is intriguing and probably accounts for the woodland aspect to the animal husbandry. This may mean that the sites were a distinctive and relatively specialised element in the settlement system, the exploitation of woodland products being an obvious possibility. It is worth noting that pigs are reported to be relatively common on high-status sites in eastern England, where they account for 20–50% of the three main food species (King 1991, 16–17). It has been suggested that pork was a high status, possibly 'gallicised' food in the late Iron Age. There are clearly problems with using animal bone assemblages as an indication of status, since for significant variation to be present the particular status food would need to be dominant in the assemblage, implying that the status applied to most consumers on the site rather than a minor elite. Neither Bagendon nor Ditches yielded particularly large numbers of pig bones and an ecological rather than status-related explanation of animal husbandry may be preferred at the Duntisbournes. However, the two interpretations are not mutually exclusive. Pliny the Elder's remark that the Druids of Britain worshipped in oaktree groves (Pliny NH, XVI, 249) indicates that woodland sites may have had a specifically religious role and concomitant political importance. The initial, late Iron Age, ditches of the Uley Shrines were apparently dug in woodland (Meddens 1993, 253–4).

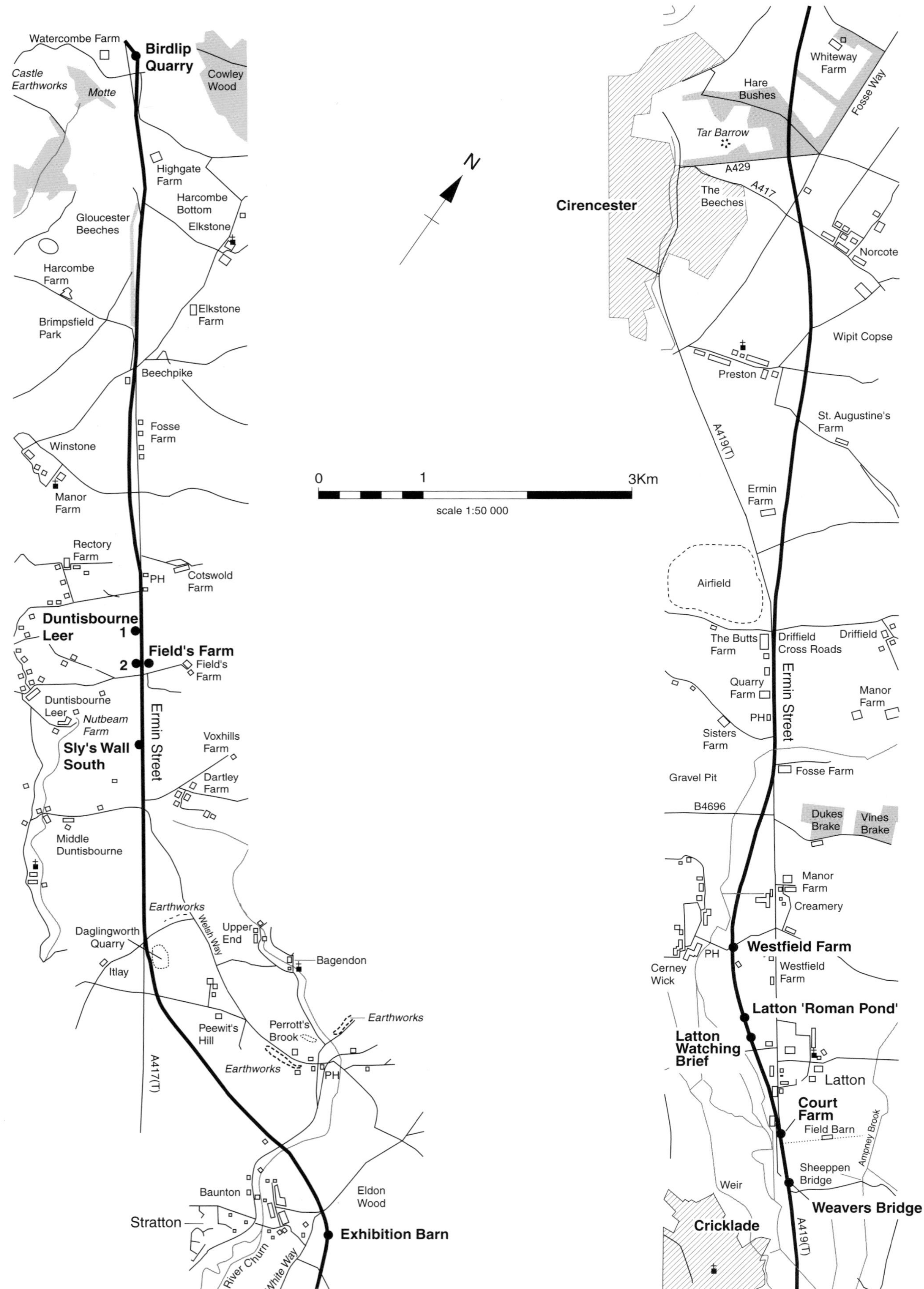


*Figure 4.1 Locations of Roman sites.*

# Chapter 4: The Roman Period

## INTRODUCTION

Sites of the Roman period were well represented on the project and varied in character and date (Fig. 4.1). They included features within both Scheduled Ancient Monuments at Latton. South of Westfield Farm, other features were preserved *in situ* following the redesign of the road (after the Stage 2 evaluation) where it crossed the scheduled area (Scheduled Ancient Monument 899). No major new sites were discovered, most having been identified or suspected from cropmarks and the Stage 1 and 2 work. There was, however, important new information from the excavations, particularly from the roadside settlement at Birdlip Quarry (Glos. SMR 11200) where the most extensive excavation on the project took place. This chapter presents and discusses all the sites with a significant Roman element, with the exception of the trenches across Ermin Street and Fosse Way / Akeman Street, which, together with other sites relating to communications, are contained in Chapter 5.

The square roadside enclosure at Field's Farm, Duntisbourne Abbots was almost certainly a funerary monument dating to the 1st or early 2nd century AD. Adjacent features examined included trackway ditches serving Ermin Street at Field's Farm and at Duntisbourne Leer, which are described in this chapter. At Court Farm, a large area of roadside quarrying was shown to be of Roman date, and its relationship with the trackway leading to the Roman settlement at Field Barn (Wilts. SMR SU09NE303; Scheduled Ancient Monument 900) was examined. A number of possible Iron Age gullies were also identified and these are dealt with in this chapter. Palaeo-environmental deposits at Latton 'Roman Pond' (Scheduled Ancient Monument 899) were shown to be largely pre-Roman, although the subsequent sequence of ploughsoils and alluvial episodes, and a series of associated ditches, relates to land use in the Roman and later periods. These features and deposits are described in this chapter while the details of the palaeo-environmental evidence are presented in Chapter 8. Further aspects of Roman land use in this area are described from the site at Westfield Farm, which also contained medieval and later features (Chapter 6). Roman features east of Latton 'Roman Pond' are also presented along with miscellaneous Roman field boundaries from other sites. At Weavers Bridge, near Cricklade, part of a late Roman site was examined which lay close to the point where Ermin Street would have crossed the river Churn.

## FIELD'S FARM

*By Steve Lawrence with Andrew Mudd*

### Introduction

The excavation at Field's Farm comprised a rectangular area measuring 82 m x 9 m positioned to examine a series of cropmarks adjacent to Ermin Street (Fig. 4.2). These had previously been subject to evaluation (Glos. SMR 4682 and 4683). Following the removal of the topsoil and a sparse covering of subsoil, a number of Roman features and evidence of extensive post-Roman wheel ruts (Chapter 6) were revealed. A further area of 20 m x 8 m was also stripped of topsoil immediately to the north-west confirming the continuation of the Ermin Street roadside ditch but no further excavation was undertaken on this area.

The Roman features primarily consisted of a variety of linear ditches and quarry pits (Fig. 4.3). Three sections of ditch formed the sides of a small enclosure at the south-eastern end of the site. This is interpreted as a Roman funerary monument. A possible central cremation had been located in the Stage 2 evaluation trench. However, this partially excavated feature, along with the fourth side of the enclosure, lay outside the limits of the excavation, preventing a comprehensive interpretation of the site.

Two of the linear ditches, 139 and 140, formed a trackway aligned off Ermin Street at an angle towards an area of cropmarks and earthworks representing a probable Roman settlement located some 400 m to the east (Glos. SMR 4682; RCHME 1976, 48). A junction between this trackway and Ermin Street was provided by a gap in the roadside ditch (138). This junction was effectively made redundant at a later date when a short ditch section (141) was dug between the trackway ditches linking the ends of the roadside ditch.

A small spread of limestone cobbles (14) sealing an earlier backfilled quarry pit was located to the south-west of the roadside ditch and may represent the edge of an Ermin Street road surface. Further areas of worn limestone cobbles present along the south-western side of the roadside ditch are less likely to represent Roman road surfaces, although this was not demonstrably the case. The use of this corridor of land parallel to Ermin Street resulted in extensive post-Roman wheel ruts and wear of the natural brashy limestone surface and, as a result, this may have acquired the appearance of a worn cobbled surface.

### Square ditched enclosure 137 (Figs 4.3–4.6)

Three sides of ditched enclosure 137 with an internal width of 10 m were exposed adjacent to the line of Ermin Street. The north-eastern side of the enclosure ditch lay outside the road corridor and consequently outside the excavation area, thus it was not possible to demonstrate the full dimensions of the enclosure. Despite this, the aerial photograph of the site indicates that the feature may be rectangular with a north-east to south-west internal length of *c.* 11 m (Plate 4.1).

The ditch consisted of a single continuous cut (contexts OAU 15, 16, 23 and 115, Glos. 614 and 621) which had been dug through the upper brashy limestone and into the more solid rock of the Great Oolite series which was generally encountered 0.6 m

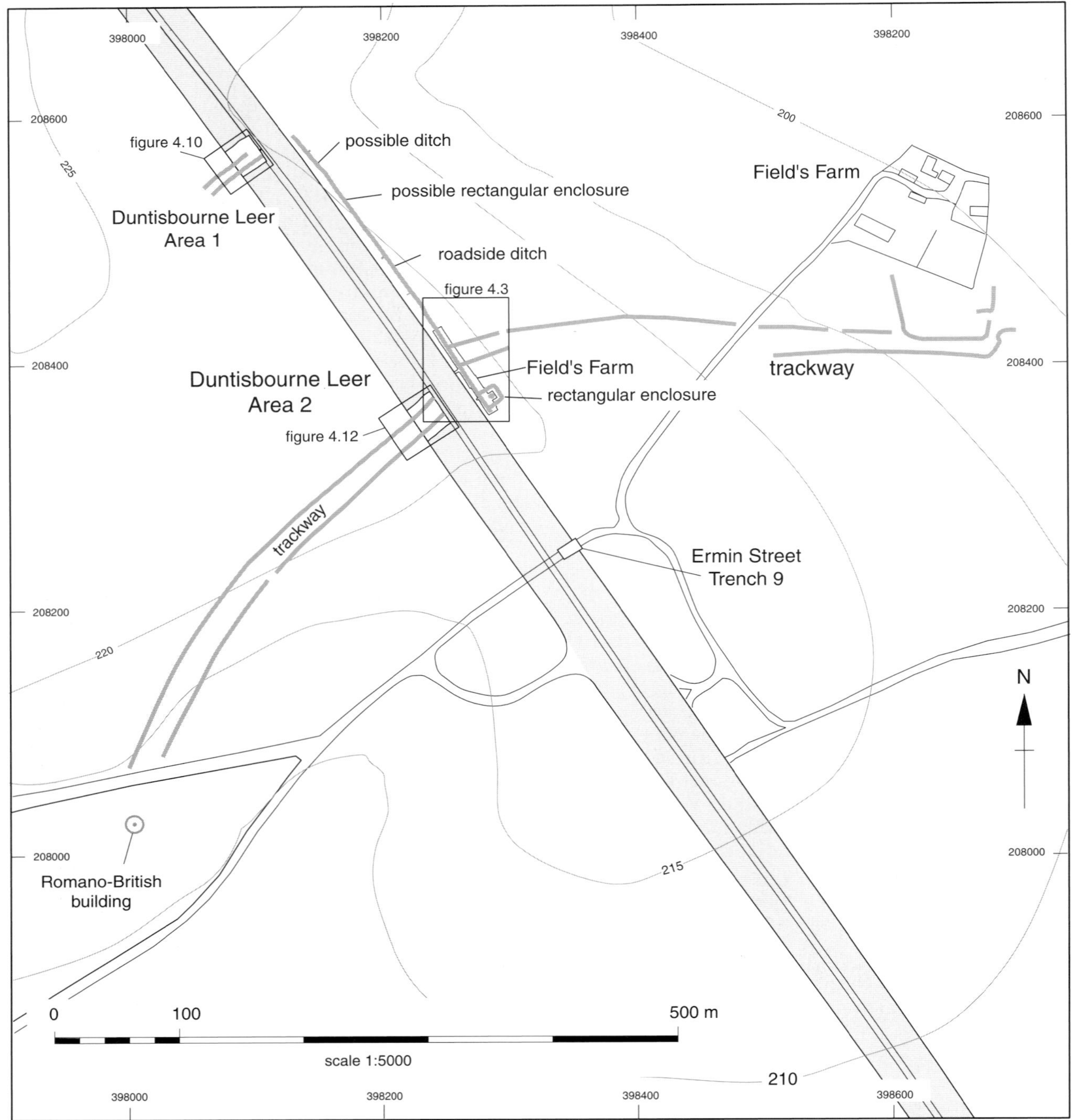


*Figure 4.2 Field's Farm and Duntisbourne Leer, location of sites and cropmarks.*

below the surface. This resulted in a characteristic profile with the base of the ditch acquiring edges of a more angular, or often near vertical, character leading down to a flat base. The upper part of the profile was equally characteristic with the interior edge having a visibly steeper slope than the outer edge of the ditch. Indeed, the interior side of the ditch was consistently 15–20° steeper than the outer edge giving the interior area an upstanding visual appearance. (Fig. 4.5, section 17 and Glos. section; Fig. 4.6, section 20).

At 3.8 m wide at its lip and 1.4 m at its base, the north-western side of the ditched enclosure (Fig. 4.5, section 8) was the widest whilst, at a depth of only 0.85 m, this was also the shallowest, stopping shortly after encountering the more solid limestone bedrock below the 'brashy' surface rock. The remainder of the ditch circuit measured between 3–3.5 m wide at the surface and 1 m wide at its base with a consistent depth of 1.1 m cutting into the solid limestone. Although the differences in the dimensions of the ditch

*Plate 4.1 Square roadside enclosure at Field's Farm and adjacent Roman trackways, Duntisbourne Abbots. The central burial pit is clearly visible as are several of the roadside quarry pits. Reproduced by permission of RCHME (ref. NMR 824/257).*

varied between the north-western side and the rest of the enclosure, the profile remained consistent with that described above - the bases at different depths merging in a gently sloping fashion.

Each side of the enclosure contained a broadly similar sequence of fills representing the consistency of the conditions or activities that occurred in its immediate vicinity. Primary silting of the ditch base was represented by a mid brown clayey deposit containing occasional pieces of degraded limestone (112 and the lower part of 62 and 618). This was present in patches of varying thickness mostly sitting in the base and up the lower edges of the ditch in a manner characteristic of the weathering of a freshly dug open ditch. Several small and abraded fragments of identifiable pottery from this deposit fell within a late 1st–2nd century range.

Following an initial phase of primary silting, the lower part of the ditch was filled by a mixed limestone rubble and silty clay deposit to a depth of 0.3–0.4 m (62, 111). Although originally thought to represent deliberate backfilling by the levelling of a bank, this appears unlikely as the rubble deposits were separated in several cases by relatively stone-free lenses of brown silt clay (eg. silty lenses included within layers 111 and 616/617). These indicate that the rubble fills were allowed to accumulate over a period of time interspersed by more stable periods of silting. Such a sequence is more suggestive of the rubble deriving from a sporadically unstable surrounding such as a

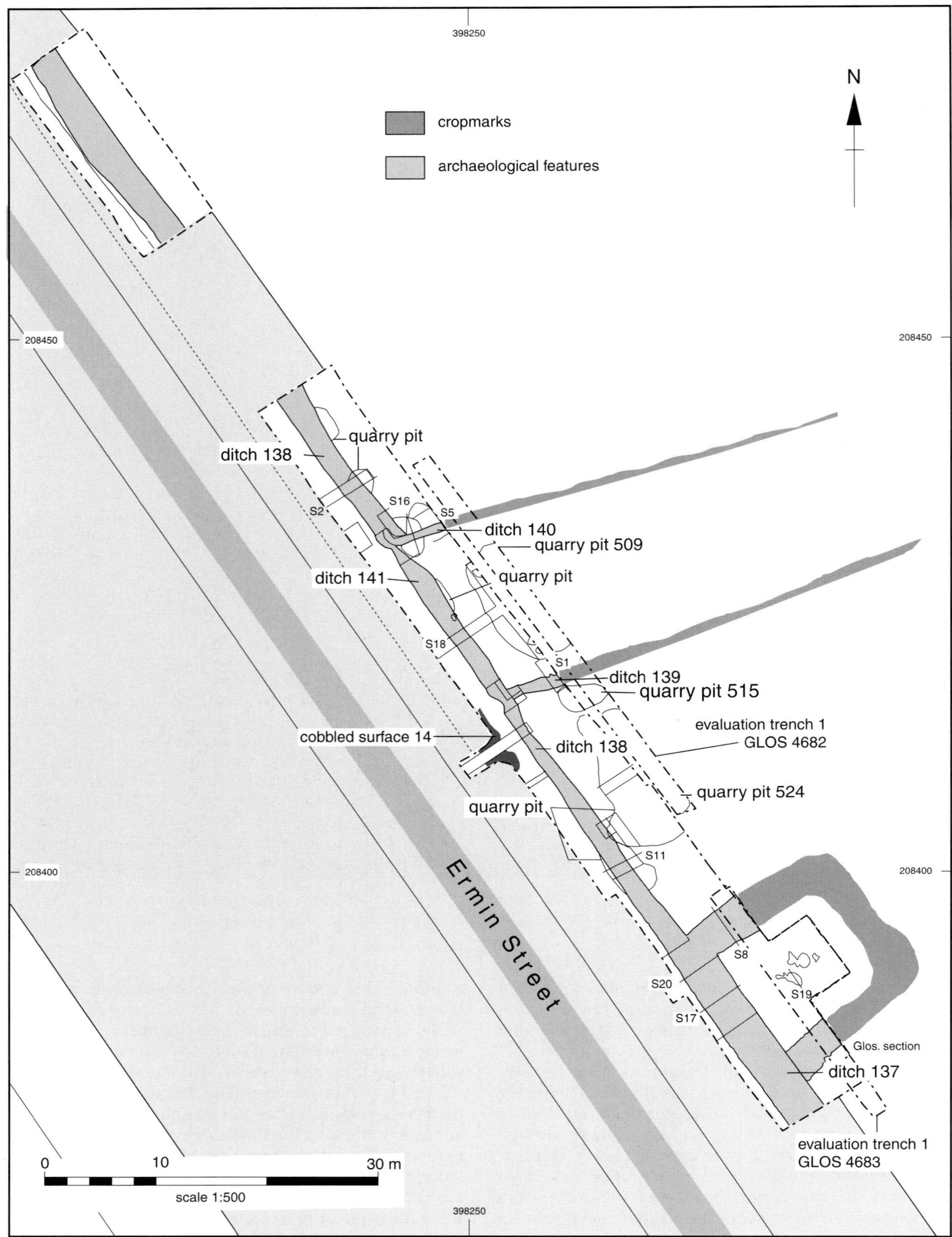


*Figure 4.3 Field's Farm, excavation areas and evaluation trenches.*

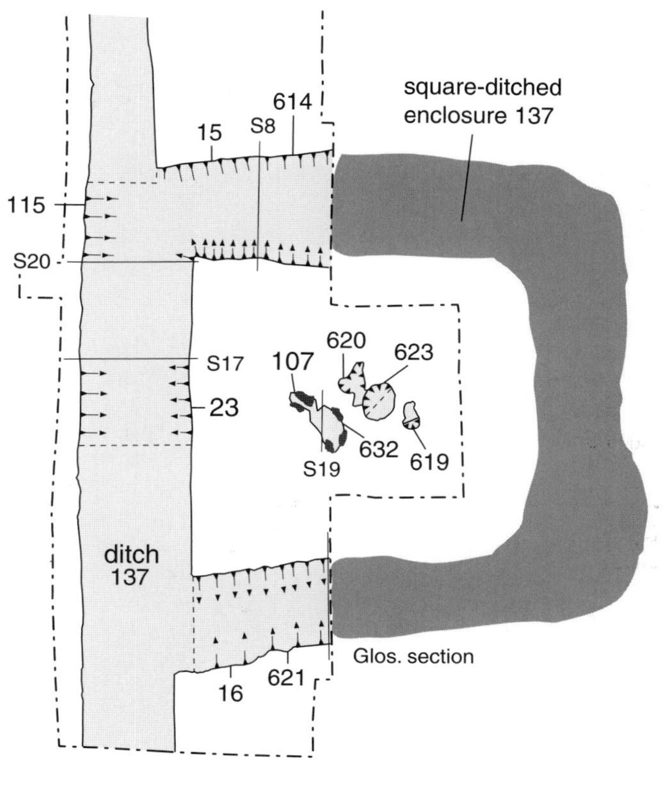


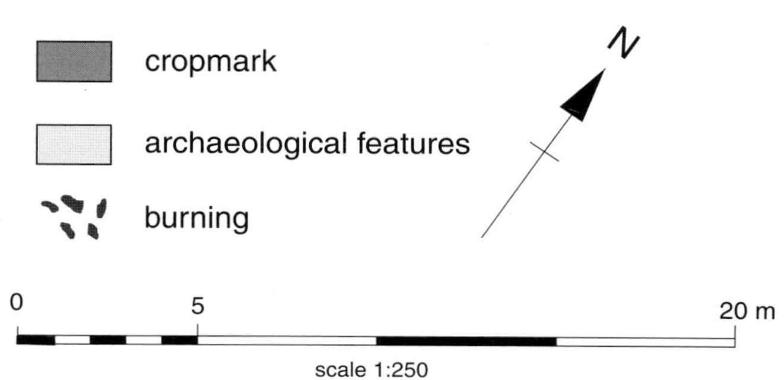


*Figure 4.4 Field's Farm, plan of square ditched enclosure 137.*

decaying and collapsing bank which would eventually achieve an equilibrium that would not result in further slumping or erosion into the ditch.

The presence of a friable brown silt clay deposit 0.3 m thick (61, 606/627) sealing the lower rubble fills marked the transition from the unstable surroundings to a period of silting accumulating in the remaining ditch void. Occasional small pieces of limestone forming thin stone horizons were present within the fill (eg. 626) presumably representing the different weathering conditions encountered during a prolonged period of silting. Several sherds from a single vessel dating to the 2nd century were recovered from this deposit (606) along with a thin folded strip of copper alloy. A subsequent layer of more stony and compact silty clay (60, 605) sealed the thick silting deposit across the width of the ditch before a final compact clayey silting layer levelled the remaining hollow (21, 601). Small crushed pieces of limestone were incorporated into the upper fill as a result of deep wheel ruts running across the fully silted ditches to a depth of 0.2 m.

The preservation of molluscs within the ditch fills was variable although high concentrations were recovered from the lower rubble fills in the base of the ditch. The species present indicate a dry open habitat immediately surrounding the ditched enclosure (see Robinson, Chapter 8). This suggests that the ditched enclosure would have been a conspicuous feature in the surrounding landscape.

Roadside ditch 138 also ran along the alignment of the south-western side of the enclosure ditch. The silting sequence, dating and alignment of this ditch at the point where it encounters the enclosure ditch demonstrates that 138 was cut prior to the commencement of the main period of silting represented by deposits 61 and 606/627 and thus existed as a contemporary feature within the life span of the enclosure ditch. The enclosure ditch had, however, already become partially silted by the primary weathering and lower rubble fills at this point which necessitated the partial removal of the thicker deposits of rubble (111) along the south-western ditch to maintain a continuous even base along the line of the roadside ditch.

### *Internal features (Fig. 4.4)*

A combined area of 77 m˝ of the interior of the ditched enclosure was exposed by the stage 2 evaluation and excavation, representing 80% of the total estimated interior area. A number of features were identified, the central focus of which was a roughly circular pit (623) surrounded by irregular spreads of remnant subsoil. Significantly the spreads of remnant subsoil showed signs of burning with the largest containing pockets of charcoal over-lying the brashy limestone surface which had been scorched *in situ.*

#### Pit 623

A roughly circular pit with a diameter of 1.15 m was partially investigated during the 1990 evaluation. It was situated slightly off-centre towards the north-eastern side of the enclosure and excavation of the upper 0.14 m of brown clay silt fill, 609, produced a single small fragment of calcined bone and occasional inclusions of burnt stone. The upper part of the profile was well defined but the pit was not bottomed. However, the aerial photograph of the cropmark shows a dark 'central' feature within the ditched enclosure which corresponds to the location of pit 623. For such a feature to show up as a cropmark indicates that it is at least as deep as similar features showing to the same level of clarity on the aerial photograph (Plate 4.1). These include some of the shallower quarry

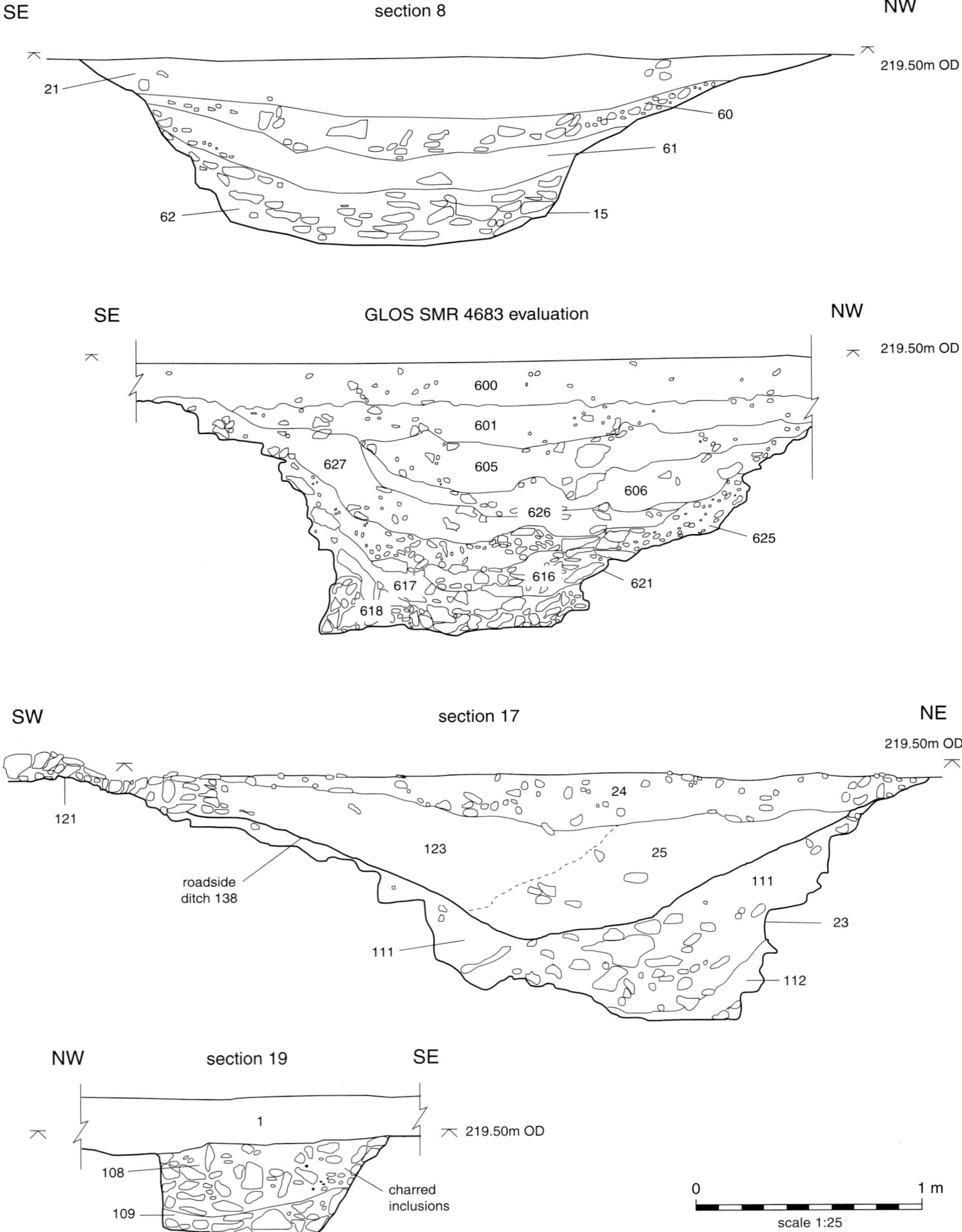


*Figure 4.5 Field's Farm, square ditched enclosure 137, sections.*

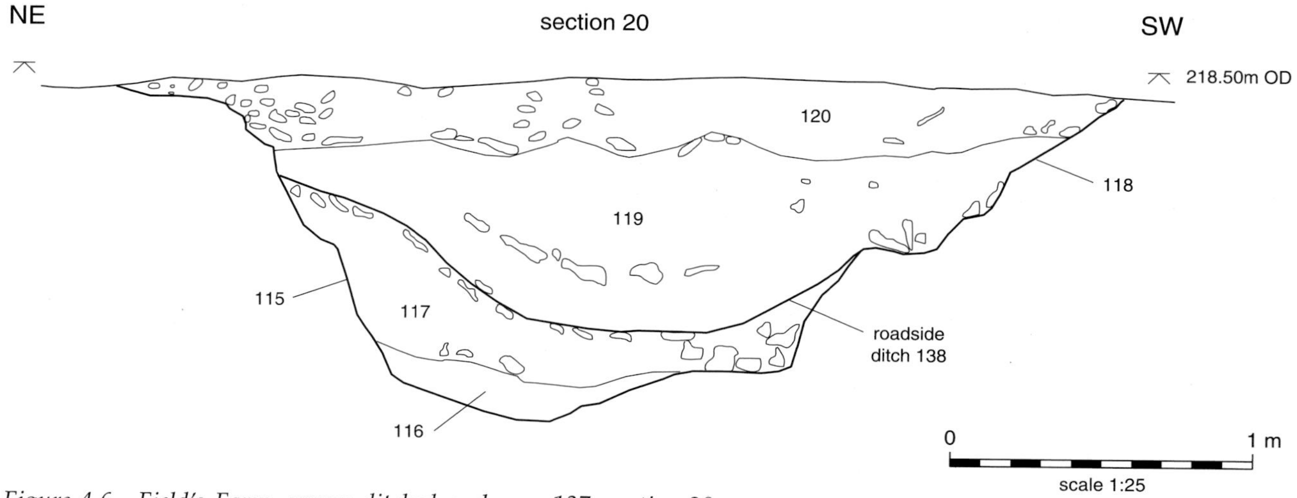


*Figure 4.6 Field's Farm, square ditched enclosure 137, section 20.*

pits excavated with a minimum depth of 0.3–0.4 m suggesting the pit was of similar depth.

*Remnant subsoil spreads*

Several irregular spreads of reddish brown silty clay subsoil were identified towards the centre of the ditched enclosure. These primarily consisted of two larger spreads (620 and 632/107) around the southern edge of pit 623 with a smaller area (619) situated to the east. Spread 620, measuring 1.6 m x 0.8 m, consisted of a clean reddish brown clay surviving in a slight undulation in the limestone surface around the western edge of pit 623. No evidence of scorching or burning was discovered in association with this deposit. Spread 619 also filled a similar irregular shallow depression to a maximum depth of 0.1 m and contained occasional flecks of charcoal.

Potentially the most interesting area of remnant subsoil was the largest measuring 2.3 m x 1 m filling hollow 632/107 and containing several identifiable deposits. The largest component of this area was the reddish brown silty clay subsoil as described above. Here, however, it consisted of a distinctly darker soil. It contained charcoal flecking and occasional small pieces of scorched limestone consistent with exposure to a high temperature. Several patches of charcoal (108, 630 and 631) were present within this deposit, directly overlying areas of scorched limestone natural demonstrating that the burning had occurred *in situ*.

Further excavation and sampling of the extreme south-western edge of charcoal deposit 108 failed to produce any charred remains. The fully excavated depth of the hollow reached 0.5 m containing a degraded limestone fill (109) in its base. Such a sequence of deposits and the irregular nature of the feature is more consistent with a burnt-out tree-throw hole which would account for the presence of charcoal and the scorched *in situ* surface of the brashy limestone. An alternative possibility is that the deposit represents *in situ* cremation or at the very least a dump of pyre debris. However, the limited excavation of this feature means that such an interpretation cannot be made with complete certainty.

**Roadside quarry pits and quarrying** *(Figs 4.7–9)*

Several areas of quarrying were located on the site ranging from relatively regular sub-circular and oval quarry pits up to 3.5 m in diameter to large irregularly shaped quarrying areas in excess of 20 m across and up to 0.8 m deep. The depth of the quarrying rarely exceeded 0.3–0.4 m suggesting that the extraction was largely targeted at exploiting the easily removable and ready-graded brashy limestone encountered in the upper 0.4–0.6 m of the sub-surface geology. Indeed a large quarry area (29) 11 m wide and located between the two trackway ditches only attained a depth of 0.3 m barely skimming the uppermost layer of limestone.

The sub-circular and oval quarries formed a roughly linear arrangement of five unevenly spaced pits located parallel to Ermin Street. Orientated north-west - south-east, each of these had been extracted to a depth of 0.3–0.4 m and backfilled with the remaining mixed overburden and residue of crushed limestone and silt. Due to their proximity to Ermin Street each of the backfilled pits had subsequently been cut through by the roadside ditch (eg. pits 37 and 82 cut by ditch segments 4 and 81 respectively). Only pit 95 situated at the junction between the roadside ditch and trackway ditch 140 remained as a broad shallow hollow when these ditches were cut.

In contrast to the pits, the larger area of quarrying (88, 515 and 524) located between trackway ditch 139 and the north-western side of the ditched enclosure (15) remained open during the life span of these ditches. This was particularly well demonstrated by quarry 515 located on the southern edge of trackway ditch 523 (Fig. 4.7). With a broad U-shaped profile 3 m wide and 0.8 m deep, this formed the northernmost component of the large quarry group. Backfilling with the mixed overburden and crushed limestone residue covered the base of quarries 88 and 515 to a depth of

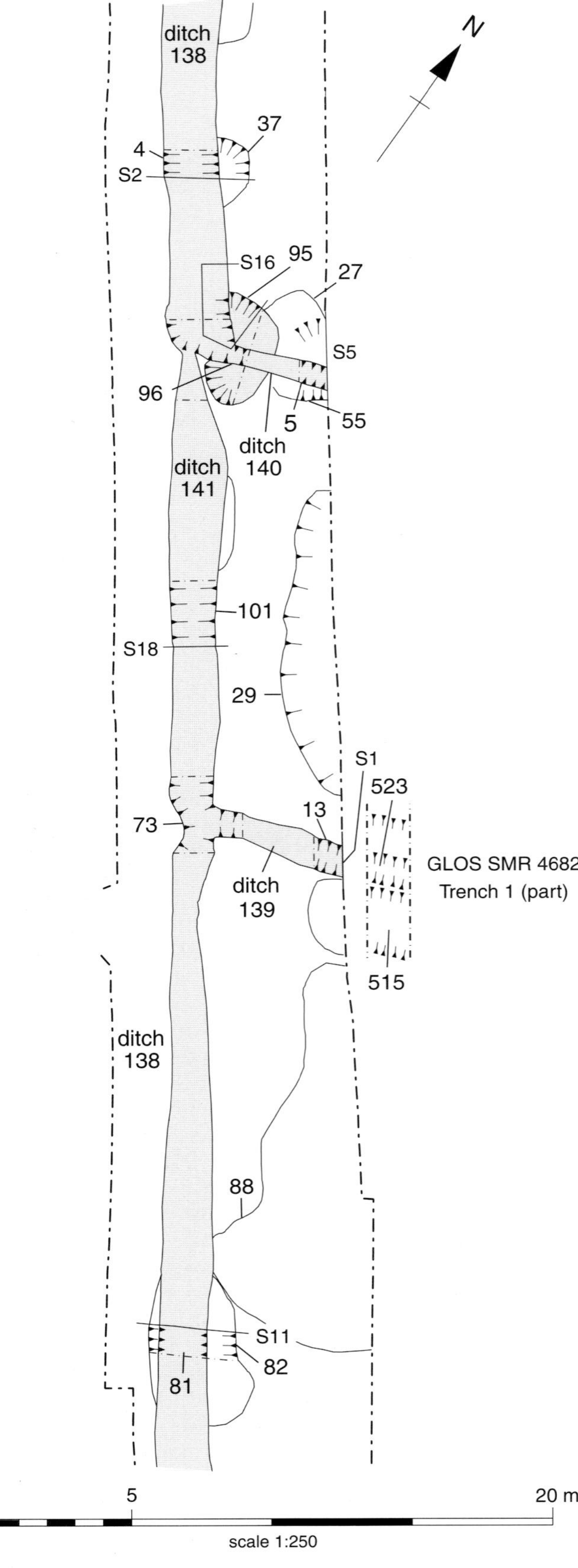


*Figure 4.7 Field's Farm, roadside ditches, trackway ditches and quarry pits.*

0.25 m leaving a void up to 0.6 m deep over a considerable area. A subsequent layer of trampled limestone fragment, 513, deriving from the construction of the trackway ditch along the northern edge of the quarry sealed the primary backfills within 515. The lack of a silting deposit between the backfill layers and the trample layer suggests that the construction of the trackway ditch occurred shortly after the extraction and initial backfilling of the quarry.

A thick silting deposit, 89/512, represented by a relatively stone-free layer 0.3 m deep, filled most of the remaining void, leaving only a shallow depression. This reflects the period of silty accumulation present in the upper part of the roadside and enclosure ditches across the site attesting to the contemporaneity of infilling of the features. This was further substantiated by the occurrence of pottery with a 2nd-3rd-century date range within layer 89. An upper rubble backfill 0.15 m thick (511) was spread across the silted quarries and trackway ditch before a final accumulation of silt (90 and 503) 0.2 m thick levelled the area.

**Roadside and trackway ditches** *(Figs 4.7–9)*

The 17 m-wide trackway was defined by two paired ditches, 139 and 140, aligned east-north-east off Ermin Street towards an earthwork and cropmark complex to the east. No surfacing was located along the exposed length of the trackway which was occupied by an area of brashy limestone. Shallow quarrying had extracted the upper 0.3 m of its surface. By respecting the position of the trackway, the accompanying Ermin Street roadside ditch (138) provided a junction between the minor trackway and major road route. This junction was subsequently blocked by a ditch segment, 141, excavated between the trackway ditches to effectively make the roadside ditch a single continuous ditch.

**Trackway ditch 139** *(Fig. 4.8, section 1, Glos. SMR 4682 Tr. 1 section)*

Ditch 139 defined the southern side of the trackway and was traceable as a cropmark for a further 35 m to the east of the excavated area, running roughly parallel to ditch 140. The southern ditch had near vertical edges with a flat base 0.5 m wide and with the upper 0.15 m of the ditch splaying to 1.4 m wide at its lip (Fig. 4.8, section 1). It was 0.5 m deep, sloping up to a depth of 0.3 m below the surface of the limestone at the junction with the roadside ditch (see below). The difference in the excavated depth of the ditches may relate to the northern ditch largely being cut into an area of quarry pitting. Indeed, further to the east the southern ditch (523) does run through such a partially backfilled quarry pit and along the northern edge of a large deep quarry (515), resulting in the ditch being dug to the greater depth of 0.6 m (Fig. 4.8, Glos. section).

A silty weathering deposit (18) containing pieces of limestone spilling off the edge of the ditch filled most of it with a secondary limestone rubble backfill levelling the ditch to the east (17 and 511). This same rubble layer could also be seen running across the partially backfilled quarry 515 demonstrating that this large pit had remained open throughout the life span of the trackway ditch.

***Trackway ditch 140*** *(Fig. 4.9, sections 5 and 16)*

Like the southernmost ditch, the northern side ditch consisted of a single cut (segments 5 and 96) running east-north-east – west-south-west off the line of Ermin Street and roadside ditch 138. In contrast to ditch 139 this can clearly be traced as a distinct cropmark sweeping eastward for 400 m towards the probable Roman settlement near Field's Farm (Glos. SMR 4682).

With a narrow steep-sided U-shaped profile 0.5–0.6 m wide the ditch differed from the more V-shaped dimensions of the roadside ditch (138) as this turned to the east and ran into the trackway ditch. The upper 0.3 m of the ditch splayed to a broad shallow profile of varying width as a consequence of being cut through a series of partially backfilled quarry pits (eg. pits 27 and 95). In a similar fashion to trackway ditch 139, this ditch was also shallowest at its junction with the roadside ditch (138) where it measured 0.5 m. This depth increased sharply over a distance of 2 m to a maximum of 1.1 m largely due to it being cut into the partially backfilled quarry pits.

The sequence of deposits filling the roadside ditch also continued east into the trackway ditch (Fig. 4.9, section 16). This primarily consisted of the lower compacted silt and rubble deposit (48 and 97, Fig. 4.9, section 5) filling the steep-sided lower 0.4 m to 0.6 m of the base. A subsequent layer of silting, 98, containing a number of sherds dating to the 2nd century, accumulated in the remaining void to a maximum depth of 0.5 m thinning to only 0.1 m deep towards the east. This levelled the trackway ditch to the surface of the partially backfilled quarry pits leaving a broad shallow hollow approximately 3 m wide and 0.2 m deep along its length. A further silty layer (49 and 110) containing small pieces of limestone levelled the remaining shallow hollow.

***Roadside ditch 138*** *(Fig. 4.8, section 2 and Fig. 4.9, section 11)*

Two linear ditches formed an alignment along the south-western edge of the site parallel to Ermin Street. They were separated by a 17 m wide gap where they joined the northern (140) and southern (139) trackway ditches (above) at their junction with the Roman road.

The north-western stretch of the ditch consisted of a single cut (4) 2 m wide and 0.85 m deep with a flat based V-shaped profile cut through several infilled quarry pits (Fig. 4.8, section 2). As seen elsewhere on the site, the ditch assumed vertical sides towards the base as the more solid limestone was encountered beneath the brashy surface. The ditch subsequently slopes up to a shallower depth of 0.5 m at its south-eastern end where it turned sharply to the east into the northern side ditch of the trackway (96). Consequently, as the ditch only cuts the brashy

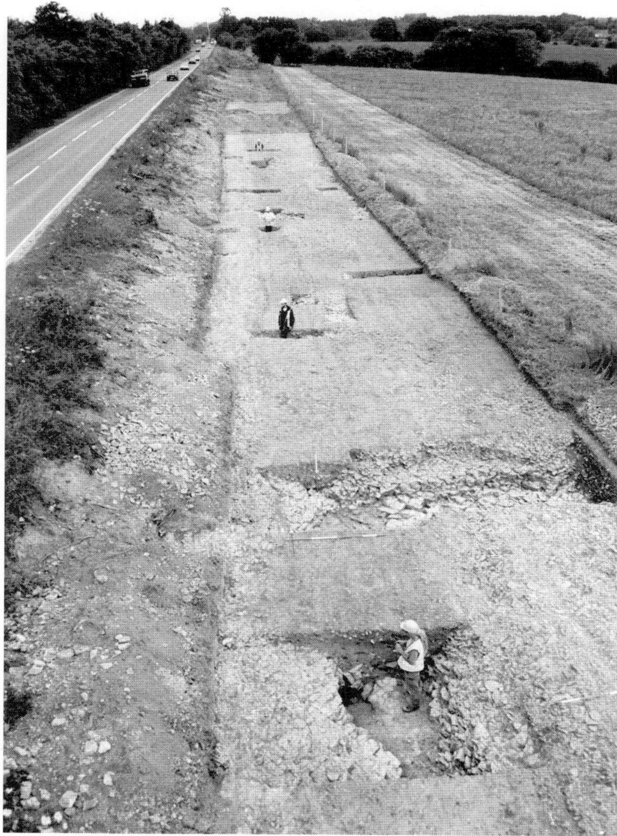

*Plate 4.2 The roadside ditch at Field's Farm which cut the square enclosure in the foreground.*

limestone at this depth, a more rounded profile was adopted with an uneven base. A primary deposit of compacted silt and rubble filled the ditch to a maximum depth of 0.4 m thinning to 0.2 m where it ran into the trackway ditch. A more substantial silting layer (41 and 98) 0.4 m thick sealed the primary fills levelling the remaining hollow across the width of the ditch.

The south-eastern extent of the ditch varied more both in its width and its profile. As with the north-western extent, the shallowest point was at the junction with the respective trackway ditch (139) running to the east. At only 1 m wide, the roadside ditch was also at its narrowest here, gradually widening to 2.15 m as it approached the south-western side of the ditched enclosure (137) and gradually deepening from 0.3 m to 0.65 m. Again the deeper sections of the ditch cut into the more solid limestone displaying near vertical edges towards the base. However, a stepped area along either edge of the ditch was also present at the uppermost level of the bedded limestone. This was due to the ditch being cut into the

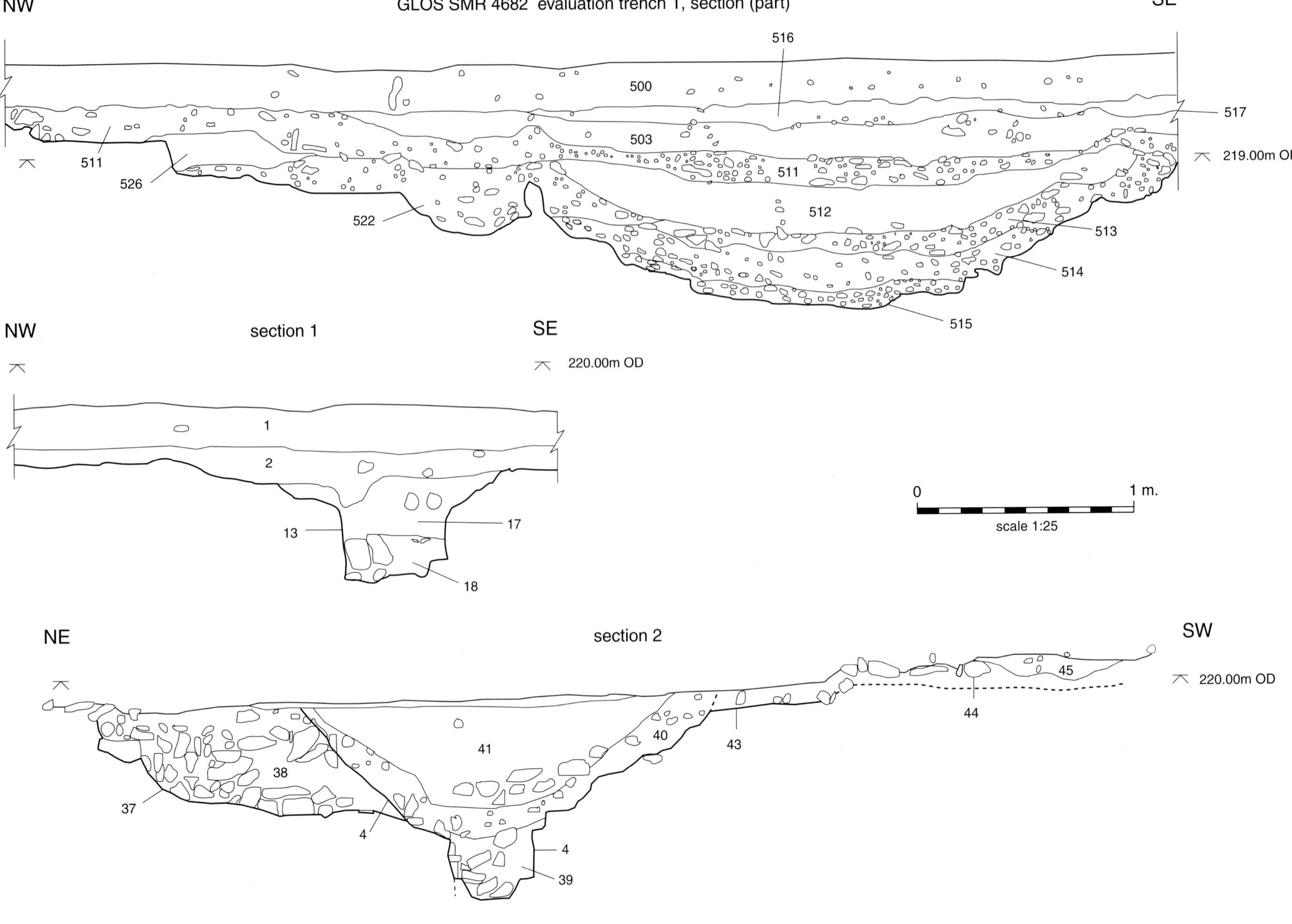


*Figure 4.8 Field's Farm, roadside and trackway ditches, sections.*

relatively easily removed fills of the quarry pits which had mostly been excavated to exploit the brashy limestone. Upon encountering the solid limestone it was only then necessary to cut a narrow slot for the base of the ditch.

A primary silty weathering deposit 0.15 m thick (79) containing occasional degraded limestone pieces filled the base of the ditch along its length (Fig. 4.9, section 11). This was subsequently sealed by a layer of crushed and degraded limestone fragments 0.2 m thick (78). This appears to have derived from the wear and weathering of the Ermin Street road surface and contained the remains of a single vessel dating to the mid 2nd century which had been broken *in situ*. A final silting layer (76) 0.35 m thick and equivalent to layers 41 and 98 to the north-west filled the upper part of the ditch levelling the remaining hollow. A thin stone horizon was situated towards the base of this deposit.

Silting deposits 76 (Fig. 4.9, section 11) and 119 (Fig. 4.6, section 20) were common to both ditches 138 and 137, demonstrating that the enclosure ditch (137) already existed as a partially silted ditch which was incorporated into the line of the roadside ditch (Fig. 4.5, section 17). Here the broad profile, 3.5 m wide and 0.7 m deep, of the open enclosure ditch was assumed by the roadside ditch. The silting deposit, 25/123, filling the majority of this length of ditch was generally thicker (0.6 m) but similarly contained a distinct stone horizon towards the base, encountered along the remaining length of the roadside ditch. The deposit was thicker to the south-west, indicating that it was mostly derived from the roadward side of the ditch. Some worn cobbles presumably deriving from the use of the Ermin Street road surface were also incorporated into this layer along the south-western edge. Sherds of Oxford Colour-Coated Ware from deposit 25 indicate that the ditch was still filling in the late 3rd–4th century.

### *Roadside ditch segment 141* (*Fig. 4.9, section 18*)

Ditch 141 consisted of a single 17 m-long segment varying between 1.5 m and 2 m wide tapering to a narrow terminal at either end. Situated in the gap in the roadside ditch, this effectively blocked the junction of the trackway with Ermin Street.

A profile differing from the main roadside ditch was also maintained along its length, with a much broader well-defined flat base 0.8 m wide, and with edges that varied from near vertical to more irregular sloping sides. This was 0.5 m deep at its centre becoming shallower at 0.3 m towards the termini and was filled by a single silty deposit containing a higher percentage of limestone towards the base (70, 100 and 127). Only a small area at the south-eastern end of the ditch exhibited a secondary upper fill (69). Containing some small worn cobbles, this probably represents weathering of the Ermin Street road surface to the immediate south-west. Combined, these deposits demonstrate that the ditch was allowed to silt up naturally after its excavation.

Ditch segment 141 was cut while ditch 138 was an open feature along the road verge. As the main roadside ditch and the trackway ditches were contemporary, with the same silting sequence filling the ditches, it appears that the trackway was effectively made redundant after only a relatively short life span and prior to the full silting of ditches 139 and 140. It is possible, however, that the blocking ditch was bridged to keep the trackway in use.

### Ermin Street road surface (*Fig. 4.3*)

The remnants of a possible cobbled surface, 14, were found within a sondage cut into the modern road embankment to the south of the site. The surface survived to a width of 1.4 m across the sondage. It consisted of a single course of rounded limestone fragments up to 0.10 m in diameter, set into an orange brown sandy layer, 22, the sole fill of quarry pit 6, which contained some undiagnostic Roman pottery. Further areas of cobbling were found in the main excavation area just outside the sondage and also in a zone close to the southern end of the trench up to 3 m long and 0.40 m wide. It is possible that some of the areas identified as cobbling were in fact natural outcrops of worn stone. However, the concentration of stones above a filled quarry is evidence for a metalled surface which, while unlikely to be a remnant of the 1st-century road, appears to be a later surfacing parallel to Ermin Street. On the surface was a coin of Constantine dated to between AD 330–335 (cat. 217) which, if *in situ* suggests that the surface was in use in the 4th century. The coin, however, may have been redeposited.

### *Post-medieval wheel ruts*

A large number of parallel linear ruts with a steep-sided U-shaped profile cut the surface of the brashy limestone and the upper fills of all the features located on the site. As seen elsewhere along the road corridor, most notably at Middle Duntisbourne, these were aligned parallel to the line of the modern A417 and the silted Ermin Street Roman roadside ditch (138) on a north-west to south-east alignment.

The location and orientation parallel to Ermin Street suggests that the wheel ruts were a result of traffic slewing off the line of the previous Roman road surface situated to the south-west of ditch 138. This occurrence clearly post-dates the Roman activity on the site since each rut cut across the fully silted ditches and quarries. A well-preserved horseshoe of late Saxon/early Norman-type came from the wheel ruts running across the upper fills (20 and 50) of the square-ditched enclosure.

## Discussion

### *Sequence and dating*

Despite a shortage of pottery and other dateable finds at Field's Farm, the stratigraphic sequence provides a

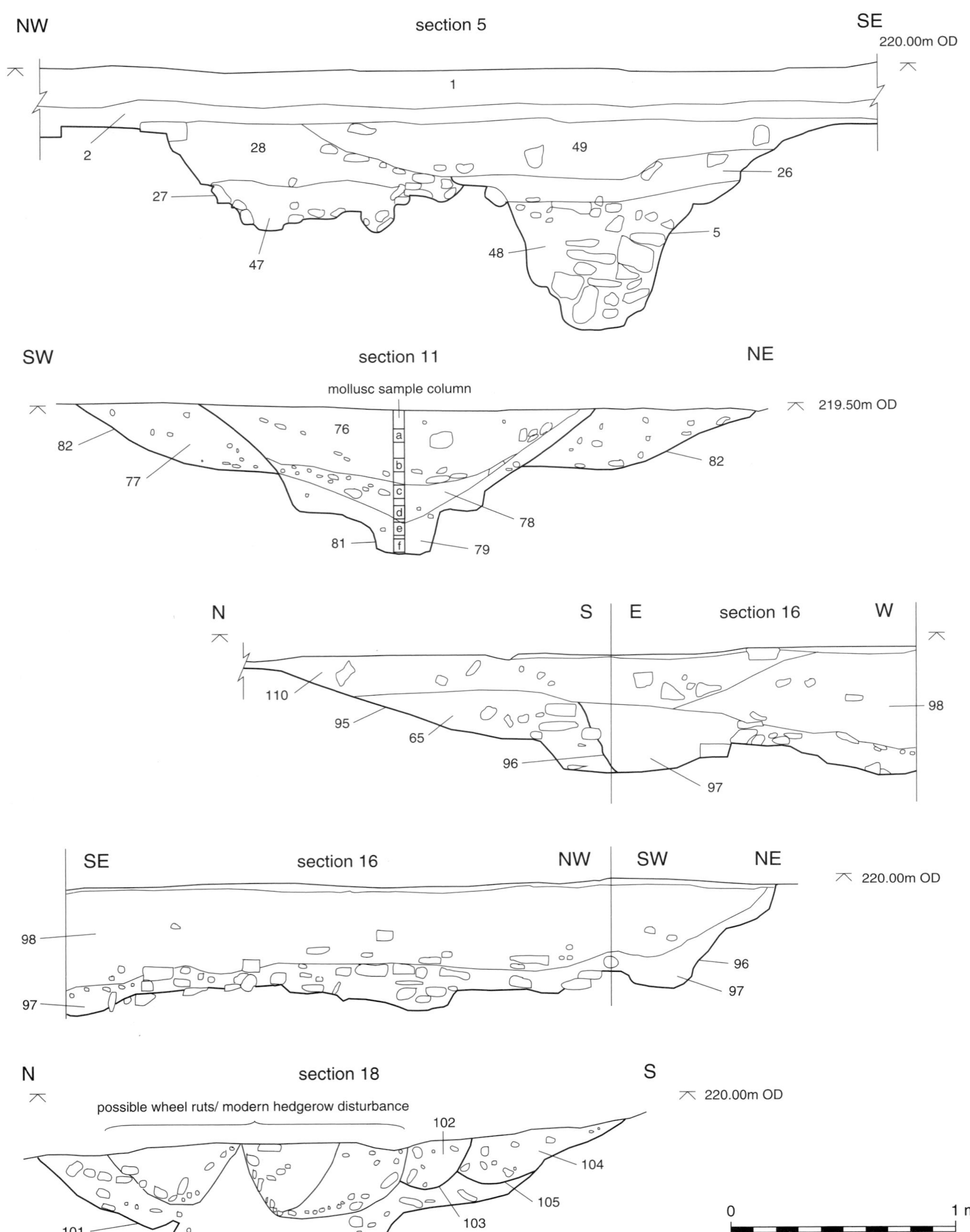


*Figure 4.9 Field's Farm, roadside and trackway ditches, sections.*

basis for an interpretation of the development of the site.

The earliest activity was the excavation of the roughly linear arrangement of quarry pits, which were shown, for the most part, to have been infilled before the roadside ditch (138) was cut. These pits may relate to the original construction of Ermin Street although, to judge by the excavated sondage in the modern road embankment, the pits appear to have been set back between 5 m and 10 m from the edge of the Roman road. There was no dating evidence from the pits themselves. It seems clear, however, that the larger pits (88 and 29), still further back from the road, were later. They were still open when the trackway ditches (139 and 140) were dug, and these can be shown to have filled in at the same time as the roadside ditch. It would be logical to see quarry 29 as the latest of all since it effectively blocked the trackway and appears to have infilled at the same time as the trackway ditches rather than earlier.

It is worth noting that the square enclosure (137) was not cut through any quarries. This was evident both from the excavation and the cropmarks, which show that the quarrying avoided the enclosure, or vice versa. This may be taken to imply that the enclosure pre-dated the earliest quarrying identified in the excavation. Since the quarrying may not have been connected with the original construction of the road, it need not follow that the enclosure was as early as the mid 1st century, although this is quite likely. The only finds from the enclosure ditch came from fill 112, and these suggest a late 1st-century (or later) initial infilling. It is unclear how much reliance should be placed upon these sherds, but it can probably be concluded that the enclosure was dug within a few decades of the road construction.

Ditch 138 was cut through the enclosure ditch, on the same alignment, when the latter had partly infilled. A vessel from fill 78 (Fig. 4.9, section 11) indicates that the ditch was probably dug in the first part of the 2nd century (unless any cleaning out had removed earlier deposits). The trackway ditches 139 and 140 were clearly respected by ditch 138, which shallowed at its junction with them. At face value, this indicates that the trackway pre-dated ditch 138. However, since the terminals of the trackway ditches coincided with the alignment of 138 quite precisely it is possible that the layout was designed as a unit. This is plausible if ditch 138 is seen as a property boundary associated with the settlement which the trackway served, rather than a 'roadside ditch' in an exclusive sense. Pottery from fill 25 (Fig. 4.5, section 17) indicates that the ditch was still infilling in the late 3rd century. This seems a long duration for the feature unless it were maintained by recutting or cleaning.

The blocking ditch (141), which appears to have put the trackway out of use, was cut while ditch 138 was still open and it filled in together with the other ditches. This would appear to indicate that the trackway was in use for only a short time, although a longer period may be allowed for if ditch 138 had been kept clean. The position of quarry pit 29 may also be taken as indication that the trackway was not used for long, although the dating evidence required to substantiate this is not available.

The latest Roman activity in this area was probably the metalled surfacing, 14, found within the sondage close to the modern road. On the basis of a single coin, this may well have been a 4th-century feature. A projection of the line of the Roman road from Ermin Street Trench 9 (Burcombe Lane) suggests that this metalling extended for up to 8 m from the original line of the road itself. This represents a substantial widening of the road here, albeit in a rudimentary fashion. It is directly comparable to the 4th-century metalling at Birdlip Quarry, although the evidence from Field's Farm is admittedly flimsier.

### *Square ditched enclosure 137*

The excavation of a square ditched enclosure (137) at Field's Farm provided the rare opportunity to examine a little known class of monument in southern England. Previous evaluation of the cropmark had defined a central pit (623) thought to represent a cremation burial although this was not conclusively demonstrated by full excavation (Hoyle 1990, 49). The tradition of placing a cremation within a square, or roughly square, ditched enclosure was an uncommon burial rite in Roman Britain with few direct parallels. However, differing types of square or rectilinear enclosures are recognised as being used as funerary monuments at varying times spanning the late Iron Age to late Roman periods. These can broadly be separated into three periods represented by differing classes of enclosure. The earliest of these dating to the immediate pre- and post-Roman conquest periods were the richly furnished cremation deposits of the late Iron Age often set within rectilinear ditched enclosures exhibiting entrances. Such examples can be seen at King Harry Lane, St Albans (Stead and Rigby 1989) and Skeleton Green (Partridge 1981) although both these enclosures are larger than the example at Field's Farm and contain groups of cremations rather than a single one. The arrival of Roman burial rites witnessed the introduction of a variety of funerary practices including the placing of a single cremation within a ditched enclosure. An excavated example bearing close similarities to the monument at Field's Farm is the continuous square ditched enclosure at Roughground Farm, Lechlade (Allen *et al.* 1993), which contained a central cremation in a pottery jar dating to the early 2nd century. Later examples of funerary enclosures include a small, 3 m-square enclosure of the late 3rd-4th century containing several cremations at Barrow Hills, Radley, Oxon. (Boyle and Chambers in prep.); and inhumation burials within continuous square enclosures possibly as late as the early 5th century at Queenford Farm, Dorchester-on-Thames (Chambers 1987). At Poundbury, Dorset, there are three examples on the outskirts of a large late Roman cemetery, probably occupying a roadside location (Farwell and Molleson 1993).

The interpretation of the monument must be tempered by the fact that the central feature was only partly excavated and could only be tentatively defined. However, the example at Roughground Farm provides strong comparative evidence that the enclosure at Field's Farm was a funerary monument associated with a cremation burial rite practiced from the 1st-early 2nd century. At Roughground Farm a continuous ditched enclosure measured *c.* 6 m and is comparable not only in plan and date, but also as the interior displayed evidence that the soil within the enclosure may have been removed as part of the burial rite. This was followed by the burning of a structure around the cremation leading to the deposition of a dark spread of soil around the backfilled cremation pit (Allen *et al.* 1993, 53). Burnt patches of soil and limestone present within enclosure 137 suggest that a similar burial rite may have taken place.

A comparable cropmark exists to the south-east at Daglingworth Quarry (Glos. SMR 4783) positioned on the north-eastern side of Ermin Street. This exhibits the same characteristics as the Field's Farm cropmark with a central feature set within a roughly square continuous enclosure 11–12 m across. The cropmark at Daglingworth Quarry occupies a roadside location set back some 20–30 m from the actual edge of Ermin Street on a slight rise in the ground. Situated only 3° km outside Cirencester on the route along Ermin Street to Gloucester, this enclosure would have been a conspicuous feature in the landscape. It has been suggested that the Tar Barrows, situated 0.5 km north-east of the *Verulamium* gate of Cirencester may also be early Roman in date (Darvill and Holbrook 1994, 53), although this interpretation, often made in order to support speculation that the original line of the Fosse Way ran this way, lacks concrete evidence.

The placing of cemeteries and monuments along major routes, that is, outside towns and on the entry to villa estates, was a regular practice throughout Roman Britain (Jessup 1959; Collingwood and Richmond 1969). The visual role of a roadside funerary monument was clearly an important aspect governing its construction and the Ermin Street roadside location was one of the most prominent characteristics of the enclosure at Field's Farm. Also, a trackway was located to the immediate north of the enclosure running towards a small settlement (Glos. SMR 4682) some 400 m to the east (Fig. 4.2). Thus the ditched enclosure was situated on a major route in and out of Cirencester and at the junction with a trackway leading to a contemporary settlement. The visual function of the monument was further established by the profile of the enclosure ditch. Being dug into the white limestone this would clearly have been a very visible feature, and this was further enhanced by the much steeper internal edges of the enclosure giving the central area a prominent appearance.

Of similar interest is a poorly understood example of a cremation set within its own square walled enclosure located to the north-west of Bath Gate just outside Cirencester (McWhirr *et al.* 1982, 21, fig. 2, *mf 5/5*). This consisted of a late 1st-century cremation placed within a pottery urn which had been set below a thin platform spread of stones and surrounded by a small walled enclosure measuring approximately 6.5 m x 6 m. The enclosure was situated some 20 m off the line of the road leading north-west past the amphitheatre on the western side of the town and the cremation was placed towards the north-eastern side of the enclosure. Several similarities with the Field's Farm monument are apparent. Although the overall monument constructed around the cremation differed, the construction of a square walled enclosure effectively mirrors the construction of the ditched enclosure above the ground, except with a limestone wall instead of a ditch cut into the limestone. The similar date and appearance of these monuments suggests that they probably derived from the same or similar customs defining a cremation funerary ritual in the late 1st to early 2nd century.

The examples discussed above are all from a relatively limited geographical area within Gloucestershire. Comparative examples further afield are very rare. The only example of probable early Roman date is that at Handley, Dorset (White 1970) where a square-ditched enclosure containing a central cremation was covered by a slight barrow mound. This was situated on the edge of a trackway leading into a ditch and bank earthwork at Gussage Hill. Again the monument was placed in a very prominent position attached to the side of a trackway at the entrance to an earthwork enclosure complex. Although the excavator remained uncertain of the date of the monument, he attributed it to the local cultural groups because of the assumed slow rate of Romanization on Cranbourne Chase (White 1970, 31). A contrasting view may see it as an outward display of Roman influence in the area.

The large earth barrows containing single cremation deposits are often associated with a wealth of grave-goods. This, combined with their spaced distribution, led to the early suggestion that they were the graves of the local aristocracy descended from the local tribal chiefs or notables (Collingwood and Richmond 1969, 169). The late Iron Age cremation burial traditions as seen in Catuvellanian sites at Skeleton Green, Puckridge and King Harry Lane, Hertfordshire (Partridge 1981; Stead and Rigby 1989) also demonstrate the commemoration of burial within ditched enclosures. However, these burials display a markedly different burial rite. The groupings of cremations within enclosures with a primary cremation as a focus suggests that some form of social or familial relationship was maintained after death and represented in the placing of the burial within the enclosure. Essentially the cremations can be seen to represent family and kinship ties. The individual cremations and roadside monuments of the early Roman period, however, show a clear break from the native tradition and in doing so display a clear message to the observer of the Roman nature of the burial. Philpott (1991, 217) defines this difference between native pre-Roman cremations and those of Roman influence in terms of the items included in the grave and the commemoration of that grave.

Continental grave furnishings and cinerary urns not normally used in native cremation groups are taken as the primary indicator of a Roman grave with a greater emphasis tending to be laid upon the commemoration of the dead in the form of a surface monument . In addition the occurrence of immigrant grave furniture and burial rites is taken as an adoption of Roman culture by the native population. Although lacking grave goods other than a Roman cinerary container, the occurrence of the ditched enclosure monuments within roadside contexts would appear to form part of the adoption of a Roman way of life in the region. The placing of such a monument at a key point along Ermin Street ensured that it was viewed on a regular basis, with the monument being imposed on the passing observer rather than requiring special occasions to visit it. In doing so a very clear message was being communicated of the Roman affinity of the monument. It is likely, although it cannot be demonstrated, that this was an aspect of the Romanization of local traditions rather than an expression of imposed Roman authority.

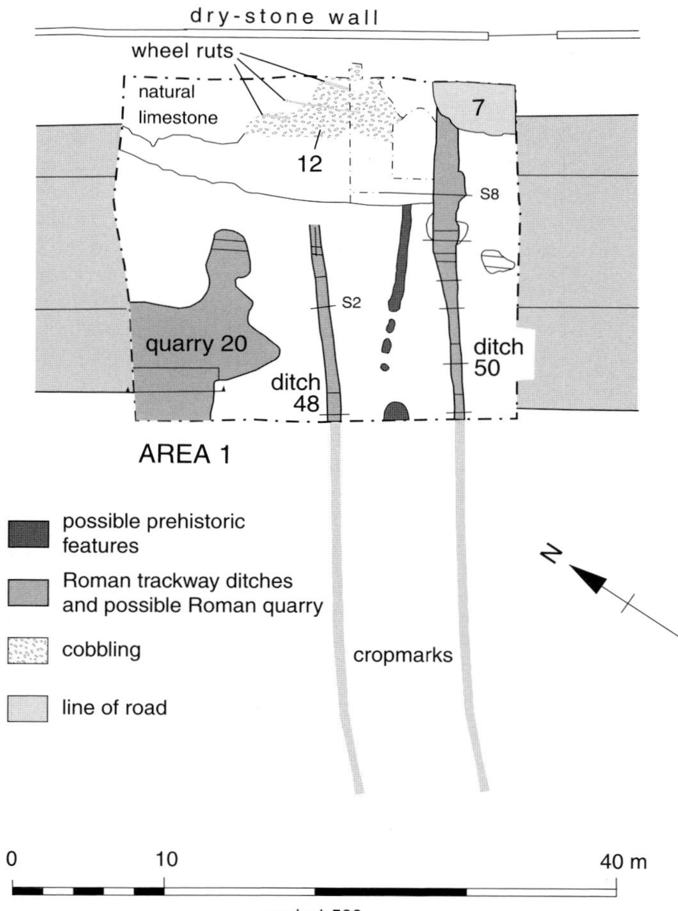


*Figure 4.10 Duntisbourne Leer, Area 1, plan of excavated features.*

## DUNTISBOURNE LEER: ROMAN TRACKWAYS

*By Steve Lawrence with Andrew Mudd*

### Introduction

Two separate areas, Area 1 (23 x 21 m) and Area 2 (23 x 30 m) were situated 223 m apart and excavated to examine two pairs of parallel linear ditches which aerial photographs and the Stage 2 evaluation demonstrated were trackways or minor roads running at right angles to Ermin Street (Fig. 4.2). The cropmarks show that the trackway ditches in Area 2 (Glos. SMR 4677) continue some 200 m south-west to a Romano-British building (Glos. SMR 3644). Those in Area 1 (Glos. SMR 11203) appeared to be more complex with several recuttings. The prehistoric features encountered in Area 1 are described in Chapter 2.

### Area 1 *(Fig. 4.10)*

#### *Trackway ditches 48 and 50*

Two parallel linear trackway ditches were cut into the limestone bedrock. The internal distance between the two ditches measured 7.5 m. Ditch 48 was exposed for 13.9 m and petered out at its north-eastern end where it had probably been truncated by later ploughing. Three segments were hand-excavated and showed the ditch to be about 1 m wide and up to 0.48 m in depth (Fig. 4.11, section 2, segment 16). It was filled with a reddish brown silt with 20–50% inclusions of natural limestone and contained no finds.

Five segments were hand excavated across ditch 50. The south-western half of the ditch was similar in character to ditch 48, (*c.* 0.72 m wide and 0.30 m in depth). Midway along its length it gradually widened and deepened to a maximum of 2.2 m in width and 0.50 m in depth. The deepest section at the north-east end revealed some gradual filling followed by the latest fill, 21, a substantial number of large slabs of natural limestone (Fig. 4.11, section 8, segment 25). These limestone slabs (up to 0.35 m across) were steeply angled into the ditch and perhaps deliberately deposited. The steep profile into which the limestone slabs were pitched may have been the result of recutting/ cleaning at the north-eastern end of ditch 50, although this is not entirely clear. There were no finds in the ditch. Its north-eastern end was cut away by a modern feature (7) with a fill of topsoil.

#### *Cobbling 12 (Fig. 4.10)*

An area of worn limestone cobbling, 12, was exposed in a slight hollow at the bottom of the slope adjacent to the present drystone boundary wall. The cobbling (10 x 5 m) appeared to be confined to a natural silty hollow. Further west the surface could be traced by wear in the top of the exposed limestone bedrock and the continuation of the wheel ruts cutting into the natural limestone. The cobbles varied in size but were

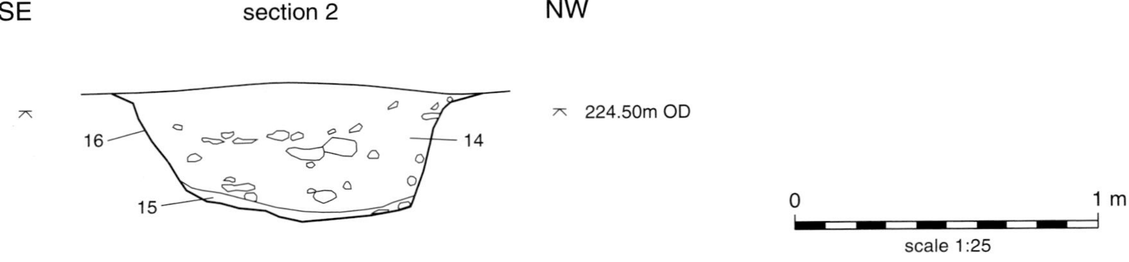


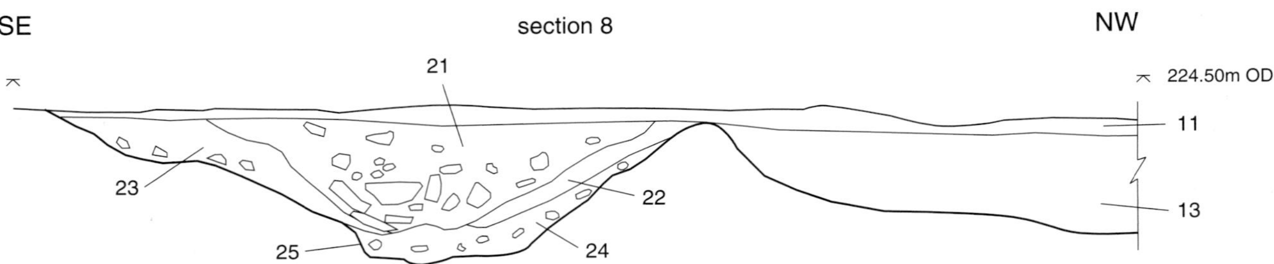


*Figure 4.11 Duntisbourne Leer, Area 1, sections.*

typically 60 x 60 x 30 mm. Manganese staining had turned the upper exposed surface of many cobbles a dark grey colour. The scars of wheel ruts were orientated north-north-west – south-south-east running approximately parallel to the present dry stone boundary wall. They were too shallow (30 mm) to have any distinct profile but were 0.10–0.15 m in width. The longest rut was traced for 5.5 m. A section through the cobbles exposed the natural silt deposits below and illustrated that these cobbles were a laid surface rather than the result of traffic wearing the natural limestone surface.

The cobbled surface was originally thought to be the remains of metalling associated with the two trackway ditches (48 and 50). However, the cobbling and worn bedrock ran across the projected line of trackway ditch (48), and, if the ditch originally continued in this direction, this would indicate that the cobbling post-dated the trackway. It seems likely that later ploughing had truncated ditch 48 as well as some of the cobbling and the location of the original terminal of the ditch remains unknown. Isolated patches of cobbling were also seen on the edge of ditch 50 but the relationship between the two was unclear. Later ploughing had probably removed any other cobbles in this area. In the hollow the cobbles were sealed by a ploughsoil, 11 (Fig. 4.11, section 8), which contained a medieval pottery sherd (late 12th–14th century) and in another ploughsoil (5), possibly the same as 11, there were two post-medieval sherds and an undated iron hook.

There seems little doubt that the rutting and smoothing of the cobbled surface and natural limestone can be attributed to medieval and later traffic on the margin of Ermin Street. The wheel ruts ran approximately at right-angles to the trackway and are clearly unrelated to it. However, the date of the cobbling itself is less clear. Although it lies on the projected alignment of trackway ditch 48, it is by no means clear that the ditch ever extended that far and the cobbling may have been more or less contemporary with the ditches, providing a firm surface near the junction of the trackway and Ermin Street. Alternatively the cobbling may be post-Roman, and within the context of road construction in this area, it is likely to date to the turnpike era (ie. 18th century) rather than being substantially earlier.

### *Quarry 20* (Fig. 4.10)

A large quarry feature was situated 3 m north of trackway ditch 48. It was irregular in plan and measured over 13 x 10 m, its full extent was unclear as it continued beyond the limit of Area 1. A large section (5.5 x 1.6 m) revealed a wide irregular bottomed feature measuring 0.62–0.86 m in depth. A mixed fill of decayed limestone and lumps of limestone (19) was overlain by a mix of silt and limestone which formed a distinct horizon and occurred either flat or at a slight angle, suggesting deliberate backfilling. In contrast, the latest fill (17) was a limestone-free deposit which produced an undated abraded tile fragment. No other finds were recovered from 20. The 1990 evaluation section across this feature (Trench 3, cut 444) mistook the quarry for the northern most trackway ditch and two abraded Roman pottery sherds were found. The date of the original quarrying may, therefore, be Roman, although a post-Roman date is also possible.

**Area 2** *(Figs 4.12–4.13)*

***Trackway ditches 238 and 239***

Two parallel linear trackway ditches were cut into the limestone bedrock and ran north-west - south-east at right angles to Ermin Street. The internal distance between the two ditches measured between 12 and 13.7 m. Ditch 239 measured 1.5 m in width and 0.60 m in depth. Three hand-excavated sections across it revealed a V-shaped profile with a deeper 'trough' in the bottom which contained the primary fill. The primary fills had a high proportion of limestone and were typically a 50/50 mix of reddish brown silt and lumps of natural limestone. The fill of the deeper trough was very similar to the natural bedrock and it was not immediately apparent as a fill until finally excavated. Interestingly, the mid-section of ditch 239 (Fig. 4.13, section 16, segment 208) contained a thick lens of redeposited natural light green clay, 206, sloping in from the south side. Superficially this appeared to be the bottom of the feature but further excavation revealed the deeper profile and fill 207. Although possibly caused by natural erosion the clay did not have an obvious derivation. The later fills, in contrast to the primary fill, had fewer limestone inclusions. A 1st-century sherd of early Severn Valley ware was recovered from fill 205, some way down the ditch profile above the primary fill. One early Saxon pottery sherd from the latest fill (229 in segment 233) indicate that the ditches must still have been open in the period AD 450–850.

Three hand-excavated sections across ditch 238 revealed a slightly irregular U-shaped profile. Two of the sections (furthest away from Ermin Street) indicate recutting on the outside of the ditch. The sections suggest the earliest cut was similar to the other ditch (239), as it had a steep V-shaped profile with a depth of 0.80 m. The recut resulted in a shallower ditch 0.50 m in depth and 2.2 m in width with a wide U-shaped profile and a slightly rounded bottom. This recut was not apparent in the section nearest to Ermin Street where the ditch narrowed to 1.3 m. The primary fill of ditch 238 yielded one tiny Roman pottery fragment and the latest fill (214) contained fragments of a probable hipposandal (Table 7.51) and a sherd dated no earlier than the 2nd century AD.

Superficial discrete remnants of a cobbled surface, 234, occurred on the inside and outside of ditch 238, but the relationship with the trackway ditch was unclear. The cobbling probably corresponds to that identified in the evaluation and recorded in the ditch section as well as between the two ditches. Since the cobbling post-dated the partial silting up of the ditch it was suggested that it represented a re-surfacing of a well-used roadway or the improvement of an unmetalled trackway. None of the ditch sections excavated in Area 2 contained well defined bands of cobbles within their upper fills and no further evidence of a cobbled surface was seen. It therefore seems that the metalling was either quite localised and random, or largely eroded away. It does, however, seem likely that it belongs, with the trackway ditches themselves, to the Roman period. The trackway is traceable as far as the present minor road to Duntisbourne Abbots, ignoring both medieval and post-medieval landscape features, and it seems unlikely that it was re-used in these later periods. However, the presence of early Saxon pottery shows that the ditches were still partially open in the post-Roman period.

## Discussion

The excavations have confirmed a Roman date for the trackway in Area 2 (Glos. SMR 4677), which can be interpreted with reasonable confidence as a minor road linking a Romano-British site of uncertain, but presumably not insignificant, status (Glos. SMR 3644) to Ermin Street (Fig. 4.2). The width between the ditches (over 12 m) would have allowed for two-way traffic. There is little doubt that the surface of the road was

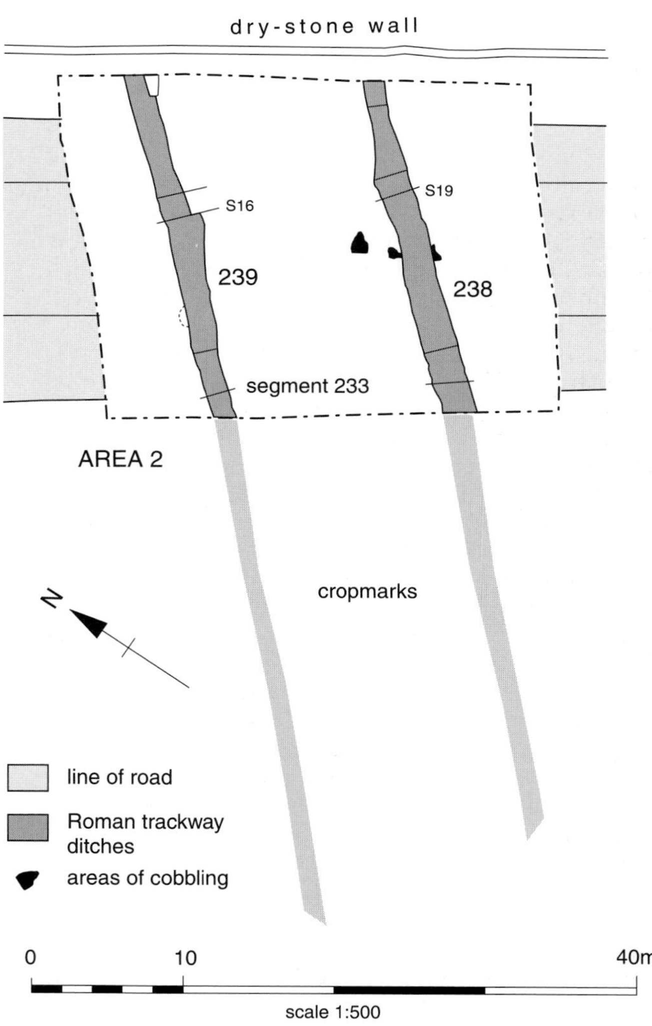


*Figure 4.12 Duntisbourne Leer, Area 2, plan of excavated features.*

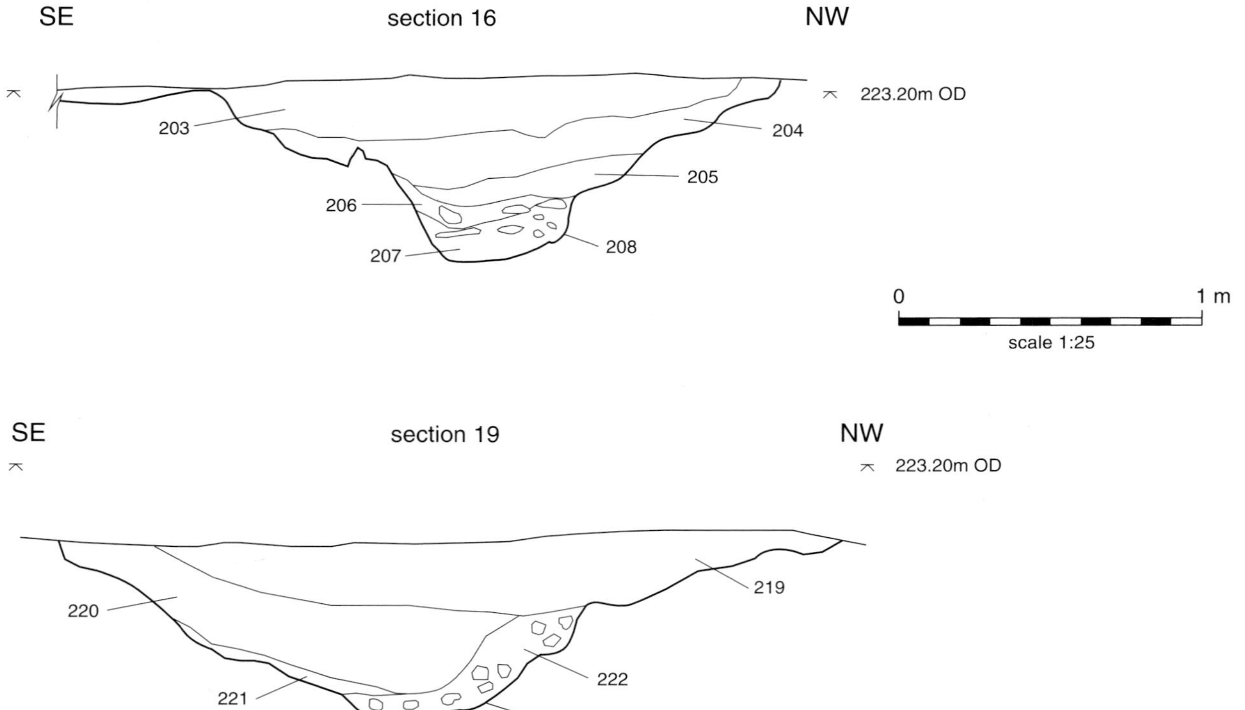


*Figure 4.13 Duntisbourne Leer, Area 2, sections.*

metalled to some degree, but the surviving metalling was found to be extremely limited and it remains unclear whether it was originally continuous between the ditches, and whether it was part of the original construction or a later improvement.

The dating evidence was limited to a few sherds, but there is some indication that the roadway was long-lived. There seem to have been at least two episodes of ditch digging, the initial, deeper ditch having at least partly silted up before being redug. There is no good dating for the first episode, but it probably took place in the 1st or 2nd century on the basis of the pottery. The 1st-century sherd from the later cut can be assumed to have been redeposited, but this is not certain, and it remains possible that the first episode was both very early and short-lived. The ditches were then recut, probably in the later Roman period. The early Saxon pottery from the upper fill indicates that the maintenance, if not the actual re-instatement, of the roadway could have been very late indeed. Any further confirmation of the dating can only come from an examination of the Roman settlement which the roadway served.

The results of the excavations in Area 1 (Glos. SMR 11203) were inconclusive and, although a Roman date for the trackway ditches appears likely purely on the basis of the site's type, no supporting evidence was retrieved. There are as yet no indications of a Roman site which the trackway might have served, which means that there is not even any circumstantial dating evidence and further investigations are required to clarify its date and function.

## COURT FARM

*By Steve Lawrence with Andrew Mudd*

### Introduction

The site, situated immediately opposite Court Farm, Latton, fell along the extreme south-western boundary of Scheduled Ancient Monument (SAM) 900. The known remains within this portion of the road corridor spanned the Neolithic to post-medieval periods, although the vast majority of archaeological remains related to Roman activity on the site. This primarily consisted of very dense quarry pitting along the edge of Ermin Street and the south-western end of a trackway defined by a recut pair of ditches. The trackway led to an extensive area of settlement cropmarks concentrated 450 m to the north-east in the corner of the SAM boundary (Wilts. SMR SU09NE303). Both the position of the main trackway ditches and the extent of the dense quarry pitting had been previously demonstrated by aerial photography (Plate 4.3) and geophysical survey (CAT 1995; GeoQuest 1995) and are shown on Figure 4.14.

Earlier activity on the site was represented by the occurrence of residual prehistoric pottery within the fills of the Roman quarry pits and trackway ditches. Several early prehistoric sherds were present although these were generally very small and abraded. The larger component of the prehistoric assemblage covers the middle to late Iron Age and the quantity of this, albeit mostly in residual contexts, suggests that features of this date were present prior to being removed by the dense quarry pitting. Indeed, several

*Plate 4.3 Roman settlement at Field Barn near Court Farm, Latton. Dense Roman quarrying can be seen flanking Ermin Street (top right) and respecting the ditched trackway leading to the settlement. Reproduced by permission of RCHME (ref. NMR 973/219).*

gullies and probable pits of Iron Age date had survived truncation at the south-eastern end of the site where the quarry pitting became more dispersed (Fig. 4.15). Further possible pre-Roman gullies were located towards the centre of the site although these were not visible on the surface plan due to being masked by the increasingly dense quarry pitting.

A variety of linear features post-dating the Roman activity were also located across the site, most of them probably representing cultivation furrows. These were aligned north-east to south-west perpendicular to Ermin Street cutting across the infilled quarry pits. Each had been subsequently truncated by the construction of the Thames and Severn canal along the north-eastern edge of Ermin Street. Further features associated with the canal were situated parallel to its north-eastern edge. Of these, a well constructed stone field-drain coincided with the location of two SMR entries (Wilts. SMR SU09NE304 and 305) which had previously recorded the presence of a stone building of Roman date. These records can now be regarded as erroneous as the present excavations have demonstrated an absence of surviving Roman structures in this area.

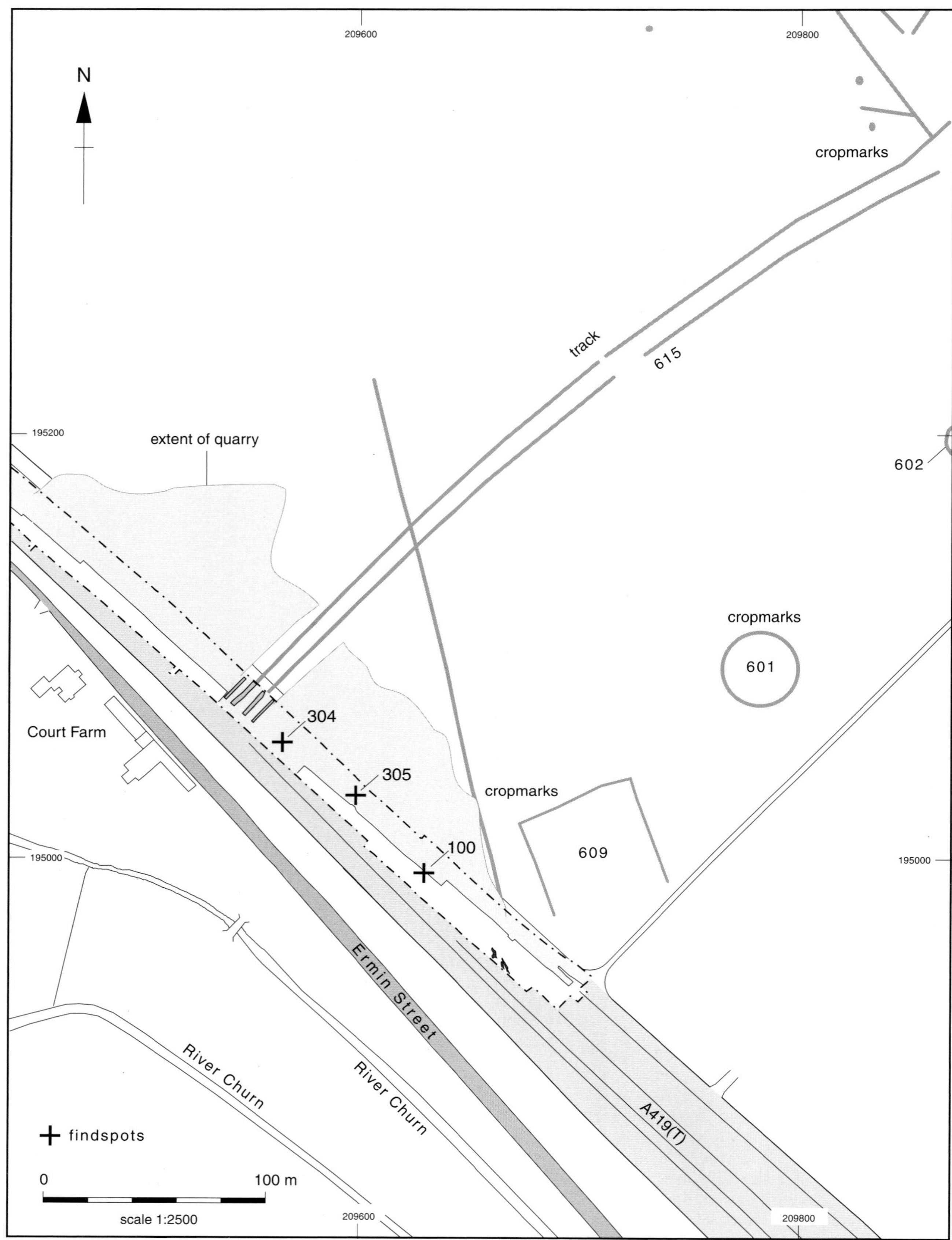


*Figure 4.14 Court Farm, location of site and cropmarks.*

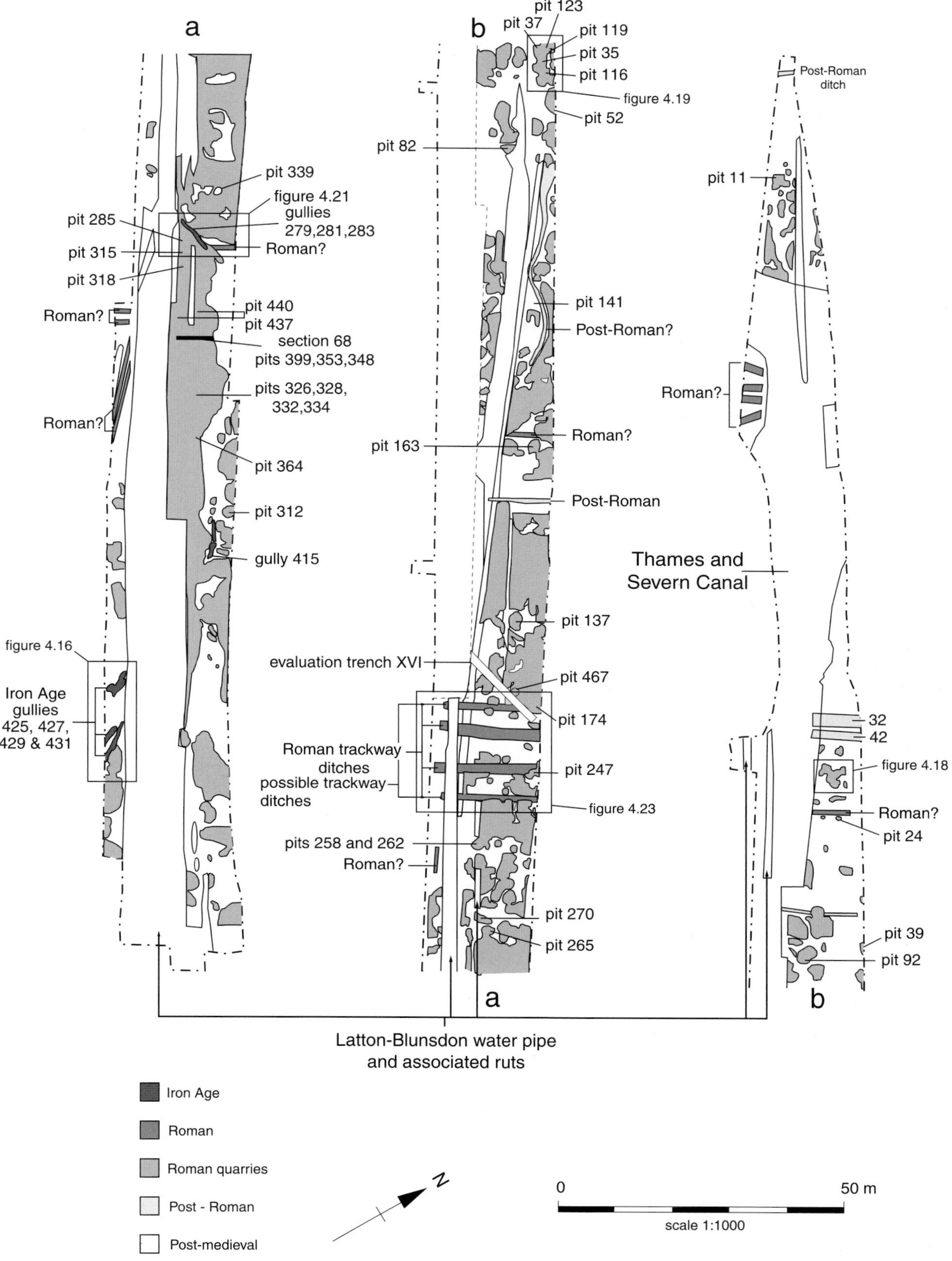


*Figure 4.15 Court Farm, general site plan.*

## Residual prehistoric pottery

A number of residual sherds spanning the early and late prehistoric periods were recovered from a variety of Roman contexts across the site. The early prehistoric period was represented by only four sherds (see Barclay, Chapter 7). Each of these was poorly preserved, small and abraded and located in residual contexts. Similarly, five small undiagnostic flint flakes were recovered from later contexts across the site. Although the occurrence of such a small group of artefacts in residual contexts is of little value in furthering an understanding of this period, it does add to a growing amount of evidence of early prehistoric activity in the immediate area. This has previously been demonstrated by the discovery of a Neolithic pit containing flints and burnt fragments of antler (Wiltshire Archaeology and Natural History Magazine 1977/78, 203; Wilts. SMR SU09NE100). Cropmark and geophysical evidence may suggest a ritual aspect to this activity with ring ditches located to the north-east of the pit (Fig. 4.14, Wilts. SMR SU09NE601 and 602).

The later prehistoric assemblage consisted of a larger and more coherent group of pottery. The majority of this was represented by middle-late Iron Age forms although two decorated vessel sherds recovered from the fills of trackway ditch 490 (segment 243, Fig. 4.23) were suggestive of an early Iron Age element. The considerable quantity of residual sherds representing the middle-late Iron Age were mostly found within Roman 1st-century quarry pits and often exceeded the quantity of Roman finds. With this level of residual material it is clear that the quarry pitting had truncated and removed earlier features across the area. As the site was only subject to sample excavation it is also apparent that a number of features, rather than a few isolated ones, must have existed for such a residual assemblage to occur with this consistency across the site. A suggestion of the type of activity was demonstrated by the presence of several features of probable pre-Roman date located towards the edge of the quarry pitting. These for the most part consisted of shallow gullies truncated by quarry pits although some of the pits may also have been of pre-Roman date.

## Late prehistoric curvilinear/linear gullies

*(Figs 4.16–17)*

Several linear and curvilinear gullies were located towards the south-eastern end of the site. The main group of these, clearly visible on the surface plan, consisted of four linear gullies forming two probable phases of paired gullies each terminating at their northern end. The primary phase, 425 and 429, extended 7 m into the excavation area from the southern edge. Of these, the eastern gully (425) was slightly wider at 0.75 m tapering to 0.5 m wide whereas the western gully (429) remained consistently 0.5 m wide along its length. Both attained a maximum depth of 0.2 m with a rounded profile and were filled with a single brown silty clay deposit. Although it was not

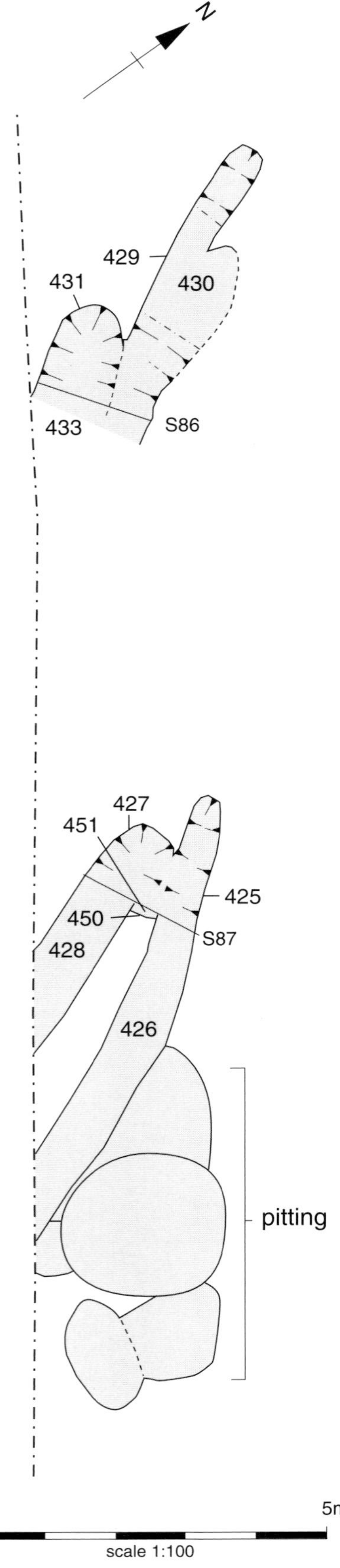


*Figure 4.16 Court Farm, plan of later prehistoric gullies.*

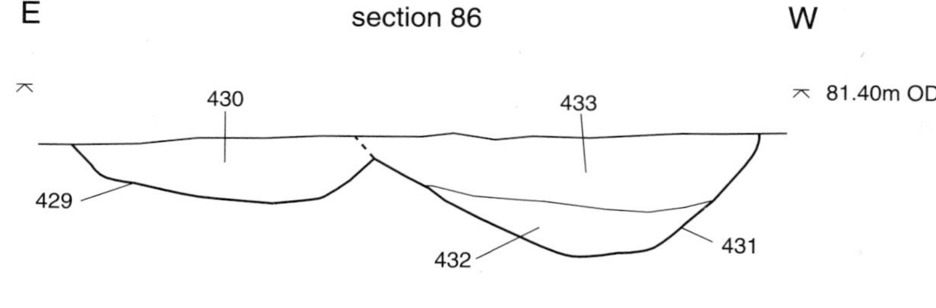


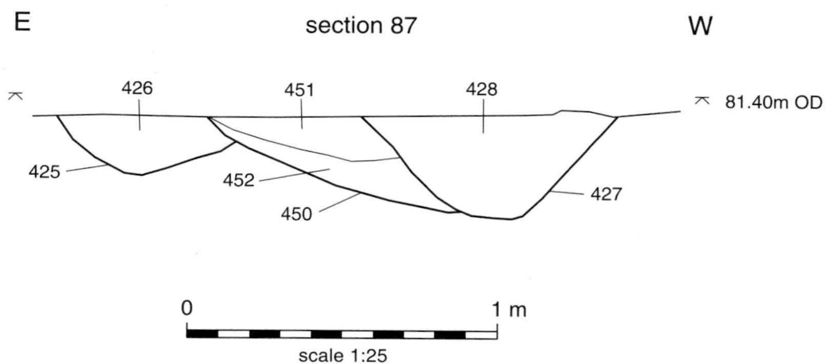


*Figure 4.17 Court Farm, sections through later prehistoric gullies.*

possible to demonstrate conclusively that these gullies existed as a pair, the similarities in dimensions, alignment and fill type would suggest that they were associated. The subsequent recutting of both gullies along their western edges similarly suggests that these were paired features.

The recut gullies, 427 and 431, were slightly more substantial than their predecessors at 0.95 m and 1.1 m wide respectively and 0.3 m deep. Both gullies, displaying similar rounded profiles, terminated to the north short of the primary phase gully terminals. A primary weathering deposit (432) and a secondary fill (433) were contained within the slightly larger gully whilst a single deposit filled the eastern gully (428). Of these, the upper fill in gully 431 consisted of the same brown silt clay deposit as encountered within gully 427. Over twenty Iron Age limestone-tempered sherds were recovered from the terminal of gully 427 supporting a pre-Roman date for these features. More significantly, the orientation of these gullies in relation to Ermin Street suggests that they probably pre-date its construction as later linear features generally respect its alignment either in a parallel or a perpendicular fashion.

Towards the south-eastern end of the dense quarry pitting a number of pits and postholes were located around the gullies. The surface plan shows that at least one of these pits was truncated by gully 425 whilst a further small pit, 450, truncated gully 425 but predated the recut gully 427. The group of pits along the eastern edge of gully 425 was not excavated. As a result it was not possible to demonstrate any substantial difference between these pits and the 1st-century quarry pitting.

Further gullies of a similar character were located towards and within the area of dense quarry pitting. Of these an isolated 7 m long section of curvilinear gully (415) was located 25 m to the north of the paired gullies and just before the main concentration of the quarry pitting. Gullies within the area of dense quarry pitting were only identifiable through excavation as they were not visible at surface level due to extensive truncation by the quarrying. As a result only very limited remains of these survived (Fig. 4.21, Fig. 4.22, sections 66 and 74, contexts 279, 281 and 283) and no finds were recovered. However, the fills of the quarry pits truncating these did contain a proportionally larger number of Iron Age sherds than other more isolated quarry pits.

### Quarry pitting

*(Fig. 4.20, sections 30 and 68)*

The largest group of features revealed across the site consisted of intercutting gravel quarrying pits. Although these extended along the length of the excavation parallel to the line of Ermin Street, the densest areas were situated either side of the primary trackway ditches 489 and 490 (Fig. 4.23). Due to their density only a selected sample were excavated to demonstrate their morphology, date range and extent.

Possibly the most conspicuous feature of the quarrying was its extensiveness with a concentration within 120–150 m either side of the trackway. Its extent was only partially revealed in the excavated area, but an earlier geomagnetic survey of a wider area had identified a mottled geophysical terrain across the centre of the site. This clearly corresponded to the quarry pitting, showing that it extended up to 100 m along the length of the trackway occupying the angle between either side of the trackway and Ermin Street (Fig. 4.14). This is also apparent from cropmark evidence (Plate 4.3). The line of the trackway was respected by the pitting although this did extend up to the edge of the ditches, even truncating the earlier phase in the case of pit 213 (Fig. 4.24, section 64) which probably hastened the infilling of the primary ditch.

The sequence of pits, where they intercut, displayed a pattern of a new pit being dug in close proximity to the backfilled remains of another, resulting in the complexity of the surface plan (Fig. 4.18). Indeed, in many circumstances the overburden from the newly excavated pit was used to backfill the earlier pit. As a result one edge of the earlier pit was truncated by its successor and this ensured that the maximum quantity of gravel was extracted from the immediate vicinity. This also created a rather general pattern of

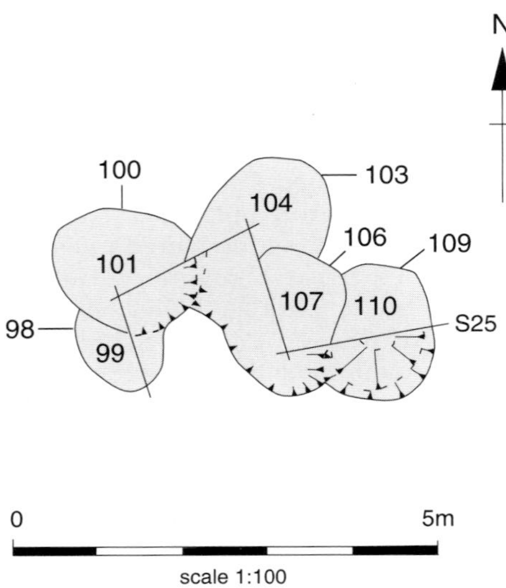


*Figure 4.18 Court Farm, plan of pit group 99–109.*

pitting not immediately clear on the surface. Section 68 (Fig. 4.20) clearly demonstrates this with a progression of the quarrying from north to south as each pit was excavated in turn. Although this was not a rigid pattern of extraction, a similar method also produced arcs of pits such as can be seen with pit group 35, 37, 114, 116, 119 and 126 (Figs 4.19–4.20).

All of the pits were sub-circular or oval in plan although they did vary considerably in size and depth. The smaller pits, of less than 1 m diameter, tended to be more circular with a shallow bowl-shaped profile. These were only excavated 0.1–0.3 m into the gravel often containing two distinct fills. The shallow primary fills covering the base of the pits consisted of a loose silty gravel resulting from the disturbance of the natural during extraction (eg. Fig. 4.20, 118, 121, 122, 125 and 128 – section 30). A single backfill of a mixed gravelly brown silt clay levelled the remainder of each pit. The largest pits often attained a diameter in excess of 3.5 m and differed from their shallow counterparts with near vertical or steep sloped sides and a very regular flat base. However, these also displayed the same sequence of fills representing backfilling with the mixed overburden soil. Due to their size, the larger pits contained a series of backfills and tip layers clearly exhibited by pit 348 rather than a single event.

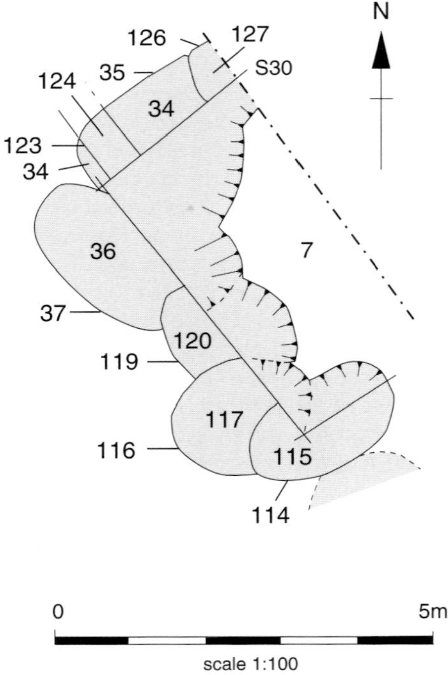


*Figure 4.19 Court Farm, plan of pit group 35–126.*

Finds were generally sparse within the backfills with only seven contexts producing more than ten sherds. However, a consistent assemblage of pottery was represented with most sherds being closely datable to the 1st century AD. Few other finds were recovered, although these include a well-preserved, complete penannular brooch (Fig. 7.22.523) from fill 132 of pit 174 (Fig. 4.15). A similar example has been discovered from Cirencester in a context dating to between AD 49 and 70/5 (Mackreth 1982, 92, fig. 27, 17).

### Trackway ditches 489 and 490, and surface 304
*(Figs 4.23–24)*

A series of distinct paired linear features aligned north-east - south-west were clearly visible following the stripping of the topsoil and buried ploughsoils. The larger of the features, 489 and 490, corresponded to the location of a previously identified cropmark (Wilts. SMR SU09NE615). This consisted of a 5 m-wide ditched trackway running from Ermin Street towards a rural settlement located 450 m to the north-east at Field Barn. After becoming fully silted the primary phase of ditches 489 and 490 were recut along their length removing all but the outer edges of the earlier ditches. Faint traces of wheel ruts were also present associated with the narrow trackway of ditches 489 and 490.

A third pair of shallower features, 488 and 491, may have defined a much broader phase of trackway 15 m wide that remained centered upon the primary trackway. These 'ditches' had not been previously located on the aerial photographs and it seems they may not have extended the full length of the earlier trackway ditches. They were stratigraphically late features and it is possible that they were plough furrows rather than ditches, although they were deeper than any of the other furrows identified on site and their symmetrical location with respect to trackway ditches 489 and 490 is remarkable. They are regarded as possible ditches although more evidence is required to confirm this status.

#### *Primary trackway ditches 489 and 490*

A parallel pair of linear ditches running north-east - south-west defined the primary trackway between

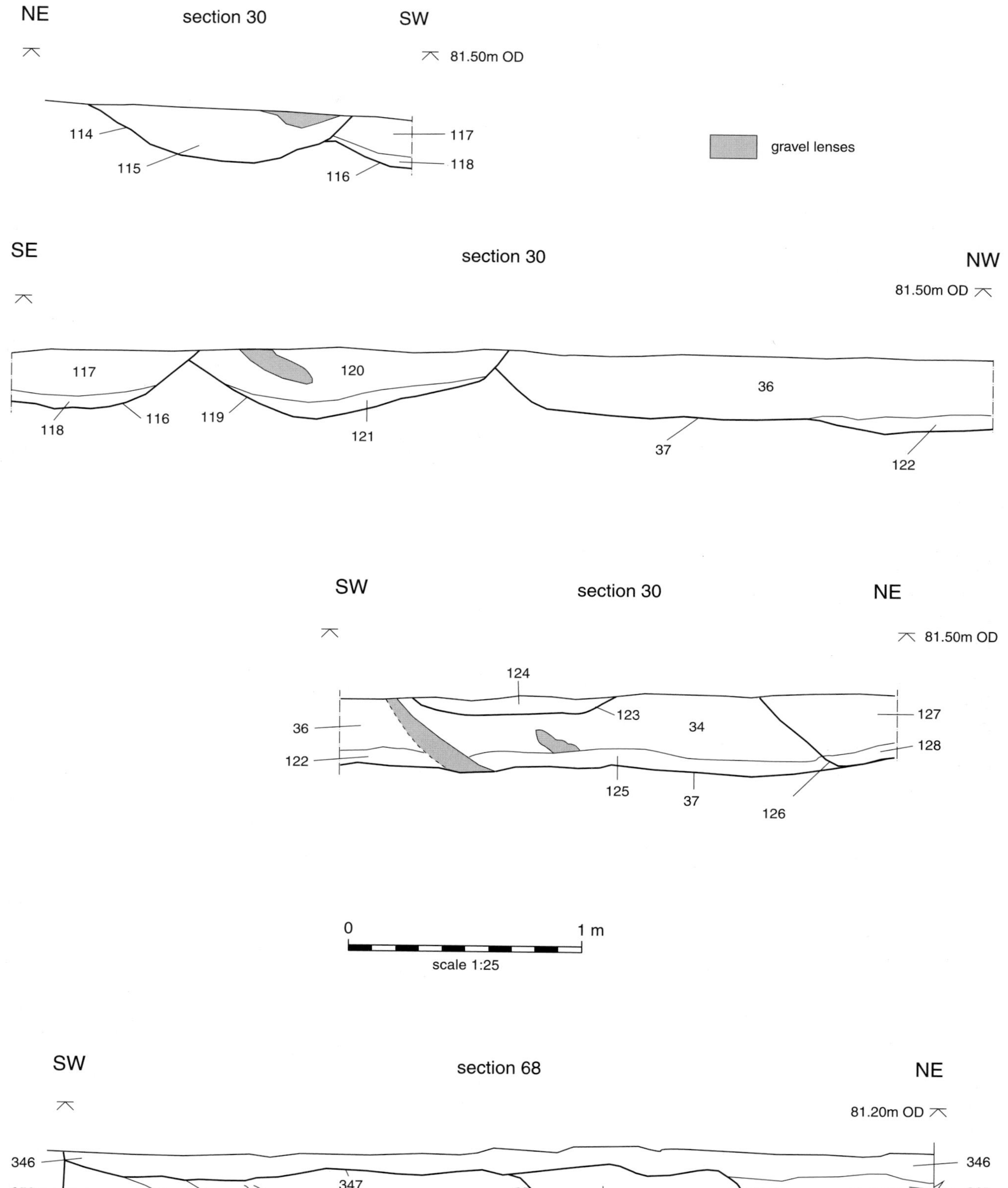


*Figure 4.20 Court Farm, pit groups, sections.*

*Plate 4.4 Extensive spread of Roman quarry pits at Court Farm, Latton. The Latton-Blunsdon water pipeline (unexcavated) runs the length of the trench.*

4.5–5.5 m wide. Excavation of these ditches showed that two phases of ditch were present with a secondary phase recut defining a slightly narrower trackway than its predecessor. Being recut along the line of the earlier ditches, these had also removed a substantial amount of the primary phase ditch profiles and fill sequences.

Only a 0.5 m wide section of the primary phase ditch (Fig. 4.23, Fig. 4.24, segments 195, section 64, 205 and 394, section 71) survived along the north-western edge of 489. The ditch maintained a uniform straight side sloping between 45° and 55° with a rounded base slightly flattened along the centre of the ditch. A variation in the uniform profile existed to the north-east where the ditch displayed a slightly shallower gradient along its upper edge (205). The ditch attained a maximum depth of 0.7 m at the north-eastern end gradually shallowing to 0.4 m as it approached the line of Ermin Street to the south-west.

A variety of fills were encountered within the primary cut of 489. Although the exposed length of ditch was only 17 m the individual fills were specific to each excavated section and did not form part of a consistent silting sequence stretching along the length of the ditch. However, each deposit shared a common characteristic of having a high gravel content. Of these only the primary fill, 206 (segment 205, not illustrated), consisted of a grey silty sand characteristic of the weathering of the sides in an open ditch. This coincides with the existence of a slight weathering cone along the upper edge of segment 205. The remaining gravelly deposits (196, 198, 207, 208, 395 and 396) were contained in a mixed orange-brown silt clay more indicative of backfilling or infilling occurring as a result of disturbed soil being in close proximity to the ditch. This, it would appear, was largely a result of the disturbance caused by the quarrying activity that was occurring along the edge of the ditch. As a result of this the ditch quickly became infilled with the loose spoil created by the quarrying. The only exception to this sequence was fill 197 (Fig. 4.24, section 64) consisting of a silty clay which lacked any inclusions. Although this does represent a silting period, its singularity within the fill sequence suggests that infilling occurred over a relatively short span with little opportunity for periods of silting.

The corresponding south-eastern ditch (490) of the primary phase trackway similarly survived as a 0.5 m wide section which had largely been truncated along its inner edge by the recutting of the ditch on the same alignment. This ditch was consistently shallower than its counterpart, 489, although it shared the same characteristic of being deepest at its north-eastern end and gradually becoming shallower towards the south-west. The deepest section of the ditch (243) attained a depth of 0.52 m with a neatly defined rounded base.

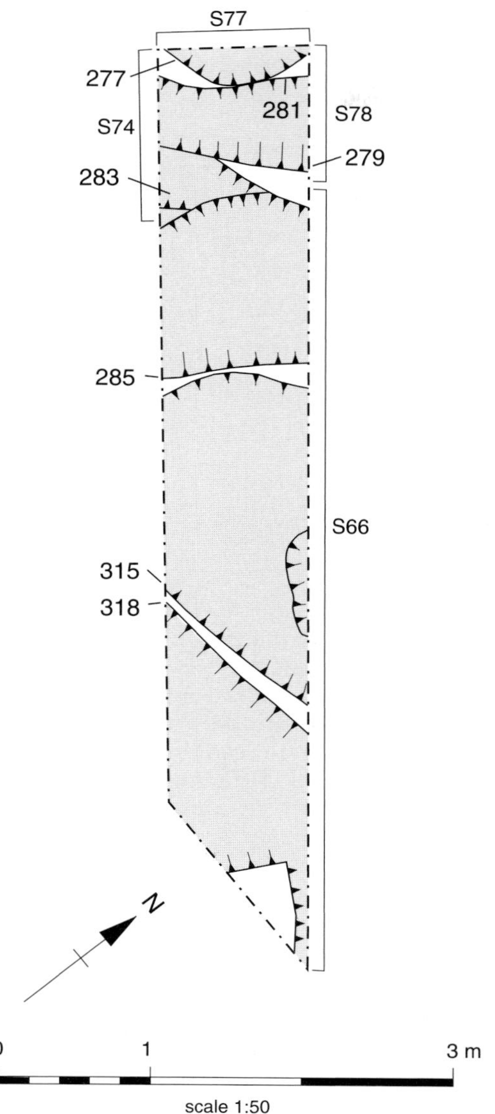


*Figure 4.21 Court Farm, plan of possible Iron Age gullies 279, 281 and 283 cut by quarry pits.*

This sloped up to 0.3 m deep at its south-western end maintaining a straight side angled at 45° along its length but with most of the base having been removed by recutting.

Fewer fills were present in the primary cut of ditch 490 than in the accompanying cut of 489. The fills were predominantly of a mixed gravelly composition reflecting the rapid nature of the infilling of the ditch as also encountered in ditch 489. Indeed a single fill, 242, was responsible for the levelling of the complete ditch void to the north-east whilst gravelly fill 406 (Fig. 4.24, section 71) similarly levelled the ditch to the south-west. Several sherds dating to AD 50–100 were recovered from the single backfill of segment 243 which also included a residual decorated sherd of possible early Iron Age pottery (see Timby, Chapter 7).

The existence of a quarry pit (213) cut into the side of ditch 210 prior to the ditch recut (217) demonstrates that the quarrying activity was occurring during the primary phase (Fig. 4.24, section 64). Also, the secondary ditch truncated all the quarry pits along its edge, further demonstrating that the quarrying predated the recutting of ditches 489 and 490. This re-inforces the view that the quarrying located along the immediate edge of the trackway primarily took place during the earlier phase which, due to their proximity and the loose mixed spoil created during quarrying, led to the rapid infilling of the ditches.

### *Recut trackway ditches 489 and 490*

Following the deposition of the upper fills which levelled the primary phase of trackway ditches, both were recut to define a slightly narrower trackway between 4.25 m and 4.5 m wide. In both cases only the outer edge of the primary phase ditch survived to a maximum surface width of 0.5 m with the recut of ditch 490 generally truncating more of the primary phase fills than that of ditch 489.

The recut of ditch 489 varied more in its profile than the primary cut although it mirrored the depth of the primary cut along its length being deepest to the north-east at 0.7 m and becoming shallower to the south-west at 0.4 m. The exterior edge of the ditch remained consistent with a straight side angled between 50–60° with a well defined rounded break of slope to the base of the ditch. The inner edge varied more between a gentler slope (segment 232) and a much steeper, near-vertical edge (Fig. 4.24, section 71). In each case the base of the ditch was rounded, undulating slightly across its width. In spite of the variation in profile, the ditch maintained a width of 1.8–1.9 m narrowing to 1.4 m towards the south-west corresponding with the shallowing of the ditch.

In contrast with the sequence of gravelly deposits infilling the primary cut, the recut ditch contained a sequence more representative of prolonged periods of silting. The number of individual deposits in each section varied between two and four although all were silty, with sandy and gravelly lenses sitting in the base of the ditch to a depth of less than 0.1 m (233, 398, 571). These were followed by secondary and tertiary fills of a similar character with an increasingly higher clay content and lesser amounts of gravel, each forming an evenly deposited layer between 0.15–0.2 m thick in the ditch (234, 235 and 399, 400). As the south-western end of the ditch was shallower than the remainder, fill 400 levelled the void at this end. A final layer, 236, levelled the ditch to the north-east. This sequence of silting fills also existed in the central section of the ditch although only two fills, both 0.3 m thick, represent the entire sequence at this point (202 and 203) with very little gravel in either deposit (Fig. 4.24, 564).

The accompanying recut of ditch 490 was similarly dug 0.5 m inside the line of the primary phase ditch. This also matched the north-western ditch in its dimensions being 1.7–1.9 m wide and 0.65 m deep

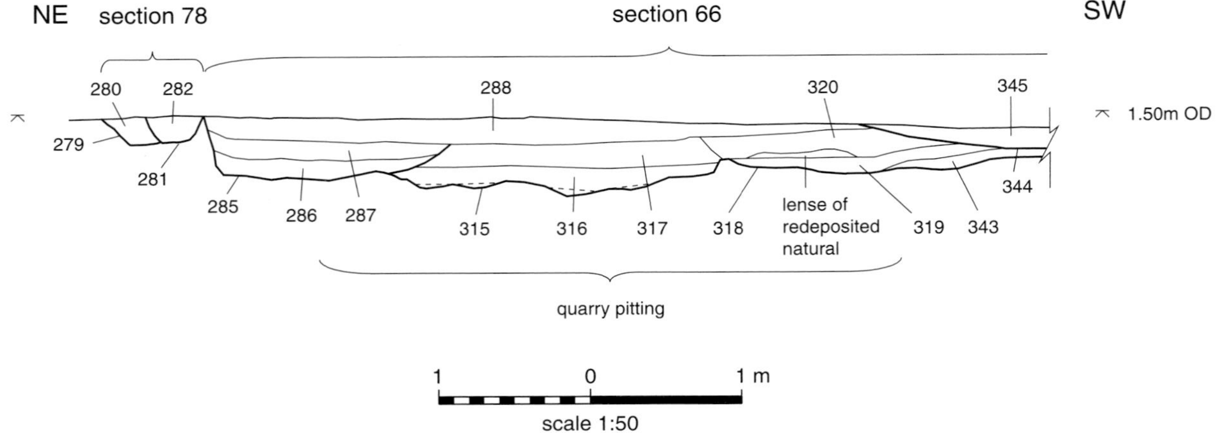


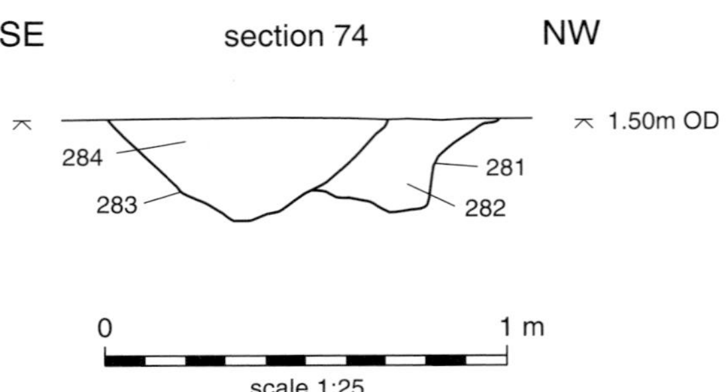


*Figure 4.22 Court Farm, possible Iron Age gullies, sections.*

(225) narrowing to 1.2 m wide and 0.4 m deep at its south-western end (401) (Fig. 4.24, section 71). With a broad splayed U-shaped profile this recut maintained a more symmetrical profile than its counterpart. A generally flattened base existed along its length being slightly more rounded in cut 225 than in the well defined flat base of cut 217.

A similar sequence of silting fills was present in the recut of ditch 490. Here the primary fill varied between clayey (218 and 402) and more sandy (224) deposits but with each containing distinctive lenses of gritty sand and gravel demonstrating the process of silting and weathering throughout the ditch. A secondary fill (219) similar to the primary silting was deposited in cut 217 before a thick layer (220 and 223) up to 0.4 m deep sealed the lower fills levelling the north-eastern end of the ditch. This sequence of upper fills did not continue through to the south-western end of the ditch where two gravel fills (403 and 404), probably deriving from the truncated primary phase fills, levelled the ditch.

### *Trackway ruts and repair surfacing 304*

A series of narrow parallel linear ruts (305) were located between trackway ditches 489 and 490. These directly cut the underlying natural gravel to a maximum depth of 0.15 m varying between 0.1 m and 0.3 m wide. Each of the ruts was filled with a loose silty gravel deposit 304 which may have formed a repair surfacing deposit between the trackway ditches. This was not a consistent deposit along the length of the trackway, however, and most of the loose silty gravel present probably represents the churned upcast of the natural substrate resulting from traffic, rather than any purposeful surfacing. No other traces of surfacing were present along the length of the trackway.

### *Possible trackway ditches 488 and 491*

Linear features 488 and 491 were both cut into the dense backfilled quarry pitting that lined the edges of the earlier phase trackway. These features appeared to define a much broader trackway 15.5 m wide, centered upon the earliest trackway.

Feature 488 comprised a single cut 1.2 m wide truncating a series of backfilled quarry pits to a maximum depth of 0.3 m. The feature maintained a sharply defined profile with straight sides sloping at 45° and a flat base varying between 0.5 m and 0.6 m wide. This terminated to the south-west as an ill-defined shallow rounded hollow only 0.1 m deep. A single mid-brown gravelly silt clay (173 and 139) filled the length of the feature, becoming slightly more gravelly towards the base of the fill where it was cut directly into sand and gravel natural rather than into the backfilled quarry pits (136).

The accompanying south-eastern feature (491) had a matching profile and fill sequence along its length, with a shallow terminal at its south-western end. Only the very base of the ditch survived at the extreme north-eastern excavated section due to later plough furrow disturbance (293) but the rest of the feature attained a depth of 0.22 m and was 1 m wide. A similar gravelly mid-brown deposit filled the length of the feature (276, 296 and 410/412). Again a more gravelly silting fill, 275, existed as a primary weathering deposit at the point where the feature was cut directly into gravel (274).

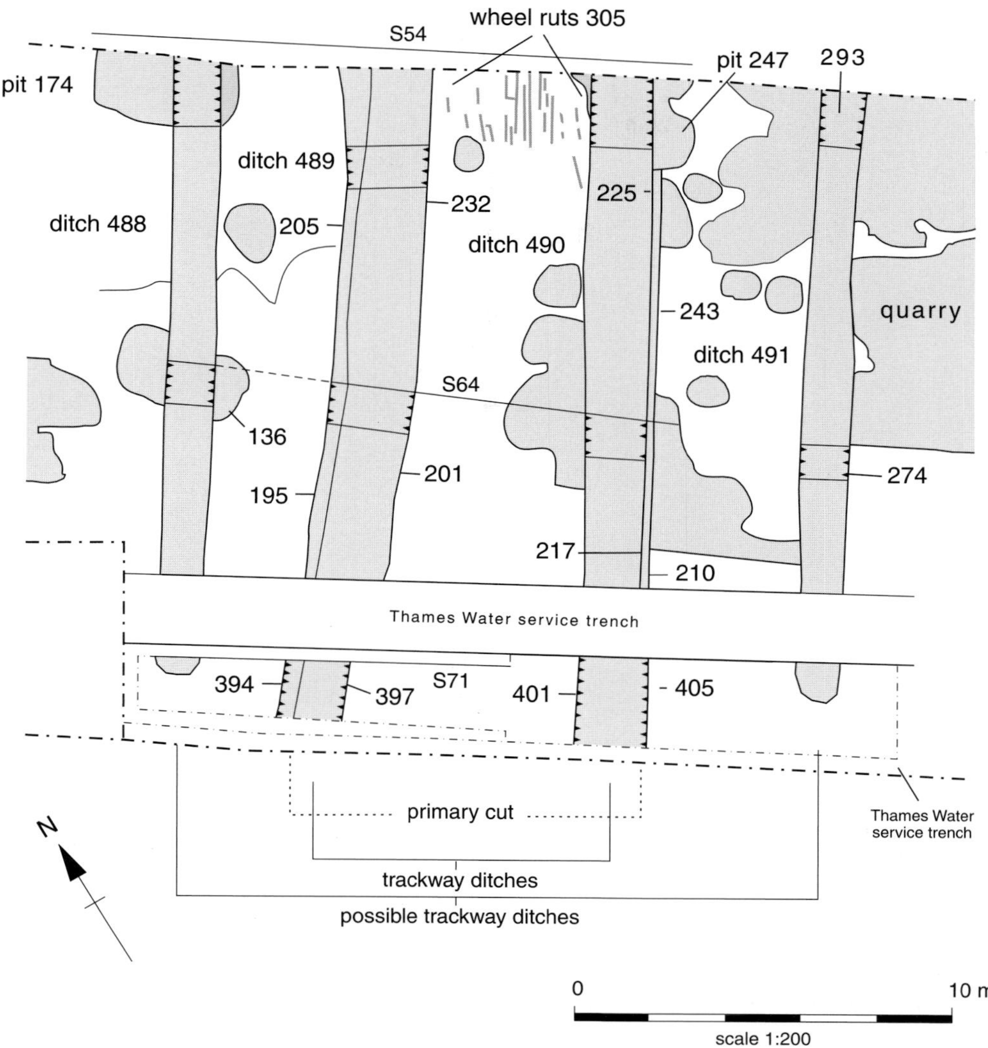


*Figure 4.23 Court Farm, plan of trackway ditches.*

It remains unclear whether these features were Roman or later, and whether they were ditches or plough furrows. Their depth and symmetrical disposition with regard to trackway ditches 489 and 490, led to their interpretation in the field as later trackway ditches. However, a broader view of both the geophysical and cropmark evidence indicates a clear pattern of plough furrows, approximately 15 m apart, across the field. It is possible that the features were relatively deep and narrow examples of these although the individual features are not evident as cropmarks or geophysical anomalies.

## Discussion

### *Quarrying*

The excavations at Court Farm principally revealed a dense alignment of quarry pits alongside Ermin Street. These were selectively sampled, and the evidence was sufficient to demonstrate that at least a substantial amount, if not all, of this quarrying was of Roman date. This conclusion is supported by the way in which the quarrying respected the ditched trackway which led from Ermin Street to the Roman settlement at Field Barn (SAM 900; Wilts. SMR SU09NE303). Circumstantial evidence would indicate that the quarrying was related to the construction and/or repair of Ermin Street and can be assumed to have started in the mid 1st century AD, although this cannot be demonstrated archaeologically. The date range of the Roman pottery can be accommodated within the Neronian/Flavian period but may extend to the early 2nd century at the latest. It is reasonable to assume that this is indicative of the general date of the quarrying, although, of course, it could reflect the background scatter of rubbish available for redeposition, and the quarrying itself may have continued without new finds being incorporated. On the whole this appears unlikely. While a few quarry pits contained exclusively Iron Age pottery (Table 7.12), this was shown stratigraphically to be residual like most of the other Iron Age sherds.

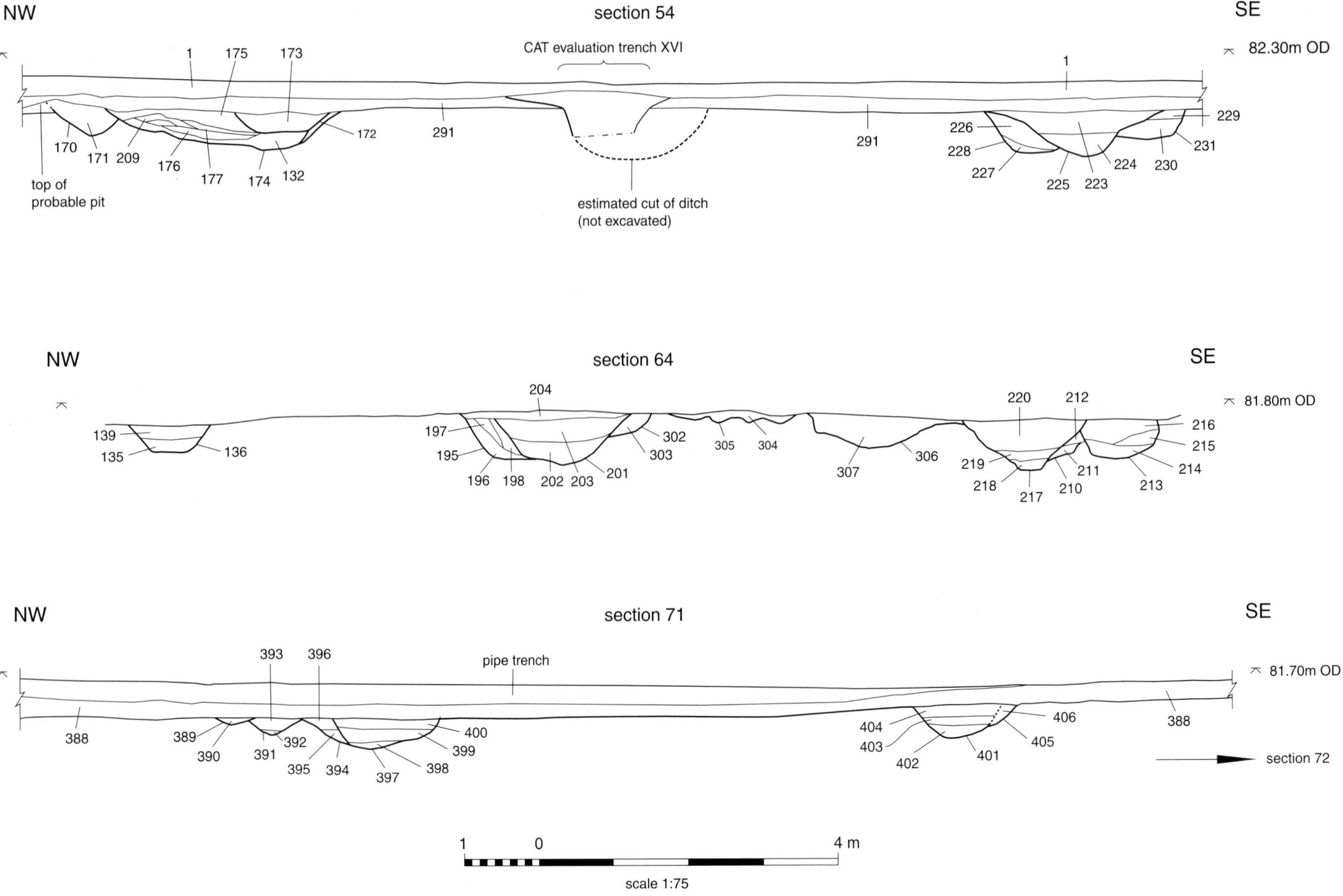


*Figure 4.24 Court Farm, trackway ditches, sections.*

The Roman quarry pits were generally small and shallow, and sub-circular or irregular in shape. This suggests a fairly small-scale, *ad hoc*, approach to gravel extraction which may be accounted for by the desire to move the material a minimal distance to where it was needed as the road progressed, rather than working a 'face', which would perhaps have been the more efficient method of actually acquiring the material. It is interesting to note, however, that the cropmark and geophysical evidence indicates that the quarrying was concentrated, both in extent and density, either side of the trackway which led to the settlement at Field Barn. This probably indicates that the quarrying was intended to supply a surface for the trackway (for which there is some, but very little, surviving evidence), as well as Ermin Street. It could further imply an association between the settlement and the road, through, for instance, the owner allowing, or being in a position to benefit from, the extraction of gravel from his land.

#### *The trackway*

The pair of recut trackway ditches defined a narrow trackway, 4.5–5.5 m wide, which cropmarks show running to the Roman settlement at Field Barn. Although little useful dating evidence was recovered from their fills, the ditches were respected by the quarry pits and must be within the general chronological range of those features, if not earlier. It is difficult to disentangle the elements of the cropmark complex which the trackway served. It is reported that the settlement probably contained two buildings (information from Wilts. SMR), although these, and the 'pavement' recorded by Aubrey in 1676, may belong to the later phases of settlement. Part of a triple-ditched possible enclosure is clearly visible on aerial photographs. Whatever the form or nature of the settlement, it may, on present evidence, be assumed to have had 1st-century (or even earlier) origins and to have regarded its links with Ermin Street to be of some importance.

## LATTON 'ROMAN POND'

*By Steve Lawrence with Andrew Mudd*

### Introduction

Situated within Scheduled Ancient Monument 899 to the west of Latton village, the 'Roman Pond' site lay on the first gravel terrace approximately 200 m north of the river Churn. The site occupied a low depression defined until recently by two curving field boundaries (Plate 4.5; Fig. 4.25). The western boundary has since been straightened. An evaluation trench excavated as part of the Stage 2 programme of works (CAT 1991b, Trench XIII) had identified a peaty layer up to 0.5 m thick extending along the base of the low lying ground. This had been interpreted as the basal fill of a pond with a number of Roman sherds found within it spanning the 1st–4th centuries suggesting contemporaneity with the rural settlement complex to the north (Wilts. SMR SU09NE351; Plate 4.4 and Fig. 4.25). Due to the potential importance of the relationship between the settlement and the possible pond, the peat deposit was to be excavated as three longitudinal strips 10–12 m wide and 120 m long within the line of the road corridor (a southern, central and northern strip labelled as areas S, C and N respectively – Fig. 4.26). Each strip was separated by 1 m-wide baulk sections with further baulk sections across the width of the centre strip to demonstrate the full extent and the vertical stratigraphy of the deposits. In addition each strip was excavated in two stages, initially down to the level of the peat deposit which was recorded *in situ* followed by a secondary strip to the level of the gravel.

The excavations indicated that the 'pond' was actually part of an extant palaeochannel which had been subjected to prolonged waterlogging and episodic flooding. This was reflected not only in the peat deposit but in several episodes of alluviation above and below the peat. The peat deposit was found to be a largely pre-Roman feature without significant finds. The only archaeological features identified within its limits were three ditches, each filled with organic peaty deposits and alluvial clays. Further sequences of ditches were found to the west, defining the boundary between the higher gravel terrace and the lower ground occupied by the relict stream course to the east.

Although this re-interpretation meant that much of the significance of the peat deposit in relation to the Roman settlement was lost, the environmental potential of the pre-Roman deposits was high. Incremental samples for macroscopic plant remains and mollusca, and column samples for pollen were taken and are reported on elsewhere (see Robinson and Scaife, Chapter 8). These were taken independently of the main excavation and were recorded separately. An interpretative summary of the stratigraphic and environmental sequences from the analyses is presented below in Figure 4.30. The stratigraphic units used in these reports are designated below *Macro* and *Pollen* respectively. A radiocarbon sample of seeds from the base of the peat (*Macro 506*) gave a date of 2943 +/- 63 BP (1365 to 929 cal BC at 95% confidence level, NZA 9119, R24151/19).

### Environmental sequence and soil accumulation

*(Figs 4.27–30)*

Two distinctive sequences of layers were present across the site divided by the recut series of ditch boundaries (boundary group 430, Fig. 4.26). The position of this boundary defined the line between marginal and good land in terms of its arable quality and this was reflected by the differing soil types located to either side. The western side was exclusively occupied by a series of ploughsoils dominated by two thick upper horizons, 107 and 108, with the thin remains of two further ploughsoils surviving beneath these. Several plough furrows were also associated with these soils, running up to the line of the boundary ditch.

*Figure 4.25 Latton 'Roman Pond' location of excavation area.*

*Plate 4.5 Cropmarks of the Iron Age and Roman settlement south of Westfield Farm, Latton. The 'Roman Pond' is the area of rough ground defined by curving field boundaries. The focus of Roman occupation is clearly visible in the centre of the picture. To the left, the rectangular enclosure on a different alignment is Iron Age. Reproduced by permission of RCHME (ref. NMR 883/195).*

In comparison, the layers occupying the low lying area of the shallow palaeochannel to the east of the boundary were more diverse. The lower layers consisted of a main peat deposit, 113 (Fig. 4.27. sections 1, 22, 26 and 40), and several alluvial clays. There is evidence that the upper surface of the peat was ploughed. However, the marginal nature of this ground for arable agriculture remained and was reflected by the occurrence of an alluvial layer, 140 (Fig. 4.27, sections 1, 22 and 26), overlying the lower ploughsoil. Later the area was subject to occasional inundation and appears to have remained wet pasture or meadow.

#### *Ploughsoil sequence to the west of boundary ditch 430*

The earliest ploughsoil to the west of the ditch sequence was represented by a 0.15 m-thick disturbed interface with the underlying gravel (contexts 201, 291/298, 359). This had a mixed clayey gravel composition deriving from the patchy clay alluvium existing to the west of the ditch boundary on the gravel terrace. The westernmost group of ditches, 429 (Fig. 4.26) (below) cut this soil layer, as did a number of broad furrows filled with a gravelly ploughsoil which were aligned perpendicular to the ditch. Ditch 299 and posthole alignment, 425, were also cut through the surface of this layer within area S1. A second similar ploughsoil, 146/349, with fewer gravel inclusions overlay the lower ploughsoil in the central and northern areas partially sealing the infilled primary ditch 165/383 in boundary group 430.

The most substantial ploughsoil horizon, layer 108, sealed both the furrows and the two earlier ploughsoils attaining its greatest depth of 0.4–0.5 m at boundary ditch 430. This boundary was represented by six ditch cuts (below) and the ploughsoil was truncated by the latest ditch in the sequence, 326/403, while clearly sealing the third ditch, 166/299/415. It remains unclear whether this ploughsoil horizon relates to the fourth or fifth boundaries or, indeed, both.

A modern arable ploughsoil, 107, constituted the uppermost layer. As a 0.3 m thick homogenous mid greyish brown friable soil darker than the underlying ploughsoil, this was clearly distinguishable extending up to the line of the modern field boundary which marked its eastern extent. The two upper ploughsoils over the gravel at the north-western end of the site generally had a lower clay content than those to the south-east which, being situated across the low-lying area of the extant palaeochannel, consisted largely of alluvial clays.

### *Peat deposit 113, alluvial layers and buried ploughsoils*

Lying to the east of ditch series 430, the relict stream course was shown to have a shallow profile, approximately 80 m wide and 0.6 m at its deepest, dipping slightly from the north-east towards the main channel of the river Churn lying to the south-west.

The base of the channel was occupied by a 0.2 m-thick layer of yellowish brown alluvial clay, 191/364/*Macro 507/Pollen 515*, which graded up to a greyer clay, 181/263/363/*Macro 506/Pollen 514*, towards the peat horizon above (Fig. 4.30). The alluvial clay lay mainly in the base of the channel where it remained unbroken as a thick layer, whereas to the west of ditch boundary 430 it became patchy and thin, demonstrating that the fields to the side of the channel largely remained above the water level. Plant remains indicated that a dry fen scrub or carr had existed within this hollow.

Following the deposition of the alluvial clay, persistent wet conditions prevailed and a rise in the water table resulted in waterlogging. This led to the accumulation of a distinctive dark brownish black clayey peat (layer 113/macro 505/pollen 513) which reached a maximum depth of 0.3 m within the lowest lying ground of the palaeochannel. The pollen evidence indicates an episode of general tree clearance in the catchment area while the peat was forming. A number of sherds, spanning the 2nd-4th centuries, were recovered from the surface of the peat deposit, showing that the final phase of peat accumulation occurred during or shortly before the Roman occupation represented by the cropmarks to the north of the site. A second phase of tree clearance, marking the transition to Pollen Zone 3, took place at around this time although it is not possible to place it precisely. Ditch 427 (below) was dug through the surface of the peat towards its western edge with an embankment along the drier side.

A distinctive mixed ploughsoil (112), extending up to the line of boundary ditch 430, sealed the peat deposit. This had a mottled appearance consisting of three very clear components, a yellowish brown silty clay, a grey clay and pockets of peat to a total thickness of 0.2 m. The peat component had been dragged up by the plough from the surface of the underlying layer but the two further clay deposits must have accumulated above the peat before further ploughing. With their homogenous appearances and lack of inclusions the clays may represent at least two individual alluvial episodes post-dating the peat. Although a relatively large assemblage of Roman sherds (35 sherds, 364 g) was recovered from 112, it remains unclear if these were solely derived from the surface of the underlying peat or were incorporated during Roman or later ploughing. A single, tiny post-medieval sherd can probably be ignored as intrusive. Certainly 112 was associated with one of the earlier ditches in boundary series 430 as a subsequent alluvial layer, 140, had been deposited before the fourth ditch in the sequence (ditch 168/329/409) was cut. However, the association between boundary and ploughsoil had been removed by the recuts.

The marginal nature of the area was demonstrated by a further alluvial episode, layer 140/Macro 504? and 503/Pollen 512, sealing the early phase of arable cultivation on the low lying ground represented by mixed ploughsoil 112. This siltier orange brown alluvium was present across the area, being thickest at 0.15 m along its north-western extent and becoming patchy across the centre of the palaeochannel, where most of the deposit had been incorporated into the overlying soil 149.

Unlike the earlier ploughsoil, the alluvially derived soil 149 (Macro 502/Pollen 511), above 140, formed a consistent layer 0.2 m thick across the site. Although this overlay the infilled ditch 168/329/409 (ditch group 430) and the recut 328/404, it probably formed throughout the life-span of these boundaries. The uppermost layer consisted of similar clayey soil, 160 (Macro 501/Pollen 510). Up to 0.3 m thick, this too had an alluvial origin, being noticeably more clayey than its counterpart on the western side of boundary 430. The molluscan evidence indicates that both these upper soils formed under damp grassland, prone to occasional flooding. However, both soils contained an even distribution of fine stones, and had clearly been ploughed, although, as the snails indicate, the field had never been under an arable regime. The RCHME aerial photograph, taken in 1975, (Plate 4.5) shows that the land had not been ploughed at that stage. It is likely that ploughing relates to the more recent cultivation of improved grassland.

### Linear ditches and field boundaries

A number of ditches of varying size ran across the site. The largest of these was a sequence of six successively

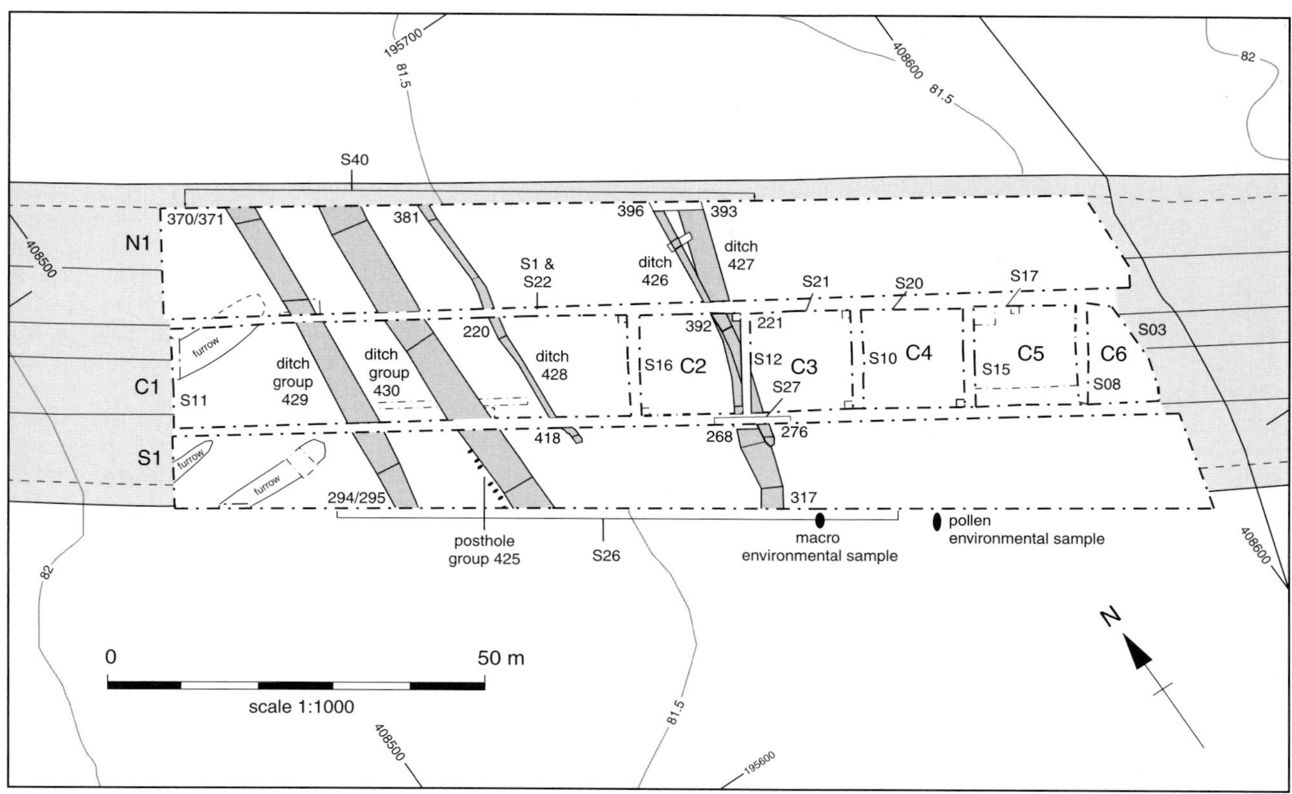


*Figure 4.26 Latton 'Roman Pond', plan of excavated features.*

recut ditches, ditch group 430, defining the same boundary between the higher gravel terrace to the west and the lower lying ground to the east. These ditches formed a consistent boundary with each ditch being cut from a higher level than the previous one as successive ploughsoils accumulated to the west while, alluvially derived soils accumulated to the east. Remaining in the modern landscape until very recently, this boundary had been represented by a hedge line. The eastern limit of the former channel was defined by an active drainage ditch similar to those in ditch group 430. The only other ditches situated on the rise of the gravel terrace were two intercutting broad shallow ditches, group 429, located 7 m to the west and following the same north-south alignment.

Three further ditches, 426, 427 and 428, were situated to the east of group 430. Each of these was cut into the peat that had accumulated along the line of the relict channel, although only ditch 427 was cut from its surface, and a thin ploughsoil had accumulated before ditches 426 and 428 were cut almost parallel to it.

### *Ditch 427 (Fig. 4.27)*

A continuous broad linear ditch, 427, (segments 221/268/317/393), aligned slightly more east-west than the other north-south ditches, was cut through the surface of peat deposit 113 along the centre of this area of low-lying ground. It was accompanied by a slightly raised peat bank, 248, (Fig. 4.27, section 22) along its western edge derived from the ditch upcast. Extending up to 2.6 m from the edge of the ditch, subsequent ploughing represented by buried ploughsoil horizon 112 had spread this deposit over a wider area whilst similarly removing the full height of the bank. The ditch generally maintained a uniform profile 0.5–0.6 m deep and 2.1–3 m wide with a broad flattened base and uniformly sloped sides. The exception to this was at the extreme northern end of the ditch (393) where it widened to in excess of 5 m whilst becoming shallower at 0.3 m deep.

A peaty deposit (224/270/316/394) filled the length of the ditch. Two fills were differentiated towards the southern end where the lower part contained slightly more inclusions of sand, gravel and limestone flecks. The occurrence of peat in the ditch suggests that standing water was present throughout its existence. Occasional moving water would have passed along the ditch during wetter periods accounting for the coarser inclusions in the deposit. This also occurred in ditch 428 situated at the edge of peat layer 113 to the west, and in the accompanying ditch 426 which was recut along the line of 427 after ploughsoil horizon 112 had sealed the previous ditch and bank. Eleven sherds (109 g) of pottery, dating to the 2nd–4th centuries, were recovered from the peat filling the ditch (270 and 394). Three similarly dated sherds were recovered from the surface of the peat layer 113.

***Ditches 426 and 428*** *(Figs 4.28–29)*

Two parallel linear ditches (426 and 428) aligned north-south and spaced 23 m apart were cut through the surface of buried ploughsoil horizon 112 and into peat deposit 113. The eastern ditch, 426 (segments 276, 392, 396), crossed the line of earlier ditch 427 cutting its fills and the bank along its western edge before terminating 2 m into the southern area (276). The western ditch, 428 (segments 220, 381, 418), similarly terminated to the south (418), 4 m into the southern area of excavation. Ditch 428 maintained a well defined U-shaped profile 1.5 m wide and 0.45 m deep filled with a dark silt (226/391). This slightly peaty fill was interleaved with a band of grey alluvial clay demonstrating the wet character of the contemporary surroundings.

The eastern ditch, 426, was less well defined than its western counterpart (428) with a general depth of only 0.2 m and a variable and often uneven profile. In spite of this, the ditch had a consistent width of 1–1.2 m. It did attain a depth of 0.5 m through the central area with a more uniform U-shaped profile resembling that of the western ditch, 428. However, this was only present for a short section where it crossed the line of an earlier ditch, 427, and terminated (276). It contained a silty clay, similar to that in the western ditch.

***Ditch group 430*** *(Fig. 4.28)*

A series of six intercutting ditches formed the major land division across the site at the topographical divide between the raised gravel terrace to the west and the lower lying ground to the east. The difference in height was demonstrated by the comparative level of the underlying gravel surface which sloped up from 80.60–80.98 m on the western side of the ditches, whilst sloping down from 80.57 m to 80.21 m to the east. This difference marks the distinction between fertile and marginal land in terms of its potential for cultivation, with the differing sequence of layers present either side of the ditches clearly showing that this remained the case throughout history. The boundary was successively re-established from its creation until the present day where it remains as a division between arable land and pasture matching a corresponding boundary on the south-eastern side of the relict stream channel (Plates 4.4–5).

Ditches 165/383 and 180/322/382 were the earliest in the sequence and the associations between the ploughsoil horizons and the ditches suggested that 180/322/382 was the primary cut of the two. Ditch 165/383 truncated an earlier ploughsoil which may have related to the earliest ditch.

The primary ditch (180/322/382) had a distinctive broad flat-based profile 1.8–1.9 m wide penetrating the underlying gravel to a depth of 0.5–0.6 m. This was filled by a single dark grey clayey deposit suggestive of frequent flooding along the ditch. This was a regular occurrence as subsequent ditches often exhibited similar clayey fills with clear alluvial episodes repeatedly present in the layer sequence to the west of the boundary, represented for instance by layer 140.

The subsequent recut, 165/383, was only identified in the northern and central excavation areas. Its southern extent had been truncated by later ditches as the boundary was successively recut. At 1.5 m wide this was one of the smaller boundaries in the sequence although it attained a similar depth to the other ditches at 0.3–0.4 m with a splayed U-shaped profile. A grey clayey deposit, 171/399, filled the base of the ditch to a depth of 0.2 m again suggestive of regular or prolonged flooding. A further silty clay alluvial fill occupied the top of the ditch and was sealed by a thin clayey ploughsoil horizon, 146/349.

Situated between the two earlier boundaries, the next ditch in the sequence (166/299/415), possessed a very similar profile to that of the earliest with a distinctive well defined flat base and straight sides. Again the primary fill of this was similar to the deposits contained within the previous ditches with a predominately clayey composition containing some humic material (238/339/416). However, it was at this point that the sequence changed from exclusively alluvial to mostly plough-derived deposits. With a much more silty composition and a distinctive reddish appearance the upper fills (237/338/413) contrasted with the grey clays of the alluvial sequence. This process was vividly demonstrated by the existence of a later ploughsoil, 108, up to 0.35 m thick sealing the ditch and of similar appearance to its upper fills. Two post-medieval pottery sherds were recovered from the ploughsoil.

Replacing ditch 166/299/415, the largest boundary in the sequence had a 3.2 m wide and 0.55 m deep uniform rounded profile (168/329/409). The greater breadth may have been a response to the previous ditch having become quickly filled with ploughsoils. Indeed, after becoming partially silted with darker more organic ploughsoils, the ditch was cleaned out along its centre to the same depth producing a distinctive V-shaped recut (328/404) which was almost certainly also present in section 1 (fills 172–175) (Fig. 4.28). This contained a number of clayey fills in its base indicative of prevailing wetter conditions before a thick ploughsoil derived deposit, 327/405/175, sealed the remaining 0.3–0.4 m deep ditch void.

Soil horizon 149 sealed the upper fills before the final boundary in the sequence (403/326) was cut along the western edge of its predecessor. This had a distinctive profile 0.4 m deep and 1.3–1.6 m wide with a flat base and steep sides giving the ditch a trench-like appearance. Again this was filled along its length with a homogenous mid brown ploughsoil deposit.

***Posthole alignment 425*** *(Fig. 4.26)*

A linear arrangement of nine postholes were located along the western edge of ditch series 430 within the southern excavation area (S1). Mostly spaced at 0.8 m intervals, these were aligned roughly parallel to the ditches 1 m away from their western edge converging

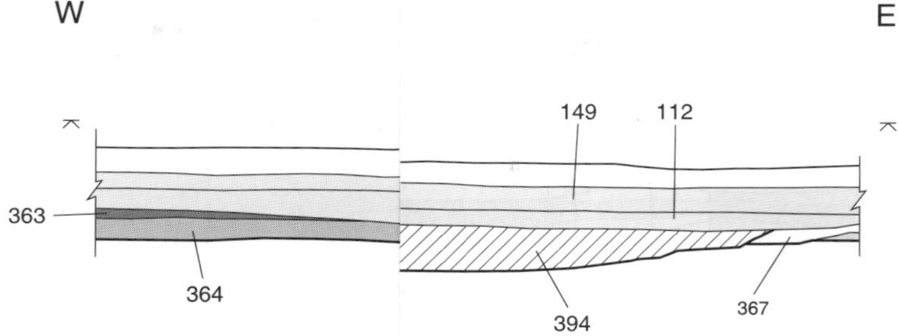





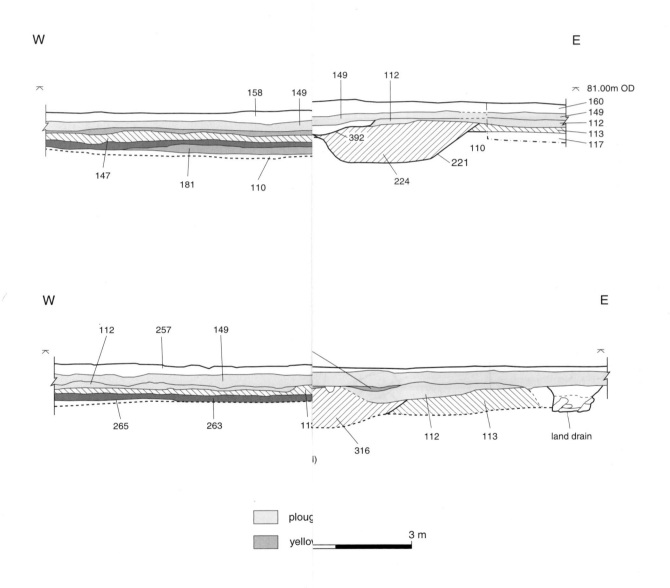


*Figure 4.27 Latton 'Roman Pond', ditch group 429, sections.*

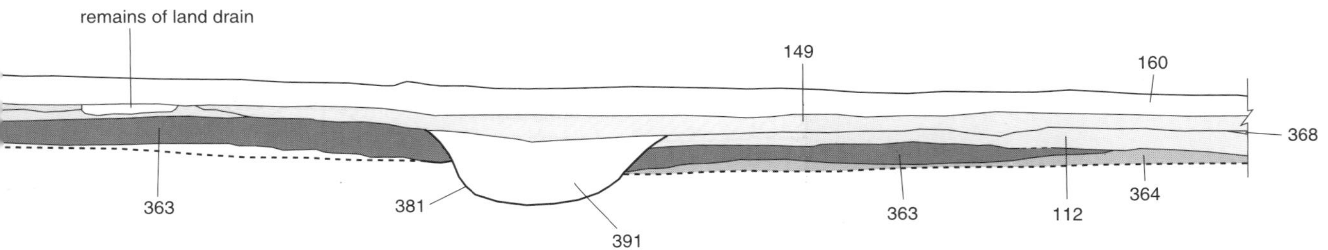
E
81.50m OD
remains of land drain
149
160
368
363
381
391
363
112
364

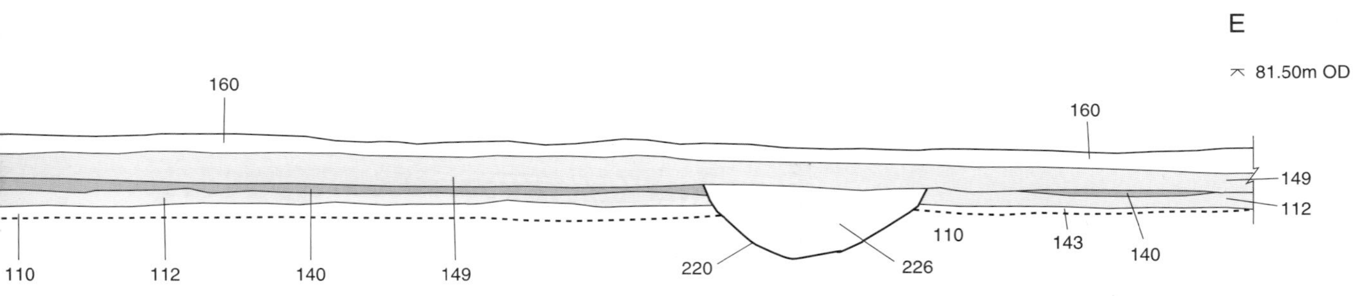
E
81.50m OD
160
160
149
112
110
112
140
149
220
226
110
143
140

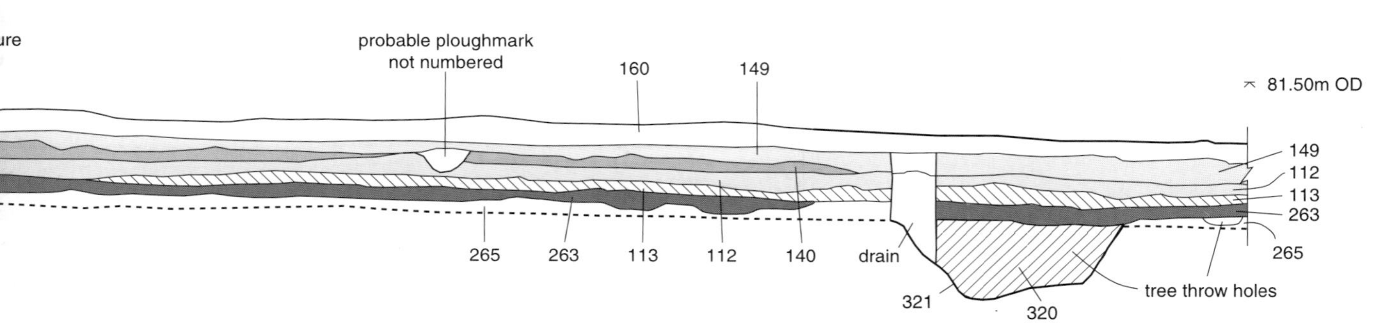
W
ure
probable ploughmark
not numbered
160
149
81.50m OD
149
112
113
263
265
265
263
113
112
140
drain
321
320
tree throw holes

1
0
3 m
scale 1:50

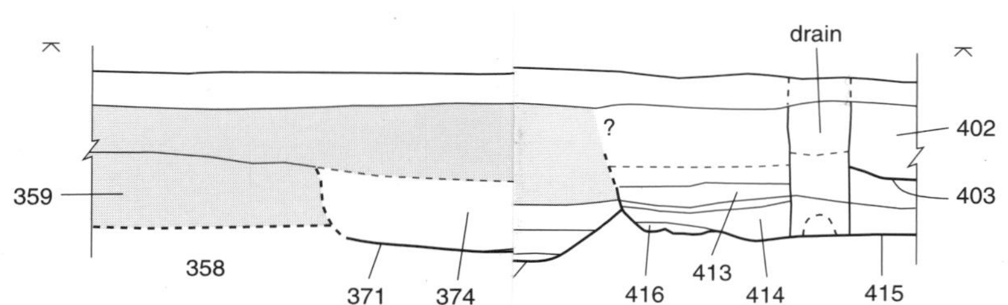


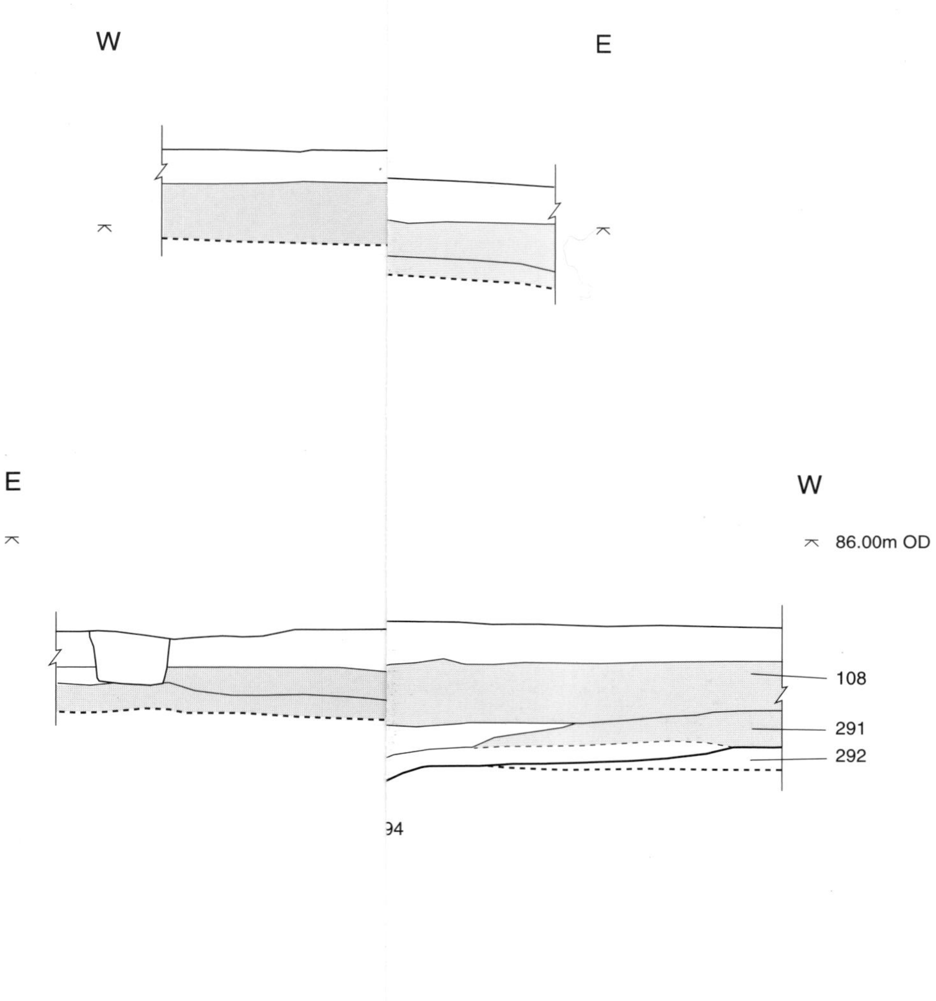


3 m.

29 *Latton 'Roman Pond', ditch groups 426 and 427, sections.*

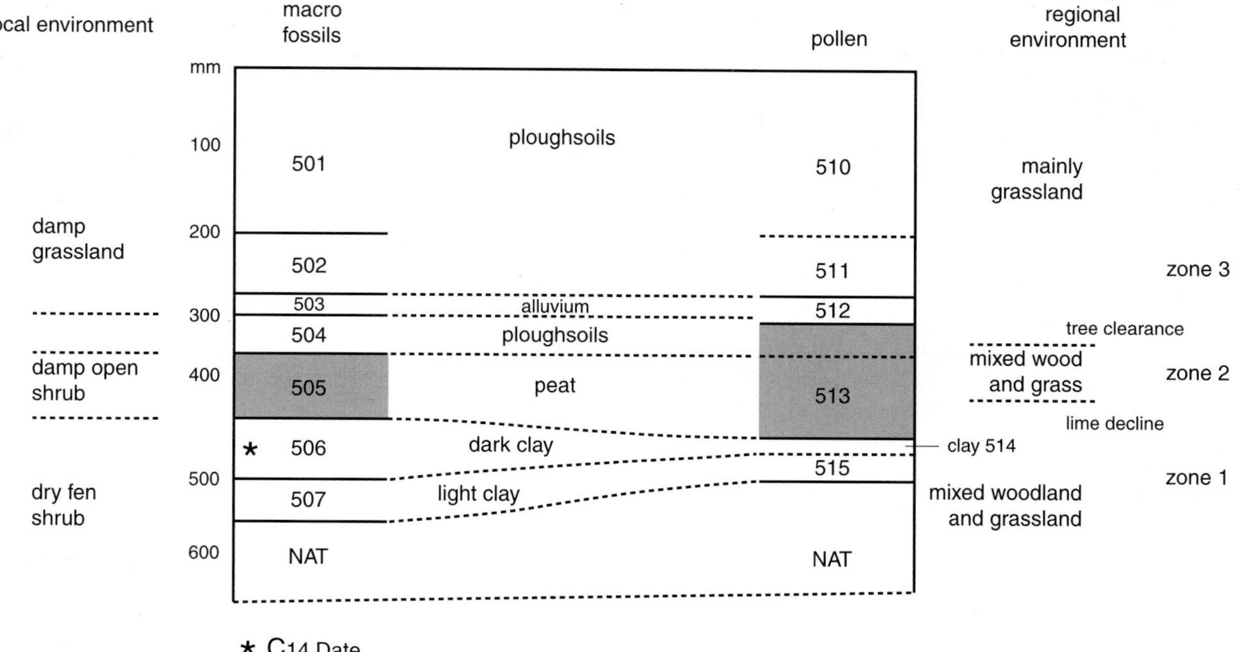


*Figure 4.30 Latton 'Roman Pond', sedimentary sequence.*

to 0.3 m at the northern end. The northernmost posts (304, 304 and 306) were only spaced at 0.3–0.5 m intervals. A further single example, 312, was situated central to the alignment 0.75 m to the west. The postholes had similar profiles, with vertical or near vertical sides and a flat base. Most penetrated the gravel to a depth of 0.4 m although the deepest was 0.6 m deep. Of these, posthole 318, located in the baulk section, demonstrated that they were cut from a higher level through buried ploughsoil layer 291. This gave a total depth of 1.1 m from the surface of layer 291 suggesting that each of the postholes was up to 0.5 m deeper than the cut into the gravel indicated. The fact that the four southernmost (287, 300, 314 and 318) contained the remains of poorly surviving posts in their bases (in an absence of general waterlogging of the soil) suggests the post alignment was relatively modern. Two sizes of flat-based posts, each of oak, were present, arranged in an alternate manner with the larger having a diameter of 0.3–0.4 m and the smaller 0.2 m. They presumably served as a fence-line, albeit a surprisingly substantial one (see Mitchell, Chapter 7).

### *Ditch group 429 (Fig. 4. 27)*

The westernmost boundary consisted of a series of two shallow intercutting linear ditches (group 429) aligned parallel to the successive sequence of recut ditch boundaries, 430, and located 7–8 m to the west. No conclusive sequence was established largely due to the similarity of the fills, although section 40 does suggest that the eastern ditch was the earlier. As demonstrated by section 26, the period between cuts was not sufficient to allow the earlier ditch to have become fully infilled.

Both ditches varied considerably in width with the eastern ditch, 294/370, varying between 1.45 m in the northern area and 1.85 m in the southern area. This maintained a depth of 0.4 m, with a broad flat base and gently sloping sides. A single mixed gravel and clayey silt deposit, 293/372, filled the majority of the ditch extending 2–4 m over the eastern lip. This suggests that the deposit was derived from ploughing up to or probably over the edge of the ditch with ploughsoil subsequently spilling into the ditch as the boundary was moved further to the east.

The western ditch (295/371) was also 0.4 m deep although this had a maximum width of 2.2 m narrowing to only 0.8 m wide towards the south. It had a well defined flat base and slightly steeper edges than its eastern counterpart. A primary gravelly fill (373) sealed a single mixed gravelly deposit (296/374), 0.2–0.35 m deep. A plough-derived deposit, 297, filled a remaining shallow depression over the ditches to the south before subsequent ploughing, represented by post-medieval layer 108, respecting the later ditches of boundary 430, sealed the ditch fills.

## Discussion

The environmental and sedimentary sequence provides important new information on the development of the landscape both locally and regionally. This is discussed more fully below (see Scaife, Chapter 8). By way of a summary, it can be said that waterlogging in the hollow of the palaeochannel started with a rising watertable in the later Bronze Age. The subsequent development of peat shows an episode of tree clearance marked by a decline in lime (Pollen Zone 2), although tree pollen was still around 50%. There was then a more thorough clearance towards the top of the peat sequence when tree pollen was reduced to less than 5% and grasses increased to 75%. This can be broadly dated to the Iron Age, and, viewed within the sequence as a whole, may have been relatively late. Roman activity is represented by pottery from the top of the peat which appears to have been associated with the initial digging of boundary and/or drainage ditches. The specific interpretation of the features encountered in the excavation is presented below.

The sequence of six recut ditches (ditch group 430), dividing the gravel terrace from the 'Roman Pond' shows that this has been a persistent boundary. There can be little doubt that the earliest of these ditches is Roman in date despite a deficiency of supporting artefactual evidence. Leaving aside a post-medieval sherd from segment 382 (Fig. 4.28, section 40), which is most plausibly intrusive, the pottery recovered from these ditches comprises a 2nd- or 3rd-century sherd from the same context and two undiagnostic Roman sherds from segment 165 (Fig. 4.28, section 1). A tiny scrap of post-medieval pottery from the surface of segment 299 (fill 336) is of unreliable provenance, although it may suggest that the third ditch in the series was not finally filled until the post-medieval period. The fourth ditch (409/168/329) and its recut are undoubtedly post-medieval on stratigraphic grounds, while the sixth (326/403) is relatively modern. The cropmark plot (Fig. 4.25) shows that a ditch associated with the adjacent Roman settlement runs into this area, although it is not possible to tell which excavated example it corresponds to.

Ditch group 429, running parallel to ditch group 430 to the west, is of unknown date. The two ditches do not appear to be aligned with any of the cropmark features and it is not clear how far north they continued. They were presumably contemporary with one or more of the main boundary ditches, and perhaps make sense as defining a trackway leading up the side of the field. A Roman date is unlikely on present evidence, particularly as the ditches appear to cut the lower ploughsoils (146 and 201) and their broad shallow form is untypical of Roman ditches. They are respected by the plough furrows recorded in the excavation (Fig. 4.26) and are more probably medieval.

Ditch 427, lying more or less centrally within the palaeochannel, is an intriguing feature. It cut the peat deposit 113 and was sealed by the earliest ploughsoil, 112. It furthermore contained exclusively Roman pottery, and there is no *prima facie* reason for arguing that it is not of Roman date. That there was Roman activity in the 'pond' is suggested by the amount of Roman pottery from layers 113, 112 and ditch 427, which, at 49 sherds (506 g), can be considered large for 'off-site' deposits and accounts for over half the pottery from the site. The presence of a Roman ditch here suggests that there was an attempt to drain or demarcate this area of land for some purpose.

The air photographic evidence shows that a ditch still existed as a slight earthwork in this location in 1975 (Plate 4.5) before the 'pond' was ploughed. It is not certain that this is the same ditch, partly because the alignment is not unequivocally the same, though undeniably close, and also because of the difficulty of envisaging such longevity for a relatively slight feature. However, the only other ditch found in this location in the excavations was the extremely shallow 'ditch', 426, which can surely be dismissed as a contender unless the excavated evidence is totally misleading or the feature had been quite drastically truncated. It is tempting to see the photographed ditch as Roman because, at the northern end of the field, it crosses the curving boundary of the 'pond', which itself is surely the fossilisation of the medieval headland and respected by all subsequent cultivation. Like ditch 427, the ditch seen from the air also had a bank on its western side. If it were the same feature as ditch 427 it must be assumed that ploughing since 1975 had been severe enough to completely obliterate any trace of the earthwork, and that both upper soils in sections 40, 22 and 26 must therefore be modern, as the evidence from the soils themselves suggests. The fact that the ditch cut a straight line without any apparent regard for the local topography suggests that it was primarily concerned with land division rather than drainage. However, the cropmarks suggest that this ditch was part of a field pattern of slightly different alignment to that associated with the Roman settlement, lying as it does approximately parallel to another long straight ditch about 120 m to the west. These ditches give the appearance of being later than the main Roman system and may respect the modern cross boundary to the north. The air photographic evidence for their Roman origin is not therefore decisive, but combined with the results of the excavations, it give some grounds for considering this a serious proposition.

After ditch 427 went out of use and became choked with peat, the field was ploughed. The horizon of ploughsoil (112) extended over 427 and across most of the field to the east. There is no particular reason to consider this to be a Roman event, (although there is no direct evidence to contradict this). Detailed examination of 112 showed that alluviation had preceded the ploughing, and the soil perhaps fits better within the context of the medieval expansion of arable. Subsequent flooding (alluvial layer 140) must have ended the arable experiment and the molluscan evidence (Macro 503) suggests that the area became damp grassland or meadow which persisted until recent times (Macro 502, 501).

The purpose and date of ditches 428 and 426 within the 'pond' are unclear. Both terminated within the excavation area and are unlikely to have functioned as drains, at least not effectively. Ditch 426 was very shallow and was conceivably a medieval furrow rather than a ditch, an interpretation which its slightly sinuous course may support. Ditch 428 mirrored 426 in plan but was more substantial and more convincingly related to land management. It appeared to cut alluvial layer 140, and was therefore more or less contemporary with the later ditches in group 430. This suggests that it was late or post-medieval, rather than any earlier, and probably not therefore connected with arable farming. These two interpretations are somewhat difficult to reconcile, but for want of further evidence a more conclusive explanation remains elusive.

## WESTFIELD FARM

*By Helen Drake and Andrew Mudd*

### Introduction

The site comprised two trapezoidal areas (Areas 1 and 2) on either side of the Cerney Wick road to the west of Westfield Farm (Fig. 4.31). The site lay a few metres outside the Scheduled Ancient Monument (SAM 899). In the Stage 2 field evaluation an oval ring ditch and several undated linear ditches had been examined approximately 50 m north-east of Area 2 (CAT 1991b, Trench VII). Due to a subsequent repositioning of the alignment of the new road, this area was taken out of the route corridor. The excavation was designed to investigate a single linear ditch and traces of ridge and furrow seen on aerial photographs which hitherto had not been examined (Plate 4.5).

In Area 1 the features revealed comprised post-medieval field boundaries and traces of ridge-and-furrow. In Area 2 two phases of ridge-and-furrow cultivation were recorded. However, a recut boundary ditch and a group of quarry pits are likely to be Roman. These are described below while the medieval and later features are presented in Chapter 6.

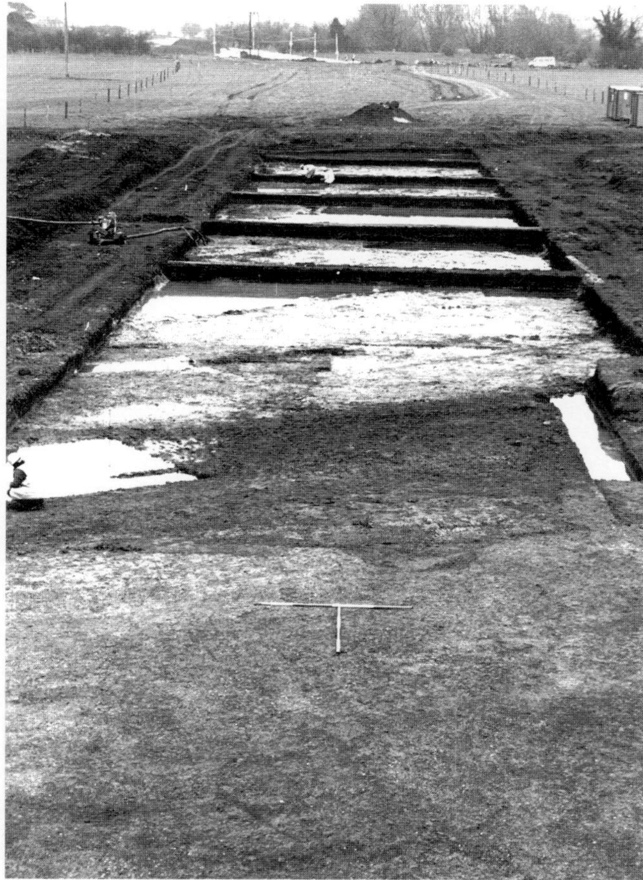

*Plate 4.6 Latton 'Roman Pond' after the first stage of stripping looking south-east. Ditch group 430 is the large ditch in the foreground.*

### Ditch 31/32

In the north-east corner of Area 2 a ditch and later recut were found running on a north-west - south-east alignment. They did not exactly follow the line of any of the ditches in Area 1 and are not considered to form part of the same field boundary system. The initial cut, 32, was 0.94 m wide and 0.38 m deep. A single fill (36) of silt clay yielded a fragment of a South Gaulish samian cup (Dragendorff 27), probably of Flavian date.The ditch was cut on its western edge by a wider and deeper recut, 31, which had a broad U-shaped profile 0.43 m deep, in contrast to the earlier cut which had a much flatter base. Three fills were present, with the earlier two producing no finds. The initial fill (57) constituted a thin layer of silt clay with a green cast to it. The second fill (35) was similar to the primary fill but contained fewer gravel inclusions. The latest fill, (30), was only present in part of the ditch and represented material that had collected within a depression in the infilled ditch. A large number of fragments (127 g) of a Roman greyware vessel were present in this deposit. This is not closely dateable but does suggest that the ditches had gone out of use in the Roman period.

### Quarry pits

A number of irregularly shaped pits were recorded in Area 2, the majority of which were clustered in the south-east corner of the trench without inter-cutting. These pits were probably dug for the extraction of gravel, although it is not certain that they all belong to the same period of activity. One of the pits (39) was cut by ditch 31 and therefore appears to be Roman or pre-Roman. The others are probably of the same date. Roman pottery was recovered from pit 46. Only one probable quarry pit (33) appeared to post-date the post-medieval plough furrows but it is likely that this was either an isolated case or misobserved. Seven pits were examined by excavation. They were generally small and shallow (up to 0.4 m deep), although pit 22 was 10 m long and 0.75 m deep.

### Discussion

The recut Roman ditch (31/32) in Area 2 is almost certainly the feature visible as a cropmark running more or less parallel to Cerney Wick Road (Plate 4.6; Fig. 4.31). An alternative is that it is the ditch approaching the excavation from the south-east, which forms part of the irregular field system on this alignment, but if this were the case both ditches ought to have been present in the excavated area, which they were not.

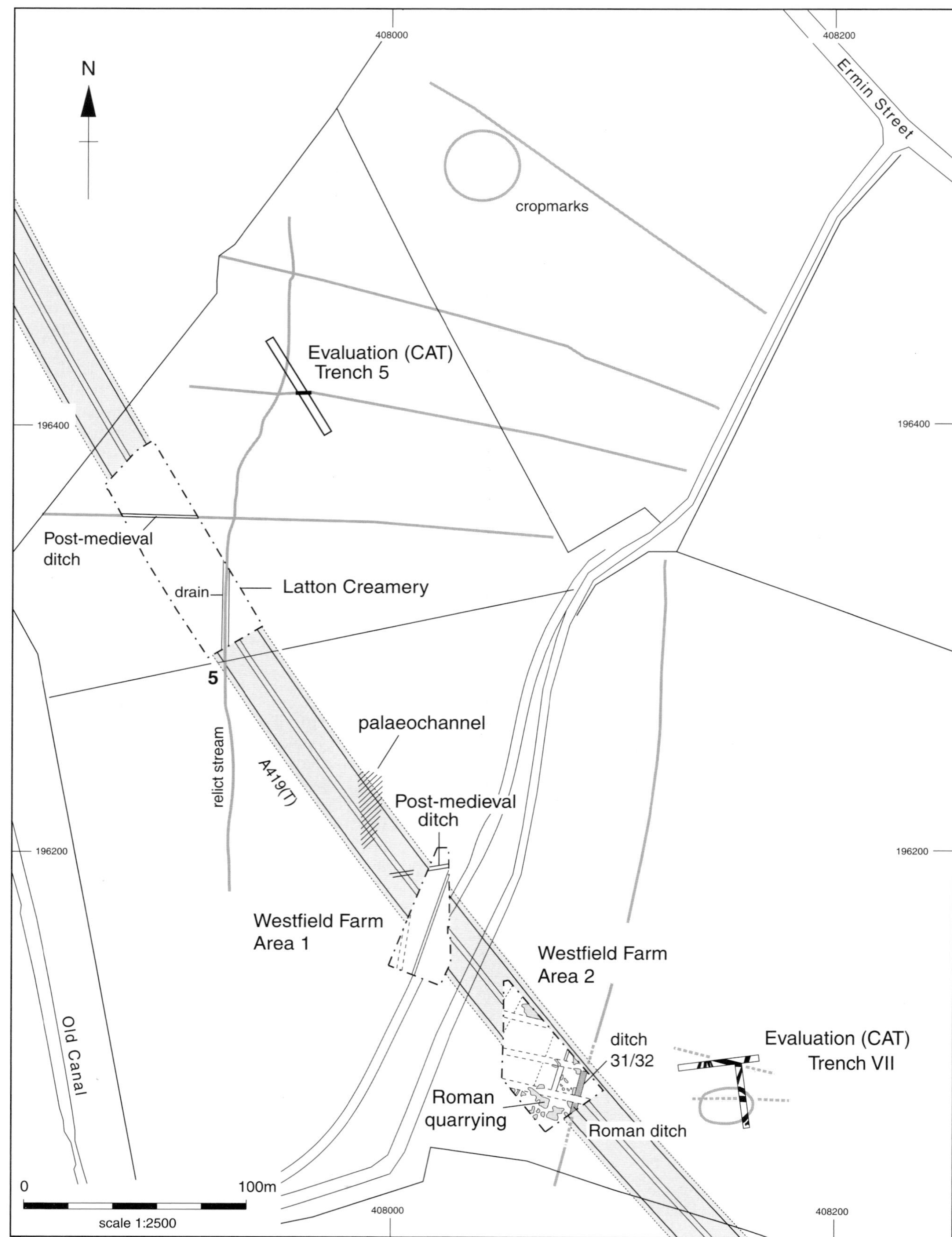


*Figure 4.31 Westfield Farm, site location and cropmarks.*

*Plate 4.7 Cropmarks east of Latton 'Roman Pond'. Reproduced by permission of Bryn Walters (ref. SU 08619572).*

Perhaps the most significant feature about this ditch is that it appears to form a boundary to the quarrying, which is confined almost exclusively to the west of it. This pattern was not particularly evident from the small area excavated, but the cropmark broadens the picture considerably, showing an extensive band of pits running along the western boundary of the field. This respect for the Roman ditch would, in itself, suggest that the quarrying was Roman in date, although the artefactual evidence (such as it is) and the general character of the pits (which is similar to that observed at Court Farm) provide some corroboration.

The reason for such extensive quarrying alongside Cerney Wick Road is not immediately apparent. It may suggest a Roman origin for this road, although other evidence would be required to substantiate this. In particular, it is not clear whether the quarrying extends under the road, or respects it. The road itself is not straight, and there is no cropmark evidence to suggest that it originally was. In fact the kink in the road coming from the north-east suggest that it deliberately avoided the area of quarrying which may therefore have remained rough ground in the post-Roman period, and would indicate a post-Roman origin for the road.

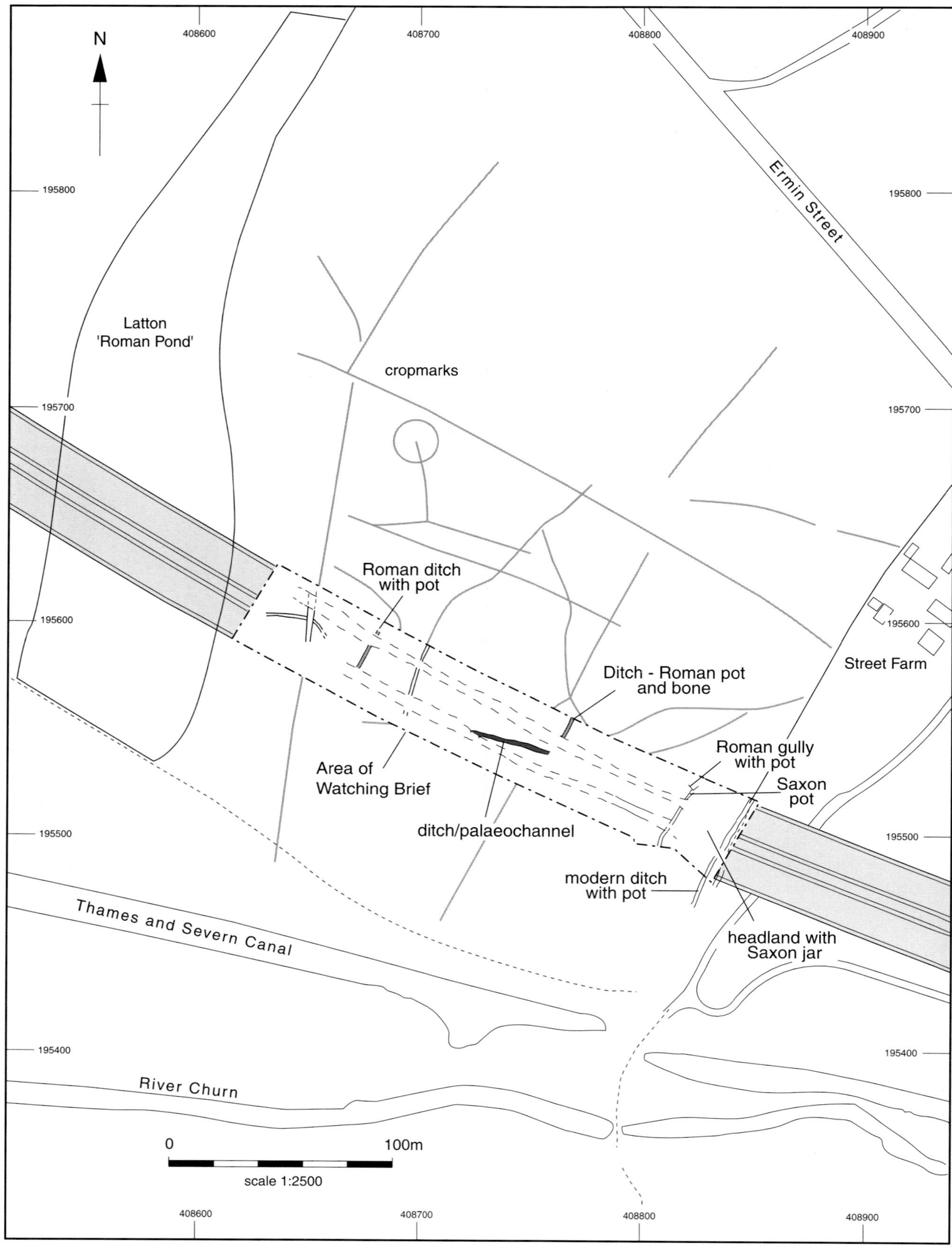


*Figure 4.32 Field Between Latton 'Roman Pond' and Street Farm, features located in watching brief and cropmarks.*

*Plate 4.8 Area of field boundaries and quarrying south-west of Westfield Farm. Reproduced by permission of RCHME (ref. NMR 4763/35).*

## FIELD BOUNDARIES BETWEEN LATTON 'ROMAN POND' AND STREET FARM

*By Andrew Mudd*

The watching brief maintained during topsoil stripping in this sector afforded the opportunity of investigating a number of boundary ditches and a palaeochannel in this field (Plate 4.5, Fig. 4.32). Two of the ditches and one small gully yielded exclusively Roman pottery and it seems that a Roman field system is present in this field. However, it is not entirely clear whether this corresponds to the irregular pattern of ditches visible as cropmarks. The Roman ditches were very shallow (up to 0.25 m deep) and it is possible that they do not correspond to any of the visible features, although there were no other ditches present to account for the cropmarks. A much larger ditch on the western side of the field is clearly the major medieval or later boundary.

Of some interest is the discovery of earlier Saxon pottery on the eastern side of the field. One sherd came from a shallow ditch on approximately the same alignment as the probable Roman ditches to the west, while two other fragments came from an adjacent soil interpreted as a medieval headland.

## NORCOTE FARM

*By Andrew Parkinson with Andrew Mudd*

In addition to the boundary ditch which was probably later prehistoric in date (Chapter 3), a series of shallow ditches ran at right-angles to the earlier feature (Figs 3.31–3.32).

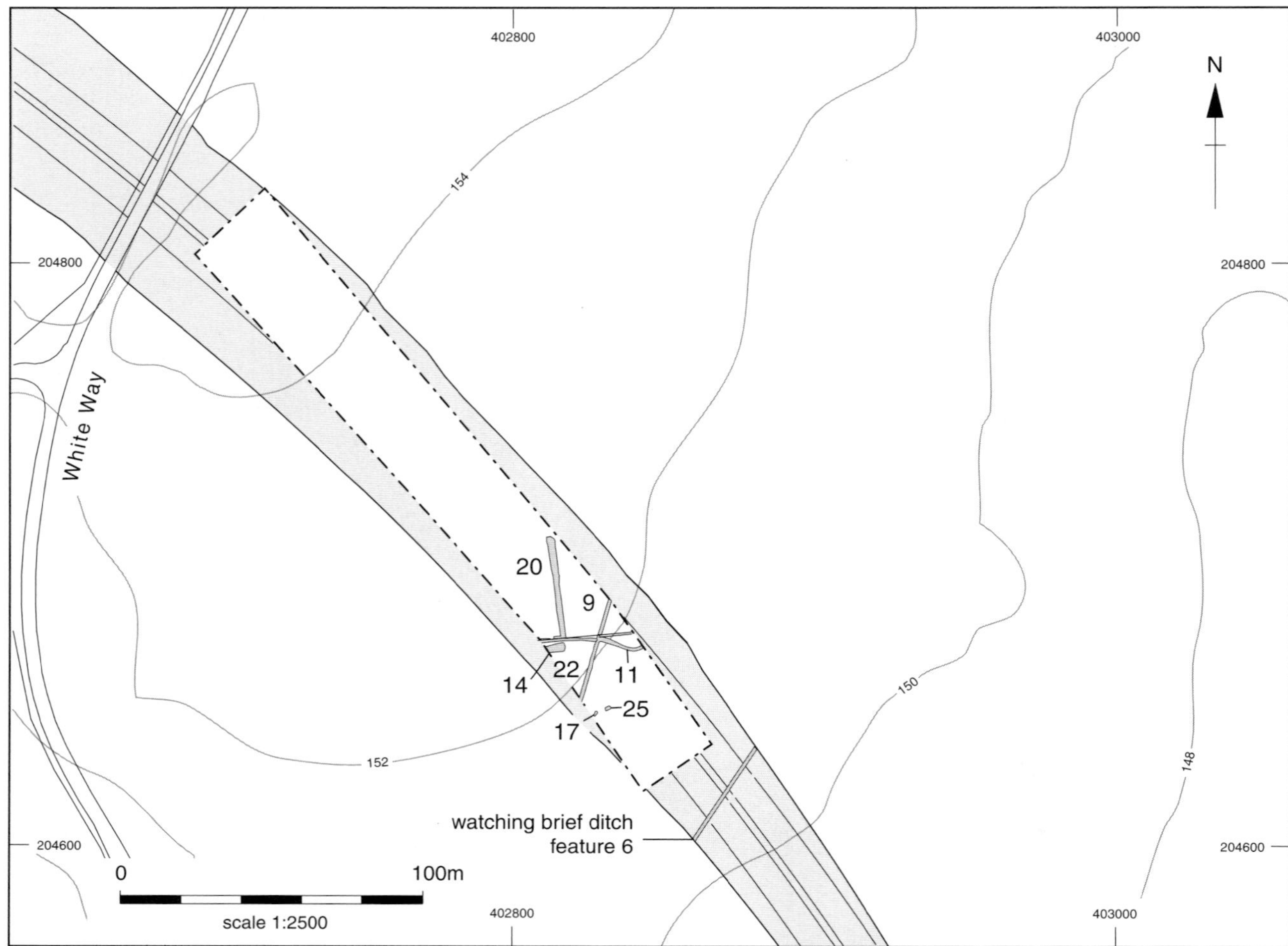


*Figure 4.33 Exhibition Barn, trench location.*

### *Ditches 240, 241, 242 and 243*

Four small ditches ran east-west across the site. All were similar in size, typically about 1 m wide and 0.3–0.4 m deep, and slightly irregular in plan. In the western half of the site they ran within a slight hollow at the bottom of a north facing slope, a topographic feature which continued west beyond the CPO boundary. The remnants of a ploughsoil (146) were present in a slight hollow between the ditches. The relationship between the ploughsoil and the ditches was unclear although they clearly pre-dated the medieval ridge-and-furrow. A single Roman pottery sherd came from the surface of the southernmost ditch (240) and two iron hobnails came from the northernmost ditch (243), suggesting a probable Roman date. The ditches cut across the top of an earlier north-south ditch, 239, which, although without finds, is considered to be later prehistoric.

The east-west ditches were too shallow to give any clear stratified relationships and badly truncated by later ploughing. However, the layout would suggest they are near contemporary in date. They probably represent a sequence of shallow boundary ditches, perhaps associated with hedgerows, although it is possible that they bounded a trackway of two or three phases. If they marked the line of a routeway it may be no coincidence that the Roman ditches cross the earlier ones near a narrow gap, suggesting the position of a long-lived entrance way. There does not seem to have been a Romano-British settlement nearby although one is known to exist at Witpit Copse *c.* 600 m to the east (Glos. SMR 3176) towards which the ditches may have been heading (Fig. 3.31). It is noteworthy that the programme of sieving 40 test pits prior to topsoil stripping produced only one Romano-British pottery sherd.

## EXHIBITION BARN

*By Helen Drake and Andrew Mudd*

### Introduction

The area investigated lay to the east of White Way (Glos. SMR 2039), which is a ridgetop route also known as Salt Way or Salt Street and thought to be of Roman or even earlier origin now followed by the line of a modern road (Fig. 4.33). North of Exhibition Barn the route deviates from a remarkably straight course as it approaches Cirencester. It has been suggested that this deviation is a medieval modification of an originally straighter course (Darvill and Holbrook 1994, 52). Fieldwalking by Cotswold Archaeological Trust in 1991 found mainly scatters of post-medieval and modern pottery (CAT 1991a, 53–4). Pottery and flintwork, tentatively dated to the Neolithic, were also recorded. The Stage 2 assessment involved the excavation of a 90 m trench (Trench 1991/507) to examine the area of the possible original alignment of White Way to the east of the road's present course. The results of the evaluation proved inconclusive although a ditch of uncertain date was discovered running on approximately the correct alignment.

An area 250 m long and 40 m wide was stripped down the centre of the road corridor in order to clarify the potential for prehistoric features and the possible course of White Way. Archaeological features were limited to a series of intercutting linear ditches, two quarry pits and a possible Roman hearth (Fig. 4.34). The quarry pits were of medieval and/or post-medieval date. The underlying site geology is limestone of the Great Oolite series.

**Roman and medieval field boundaries**

During stripping a number of intercutting ditches were revealed representing part of an evolving field boundary system. Dating this sequence is problematic, as little artefactual material was recovered.

***Ditch 9***

This linear feature, which ran on a north-south alignment across the site was identified as the primary ditch within this series. One excavated section had revealed a flat-bottomed, steeply-sided profile, 1.17 m wide and 0.64 m deep. It contained two fills, the earliest of which yielded one sherd of Roman pottery. The later fill, which contained significantly more silt and was up to 0.2 m deep, was very similar to the subsoil which overlay the natural and may represent the gradual silting of the top of the ditch with ploughsoil. This deposit (8) yielded 28 Roman sherds which are thought to have come from a single vessel. One other pottery fragment tentatively dated as medieval came from within this fill. It is, however, a small abraded sherd, and the date is by no means certain. A copper alloy hooked strap-end from the same fill has not been identified and neither its function nor the date are certain.

A further ditch, which was revealed during the watching brief 75 m to the east (Fig. 4.33), possessed a similar form and dimensions. It is highly likely that this was part of the same field system although no dating evidence was recovered.

***Ditch 11***

Only approximately 15 m of this ditch was revealed by stripping, the eastern end continuing beyond the edge of excavation. Sinuous in plan, it measured 1.5 m wide and 0.40 m deep and ran on a broadly east-west alignment. Its western terminal cut into the lower fill of ditch 9 but not across the ditch. Its profile and two fills were very similar to those of ditch 9. Only one find was present, a fragment of tegula, from the earlier fill (19).

***Ditch 22***

Ditch 22 also ran on an east-west alignment, with its eastern terminus cutting ditch 9 opposite ditch 11. It was identified as clearly different from ditch 11. It was closely followed by the line of the modern field boundary (by which it was truncated). This ditch was slightly smaller than the two earlier ditches, measuring only 1 m wide and 0.30 m deep, and had a broadly U-shaped profile. It contained only a single fill with a high silt content, similar to the later fills (8 and 10) in ditches 9 and 11. One sherd of poorly preserved limestone-tempered ware was present, probably dating to the medieval period.

***Ditch 20***

Ditch 20 ran on a north-south alignment roughly at right angles to ditch 22 with its terminal cutting the edge of the latter. It again was filled with a single deposit, and was 0.42 m deep. It was much wider than the other ditches being almost 2 m in width. No dating evidence was recovered.

***Dating evidence***

The dating evidence for this series of ditches was sparse. It is apparent that in the sequence of ditch cutting, each ditch respected the presence of the earlier one as the pattern evolved. This extended to the location and alignment of the present hedgeline, which ran across the terminal of ditch 20 at right angles to it, thereby closely following the course of the earlier ditch 22. It appears likely that these two late ditches are medieval or later in date, a view which receives some support from the possible medieval sherd from ditch 22, the shallow form of both the ditches, and the silty nature of their fills.

The earlier ditches, 9 and 11, were of a different form, being deeper, steep-sided and flat-based. Both contained a rubbly main fill under a thinner, silty upper fill. The main fills were devoid of finds with the exception of a Roman sherd and fragment of tegula. While it is possible that these were residual in later features, the concentration of pottery (possibly from a single vessel) in the upper fill of ditch 9 suggests that this ditch, at least, was of Roman origin and was being infilled in the Roman period. The single possible medieval sherd from the same context may have derived from the final silting of the upper levels and does not provide a convincing *terminus post quem* for the ditch itself. Ditch 11 seems likely to have been a later addition to ditch 9, its sinuous form perhaps suggesting surface features to which it had to adapt.

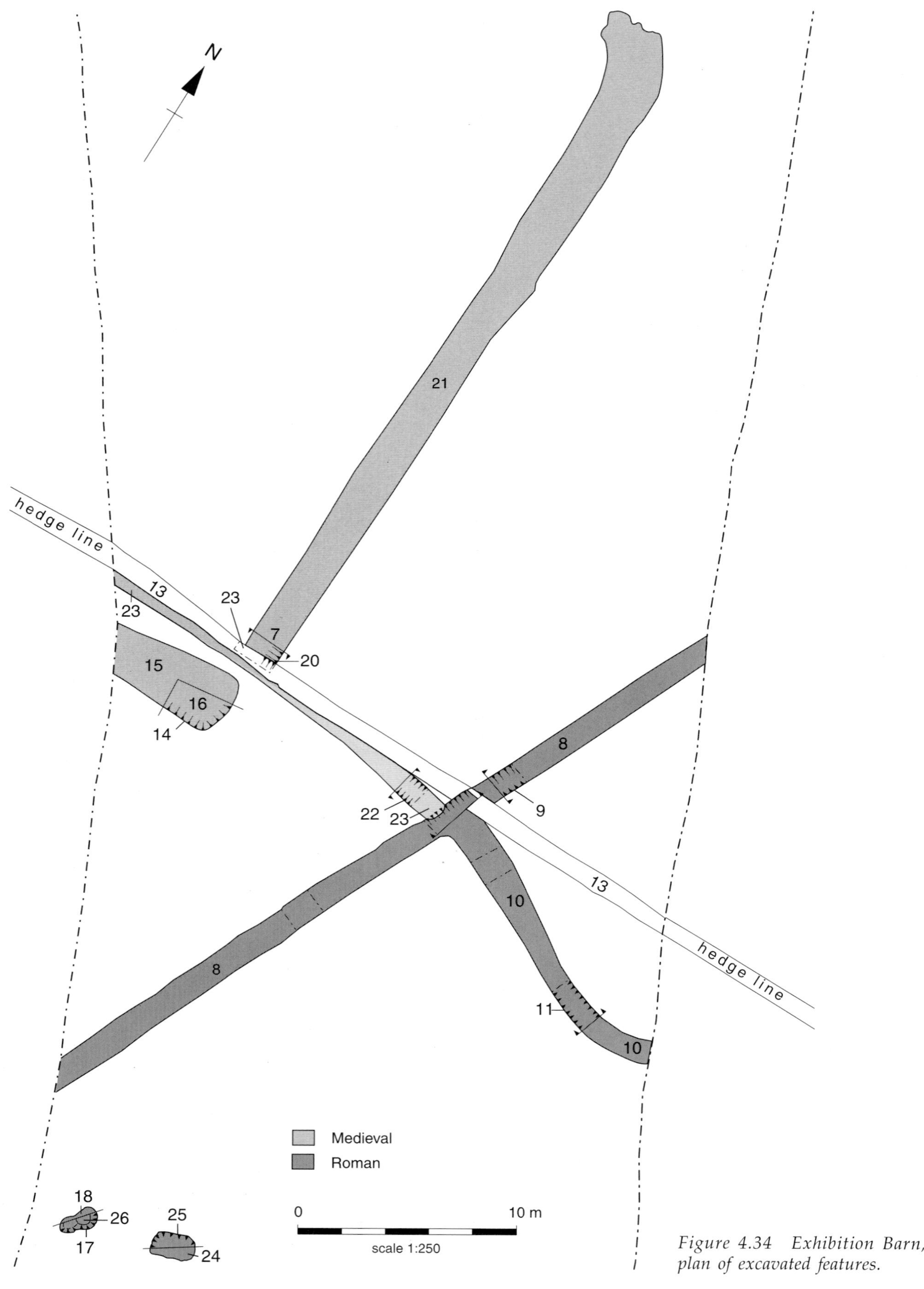


*Figure 4.34 Exhibition Barn, plan of excavated features.*

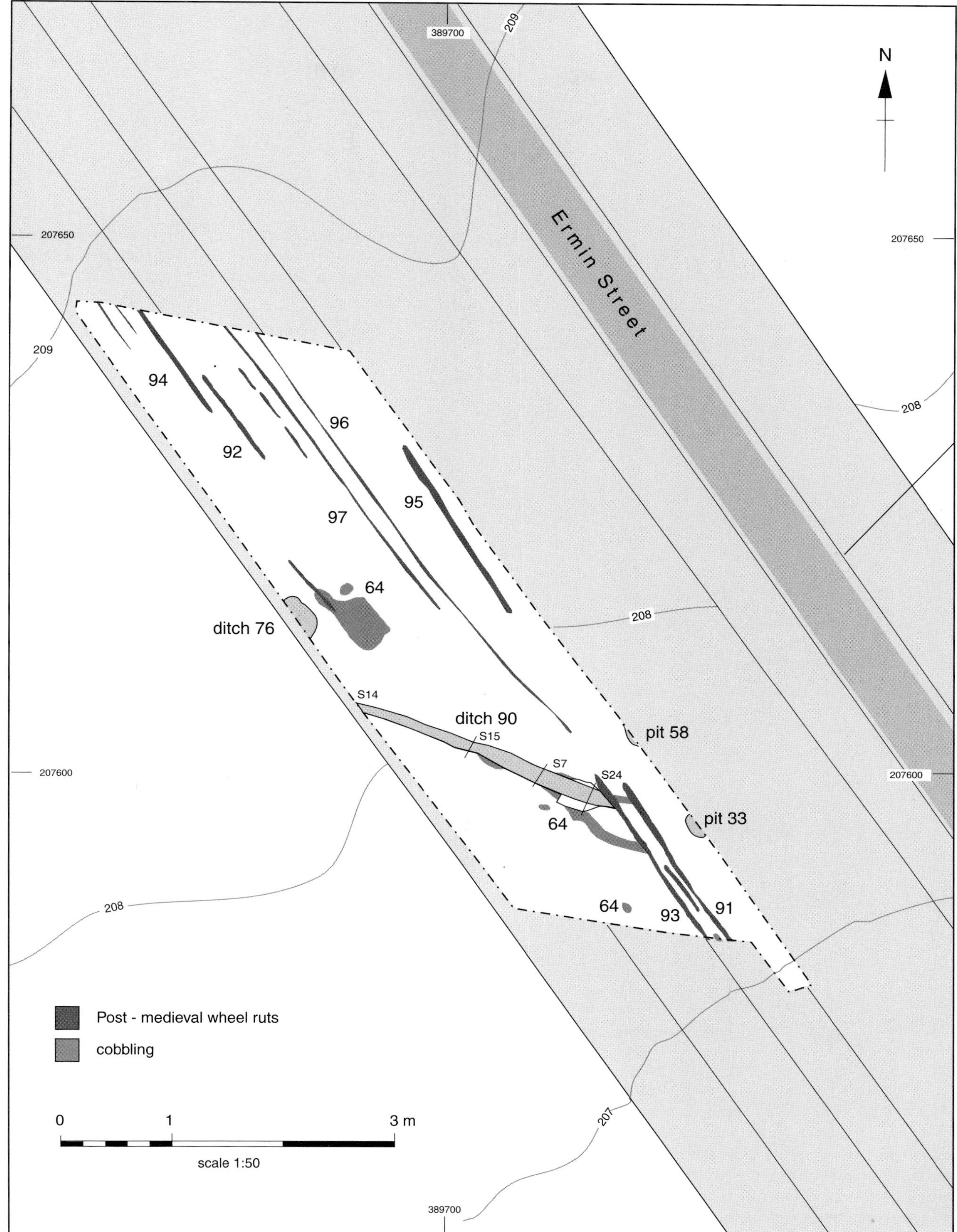


*Figure 4.35 Sly's Wall South, plan of excavated features.*

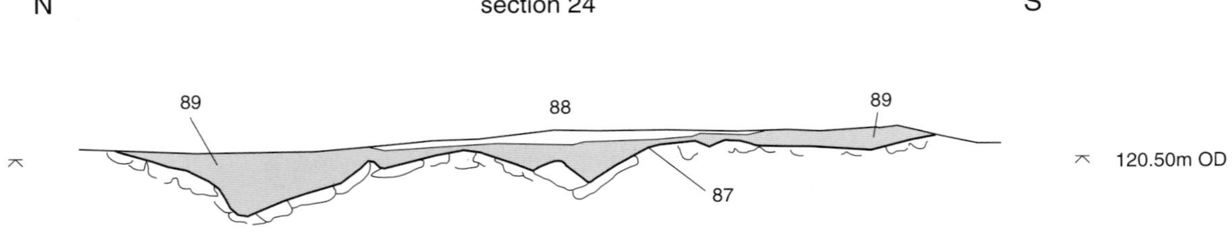


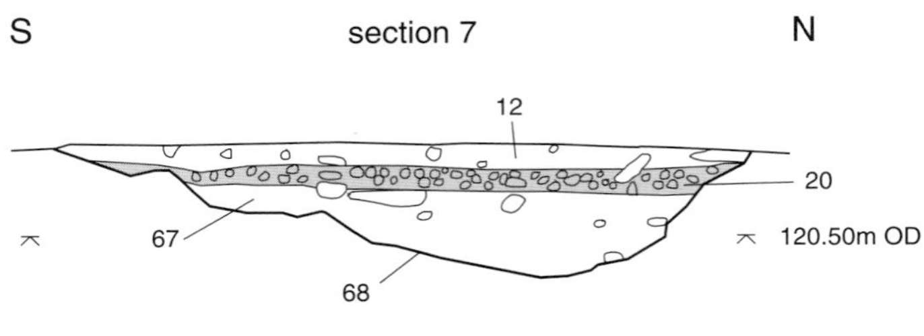


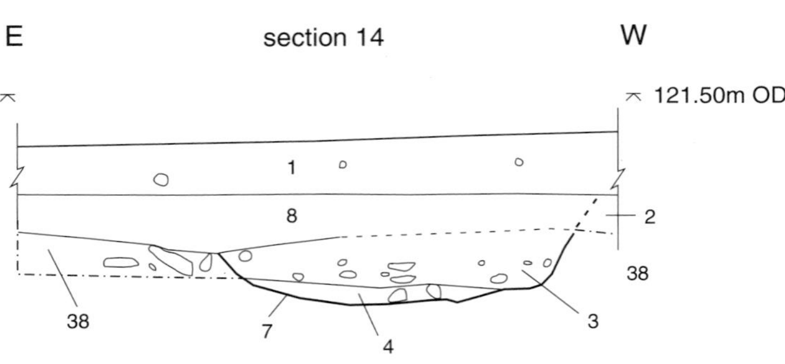


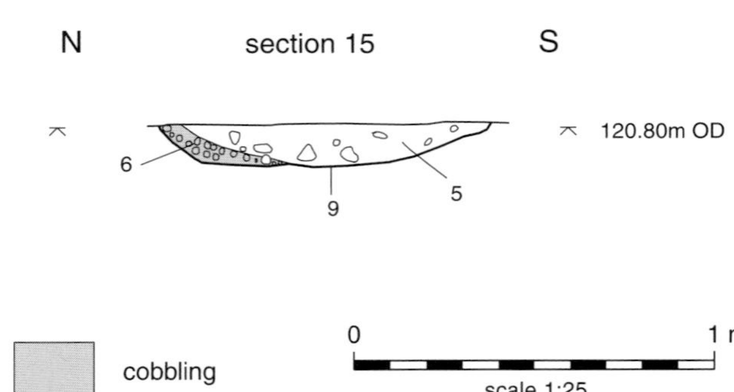


*Figure 4.36 Sly's Wall South, sections.*

Some sort of occupation in the vicinity would at least provide a context for the pottery in the ditches although the location of this occupation is by no means clear. No pottery was recovered in the Stage 1 surface collection survey.

The way in which the medieval ditch, 22, respected the Roman ditches, 9 and 12 is remarkable and must indicate that their positions were still evident, perhaps as slight earthworks or because of associated hedgerows.

**?Roman hearth 25** *(Fig. 4.34)*

A small ovoid feature (25) was excavated to the south of the field boundary system, measuring 2.13 m x 1.14 m with a depth of 0.19 m. Its single fill yielded a large quantity of burnt limestone, together with charcoal flecking. A soil sample contained predominantly cereal grain with the two most common grains being *Triticum spelta* and *Hordeum* sp. The cereal assemblage as a whole is typical of the Roman period and one pottery sherd of Roman date was found on the surface of this feature. The natural subsoil surrounding and underlying this feature did not show any signs of having been affected by heat from *in situ* burning. The interpretation of this feature as a hearth is therefore by no means certain and it may instead represent a burnt stone deposit.

**Feature 17** *(Fig. 4.34)*

A little to the west of this deposit lay a kidney-shaped feature (17), measuring 2 m x 1 m, with two fills, 18 and 26, containing small inclusions of burnt limestone and charcoal. A sample of this material revealed no further information. This feature may be a burnt tree-throw hole.

## SLY'S WALL SOUTH

*By Steve Lawrence with Andrew Mudd*

### Introduction

A trapezoidal area of approximately 0.19 ha. was investigated at Sly's Wall South (Fig. 4.35) which lay in the field immediately to the south of Sly's Wall Plantation. The site lay to the west of the Ermin Street and 1.5 km to the north of Duntisbourne Rouse village.

The site was originally evaluated in 1990 by Gloucestershire County Council in order to investigate the presence of a single linear cropmark identified by aerial photography (Glos. SMR 9432). One trench, measuring 30 m x 1.6 m, was positioned across this feature which proved to be a broad shallow ditch, 90, running on an east-west alignment. It was interpreted as a probable Roman trackway ditch. No finds were recovered but a thin horizon of rounded limestone cobbles was recorded in the latest fill which implies a later phase of metalling. A number of narrow linear grooves underlying the topsoil were also found cutting the limestone bedrock.

An area extending either side of ditch 90 was stripped. Any association with Ermin Street could not be determined as the ditch petered out within the excavated area. Four sections excavated through the ditch revealed similar profiles to those observed during the evaluation phase (Fig. 4.36). A number of other features were also revealed including two pits, 58 and 33, one possible ditch terminus, 76, and several narrow linear features thought to be wheel ruts. Additional features proved on examination to be irregular-shaped natural hollows filled with a homogenous red brown silt.

### Ditch 90 *(Figs 4.35–4.36)*

Approximately 25 m of the ditch, running east-west, was revealed in the excavation area. The western end was seen to continue beyond the edge of excavation but the eastern end petered out in an area of wheel ruts. In general the ditch presented a broad U-shaped profile. The dimensions of the ditch cut did, however, vary along its length becoming wider and shallower as it petered out. Ditch segment 7 (Fig. 4.36, section 14), placed against the western baulk, measured 0.65 m wide and 0.32 m deep and contained a single main fill of a stone-free reddish brown silt (3), which overlay a thin stony primary silt (4). The later fill (3) yielded a fragment of clay pipe, although this is thought to have possibly derived from an intrusive plough/wheel rut. At the opposite end of the ditch, segment 87 (Fig. 4.36, section 24) demonstrated that the feature had widened out to 2.4 m, but was only 0.20 m deep. It was filled largely with rounded pebbles (89) which resembled cobbling. This corresponded to fill 309 of the evaluation trench and was also seen in segments 9 and 68 (Fig 4.36, sections 15 and 7), although in the latter it formed the middle fill (20) which overlay a largely stone-free silt.

### Pits 33 and 58 *(Fig. 4.35)*

Two pits protruding from underneath the eastern edge of excavation contained a similar sequence of deposits to each other. Pit 33 was the larger of the two, 1.10 m in diameter and 0.36 m deep, in contrast to pit 58 which was only 0.66 m in diameter and 0.22 m deep. Both were oval-shaped with an uneven but generally flat base and contained three fills. The earliest fills (32 and 36) consisted of a mid orange-brown silt loam with sparse limestone fragments. These were overlain by fills 31 and 35 which included frequent cobbles similar in appearance to the cobbling fills seen in ditch 90. This cobbling was overlain in both cases by an orange-brown silt that had been disturbed by ploughing. One pottery sherd apiece was recovered from the primary fills, an indeterminate Roman sherd from 32 and a fragment of Oxford colour-coated mortarium, of probable 4th-century date, from 36.

### Ditch terminus 76 *(Fig. 4.35)*

A length of only about 3 m of this feature was revealed possibly forming the terminal of a ditch oriented at approximately right-angles to ditch 90. Alternatively it may have been a pit. It had a steep-sided, flat-bottomed profile 1 m wide and 0.68 m deep, containing five fills. The earliest of these was a mid brown-grey silt clay which included 80% limestone fragments. This was overlain by a thin layer of silting which had accumulated against the north-eastern edge of the cut and was in turn overlain by a second stage of stone slumping (84), similar in appearance to the primary fill, 86. A further stage of silting, again lying against the north-eastern edge, contained only 5% limestone. Sealing these deposits was a layer of cobbling (61), similar to that seen elsewhere on site. No dating evidence was recovered and a sample taken from fill 85 for palaeo-environmental analysis did not produce any further information.

### Cobbling 64 *(Fig. 4.35)*

A roughly rectangular area of cobbling was exposed during stripping lying close to the possible ditch terminus 76. Other smaller areas of similar appearance were noted near ditch 90 and wheel ruts 91 and 93, and were also contained as fills in ditch 76 and 90 and pits 33 and 58.

The main patch of cobbling (64) covered an area of approximately 2 m x 5 m and was 0.06 m deep. It was seen to directly overlie the natural limestone bedrock and had been cut by later wheel ruts. The smaller areas of cobbling found near to ditch 90 and wheel ruts 91 and 95 were similar to deposit 64 with the cobbles typically measuring 0.10 m in diameter. These areas may represent the remains of a cobbled surfacing associated with a wider alignment of Ermin Street during the medieval/post-medieval period. The majority of the surface was probably truncated by later ploughing, the only remains surviving where it had partially sunk into softer underlying features such as the ditch and pits.

### Post-medieval wheel ruts *(Fig. 4.35)*

A number of narrow linear features ran parallel to the line of Ermin Street. These were similar in form and profile to those seen during the evaluation phase which were originally interpreted as plough marks. Subsequent work at sites such as Middle Duntisbourne, however, strongly suggests that they are wheel ruts caused by vehicles slewing off the line of Ermin Street as they ascended the hill from the south.

A number of the ruts were examined (features 91–97). All ran on a similar alignment and had a narrow U-shaped profile. They varied in width from 0.38 m to 0.65 m wide with a maximum depth of 0.26 m.

A single fill was present which in all cases consisted of an orange-brown silt-clay with occasional small limestone fragments, very similar to the subsoil (2) which was probably plough-derived. No dating evidence was recovered but rut 93 cut ditch 90 and a late medieval or post-medieval date is likely.

### Discussion

There is no clear evidence for the date or function of ditch 90. The evaluation suggested that it was a single ditch associated with a cobbled trackway, and a superficial similarity with the Roman trackway and cobbling at Duntisbourne Leer Area 2 is apparent. The absence of an adjacent ditch, at least on the western side, is puzzling but does not rule out its association with a trackway since (as the excavations at Duntisbourne Leer Area 1 showed) paired ditches can be of radically different dimensions and a shallow ditch could have been lost to the plough. Alternatively, it may simply not have been required. If it were not a trackway ditch, a field boundary is another possible interpretation. Its oblique alignment to Ermin Street represents a problem of interpretation whatever the purpose or date of the ditch (unless it were prehistoric, which can probably be discounted on present evidence). There are no obviously associated features. Four cropmark features to the north-west, on a very similar alignment to this ditch, were evaluated and found to be geological anomalies (GCC 1990, fields 42 and 43, trenches 2, 3, 5 and 6).

A Roman date for ditch 90 is by no means certain. Much depends upon the interpretation of the patchy cobbling and whether it can be treated as a single deposit. The fact that it extends both sides of the ditch would suggest that it was not a surface associated with a trackway, although the small areas involved would make it possible that some, or all, of the cobbling was in fact redeposited. It appears, however, that the ditch was partly open when the cobbling was being deposited or redeposited, layers of cobbling having been found in the lowest part of the shallower ditch segments. Significantly, cobbling was found in the upper fills of pits 33 and 58 and ?ditch 76, slightly sunk into the tops of these features. The diagnostic sherd of 4th-century pottery from the lower fill of pit 58 would appear to indicate that the overlying cobbling, and hence ditch 90, must be either very late Roman or post-Roman.

However, considerable disturbance by wheeled and presumably other kinds of traffic from the medieval period onward could have resulted in the redistribution of cobbles into the ditch. It is also possible that the ditch was partly redug and filled with cobbles to consolidate the ground. The largely stone-free lower silt in segment 68 (Fig. 4.36, section 7) does suggest that the ditch's origin predates the cobbled surfacing. Nevertheless, bearing in mind the pottery dating available, a 4th-century or later origin for the feature now seems most likely.

The cobbling itself may be much later. It extended for up to 20 m from the line of Ermin Street and seems most likely to have been spread from the road by traffic, or been intentionally distributed on a random basis to help consolidate the ground where it was needed. If it represents a deliberate surfacing, it is possible that the cobbling was late Roman, but it seems more likely to have been post-medieval. Actually it is by no means clear that the cobbling at Sly's Wall was a deliberate deposit. The fact that deposit 64 directly overlay the natural limestone did suggest that it was essentially a natural deposit eroded and rounded through wear, rather than a deliberate surfacing. If so, it may represent a gradual accumulation of worn stone from medieval times onward.

## WEAVERS BRIDGE

*By Helen Drake and Andrew Mudd*

### Introduction

An area of *c.* 0.50 ha. was excavated at the southern end of the scheme, approximately 0.5 km north of Cricklade. The site lay about 200 m east of the point at which the old A419 crossed the river Churn at Weavers (or Cricklade) Bridge on the Churn floodplain near its confluence with the Thames. The location and shape of the excavation was determined by the form of the Marston Meysey slip road (Fig. 4.37).

The area had been identified as being of archaeological interest due to the probable presence of the original course of Ermin Street, which is considered to have run in a direct line from Weavers Bridge to Calcutt (CAT 1991c). The site was evaluated by the Cotswold Archaeological Trust in 1994 (CAT 1994). Three trenches on north-east - south-west orientations were subsequently excavated with Trench 1 revealing a sequence of recutting linear features lying north-east of what was interpreted as the Roman road (Fig. 4.38). This was poorly preserved, but consisted of a remnant surface of limestone lying on a low bank of alluvial clay about 7 m wide, itself built on alluvial deposits. A dark Roman "agricultural" soil was recorded at the north-eastern end of this trench. A number of finds were recovered from this including pottery, coins and glass all dating to the late Roman period. An auger survey suggested it was a localised deposit covering an area approximately 12 m x 9 m. No archaeological deposits were found in the two other trenches.

For the excavation, an area of 155 m x 30 m was stripped to the north-east of the Roman road. The area of dark soil (interpreted in this report as a midden) was exposed in the southern part of the site. However, most of the rest of the site was covered with drainage ditches and stream channels of medieval and later date, the majority of which ran on a north-south alignment. These are described in Chapter 6.

### Midden deposit *(Fig. 4.39)*

A spread of dark silt-clay (57) which contained a scatter of artefactual material dating to the late Roman period was found at the southern end of the site. A rather lighter and browner soil (51) extended south

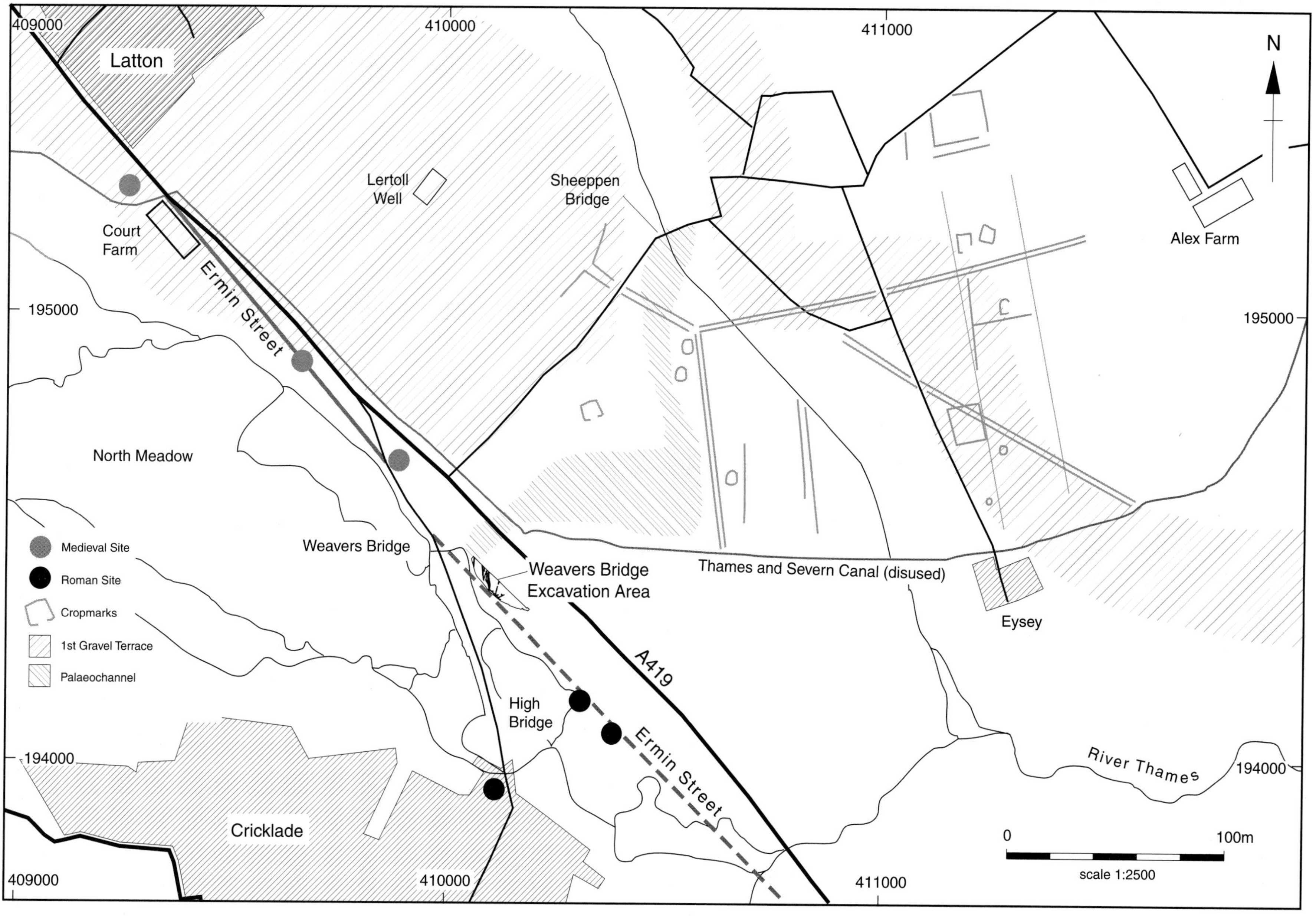


*Figure 4.37 Weavers Bridge, site location in relation to known find spots.*

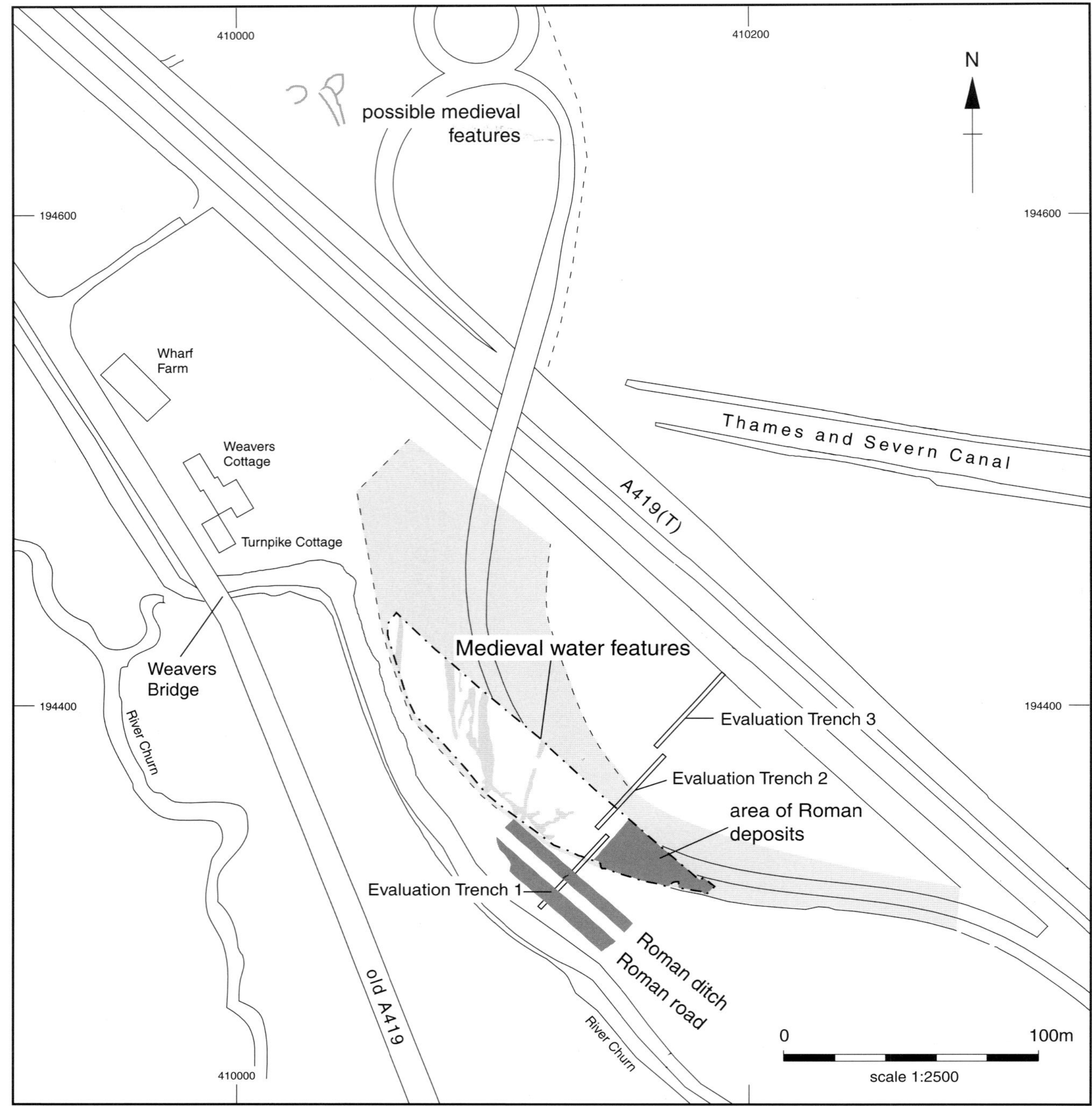


*Figure 4.38 Weavers Bridge, detailed location.*

and east of this deposit partly overlying 57. It also infilled the tops of the ditches in this area. Both these deposits overlay layer 58, a blue-grey alluvial clay containing abundant water snails (see Robinson, Chapter 8). This layer was limited to the southern end of the site. All the Roman features cut this layer.

**Layers 51 and 57** *(Fig. 4.39)*

Layer 57 consisted of a dark grey-brown silt-clay containing high concentrations of burnt material. Measuring 0.10 m deep it covered an area approximately 10 m x 11 m extending south-eastwards from the location of Evaluation Trench 1 (and equivalent to deposit 103). Approximately one-third of this deposit was excavated and yielded large quantities of pottery, animal bone and other domestic artefacts, along with a total of 40 coins (cat. 236, 239, 249, 252, 255, 257, 260, 262, 265). Only four of these coins were minted before AD 330, and none are earlier than AD 275 (see Davies, Chapter 7). The majority date to between AD 330–348, exhibiting a tight chronological range, with one later coin struck between AD 354–64, effectively providing a *terminus post quem* for the end of the

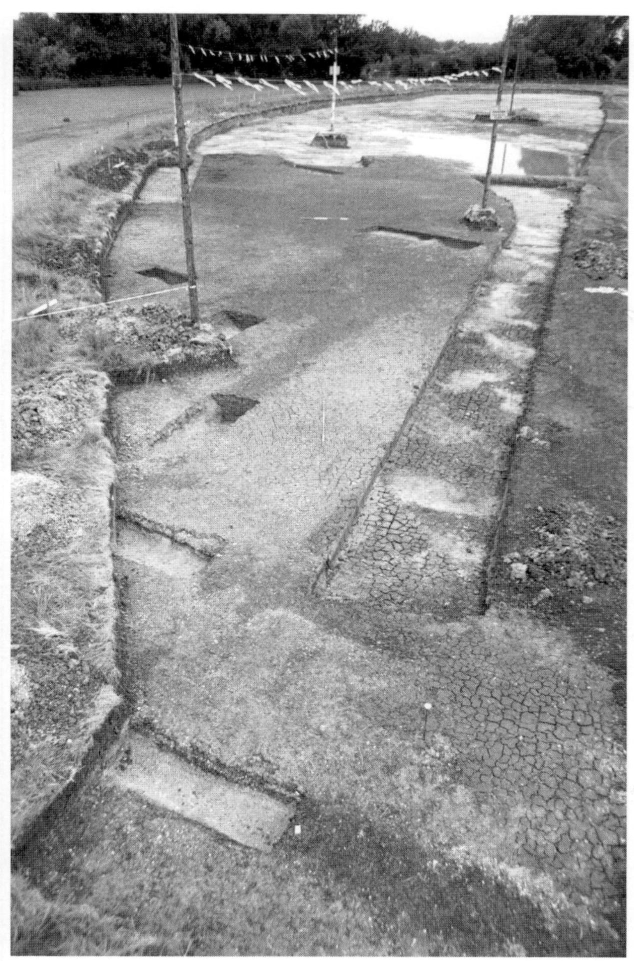

*Plate 4.9 Weavers Bridge. The site looking from the north-west. The late Roman midden is in the dark soil in the centre of the picture.*

occupation. This is effectively the same date range as that provided by the three 4th-century coins from the evaluation, the latest of which was dated to AD 350–360. The four earlier coins may be residual. The range of pottery fabrics present suggested a similar dating to that indicated by the coinage, with the majority dating to the late 3rd–4th centuries (see Timby, Chapter 7, Fig. 7.12.137). The presence of abraded sherds of Savernake ware in the assemblage points to late 2nd-century activity nearby. The average sherd size in general was quite low for Roman material and particularly for a midden deposit where larger and better preserved sherds would be expected. This might suggest that the material was either deliberately broken up or redeposited from another context. Two loomweight fragments (Table 7.54) and part of a decorated bone handle for a whittle tang implement (cat. 659) were also recovered along with a quantity of animal bone. A sample taken for environmental analysis yielded a total of 154 oyster shells with similar numbers of upper and lower valves.

The later deposit, 51, also consisted of a silt-clay but was more yellow in colour with the appearance of a ploughsoil rather than a midden. A less substantial deposit than layer 57, it only reached a depth of 0.05 m and became shallower towards the south. While a large quantity of charcoal was present, the finds were sparser than those in layer 57. As with 57, the pottery dated from the late 3rd–4th centuries, and the presence of a stamped bowl of the Oxfordshire industry suggests activity continued well into the 4th century. Late 2nd-century samian ware was also present indicating earlier activity in the area. Ten copper alloy coins were retrieved with almost identical date ranges to those found in layer 57 (cat. 232, 234, 237, 242, 247, 251). Only three dated to earlier than AD 330, with none dating to earlier than AD 260. As with layer 57, the latest coin was dated to AD 354–64. The majority of the coins were located close to layer 57.

Both deposits suggest a significant level of settlement activity nearby during the late Roman period. Although no direct evidence of a settlement was found, the density of finds is too high to belong to a general manuring scatter. Layer 57 is considered to be a rubbish midden with an adjacent soil, 51, which may have derived from later alluviation, incorporating a number of residual finds.

### Ditches *(Fig. 4.39)*

At the southern end of the site a total of six ditches were revealed, four of which yielded finds dating to the late Roman period. Running on differing alignments they are believed to represent at least three distinct phases. All were cut through layer 58, and were overlain by layer 51, the later of the two artefact-rich deposits.

#### *Ditch 134*

Running on an east-west alignment for at least 15 m, this was stratigraphically the earliest ditch present. One machine-cut section through it revealed a broad U-shaped profile, 2 m wide and about 1 m deep. Three fills were present, all of which consisted of a grey-brown silt-clay distinguished only by the amount of gravel present within each deposit. The earliest and latest fills, 126 and 124 respectively, were relatively clean, in contrast to the middle fill (125) which included 30% gravel, perhaps derived from edge slippage. No dating evidence was recovered, but the feature was cut by ditches 132, 133, 135 and 136, three of which contained material dating to the late Roman period.

#### *Ditch 133*

This ditch entered the trench from the north on a north-south alignment but then turned south-eastward close to the north-eastern edge of excavation. Two sections were hand-excavated, one located close to the south-western baulk and the other over the point where it began to swing east. Both contained two fills and showed a U-shaped profile about 1 m wide and 0.5–0.7 m deep. The early deposit, 104 and 114,

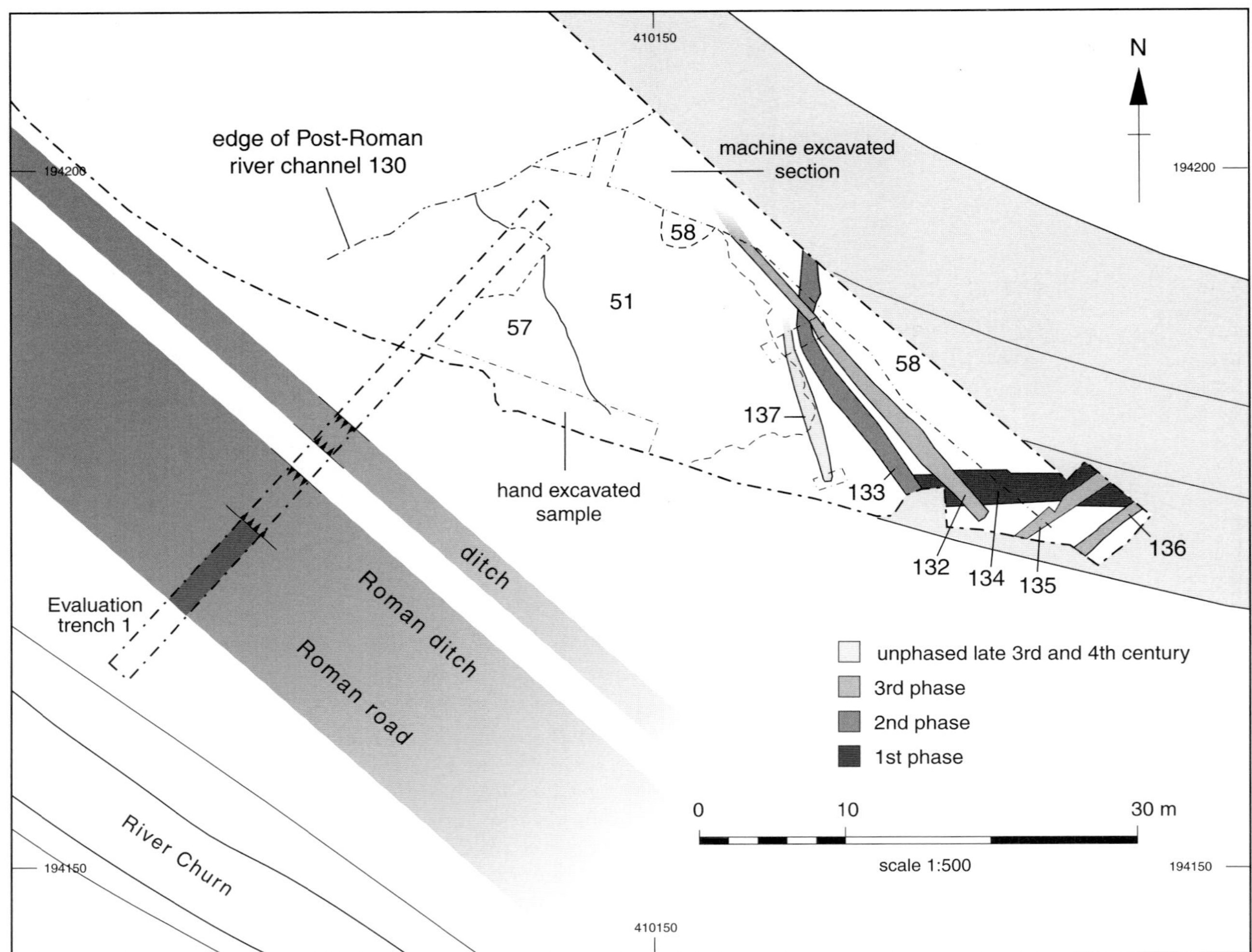


*Figure 4.39 Weavers Bridge, detailed plan of excavated features.*

consisted of a blue-grey silt-clay with the gravel content increasing from 2% to 30% as the ditch turned. The later fill was a consistent yellow-brown silt-clay. No dating evidence was recovered although the ditch was cut by ditch 132.

### *Ditches 132, 135 and 136*

Ditches 135 and 136 ran on approximately parallel north-east - south-west orientations in the extreme south-east corner of site. They were 2 m apart. Both measured 1 m wide and about 0.4 m deep, with similar cross-profiles of concave, steeply-sloping sides and rounded bases. Ditch 136 contained two fills of blue-grey silt-clay, with the earlier deposit, 82, having a high humic content. Three sherds of 1st–3rd-century pottery were recovered from the later fill, 62. Three fills were identified in ditch 135, with a single sherd of late Roman pottery recovered from its latest fill, 60. The primary fill, 73, contained a high gravel content resulting from slippage on its south-eastern edge indicating the possibility of a gravel bank. It was impossible to tell whether the ditches were coeval or sequential.

Ditch 132 ran at a right angle to ditches 135 and 136. Measuring 1 m wide and 0.42 m deep, it had a narrow flat base with steeply sloping, almost vertical, sides. Two sections were excavated, with segment 109 revealing a thin band of gravel slip located on its eastern edge that was not present in segment 74. Two further deposits were present both consisting of blue silt-clays with the latest fill, 112, yielding four sherds of late 3rd- / 4th-century pottery. The ditch terminated shortly before reaching the south-eastern edge of excavation, suggesting a possible entrance between it and ditch 135.

### *Gully 137*

Measuring 0.70 m wide this ran on an approximately north-south alignment, its southern end terminating within the excavation area. The terminal was 0.5 m deep with steep, almost vertical sides. Its base lay below the water table and it contained two silt-clay fills. From the terminal it could only be traced a short distance in plan but was identified in section further to the north under layer 51. Here it had shallowed to 0.26 m and only contained a single fill of blue-grey silt-clay (111). Two sherds of late 3rd-4th century pottery were recovered.

### Discussion

The excavations revealed what must be regarded as part of a late Roman settlement on the floodplain of the river Churn close to Ermin Street. Although no structures were found, the quantity of material from layers 57 and 51 indicates that these were probably middens and that structures almost certainly existed nearby, if not within the excavated area. The evidence for 4th-century buildings can be notoriously elusive despite abundant finds, as the excavations at Birdlip Quarry and other sites testify. Despite the suggestion that the material may have represented dumping from further afield (CAT 1994), the siting of middens at a distance from settlements is not a known practice in the late Roman period and a derivation of this material from an adjacent settlement is far more likely.

The date range from the coins indicates that the main part of the occupation here was relatively brief, perhaps just for the first half of the 4th century, although a few earlier coins and pottery suggest that there may have been activity here from the later 2nd century. The ditches are thought to represent three phases but it is unclear whether or not any of them were strictly contemporary with the midden. The only 4th-century pottery came from the upper fills of the latest ditches in the sequence (ditches 132, 135 and gully 137) which may therefore have been out of use at this time. The earliest ditch (134) is presumed to be Roman, although it contained no finds. The later ditches were approximately parallel or perpendicular to Ermin Street, but it is unclear whether the association between road and settlement was a close one. A single ditch, running parallel to the roadside ditch and about 2 m from it, was revealed in Evaluation Trench 1 and this may have been settlement-related. Its recut or upper fill contained some 4th-century pottery. There was no evidence for a building fronting the road in this trench, although the limitations imposed by a single evaluation trench inevitably mean that this absence cannot be regarded as definitive. However, the absence of Roman deposits or features within Evaluation Trenches 2 and 3, which effectively formed a continuous transect between the Roman road and the A419, suggests that the occupation was genuinely sparse, perhaps representing no more than a single dwelling (although the truncation of ground to the north-west by later stream channels needs to be borne in mind).

The excavated evidence was insufficient to define the nature of the site; although it was located near both road and river, there is no suggestion of a function related to either. It is worth mentioning that the Roman deposits overlay a substrate of alluvial clay, which suggests that the site may represent a late colonisation of somewhat marginal land (as has been suggested for the settlement at Birdlip Quarry, which in other respects was in a radically different location, but nonetheless a relatively well sheltered one). There is abundant evidence for Roman activity in the Upper Thames/Lower Churn area although no sites in the immediate vicinity are clearly defined (Fig. 4.37). A similar site may exist *c.* 400 m to the south-east on the line of Ermin Street (Wilts. SMR SU19SW309 – east of High Bridge) where areas of dark soil appear to be closely associated with finds of Roman metalwork (Wilts. SMR SU19SW310). The extensive, rectilinear, ditched trackways east of Weavers Bridge are undated although highly likely to be Roman given their disregard for the modern lanes and villages. They appear to be associated with individual sub-rectangular enclosures for which, again, there is only cropmark evidence, but which are plausibly Roman. At face value this may suggest an intensive exploitation of the lower terrace and floodplain, perhaps associated with a distinctive type of small, scattered settlement. A specialised pastoral emphasis to this occupation would seem a reasonable assumption on locational grounds, although much remains to be done to confirm this speculation.

## BIRDLIP QUARRY
*By Andrew Mudd*

### Introduction

The excavation of the Romano-British settlement at Birdlip Quarry was the largest on the road project. It took place within the footprint of the roundabout at the northern end of the development, just south of the modern quarry (Fig. 4.40). The site lay between 260–266 m OD occupying a south-facing slope, which included a shallow dry valley. It lay adjacent to the A417 which follows the course of Ermin Street. Due to an alteration of the road alignment and the position of the roundabout between the evaluation stage and the commencement of excavation, much of the excavated area had not been evaluated.

Approximately 1 ha was excavated in several stages (Fig. 4.41). The main area excavation which incorporated occupation Areas A–E was followed by two small trenches examining the course of Ermin Street to the north-west (Areas 1 and 4), the line of a new culvert (Area 6), and areas between the main excavation and Ermin Street (Areas 2A–C). Other deposits between the main excavation and the A417 either lay outside the development corridor, or were to be preserved *in situ*. However, another occupation area (Area 3) was found further south during a watching brief on the line of the slip road. This was subsequently extended to examine a late Roman road surface (Area 5). In addition to these excavation areas, two trenches (Ermin Street Trenches 3 and 4) were excavated as part of the programme specifically designed to examine Ermin Street. These are included in this section.

Extensive Romano-British occupation was found both on the hillslope and in the dry valley. A thin scatter

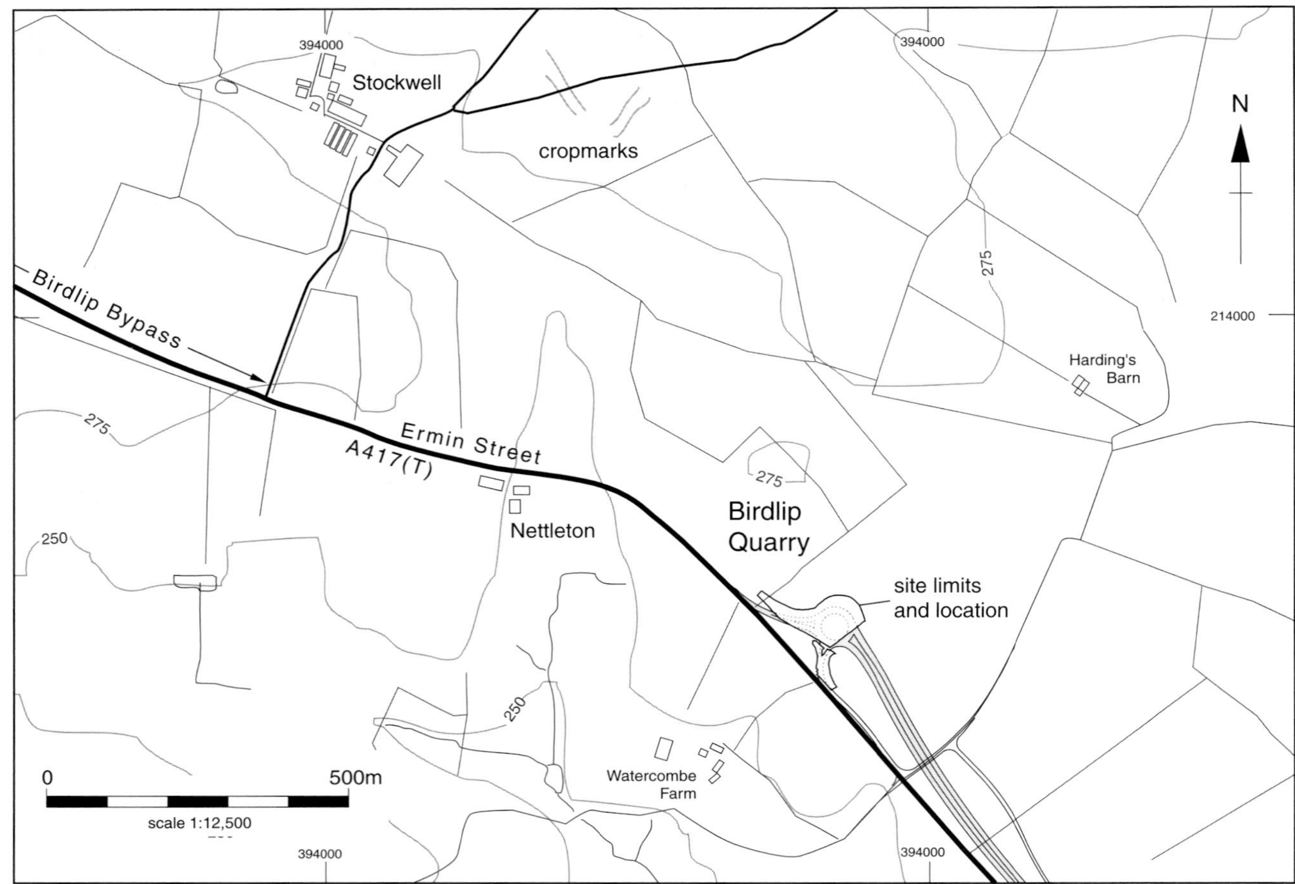


*Figure 4.40 Birdlip Quarry, site location.*

of prehistoric pits was also uncovered (Chapter 2, Fig. 2.2). The hillslope was cut on the eastern side of the site by a regular series of medieval plough furrows which became less substantial towards the top of the slope (Chapter 6, Fig. 6.8). These were probably medieval and had truncated Roman features locally. Deep ploughing was also evident at the western end of the site and ploughmarks were evident elsewhere. This later cultivation had resulted in some truncation of Roman deposits, although generally those deposits within the dry valley were exceptionally well preserved.

## Site layout

The main elements of the Romano-British settlement consisted of several discrete areas containing occupation debris (Areas A–E in the main excavation, and Area 3) concentrated particularly on the lower hillslope. These were interspersed with a pattern of shallow-ditched boundaries and enclosures. Other features were relatively sparse but included a corn dryer, three wells and a small number of pits and gullies. Evidence of structures was found within all the occupation areas, except Area B. Those on the hillslope were shown to have been located on shallow terraces.

Throughout the life of the settlement the main focus of occupation was within the dry valley in Area A where a sequence of buildings developed, set back a little from the Roman road. The sequence started with circular wooden buildings, which were later replaced by stone-founded structures, initially of circular and, in the final phases probably rectangular, form (Figs 4.44, 4.73 and 4.89). There were few ancillary features, but to the east of Area A was a small enclosure attached to a ditched trackway which ran up the hill. Both these features became redundant later on.

Another structure of apparently quite rudimentary, partly circular, form was sited in Areas C and 2C. This structure was associated with a series of ovens and a stone surface. Area D on the hillside in the centre of the site was the location of another partly circular structure which was later replaced by a structure of circular or semi-circular form. The structures were sited in the corner of a partial enclosure and were associated with a smaller probable structure of similar form to the north, and a well to the east. Area E was the site of another sequence of two rudimentary circular or partly circular buildings, again associated with a well. Part of another probable structure, this time of rectangular form, was located in Area 3, close to the edge of Ermin Street. The only other evidence of rectangular structures lay west of Area A, well back from the line of the road, although the evidence was very slight.

A possible ditched track running east-west divided the main part of the site from an enclosure to the north. The enclosure contained another well and, while without direct evidence of structures, buildings were probably located just outside the excavation area to the north-west where occupation had been suggested from the results of the evaluation.

Settlement probably did not extend significantly further west, beyond Area A, although there was greater plough truncation here. There were no significant finds or features to the east of the site.

### Phasing

The nature of the site and the way in which it was excavated in stages, required each of the separate excavation areas and each of the 'complex areas' of the main site, to be phased individually. Each 'Phase' in the following site description is therefore unique to each of the excavated areas (eg. Area 2A, Area 3, Area 4) or each of the 'complex areas' within the main excavation (eg. Area A, Area B, Area C). The latter were more or less discrete areas but were not defined physically. It was not assumed at the outset that changes and developments across the site were synchronous. The phases within each area did not include all the details of development which could be detected, but did reflect significant changes in the organisation of the settlement, including the use and abandonment of structures and areas of the site.

At the next stage the whole site (with the exception of certain areas which remained unphased) was divided into two higher order Periods. This division appeared to reflect site-wide changes which could be dated to around the middle of the 3rd century AD. Period 1 was given a start date of around AD 180 since any earlier occupation was light and the presence of structures much before this is doubtful. There were, however, deposits in Area A which pre-dated the earliest structure here and these probably dated to earlier in the 2nd century (Pre-Period 1). Period 2 started around AD 250, but this is not to say that the changes across the site need be synchronous since the dating evidence was not precise. At a later stage of analysis it was decided that subtle but significant site-wide changes could be detected within Period 2, which was consequently divided into sub-Periods 2A and 2B. The latter reflected the latest phases of the accumulation of material when most of the structures appear to have gone out of use except the third phase of building in Area 3 and those represented by the linear walls in Area A. The date range of Period 2B is difficult to estimate and again there is no compelling reason why the phases in each Area need be exactly the same. The best dating evidence comes from Area 3 where the beginning of Phase 3 has been placed in the 320s. In Area A, Phase 6 is thought to have started slightly later, at around AD 340. A compromise would suggest a site-wide change in occupation marking Period 2B can be given a start date of around AD 330.

*Plate 4.10 The Romano-British settlement at Birdlip Quarry, Cowley. The site lay beside Ermin Street (now the A417) which runs south toward Cirencester. The stonework in Area A is clearly visible, as are the medieval lynchets. The picture was taken before Areas 2, 3 and 5 had been opened up. The Iron Age site at Highgate House lies in the middle distance. Reproduced by permission of RCHME (ref. NMR 15424/03).*

*Table 4.1 Birdlip Quarry, a concordance of the phases for each Area*

| AREA | PERIOD 1 Phase | PERIOD 2A Phase | PERIOD 2B Phase |
|---|---|---|---|
| A | 2 | 3–5 | 6 |
| B | 1–3 | 4–5 | 6 |
| C | 1 | 2 | 3 |
| D | 1 | 2 | 3 |
| E | 1 | 2 | 3 |
| 1 (Ermin St) | 1–3? | 3? | 3? |
| 2A (Ermin St) | 1–2? | 2–3 | 4 |
| 2B–2C | 1–2 | 3–5 | 6 |
| 3 | 1 | 2 | 3 |
| 5 (with Ermin St Tr.3) | 1 | 2 | 3 |
| 6 (Ermin St) | 1 | 2 | 3 |

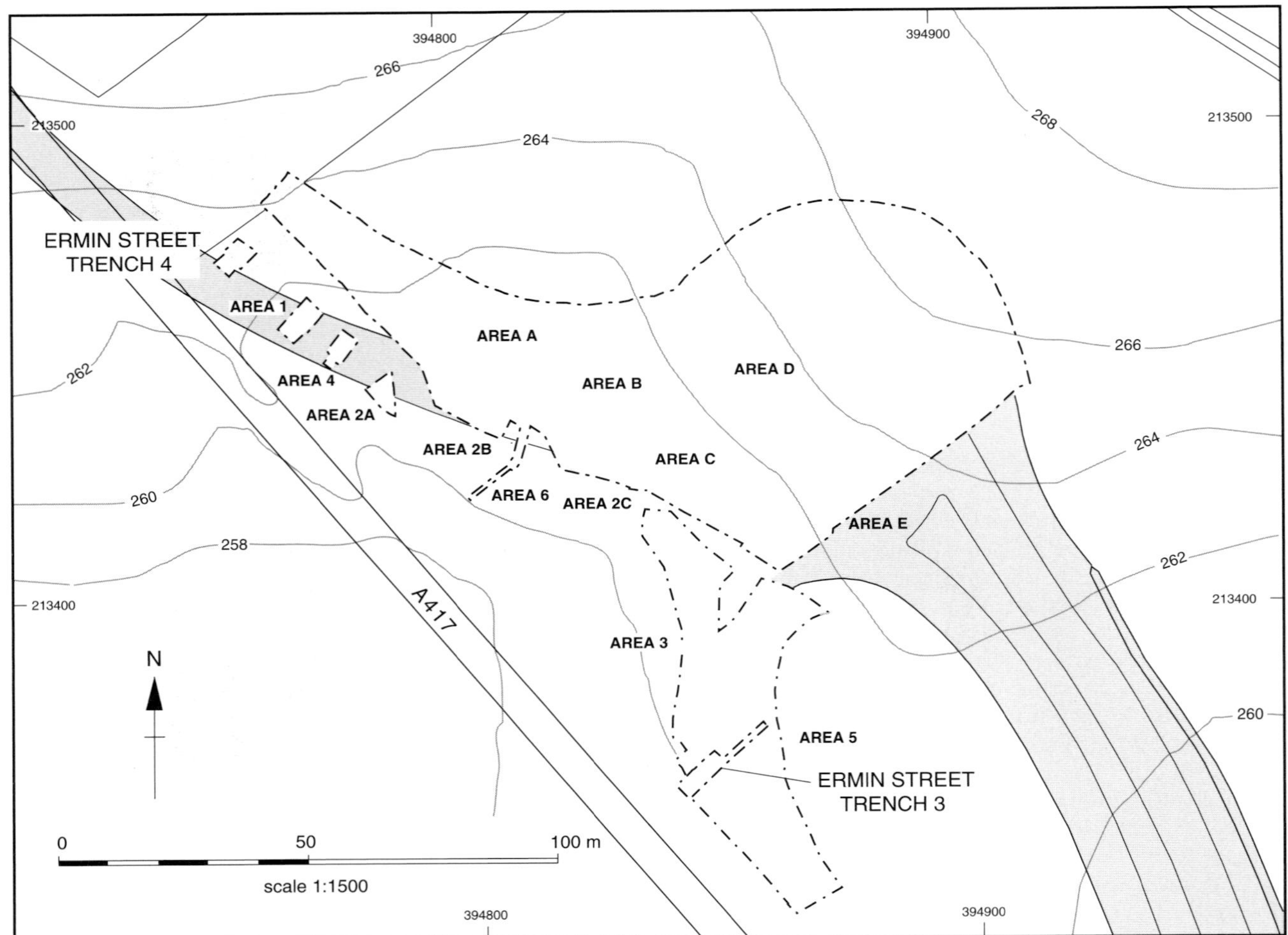


*Figure 4.41 Birdlip Quarry, site plan showing individual excavation areas (1–6) and foci of occupation in the main site.*

The end date is thought to be not much later than AD 370/380, although this might be pushed forward to *c.* AD 390 taking the single Theodosian coin as evidence. The approximate dates are therefore: Period 1 AD 180–250, Period 2A AD 250–330, and Period 2B AD 330–380.

**Structure of report**

The following description of the site is ordered chronologically as far as possible. The trenches which examined Ermin Street are described and discussed at the end of the section, since, with the exception of Area 5, their phasing does not neatly tie in with that from the main site and they form a convenient group. The descriptive section is followed by a discussion of the finds in relation to the site. The interrogation of the database and the plotting of spatial data was undertaken using Dominic Powlesland's G-sys GIS/GDMS programme. Some of the results are discussed as a demonstration of the potential of this technique for the examination of site data in a way which is seldom attempted on sites of this period. It was also felt that the unusual quality of preservation of deposits in the dry valley justified particular attention to the distribution of finds in and around the structures in Area A. The spatial analyses indicate the value of this line of enquiry as a tool for identifying some characteristics of site deposits, and as an aid to understanding the nature of the settlement and its inhabitants.

**Pre-period 1: 2nd century AD?**

Activity was represented by a probable hollow way and a small group of features which pre-dated the earliest structure in Area A.

***Areas A, 2B and 2C: Phase 1***

*Hollow way (Fig. 4.42)*

A discontinuous and diffuse layer of stones, 1151, lay in a slight hollow in the natural silt-clay on the western side of the dry valley. The hollow ran up hill, north of the later penannular ditches, with the stones continuing as layer 1148. Layer 1139 was probably part of the same spread although the fact that it formed a more solid surface outside the later ditch 1450, suggests that it was also associated with the first

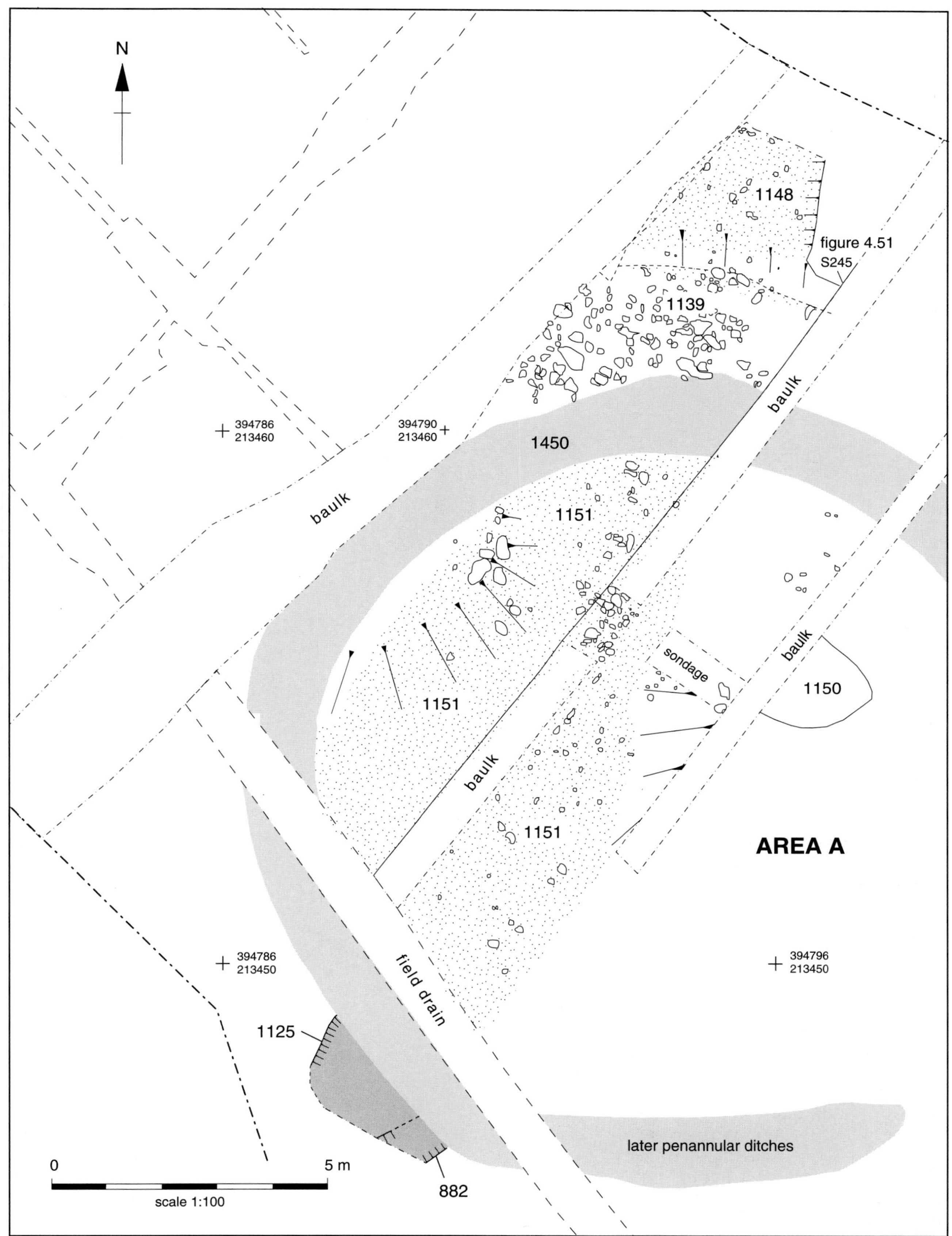


*Figure 4.42 Birdlip Quarry, pre-period 1 hollow way and other features in Area A.*

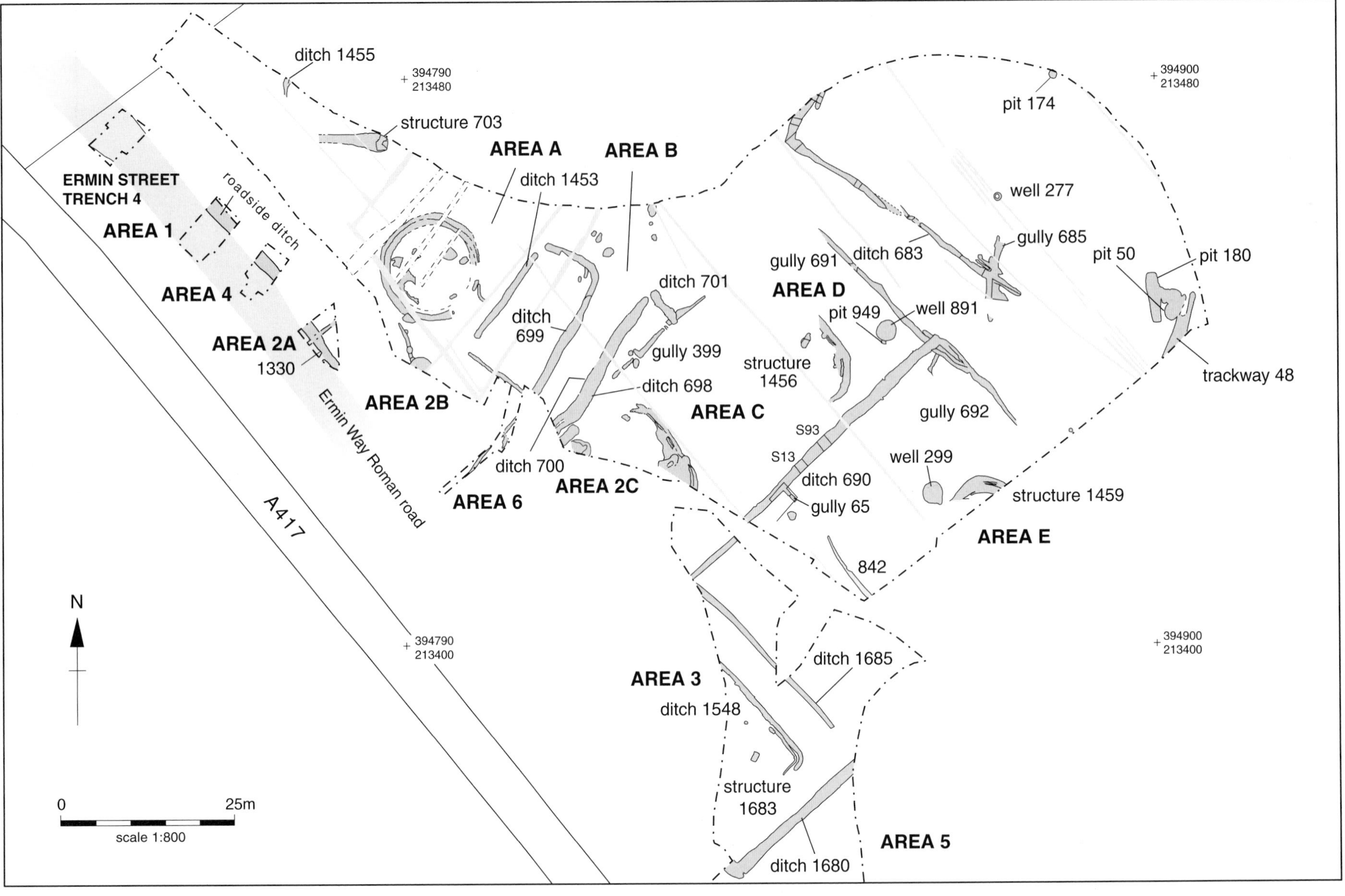


*Figure 4.43 Birdlip Quarry, plan of excavated features, period 1.*

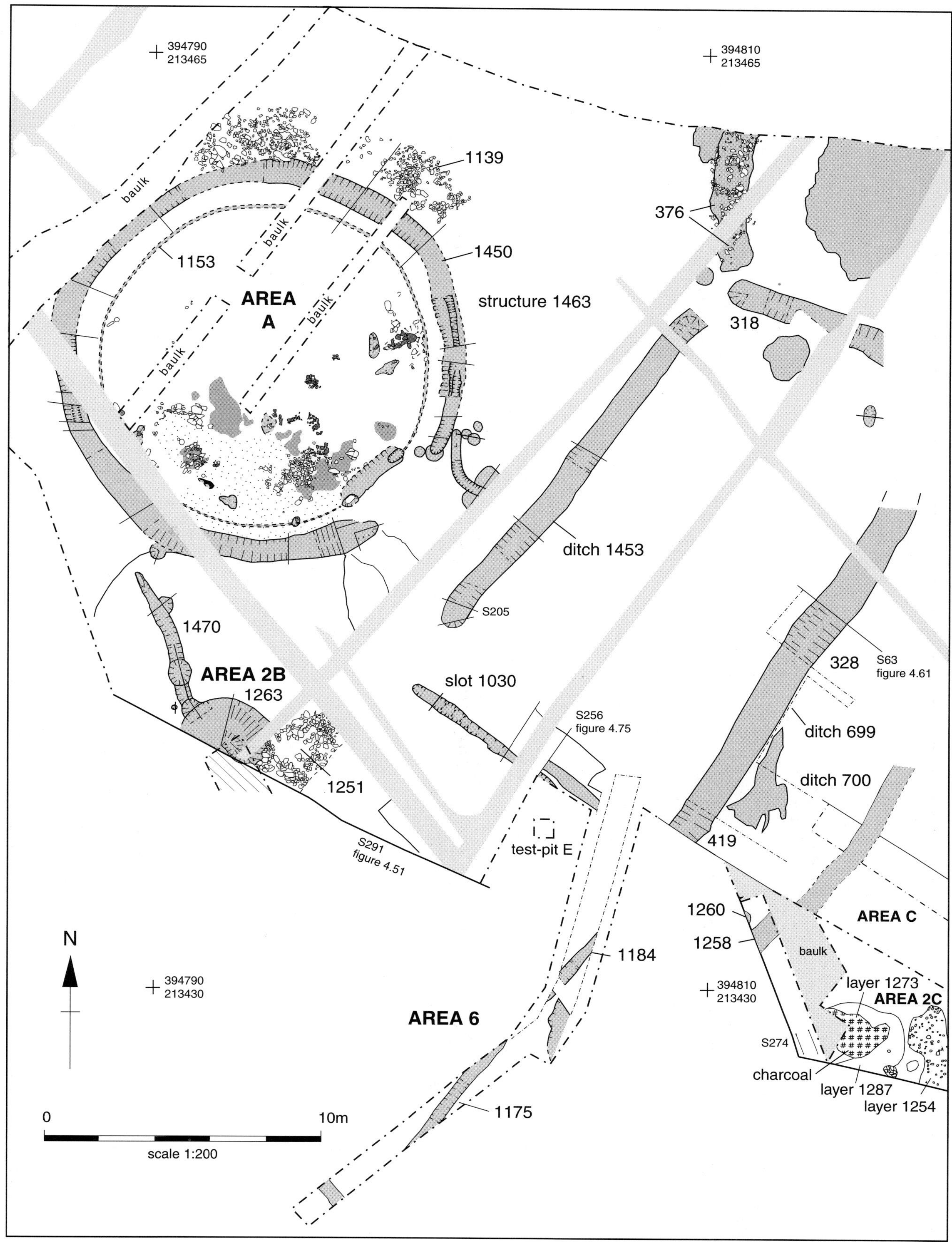


*Figure 4.44 Birdlip Quarry, period 1, phase 2A, structure 1463 (Area A).*

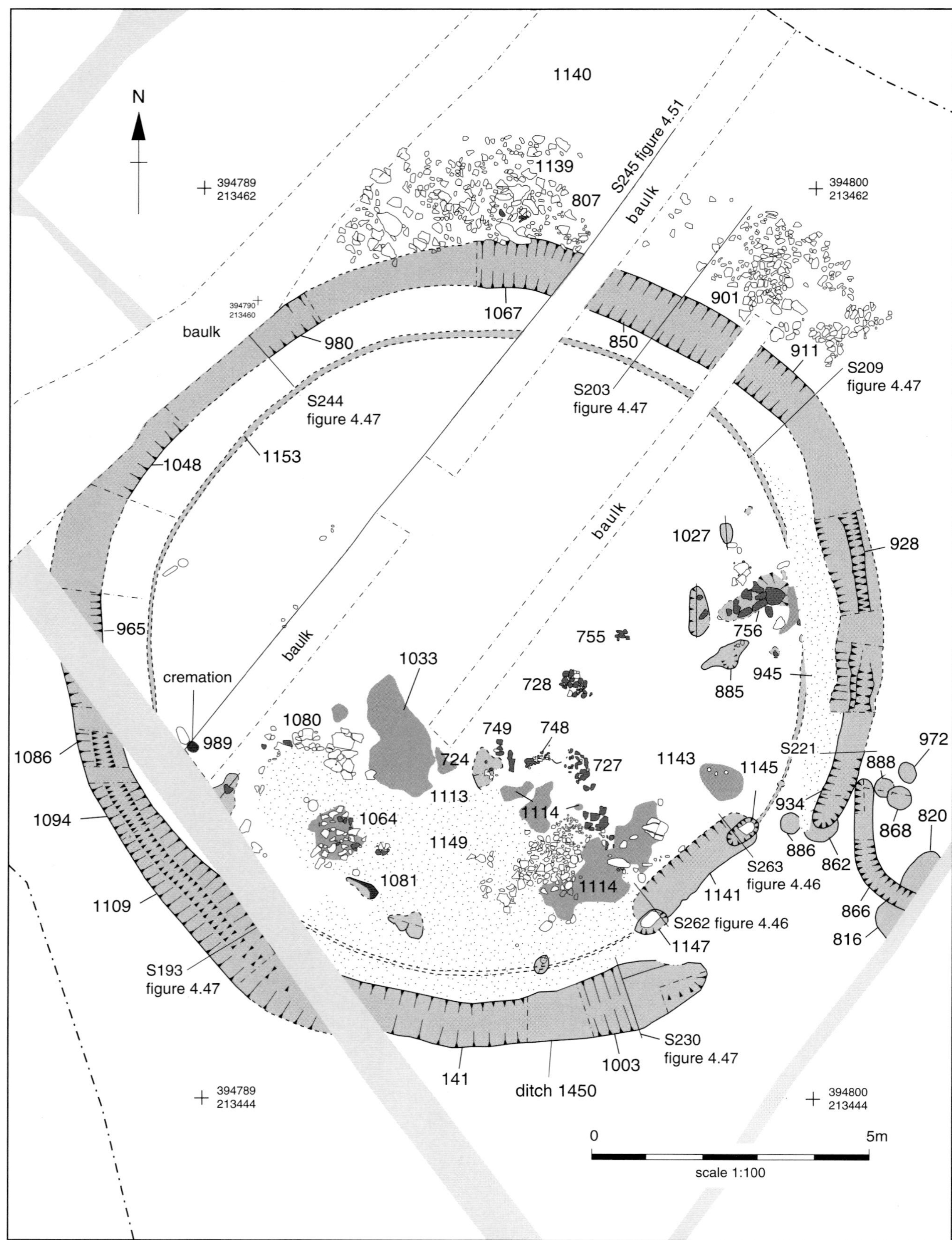


*Figure 4.45 Birdlip Quarry, plan of structure 1463.*

building here (below, Phase 2A). The hollow itself is interpreted as an eroded 'hollow way' leading up the slope. The stones in layer 1151 were angular or sub-angular without indication of wear, suggesting that they were a later surfacing within the hollow, although it is possible that they were a more fortuitous accumulation caused by erosion higher up the slope.

The hollow was filled with a largely stone-free yellowish brown clayey silt with grey mottles (layer 994) which was 0.1–0.2 m thick, homogeneous and appeared to represent a natural accumulation (Fig. 4.51, section 245). The deposit contained pottery of the 2nd century AD and animal bone. Close dating of the pottery is not possible, but it may be of the mid, or even earlier 2nd century in order to accommodate a natural infilling of the hollow way before the first structure was built. Alternatively, the deposit might have been made ground to fill the hollow immediately prior to the construction of the first structure. A logical explanation would see it as having been derived from cutting into the hill face to create the terrace on which the structure was to stand, but in terms of the observed soils, layer 994 did not appear to be dumping and did not contain stones as surely it would have if it had been derived from terracing. A similar deposit, 1150, occupied a hollow of negligible depth to the east. The evidence seems to indicate a period of abandonment of the use of the hollow way in the earlier 2nd century AD and natural infilling.

The date of the use of the hollow way cannot be estimated. Pottery from colluvial layer 1140 (which appeared to slightly overlie the stony layer 1148 shown on Figure 4.42) contained an assemblage of pottery which may belong to the earlier 2nd century (possibly relating to activity further up the hill), but the hollow way may have had its origin much earlier.

*Pit 1125 and feature 882 (Fig. 4.42)*

The sharply rectangular corner of a probable pit, 1125, was revealed on the south-western edge of Area A. It was estimated to have extended for about 3 m in a north-west – south-east direction although it had been truncated on its northern side by penannular ditch 1450 and on its southern side by feature 882. It was 0.4 m deep and flat-based and it was filled with a notably pale yellowish brown silt-clay (1124) without diagnostic finds. Its date is unclear but it may be early Roman.

Feature 882 was heavily truncated by the penannular ditches of the later structures. It was of indeterminate shape but considered likely to have been a shallow ditch (0.23 m deep) running south-west – north-east. It may have been connected with the later penannular ditches as its upper surface (712) contained a few sherds of 3rd-century pot. Its primary fill (890) was without finds. It was not traced any further south-west in Area 2.

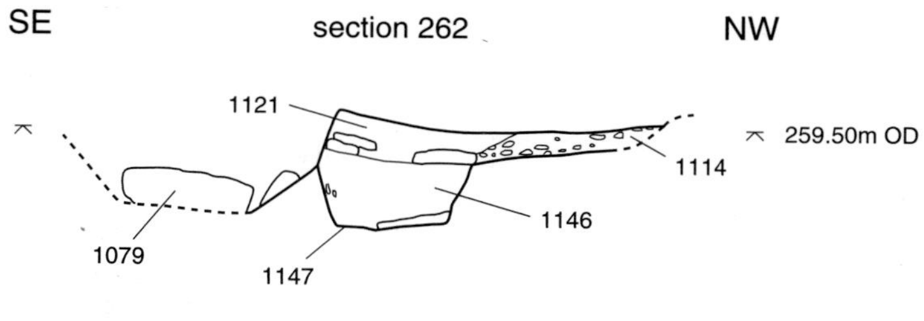


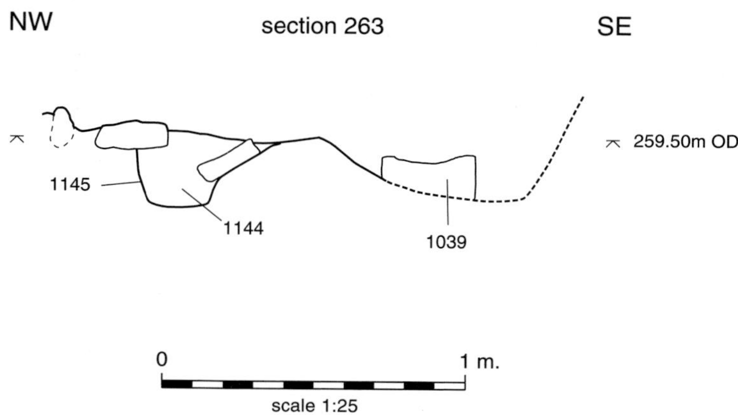


*Figure 4.46 Birdlip Quarry, entrance postholes, sections.*

*Soil layers in Areas 2B and 2C*

In these areas there was no clear indication of features pre-dating the roundhouses of Phase 2. This absence includes the hollow way which was not definable south of Area A and may have become much more diffuse. Instead the area contained a series of soil layers with few finds overlying undisturbed colluvium. These were compact light brown, mottled mid brown silts with progressively more orange-brown flecking towards the base of the sequence. The earliest soils, 1283 and 1284 were undated (Fig. 4.51, section 291). These may be identified with a general early soil horizon, which includes 1126 (datable to the 2nd century) further north (Fig. 4.75, section 256). Layer 1268 (Fig. 4.51, section 291, North) is approximately equivalent and yielded an assemblage of pottery dated to AD 150–250. A coin (cat. 292) of AD 193–211 was recorded as coming from the top of this layer at the interface with 1225.

**Period 1: c. AD 180–250**

The main occupation on the site started in this Period. It consisted of a layout of structures and ditches across the hillside (Fig. 4.43).

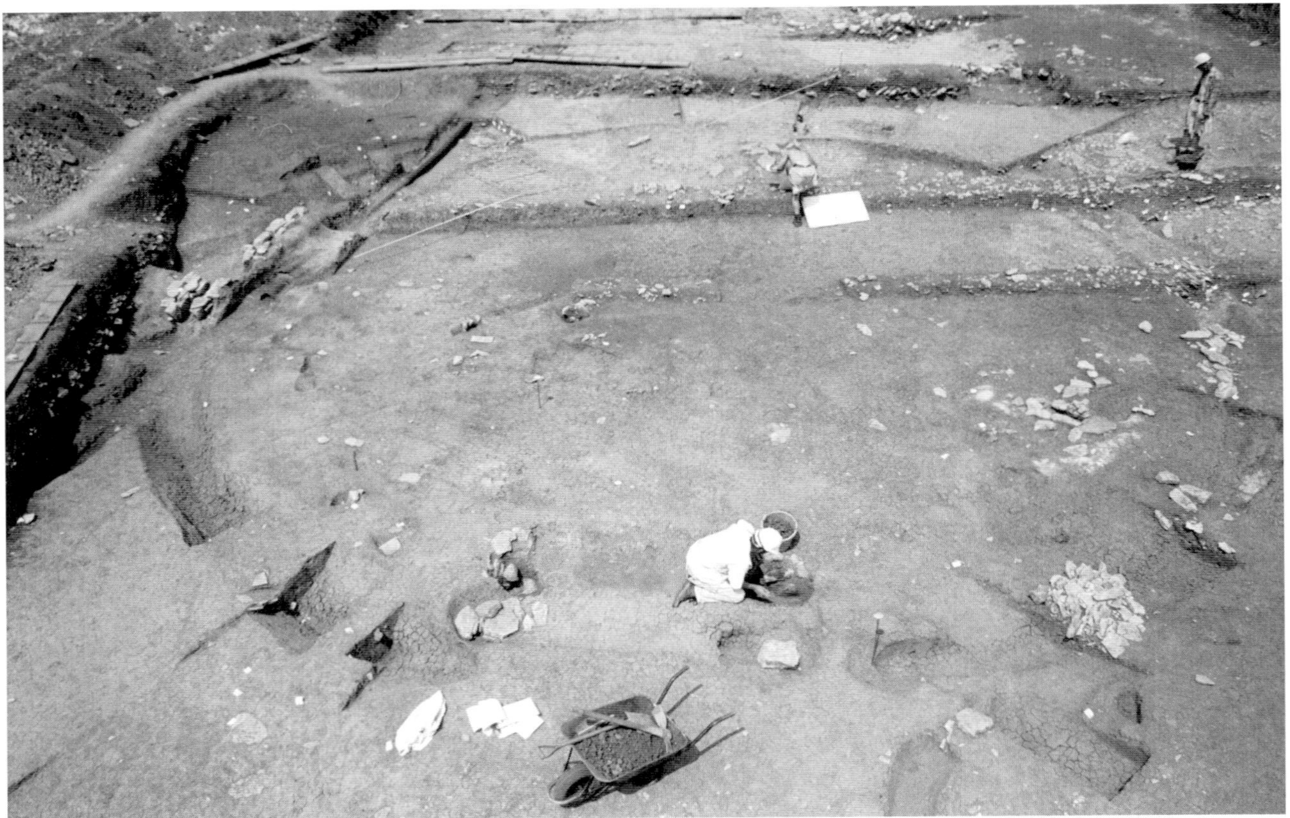

*Plate 4.11 Area A roundhouses. The earlier pair of entrance postholes under excavation (structure 1463) lie inside the later pair (structure 1464).*

***Areas A and 2B: Phase 2A** (Figs 4.44–45)*

The silting up of the hollow way was followed by the cutting of a terrace for a roundhouse platform, the construction of the first roundhouse (structure 1463) and the excavation of the first penannular drainage ditch (1450).

*Stony layer 1139 (Figs 4.44–4.45)*

Stone layer 1139 formed a skirt around the outside of ditch 1450 (segment 1067 in this part of the site) and appears therefore to have been associated with the ditch although it lay partly within the hollow way. However, rubble layer 1128 and layer 807 (Fig. 4.51, section 245), a dark yellowish brown clay-silt with some stones, which were both interpreted as upcast from the ditch, overlay 1139 showing that the excavation of the ditch put the stone surface out of use. Layer 1139 may originally have been related to the hollow way but appears to have been repaired and extended for use during the construction of the roundhouse. It had a rather more worn appearance than layer 1151 (the stones within the hollow way). It was then cut through and covered over when the ditch was dug. Layer 901 of larger stone slabs appeared to seal ditch upcast and was probably contemporary with the ditch.

*Structure 1463 (Fig. 4.45)*

The drainage ditch 1450 formed a near-circle of about 13 m in diameter internally with an entrance gap to the south-east. The ditch was from a little under 0.3 m to 0.4 m deep (being shallower on the northern side) with a generally steep-sided and round-based profile (Fig. 4.47, sections 193, 230, 244, 209 and 203). Although the later recut 1451 resulted in some truncation, 1450 was the deeper and its course was reasonably clear even on the southern side where the later cut followed the alignment of 1450 precisely.

Within the enclosure formed by the ditch was the trace of a circular wall of stakes (1153), 12 m in diameter, which butted a pair of door posts (1147 and 1145). The stake wall was a subtle feature which only became apparent under favourable moisture conditions. It was not visible as a continuous ring, but enough survived to be sure of its interpretation. On the northern side, the excavation of the underlying layer 994 had already commenced before the stake wall was recognised. Although initially a ring of postholes was also suspected, exploratory investigations failed to identify any convincing ones. The line of stakeholes did not appear to be set in a gully but formed a ragged line through the stakes having been driven into the ground close together. The 'gully' effect was therefore created by the disturbance of the upper part of the stakeholes,

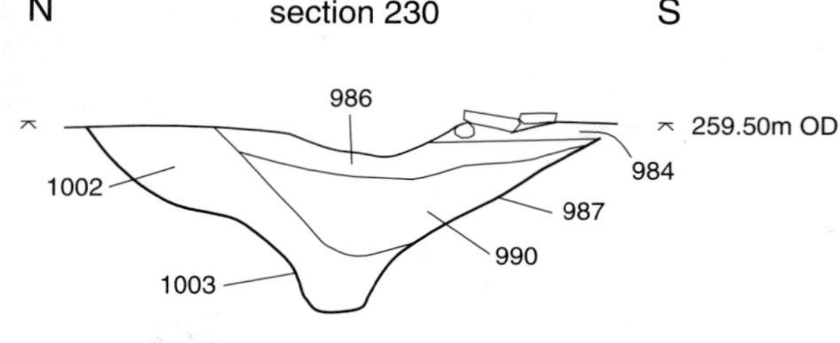


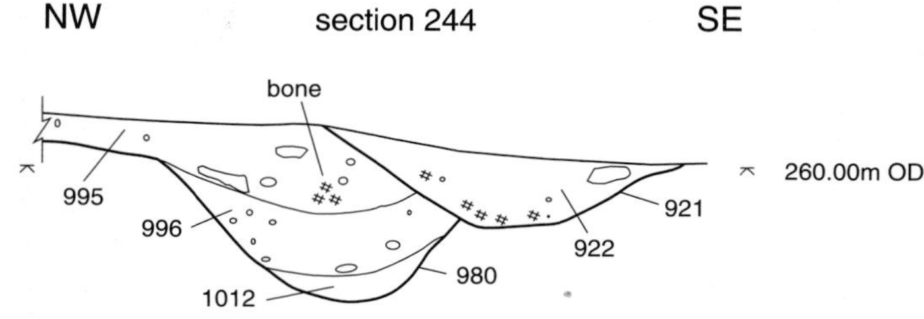


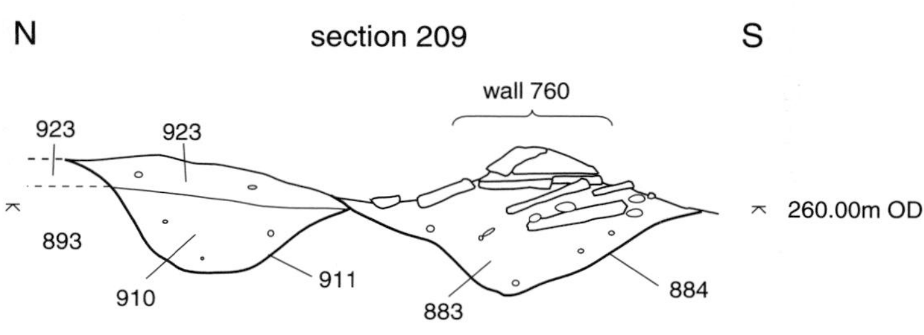


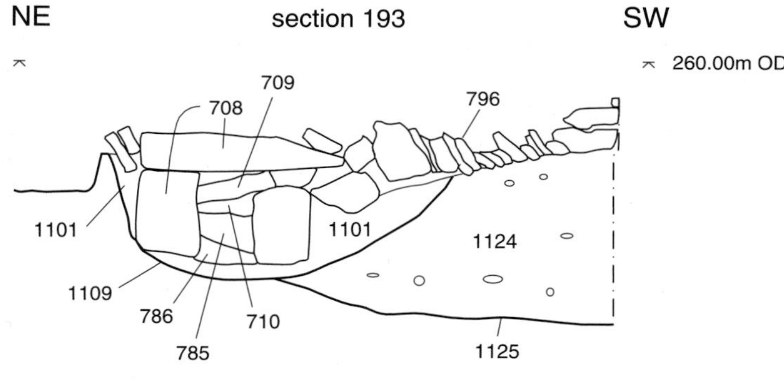


presumably when the stakes were removed. The stakes had been driven to a depth of *c.* 0.2 m through a low mound on the inner lip of the ditch (layers 945 and 1149). This mound was not considered to be upcast spoil but probably an area of relatively protected ground at the edge of the sequence of roundhouses which had not been subjected to wear like the interior area.

There was no indication of any roof supports. The door-posts (Fig. 4.45–4.46), to which the stake wall would have been attached, were set in postholes 2.2 m apart and 0.25 m deep linked by a shallow threshold or sill (1141). The postholes themselves were oval in shape (0.3 m by 0.6 m) suggesting that they each might have held a pair of posts. The door frame might then have been separate from the wall posts to which the stake wall would have been attached. However, each posthole contained a single flat stone post-pad and it is possible that it contained just the one post. Although the postholes were quite shallow, it must be assumed that the door frame was sufficiently rigid when attached to the stake wall. The threshold was very shallow (0.07 m at the most) and was filled with flagstones which had been pressed into the natural clay-silt. The relationship between these threshold stones and the postholes suggested that the stones represented an infilling of a shallow slot which may well have held a wooden sill beam. This may have been joined to the door frame to help maintain rigidity. The stones themselves would therefore relate to the consolidation of the ground in the subsequent structural phase.

Gully 866 (=818) formed a small 'antenna' at the entrance. It had unclear relationships with adjacent features. It was probably more or less contemporary with pit 862 which may have been a recut of the terminal of 1450 (segment 934) rather than a pit. A number of other shallow pits clustered in this area (pits 886, 868, 888, 972, 816 and 820). The latter two contained abundant limestone (like

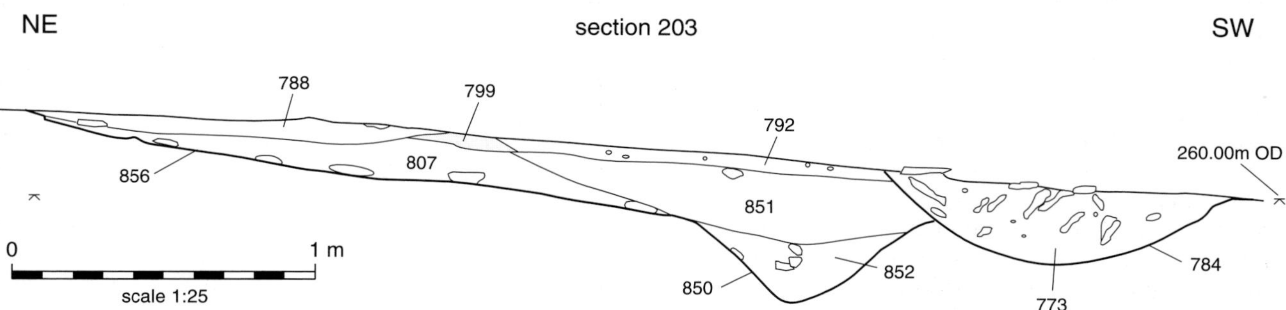


*Figure 4.47 Birdlip Quarry, penannular ditches, 1450 and 1451, sections.*

*Plate 4.12 Area A roundhouse. The picture shows the later entrance postholes and interior flooring.*

gully 818) and may have been infilled immediately prior to laying floor 802 in the subsequent phase. The phasing of the others is unclear. The purpose or purposes of these pits are not known. They may have held small posts, probably free-standing since they form no pattern. However, a probable storage or dedicatory vessel 943 came from a similar-sized pit in this area (below, Phase 4 pit 942), and it seems possible that these pits contained stored items or dedicatory deposits of a perishable nature.

On the south-western side of the interior of the roundhouse a substantial part of a 2nd-century greyware vessel (978) containing a small quantity of cremated human bone was discovered in a pit (989) close to the wall line (Fig. 4.45). The rim of the vessel was missing suggesting that it had protruded above the original ground surface. It is possible that this deposit was associated with a 'back door' although it is unclear whether or not the stone culvert 708 (assigned Phase 2B – Fig. 4.49) existed in the first phase of penannular ditch. Alternatively the cremation may have been deposited in Phase 2B and associated with the culvert itself, although this may be stretching the dating evidence somewhat.

In general it was impossible to be sure whether interior deposits and features were associated with the first or second of the roundhouses. The dating evidence from artefacts was not precise enough to discriminate between the two phases. However, there was some suggestion of relative phasing from the stratigraphy of floor deposits and burnt areas and those relating to the earlier phase are shown in Figure 4.45. The occupation layers overlying the floors can be shown to be related to the Phase 2B roundhouse (structure 1464), and these are described below. It appears that the interior of structure 1463 was generally kept clean, or had been cleaned out at the end of the occupation.

There were traces of prepared floor layers within the roundhouse although none was extensive and their distribution was patchy. It is unclear how extensive the original flooring was, but it seems unlikely that it ever covered most of the interior of the building. A 'mortar' floor of fine crushed limestone mixed with yellowish silt was laid just inside the main entrance (layer 1114) and also on the south-west side (layers 831 and 836, shown as Phase 2B – Fig. 4.49). This floor also had a surfacing of small, flat limestone pieces near the main entrance (layer 925). Layer 1009 (shown as Phase 2B – Fig. 4.49) towards the back of the structure was a much more mixed deposit of compact brown silt with patches of 'mortar', burnt clay and burnt stone. It was interpreted as a mixed and trampled floor layer, which had perhaps been subjected to heavy wear.

Hollow 1064 was a roughly circular depression on the south-western side of the roundhouse. It reached a depth of only 0.02-0.03 m and is likely to have been an eroded hollow rather than a cut feature. It contained a concentration of limestone slabs and tegulae within a matrix of greyish brown silt (Fig. 4.45).

Three patches of fire-reddened clay floor, 724, 1033 and 1080, were found close together in the south-western area of the roundhouse and are likely to belong to the same event (Fig. 4.45). They may originally have been contiguous. This was the largest area of burning within the roundhouses. It was strati-graphically very early, underlying floor 836 and was certainly of Phase 2A, conceivably earlier. No deposits or finds were associated with this activity and it appears that the area had been swept clean before floor 836 was laid.

Hearth 756 was an area of burnt limestone slabs on the north-eastern side of the floor. The feature had been almost completely destroyed with one large fractured slab and two possible edging stones the only remaining parts of the structure still *in situ*. The soil under and among the stones (1127) had been burnt red and appeared also to have filled a small slot at the base of the feature. Dark ashy soil with burnt stones (918) was spread around the feature and similar material was present in nearby hollows which showed no sign of *in situ* burning and are therefore likely to have been filled with debris from this feature. The feature therefore appears to have been abandoned and possibly deliberately destroyed relatively early, although there is no specific reason why it should be associated with Phase 2A rather than 2B.

Hearth 727 comprised several patches which were probably all part of the same spread of quite small, burnt stones forming a crescent. They overlay a spread of burnt material, 1104. The hearth was cut by a pitched stone 'setting' 747 (assigned to phase 4), and could belong with Phase 2A or 2B (Fig. 4.45).

Hearth 728 was a small circular patch of burnt stone within a shallow cut (1032). It had no relationship with adjacent unburnt stone patches.

Hearth 749 was a very small patch of fire-reddened stone probably cut by posthole 1113 (assigned Phase 2B) and overlain by floor 722 (Phase 4).

Deposit 755 (=1022) was a small collection of burnt stones, although since there were a few unburnt ones present it is possible that the burning was not *in situ* (Fig. 4.45).

### *Dating evidence*

There was little dating evidence from the primary fills of ditch 1450, even where it was distinct from ditch 1451 and where primary and secondary fills could be distinguished. From segments 1067 and 850 a total of ten sherds from the primary fills are of broadly 2nd-century AD date. Later the ditch appears to have been infilled deliberately. The best evidence for this comes from segment 1067 (Fig. 4.51, section 245) where fill 915 was essentially a dump of natural clay-silt which filled the ditch and was spread over the outer edge, presumably to raise the ground level. An assemblage of 19 sherds suggested a date of *c.* AD 180–250. Similar material from segment 980 (fill 995) yielded a more general 2nd / 3rd-century date, while terminal 934 contained nine 2nd-century sherds and levelling layers 792 and 788 (Fig. 4.47, section 203) contained eight 2nd-century sherds each. The pottery cannot provide dating precision, but the overall conclusion that the building went out of use around AD 200, is consistent with the evidence for the later chronology. The date of the construction of the roundhouse is even more difficult to estimate. The entrance postholes were filled with stony greyish brown silts with yellowish patches suggesting that they had been infilled after the posts had been removed. There was no indication of a post-pipe. The pottery from 1146 (posthole 1147) was datable to the late 2nd / early 3rd century which is consistent with the date for the dismantling of the building. The ditch upcast layer 807 which contained an assemblage of 42 sherds was only broadly datable to the later 2nd / early 3rd century. If a 20-year lifespan for the building is considered reasonable, it may have been constructed around AD 180, although the evidence could accommodate a date of 20 years either side of this.

### *Ditch 1453 (Fig. 4.44)*

To the east of the roundhouses, the earlier of two phases of ditch ran north-west – south-east for 15 m. This was dug slightly deeper than its replacement, but it was truncated along its entire length and there was little or no dating evidence from most of the segments. Its infilling can, however, be dated to *c.* AD 180–250 (fill 998) so it appears to be broadly contemporary with the Phase 2 structures.

### *Slot 1030=1282/1169 (Fig. 4.44)*

A narrow, well-defined slot (1030) ran along the southern edge of Area A. This was later defined as feature 1169 in Area 6 and feature 1282 in Area 2B where it cut soil layer 1283 (Fig. 4.51, section 291). Here it was examined in a small section on the edge of the previously-excavated Area A (Fig. 4.75, section 256). It had very steep, straight sides and a flat base and ran south-east from a clearly-defined terminal for more than 10 m. The function of this slot remains unclear. It was initially thought to be a beam-slot, but the later excavation showed it to be unassociated with any structural features either parallel or at right-angles to it. It is probably best interpreted as a drainage gully, but its sharp profile indicates that it is likely to have been timber-lined. Although its relationship with ditch 1182 (= 1184 / 1175 in Area 6) lay outside the excavation, it is considered likely that it ran into this larger ditch or its earlier version 1186 at right-angles. The slope of 1030 was very gentle, dropping only about 0.10 m over its exposed length.

In Area A the feature was demonstrably strati-graphically early and the primary fill 1061 of 1030 yielded 2nd-century pottery. Two coins dated to AD 193–211 (cat. 290 and 293) were recorded as coming from just above this fill in Area 2B (layer 1266), but the levels suggest that they might have come from the top of the fill. It is possible, then, that the gully went out of use around or shortly after AD 200. Two fragments of a late 3rd- / 4th-century jar were recorded as coming from the upper fill of 1282 (1281) but seem more likely to have derived from an overlying layer, 1227. There appears to be some unreliability in the provenance of finds from segment 1282. A glass bead (cat. 663), was also recorded as coming from this fill although its level indicates that it must have come from higher up. In Area 6, 1169 cut a clean, light yellowish brown subsoil, 1180 (Fig. 4.100, section 268). It was also recorded as cutting an undifferentiated dark brown 'occupation' layer 1168, although since this layer (=1167) was generally dated to after the mid 3rd century, there is an obvious inconsistency here and it is possible that this relationship was not correctly observed.

*Gully 1407 (Fig. 4.44)*

A shallow, slightly sinuous gully, just 0.08–0.11 m deep, ran south-east from an ill-defined terminal just south of the roundhouses. It was excavated in several segments as it was initially thought to represent a series of discrete features, but is best interpreted as a single gully with irregular edges. Its function is obscure and its stratigraphic position somewhat uncertain. It appeared to be cut by pit 1263 (whose date of origin is not clear but which is assigned to Phase 2B, Period 1, and its infilling to Phases 3–4, Period 2). The gully is thought likely to have cut layer 1268, although its edges were not at all clear until 1268 had been removed. A date in the late 2nd or early 3rd century would fit reasonably well in the overall stratigraphic sequence although it cannot be determined to which sub-phase it belonged. If it were contemporary with the use of pit 1263, it may be seen as the trace of a walkway, perhaps originally of wood, between a back entrance of structure 1463 and the pit.

*Stone surface 1251 (Fig. 4.44)*

A small spread of stone (1251) overlay soil layer 1268 on the southern edge of Area 2B extending beyond the excavation area (Fig. 4.51, section 291). The feature was cut by pit 1263 and possibly by gully 1293. The stones lay mainly flat and were worn on the upper surface. While apparently serving as some sort of surface, their precise purpose is unclear and they do not appear related to any other features here or in Area A.

***Areas A and 2B : Phase 2B** (Figs 4.48–50)*

After structure 1463 had gone out of use and the penannular ditch had been infilled, it was replaced in an almost identical position by structure 1464. A new penannular ditch was dug and a floor of stone flags laid at the entrance.

*Structure 1464 (Fig. 4.49)*

The new penannular ditch (1451) was located slightly inside the earlier ditch on the northern and western sides but almost precisely cut it elsewhere. A new pair of door posts (1079 and 1039) were positioned just inside the earlier pair (Fig. 4.50, sections 239 and 247). Although there was no trace of a stake wall associated with the new ditch, it is certain that the whole structure would have been replaced as the new ditch cut the earlier stake wall alignment. The new ditch was generally shallower and with a more rounded profile than the earlier one. Each segment also tended to have a single homogeneous fill which appeared to represent a deliberate infill. In particular the pitched stone in fill 773 (segment 784) would seem to be clear evidence of this (Fig. 4.47, section 203).

On the south-west side a stone-lined culvert (708), inserted into the ditch circuit, is likely to be of this phase, although at this point the ditches of both phases coincided. It is possible that the culvert was simply inserted into the earlier ditch. The culvert was 3.5 m long, constructed of parallel rows of roughly squared limestone blocks set on edge. Capstones were present at the southern end and are likely to have been robbed from elsewhere. There was no bonding but a number of the stones had been wedged upright with smaller stones. Eight of the larger stones showed fire-reddening, generally, though not exclusively, around the bottom edge. Since the wedging stones were not reddened it seems likely that the burning relates to an earlier use. The culvert was filled with layers of greyish brown and orange-brown silts, probably representing *in situ* accumulation.

Stone floor 802 *(Fig. 4.49)*

A floor of limestone slabs (802) was laid at the entrance to the roundhouse sealing the 'antenna' gully 866. The pottery from beneath this floor was quite plentiful (66 sherds) and exclusively 2nd-century. It was interpreted as a deposit of rubbish associated with the earlier structure.

Midden deposits 986, 984, 803, 780 *(Fig. 4.49)*

A series of dark soils outside and on the southern side of the entrance are interpreted as a midden associated with structure 1464. Layer 984 contained worn fragments of horizontally laid limestones and may have been a remnant floor layer associated with the roundhouse. Above it layer 803 consisted of more tightly-packed stones although those did not form a good surface and may represent dumping. Although they form a stratified sequence which filled the top of ditch 1451, and were therefore initially assumed to belong to the later phases of occupation here, the dating of the large assemblages of pottery from each of these deposits consistently falls within the period AD 180–250 and must therefore belong with Phase 2. It must be assumed that the midden material was used to infill the top of the adjacent ditch to consolidate the ground at the end of Phase 2. A deliberate infilling accords with the evidence from the other ditch segments.

An alternative explanation is that all these layers represent a continuous *in situ* accumulation of rubbish during the life of the structure 1464. This seems less likely, particularly as stone layer 803 appeared to have been deliberately packed into the ditch and the infilling would effectively have put the ditch out of use as a drainage feature.

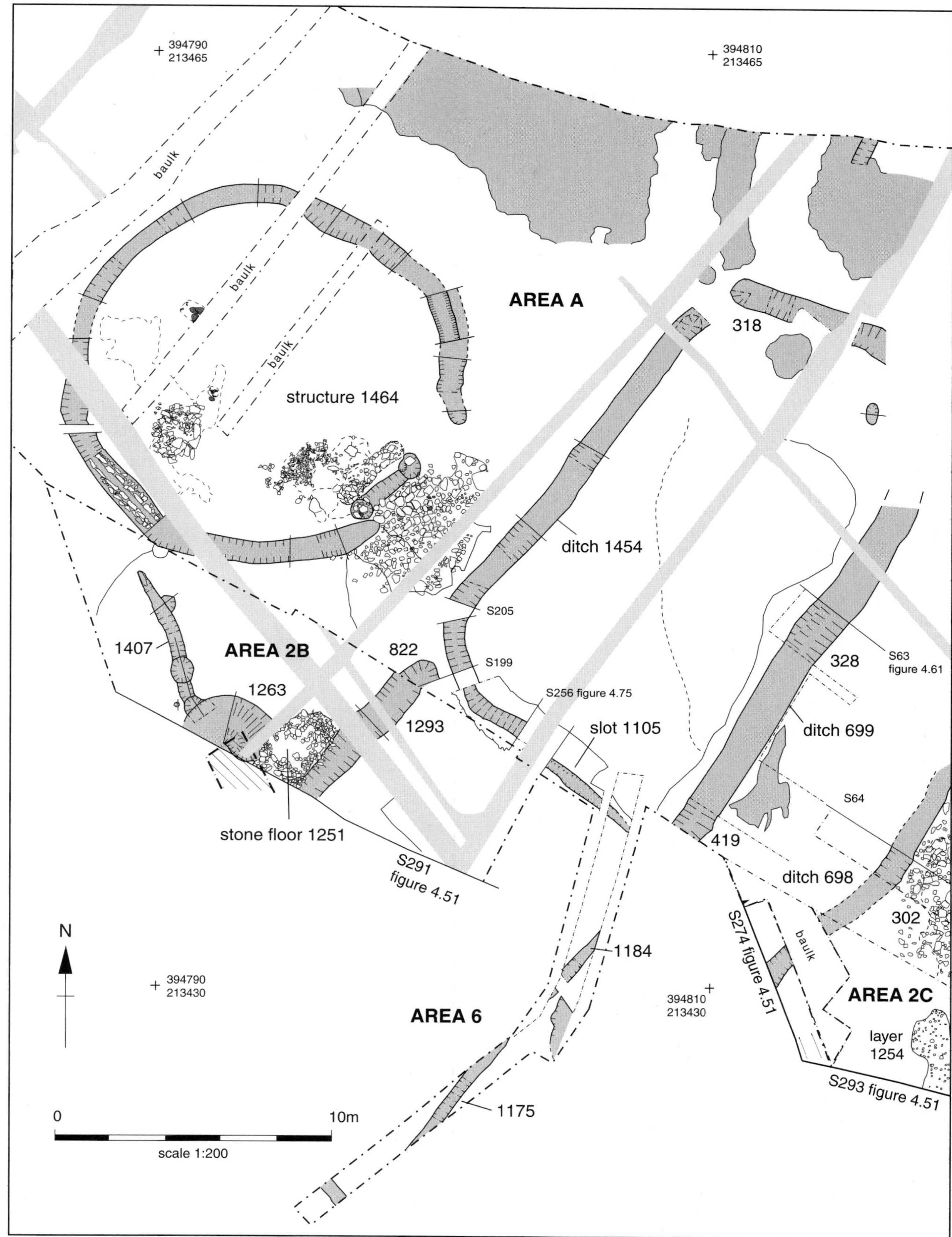


*Figure 4.48 Birdlip Quarry, period 1, phase 2B, structure 1464 (Area A) and nearby features.*

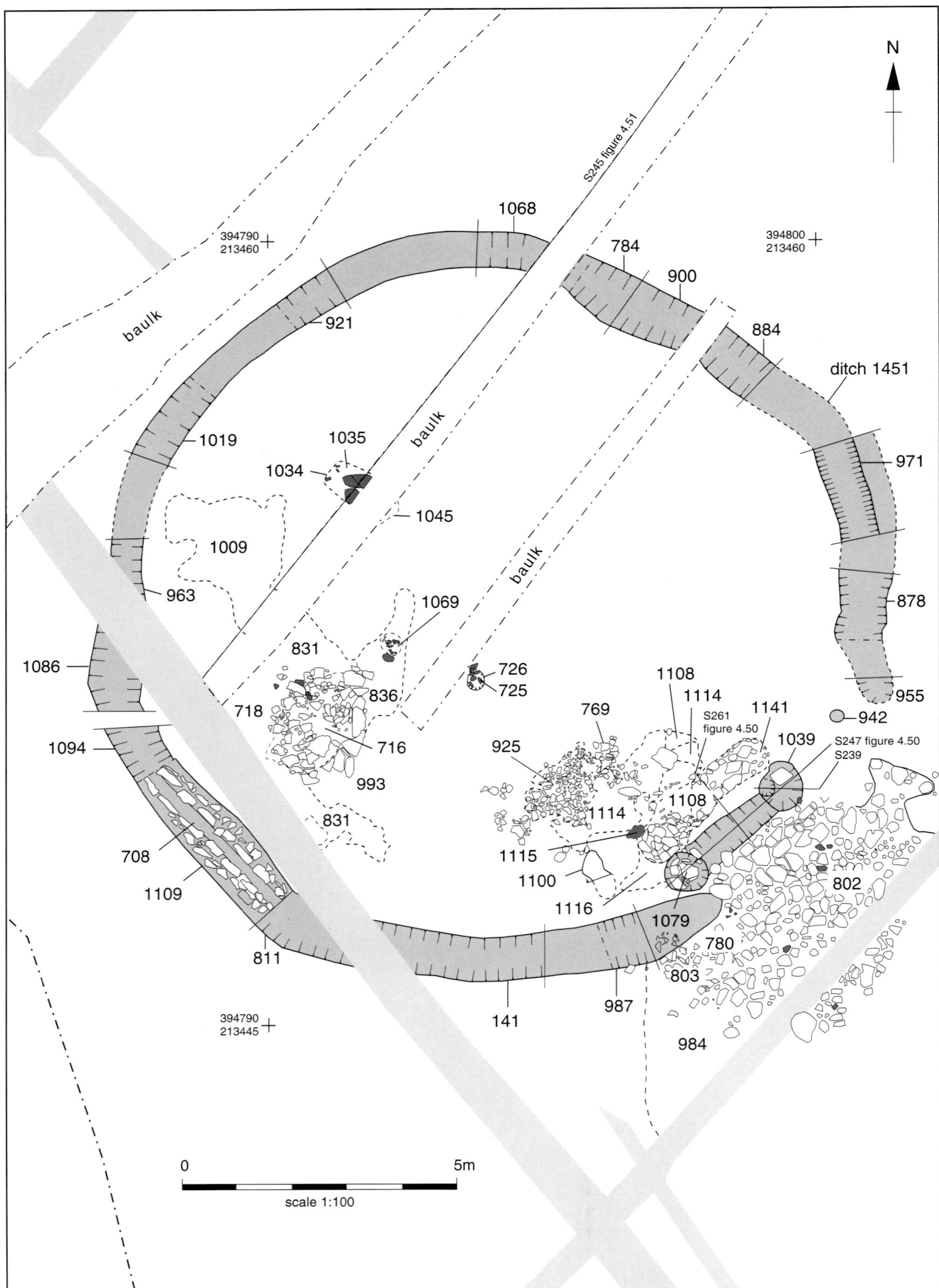


Figure 4.49 Birdlip Quarry, plan of structure 1464.

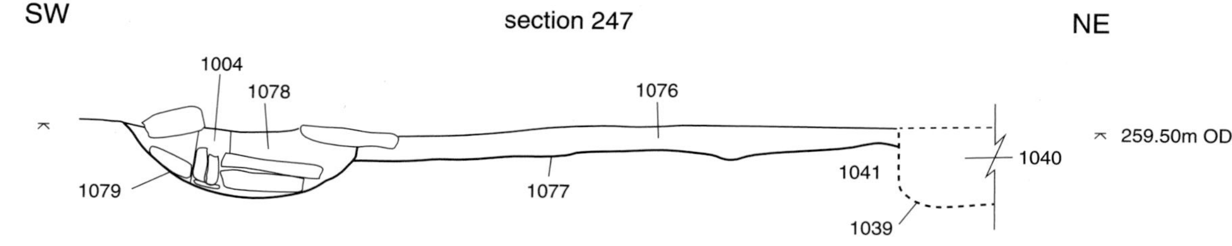


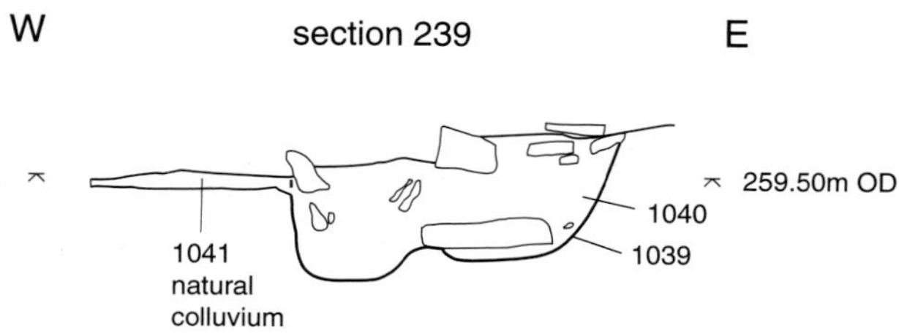


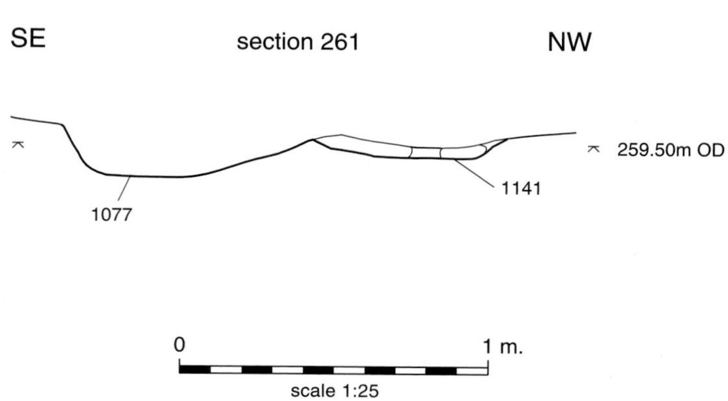


*Figure 4.50 Birdlip Quarry, entrance features of structure 1464, sections.*

### Occupation layers *(Fig. 4.49)*

Excepting those deposits filling features within the roundhouses, layers which could be interpreted as contemporary with the occupation of the buildings were not widespread and tended to be located immediately inside the main doorway. Layer 1116 was a compact mixed deposit of yellow clayey silt and grey silt with charcoal, no more than 0.04 m thick. It was contiguous with floor 1114 and overlay both the stone 'sill', 1141, and posthole 1145 of the doorway of structure 1463, and so was demonstrably associated with the Phase 2B occupation. Layer 1116 was overlain by a patch of darker silt with charcoal, 1108, which may have been essentially part of the same layer. The latest layer associated with Phase 2 was a dark grey-brown silt with small, flat, limestone slabs, 1013. This overlay 1116. It did not form a good surface, but it is considered likely that it represented late flooring overlying occupation debris, which had become broken up after abandonment, possibly during the use of the later, Phase 4, occupation. None of the finds from this layer need be later than the mid 3rd century.

### Stone structure 718 *(Fig. 4.49)*

The structure survived as no more than a collection of limestone blocks within a shallow hollow on the south-western side of the structure. It was associated with 993, a thin dark silt around and among the stones which may have been an occupation layer associated with the stones. A large number of nails and an iron reaping hook (cat. 590) were found in this deposit. It was unclear to which building this feature was related, but the fact that some of the stones were embedded in floor layer 836 indicated that it was probably contemporary with structure 1464 and had subsequently been demolished or modified for use at a later stage. On the eastern side of 718 was an alignment of larger limestone blocks, 776, apparently forming a rough wall. These directly overlay 718 and may have formed part of the same structure. However, they would have stood proud of the contemporary floor surface and may have been a later construction. They were, in fact, level with the floor surface of the later structure, 1452, and appear to have been incorporated into that construction, although that would not preclude the possibility that they had also formed part of stone structure 718. The soil layer butting 776 was a dark silt, 716, which was essentially very similar to 993. None of the pottery recovered from these layers need be later than the 2nd century. The function of this feature is unclear but it may have directly replaced hollow 1064.

### Hearth 1034/1045

The remains of this feature consisted of a very shallow hollow, the edges of which had been burnt dark red. On the other side of the baulk 1045 was almost certainly the same feature but here was of negligible depth. The fill of 1034 (1035), contained burnt limestone. The overlying layers, 924 and 848 (Phase 3), were charcoal-rich and must have incorporated debris from this hearth. This suggests that the hearth was associated with the Phase 2B occupation.

Hearth 1069

This was a localised circular patch of burnt clay and limestone fragments in the south-western area of the roundhouse. It overlay floor 836 and was therefore later than the burnt area 1033.

Hearth 769

This was another patch of fire-reddened stone which partly overlay floor 925.

Burning 1115

This was a very small area of burnt material. It was located just behind the doorpost of structure 1463 and for this reason is considered more likely to be of Phase 2B where it would have been sited further inside the house.

Feature 1100

This was an irregular shallow pit (0.08 m deep) which would have been located just inside the wall of the roundhouse. It contained burnt debris, including stone, together with a substantial part of a Dorset Black Burnished Ware jar. There did not appear to be any *in situ* burning and it is impossible to be sure whether the finds related to the function of the pit or represented backfill redeposited from elsewhere.

Dating evidence

Ditch 1451 appears generally to have been kept clean and then deliberately filled in when it had gone out of use. The exception was the culvert 708. This did not contain diagnostic finds although an absence of colour-coated wares from these fills could be taken to indicate an infilling by the mid 3rd century. In the other segments, particularly the terminals 955 and 987, the pottery from the main fills (954, 990, 142, segment 141; 812 segment 811; 964 segment 963) and the backfilled midden deposits (984 and 986) give a consistent date AD 220–250 for the infilling. Anomalous dating comes from fill 1020 (segment 1019) and fill 146 (segment 141) which yielded exclusively 2nd-century pottery, but it is probable that this had been redeposited. Generally, there seems to be a clear cut-off date of *c.* AD 250 for material associated with this structure and the deliberate levelling of the site appears to have taken place around or shortly before this date. The date of the construction of structure 1464 is less clear, but it seems likely, from the way it imitated structure 1463, that it was constructed shortly after structure 1463 went out of use. Post-packing (1078) from the entrance posthole 1079 (Fig. 4.46, section 262) yielded six sherds dating from after *c.* AD 220. In addition a sherd of BB1, dated after AD 230, apparently came from the lining of the stone culvert 708 (fill 1101 – Fig. 4.47, section 193). Both these dates seem rather late given the other evidence, and a construction date of AD 200–220 seems more likely if the structure was abandoned before AD 250.

*Ditch 1454 (Fig. 4.48)*

South-east of structure 1464, the curving ditch 1454 recut and extended 1453 (Phase 2A) at a shallower depth. It appeared to have been dug to drain water away from the structure and into ditch 699, but excavation showed that 1454 petered out short of 699. It may equally have served as a boundary as it was replaced in Phase 4 by wall 775. It was actually excavated out of sequence under the assumption that it was contemporary with wall 775. However, the pottery assemblage was very similar to that in the sequence of ditches 1258, 1256 and 1255 (Area 2C), and the deposits from Phase 3 in Area A, suggesting that it became infilled in the 3rd century. This seems likely to be associated with the abandonment of structure 1464.

*Slot 1105=1170 (Fig. 4.48)*

Slot 1030 (Phase 2A) was replaced by a very similar feature, 1105, on the same alignment but repositioned about 6 m to the south-east and offset slightly. Slot 1105 was a little wider and shallower than 1030 but was probably another timber-lined drain (Fig. 4.75, section 256). It had a single dark greyish brown fill (1106) without diagnostic finds.

*Pit 1263 (Fig. 4.48)*

Pit 1263 was only partly revealed within the excavated area and its overall form and depth were not recovered. It had also been disturbed by a geotechnical pit. It was probably circular with a diameter of about 3 m or a little more and had cut a notch into the stone layer 1251. It was excavated to a depth of 1.4 m. The northern edge showed a marked step. Its function is unclear but it may have been a well or storage pit.

The pit was deliberately backfilled after the middle of the 3rd century and sealed by layer 1225 (Phase 3, Period 2A). It may therefore have been dug in the earlier 3rd century, although there is no strong reason why it could not have been earlier still. The fills included a dump of ash and charcoal, 1265, which also contained some charred grain and weed seeds (Table 8.55, sample 138). The upper dark fill contained a small group of earlier 3rd-century sherds suggesting that the final infilling had used nearby midden material.

*Gully 1293 (=822) (Fig. 4.48)*

This shallow gully in Area 2B was almost certainly the same as feature 822 in the main excavation area although the latter was not well defined. It would appear to have been cut into the terminal of slot 1030, hence it is likely to have been contemporary with slot 1105. The gully deepened to 0.30 m at the southern edge of the site and may have cut through the edge of

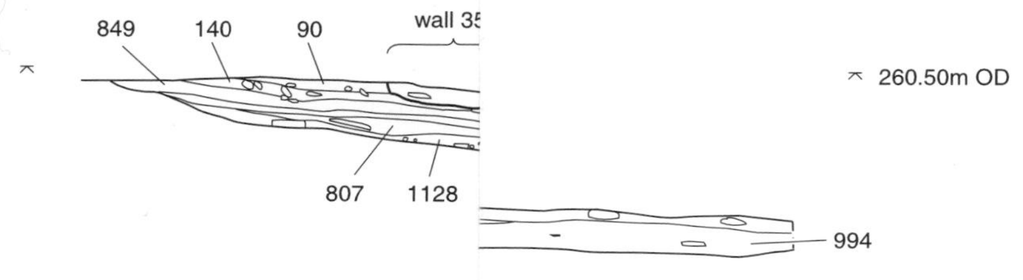


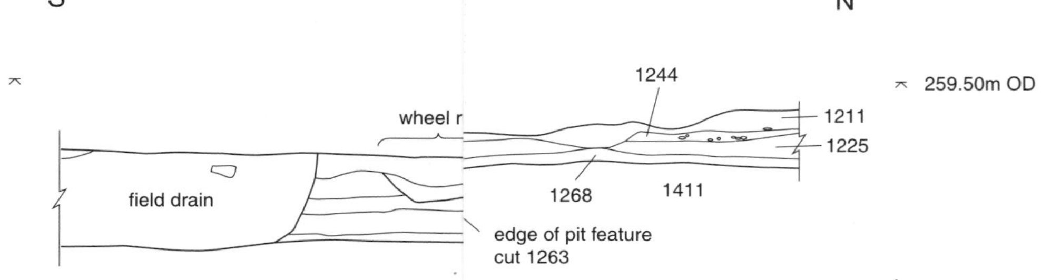


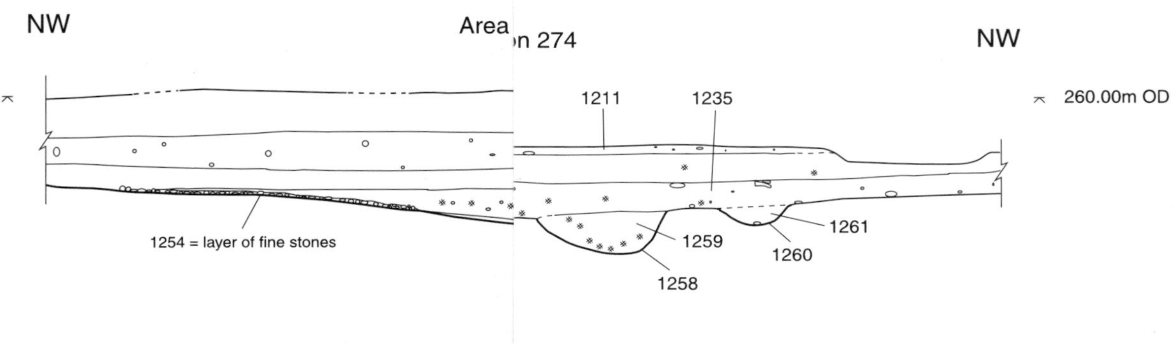


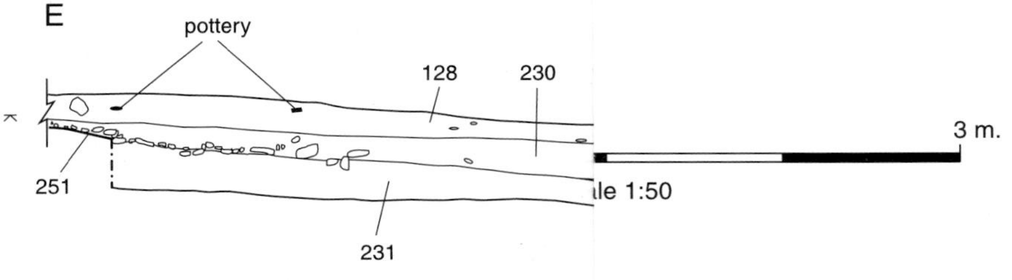


*Figure 4.51 Birdlip Quarry, main excavation, sections.*

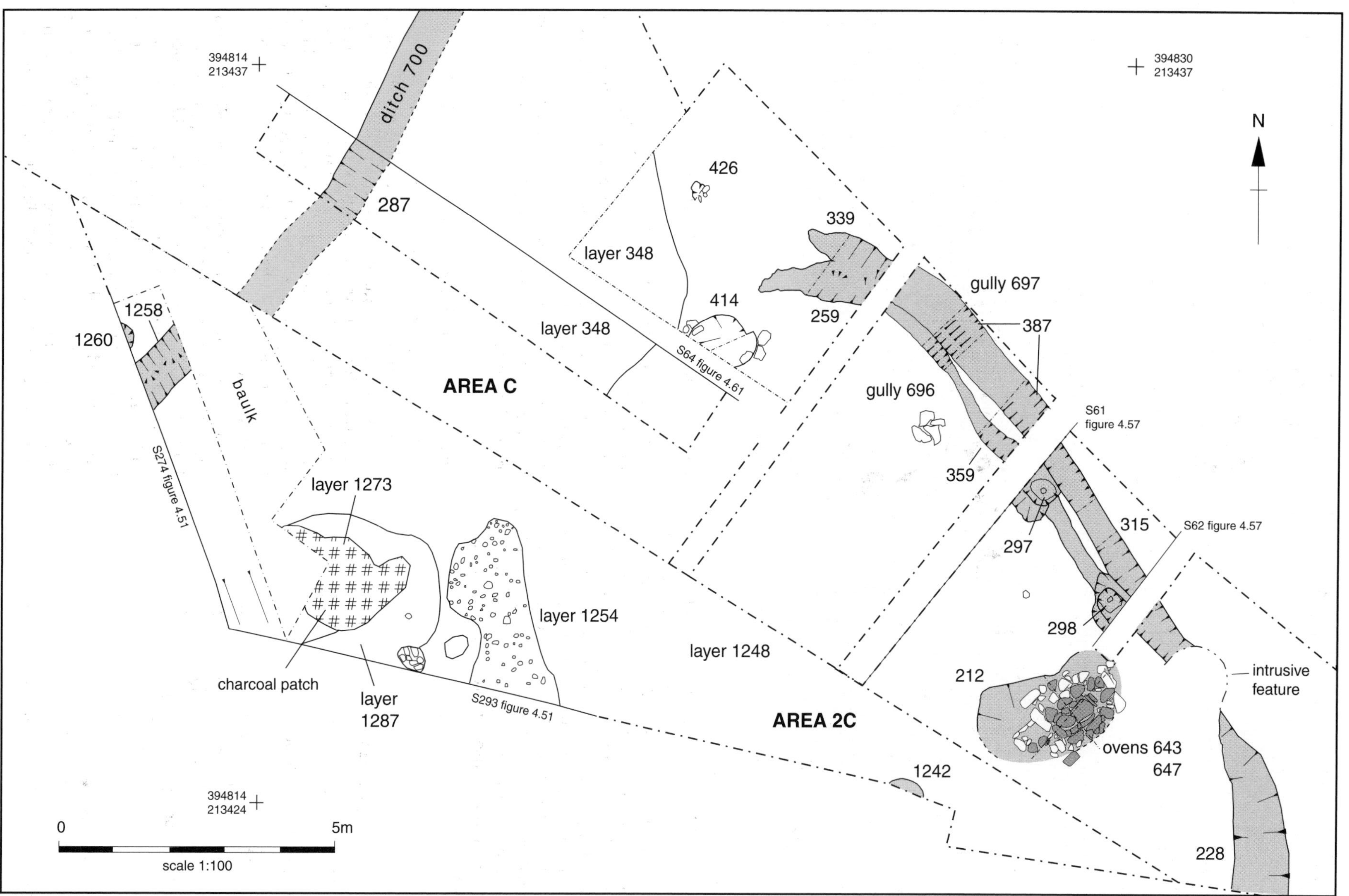


*Figure 4.52 Birdlip Quarry, period 1, early phase, features in Area C/2C.*

*Plate 4.13 Area C Oven 647. The latest in a series of ovens on this spot.*

the stone floor 1251, although it is equally possible that both were in use at the same time. The gully was partly backfilled with rubble (1292 and 813) probably early in the 3rd century (Fig. 4.51, section 291). It is unclear why this was done, but it may have been connected with providing access to structure 1464 rather than denoting the destruction of a nearby structure or floor surface. This was followed by a period of natural silting in the top of the ditch (1291) which contained post-AD 220 pottery and suggests the feature went out of use towards the middle of the 3rd century.

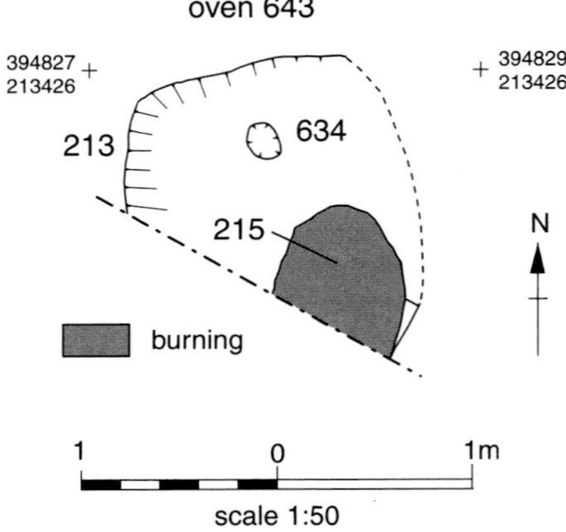


*Figure 4.53 Birdlip Quarry, Area C, oven 643.*

***Area C : Phase 1 and Area 2C: Phase 2A*** *(Fig. 4.52)*

Although excavated in separate operations, these two adjacent areas show sufficient unity to be treated as one. The main early features were a series of five ovens constructed towards the eastern edge of a shallow terrace which had been cut into the hillside. A rudimentary wall or windbreak was constructed on the northern side of the terrace, but there were few internal features.

*Ovens 643, 644, 645, 646 and 647 (Figs 4.53–57)*

All the ovens were constructed on the same spot and the group represents a series of modifications, some quite minor, to an original structure. They are described in chronological order. There was little dating evidence although nine sherds from layer 209 were dated AD 120–200 and all the pottery from these features is compatible with a 2nd-century date. Pottery from the demolition rubble 193 (Fig. 4.58) is dated to after AD 200.

There was little remaining of oven 643 except a sub-rectangular or oval pit (213=1238) approximately 1.6 m north-south x 1.2 m east-west x 0.15 m deep, with a large burnt slab (215) towards the southern end (Fig. 4.53). It is possible that 213 represents a robbing cut to remove a stone lining, but the shallowness of the edge of the pit suggests that the pit was never lined with stone like the later ones. Burning was not general over the base of this feature or on the edges. It was quite restricted, though intense, on slab

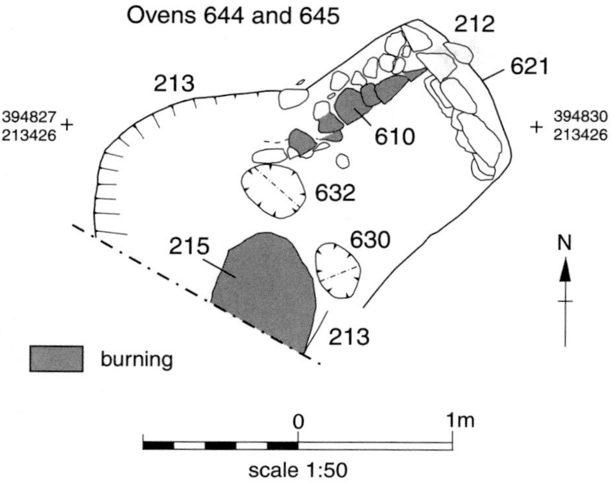


*Figure 4.54 Birdlip Quarry, Area C, oven 644 and 645.*

215, and underneath was an ashy deposit (553) which overlay burnt natural clay-silt (554). It is possible that slab 215 was a later lining, or had been moved from elsewhere. A small posthole (634) probably belongs with this structure, but its purpose is unclear. Layers 204 and 209 were similar charcoal-rich layers which probably represented debris from the oven spread around (Fig. 4.57, section 51) Samples of charred remains from both layers were analysed in detail (Table 8.53, samples 22 and 24; Table 8.56, sample 22, see Pelling, Chapter 8). The samples were actually quite different, Sample 22 consisting mostly of cereal chaff and sample 24 mostly of weed seeds. It is likely that both represented batches of material used as fuel or kindling.

Oven 644 comprised a rectangular pit, 212, of similar dimensions to the earlier oven but slightly deeper (0.27 m) and oriented north-east – south-west (Fig. 4.54). There were two substantial postholes, 630 and 632, at the south-west end. Posthole 630 was 0.35 m deep and posthole 632 was 0.2 m deep below the base of the oven and both contained some limestone fragments and reddened clay. A stone lining 621 was evident at the north-east end consisting of five rough courses of limestone bonded with a white sandy mortar. The stones were largely unburnt. The steepness of the sides of the pit suggested that it may originally have been lined on three sides. The absence of evidence for burning and the use of (presumably wooden) posts, suggests that the feature was not used as an oven, or at least that the fire was located outside the chamber. A possible reconstruction would see stone slab 215 as the base for a fire with the heat being directed between the posts and into the chamber. Even in this reconstruction the posts would have been subjected to intense heat and it is possible that the posts were of stone. The use of stone slab 215 would imply that charcoal layer 209 was associated with this oven.

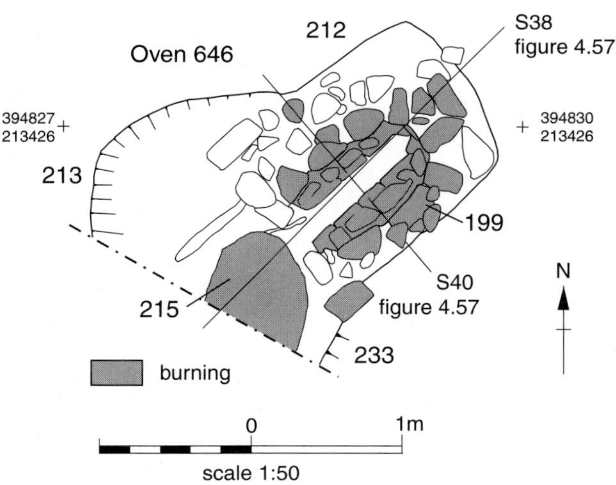


*Figure 4.55 Birdlip Quarry, Area C, oven 646.*

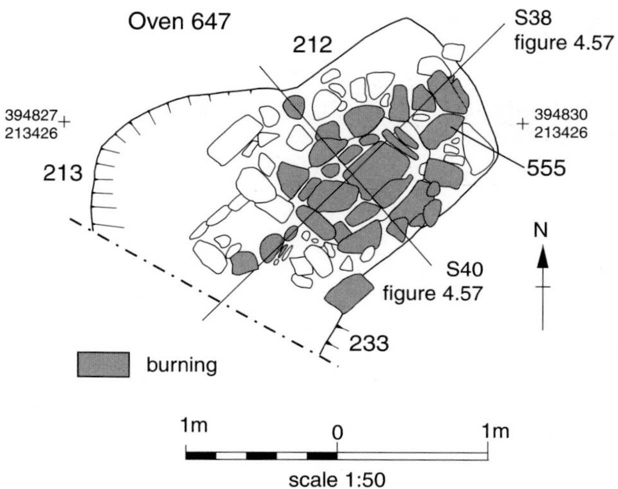


*Figure 4.56 Birdlip Quarry, Area C, oven 647.*

Oven 645 was a modification to oven 644 involving the insertion of a stone lining 610 along the north-west side, butting wall 621. Although this may have been the original form of oven 644, the new insertion was markedly more fire-reddened than wall 621 suggesting a change in use whereby fire was used in close proximity to wall 610. It is possible that the posts were not part of this structure, although they might have been used if shielded from direct flame. The general lack of reddening on the end wall still remains puzzling but it is possible that it too was shielded.

Oven 646 involved the further modification of pit 212 with the insertion of a thick stone lining 199 resulting in a much smaller, more oval-shaped oven (Fig. 4.55). The stone was neatly battered and perhaps three courses thick at the north-east end, making the base relatively narrow. The stone lining was made with shaped, round-edged stones which were heavily burnt all the way round the oven. The surfaces were partly disintegrating, and it is possible that the rounding

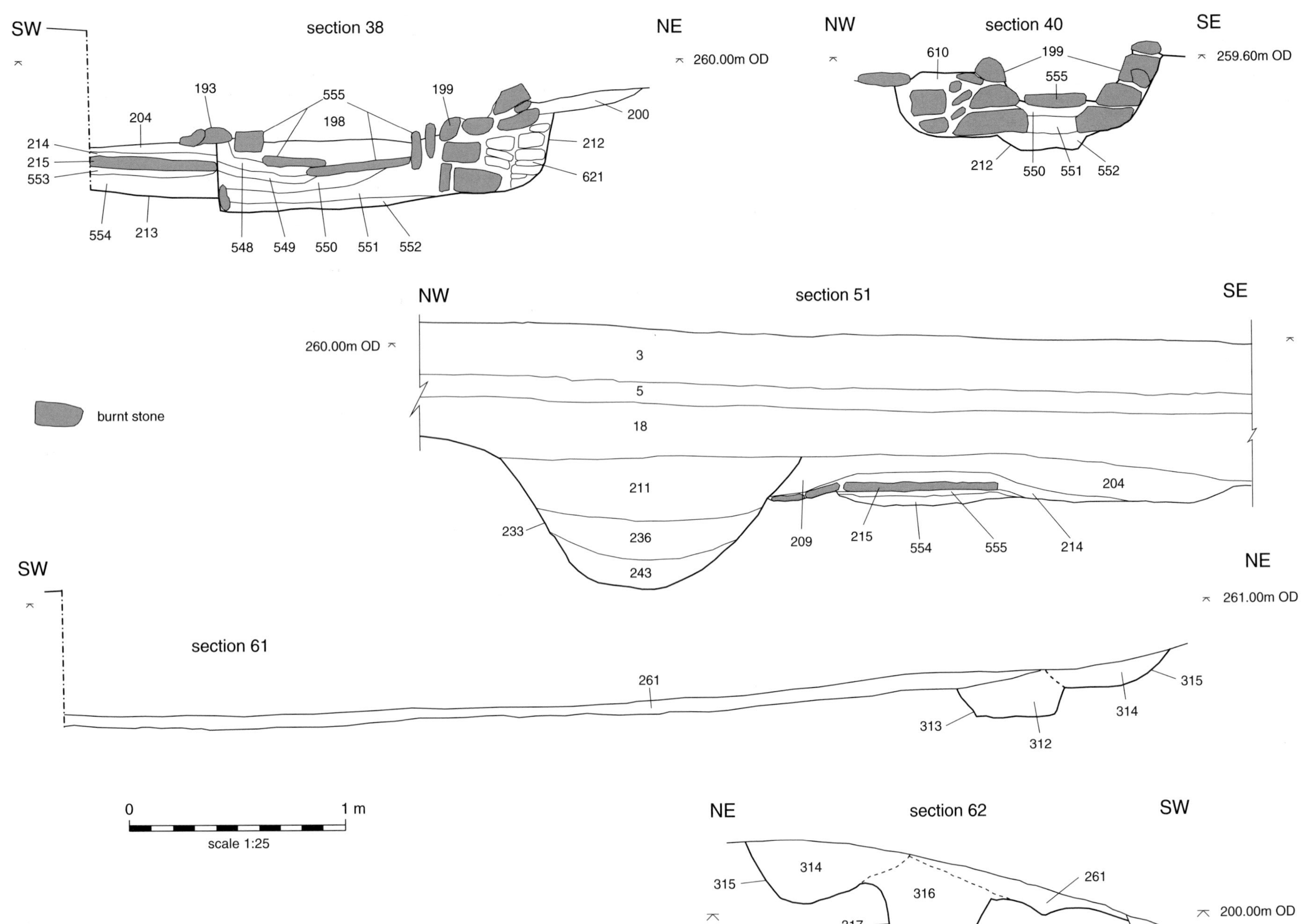


*Figure 4.57 Birdlip Quarry, oven and other features in Area A, sections.*

was due to heat-induced exfoliation. The base contained successive layers of yellowish white (551 and 549) and pinkish (550 and 548) silt. The whiter layers presumably resulted from ash mixed with burnt clay when the fuel residue was raked out. The interleaved burnt silt may represent successive resurfacing. There was little charcoal, indicating considerable care in keeping the oven clean.

The final form of the oven, 647, involved relining structure 646 with stone slabs on the base and at the north-east end (context 555) (Fig. 4.57, sections 38 and 40), and possibly also at the south-west end (although a single stone here may have been fortuitous). This reduced the size of the oven to 0.7 m x 0.5 m x 0.12 m deep. The new lining was also heavily burnt. The fill was a dark grey brown silt with charcoal (198). The carbonised material was again dominated by cereal chaff with some charcoal (Table 8.53, sample 14; see Pelling, Chapter 8).

*Gullies 696 and 697 (Fig. 4.52 and Fig. 4.57, sections 61 and 62)*

Two shallow gullies ran inside the northern rim of the terrace. There was some overlap between them and they may have been sequential features. The relationship between the two was unclear, but on the basis of the associated pottery from 338, gully 696 (segments 339 and 389) was the earlier. This was the narrower and less distinctive of the two. Two morticed limestone blocks (297 and 298) were set in shallow postholes (313 and 317) on the alignment of this gully. The blocks were roughly squared and of a similar size (0.30–0.37 m$^2$ and 0.15 m thick) with a mall square socket on the upper face. The gully was barely traceable between the two stones and it is possible that, at this point, the mortices supported a gateway in a fence. However, there were no identifiable postholes along the line of the gully and it is unclear how a fence would have been constructed.

Gully 697 was slightly more substantial and was probably the gully traceable south-east of the later ditch, 233, petering out towards the edge of the excavation (segment 228). It was not evident in Area 2C. Again its function is unclear, but it did not appear to have structural significance and is probably best interpreted as a drainage gully diverting water running down the hillside. There was no obvious sign of an associated structure, although there is no stratigraphic reason why the morticed stones 297 and 298 could not have been coeval with it. A curving alignment of post-settings is suggested by the inclusion of a shallow, stone-filled feature 414 at the end of the gully and a patch of (unnumbered) stones 2.5 m from 297 (Fig. 4.52). However, it is far from clear what kind of structure (if any) would be implied by this collection of features.

An assemblage of 32 sherds of pottery from fill 386 (segment 387) is dated to AD 180–250. A large proportion of a Dorset Black Burnished Ware jar (cat. 154) from fill 258 (segment 259) may be associated with this phase, although it could be a later insertion.

*Floor layers*

There was no good evidence of a floor layer contemporary with this phase of occupation. Pottery of 2nd-century date was common in the overlying layer 253 and it was also present in layer 227 (both Phase 3). Material associated with the first phase of occupation therefore comes from layers which are indistinguishable from later deposits. This is probably due to an absence of a prepared floor and the consequent mixing and churning of material. Layer 348, which underlay the stone surface 302 (Phase 2) contained little except fragments of an iron bucket hoop (cat. 566).

*Stony layer 1254, charcoal patch 1273 and burnt patch 1242 (Fig. 4.52)*

West of the ovens and probably, though not certainly, contemporary with them, a layer of fine stones (1254) directly overlay the reddish brown colluvium 1248 on the eastern edge of a slight hollow (Area 2C). It may have been intended as rudimentary flooring and the stones were pressed into the underlying 'natural'. However, it is unclear what this would have been associated with. It was limited in extent and it appears unlikely that it originally extended further as there was no indication of truncation or thinning out through wear. Up slope (ie. eastward) the overlying layer was a general dark soil 1210 which appeared not to have been disturbed by ploughing.

Layer 1254 was probably contemporary with charcoal spread 1273, of uncertain derivation, but apparently not *in situ*. This overlay a broader spread of greyish brown silt with charcoal, 1287. These layers were sealed by a bank of silt-clay (1272) associated with ditch 1255 (Fig. 4.51, section 293 and Fig. 4.59). At the eastern end of this area, feature 1242 represented a small lens of *in situ* burning which was recorded only in section.

*Ditch 700 (see also Area B; Phase 2A)*

A series of two boundary ditches 700 (segment 1258) (Fig. 4.52) and 698 (segment 1256) (Fig. 4.58) and a curving ditch (1255) (Fig. 4.59) were dug through the western part of Area 2C. Ditches 700 and 698 extended from the main excavation area (Area B) where ditch 700 was the earlier. No relationships between any of the ditches were evident in Area 2C. However, they were clearly sequential and are assigned to Phases 2A to 2C.

Ditch 700 was without diagnostic dating evidence from any of its segments. It appears to have been deliberately infilled and replaced by ditch 698, segment 1256 (Fig. 4.51, section 274).

### *Area C: Phase 2 and 2C: Phase 2B* (Fig. 4.58)

*Ditch 233 (=1229)*

Ditch 233 was dug against the edge of oven 647 and almost certainly put it out of use, although the structure

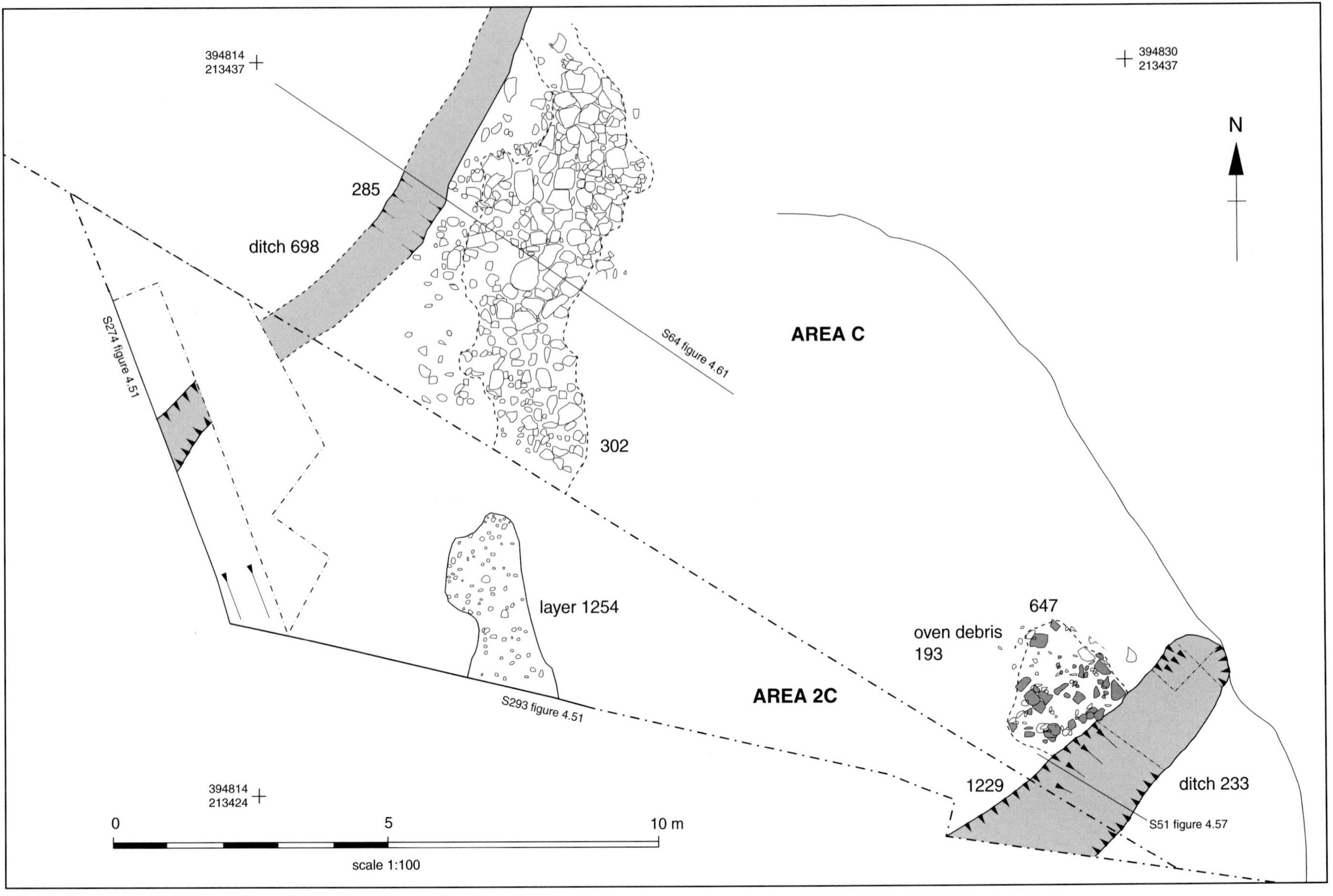


*Figure 4.58 Birdlip Quarry, period 1, middle phase, features in Area C/2C.*

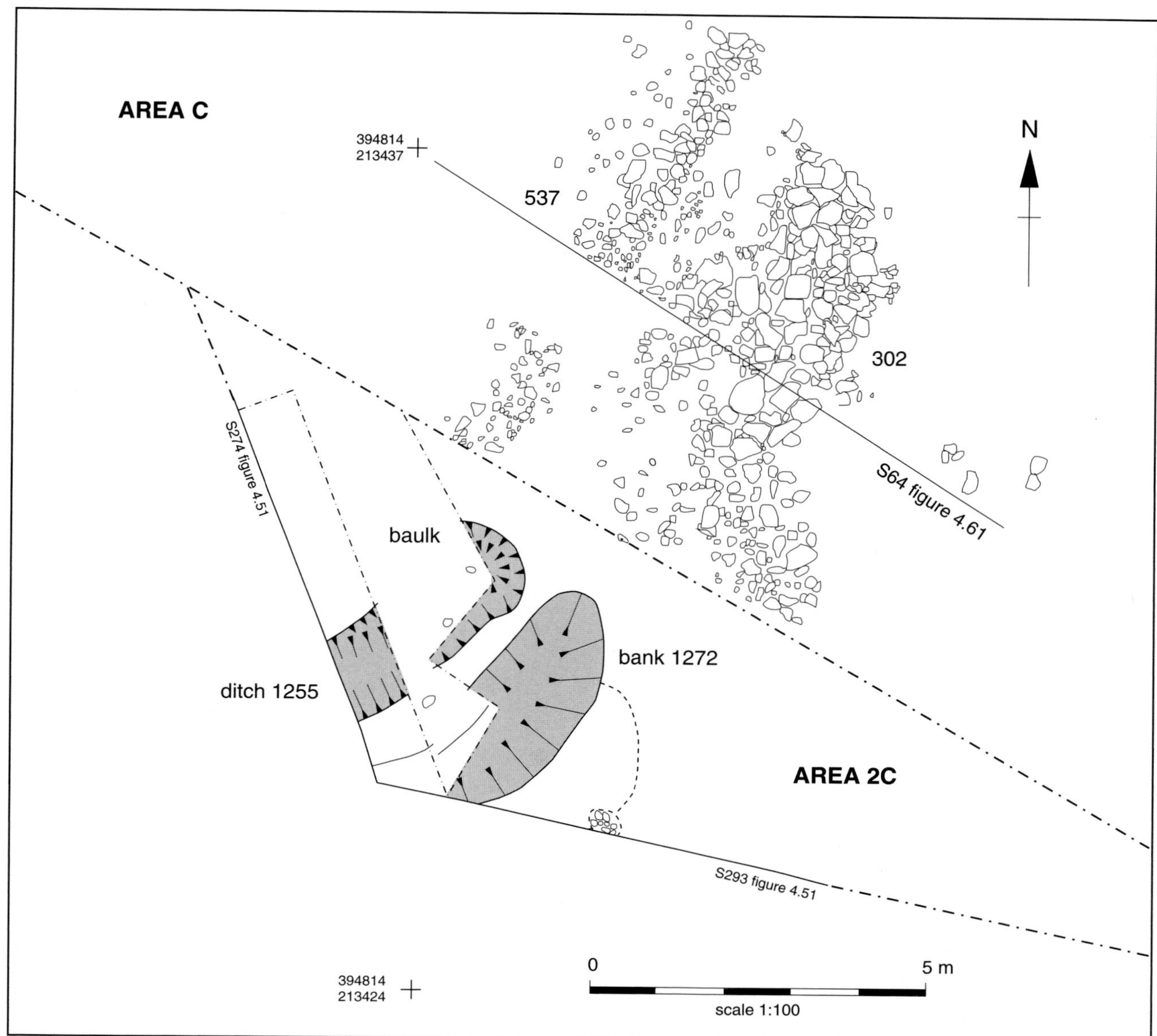


*Figure 4.59 Birdlip Quarry, period 1, late phase, features in Area C/2C.*

itself was not damaged by the ditch. There is no evidence of a significant period of abandonment before the ditch was dug and it is possible that the change of use of this area was quite rapid. It is also possible that the ditch related to the continued maintenance of a boundary here, as its terminal lay close to the edge of the terrace. The primary fill (243), a yellowish brown clayey silt, yielded 11 sherds giving a *terminus post quem* of AD 220 (Fig. 4.57, section 51). This is considered more reliable dating than that gained from fill 1230 (segment 1229) where 41 sherds were dated to the 2nd century, and it is assumed that the earlier pottery is residual. The second fill 236 was a dark brown silt with charcoal which may have eroded from around the ovens. The upper fill, a cleaner yellowish brown silt with limestone lumps, some burnt, is thought to represent natural accumulation. Abundant pottery from this deposit is dated to *c.* AD 240–300. The ditch is thus thought to have been in use during the earlier 3rd century and was left to silt in around the middle of the 3rd century, although pottery was clearly still reaching the area.

*Stone surface 302 (Fig. 4.58, Fig. 4.61, section 64)*

This was a spread of large, but not uniformly large, stones on the western side of Area C. A few stones extended south into Area 2C. These were stratigraphically distinct from layer 1254 (Phase 2A, above) but there may be some significance in the coincidence of the eastern edge of both these deposits. The stones in 302 were generally quite rounded and worn suggesting that they had been heavily used (rather than being a wall base). Some of the stones were burnt,

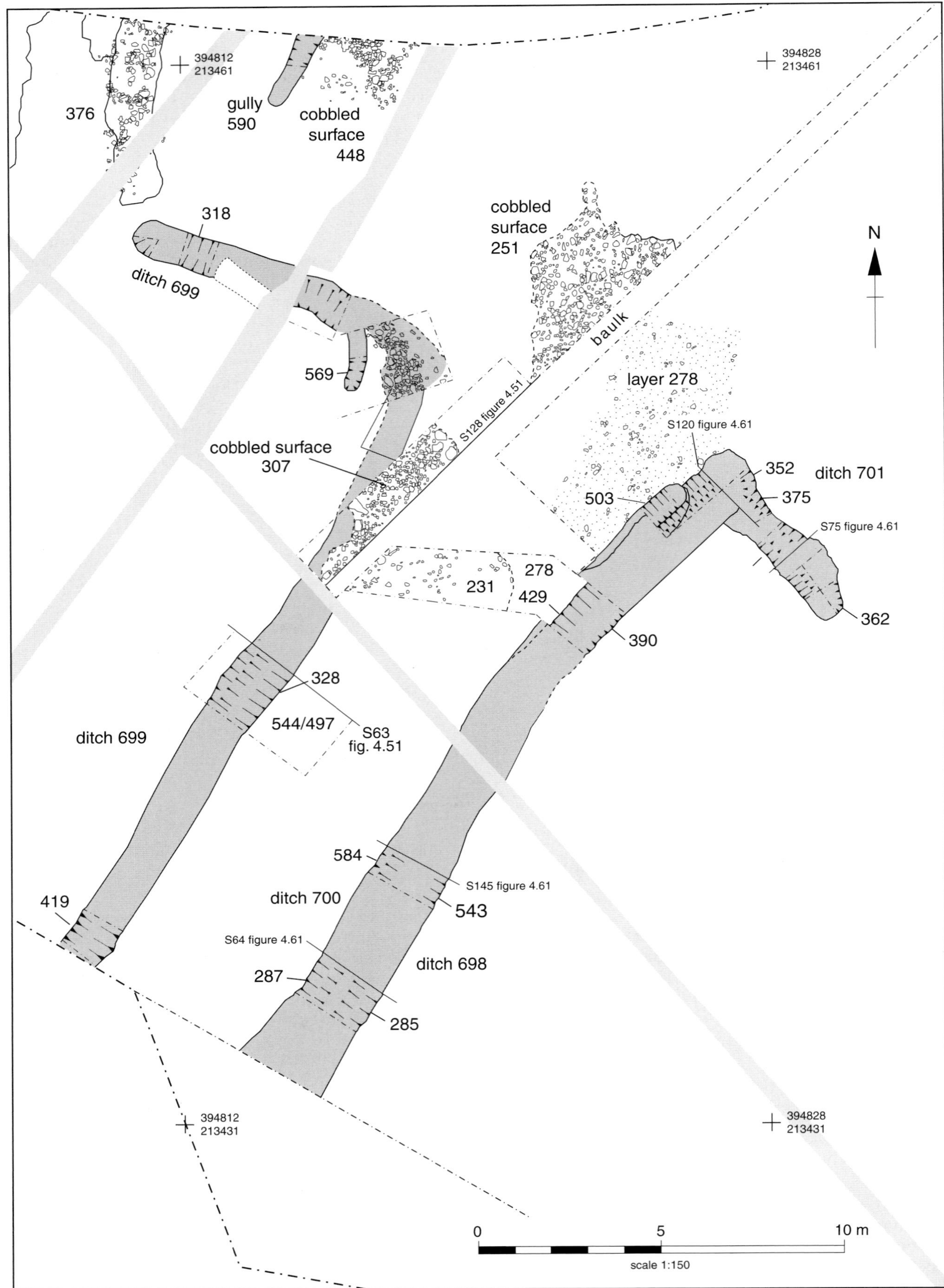


*Figure 4.60 Birdlip Quarry, period 1, Area B, phase 1–3.*

but clearly not *in situ*. The surface most likely served as an area of hard-standing although there was no clue as to its precise purpose. Its date is also unclear. Associated pottery (ie. from among and under the stones) is generally of the 2nd or 3rd century. However, it appears that the stonework respected ditch 698 (segment 543) and it may therefore have had its origin in the 2nd century and have been contemporary with the ovens. It may also be significant that a layer of stones (537) was dumped in the top of the ditch (Phase 2C) and this may represent a later extension of surface 302 in the early 3rd century.

*Ditch 698 (segment 1256) (See also Area B: Phase 2B)*

This ditch appears to have replaced ditch 700 after the latter had been deliberately infilled. The dating evidence from Area B suggests that the new ditch need not have been in use after AD 200, although pottery from the lower fill of segment 1256 (fill 1257) indicates that it was in use slightly later (Fig. 4.51, section 274).

***Area 2C: Phase 2C*** *(Fig. 4.59)*

*Ditch 1255*

Ditch 1255 was curving slightly and terminated within the area, so it may not have been a boundary ditch like ditches 700 and 698. It perhaps defined an area of occupation or a structure located outside the excavation. It had a bank (1272) on its eastern side which sealed occupation layers 1273 and 1287 of probable early 3rd-century date. Ditch 1255 would therefore post-date the other ditches and was presumably dug shortly after ditch 698 had gone out of use. Its primary fill was without finds but a considerable amount of pottery (around 250 sherds) from the upper fill (1250) and overlying layers 1236 and 1235 (Fig. 4.51, section 274), indicates that the series of ditches had gone out of use and been filled in before about AD 280. These soils probably represent a mixture of colluvial accumulation and rubbish disposal. Most finds are recorded as coming from the top of the layer, so it is possible that ditch 1255 had gone out of use in the earlier 3rd century after a very brief period of use.

***Area B: Phase 1***

*Soils and gullies 399, 569 and 590 (Figs 4.43 and 4.60)*

Phase 1 comprised deposits predating the main ditches here. In theory this included the soils and colluvial silts (497, 231, 278, 455 and 544) which the ditches in this area cut. However, the dating evidence from these layers is unhelpful and includes some intrusive material, including a medieval sherd (from 231) and late Roman shelly ware (from 278). This is probably because the finds include material from general cleaning of the 'natural', rather than being solely from the strictly sealed deposits. A fragment of a possible lead pig (cat. 645) and a bone pin (cat. 652) from 278 need not be early.

The earliest stratified feature here was gully 399 (Fig. 4.43) which yielded nine 2nd-century sherds and was cut by ditch 701. It survived as a barely traceable hollow which petered out in a collection of shallow linear scoops (560). Its character is unique on this site and it is unclear what other features it related to. Its alignment pre-figures the later boundary ditches to the west and it seems likely that it was an earlier version of ditch 700. It may already have defined the eastern side of a track or less formal route running up the hill. This was later defined by ditches and cobbling (Phases 2–3), but unless the hollow way was entirely natural, it seems that it must have had an earlier origin which only became formalised in the 2nd century AD.

Gully 569 (Fig. 4.60) may also have been an early feature, although its relationship with ditch 699 (Phase 2B) was unclear. The gully was only evident for a short distance. To the north, gully 590, which ran north-east off site, was stratigraphically early, but also of unclear significance.

***Area B: Phase 2A*** *(Fig. 4.60)*

*Ditch 701*

This was excavated in segments 362, 353 and 375. It was a short length of ditch with very steep/vertical sides and a flat base (Fig. 4.61, sections 75 and 120). Its sharp edges suggested that it might have held a timber beam, but it could not be related to anything structural. It also appears unsuitable to serve for drainage and its function is unclear. The lower fills (364 and 374) were thick deposits of yellowish brown silting, while the dark grey upper fill (363) may have been much later infilling. The feature lacked good dating evidence although pottery from the lower fills was consistent with a 2nd-century date.

*Ditch 700*

This ditch had a terminal (segment 503) a short distance from ditch 701 and ran south-west at right-angles to it. It was examined in four segments in the main excavation and also examined in Area 2C (Fig. 4.52). It contained no finds, probably partly because it was heavily truncated by the later recut 698, although where the ditches were separate the earlier one was without finds (Fig. 4.61, section 64). In segment 584 all finds were labelled with the recut because of the difficulty of distinguishing the fills at the time of excavation. It is considered probably contemporary with ditch 701, although 700 was more obviously a drainage feature with more moderately sloping sides and a variable flattish or rounded base (Fig. 4.61, sections 64 and 145). The method of infill was not entirely clear, but greyer cast to the upper fills could be interpreted as showing deliberate infill (fills 286, 581 and 582) following natural primary silting (fills 373 and 583).

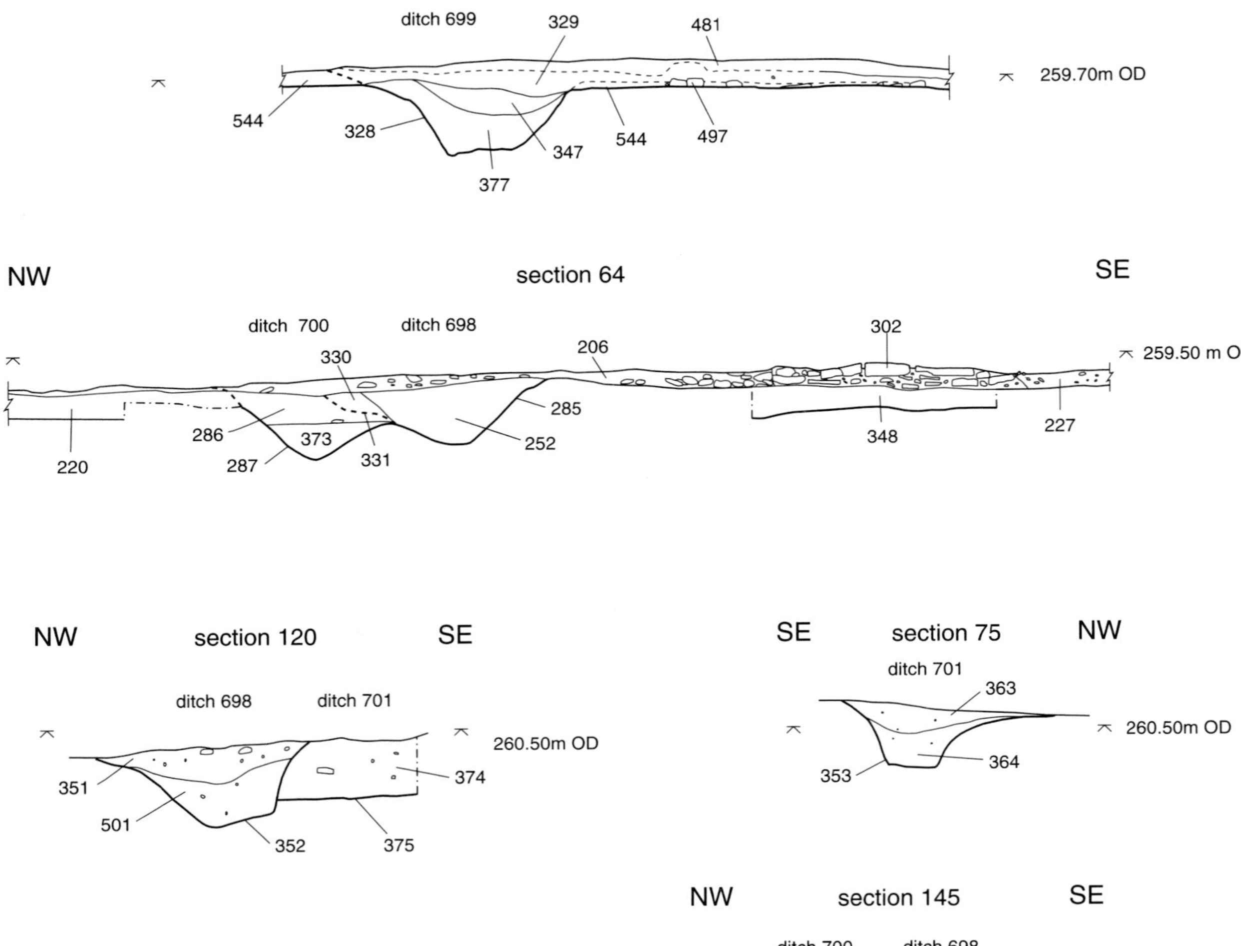


*Figure 4.61 Birdlip Quarry, period 1, Area B, phase 1–3.*

***Area B: Phase 2B*** *(Fig. 4.60)*

*Ditch 698*

This ditch represents a recut of ditch 700 and was very similar to the earlier cut in size and shape. Its terminal cut ditch 701. Again its fills could be interpreted as relatively clean primary silting, followed by deliberate infilling. This is clearest in the terminal (Fig. 4.61, section 120, segment 352) where the upper fill (351) contained a dump of stones, and also in segments 285 and 543 where the infilling was completed with a deposit of stones (537), which appeared to represent a consolidation of the ground in the vicinity of Area C (Fig. 4.59).

Assemblages of pottery from three of the segments indicate a 2nd-century infilling. Pottery from segment 390 (fill 410) and from segment 1256 (fill 1257) in Area 2C appears to be slightly later, and a compromise would suggest that the ditch went out of use at the end of the 2nd or beginning of the 3rd century AD.

*Ditch 699*

This ditch ran south-east from a narrow terminal and then turned sharply south-west approximately parallel to ditch 698. It is almost certainly the same as the ditch running the length of Area 6 (Fig. 4.48, segments 1184, 1182 and 1175). The profile of the ditch was varied but

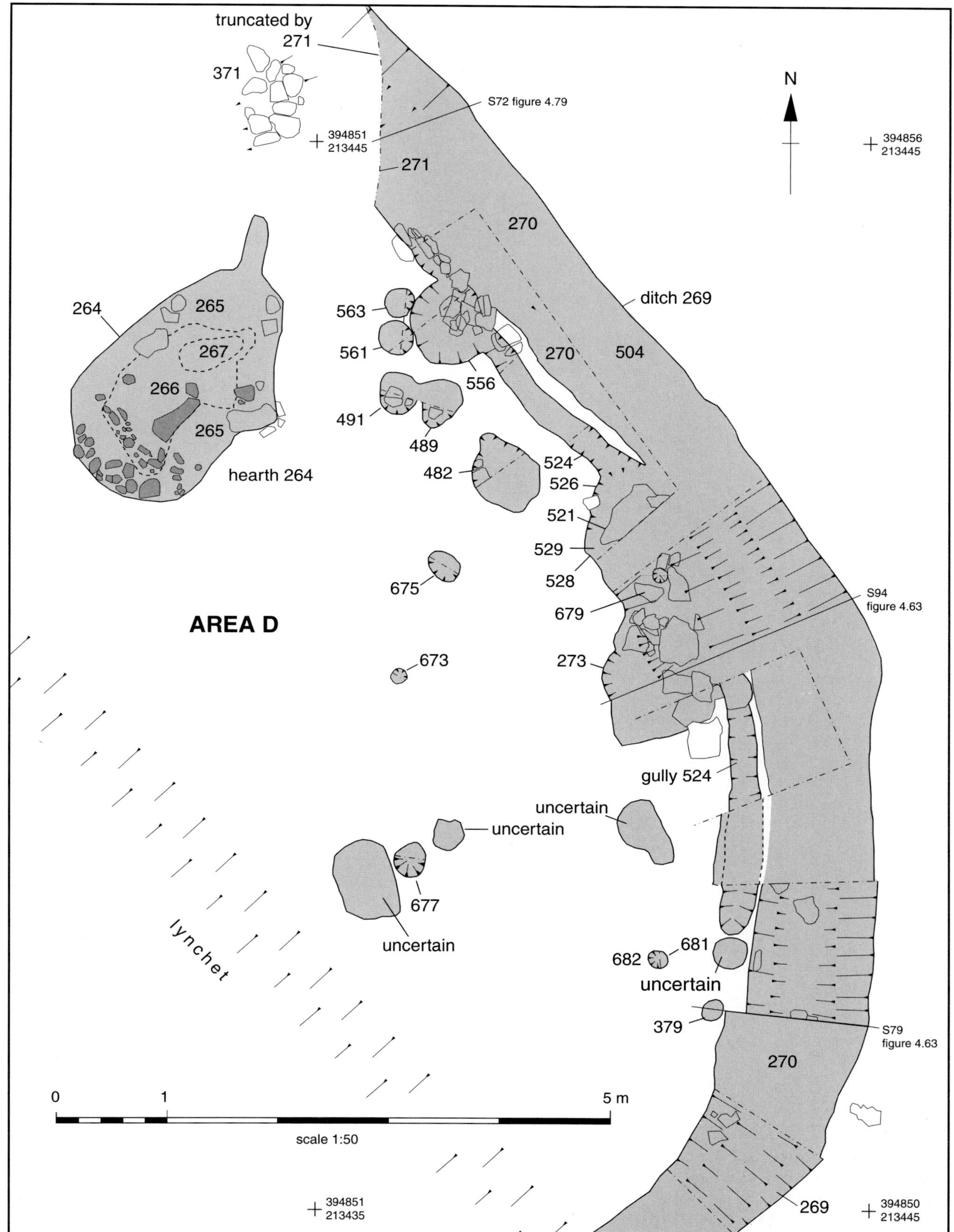


*Figure 4.62 Birdlip Quarry, period 1, structure 1456.*

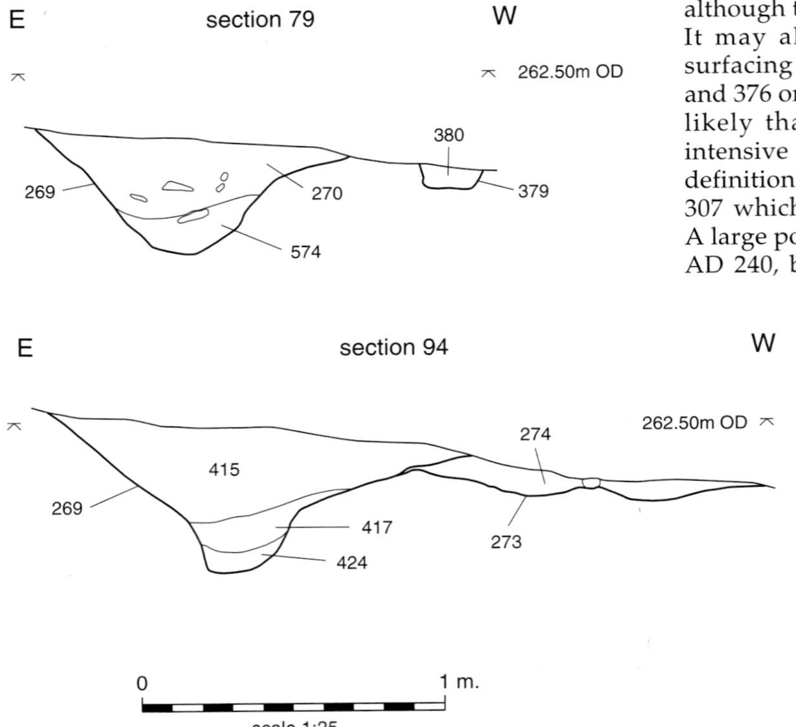


*Figure 4.63 Birdlip Quarry, period 1, structure 1456, ditch 269, sections.*

with a tendency to be deeper than ditch 698 and with a narrower base. All the sections in the main excavation (segments 318, 328 and 419) showed two fills - a deep orange-brown clayey silt overlain by a greyer fill which may have been deliberately deposited (Fig. 4.61, section 63). The segments in Area 6 showed only a light greyish fill, perhaps because the ditch had been kept clean.

There was little dating evidence. Pottery from the lower fill (309) was consistent with a later 2nd-century use of the feature. The upper fill (347) was spot-dated to post-AD 200 and fill 296 (segment 318) contained a Dressel 20 amphora rim of late 1st/early 2nd- century type. There were no diagnostic finds from the segments in Area 6. The ditch could therefore be contemporary with 698, going out of use in the early 3rd century. The ditches are likely to have defined a trackway running up the hill.

### *Area B: Phase 3* (*Fig. 4.60*)

#### *Cobbled surfaces 307, 251 and 448*

The upper fill of ditch 699 in segment 318 was immediately sealed by a layer of limestone 'cobbles' 307 which occupied the deepest part of the hollow way and spread out over the surrounding 'natural' clay-silt. The stones were sub-angular or rounded with a maximum size of about 0.30 m but with many smaller stones and chippings between the larger ones. Many of the stones were burnt. This layer was likely to have been coeval with layer 251 slightly higher up the slope although there was no relationship between the two. It may also have been part of a larger area of surfacing which included surviving remnants 448 and 376 on the edge of the site to the north-west. It is likely that this cobbling was related to a more intensive use of the hollow way, or a more formal definition of it. There was little dating evidence from 307 which was the more deeply stratified deposit. A large pottery assemblage from 251 is dated to after AD 240, but it is not really possible to distinguish what was truly within the layer from material which accumulated during its use or even after its abandonment.

### *Area D: Phase 1* (*Fig. 4.62*)

#### *Structure 1456*

Structure 1456 was situated on a shallow terrace which had been cut into the hillslope on the central part of the site (Fig. 4.62). The southern part of this structure had been cut away by a lynchet and its overall form is uncertain as a result. It comprised a curving ditch (269) with a shallow gully or slot (524) close to its inner lip. There were a number of small shallow pits/postholes associated with this gully. Others may have been contemporary, or associated with the later structure 1457. Overall, there were few internal features although hearth 264 belongs with this structure.

#### Ditch 269

The original extent of ditch 269 is uncertain since both terminals were truncated, the southern one by a lynchet and the northern one by ditch 271 of the later structure 1457. The northern terminal is thought to have terminated just north of section 147 (Fig. 4.79) although this was not observable. While two ditches emerge in truncated form on the north-west side of structure 1457 (466 and 468), neither were on the alignment of ditch 269 as revealed in section 72 (Fig. 4.79). Unless the course of the ditch were irregular, or the excavated section misleading, it seems that 466 and 468 must represent two sub-phases of the later structure 1457. Ditch 269 therefore would have formed a partial enclosure, presumably for drainage and serving to divert water running down the hillslope around an area of occupation. It had a quite consistent composite profile with a shallow upper slope plunging towards a flattish base (Fig. 4.63, sections 79 and 94 and Fig. 4.79, section 72). This may have been due to prolonged erosion of the edges while the ditch was open, or perhaps caused by the thorough cleaning out of an originally shallower ditch. The ditch generally had two or three fills in its deeper segments. The lowest fills (574, 573 and 424) were reddish or greyish brown silts. Where present, the middle fills (417 and 370)

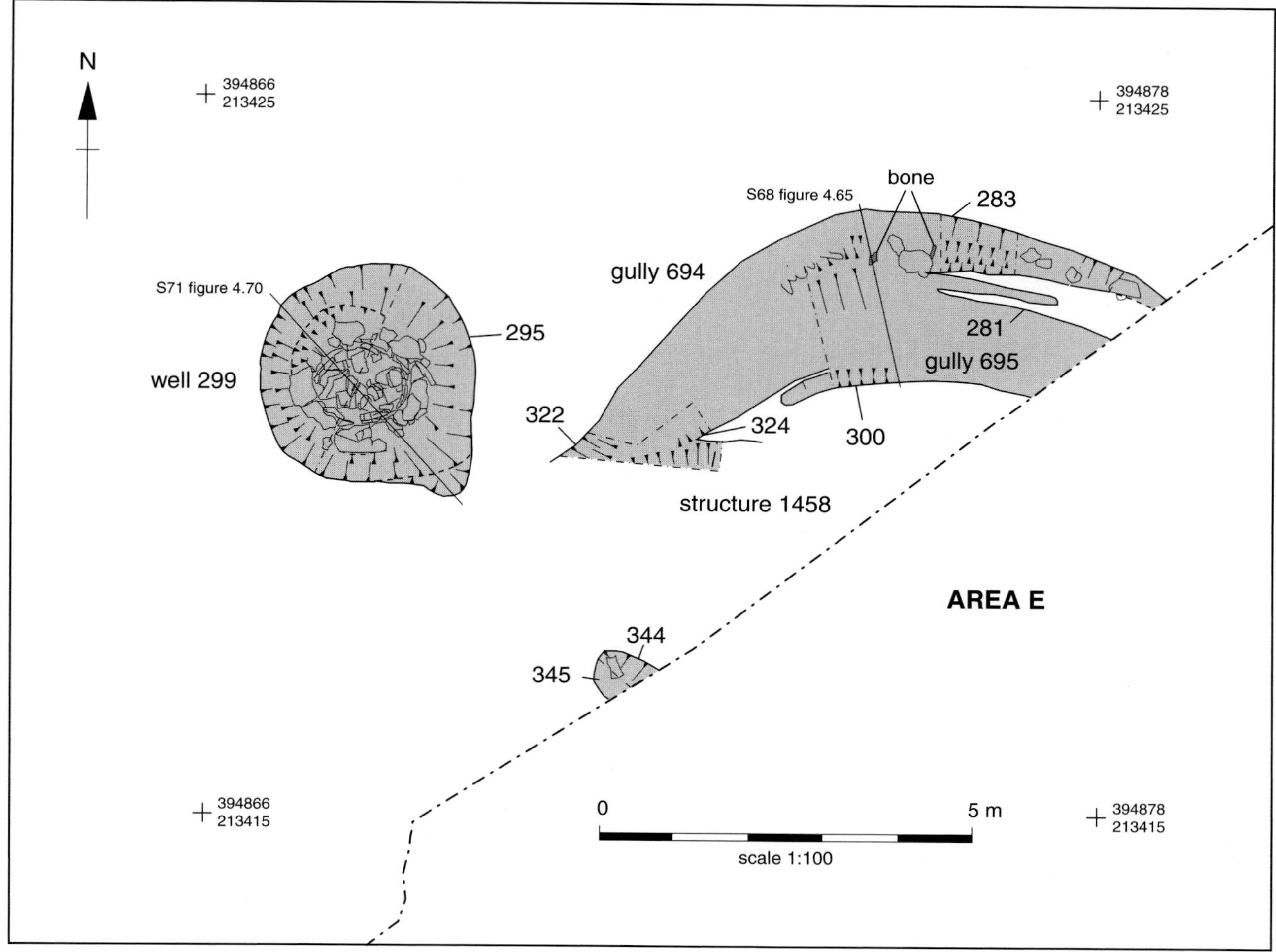


*Figure 4.64 Birdlip Quarry, structure 1458, and well 299.*

were darker with more charcoal, perhaps representing dumping towards the end of the occupation. The upper fills (270, 504 and 415) were a lighter reddish brown with fine limestone fragments, suggesting a period of natural infilling with ploughsoil.

### Gully 524

Gully 524 was an insubstantial feature running just inside and parallel to ditch 269. It was no more than 0.07 m deep with a rounded profile. It is considered likely to have been a feature of some sort of structural significance, perhaps to hold a wall or fence. The small pits and possible post/stakeholes which clustered along this alignment were similarly insubstantial and without apparent pattern. The structural evidence is quite similar to that in Area C/2C and seems to indicate a rudimentary building open to the west or south-west.

### Hearth 264

This hearth was an oval or sub-rectangular area of heavily burnt soil and stones measuring 2.2 m x 1.3 m x 0.12 m deep. There was no evidence of a stone base. The burnt stone indicated the former presence of a lining of some sort, but very little appeared to be *in situ* and the form of the original construction is unclear. It may possibly have been an oven with a superstructure. The hearth hollow was filled with burnt clay-silt (640) and was overlain by spreads of burnt stone, soil and charcoal (265, 266 and 267). The hearth was cut through by gully 340 and associated postholes (Period 2A). However, the degree of disturbance appears to be more than can be accounted for by the insertion of the later structure, and it is probable that the structure was demolished when the new building was erected.

### *Dating evidence*

The date of structure 1456 is not entirely clear and the evidence is equivocal. Nearly all the associated pottery comes from ditch 269. The primary fills yielded 18 sherds all of which indicated a 2nd-century AD date. The middle fills contained nothing diagnostic. The upper fills produced somewhat conflicting evidence with 415 containing a 2nd-century assemblage (31 sherds) while a DORBB1 flanged bowl from 270 would belong to the late 3rd century onwards. Similarly, the upper fill 369 (Fig. 4.79, section 72) yielded a late 3rd-

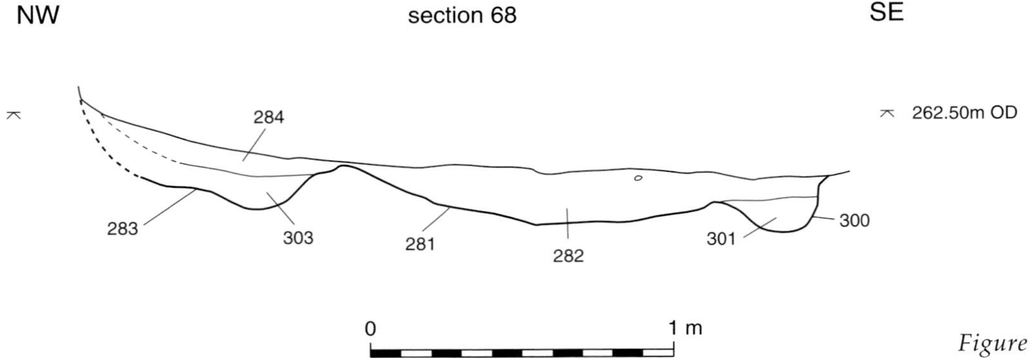


*Figure 4.65 Birdlip Quarry, structure 1458, section.*

or early 4th-century assemblage, although this fill was uncharacteristically dark and may belong with the later phase fill 272, possibly related to a cut of the later ditch, 271, of Period 2A. The disparity in the dates from these two contexts compared with the evidence from the other ditch fills does suggest that the late pottery is intrusive or misattributed during excavation. Thus it would be preferable to see a lack of ditch maintenance from the late 2nd century or at the beginning of the 3rd century and the ditch left to silt up until reoccupation in the later 3rd century. A compromise to accommodate the later dating would suggest that gradual infilling was still taking place in the later 3rd/early 4th century.

### *Area E: Phase 1* (*Fig. 4.64*)

#### *Structure 1458*

Structure 1458 occupied a terraced platform on the eastern edge of the site which was only partly within the excavation area. It consisted of an outer gully (694) and an inner groove (300) with a broad gully (695) between them (Fig. 4.65, section 68), probably indicating a semi-circular structure open to the south/south-west. The gullies are thought to represent an inner wall line, an outer eaves-drip gully and a feature of unknown origin between them. Gully 695 may have had structural significance or it may have resulted from the dismantling or destruction of the structure. The north-west segment of the outer gully (segment 283) had an irregular line of large stones on the surface of the fill (284) suggesting that they had tumbled in from a rudimentary wall on the outer lip of the gully (which here coincided with the top edge of the terrace.) This, like the gully itself, may have been intended to discourage water from running into the structure. There was no indication of an internal surface, although, had one existed, it would be expected to have survived within the area of the terrace. The 'natural' here was quite mottled suggesting that it had served as the floor. A shallow hollow 344 may have belonged with this or the later structure 1459. There was no good dating evidence for this structure, but nothing inconsistent with a 2nd- to 3rd-century date. Adjacent well 299 also belonged to this phase and is described below.

### *Area 3: Phase 1* (*Figs 4.66–67*)

#### *Possible sub-rectangular structure 1683*

There is some suggestion of occupation in this area before the construction of a rectangular stone-based structure in Phase 2. The evidence was slight and not clearly identified during the excavation, although the gully which defined the structure on its northern side was initially given two phases which the current interpretation suggests was valid. The main evidence for this comes from the pottery which contains a late 2nd/early 3rd century component in the Phase 2 gully segment 1528 (fill 1527), and in segment 1548 (fill 1526) which can now be interpreted as an earlier cut of the same gully (Fig. 4.83, section 300). There are also some features of a relatively early phase which are thought to be related to this occupation.

Phase 1 would therefore include an early phase of north-west – south-east gully (1548 = 1668) which was almost entirely removed by the later recut. This contained a light brown fill which contrasted with the dark grey later fill. There is also the line of a possible beam-slot (1561 = 1606) which was only clear on the southern side where it turned a corner, but which underlay wall 1605 of Phase 2 and originally may have continued running parallel to gully 1548. A possible hearth 1635 appeared to have been sealed by the later stone floor or make-up layer 1512, and a pit 1612 which contained burnt stones was sealed by the pitched stone surface 1504. Both are likely to be part of the earlier phase. The evidence may therefore indicate a rectangular or sub-rectangular, timber-framed structure of indeterminable dimensions, with an earthen floor and a hearth.

The structure can only be broadly dated to the late 2nd and 3rd centuries AD. There was a possible dedicatory jar (1536) in Wiltshire sandy ware fabric buried near the later entrance, but this is imprecisely datable to the 2nd and 3rd centuries and could therefore belong with either phase. A denarius of AD 218–22 was sealed by the wall 1503 of the later structure. This does not help to date the subsequent phase, but perhaps furnishes some further evidence of occupation in Phase 1.

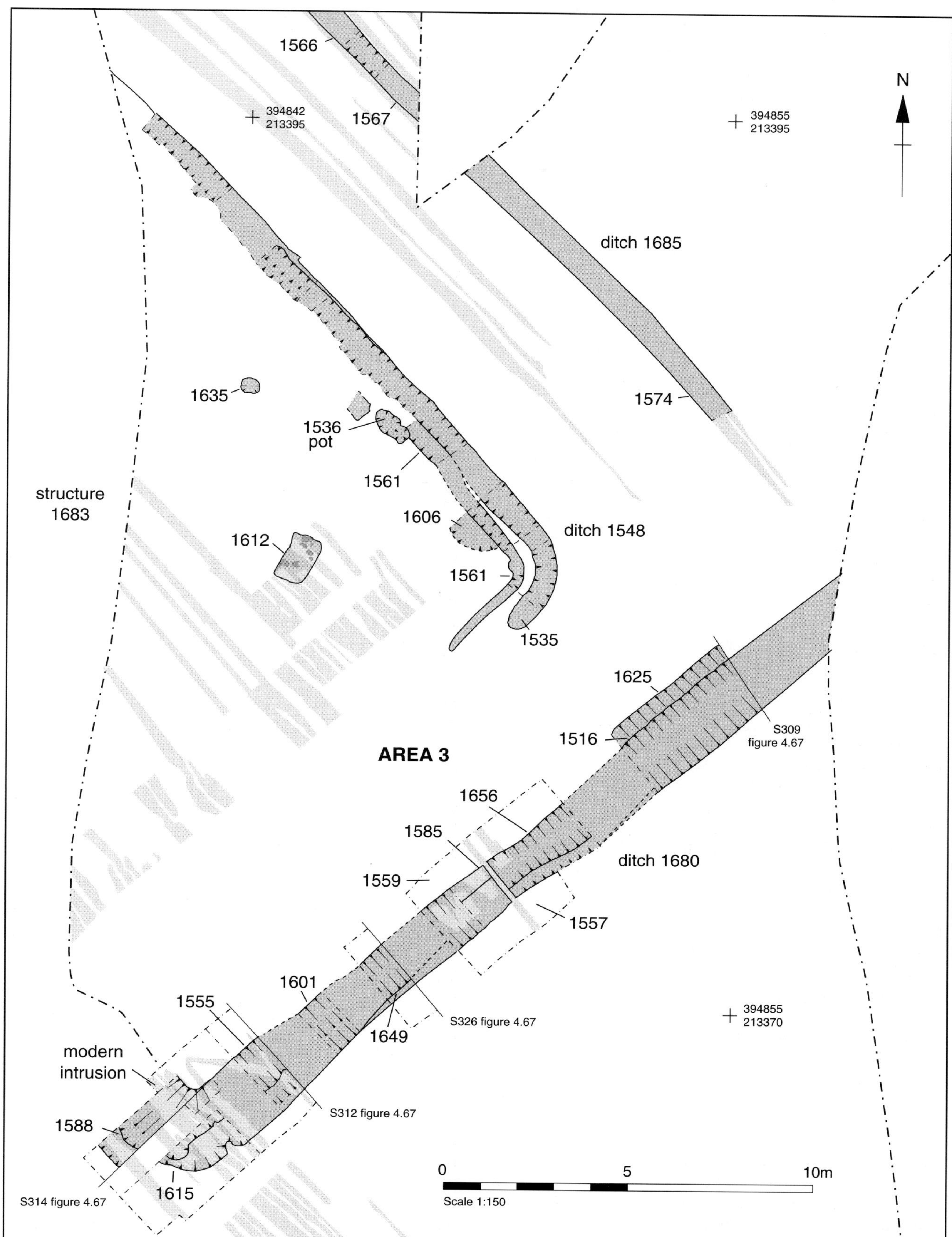


*Figure 4.66 Birdlip Quarry, period 1, structure 1683 and ditch 1680.*

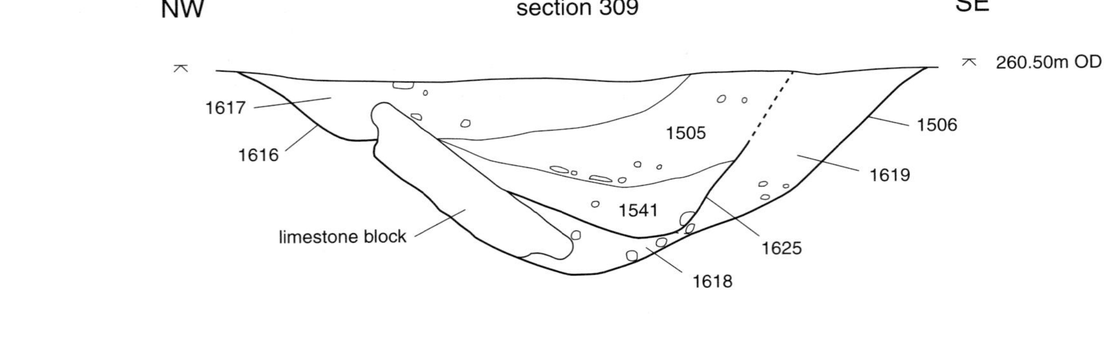


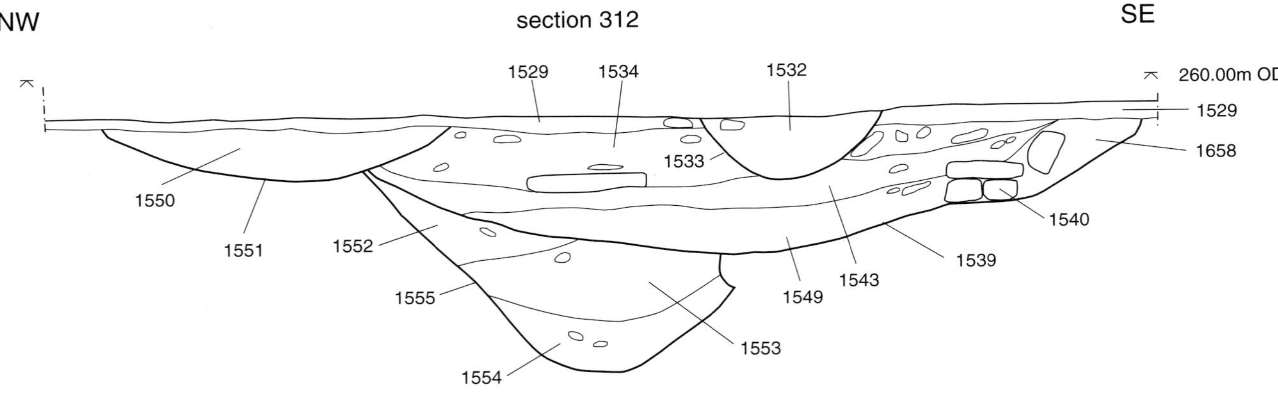


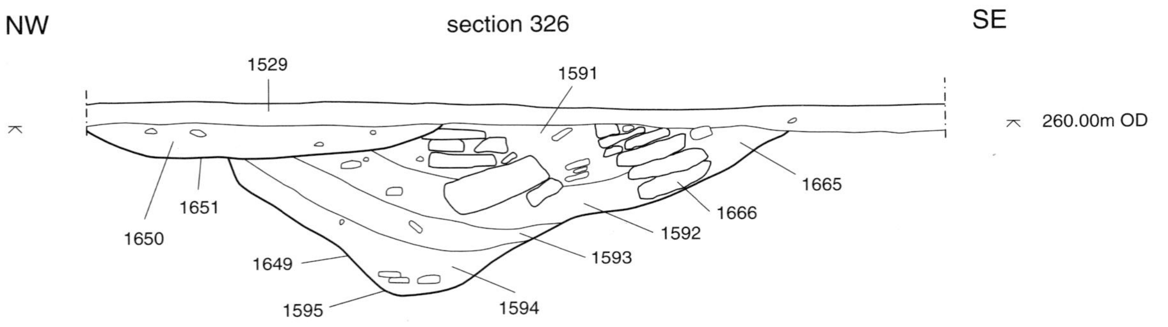


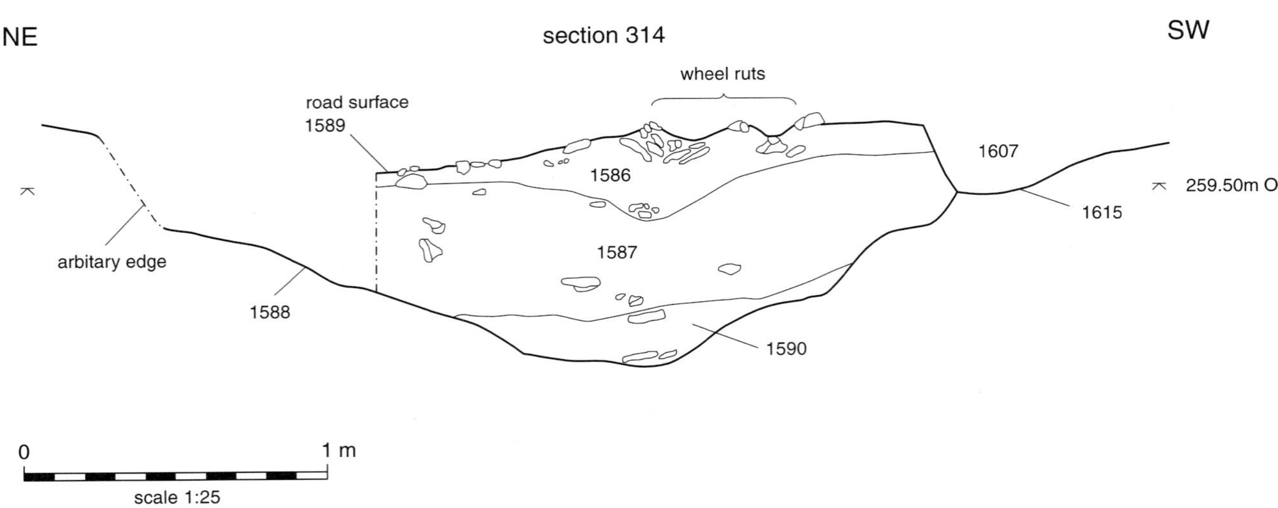


*Figure 4.67 Birdlip Quarry, Area 3, ditch sections.*

*Boundary ditch 1680 (Figs 4.66–4.67)*

The first of three phases of boundary ditch ran north-east – south-west, south of the rectangular structure. The south-west corner turned a right-angle to run north-west, presumably acting as a roadside ditch, although it was overlain by a later re-surfacing which formed a lateral extension to Ermin Street. The dating evidence is insufficiently precise to confirm that the ditch was strictly contemporary with the structure, but the dates are broadly compatible. Ditch 1680 was the deepest in the sequence of ditches, about 1.5 m wide and 0.7 m deep (Fig. 4.67, sections 309, 326, 312 and 314). The upper part was heavily truncated by the Phase 2 ditch 1681, and it was sometimes difficult to know to which ditch a particular fill should be assigned.

Segment 1506 was excavated as only one ditch, but the section was substantially re-interpreted in the light of evidence from the other segments, which made it likely that the later ditch, 1681 (segment 1625), had largely removed 1680 (Fig. 4.67, section 309). However, there are certain observations which sit uncomfortably with this re-interpretation, namely the absence of a Phase 2 revetment wall in this section, and a late 2nd/3rd-century assemblage of 20 sherds from 1505, which would be considered to be redeposited if it came from a Phase 2 fill. It is therefore still unclear whether Phase 2 is represented at all in this segment and it is possible that the later ditch terminated further south-west.

The fills of ditch 1680 were light mottled orange-brown and grey silts, tending to be darker and greyer higher up. They were interpreted as representing natural silting with more cultural material being incorporated into the higher fills. Infilling may well have taken place over a long period but there was no indication that the area had been abandoned. Pottery from the fills of ditch 1680 gives rather inconsistent dates. There is no real evidence as to when the ditch was first dug. A 2nd/3rd-century assemblage from the primary fill 1584 (segment 1585) appears to give a broad date for the use of the ditch. Late 3rd/4th-century pottery comes from the main fill 1553 (segment 1555; Fig. 4.67, section 312) which may indicate that the ditch was still in use at this time. Three late 3rd-century sherds from 1594 (segment 1649; Fig. 4.67, section 326) would on the face of it, support a very late use of the ditch, but the problem of distinguishing fills from the earlier and later cuts may mean that the finds were mis-assigned.

*Ditch 1685 (Fig. 4.66)*

This feature formed a boundary north-east of structure 1683. It was only up to 0.58 m deep, shallowing to an ill-defined south-east terminal and was without diagnostic finds. Its mid to light yellowish brown fill

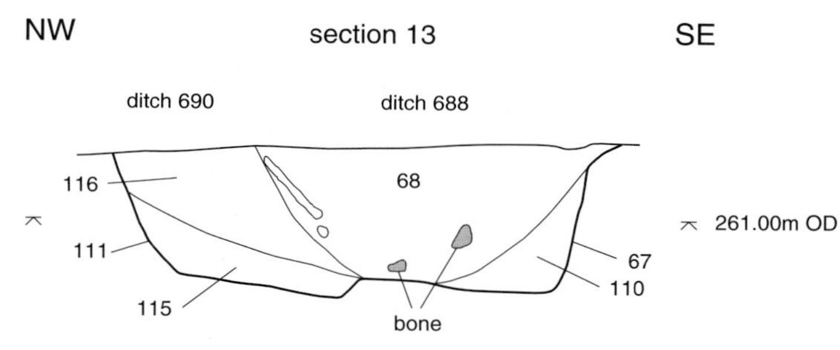


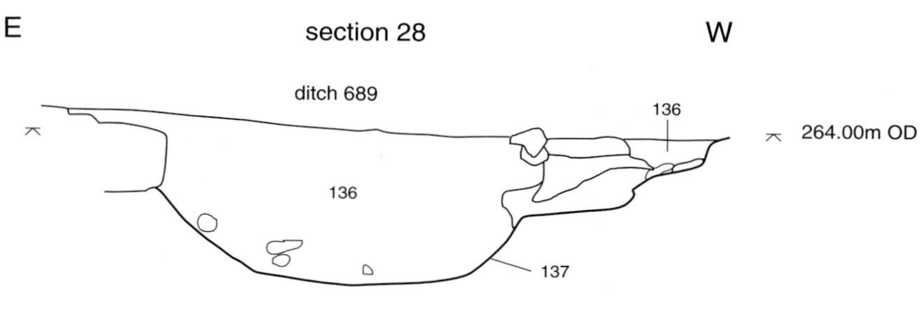


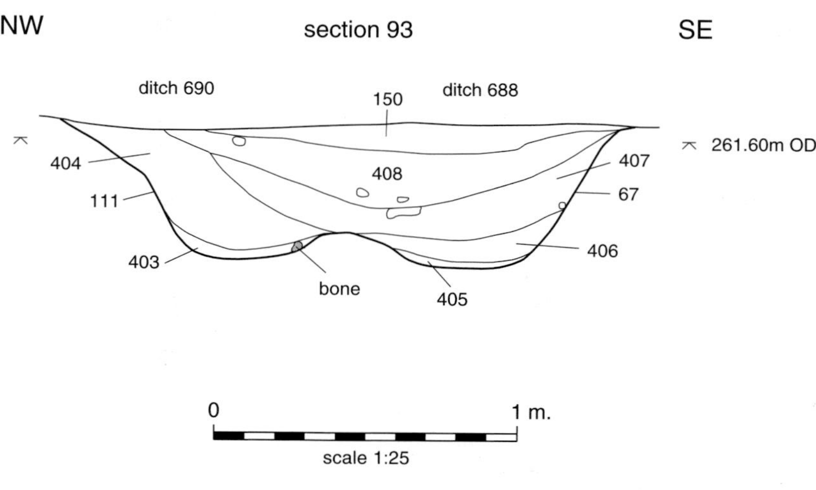


*Figure 4.68 Birdlip Quarry, main site, ditch sections.*

lacked the greyness typical of the later phase features in this area, which suggested that the ditch belonged to Period 1.

### *Main site boundary ditches: Phase 1* (*Fig. 4.43*)

A pattern of linear ditches and gullies can be identified suggesting that field/property boundaries were established in the earlier period. These include the ditches already discussed under Areas A, B and C. Finds were generally sparse and features were frequently truncated by recutting, so the dating evidence and the overall pattern of activity were somewhat hazy.

*Ditch 690*

This was the earlier cut (segment 111) of the main north-east – south-west linear ditch. It was largely truncated by the recut 688 and there was no good dating evidence from the fills (Fig. 4.68, sections 13 and 93). All the fills, which tended to be light orange-brown silts, may be interpreted as natural silting implying a long period of use or possible abandonment since the ditch appears to have filled com-pletely before being recut on its eastern side. It was traced southward into Area 3, but its junction with ditch 1685, which ran at right-angles, was not within the excavated area.

*Gullies 691 and 692*

These gullies formed a sequence of stratigraphically early features running north-west – south-east in the complex of intersections at the northern end of ditch 690. Gully 692 appears to have replaced 691 and then have been replaced by 689 (Period 2A) although it is considered possible that a 689 was partly coeval. The north-west end of the gullies was cut by a lynchet, but it seems probable that they terminated at this point anyway. To the south-east they faded out in an area of outcropping limestone. There was little dating evidence.

*Ditch 683*

Ditch 683 in the northern part of the site seems to have had an early origin and was probably con-temporary with gullies 691/692 defining a space 8–9 m wide running north-west – south-east The ditch was generally about 1 m wide and under 0.3 m deep. It became shallower toward the south-eastern terminal and it is unclear whether or not it originally extended further in this direction. The south-east sections (segment 138) showed a single orange-brown fill containing an assemblage of 18 sherds of 2nd-century date. To the north-west a number of recuts were identified. The dating evidence from this area appears somewhat mixed, but redeposited 2nd-century pottery was present (fill 505, segment 567) and it is likely that the original ditch was followed by the line of later recuts and turned north-east. The earliest ditch, segment 475 which had a light yellowish brown lower fill, was probably equivalent to segment 138, although the dating from the main fill 568 suggests a slightly later infilling in the 3rd century.

*Gully 685*

This was an early version of the long linear gully 684 (Period 2A) running north-north-east – south-south-west, but only present at the corner of this enclosure. It shallowed northward and it is unclear how far it originally extended. It was cut by ditch 683 but was without finds.

*Gully 65 (=842)*

A segment of a small gully lay in the south-east corner of the site. It was perhaps contemporary with ditch 690 as the gully did not extend beyond it to the north-west. It had a clear south-eastern terminal. Gullies 65 and 842 were not connected but were on the same alignment and are likely to have been the same feature. There were no diagnostic finds.

### *Wells*

*Well 277 (Fig. 4.69)*

This well was located in the north-eastern part of the site apparently somewhat isolated from contemp-oraneous features (Fig. 4.43). It was excavated, in stages, to a depth of approximately 4 m (the engineering formation level) without the bottom being reached or waterlogged deposits being found. The upper 3 m had been disturbed by a geotechnical pit which had more or less half-sectioned the feature. The pit was re-excavated in two stages by machine. The section was recorded at each stage and the remaining half of the well dismantled by hand. Few finds were retrieved from the upper 3 m as there was little *in situ* material. The lowest metre of undisturbed fill was excavated by hand.

The well had a dry-stone lining (293) which was perfectly circular in form with an internal diameter of 0.6 m. The structure had been slightly damaged by the geotechnical pit but it was clear that it had survived up to the modern ground surface. There was no regular coursing evident. Below about 3 m the stone lining was seen to be tightly packed against the construction cut 288 which was funnel shaped and narrowed from a diameter of about 3 m at ground level to 1.2 m at 3 m depth. The main fill behind the stones was a redeposited silt-clay with limestone (291) although the upper packing was more mixed (289 and 290). The fill of the well-shaft below the modern infill (292) comprised grey silts mixed with large but diminishing quantities of rubble (349, 368 and 381). It is probable that this all represents infilling after the well had ceased to function. The fact that the structure of the well had survived intact until modern times would suggest that it had been deliberately infilled to the surface, the rubble having been brought from elsewhere. Among the finds from 349 was a fragment of a jet finger ring (Fig. 7.40.678). A large assemblage

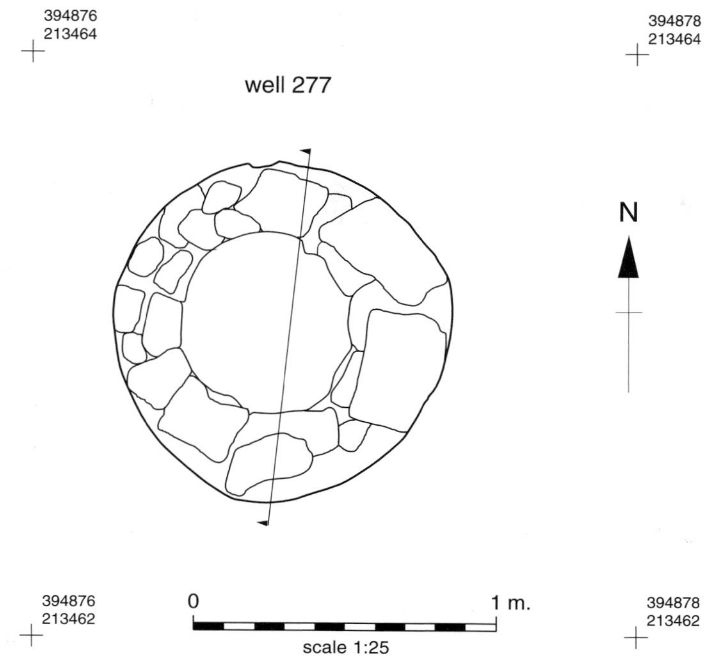


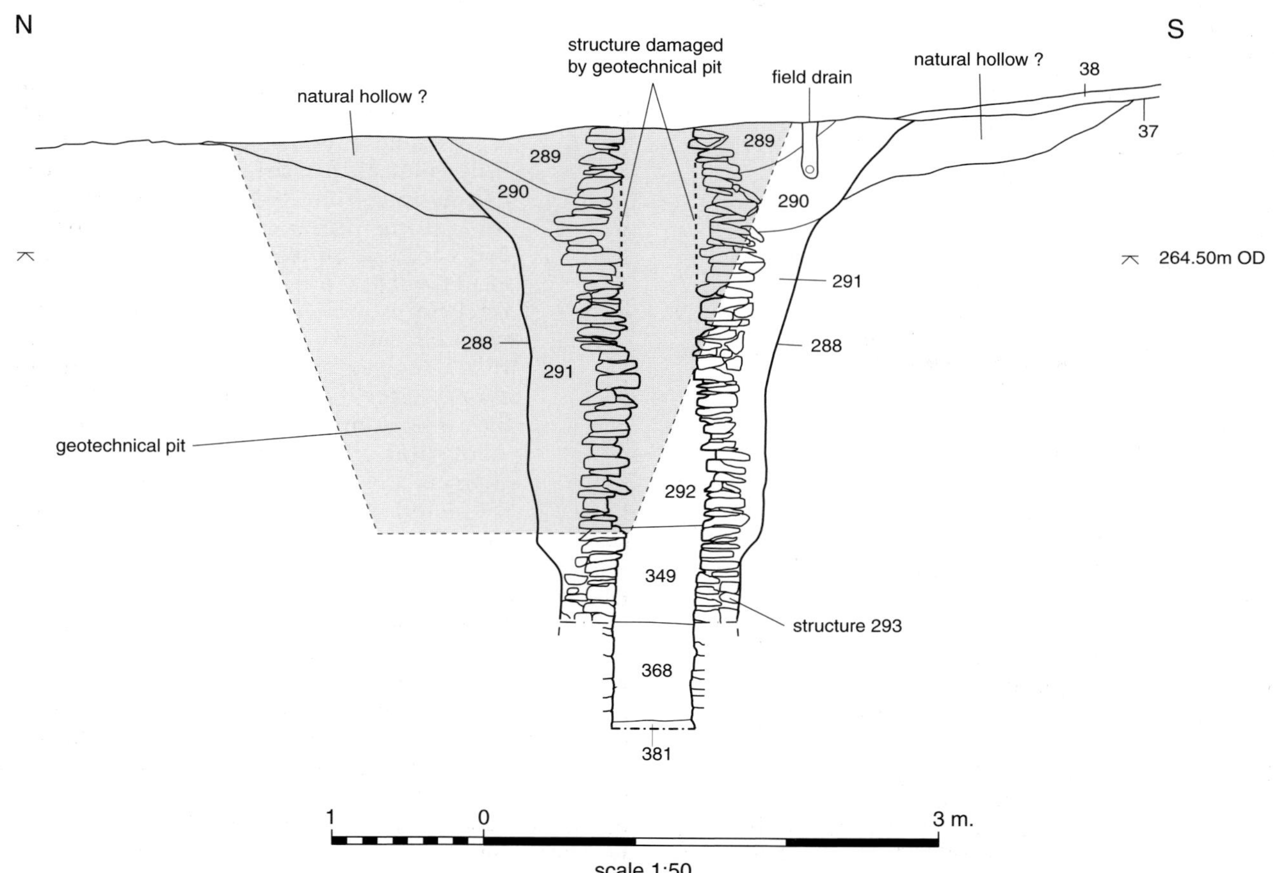


*Figure 4.69 Birdlip Quarry, period 1, well 277, plan and section.*

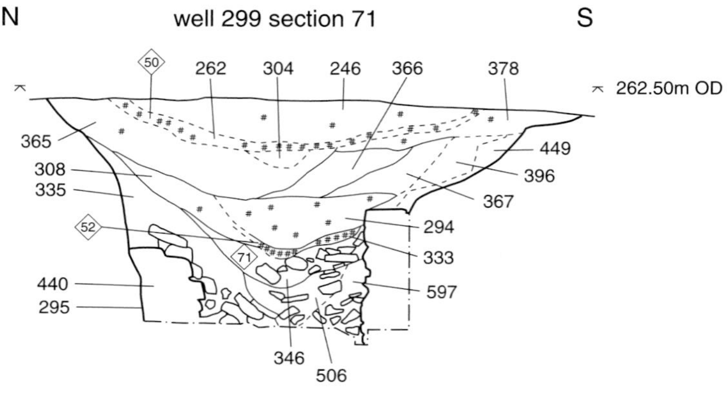


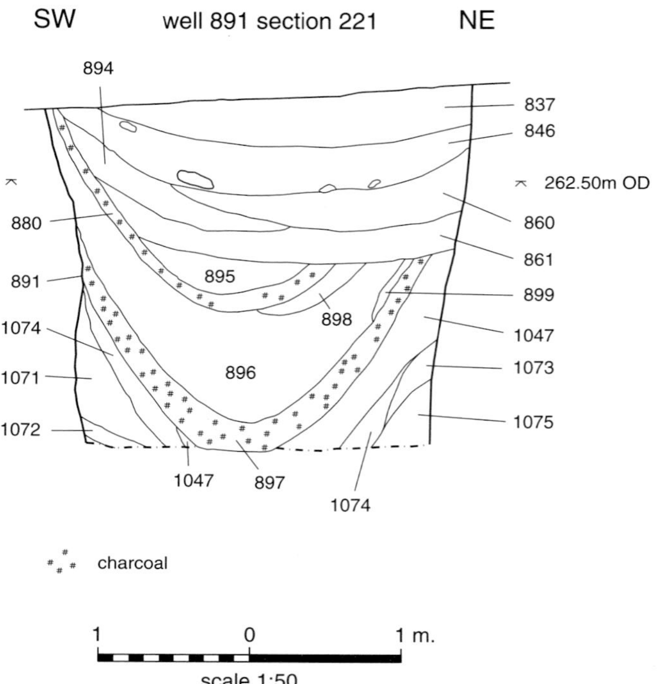


*Figure 4.70 Birdlip Quarry, sections through wells 299 and 891.*

(160 sherds) of 2nd and 3rd-century pottery came from fill 368. Carbonised plant remains from the same fill consisted mostly of wheat chaff (Table 8.53, sample 48; see Pelling, Chapter 8).

*Well 299 (Figs 4.64 and 4.70)*

This well was situated just west of Area E. It was excavated by hand to engineering formation level which was about 1.5 m below ground level. The upper part of the feature (cut 295) was a weathering cone about 3.4 m in diameter and up to 1 m deep which had been filled with dumps of domestic debris datable to the 4th century. Below this the well cut narrowed and the dry-stone lining (440) was found partly intact. It formed a roughly circular shaft about 1 m in diameter. The series of fills within and over the structure consisted largely of rubble which is likely to have derived from the upper part of the structure. Pottery from these fills was exclusively 2nd-century in date suggesting that the well had gone out of use relatively early in the life of the settlement. There was no evidence for the date of its construction. It may have been contemporary with structure 1458 (Area E) although the latter lacked good dating evidence. The radically later date for the upper infilling suggests that the area had been abandoned for much of the 3rd century, although this does not comfortably match the evidence from structure 1459 (Area E, Phase 2) which appears to have been occupied for at least part of this time.

*'Well' 891 (Fig. 4.43 and 4.70)*

This feature was situated just north-east of Area D. It was a circular pit 2.8–3.0 m in diameter. It was excavated to engineering formation level, a depth of 2.4 m, and the sides were still almost vertical. Although no stone lining was found, it is likely that the feature was another well and that the stone lining had either been removed or had collapsed further down the shaft.

The lower fills (1047, 1071–5) were largely redeposited natural silt-clays, which represented edge-slumping, mixed with a little cultural material. A few large blocks of limestone from 1073 may have been part of a stone lining. Sherds of probable 3rd-century pottery came from 1047 along with a horse's skull which is of uncertain significance. These deposits were succeeded by a series of steeply tipping fills which appear to represent infilling shortly after the collapse of the sides. Fill 897 was a thin, charcoal-rich deposit. Above this were a series of grey silts with charcoal and abundant cultural debris (896, 880) interleaved with yellowish brown silts (899, 898, 895). The large pottery assemblages from 896 and 880 suggest an infilling around the middle to late 3rd century.

The final levelling up of the hollow may have taken place in two stages. The initial fills 861, 894 and 860 were yellowish brown silts which may represent a period of natural silting, although finds were still present in reasonable quantities. This was followed by dumps of brown or grey-brown silts with limestone lumps and cultural debris (846 and 837). A partially articulated dog skeleton came from 846.

These upper fills are broadly 4th century in date, although if the pit was infilled in the mid 3rd century, a later 3rd century start for the final filling is plausible. The date for the construction of the well is not known,

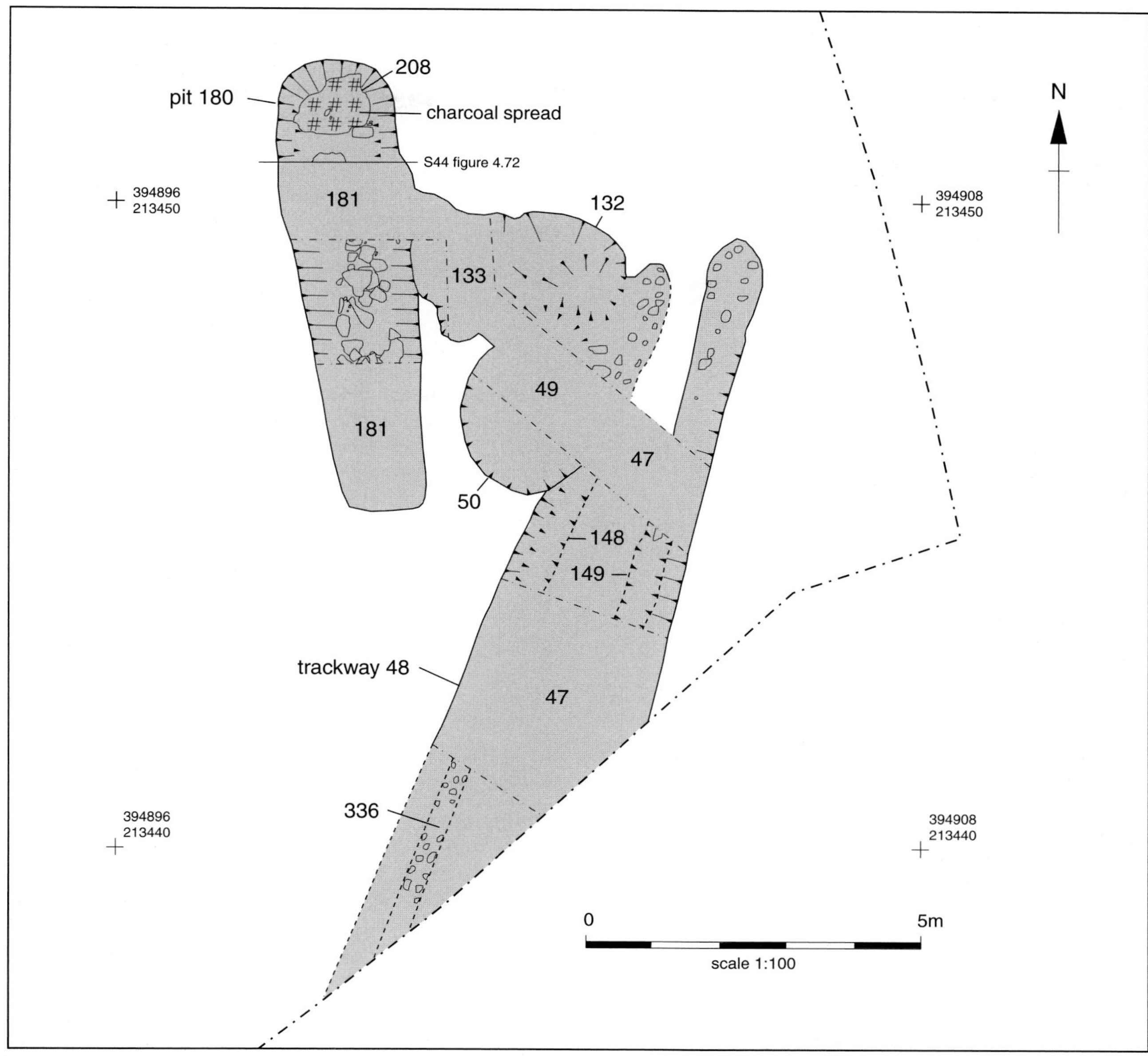


*Figure 4.71 Birdlip Quarry, period 1, plan of pit 180 and trackway 148.*

but it would be reasonable to see it as contemporary with structure 1456 (Area D) and probably dug in the later 2nd century. Its collapse and abandonment in the middle of the 3rd century is entirely compatible with the evidence for the abandonment of Area D, which was then re-occupied in the later 3rd century.

***Pits*** *(Fig. 4.43)*

*Pit 180 (Figs 4.71–72)*

This was a curious elongated sub-rectangular pit sited on the hillslope next to the trackway (48) in the north-east corner of the site. It was over 7 m long and up to 0.6 m deep with moderately or gradually sloping sides and a flattish base (Fig. 4.72, section 44). Over a thin skim of primary silting (226), the terminal contained a charcoal spread, 208, which comprised a high proportion of germinated grains, suggesting a by-product of malting (Table 8.54, see Pelling, Chapter 8). This was sealed by thin clean deposits of silt (225, 224) which may have been further natural infilling. Another thin deposit of charcoal, 207, spread for about 2.5 m along the ditch. This contained a high proportion of chaff, indicative of cereal processing waste. The middle fill of this feature, 189, was a deposit of large limestone blocks within a grey-brown silt matrix, possibly intended to put the feature out of use. The final fill, 181, was a conspicuously dark grey-brown silt with rubble and cultural material. This appears to represent a dump of occupation debris. Charred remains included a relatively high proportion

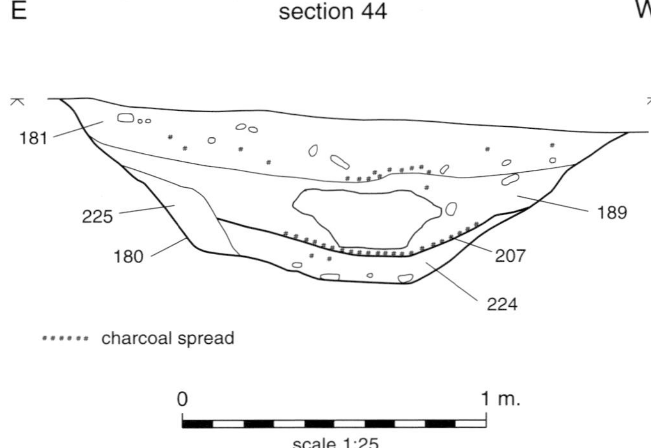


*Figure 4.72 Birdlip Quarry, pit 180, section.*

of wheat grains probably derived from the accidental burning of the crop.

A large group of pottery from 181 suggests that the feature had gone out of use before the middle of the 3rd century. Three sherds from the charcoal layer 208 are consistent with a 2nd-century use of the pit. Although it is possible that the pit was a form of corn dryer, on the whole it seems unlikely that the charcoal relates to the pit's primary purpose. There was no suggestion of burning within the pit, nor any associated with the rubble infill and the pit might have been merely a suitable repository for waste material. The function of the pit therefore remains unclear. Its position close to trackway 48 may be significant and it seems likely that it served to store crops or fuel. The stones which were later used to backfill the pit may have been from some sort of containing structure although this is far from certain.

*Pit 50 (Fig. 4.71)*

This was a shallow circular feature between pit 180 and trackway 48. It was in an area of irregular shallow scoops (which may have been tree-throw holes or quarry pits) and it is uncertain whether this might be part of the same activity. It did not have a clear relationship with the trackway and it is possible that they both filled in at the same time. A few animal bones came from the upper fill, 49. Its purpose is unclear.

*Pit 174*

This was a well-defined circular pit near the northern edge of the site (Fig. 4.43). It was 1 m in diameter and almost 1 m deep with vertical sides and a rounded base cut into bedrock. Its function is uncertain, but it may have been a storage pit. Over a thin greyish lower fill (263), the main fills 173 and 172 consisted chiefly of yellowish brown silt-clay with limestone fragments which may represent natural infilling. Pottery from 263 and 173 is consistent with a 2nd-century infilling. A single sherd from the top fill 172 is datable to after AD 200, but this is not incompatible with a use of the pit in the 2nd century.

*Pit 949*

This was a sub-rectangular pit with steep sides and a flat base, cut by 'well' 891 (Figs 4.43 and 4.70). It had been truncated by a lynchet and only survived to a depth of 0.04 m. It was without finds.

***Trackway 48*** *(Fig. 4.71)*

In the north-east corner of the site part of a probable cobbled trackway was exposed running approximately north-south. It consisted of a shallow (0.1 m) depression with a pair of wheel ruts (148 and 149) along the edges about 1.7 m apart (centre to centre) and up to 0.15 m deep. A scatter of sub-rounded limestone cobbles lay on the surface of the trackway. These were more tightly packed within the ruts suggesting a deliberate attempt to provide firm ground.

A small group of pottery from the fill of the trackway (47) is dated to after AD 200. However, this is likely to be later than the period when the trackway was in use which is likely to have started in the 2nd century, and continued for an unknown length of time.

## Period 2A: *c.* AD 250–330

During the mid 3rd century the structures of Period 1 went out of use and were replaced by slightly different structures on the same sites. The main site boundary ditches were also re-dug (Fig. 4.73).

***Areas A, 2B and 2C: Phase 3*** *(Fig. 4.74)*

*Soil layers 849 and 840 and contemporary deposits*

Following the abandonment of structure 1464 of Period 1, the penannular ditch 1451 was deliberately infilled. Later there was an accumulation of soil over this area. This was clearest on the western side where layer 849 occupied the deepest part of the terrace hollow to a maximum depth of about 0.10 m (Fig. 4.51, section 245). This layer was a very uniform mid greyish brown clayey silt with variable olive-brown mottling and abundant fine weathered limestone grains. It thinned out towards the east. There was not much evidence for this horizon inside the area of the buildings, but it is probable that it was worn away by use associated with the later structure 1452. It was probably thinly present overlying layer 731, which was the earlier subsoil in the central part of the area, although it could not be differentiated from the latter during excavation. However, it is significant that the wall (730) of structure 1452 was constructed on a very similar soil 840, and it appears likely that this is the only place on the eastern side of the later structure where this soil remained protected. Outside the later

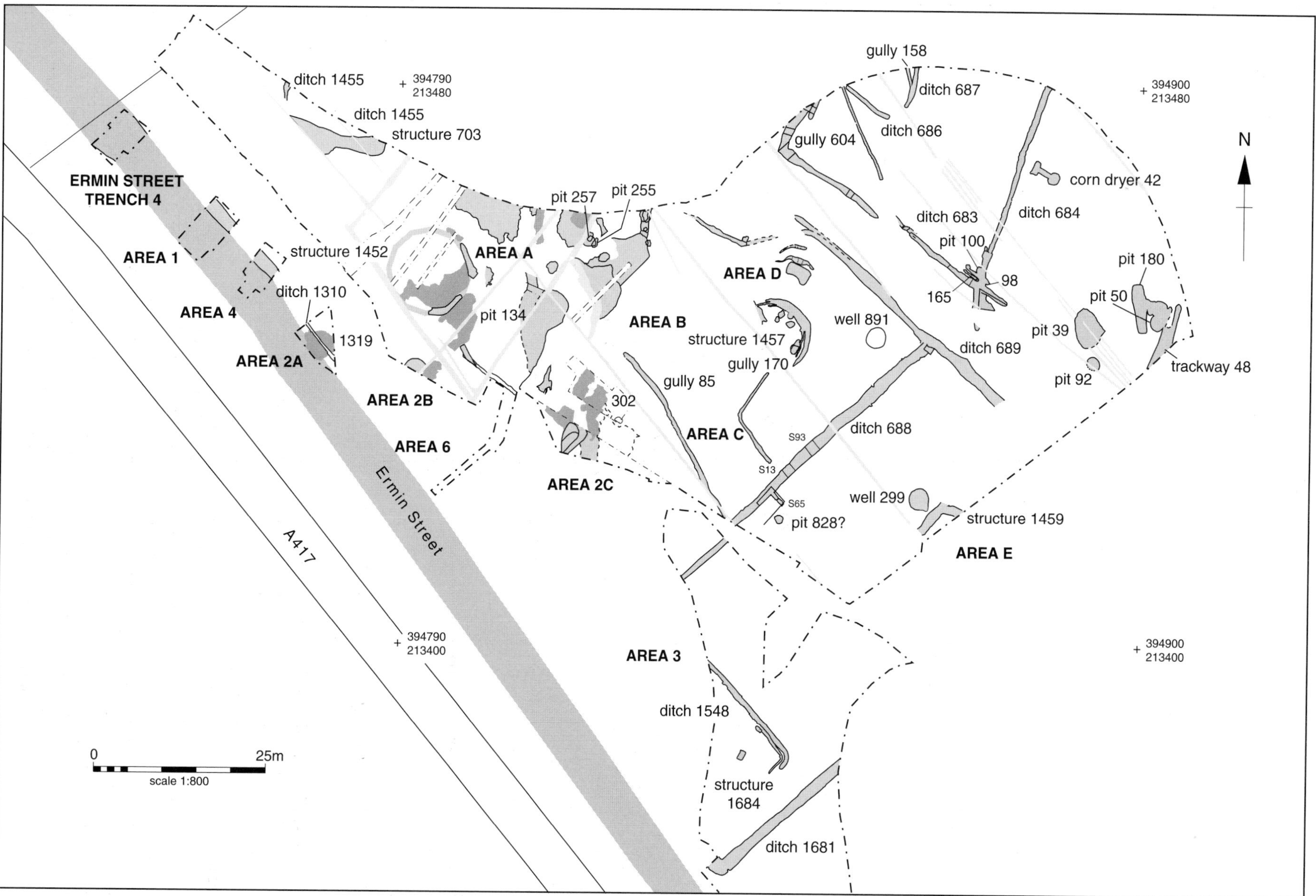


*Figure 4.73 Birdlip Quarry, period 2a , site plan.*

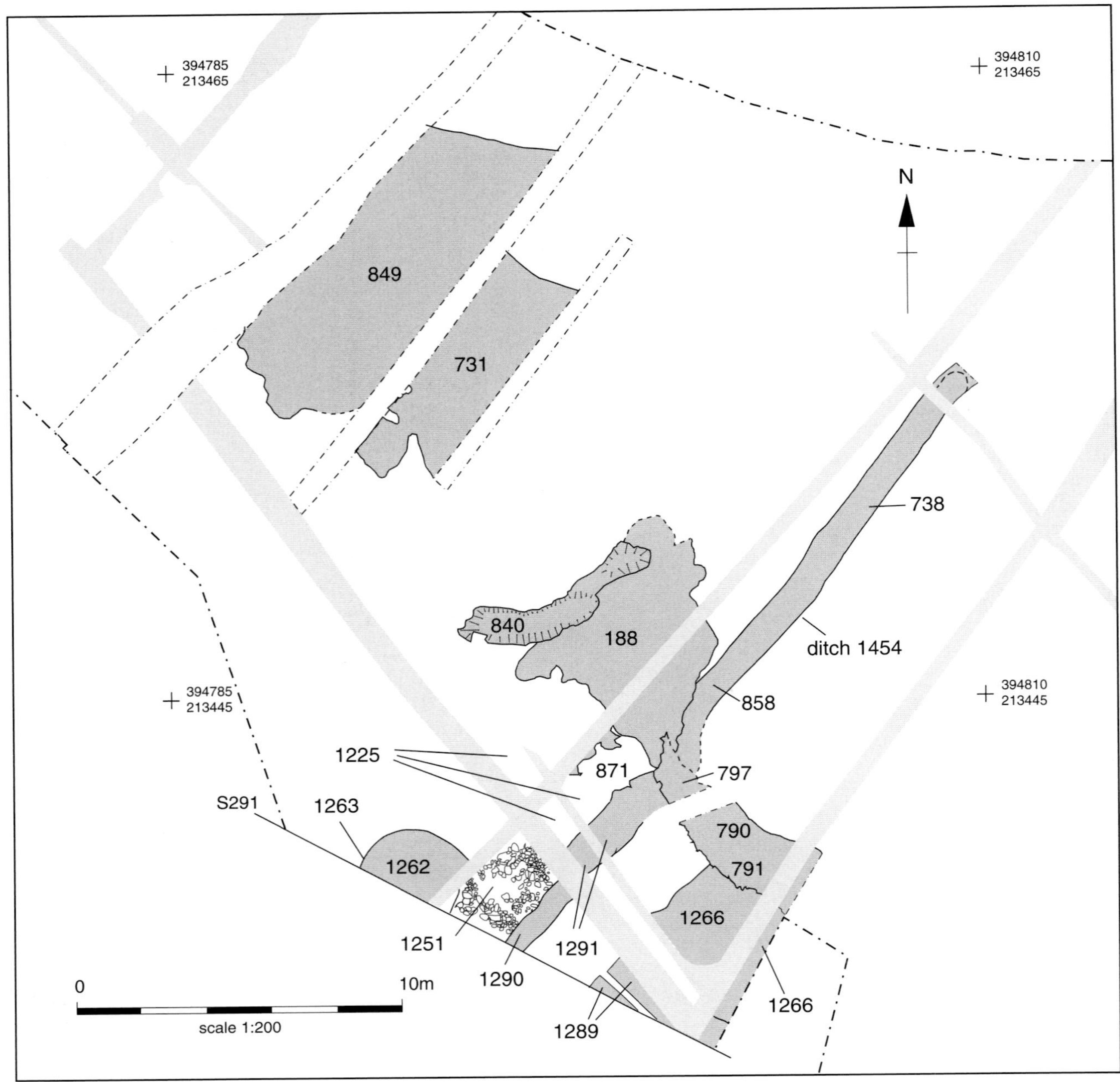


*Figure 4.74 Birdlip Quarry, period 2a, Areas A and 2B, phase 3.*

building, the soil under the later stone flagging 188 was a darker silty loam, but the assemblage of pottery shows a similar later 3rd-century date range and it is considered likely that this soil belongs to the same post-abandonment horizon, albeit perhaps mixed with earlier occupation material.

A large amount of pottery (508 sherds), datable to AD 240–300, came from layers 849, 840 and 188. It is clear that occupation continued nearby and the area was perhaps not so much abandoned as turned over to a different use.

In the south-east part of Area A, ditch 1454 had become infilled by this time with pottery from fills 738, 858, 734 and 732 of a similar character to that from the layers over structure 1464 (Fig. 4.75, section 199). There continued a development of soil beyond the confines of the ditch with layers 791 and 797 containing 3rd-century pottery.

There was little identifiable activity in Areas 2B and 2C from after *c.* AD 220. In Area 2C, the filling of ditches 1255, 1256 and 1258 was followed by a deep accumulation of soil 1235, 1236 and 1253 which yielded a large quantity of pottery (around 250 sherds) dated to AD 180–250 (Fig. 4.51, sections 293 and 274). The layer above, 1210, was a general spread of grey-brown clayey silt. The upper part of this layer was seen to be very 'clean' and was partly removed by machine, but a large number of finds came from towards the base of the layer, including 941 sherds of pottery dated to *c.* AD 180–300. It appears that the area was used as a rubbish midden until around AD 300, after which it was effectively abandoned without finds reaching it in significant quantities.

Similarly, in the western part of Area 2B, layer 225, which was a dark greyish brown silt, contained a large assemblage (232 sherds) of 3rd-century pottery (Fig. 4.51, section 291). It partly overlay pit 1263, which appears to have been deliberately infilled after the middle of the 3rd century with nearby midden material.

Further east, the backfill of ditch 1293 (Fig. 4.51, section 291) was followed by a long period of natural silting (1291 and 1290). This is probably equivalent to the 3rd-century soil development 791, 797 and 705 in the main area of excavation (Fig. 4.75, sections 199 and 256). The upper fill of ditch 1293, fill 1290, contained moderate quantities of limestone pieces which probably derived from the stone surface 1251. This appears to have remained as a visible feature. To the east, layers 1289, 1266 and 1227 represent accumulations of soil with midden material of broadly 3rd-century date, more or less equivalent to layer 210 but with rather fewer finds (120 sherds in total).

In Area 6 the accumulation of soil over ditch 698 (layers 1167 and 1168 – Fig. 4.100) probably dates from this phase, although the pottery did not provide very precise dating.

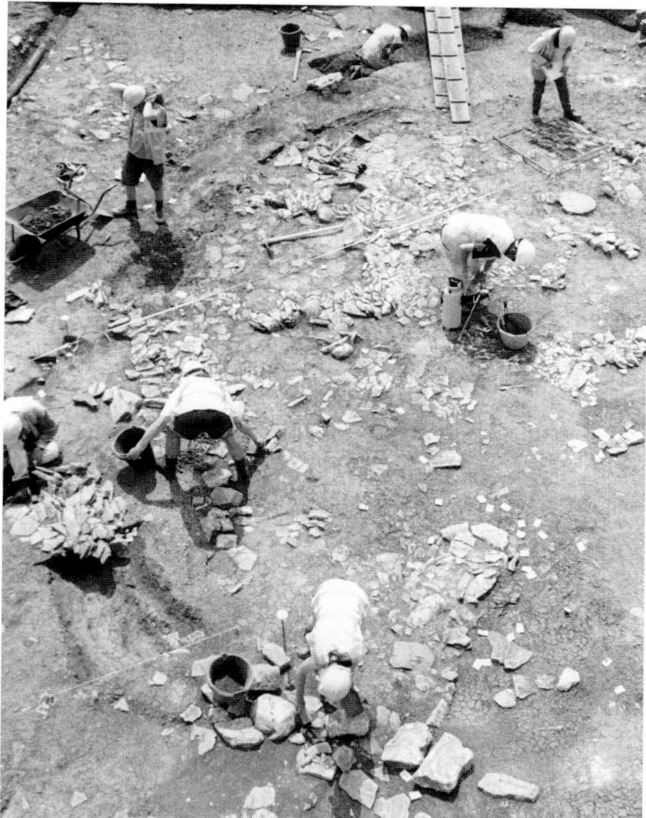

*Plate 4.14 Area A interior of superimposed structures under excavation. Stone wall footings 758 (structure 1452) in the foreground overlie the earlier penannular ditches the later of which is filled with pitched stone to the left. Hearth 756 (centre) lies close to the later wall. Patches of stone flooring occupy the interior.*

### *Areas A, 2B and 2C: Phase 4 (Fig. 4.76)*

This phase is marked by the construction of the first stone building in this area, structure 1452. This appears to have followed a period of soil accumulation (Phase 3) which was probably widespread, though only well-preserved on the western side of the area where there was less subsequent activity. The date of construction of 1452, and hence the duration of the 'abandonment', are difficult to assess. Indeed, a number of observations present problems when considered in the context of any significant period of 'abandonment'.

Firstly, structure 1452 was in almost precisely the same location and, as far as can be judged, almost exactly the same size, as the earlier structures, which implies that the intention was to copy them with a different method. From this it appears that there could not have been a significant amount of soil accumulation over this area unless the new builders were extremely tightly constrained in their choice of building type and site and the location of the new structure over the old was coincidental.

Secondly, the backfill of the penannular ditch on the north-east side (segment 784) was packed with rubble (fill 773) which appears to have served as a foundation for the wall of structure 1452 (Fig. 4.47, section 203). Indeed it appears that wall segment 758 continued into the top of ditch segment 884 as a line of wall facing-stones (Fig. 4.47, section 209). This would appear to indicate that structure 1452 was built at the same time as the penannular ditch was infilled. Generally, it would appear to make sense that the ground should be made solid in preparation for a new period of building, rather than prior to a period of 'abandonment'. Other ditch segments around the northern side of the building show pitched stone in the top fill of the ditch (sections 208 and 221) suggesting that this was a later insertion into an already infilled ditch and may have involved partial redigging of the ditch in order to provide a firmer base for the wall. Pitched stone 761, however, does not lie on the projected alignment of wall segment 758 (Fig. 4.76), and it must be considered possible that the infilling of the ditch was not connected with the construction of 1452, or perhaps a building project had been planned but had then been postponed.

#### *Stone structure 1452*

##### Walls 730 and 841

Wall 730 survived in a short section and comprised facing stones, generally one course and sometimes two courses high, with a rubble core. It was about 1 m

*Plate 4.15 Area A. Sherds of Dressel 20 amphora, almost indistinguishable from stone, lie in front of and under large facing stones of wall 730 (structure 1452).*

wide. There was no bedding for the wall, the stones had simply been laid on the ground. The facing stones had been removed in places, but the robbed void was traceable as far as a large grooved stone. Beyond this there was a gap of *c.* 3 m before the wall continued as 841 and then further north as 758–762 surviving merely as lines of facing stones.

These traces of surviving wall show a roughly circular building with an internal diameter of about 11 m. The slight angle in wall 730 indicates that it might have been a polygonal building. This would be easier to construct if using timber framing on stone footings and the insubstantial nature of the footings would seem to be more suited to timber-framing than mass construction. A 12-sided building with wall sections 2.9 m long fits the angle in wall 730, as well as the projection of wall 758, tolerably well (Fig. 4.76). Wall 841 is not really within the circuit of any regular construction and may have formed an abutment. The wall footings presumably ran all the way round but were completely robbed from the western side of the building. A projection using the model of a 12-sided polygon 11 m in diameter, shows that the wall would have run along layer 849 where this shows as a slight ridge between 'occupation deposits' 735 (=778) and 736. Beyond this the line of the wall is not traceable.

The position of the entrance is not at all clear. There may have been an entrance facing south-east between 730 and 841 but it is possible that the wall had simply been removed. Given the limited structural evidence the entrance could have been almost anywhere, but it is tempting to see one facing east-south-east between the two large grooved blocks of stone. An entrance here would also be defined by a shallow hollow, later filled with stone rubble 743, which lay just within the building. It is unclear why an eroded hollow should lie exclusively within the building rather than outside it too, but it is possible that the threshold was at one time protected by a stone alignment which was later removed. There were no entrance posts evident, but small areas of pitched stone behind each of the blocks may have been post positions lying about 3 m apart.

#### Grooved stones

Two large grooved stones formed an integral part of walls 730 and 841 (cat. 719 and 721). Both were of local limestone. That within wall 730 was 0.7 m long and 0.25 m thick with the width tapering from 0.5 to 0.35 m. It had a longitudinal groove, 0.01–0.02 m deep, cut into it, and a notch cut at one end through the thickness of the block. The piece had the app-earance of being a quarried block on which shaping or trimming had occurred.

The stone block in wall 841 was a more neatly squared slab, 1 m x 0.4 m x 70–150 mm thick. The upper surface was cut by dense parallel grooves, up to 0.02 m deep. They tended to be deepest towards the narrower edge and were well weathered. There was a later cut mark on the narrower edge and apparent tooled depressions at one end. It is possible that these had been caused by its casual use as a sharpening stone. The reverse side had been pecked smooth. The grooving is not easy to account for. It is unlikely to have been caused by ploughing since adjacent stones were unmarked even

*Plate 4.16 Area A. Squared grooved stone lying against wall 841 at the probable entrance to structure 1452.*

*Plate 4.17 Area A structure 1452. Traces of the stone-footed circular or polygonal building. The ditches and stone culvert of the earlier structures lie to the left.*

though they were at the same level. Moreover, the grooves have a marked U-shaped profile often with quite sharp ridges between them, giving the appearance of having been caused by prolonged friction with rope. This would imply that the block was tightly bound on one side and perhaps used in some kind of domestic or industrial process, but to what purpose is unclear. The absence of wear on any of the edges may imply that they were protected in some way, perhaps by adjacent stones. The only clear conclusion is that the stone's use as wall material was not related to its original function.

### Interior features

The interior features probably include most, if not all the pitched stone flooring. Although there was insufficient evidence to be sure of this, the pitched stone was never necessarily an early feature and could always be accommodated as part of structure 1452. One possible doubt concerns the position of the pitched stone surface 927 which was slightly under the stone wall 776 on the south-western side of the earlier structure. This may be sufficient reason to suggest either that 776 was a later modification or replacement of 718 rather than an integral part of it, or that the pitched stone was earlier. However, the overlap between 776 and 927 was marginal and it is considered possible that the pitched stone flooring was inserted right up against these earlier stones.

The pitched stone surfaces had a sporadic distribution, presumably related to the need to consolidate certain areas of the floor. Whether this was related to specific activities carried out is unclear. Layer 909 infilled a slight hollow which may have been at the entrance to the building. Some patches of pitched stone were very small, filling slight hollows. It is possible that these were intended as post settings for interior structures although there was no clear pattern to these features. It is possible that pit 1087 and posthole 1091 were associated with a back door, but both were very shallow and a structural significance seems doubtful. Pit 1087 contained several large sherds of a Samian bowl.

The few finds associated with this flooring are likely to have come from among and beneath the stones and therefore be related to the earlier occupation. However, at some stage there was a discontinuous re-flagging of the surface, floor 729, sealing earlier deposits which can be dated by associated pottery to the 4th century. It is unclear why this material should have accumulated on the earlier floor surface when the earlier surfaces appear to have been kept clean. The pottery from this layer was generally quite broken, although four large sherds of Savernake Ware jar suggest that some material had not been redistributed

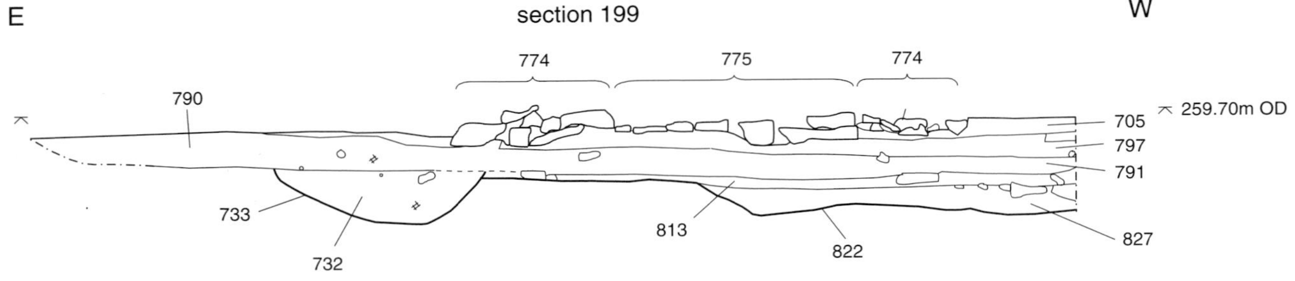


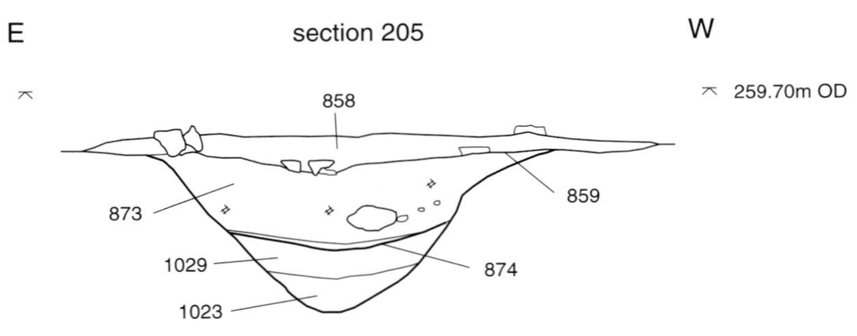


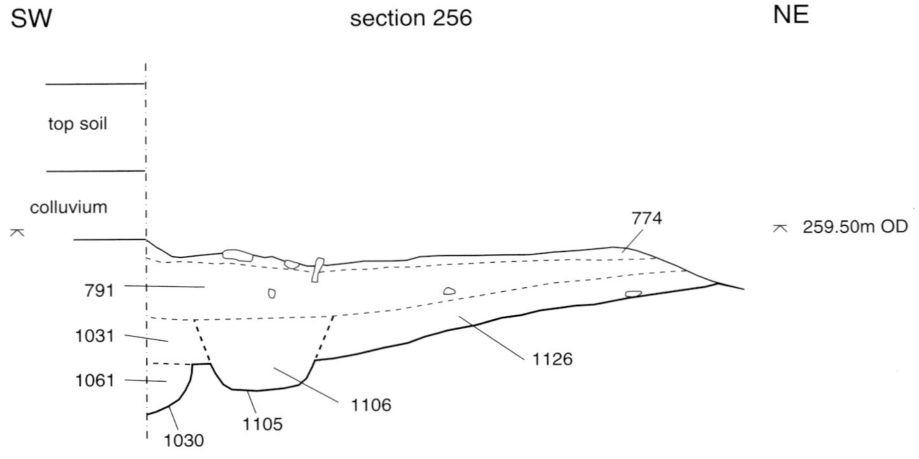

*Figure 4.75 Birdlip Quarry, ditches 1453 and 1454, slots 1030 and 1105 and associated deposits, sections.*

to a great extent. Several sherds from a DORBB1 flanged rim bowl, and from a Severn Valley Ware tankard, were also present together with the possible front loop of a hipposandal (cat. 604).

### *'Occupation layers'*

In the western part of the building the floor appears to have remained unsurfaced, although it is possible that flooring had been removed at a later date. However, there were thin deposits of dark soil with occupation material occupying slight hollows in the underlying layer (849) and sealed by Phase 5 deposits. Layers 778 and 735 would have been outside structure 1452 according to the inter-pretation presented and may have accumulated in eaves-drip gullies. Layers 736, 826, 1021 and 781 would have been largely inside the building. It is unclear why there should have been an accumulation of debris in these positions, just inside the wall and across the building, but it may have some

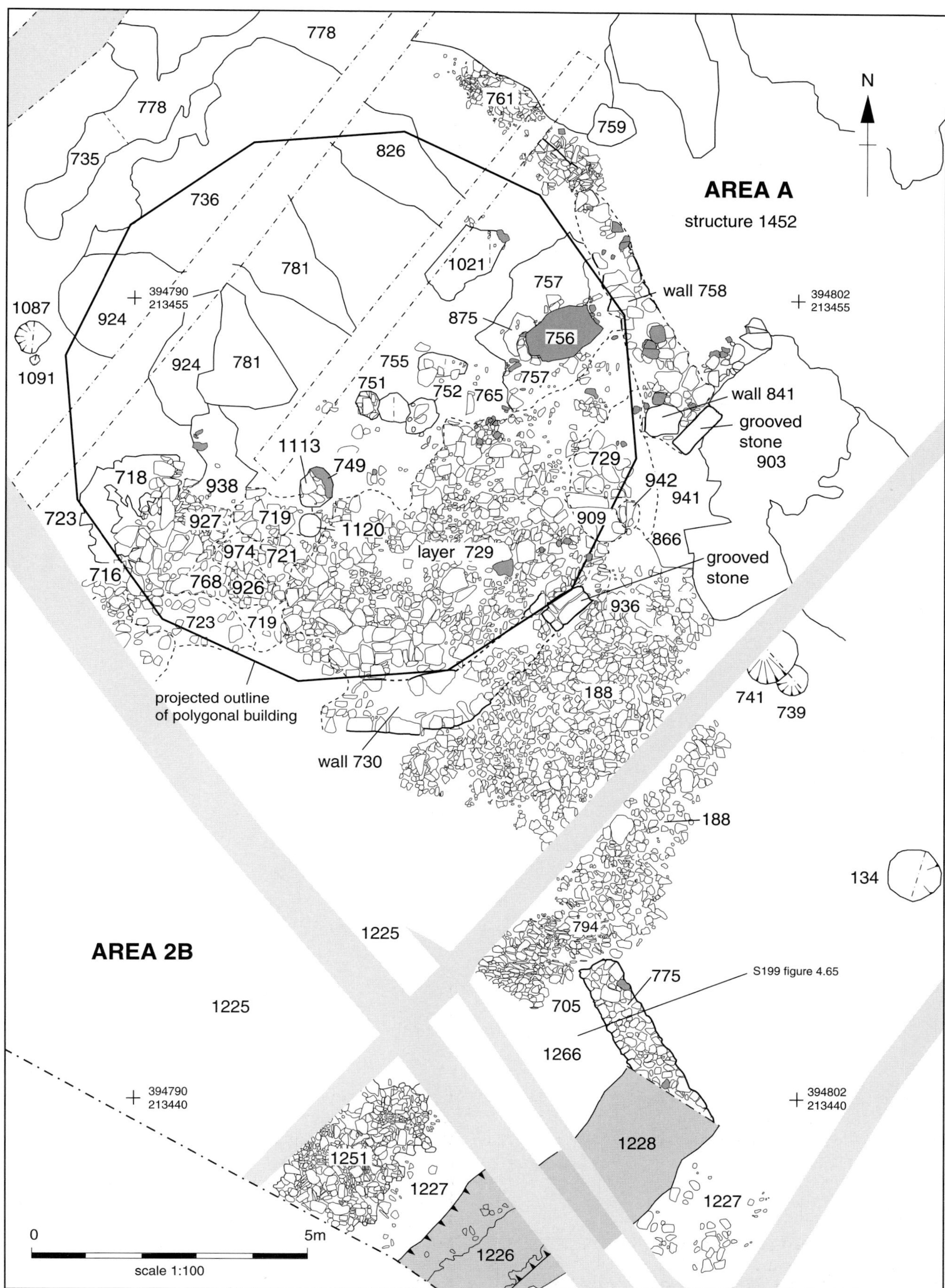


*Figure 4.76 Birdlip Quarry, period 2A, plan of structure 1452 (Area A).*

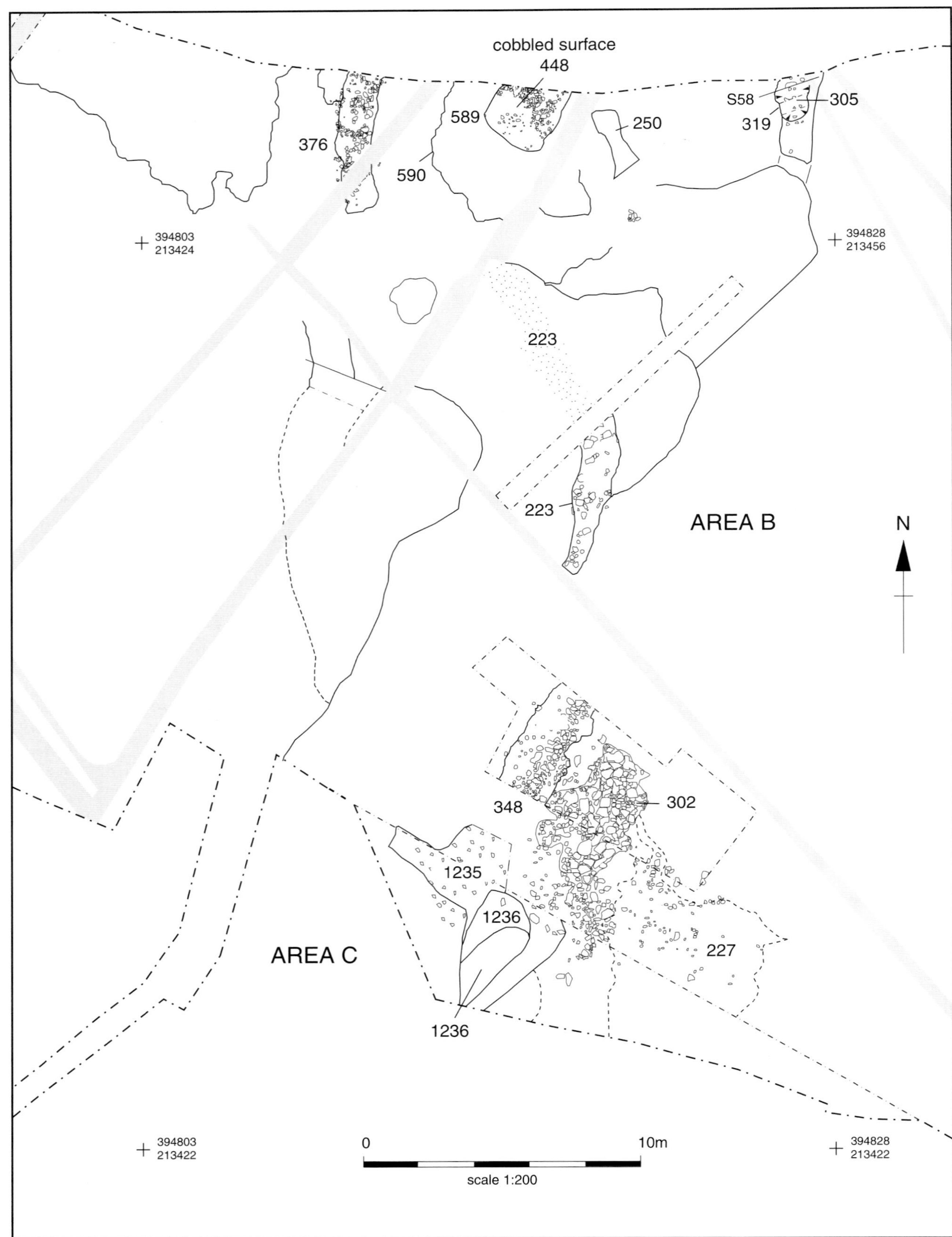


*Figure 4.77 Birdlip Quarry, Period 2a, Areas B and C.*

direct connection with activities carried out, or represent sweepings away from areas of activity. A small quantity of smithing slag came from 781. Layer 798, a more restricted concentration of dark soil and charcoal under 736, may represent *in situ* accumulation. The pottery from this layer was very fragmentary. 'Occupation layers' were also recorded in the southern part of the floor, Layers 768, 723, 924 and 938. It is unclear whether these were strictly *in situ* or material redistributed from robbing the wall or other post-abandonment disturbances.

#### Stone pavement 188

The exterior stone pavement 188 was probably all of this phase. It sealed a build-up of soil and domestic debris which was dated to AD 240–300. It was difficult to distinguish 188 from the general spreads of rubble, and although some stone flagging inside the building was initially given the same context, it is probable that this included stone flooring 729 and rubble from the walls, and that 188 was confined to outside the building.

#### Dedicatory vessel 943 (pit 942)

A DORBB1 Ware jar, substantially complete but missing its rim, had been placed in a small pit. If it were associated with the proposed interpretation of structure 1452, it would have been positioned in the centre of the doorway. Some pitched stone had been inserted into the top of the pit.

#### Dating evidence

The commencement of the occupation is difficult to estimate precisely, but was probably at the end of the 3rd century or beginning of the 4th. The pottery sealed by floor layer 729 (100 sherds) gives a generally 4th-century date for the occupation. This is confirmed by pottery from layer 798 (42 sherds) and a slightly broader date range from the later 3rd century is suggested by pottery from layer 778 (99 sherds). However, the finds from layer 736 strongly suggest that the occupation was predominantly 4th century. Notwithstanding this, a sherd of later 4th-century shelly ware from 736 and a coin of the House of Theodosius, AD 388–95 (cat. 483), which appears to be from the same level, are out of place in relation to the rest of the ceramic phasing and are considered to be from an unrecognised intrusive feature of Phase 6.

#### *Wall 775 and surface 794*

To the south of structure 1452, wall 775 consisted of two lines of facing stones and a rubble core without any form of bedding. Only one course survived. The wall appeared to respect a pitched stone surface 794. The stones were heavily pressed into the underlying soil 871 and had a fairly worn surface.

The overall pattern of these features is unclear since they did not appear in Area 2B to the south. Wall 775 may have terminated approximately under a modern pipe trench between sections 241 and 256. However, it may have been present as a group of stones in the north-east corner layer 1227, although here it did not appear as a section of wall. These stones were directly under the post-Roman colluvial layer 1211 and the intervening section is likely to have been largely lost to a combination of ploughing and machine-stripping. Stone rubble was also present in Test Pit E (shown on Fig. 4.43) and may have been the wall or wall-rubble. No trace of the wall was present in Area 6, but it is unclear whether or not it ever extended this far.

The stone surface 794 was similarly absent from Area 2. It seems unlikely that it originally extended much into this area as, in general, archaeological deposits were reasonably well-preserved here, but it is possible that the edge had been lost to machining.

### *Areas A, 2B and 2C: Phase 5*

Sometime in the mid or later 4th century structure 1452 was abandoned, the walls were largely robbed or collapsed, and there was another development of soil over the western part of the site (layer 704, Fig. 4.51, section 245). This was a grey-brown clayey silt-loam with fine weathered limestone grains and small angular lumps. Pottery from this layer was relatively abundant (200 sherds) but generally abraded suggesting that it might have been redeposited from the earlier occupation. Over the rest of the building this layer could not be distinguished from the overlying spreads of soil and rubble of the final phase although some deposits relating to the collapse of structure 1452, such as layer 815 may be of this phase. It is unclear what was happening in Area 2B. It is possible that finds were not reaching this area at this time.

### ***Area B: Phase 4*** *(Fig. 4.77)*

The cobbled surface, 307, went out of use in the 3rd century and the 'hollow way' became silted up (Fig. 4.51, section 128). Cultural material was still being deposited during this time. The lowest layer, 260, was restricted to the base of the hollow and was a uniform mottled light grey and brown silt-loam. This was overlain by 230, a light grey silt with fine weathered limestone grit which spread out more extensively. There was no indication of activity in this phase in Area C or 2C.

### ***Area B: Phase 5*** *(Fig. 4.77)*

In the earlier 4th century a deposit of fine limestone gravel, 223, was laid down running north-west – south-east across the southern part of this area. This was presumably a dump of material intended to consolidate the ground and provide a walkway. Towards the south-east the deposit became indistinct and petered out in a scatter of larger stones.

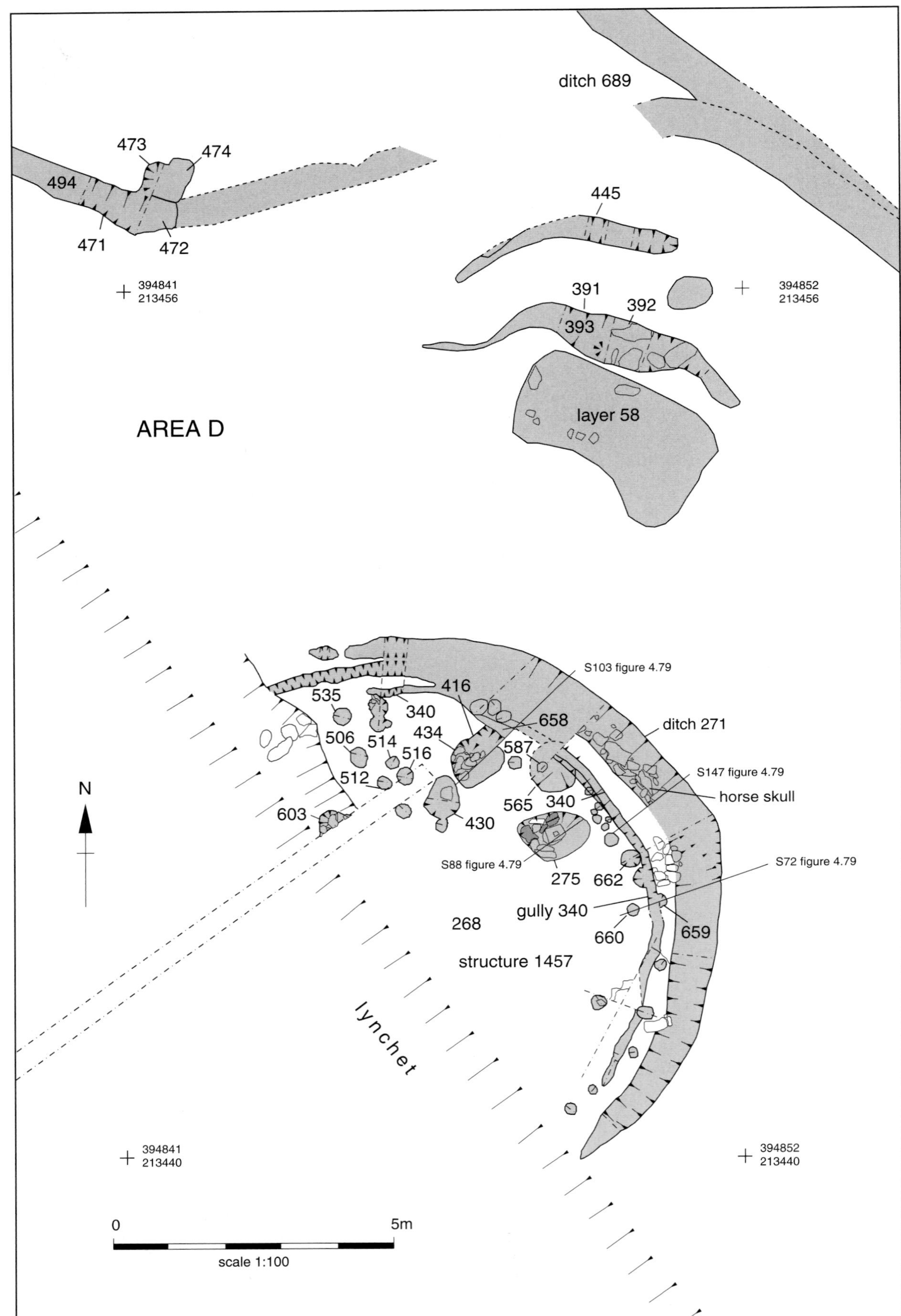


Figure 4.78 Birdlip Quarry, period 2a, structure 1457 (Area D).

Plate 4.18 Area D, structure 1457. The building has been cut away by the medieval lynchet (top).

***Area D: Phase 2** (Fig. 4.78)*

*Structure 1457*

Ditch 271

Ditch 271 was dug through the infilled earlier phase ditch 269 of structure 1456. It formed a curving enclosure with a diameter of about 10 m, although truncation by the later lynchet makes it uncertain whether its original form was circular or semi-circular. It reached a maximum depth of a little over 0.3 m on the north-east side, but shallowed considerably elsewhere and was barely evident where truncated by the lynchet. This shallowing reflects the slope of the ground since the base of the ditch was at almost exactly the same level all the way round. On the northern side the ditch split into two arms which are thought to represent two phases. No relationship between them was visible.

Ditch 271 generally had a single dark grey-brown fill (272, 469 and 467), probably representing deliberate infilling at the end of the occupation (Fig. 4.79, section 72). This contained pottery dated to after AD 240. There were also two barbarous radiates of AD 270–84 from 272, but an absence of any finds specifically datable to the 4th century. In the deepest segment north-west of section 147, a browner lower fill, 585, was also identified but was without finds (Fig. 4.79, section 147). Above this was a layer of stones, 547, which appeared represent a deliberate infilling. A horse skull had been deposited among the stones. This layer of stones was not evident in any of the other segments, but more isolated scatters of stones were present elsewhere and the concentration here may not be of particular significance.

Gully 340

Gully 340 ran inside ditch 271 as a continuous, steep-sided narrow slot with an uneven base. A concentration of shallow post/ stakeholes along this line, formed no clear pattern, but reinforced the suggestion that gully 340 was a wall-line which presumably held a row of uprights. The postholes may have provided additional support. Again there is the suggestion of two phases on the north-east side where gully 658 runs for a short distance inside gully 340 (Fig. 4.79, section 103), and some of the inner postholes may have belonged with this phase. Both the gullies and the postholes were shallow - gully 340 up to 0.17 m deep, and the postholes generally between 6 and 10 mm - and they are unlikely to have supported a roof. Gully 340 contained 12 sherds of 2nd-century pottery which is assumed to be residual from the earlier occupation.

The strip between ditch 271 and gully 340 was truncated and rather uneven. There were some quite large stones on the inner lip of the ditch tumbling into the ditch fill. These may have had some kind of structural significance, for instance to protect the base of the wall from erosion by water.

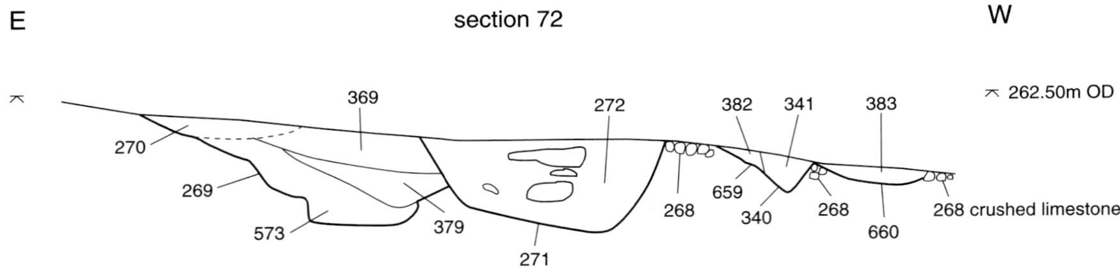


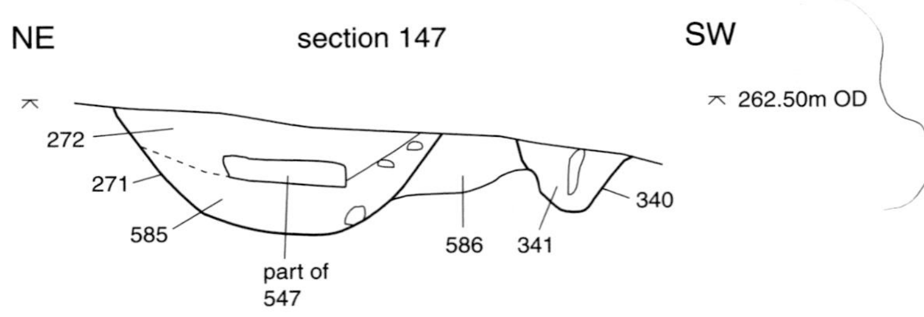


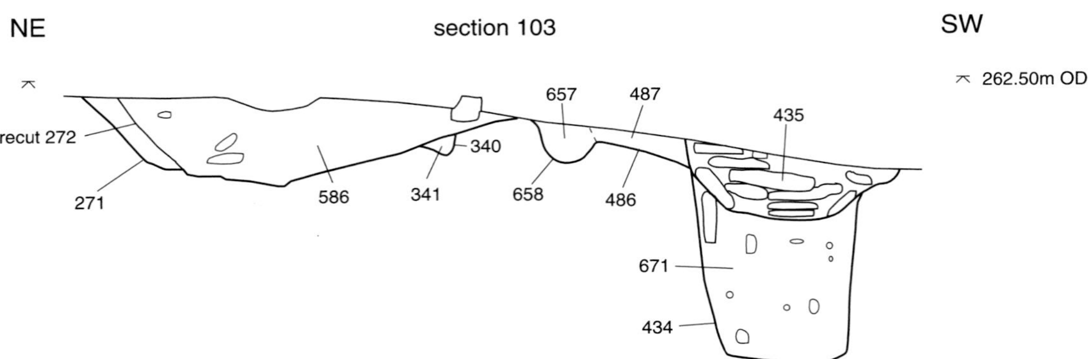


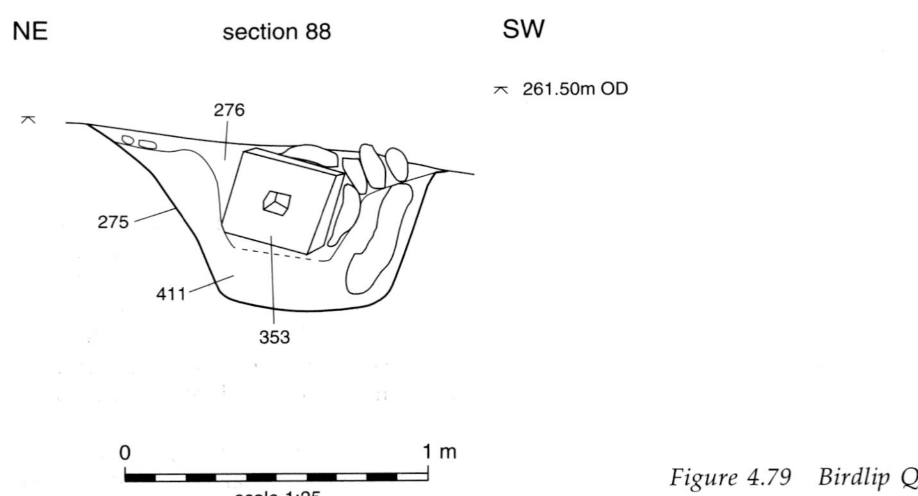


*Figure 4.79 Birdlip Quarry, Area D, sections.*

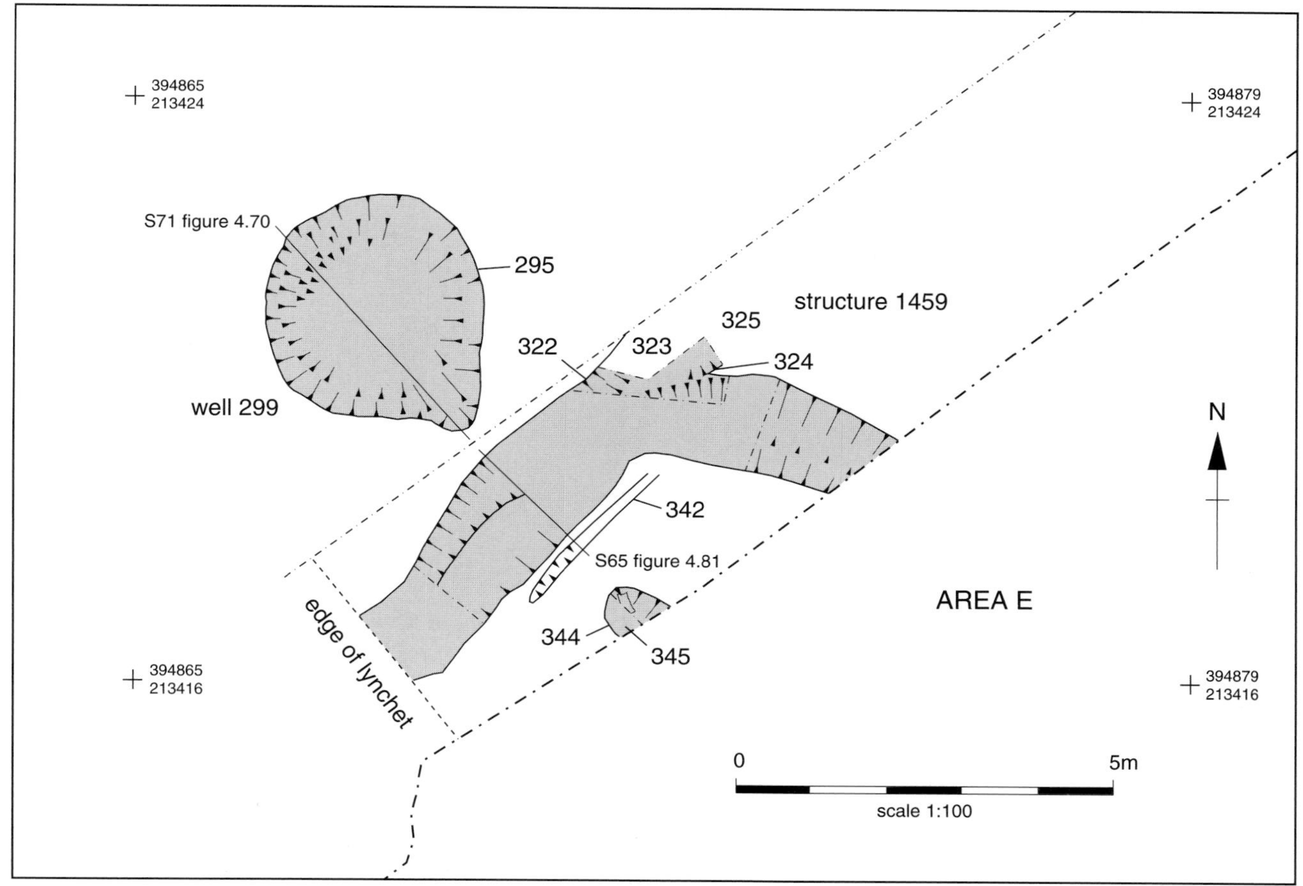


*Figure 4.80 Birdlip Quarry, period 2a, structure 1459 (Area E).*

Post-pits 434 and 275 *(Fig. 4.79, sections 103 and 88)*

Post-pit 434 was a deep feature (0.75 m) largely filled with a light-coloured silt-clay (671). This was interpreted as post-packing, although the absence of a post-void would indicate that it had slumped in once the post had been removed. The upper fill, 435, consisted of limestone rubble within a matrix of dark silt. It probably represented back-fill after the post had been removed although the density of stone suggests that it had been used as post-packing and simply put back in the vacant hole. It contained a large quantity of late Roman shelly ware which was presumably deposited after the structure had been dismantled. A slightly shallower post-pit (275) lay just a metre away to the south-east. This had a lower fill which consisted of 50% stone rubble in a yellowish brown clayey silt (411), and a darker upper fill consisting largely of stone rubble (276). Fill 276 included a large dressed block with a central square mortise (cat. 715). An iron linch pin from a cart (cat. 587) also came from this fill. Many of the other stones were wedged against the sides of the pit. Both fills may be disturbed post-packing with the upper fill containing stones from refilling the hole after dismantling the post. There was no indication of the size of the posts which the postholes held, but a post with a diameter of 0.30 m could certainly have been accommodated in each.

The function of these postholes in relation to the structure is far from clear as they occupy a position to one side of the floor. This seems to argue against them having served as roof supports. However, it is possible that an opposed pair were removed by the lynchet since, had they been dug to a slightly shallower depth than the deeper hole, 434, evidence for them would not have survived.

Floor 268

A natural outcrop of thinly bedded limestone formed the floor to the structure and had a dirty and worn appearance as a result. It probably served as the floor in both phases of occupation. Part of a Black Burnished Ware jar was found embedded into the surface just north of the earlier hearth 264. The vessel contained calcareous deposits from having been used to hold hot water, although it is considered likely to have belonged with structure 1457 rather than to have been contemporary with the hearth (section 264).

### Other internal features

There were few other internal features and none of any substance. A number of small postholes and scoops were excavated and are shown on Figure 4.78. These tended to concentrate on the northern side of the structure and may be related to internal furnishings of some kind. None were deeper than 0.1 m. Notably large sherds of Severn Valley Ware came from pit 430, and pits/postholes 506 and 535. It is unclear whether this distribution has any significance. Pit 430 also contained a mount from a bucket handle (cat. 570) and a hipposandal wing (Table 7.46).

## *Occupation north of Area D* (*Fig. 4.78*)

### *Layer 58 and gullies 391, 393 and 445*

Layer 58 was a thin patch of grey soil defined on its northern side by the surviving segments of three curving gullies. This probably marked the site of another structure although there is insufficient evidence to determine the form it might have taken. All deposits here were truncated by lynchet 123 by up to 0.15 m, although this takes no account of any terracing which might have been carried out here to accommodate the occupation. Gully 445 was just 0.1 m deep with a flattish base. It was without finds. Gully 391 was up to 0.15 m deep and contained 11 4th-century sherds. Gully 393 was shorter and without finds. It is possible that 391 and 393 marked a wall-line and that 445 was for eaves drainage, although the gullies were not precisely parallel. A circular structure with a diameter of up to 7 m could have been accommodated in the space north of structure 1457.

## *Area E: Phase 2* (*Figs 4.80–81*)

### *Structure 1459*

This structure was defined by two arms of a shallow ditch, 235 and 249, with the trace of an internal gully or groove, 342. Like structure 1458 which it replaced, the ditch had a composite profile with a deeper outer depression and a shallower inner ledge. Again the significance of this is not entirely clear, although the outer ditch is likely to have been for eaves drainage and the internal groove a wall-line. The ditch was cut by lynchet 130 and it is unclear whether or not the structure would have been open to the south. The two arms of the ditch meet at an angle of about 120° which suggests that the structure was hexagonal in plan. There was no trace of an internal floor and the only internal feature was a nebulous shallow scoop, 344, only partly within the excavation.

There were considerable quantities of pot and bone in the backfill of the ditch (234). There was also stone and tile, but insufficient quantities of either to suggest that they had any structural significance. The abandonment of the structure can be dated to after AD 220.

## *Area 3: Phase 2*

### *Rectangular stone building 1684 (Figs 4.82–83)*

The main phase of activity in Area 3 was associated with a structure with a stone wall footing and a stone floor. The stonework directly underlay the modern topsoil. This is considered likely to have formed part of a rectangular building oriented north-west – south-east, although only one wall survived. The wall-footings on the south-east and south-west sides had probably been removed. The north-west side lay outside the excavation. Deep wheel ruts of probable post-medieval date had caused considerable damage to the southern part of the structure and extended as far south-west as the line of Ermin Street. It was impossible to estimate where the walls had once been.

### Gully 1502/1528 and wall 1544

The Phase 1 gully was re-dug and the earlier deposits almost completely removed. Into this gully was inserted a dry-stone 'revetment' wall, 1544. This was wholly within gully 1502 at the north-west end where it survived as a facing structure up to three courses high (0.25 m). At the south-eastern end the wall face was on the lip of the gully and survived to just one course high. The wall face did not survive immediately in front of a large single 'threshold' stone (part of wall 1503). Here 1544 existed only as a ragged edge of stone with perhaps just two stones continuing the alignment of the wall face. It is possible that the stone facing was deliberately omitted from the entrance area, but perhaps equally possible that the facing stones had simply fallen into the ditch or had been removed. The purpose of lining the gully is unclear but, assuming it were for drainage, a lining, even if only on one side, might have helped prevent it from silting up too readily. The gully contained a large quantity of pottery of generally above average size, suggesting that it had been deliberately infilled with midden material.

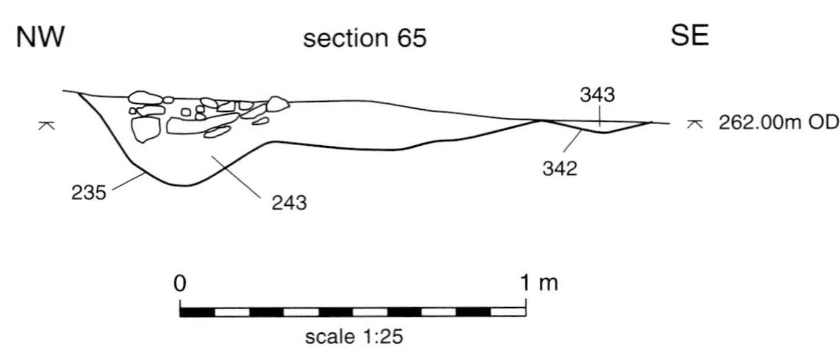


*Figure 4.81 Birdlip Quarry, Area E, section.*

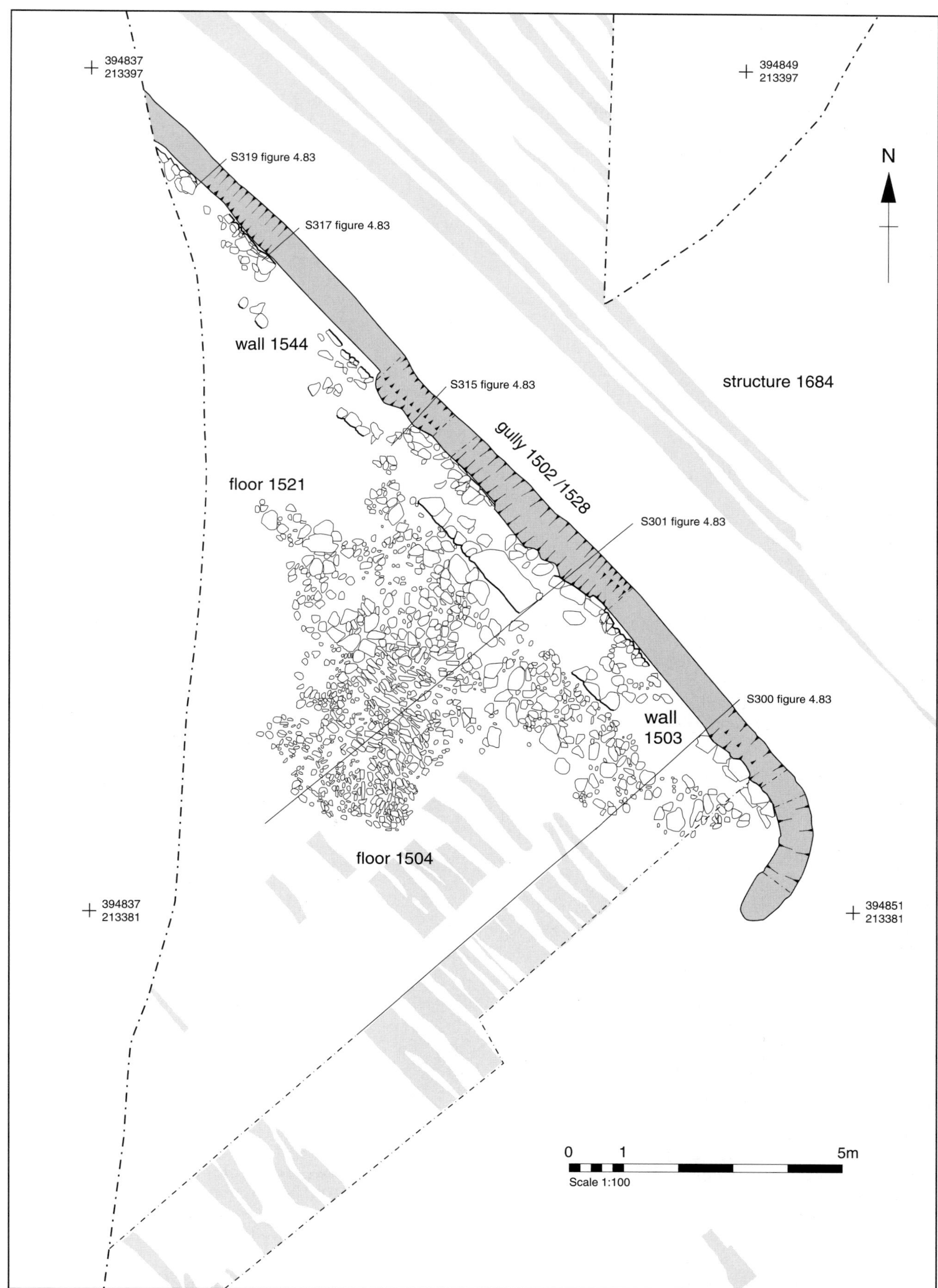


*Figure 4.82 Birdlip Quarry, Area 3, structure 1684.*

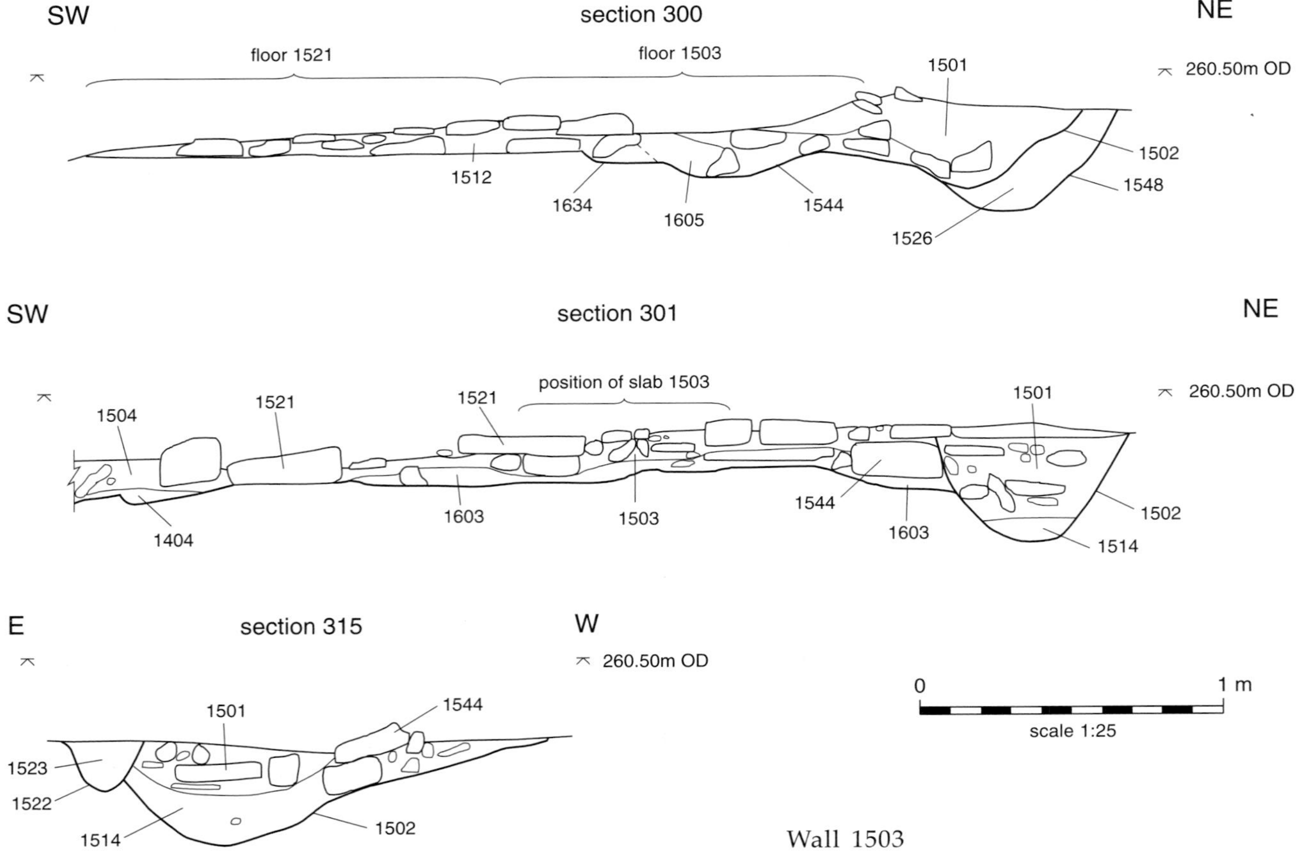


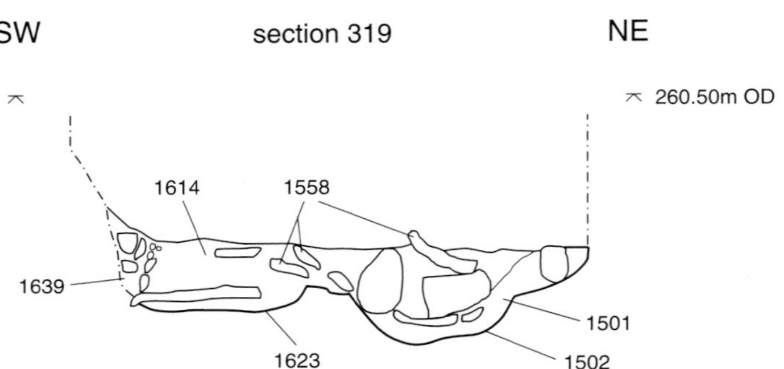


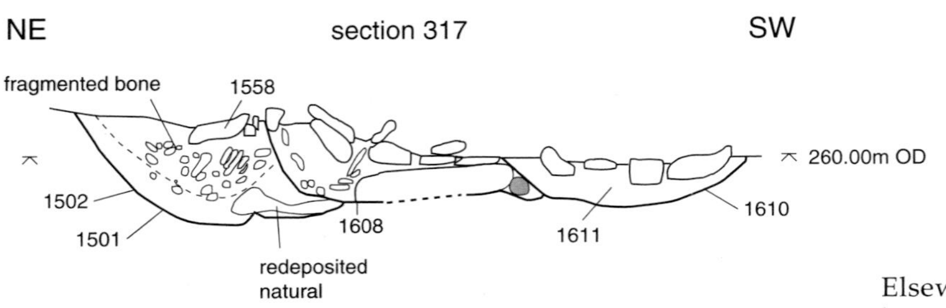


*Figure 4.83 Birdlip Quarry, Area 3, structures, sections.*

### Wall 1503

This wall formed the inner face of wall 1544. It consisted of a single course of facing stones which survived only inter-mittently. It included a single large limestone block measuring 1.65 m x 0.58 m x 0.12 m thick which was interpreted as a threshold stone although it was not noticeably worn. Between the two wall faces was a rubble core, 1605. The total width of the wall of the structure was about 1 m. Wall 1503 overlay a heterogeneous spread of stone rubble, 1512, which was probably a levelling or consolidation layer within the building.

### Stone floors 1521 and 1504

Wall 1503 was abutted by a spread of stone flagging 1521 which consisted of large stone slabs irregularly laid forming a dis-continuous surface. The stones were most tightly packed behind the 'threshold' where the flooring was occasionally two flags thick. Elsewhere the flooring was more patchy, but it is unclear whether or not this represents the original distribution of stone. A well-constructed floor of pitched stone (1504) lay in what appeared to be a central position opposite the 'threshold'.

The stones were firmly embedded into the clayey 'natural' at a steep to vertical angle. The pitched stone floor was cut by wheel ruts on three sides and again it is unclear whether the original extent of flooring is represented here. However, it can be noted that the pitched stone was physically difficult to remove and could not have been collected casually. As there was no evidence that stone had been dug up nor little in the way of outliers of damaged flooring, it appears likely that the surviving area of pitched stone more or less represented its original extent.

*Boundary ditch 1681 (Fig. 4.84)*

Ditch 1681 was a redigging of 1680 (Phase 1) after the latter had at least partly silted up. This recut was broader and shallower than the original ditch, typically 1.5–2.0 m wide and 0.5 m deep, and contained a dry-stone 'revetment' wall on the south-east side (Fig. 4.67, sections 326 and 312). It is unclear whether the ditch terminated at either end within the excavated area. No terminals were found, but in both the north-eastern and south-western segments (1625 and 1588) the 'revetment' wall was absent (Fig. 4.67, sections 309 and 314) and during the excavations it proved difficult to determine whether the fills belonged to the earlier or later ditch. However, the upper fill of segment 1588 (fill 1587) contained sherds of a storage jar from the same vessel as those found in the road make-up layers 1538 and 1589 (Fig. 4.67, section 314), strongly indicating that, in this segment at least, the later ditch was present and, moreover, had been backfilled immediately before the overlying road was constructed. Generally the other segments (1654, 1599, 1595 and 1539) showed two phases of infilling. The lower and main fills (1583, 1597, 1602, 1593, 1592, 1549 and 1543), which tended to be clean greyish brown silts, were interpreted as natural infilling, while the upper, darker and loamier silts (1531, 1534, 1596, 1591) were almost certainly levelling deposits. These contained limestone blocks from the destruction of the revetment wall. Section 312 (Fig. 4.67) shows the wall (1540) sealed by the levelling or midden material (1534) which demonstrates that the wall collapsed or was destroyed in the Roman period and not through later ploughing or rutting. After the ditch was infilled, limestone cobbling (1538 and 1586) was laid over the southern end (ditch segment 1588). This appears to represent a widening or re-routing of Ermin Street.

Revetment wall

This wall (contexts 1652, 1600, 1666 and 1540) formed a dry-stone lining on the south-east edge of the ditch where it sat on a slight ledge. It was composed of roughly dressed blocks of limestone and survived up to five courses high (Fig. 4.67, section 326), though it was generally present as two or three courses. It was a single stone wide (*c.* 0.2 m). The internal face was flush while the back edge was ragged and contained packing of smaller stones and grey silt between the wall and the edge of the ditch. It was similar to the revetment wall 1544 associated with structure 1684 (above) (Fig. 4.82) and also to the ditch revetment wall in Area 5 (Fig. 4.84).

Segment 1625

This was the first segment excavated and the section drawing (Fig. 4.67, section 309) presents a rather hypothetical recut deduced from the standing sections after the discovery of three phases of ditch in the segments to the south-west. It appears to show a recut to almost the same depth as Phase 1. Pottery (20 sherds) from the upper fill, 1505, is dated to the late 2nd to 3rd centuries, which suggests that the ditch belongs with Phase 1 although the pottery could all be redeposited. A further factor which casts doubt on this segment belonging with Phase 2 is the absence of a revetment wall on the south-east edge, nor any stone rubble within the fills. This segment is therefore untypical of the ditch and it is uncertain whether it ever extended this far.

Segment 1588

A segment excavated where the ditches appeared to run under Ermin Street and turn sharply north-west failed to demonstrate conclusively whether the ditch here belonged to Phase 1 or Phase 2 or both. The cross-profile (Fig. 4.67, section 314) was atypical of both ditches. The revetment wall had come to an end or had been removed before the ditch(es) turned the corner. Unfortunately a later cut or wheel rut (1615) on the southern side made it unclear whether the wall or wall-ledge had ever existed here. The stepped form of the southern edge did hint that there was an upper, later cut represented by fill 1587, and this appears to be supported by the presence of joining sherds in fill 1587 and the road make-up layers 1538 and 1589. This would support the interpretation of the upper fill (1587) as belonging to the Phase 2 ditch which was infilled so as to construct the road over the ditch.

*Dating evidence*

The dating evidence for Phase 2 in this area is imprecise. The use of stone revetting in both the ditch associated with the rectangular structure and the boundary ditch strongly suggests that the features are mutually contemporary and that the dating evidence can be pooled. There was no good dating evidence from the lower fills of ditch 1681. The evidence from the first phase of boundary ditch (ditch 1680) suggests that it was still silting up in the later 3rd or even 4th century. Later 3rd-century pottery also comes from beneath the pitched stone floor 1504 and is probably related to the Phase 1 occupation. This suggests that the new constructions did not start before the late 3rd century and possibly not before the 4th century. Pottery from the packing (1658) behind revetment wall 1540, dated to after AD 240, is in broad agreement with this but does not help to refine the phasing.

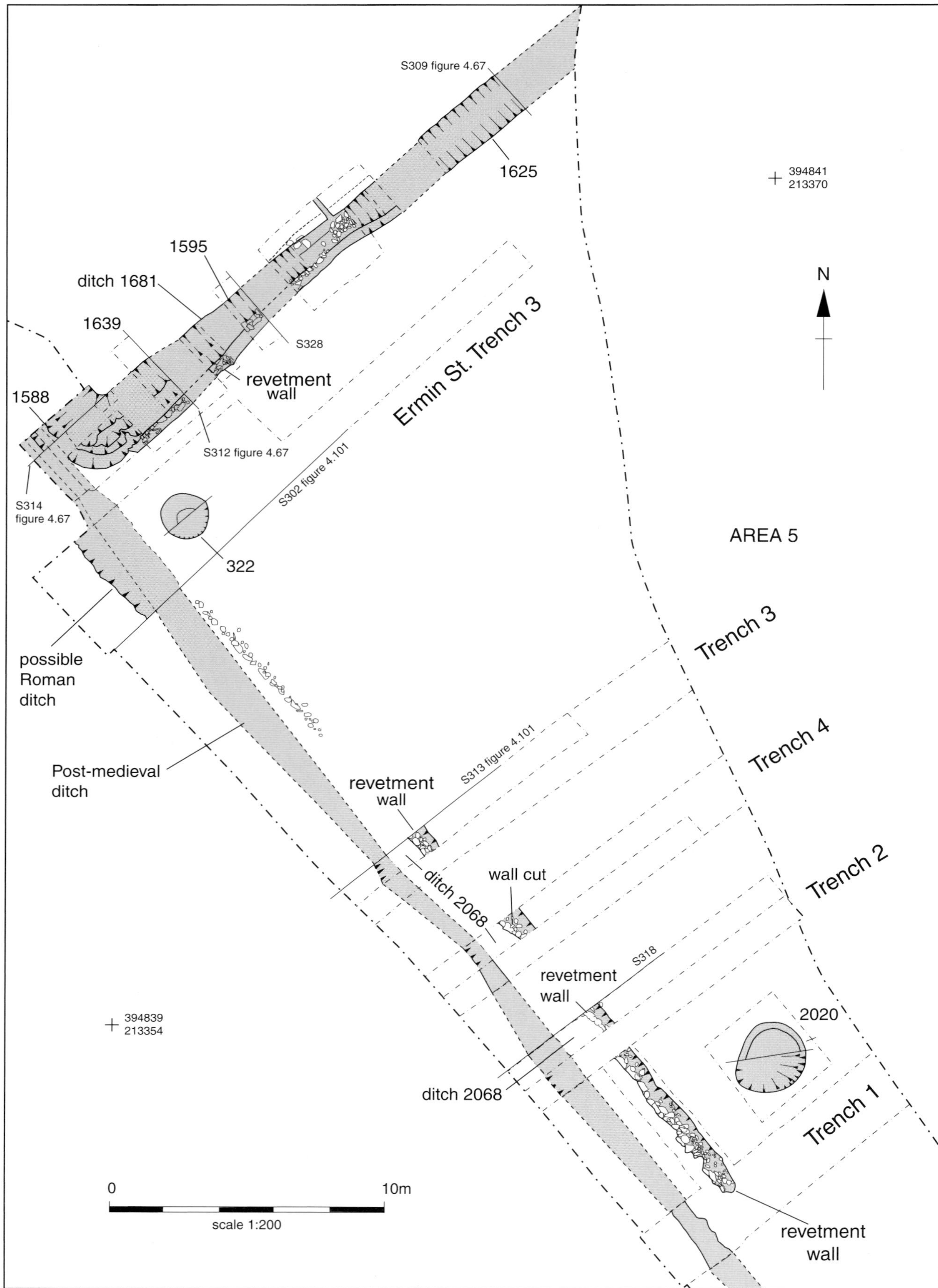


*Figure 4.84 Birdlip Quarry, period 2a, ditch 1681 and Area 5.*

A large quantity of pottery (476 sherds) came from the fill of gully 1502 (structure 1684), but can only be generally dated to the late 3rd and 4th centuries. Sherd sizes were generally above average, suggesting that the ditch had been backfilled with midden material. The pottery from the backfilling of ditch 1681 is similarly chronologically imprecise. However, it may be significant that there was an absence of late Roman shelly ware from this area and it is probable that the Phase 2 occupation was abandoned in the earlier rather than later 4th century. Coins were also sparse, the latest, from fill 1596 (segment 1599 of ditch 1681) being dated to AD 321–33. Taken with the dating evidence for the beginning of the phase, this appears to indicate that the Phase 2 occupation was relatively brief - probably not more than 50 years.

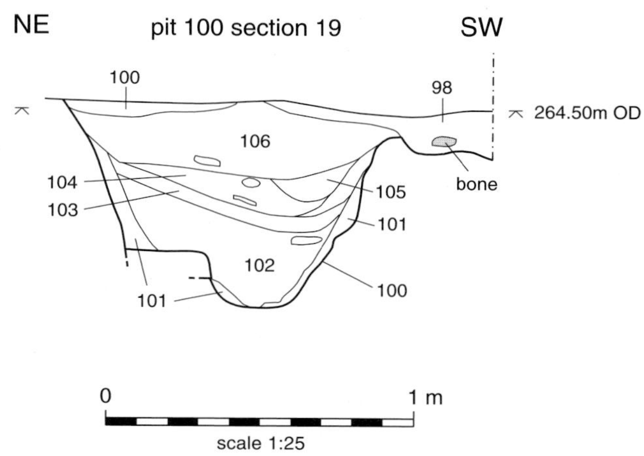


*Figure 4.85 Birdlip Quarry, period 2a, pit 100, section.*

***Main site boundary ditches: Phase 2*** *(Fig. 4.73)*

In Period 2A the main boundary ditches were re-dug and the enclosure in the northern part of the site appears to have been defined more strongly with the digging of ditch 684 and the recutting, complete or partial, of ditch 683. However, there were no replacements for ditches 698 and 699 further west.

*Ditch 688*

Ditch 688 was a recut of 690, apparently after the latter had completely silted up. It was dug to the same depth as 690, characteristically with a steep eastern edge, a rather shallower western edge and a flattish base (Fig. 4.68, sections 13 and 93). Segment 68 had a single mid greyish brown main fill (68) which contained some limestone slabs. This may have been deliberate backfill and can be broadly dated to after AD 250. It overlay lighter silting/edge-slumping (110) without dating evidence. Section 93 showed a more complex sequence but was interpretable in the same terms of lower natural silting (405 and 406), possibly followed by further natural silting (407) and deliberate backfill (408).

*Ditch 689*

Ditch 689 is interpreted as a replacement for 691 and 692. Ceramic dating for the infilling was only broadly 3rd or 4th-century although three coins from the upper part of the fill date between AD 320 and 346. Like the earlier gullies it had two cuts, but this was only evident where they separated at the north-west end (segments 137 and 80). Elsewhere it was virtually impossible to distinguish the two fills. The generally broad and shallow nature of the ditch (Fig. 4.68, section 28) suggested that two cuts might be represented throughout its length, although this proved impossible to verify.

*Ditch 683 and gullies 165 and 98*

Ditch 683 was probably recut, at least partly, in Period 2A although the dating evidence is not particularly late. Segments 575, 567 and 477 were identified as recuts. The latest dating comes from the top fill of segment 477 (fill 421) which is only broadly 3rd-century or later. Pottery of 4th-century date came from the top of ditch 577 (layer 579) although this appears to represent late dumping long after the ditch had gone out of use. At the south-eastern end of the ditch two shallow gullies, 165 and 98, ran parallel with 683 and were stratigraphically the latest features in this area. They both shallowed at the terminals and were undoubtedly originally longer. They may represent late redefinitions of this boundary.

*Gully 684*

This gully was a long linear feature running north-north-east – south-south-west and forming the eastern boundary of the northern enclosure. It cut gully 685. The southern end of the gully was cut by pit 100 and it was not identifiable in the complexity of intercutting features on the other side of the pit, so it is assumed to have terminated. It was quite shallow, 0.1–0.2 m, and contained a single fill of mid brown or greyish brown silt. Pottery from the fill was dated to after *c.* AD 240.

*Gully 85*

This was a long shallow gully in the southern part of the site seeming to delimit Area C on its northern side. It consistently contained two fills: 84, a light brown silt yielding ten sherds of pottery dating to after AD 240, and an upper dark silt, 83, which yielded large quantities of burnt stone, bone and 4th-century pottery. It was considered possible that there were two phases to this gully, but this was not really evident in any of the sections.

*Gully 170*

This was a gully of similar profile to 85, with clearly-defined terminals, and apparently forming two sides of an enclosure south of Area D. It had a lower light brown fill (183) and an upper dark fill (171) which contained broadly 3rd/4th-century pottery.

***Features in the northern enclosure*** *(Fig. 4.73)*

*Gullies 158 and 609 (unphased)*

These were two narrow rectilinear gullies, apparently parallel and running north-west – south-east. They are thought likely to be coeval. Gully 609 was more substantial, being 0.42 m deep with vertical sides and a clear terminal. Undiagnostic pottery came from the top fill (607). Gully 158 was just 0.04 m deep. It was probably cut by gully 687, although the relationship was not clear.

*Gullies 686 and 687*

These gullies formed two arms of a possible enclosure with an entrance to the south-east. They were flat-based, 686 being slightly deeper (0.25 m) than 687 (0.07–0.15 m). The fills were generally dark, and the gullies appear to have been backfilled with refuse, presumably from nearby occupation. An assemblage of 19 sherds from fill 120 (segment 119) was datable to after *c.* AD 240, while 15 sherds from fill 157 (segment 156) were more generally of 3rd- or 4th-century date.

*Pit 100*

This feature was a small sub-rectangular pit, 1.4 x 1.0 m and 0.7 m deep, with steep sides tapering to a narrow base. It was located in the south-east corner of the northern enclosure, cutting the terminal of gully 684 and cut by gully 98. Approximately three-quarters of the pit was excavated. It had quite a complex series of fills most of which can be attributed to different backfilling events (Fig. 4.85, section 19). Above a thin skim of primary silting (101), fill 102 consisted largely of a dump of stone rubble of unknown derivation. This was covered by a thin layer of greenish brown clay (103) and yellowish brown clay-silt (121) which were probably further deliberate deposits. The middle fill (104) was a deposit of dark soil with charcoal. This was overlain by a limited amount of edge-slumping (105) and a mixed brown loamy deposit (106) which was probably intended to level the ground. The uppermost deposits, 108 and 109, were thin spreads of dark soil.

The function of the pit is unclear, although a small storage pit or a latrine are possibilities. It contained few finds but pottery from 104 and 106 indicates a date after *c.* AD 240 for the backfilling.

***Corn dryer 42*** *(Figs 4.86 and 4.87, sections 3, 76 and 96)*

A T-shaped corn dryer was located in a relatively isolated position in the northern part of the site. It was totally excavated with the excavation proceeding in segments so as to obtain long- and cross-sections. The corn dryer was 4.3 m long with both the end chamber and rake-out bowl about 2 m wide. The flue and end chamber were lined with roughly squared limestone blocks (45) bonded with a yellowish sandy mortar (321). The structure survived to a depth of about 8 courses (0.6 m). The upper courses of the flue showed evidence of an arch indicating that this section of the structure was originally vaulted. Behind the upper course in both the flue and end chamber there were some pitched packing stones between the lining and the edge of the construction pit (44). The rake-out bowl was also lined with two sections of stone (438), but this was clearly a later addition and the stones were not tied with the flue lining. The building style was also different, 438 tending to be built with longer, flatter stones and bonded with grey clay (439) which was also used as packing behind the stones. The purpose of 438 was unclear but it was presumably intended as a funnel to direct airflow. Stone slabs were present as flooring at the entrance to the flue, and there were also a few in the bowl. Those in the flue were intensely burnt. Burning was also evident on the walls, fading out about 0.8 m along the flue towards the chamber end, clearly indicating that the fire was quite restricted.

The corn dryer was filled with a succession of deposits some of which were probably associated with the use of the feature and others representing debris which accumulated after its abandonment. Six samples were analysed for charred remains (Table 8.57, see Pelling, Chapter 8).

*Fill 222*

A thin, dark carbon-rich silt at the base of the structure. Interpreted as representing a primary deposit. Samples 31 and 34 yielded exceptionally high densities of charred plant remains, particularly chaff.

*Fill 221*

A more mixed deposit of grey silt with some limestone and mortar fragments. This appeared to represent debris from the final use of the corn dryer mixed with some collapsed material. Samples 32 and 33 yielded high densities of charred plant remains which included a relatively high proportion of cereal grains.

*Fill 190*

A mid brown silt with a high proportion of charcoal. This deposit appeared to include rake-out from the flue, although its thickness suggested that it may have been mixed with an accumulation of soil after the structure had gone out of use. Sample 23 included fairly abundant wood charcoal as well as chaff, grain and weed seeds.

*Fills 247 and 43*

A loose mid brown silt with limestone rubble which overlay 221 in the flue and end chamber. This represented the collapse of the flue superstructure. Fill 43 comprised generally smaller limestone pieces and probably represents a longer period of

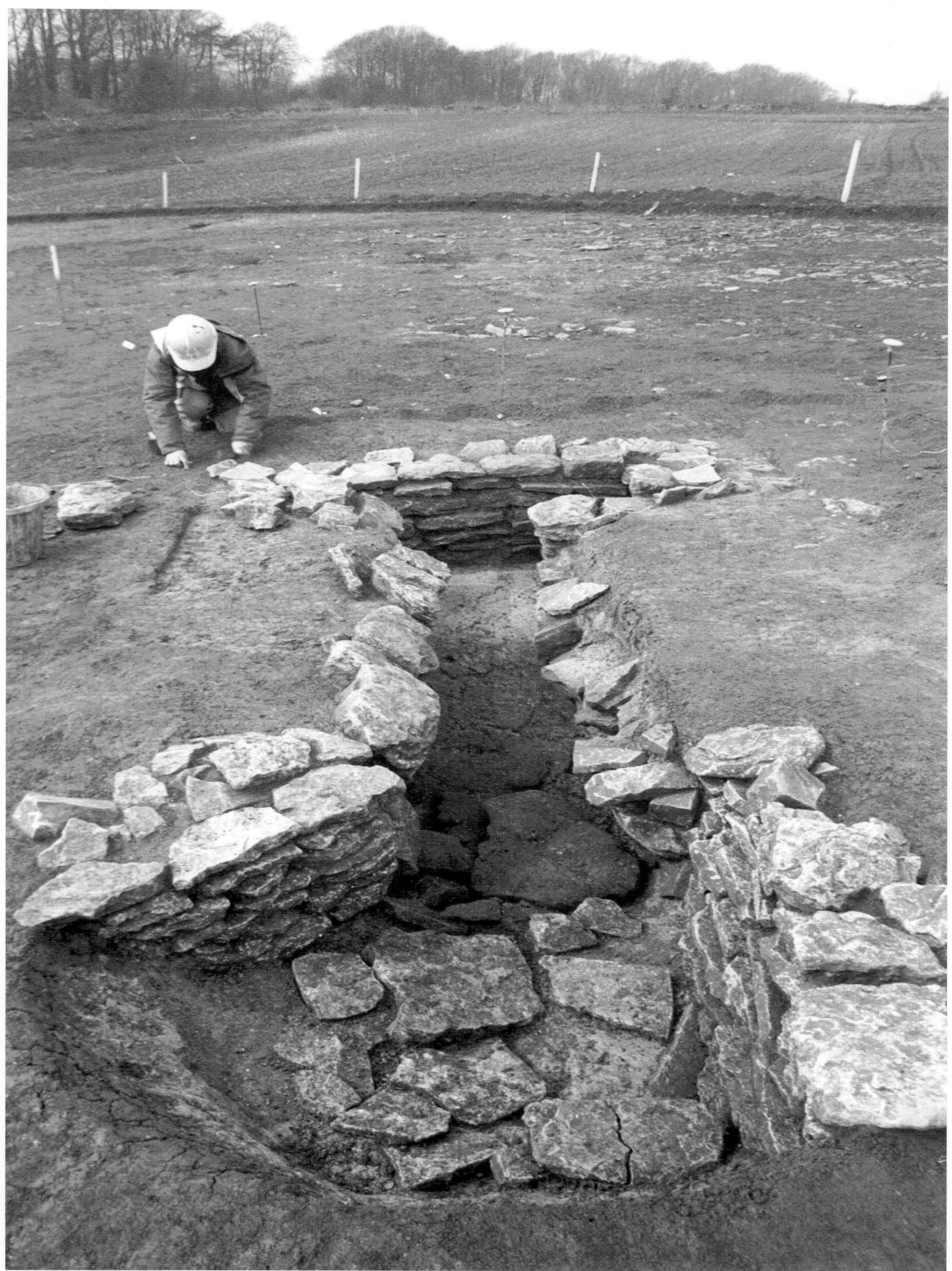

*Plate 4.19 Corn dryer 42.*

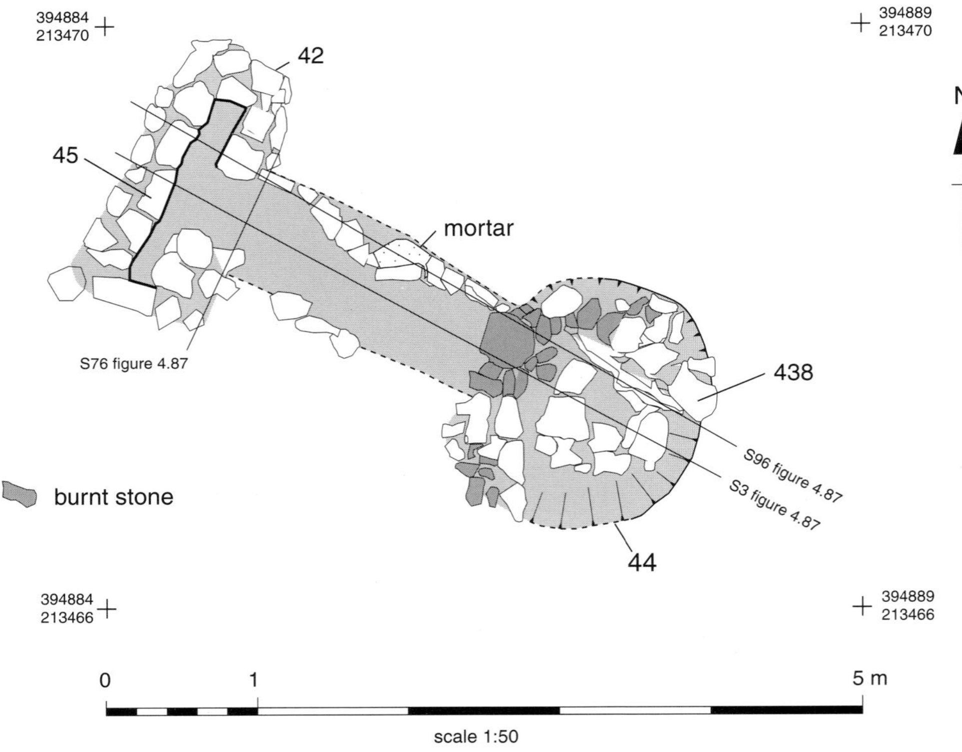


*Figure 4.86 Birdlip Quarry, period 2a, plan of corn dryer 42.*

post-collapse accumulation. Sample 3 from context 43 had a low density of charred plant remains.

*Fill 81*

A greyish brown clayey silt with limestone rubble representing backfill of the bowl. A large assemblage (87 sherds) of pottery was present. Sample 4 contained a low density of charred plant remains.

*Fill 33*

A grey silty loam with limestone rubble representing the final infilling of the bowl. It contained domestic debris including a large lump of iron slag (SF 156). Sample 1 contained charred remains of a similar character to Samples 3 and 4.

There were no chronologically diagnostic finds from the structure of the corn dryer and its date of construction is not clear. The primary fill, 222, can be dated to after AD 220 and 4th-century pottery came from 190. It is therefore likely to have been in use in the 3rd to 4th centuries.

***Pits** (Figs 4.73 and 4.88)*

*Pit 39*

This sub-rectangular pit or hollow was situated in the north-east part of the site. It had very gradually sloping sides reaching a surviving depth of 0.34 m (Fig. 4.88, section 7). The lower fill (41) was a dump of carbon-rich material which contained charred grain, chaff and weed seeds in small densities (Sample 2). It may represent rake-out from the corn dryer. The upper fill (40) was a yellowish brown clayey silt with limestone grains of uncertain derivation. It contained a fragment of iron stylus (cat 561). The dating evidence from this feature was imprecise.

*Pit 92*

South of pit 39, pit 92 was a small oval pit or hollow with gently sloping sides 0.3 m deep (Fig. 4.88, section 14). The main fill (91) was a grey-brown silty loam which contained a concentration of medium sized tabular limestone of uncertain significance. Pottery, nails and a coin were also present. The pottery was dated to after AD 250 while the coin of Constans, which came from the surface of the feature, dated to AD 347–8. 91 overlay a thin yellowish brown primary silting (107) without finds.

*Pit 134*

East of Area A, this was a small oval feature, just 0.05 m deep. It contained pottery of the 3rd century or later (fill 135).

**Period 2B: *c.* AD 330–380**

In Period 2B the structures of Period 2A went out of use. New structures are difficult to define although stone buildings appear to have been constructed in Area A. The principle elements of these consisted of a 'revetment' wall along the back of the terrace and a cross wall at right-angles which was attached to a partly circular structure of two phases. A post-built building was constructed in Area 3. There may have been structures elsewhere (Fig. 4.89).

***Areas A, 2B and 2C: Phase 6***

*Structure 985 (Fig. 4.90)*

This structure, the first of the partly circular structures, was defined by a penannular gully, *c.* 0.25 m wide and probably originally about 0.25 m deep located directly under the wall of the stone structure 713 (Fig. 4.91) , which enclosed an area with a diameter of

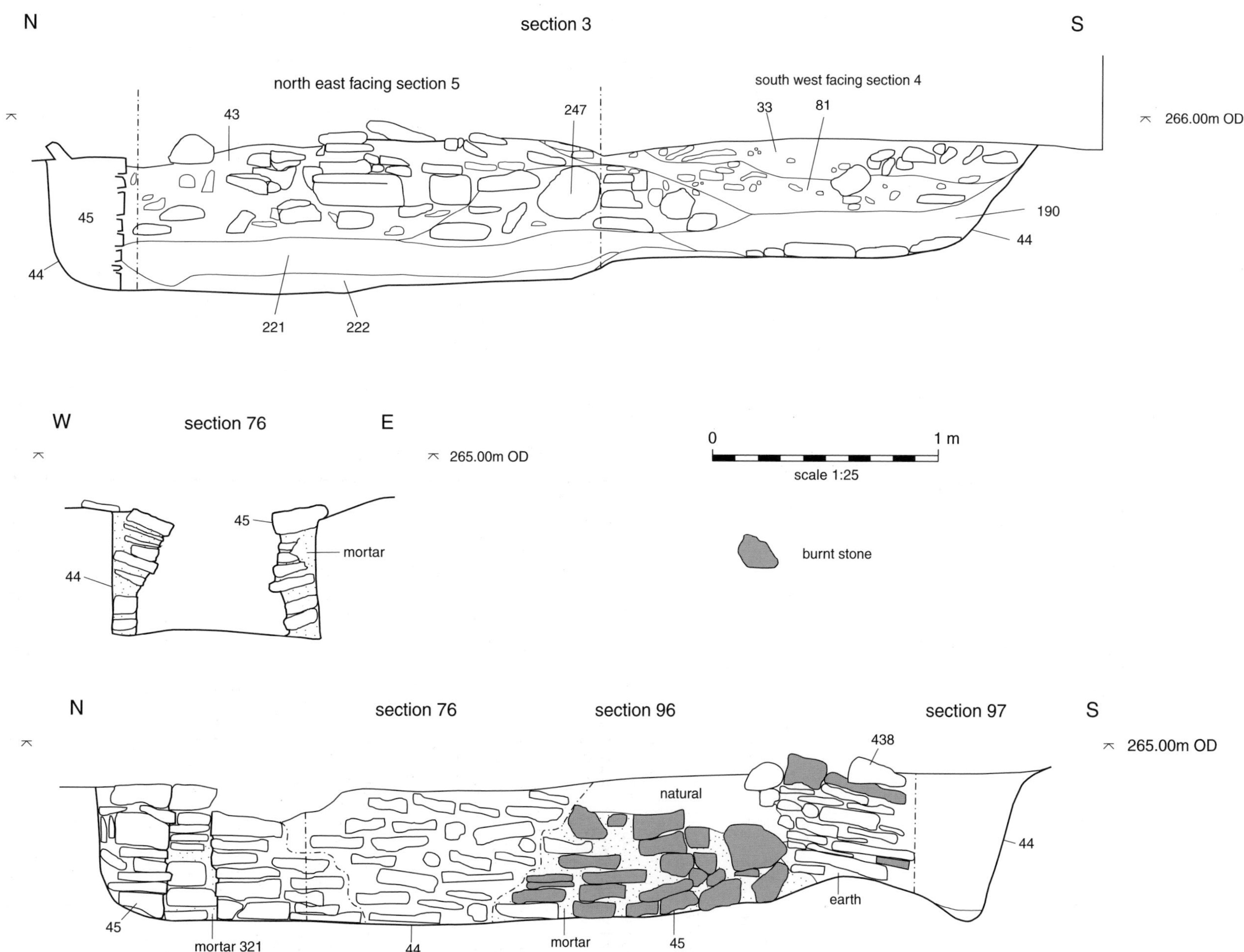


*Figure 4.87 Birdlip Quarry, period 2a, corn dryer 42, sections.*

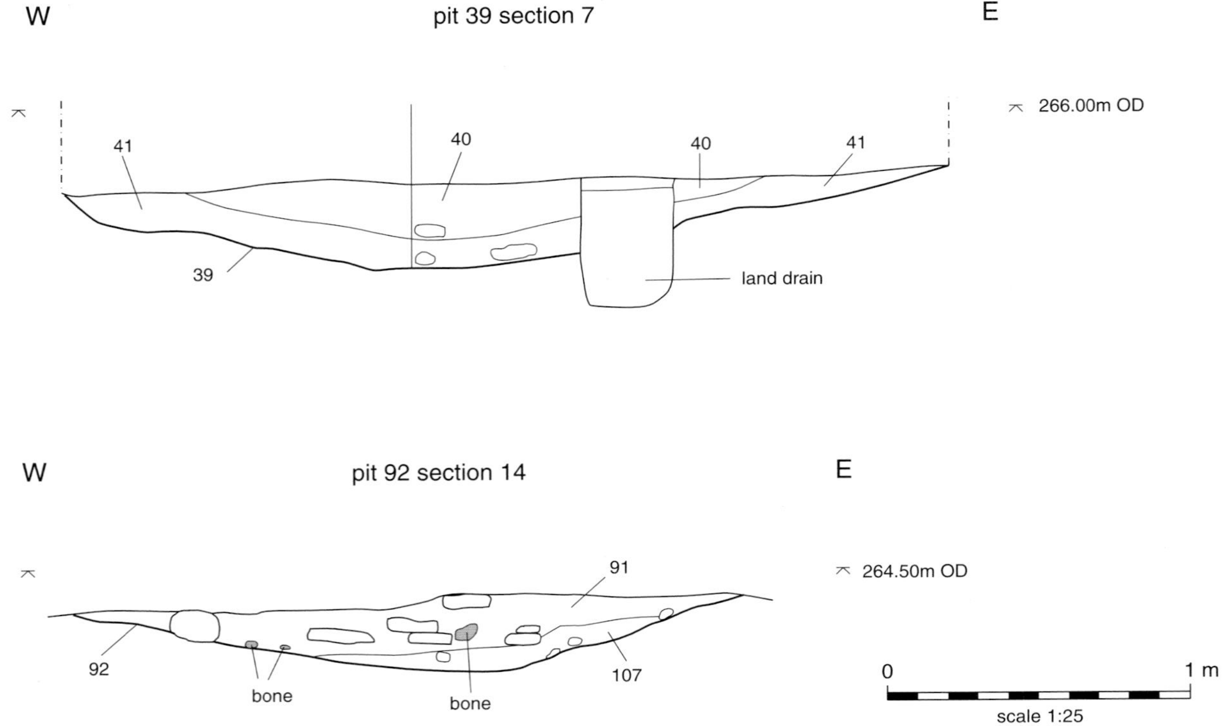


*Figure 4.88 Birdlip Quarry, pits 39 and 42, sections.*

6.3 m. It ran for *c.* 240° with quite clear terminals and it is therefore certain that it had a wide entrance (*c.* 6 m) facing south. The gully appears to have held a row of stakes or small posts although the stakeholes were not very clear individually.

The stratigraphic position of this structure was unclear. It was only fully recognised once the site had been excavated to the lighter subsoil, but variations in the soils had created certain difficulties in the excavation of the higher strata here, and it seems clear that the feature had been cut from higher up. Its position directly under the wall of stone structure 713 (below) also indicates that it was the direct precursor of 713 although it is possible to argue that it might have belonged to an earlier phase and have been standing during the period of 'abandonment' in Phase 5 while the soil accumulated around it. Despite the fact that the wall of structure 713 followed the line of 985 quite precisely, it is most unlikely that they were both part of the same structure. The construction of the wall of 713 makes it virtually impossible for a stake wall to have been incorporated with it. Furthermore the eastern side of 713 continued beyond the terminal of gully 985 indicating a difference in the plans of the two structures despite their identical size and position.

*Structure 713 (Fig. 4.91)*

Structure 713 survived as two fragments of drystone wall (714 and 122) which would have formed a circular or partly circular structure 6 m in diameter. A single course of stone was laid directly on the ground surface and there was no internal floor evident. The structure appears to have been abutted on to its northern side by wall 36, although it is possible that wall 36 had been partly demolished and the structure inserted into it. Wall 1245 (Area 2B), on a comparable alignment to wall 36, is also likely to have butted the structure. This would suggest that structure 713 was semi-circular with attached linear walls. The pitched stone surface 1224 (Area 2B) would have formed a solid surface path leading to the structure from Ermin Street. There was one late-phase posthole 833 which may have held a door post, but no opposed posthole was found.

Two patches of pitched stone (717 and 720) appeared to butt the outside of structure 713. Feature 720 stood proud of the surfaces associated with structure 1452 (Period 2A) and seems unlikely to belong with them. Feature 717 was incorporated within the angle between wall 122 and wall 36. The features may have been plinths supporting buttresses of some kind. The form of the super-structure to structure 713 is not known. It may have been roofed, although if it functioned as an animal pen it need not have been.

*Linear walls (Fig. 4.91)*

Walls 36 and 205

Wall 36 formed a cross wall running approximately at right-angles from the back of the terrace. It was of drystone construction and only surviving to one course which rested directly on the ground surface. At the north-east end it was bonded to wall 205 which

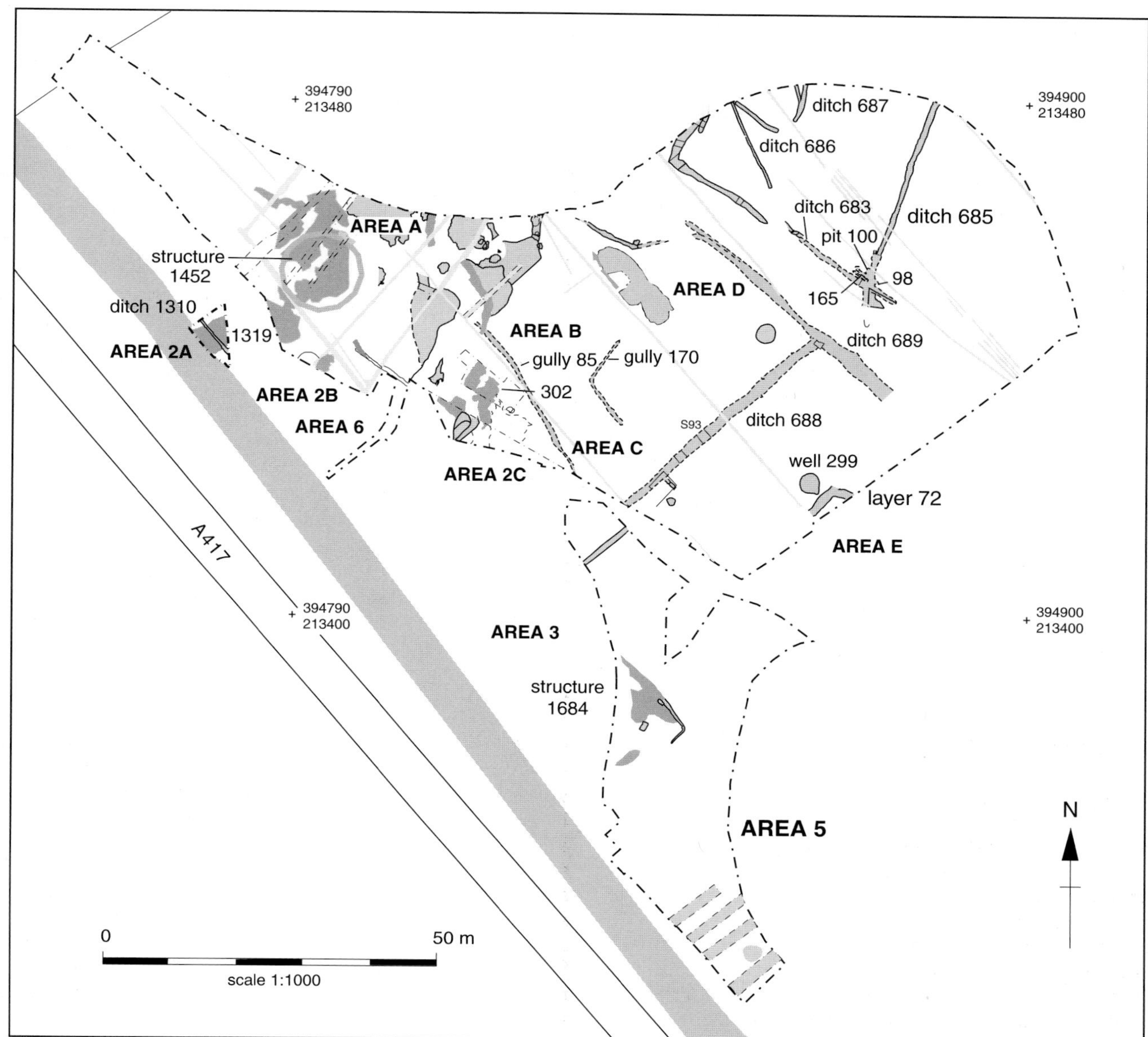


*Figure 4.89 Birdlip Quarry, period 2b, plan of excavated features.*

only survived for a short length before being cut by the water-pipe. Both walls were similar and distinct from the others in that they were constructed of relatively massive stones which tended to have interlocking faces without a rubble core. They were therefore relatively narrow (0.45–0.50 m). Wall 35 continued the alignment of 205 to the south-east but was a later addition (see below). Wall 54 to the north-west (see below) was of a different construction and its relationship with 205 is unknown. However, it seems likely that it was constructed as a separate event. Thus, while a superficial view might suggest a basic layout of just two linear features - a revetment wall at the back of the terrace and a cross-wall - it is likely that the structural sequence was more complicated and related to more than field/property boundaries.

Walls 36 and 205 may therefore have originally formed a narrow rectangular enclosure or structure with a return wall under the waterpipe baulk. The form this structure might have taken is unclear. To the north-west of wall 36 was a dense concentration of stone rubble which extended under the water-pipe baulk, but not a great deal further than that. It is unclear whether this represents the immediate post-Roman distribution of stone since there is evidence of medieval ploughing west of the baulk and stone might have been cleared from this area. However, an area of tipped stone (127) appears to represent collapsed wall lying *in situ*. The position and angle of the stones suggested that they were tumble from the top courses of wall 36. It is interesting to note that this would imply a wall height of about 2 m. This seems excessive for a boundary wall or an enclosure. A drystone wall construction to eaves height in a building may appear to be unstable, particularly given the rudimentary nature of the foundation, but this may have been a

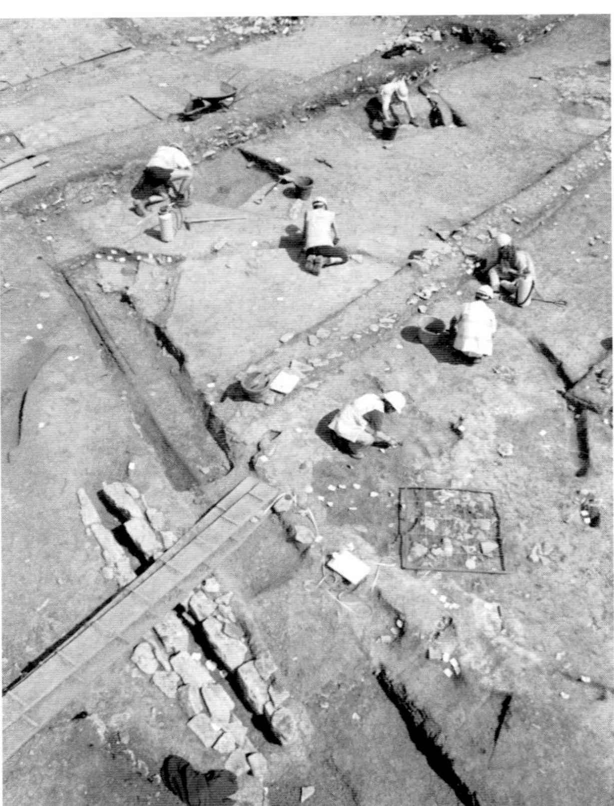

*Plate 4.20 Area A. Structure 985 is defined by a semi-circular gully. The stone culvert of the earlier penannular ditch lies in the foreground and sections through the penannular ditches are being excavated in the background.*

relatively unimportant outbuilding. It is also possible that a bonding of clay or earth was used which had weathered away.

It is uncertain whether linear wall 36 butted structure 713 or whether 713 was inserted into it. The jumble of large stones at the junction between the two structures could be interpreted as rubble from wall 36 and it may be significant that the facing stones were absent from wall 36 in this area, suggesting some disturbance caused by the insertion of 713.

### Wall 35, layers 140 and 34

Wall 35 butted wall 205. Only one course was present. It was 0.7 m wide with facing stones and a rubble core. It appears to have served as a terrace-edge revetment although the slope of the ground here was not particularly marked. It was probably contemporary with the stony surface 140 which consisted of small and medium limestone fragments tightly packed. This appeared to underlie wall 35 but did not extend south of it. South of the wall was a spread of generally medium-sized (0.1–0.15 m) and angular limestone fragments in a matrix of olive-grey silt (34). This layer had ill-defined edges except on the northern and western sides where it butted walls 35 and 36. Further south and east it could not be distinguished from the undifferentiated 'cleaning layer', 7, and the number was used for finds overlying the floor layers associated with structure 1452 (Phase 4). The nature of this layer is unclear, but it may have represented a fragmented yard surface. Alternatively, it may have been a general spread of building rubble, but it was felt that the stones were too small to have derived from structures, even allowing for weathering and post-Roman activity. A very large quantity of artefacts came from this layer including shell-tempered ware dating to after *c.* AD 350. Ten coins are predominantly later 3rd and 4th century issues, but they include the only 1st-century coin found on the site.

### Wall 54

Wall 54 was neatly constructed with facing stones and a rubble core. It survived to four courses (0.4 m high) and was 0.6 m wide without a foundation cut. Its relationship with wall 205 had been destroyed but it was on a slightly different alignment as well as being of a different construction. Its length could not have been much more than 4 m since it ended precisely where section 206 was dug.

The wall certainly appears to have served as a revetment since the slope behind the wall was more pronounced here than elsewhere. It is unclear whether the wall was cut into the hillslope or whether it was positioned at the base of a natural slope. The fill behind the wall (46) contained rubble which had presumably been used as packing. In front of the wall and butting it, layer 706 was a thin dark greyish brown silt interpreted as an 'occupation layer'. Its original extent is unclear since Roman layers were truncated by later ploughing to the south and west. It contained late 4th-century pottery and was sealed by wall rubble 53. The extent and depth of this rubble suggests that the wall was originally several courses higher. These two observations - of an associated occupation or area of rubbish accumulation, and the large quantity of rubble - suggest that wall 54 may have been part of a building. However, there is little other evidence to support this.

### Wall 177

Wall 177 continued the alignment of wall 54 to the north-west. It appears to have butted wall 54 in section 206 and its surviving length was *c.* 4.5 m. It may well have continued further north-west, but any deposits in this direction had been completely removed by later ploughing. Unlike wall 54 it was not properly constructed and consisted of no more than an alignment of rubble about 1 m wide.

### Ditch 1252 *(Figs 4.89 and 4.91)*

A broad ditch, 1252, was dug through the soil layers which had accumulated in Phase 3 (layers 1227, 1289 and 1290). This was very shallow at the northern end but deepened towards the south-west (Fig. 4.51, section 291). It was probably a drainage ditch running towards Ermin Street. There was no trace of this feature in the main area of excavation and it must have

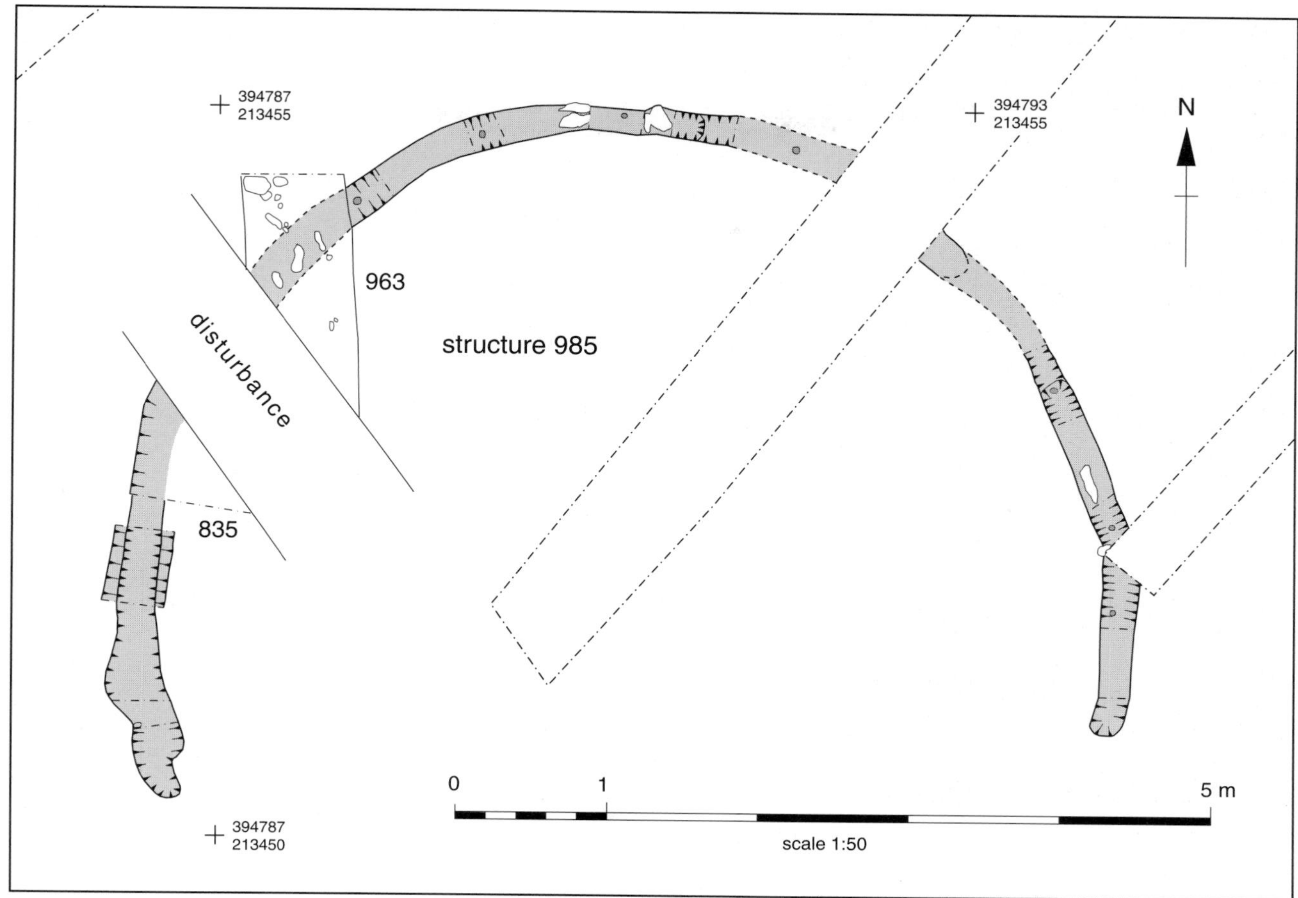


*Figure 4.90 Birdlip Quarry, period 2b, structure 985.*

terminated in the vicinity of wall 775. A projection of this wall to the south-east and a comparison of levels in the two areas suggests that the ditch was dug over the top of the wall, or perhaps up against it. The wall must have ceased to function at this stage. Occasional blocks of limestone (average size 0.2 x 0.15 m) within layer 1227 may have derived from the wall, but this is uncertain.

Initially, the ditch seems to have silted in naturally (fill 1264), but later a dump of stones, 1226, filled the entire length exposed. It is unclear what the purpose of this was, but presumably the ground needed consolidating for activity or access here.

### Wall 1245 and pitched stone surface 1224 *(Fig. 4.91)*

In Area 2B wall 1245 appears to have been constructed in a shallow trench (1269) cut into layer 1225. It was oriented towards structure 713 and it seems the two must have been linked. There was no evidence that the walls had been physically joined and, since the excavations in these two areas were carried out at different times, it is impossible to be sure how precise the alignment between the two features was. However, the wall trench may have continued into Area A as two sections of shallow gully (segments 805 and 904) up to about 0.14 m deep. These were both stratigraphically late and otherwise not accounted for. Gully 805 was conspicuously straight-edged and 904 aligns quite closely on wall 713. Neither segment contained structural stone and it seems probable that this gully is a robber trench rather than the construction cut itself. This would accord with the observation that 805 cut the pitched stone surface 796 (1224 in Area 2B).

Wall 1245 was of drystone construction, about 0.9 m wide, consisting of relatively large facing stones and a rubble core. At the north-east end it was just one course thick, but four courses survived at the south-west end. It was abutted on the western side by a well-constructed surface of pitched stone 1462 (segment 1224). This was clearly equivalent to layer 796 in Area A which extended for about half a metre further into the trench than is shown as it was partly inadvertently removed during machining. The pitched stone surface continued south-west into Area 2A (layer 1309). It clearly formed a bounded approach-path to structure 713 and the adjacent 'enclosures' (although the wall was not evident in Area 2A).

Stone surface 1224 is securely 4th-century, although the pottery dating is not particularly precise. The latest of four coins from beneath / among the stones was struck AD 337–40, giving a date of construction which effectively agrees with that provided by two coins from among the stones of layer 1311 in Area 2A

*Plate 4.21 Period 2b, Area A. Linear wall 36 butts curving wall 722 (structure 713). The pitched stone to the left may have come from the collapse of 36.*

(AD 335–40) (Fig. 4.99, section 275). There does not seem to have been any very late occupation here however. Shell-tempered ware was absent from the latest layer (1244), although both New Forest Ware and Oxford Red-slipped Ware were present. The latest coins from Areas 2A and 2B go no later than AD 347–8 (layer 1313).

### *Area B: Phase 6* (*Fig. 4.92*)

The stony deposit 223 (Phase 5) was overlain by an accumulation of very dark, almost black silt with few inclusions (128), which appears to represent midden material (Fig. 4.51, section 128). A large quantity of 4th-century pottery (529 sherds) and other finds were recovered, including a jet pin fragment (cat. 677). Eight coins give a range of date from AD 250–360 (cat. 297, 304, 366, 370, 424, 433, 443, 474). Layer 31 above was a slightly lighter and more clayey silt with an abundance of weathered stones, some burnt, of a variety of sizes. It is unclear what these stones represent. They tended to concentrate around the northern rim of this area and may have been part of a structure under 31 or further up slope. However, there was no real evidence of a structure and the weathered nature of the stone suggested that it was more likely part of a rudimentary surface or a clearance dump. The pottery assemblage of 776 sherds had a strongly late character (after AD 360/70), suggesting that layer 31 had not been heavily mixed and presumably represents a late accumulation of midden material.

### *Area C: Phase 3*

After ditch 233 went out of use, the area was characterised by the accumulation of soil layers 261, 227, 253, 206, 30 and 210. This was followed by an overlying layer of dark soil, layer 18. It is unclear how much activity is represented by these deposits, and how much represents post-abandonment accumulation . Layers 261 (Fig. 4.57, sections 61 and 62), 227 and 253 were mixed, heterogeneous greyish deposits with small patches of charcoal and containing a relatively high proportion of small, rounded limestone fragments. They were thin layers (about 50 mm) and were thought to represent rudimentary surfaces with occupation material. Finds from these layers were also mixed and included 2nd- and 3rd-century pottery as well as material of the later 3rd- and 4th-centuries. It seems that some of this material can be associated with the use of the ovens and stone surface 302, but that this had been trampled and mixed with later material. Layers 210 and 206 overlay the stone surface and are stratigraphically post-abandonment. The pottery dating is post-AD 240.

Layer 18 (Fig. 4.57, section 51) was a sealing layer of grey clayey silt which appears to represent midden accumulation. The finds from this layer were very mixed with 2nd- to 4th-century pottery present, including a single sherd of late Shell-tempered Ware. Twelve coins from the layer were mostly in the range AD 260–290 (the latest being AD 321–4), but they included two of the ten early coins from the excavations. The mixing does not appear to be due to

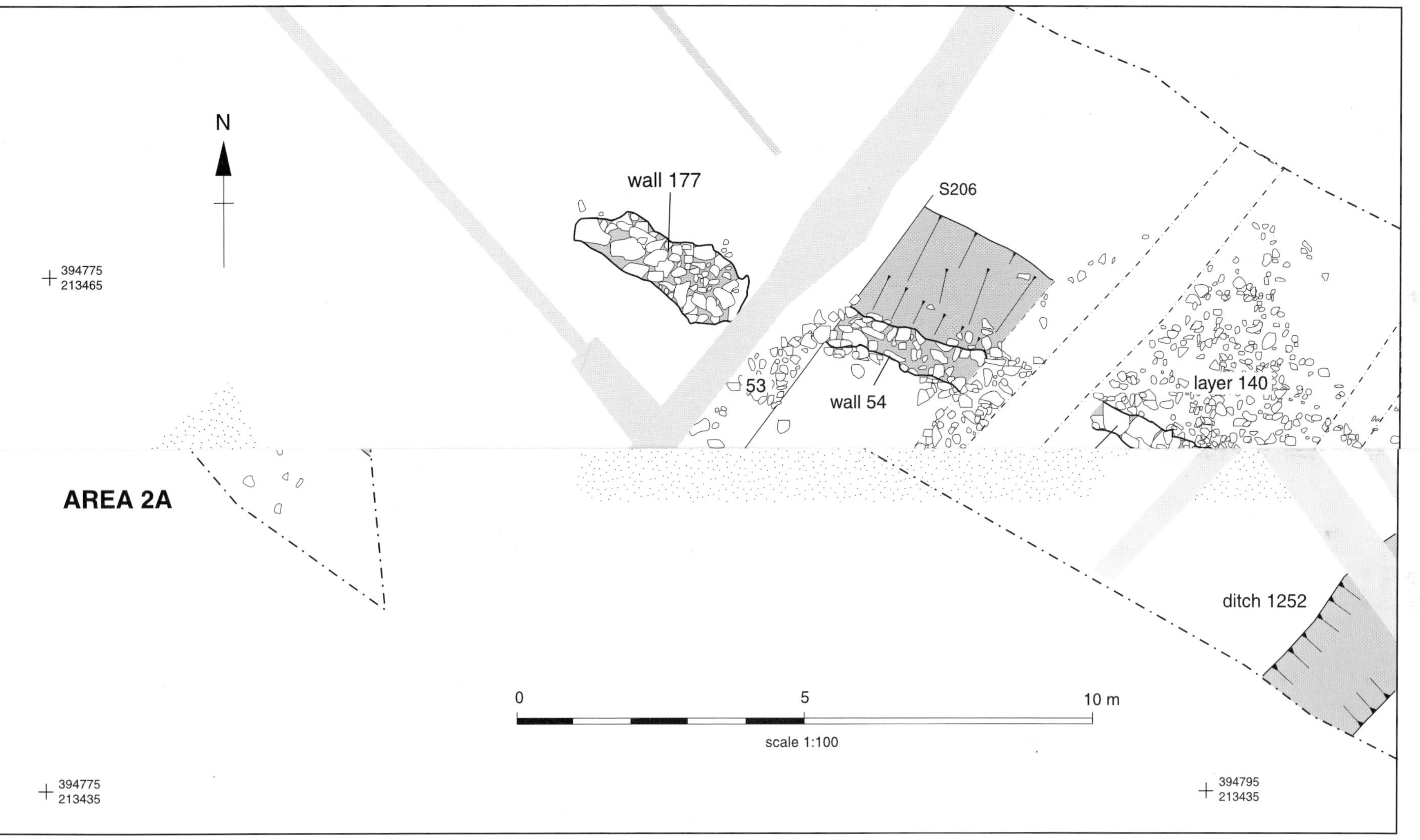


*Figure 4.91 Birdlip Quarry, period 2b, stone walls and surfaces in Areas A, 2A and 2B.*

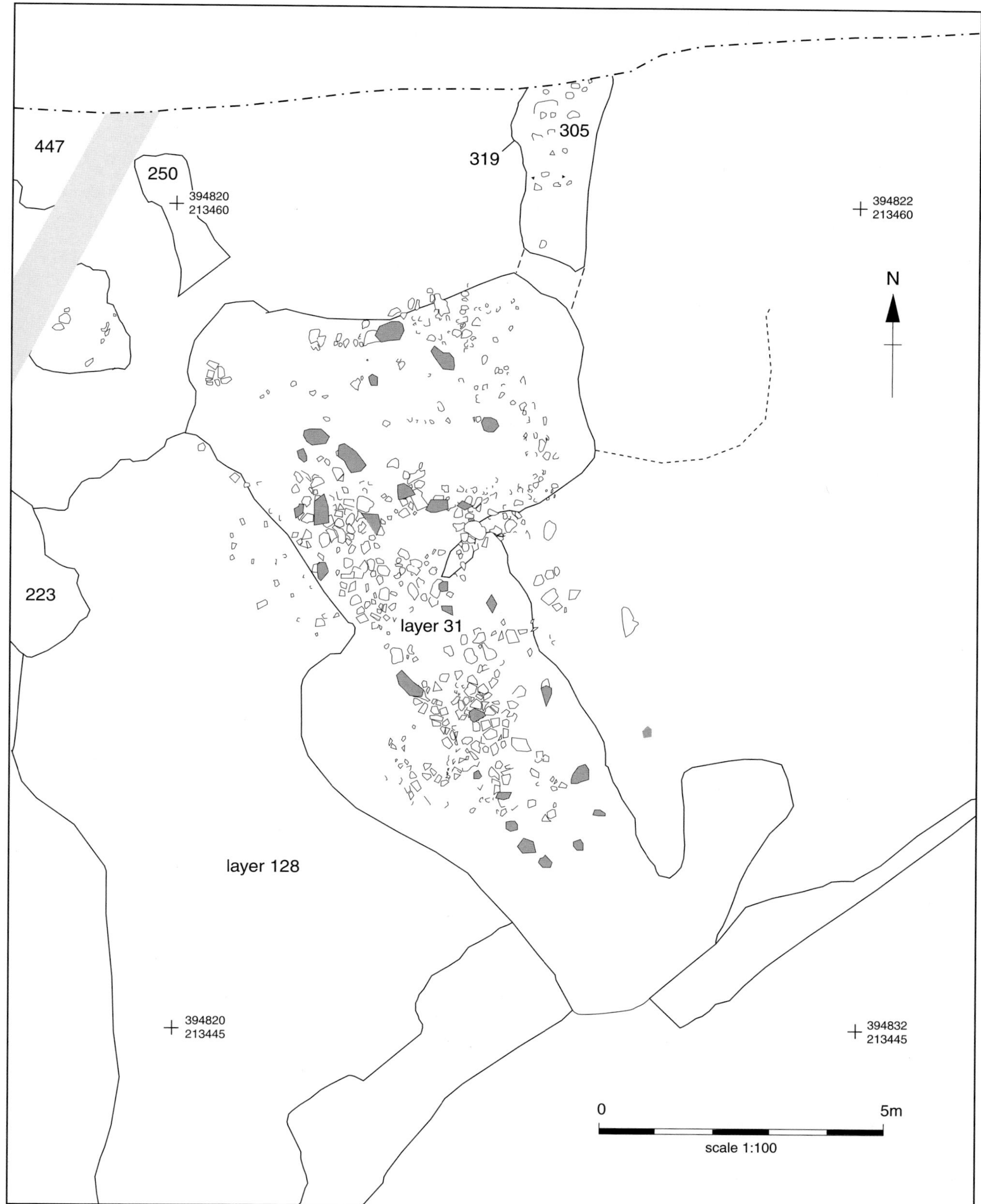


*Figure 4.92 Birdlip Quarry, Area B, period 2b.*

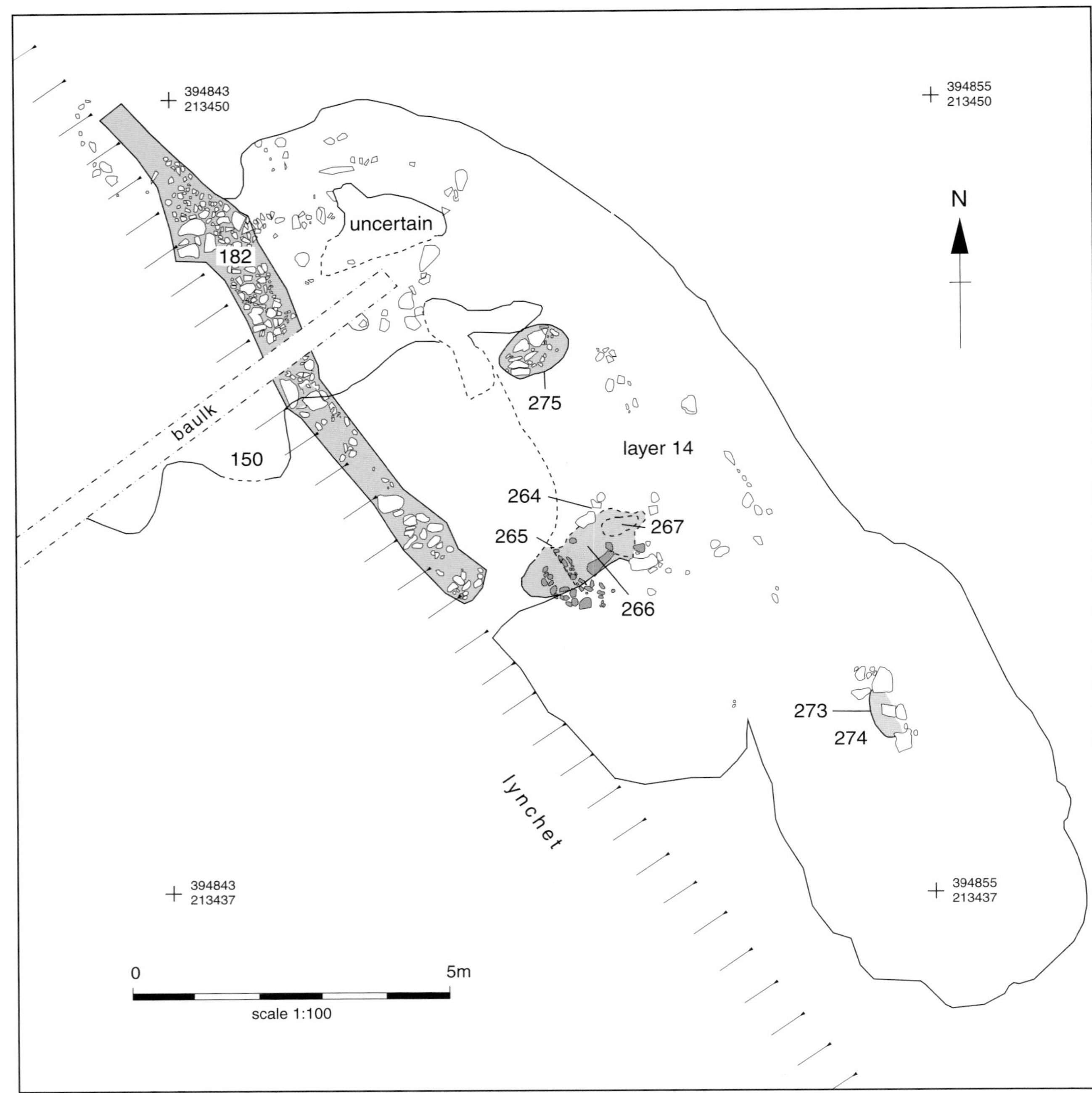


*Figure 4.93 Birdlip Quarry, Area D, period 2b.*

ploughing since there would surely have been evidence for this on the stone spread 302.

### *Area D: Phase 3 (Fig. 4.93)*

#### *Layer 14*

A dark grey silt covered the area and appeared to seal all the features relating to the previous phase. It directly underlay modern ploughsoil. It is unclear whether this material was substantially *in situ* or whether there had been a significant amount of redistribution of soil through ploughing. The layer contained shell-tempered ware dated to the later 4th century and appears to be a genuinely later assemblage (of 113 sherds) than that within the Phase 2 features, although it included some residual earlier material. This residual material appears to include seven coins dated to AD 270–84. It is unclear whether layer 14 relates to a very late occupation here after the ditches had been backfilled, or whether the area was simply used as a midden.

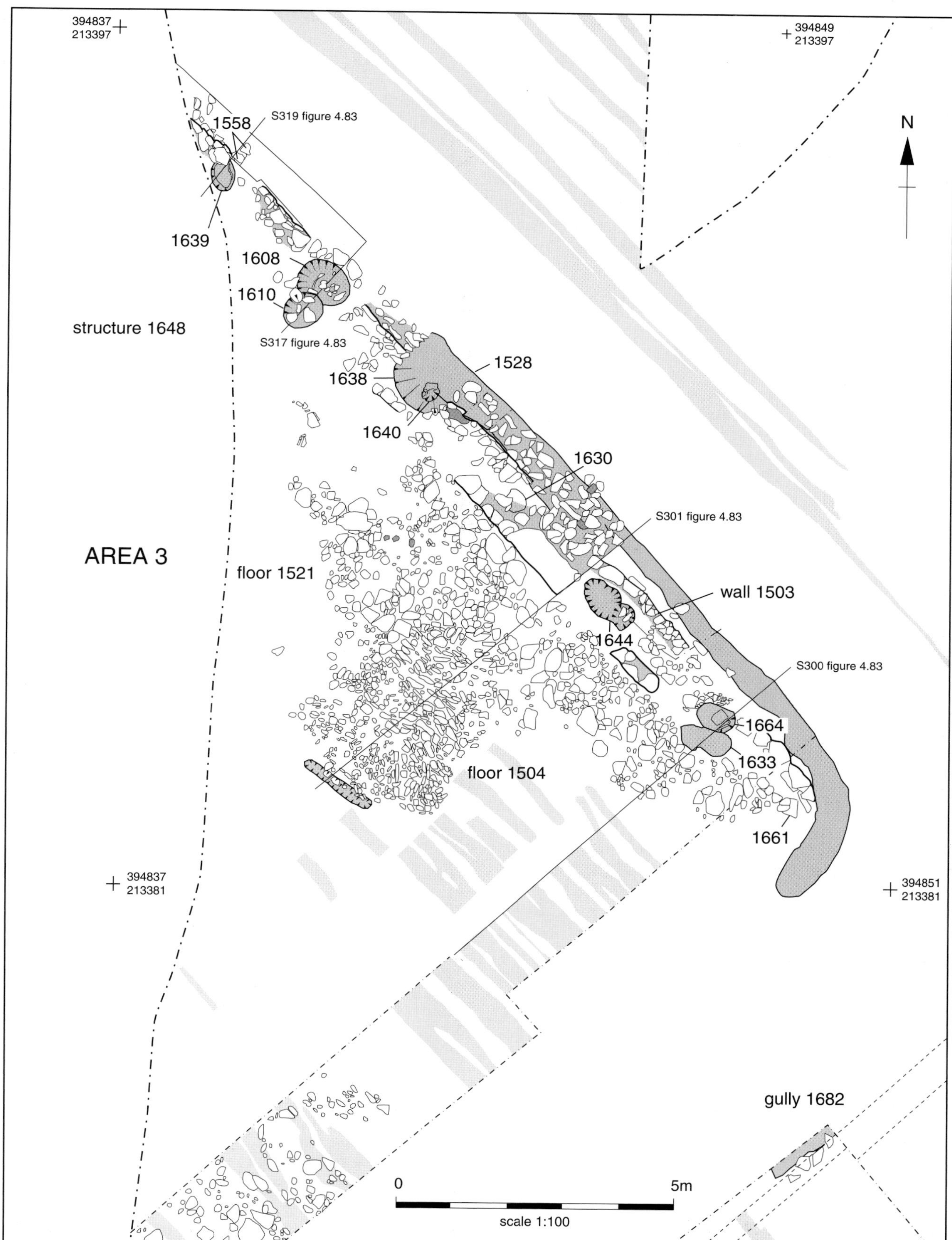


*Figure 4.94 Birdlip Quarry, Area 3, period 2b, structure 1648.*

*Possible wall remnant 182*

A line of limestone rubble lay along the top of the lynchet in a shallow trench, 602. This was a late feature cutting ditch 271 and a number of small postholes, and therefore seems to be unrelated to structure 1457 (Period 2A). It was partly covered by layer 14. Its original form is unclear as it was truncated by the lynchet to the south-east and peters out to the north-west. However, it may be a rough wall foundation. It would make most stratigraphic sense as part of Phase 3 but no related features were found and its overall purpose remains enigmatic.

***Area E: Phase 3***

*Layer 72*

The final phase of occupation in Area E was marked by the accumulation of a uniform deposit of grey silt which filled the terrace hollow. There were no recognisable features associated with this deposit and it remains unclear whether this represents occupation here or whether the area became used as a midden. There was a large quantity of pottery from this deposit (233 sherds) including shell-tempered ware of the later 4th century, and also a coin of AD 313–17. This suggests a discrete late occupation which post-dated the Phase 2 structure, although its character is difficult to assess.

***Area 3: Phase 3***

*Posthole building 1648 (Fig. 4.94)*

The rectangular stone structure 1684 was replaced by a posthole structure after the former had been demolished. The drainage ditch (1502) appears to have been deliberately infilled with pitched stone (1558) to create a surface in a segment about 6 m long north-west of the threshold stone (1503). In front of the threshold stone the ditch was filled with flat slabs.

The evidence for the structure is slight, but comes from a row of seven postholes (1639, 1608, 1640, 1630, 1644, 1664 and 1661) which cut through the earlier wall footing. Feature 1634 may be another post-base although it is out of alignment. The postholes were character-istically wide and shallow with stone post-pads at their bases. Postholes 1639, 1608, 1640, 1630 and 1644 were almost exactly 2.8 m apart while 1644, 1664 and 1661 were slightly more closely spaced. There was no evidence of opposed postholes on the south-west side of the building. The stone flooring of Phase 2 was presumably re-used.

Posthole 1639

Oval shape, 0.5 x 0.3 m and 0.2 m deep with the base occupied by a flat slab 1623 (Fig. 4.83, section 319). It cut through wall 1544 but had an unclear relation-ship with the fill of ditch 1502 since the general spread of stones here could not be differentiated. The upper fill of the posthole (1614) consisted of limestone fragments in a loose matrix of dark silty loam.

Posthole 1608

Large sub-circular pit, 0.65 x 0.70 m and 0.3 m deep with a flat stone on the base. It cut wall 1544 and also the pitched stone backfill 1558 of ditch 1502, indicating that the posthole was a later insertion rather than part of the original structure (Fig. 4.83, section 317). It appeared to be cut by pit 1610. Posthole 1608 was filled with a loose dark silt and limestone fragments (1609) some of which were pitched and could represent the remains of post-packing.

Posthole 1640

Small, oval feature in the base of a much broader but shallow pit 1638. Pit 1638 cut wall 1544 and was filled with rubble (1537). It was probably a robber pit or one dug to remove the post. The post-pad (1641) at the base of posthole 1640 consisted of a jumble of small stones pitched at angles, rather than a single flat slab.

Posthole 1630

An irregular feature defined by a gap in wall 1544, about 0.1 m deep, into which a flat stone post-pad had been placed. The fill (1631) consisted of loose small limestone fragments in a mid grey silt.

Posthole 1644

Ovoid shape, 0.5 x 0.3 m and 0.3 m deep with a flat stone on the base. It cut walls 1544 and 1503. Both the lower fill (1645) and the upper fill (1542) consisted of limestone fragments in a dark silt matrix, but the upper fill spread away from the hole proper over an area of about 0.6 x 1.0 m. The stones in 1542 tended to be pitched and crushed suggesting a deliberate insertion rather than random backfill.

Posthole 1664

Roughly circular, 0.58 m diameter and 0.22 m deep with a flat stone at the base. It cut the rubble core of the wall, 1605. The fill contained some vertically pitched stone which may have been the remains of packing around the post.

Posthole 1661

A possible posthole revealed as a flat stone, apparently in the base of a circular feature cut into the top of gully 1561. Although on alignment with the other postholes, 1661 was only about 2.2 m from 1664 and the post-pad was at a higher level than the others, leaving some doubt about its interpretation.

?Posthole 1634

A possible, but on the whole doubtful, posthole consisting of a broad, shallow depression with a flat

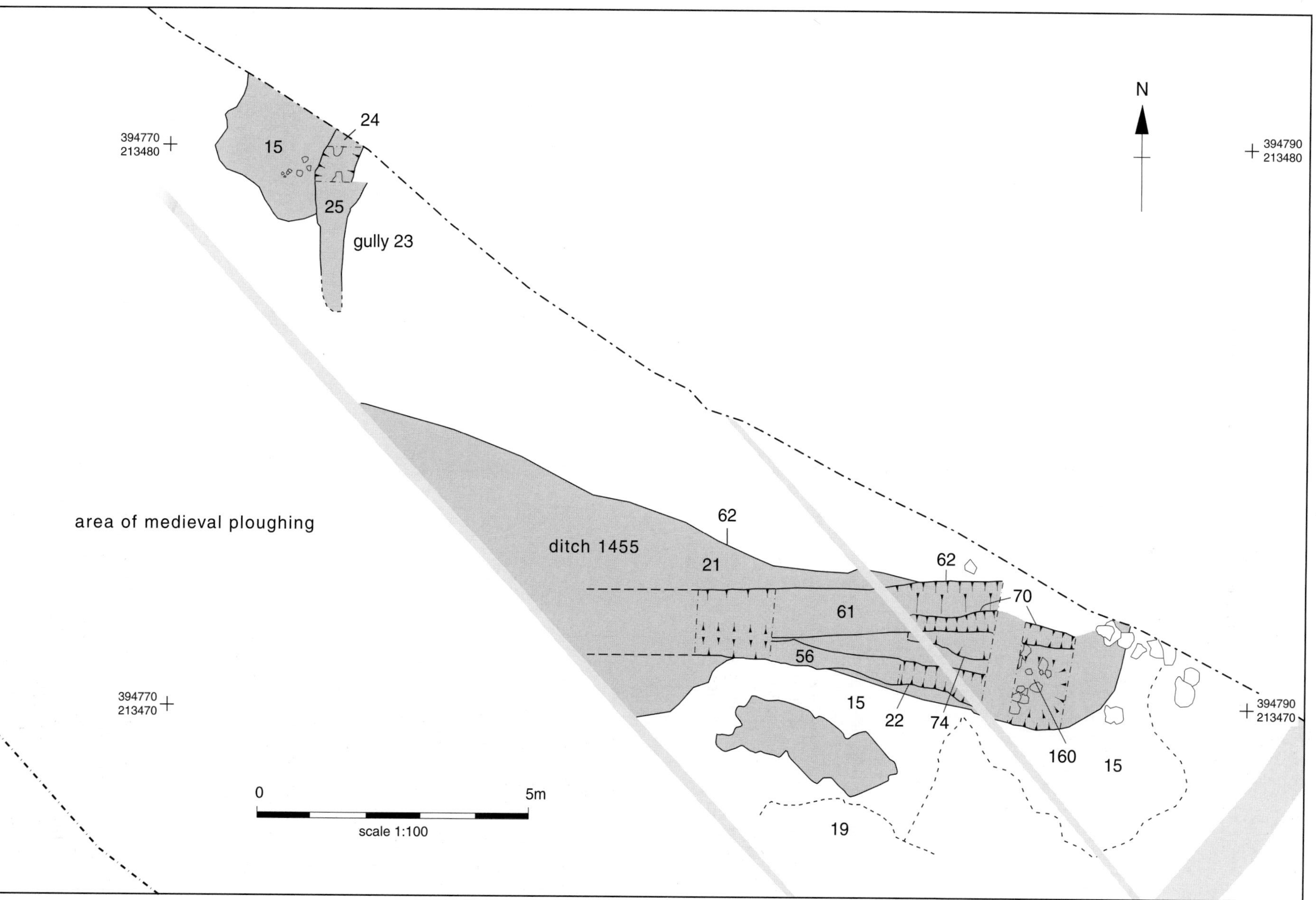


*Figure 4.95 Birdlip Quarry, unphased, ditch group 1455 and gully 23.*

stone on the base. The fill, 1633, was an area of small and medium limestones, some pitched. It at first appeared that this had been inserted through wall 1503, although excavation failed to define the edge of 1634 convincingly and its relationship to the wall remained uncertain.

*Gully 1682 (Fig. 4.102)*

Gully 1682 (segments 1616, 1551, 1621, 1655 and 1651) is interpreted as a redigging of ditch 1681 sometime after the latter had been infilled. It was a relatively broad and shallow feature, about 1.5 m wide and 0.2 m deep, and was dug on the inside edge of 1681 (Fig. 4.67, sections 309, 312 and 326). Gully 1682 had a single dark grey or grey-brown fill which was very similar to the upper fill of 1681. The relationship between the two ditches was unclear during excavation, but 1682 makes sense as the later ditch as it turned south-east to respect the edge of the new road surface 1538.

There was no good dating evidence from gully 1682, although it seems reasonable to assume that it was contemporary with structure 1648 and that both might have formed part of a rebuilding project in this area, connected with the widening of Ermin Street at this time. The best dating for this activity comes from a group of eight coins from the road surface (2012) which were grouped AD 320–4 (see section on excavations adjacent to Ermin Street, Area 5). This is effectively the same date as a coin from in the infilling of ditch 1681, and a date of construction around this time can be suggested.

## Unphased features

### *Features west of Area A*

*Ditch group 1455 (Fig. 4.95)*

This comprised two shallow ditches/gullies (22 and 62) running east-west. Their eastern terminals were under the later stone-based structure 703 while *c.* 12 m to the west they were truncated by ploughing. Gully 62 was considerably broader than 22 and had a narrow slot (70) in its base along part of its length. This contained a slightly greyer fill than the fills of 22 and 62 (fills 56 and 61) which were light reddish brown silts. Both ditches had indistinct terminals which contained rubble (160 and 94).

The interpretation of these ditches is uncertain. They may have been boundary features, although they were rather shallow. This shallowness cannot be accounted for by plough-truncation since the remains of a stone wall (structure 703) overlay the terminal of ditch 62 and had clearly been protected from the plough here. It is perhaps more likely that they represent traces of a timber-framed construction with a beam-slot (70) and an outer eaves-drainage gully (22). The width of 62 may be accounted for by the removal of the ground beam when the structure went out of use.

*Structure 703 (Fig. 4.96)*

After ditch group 1455 had filled in a layer of hillwash (21) accumulated in the remaining hollow. A dry stone wall foundation (27) was laid on top of 21. The remains of this wall consisted of a short alignment of stones within a brown silt matrix. Only the north face was clearly represented and survived up to two courses high. The south face appeared to be missing. The wall ran in a slightly more northerly alignment than the earlier ditches. Among the rubble on the northern side of the wall (28) was the possible trace of a wall running at right-angles (55). This remnant was represented by an alignment of no more than four stones. Above the rubble and butting wall 27 was a layer of grey-brown hillwash (26) which underlay the post-Roman ploughsoil (4).

Despite the fragmentary nature of the remains it appears that the walls represent the traces of a rectangular building, a corner of which had been fortuitously preserved in the hollow of an underlying ditch. The ditches are probably not directly related to structure 703, particularly as their alignments are at variance, but the location of 703 might well have been conditioned by the presence of an earlier structure.

The dating evidence is inconclusive. However, it may be significant that none of the pottery from

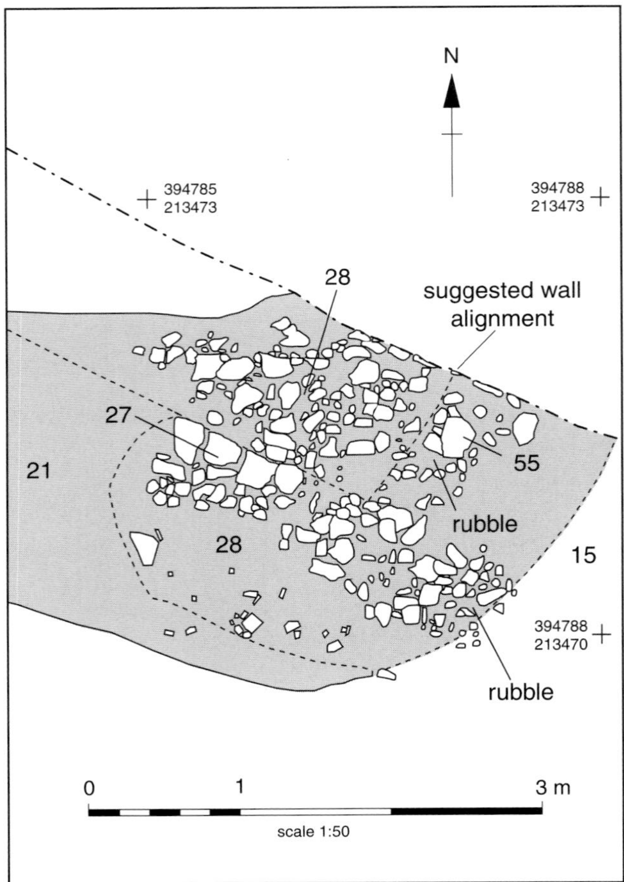


*Figure 4.96 Birdlip Quarry, unphased structure 703.*

deposits associated with structure 703 or ditch group 1455 need be later than the 2nd century. This includes a reasonably substantial assemblage (32 sherds) from layer 21. The overlying hillwash, 26, yielded exclusively 2nd-century pottery (17 sherds.)

*Gully 23 (Fig. 4.95)*

A fragment of shallow, slightly curving, gully lay near the western end of the site. It ran approximately north-south for 2.5 m before petering out. Its maximum depth at the site edge was 0.16 m. It contained a light primary fill (24) under a darker secondary fill (25) which yielded a few 2nd-century sherds. This feature would suggest that further occupation existed north of the excavation in this part of the field.

*Miscellaneous pits (Fig. 4.73)*

Pit 828

A circular pit was located just east of the boundary ditch 688 (segment 67). It was 1.4 m in diameter and 0.74 m deep with a rounded base. Its function was unclear. After a thin accumulation of light brown silt (830) it was rapidly backfilled with stone rubble (829). The pottery and a coin of *c.* AD 253–60 indicated that this had probably taken place in the later 3rd century and the feature could have belonged with either Period.

Pits 255 and 257

These were similar shallow oval features backfilled with dark brown silt and stone rubble. They were located just north-west of Area B. Pit 255 was 0.79 x 0.59 m and 0.14 m deep, while 257 was slightly smaller, 0.66 x 0.36 m and 0.05 m deep. A small amount of undiagnostic pottery was recovered. There was no evidence as to the function of these features.

**Excavations adjacent to Ermin Street: Areas 1, 2A, 4, 5, 6 and Ermin Street Trenches 3 and 4** *(Figs 4.97–102)*

A number of small excavation trenches were positioned to examine areas of the site adjacent to Roman Ermin Street, as well as part of the road itself. Five of these trenches (Areas 1, 2A, 4, 5 and 6) were excavated as part of the Birdlip Quarry site, while Ermin Street Trenches 3 and 4 formed part of the programme of excavations specifically targeted on the road.

All the trenches with the exception of Area 2A exposed part of a road surface of limestone cobbles which formed a linear feature running on the north-eastern side of the modern road. The line of the road was also traceable running up the hill north-west of Ermin Street Trench 4 and south-east of Area 5, although in both directions the surface of the road had been lost.

In some cases the sequence of deposits encountered could be tied to the phasing of the main site, while in other cases the phasing was far from clear. For this reason these trenches are considered as a group apart from the main site, although the relationship of the road to the Roman occupation is clearly of some significance and the connection between the two is examined in the following trench descriptions.

***Ermin Street Trench 4***

This trench, the furthest to the north-west, confirmed the existence of a cobbled road surface (407) continuing north-west, although it was badly disturbed and only clear on the western edge of the trench. There it was overlain by clean silts (411 and 404) which were probably imported deposits. They were truncated by modern road make-up.

***Area 1*** *(Fig. 4.100, section 270)*

*Phase 1*

The earliest feature in this trench was a shallow ditch (1220) running into the roadside ditch (1212) at right-angles. Since it was cut by 1212 it can be assumed to have been related to an earlier roadside ditch which had been completely removed. There was no dating evidence for this phase and ditch 1220 appears to have silted up naturally.

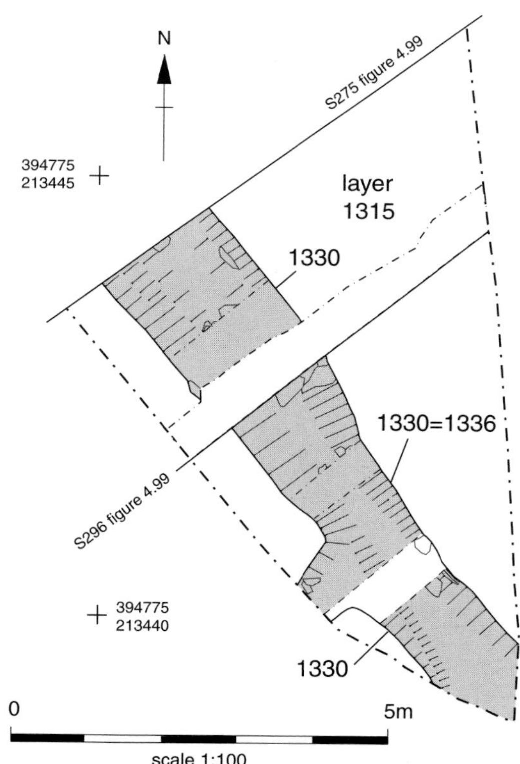


*Figure 4.97 Birdlip Quarry, Area 2A, roadside ditch 1330.*

*Phase 2*

Roadside ditch 1212 was about 1.8 m wide and 0.6 m deep with a narrow base. It respected, or truncated, the cobbled road 1208 on the south-western side. The road was exposed over a width of 4.5 m and was composed of a thin layer of local limestone which directly overlay the natural siltstone. It occupied a slight hollow, presumably caused by erosion through use, rising towards the lip of ditch 1212 where the metalling survived to its greatest thickness. The surface of the road had been much disturbed by modern tree roots.

The lowest fill of ditch 1212 (fill 1218) was a mid yellowish brown silt which appeared to represent gradual natural accumulation. It contained sherds of broadly 2nd-century date, including a sherd of East Gaulish samian, which would suggest that it was infilling in the later 2nd or early 3rd century. There were no finds from the road itself, either within or on the cobbled surfaced.

*Phase 3*

The upper fills of ditch 1212 consisted of an outer (ie. north-eastern) mid brown or slightly orange-brown silt (1215 and part of 1217) and an inner silt which had a greyish cast (1214 and part of 1217). Both probably represent natural silting although some organic inclusions are implied in the darker fill. It is possible that this darker fill occupied a recut, but the evidence from neither section was convincing.

The date for the infilling of the ditch is unclear but it is likely to be Roman. A single post-medieval sherd from 1217 is either intrusive through root disturbance, or came from an unrecognised cut in the top of the ditch, since it is inconceivable that the ditch remained only partly infilled for that length of time. A coin of AD 161–80 also came from 1217. Its significance as dating evidence is uncertain but it may imply that the final infilling of the ditch was relatively early - perhaps before the later 3rd century.

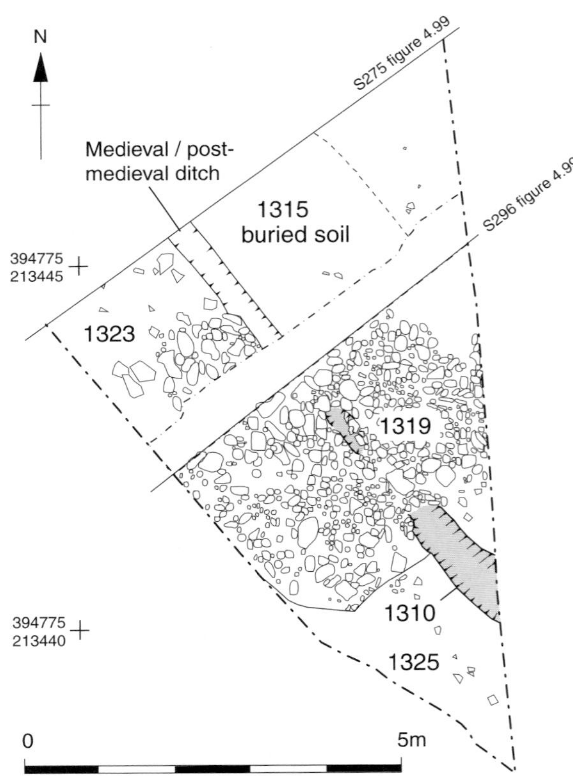


*Figure 4.98 Birdlip Quarry, stone surface 1319/1323 (Area 2A).*

*Phase 4*

The road surface was covered by a layer of clean, calcareous silt (1206). This also infilled the top of ditch 1212 (fill 1213 – not in section 270). This layer was essentially local redeposited natural silt, unlike the colluvium on the site, and implies deliberate dumping which put the road out of use. This deposit reached a maximum depth of 0.3 m on the south-west edge of the trench. Over the rest of the exposed road it had been truncated by later disturbances.

The date of this deposit was unclear. The fact that it directly overlay the surface of the Roman road suggested that it was Roman, although the implication that there was such a major remodelling of the road in the later Roman period is somewhat difficult to envisage. The same deposit was found over the road in Area 6 (layer 1163). The observation that the deposit was present in the top of ditch 1212 would also, on the face of it, support a Roman date. However, it is considered probable that there was a later recut in the top of the ditch. This has already been suggested by the presence of a post-medieval sherd and would also accord with the situation in Area 2A where a post-Roman ditch was undoubtedly cut into the top of the Roman one. The balance of evidence from this and other road sections suggests that the silt dumping comes from road construction in the early modern era (see Discussion, below).

### Area 4

This area was heavily disturbed as far as the natural silt and was abandoned after flooding. There was an indication that the roadside ditch in Area 1 continued through this trench and aligned with that in Area 2A.

### Area 2A

*Phase 1*

The earliest features in this part of the site were heavily truncated and effectively undated. The earliest surviving 'roadside' ditch, 1341, was heavily truncated by a recut (1336=1330), which followed almost precisely the same alignment, and it yielded no finds (Fig. 4.99, sections 275 and 296). Thin layers

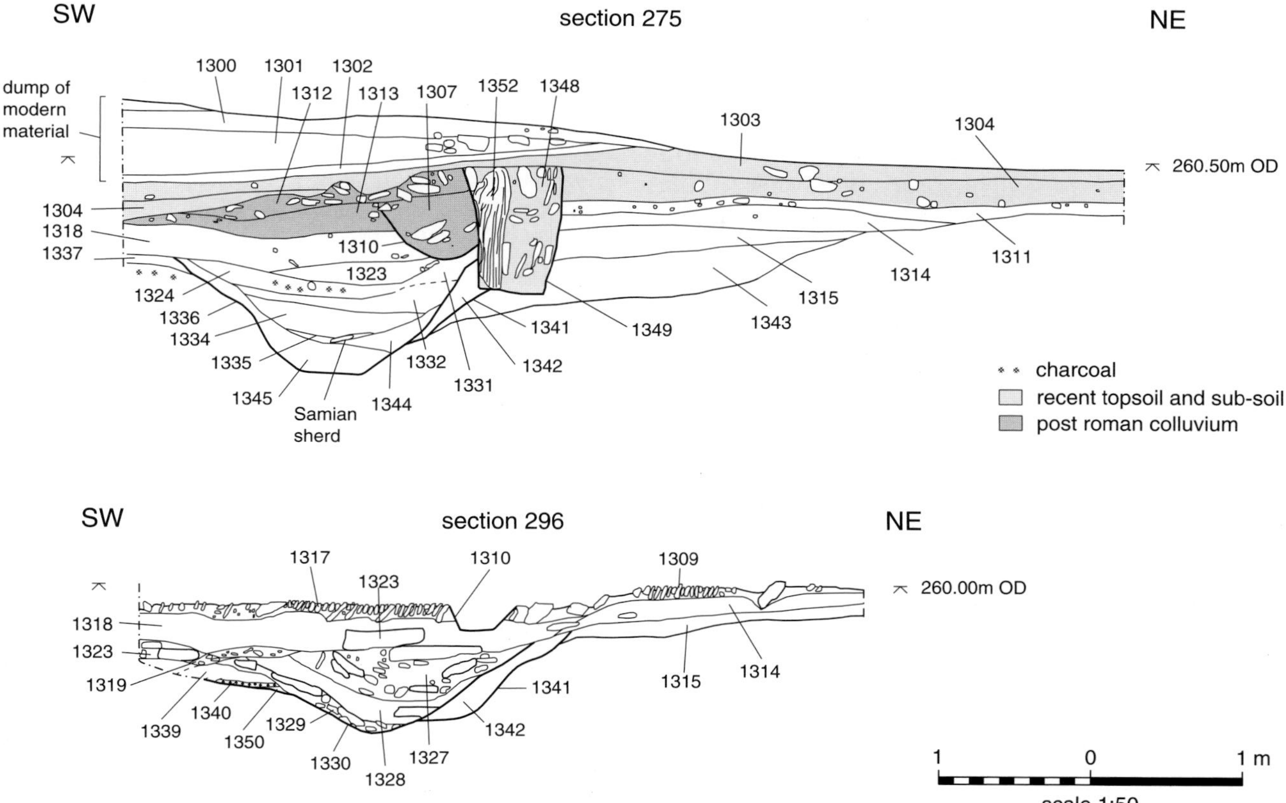


*Figure 4.99 Birdlip Quarry, Area 2A, sections.*

of charcoal, 1338 and 1340, on the south-west edge of the site directly overlay natural silt. Their origin is unclear. The road was not exposed in this trench and it is uncertain whether the layers would have predated the road itself or were related to its construction. The charcoal was covered by dumps of clean clayey silt (1337 and 1339) which probably represented upcast from one or other phase of 'roadside' ditch, but it was impossible to say which.

### *Phase 2 (Figs 4.97–98)*

The later 'roadside' ditch, 1336 (=1330), was about 1.8 m wide and 0.6–0.75 m deep. The initial silting, fills 1345, 1344 and 1346, was not particularly deep. The ditch was mainly infilled with dumped deposits (1329, 1328, 1327, 1334, 1335?, 1332, 1331 and 1324) which included a great deal of stone rubble (Fig. 4.99, section 296). This appears to have been intended to provide a foundation for the overlying stone surface 1323 (Fig. 4.98) and was probably deposited rapidly, perhaps as a single event. In the northern part of the trench layer 1324 (Fig. 4.99, section 275) was a deposit of relatively dark soil with charcoal and included a bovine skull (1326).

The stone surface 1323 was equivalent to 1319 on the south-east side of the ditch. They comprised a tightly compacted spread of large, medium and small stones, mostly laid flat but some pitched, which formed a rough surface. It appears to have been intended as a path, 2–3 m wide, running in the direction of Area A of the main site (Fig. 4.98).

Pottery from the dumping within the ditch and the stone surface itself was dated to after *c.* AD 270. There was less evidence for the date of the ditch itself, although layer 1347, possibly a subsoil which was cut by ditch 1336, yielded a sherd of Dorset Black Burnished Ware probably dating to after *c.* AD 220. From well within the ditch, possibly from the primary silting (fill 1335) came a sherd of stamped samian of mid to late Antonine date. This would suggest a rather earlier date for the redigging of the ditch, which may have taken place during Phase 2 in Area A. A late 2nd-century redigging of the 'roadside' ditch would imply a long duration for Phase 2 with the complete cycle of digging and infilling lasting about a century. Alternatively, the ditch may have been dug in the 3rd century, rather than any earlier. This would imply a long period of circulation for the samian, but this is certainly not impossible. It is possible that the infilling of the ditch was associated with the re-occupation of Area A towards the end of the 3rd century (Period 2A). In that case, there is no indication of a period of abandonment of the ditch corresponding to Phase 3 in Area A, and it appears that the ditch was kept fairly clean between its initial digging and its infilling with rubble. The re-occupation in Area A (Phase 4) would then appear to have involved the modification or repositioning of the Roman road and the provision of access to the settlement.

*Phase 3*

Later, a layer of dark soil (1322 and 1318), 0.2 m thick, developed over the stone surface. The disuse of this surface was probably only local since a large quantity of pottery (over 100 sherds) came from this soil. This phase is only broadly dated to after AD 270, although a concordance with the main site would suggest that layers 704 and 225 (Period 2A Phase 5 in Area A) are equivalent deposits, and these are more securely 4th century.

*Phase 4 (Fig. 4.91)*

Activity in this area recommenced with the reconstruction of a stone surface over layer 1318. This was a somewhat neater construction than the earlier surface, with tightly-packed pitched stones (layers 1309 and 1317) forming a solid surface over the earlier ditch, and an area of flat stones (layer 1308) to the east. It formed a path, 3–4 m wide, leading north-east and can be seen to correspond to the pitched stone surface 1224 (Period 2B Phase 6) in Area 2B which led to structure 713 in Area A.

Pottery from the surfaces themselves does not provide close dating, but two coins from stony layer 1311 to one side were struck AD 335–40. In addition there were seven coins from layer 1313 which, although an overlying colluvial layer (Fig. 4.99, section 275), contained a great deal of Roman pottery, and the coins indicate that the latest occupation in this area need not be later than AD 330-68. The absence of very late shell-tempered ware may support the impression that there were no finds reaching the area by AD 360–70.

***Road Section in Area 6 (Culvert Trench)*** *(Fig. 4.100, section 268)*

*Phase 1*

Under the road at the southern end of the trench was a mottled greyish brown and yellowish brown silt, 1179. This appeared to be a buried soil layer, but rather darker than the early orange-brown 'buried soil' 1180 further north with which it had no relationship. Layer 1179 contained a coin of AD 324–8 and eight sherds of later 3rd/4th-century pottery.

*Phase 2*

The road surface, 1164, which was laid over 1179, was composed of tightly-packed, small and medium, worn and sub-angular, limestone fragments. Its thickness only extended to one course of stones and a width of 0.8 m was exposed. It was bounded on the north-east side by ditch 1192 which was steep-sided with a narrow, flat, base. The lower fill, 1191, was a yellow-brown clayey silt without diagnostic finds, which appeared to represent natural accumulation. This was overlain by a greyish brown silt (1190) tipping in from the north-east.

*Phase 3*

Layer 1163 represents a dump of clean pale clayey silt directly over the road surface 1164. The layer was defined as 0.2–0.3 m deep in section, although it merged indistinctly with the overlying machine-excavated layer 1195, which represented a more weathered version of the same deposit at this end of the trench. The overall depth of 1163 was probably therefore in the order of 0.5 m. There is no evidence that it extended beyond ditch 1192. The final fill of ditch 1192 was a compact yellowish brown silt-clay with limestone, 1189. This appears to have been a deliberate infilling. An interpretation of the section indicates that it may have been within a later (post-Roman) cut on the same alignment as the Roman ditch, although this was not evident during excavation. Alternatively, it may have been essentially part of 1163 albeit slightly darker and with a more notable concentration of stones. The layers above 1189 comprised post-Roman colluvium (1195) and more recent road embankment deposits.

There were no finds from the deposits in this phase, although the fact that 1163 directly overlay the road surface 1164, without an intervening layer of colluvium (which might be expected in this low-lying area of the site had there been a significant period of abandonment) suggests that the dumping took place in the Roman period. However, given the early 4th-century terminus post quem for Phase 2, it appears that this activity would have been very late indeed. In common with Area 1, a remodelling of the road at this late period appears unlikely and despite some arguments for it being Roman an early modern date is considered more likely.

***Area 5 and Ermin Street Trench 3***

*Phase 1*

There were no features which could be definitely ascribed to this phase, although a number of the features which were infilled in Phase 2 could have had their origin in Phase 1.

*Phase 2 (Fig. 4.84)*

Pit 322 (Ermin Street Trench 3)

This was a circular feature, about 3 m in diameter, which was excavated to a depth of 1.46 m without the bottom being reached. The sides of the pit were vertical. The lowest fill encountered, 328, was a grey silt which may have represented a deliberate backfill. The later fills, 327, 324, 325 and 323, appear to be varying stony dumps in a slight weathering cone. These can be dated by pottery to the later 3rd/4th centuries. The feature may have been a well, although there was no trace of a lining within the deposits

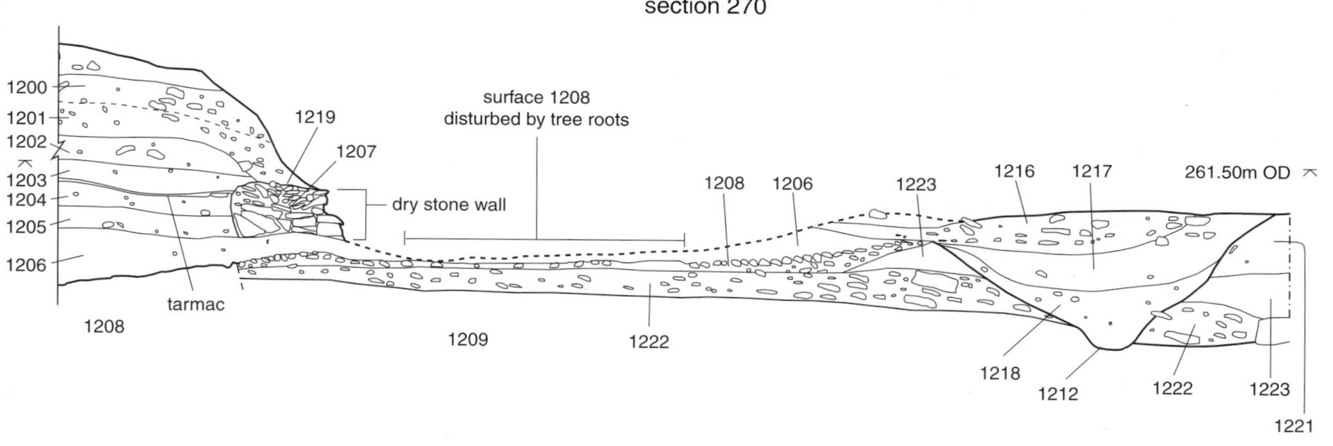


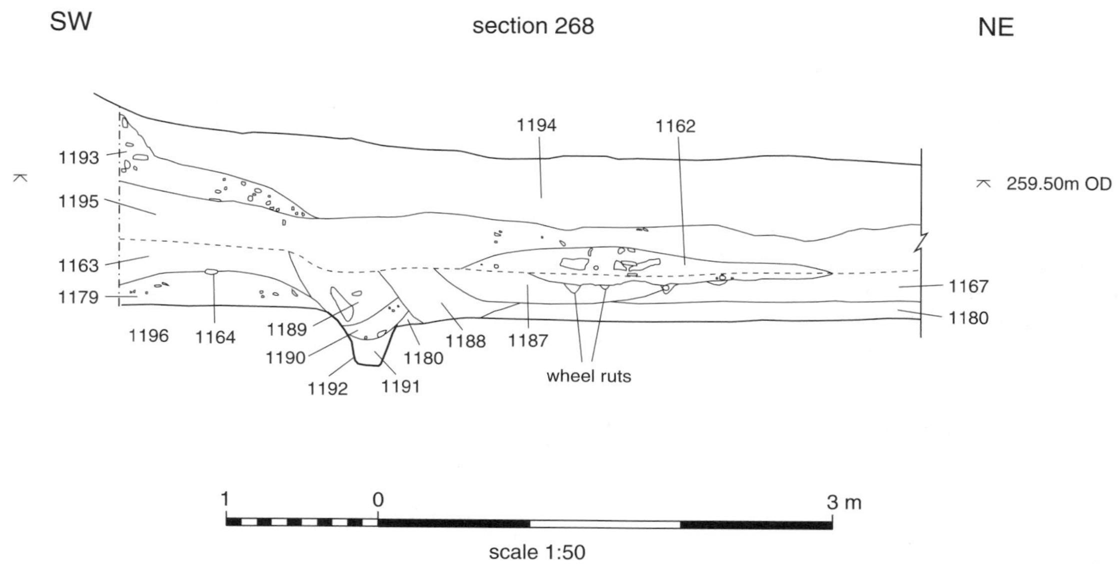


*Figure 4.100 Birdlip Quarry, Area 1, section 270 and Area 6, section 268.*

excavated. The date of origin of the feature is unknown. It was sealed by road cobbling, 309 (Phase 3), which became heavily rutted and sank into the top of the feature.

Pit 2020 (Area 5 Trench 1)

This was a sub-circular, shallow, dished feature, 2.5 m in diameter and 0.4 m deep. Above thin deposits of edge-silting (2018 and 2019) the bulk of the fill comprised a dump of rubble (2007). This may be dated to the later 3rd century. The finds included part of a substantial Savernake Ware storage jar. The feature cut an earlier, smaller, pit 2035, which was sub-circular and steep-sided. It was 1.2 m in diameter and cut to the same depth as 2020, but was without finds. Both features were sealed by the road surface 2004 (Phase 3).

Ditch 2068 (segments 2042, 2066 and 2044)

This was a shallow linear feature running through Trenches 2, 3 and 4 in Area 5. Its south-east terminal was found within Trench 1 and it appears to have been truncated by later ditches (316 and 311 – see Fig. 4.101, section 302) at its north-western end just before Ermin Street Trench 3. Its length was therefore in excess of 30 m. It was 0.3–0.4 m deep with a revetment wall (2038, 2050 and 2045) within the ditch on the north-eastern side (Fig. 4.101, sections 313 and 318). The base of the ditch was broad and flat but the opposite edge was truncated by post-medieval ditch cuts and its width is not known. The ditch was partly infilled with natural silting (2041, 2056 and 2065) and later backfilled. Trench 4 showed a recut, 2064, through 2065, but this was not evident elsewhere.

The similarity of design between ditch 2068 and ditch 1681 in Area 3, both of which contained revetment walls of identical construction, strongly suggests that the ditches were contemporary. The best independent date for the construction of ditch 2068 comes from the fill behind wall 2045 (fill 2046) in Trench 2 (Fig. 4.101, section 318), where 12 sherds are dated to the late 3rd to 4th century. This is entirely compatible with the evidence from Area 3.

The ditch was put out of use when the Phase 3 road surface 2022, 2048 and 2031 was laid over the top. However, it is possible that the ditch was contemporary with the road surface on its south-western side, and that the road was simply extended eastward over the ditch rather than being extensively re-made over its full width. Any further examination of this conjecture was not possible as the post-medieval ditches, which cut ditch 2068, had destroyed any relationship between the road surfaces on their eastern and western sides.

*Phase 3 (Fig. 4.102)*

All the Phase 2 features were sealed by road surfaces in Area 5 (layers 2022, 2048, 2031, 2004 and 2003) and Ermin Street Trench 3 (layer 309). The road consisted of a layer of small and medium sub-angular/rounded tabular limestone fragments laid directly upon the natural limestone or clay-silt, or on the fills of the earlier features. There was no contemporary roadside ditch in this area of the site. The road surface was heavily rutted from later use by wheeled vehicles. The rutting was particularly severe in the north-east area of the excavation, where it extended away from the road proper. The part of the road to the south-west of the post-medieval ditches was less heavily worn suggesting that it was out of use in the post-Roman period.

The dating evidence for the construction of the road is consistent with that from Area 3. Perhaps the best evidence comes from a group of eight coins from the silt overlying the road itself (2012 in Trench 2). These date to AD 320–5, forming a tight spatial and chronological group which is unlikely to have been redeposited and hence gives a reasonable *terminus ante quem* for the road. It can be noted that a coin in this date range came from destruction deposits associated with the revetment wall in ditch 1681 (Area 3). Evidence from this area has already been used to suggest a deliberate infilling of the ditch and a rapid construction of the road over it (Area 3 Phase 2, above).

### Discussion of road sections at Birdlip Quarry

A complete road section through Ermin Street was not available in this part of the route and observations on the nature and development of the Roman road are based upon partial evidence. Nevertheless, some interpretations can be advanced and supported with reference to the more complete sections excavated through the road (Chapter 5).

There was a fundamental difference between the sequences revealed in roadside trenches lying to the south-east of the main site, and those to the north-west, which will be discussed as separate groups. Area 6, in the middle, contained some information common to both groups.

The road surface exposed on the south-east side (Area 3, Area 5 and Ermin Street Trench 3) was clearly a late Roman construction although it had been used and heavily worn in later periods. This later use accounts for a few medieval/post-medieval horseshoe fragments found in features which are, based on the totality of the evidence, undoubtedly Roman. One came from ditch 2068 (fill 2046), one from road or repair layer 2017, and two from road 2048. The relationship of the ditch and road to the occupation in Area 3 makes it clear that they are late Roman and that the horseshoes were therefore intrusive. There was also a post-medieval horseshoe from ditch 311 (fill 310) in Ermin Street Trench 3 (Fig. 4.101, section 302), although it is still unclear whether this was part of Roman ditch 2068 or a later cut. The wheel ruts and overlying silts yielded nine horseshoe fragments and later contexts three more.

The comparative absence of wheel ruts in the road surface on the western side of the post-medieval ditch has been suggested as indicating that that this part of the road was not used in the post-medieval period. This suggestion is emphasised by the find of eight 4th-century coins, almost certainly forming a purse group, from the silts overlying the road at the western end of Trench 2. This would seem to indicate that the road here went permanently out of use shortly after the Roman period. This may also be true of the small section of road exposed in Area 6 which was also probably late Roman. It is unclear why this line, which was closest to the original line of Ermin Street (lying to the west of the site under the A417), should have been abandoned. It is evident, however, that damage caused by wheel ruts was heavy and extensive on the road surface further east and also in Area 3 as post-medieval traffic spread further away from Ermin Street and attempted to find hard ground. It is possible that this route related to the difficulties of crossing the dry valley in the post-medieval period along the original course of Ermin Street.

To the north-east of the settlement a well-worn road surface in a slight hollow way was exposed in Area 1 and Ermin Street Trench 4. It was not encountered in Area 2A and the road seems to have been running at a slight angle to the modern road taking it west of the excavation area. It was not possible to prove that this was the Roman military road, but this seems highly likely given the finds from the roadside ditch in Area 1 and the lack of an obvious alternative context for the road's existence.

There was no build up of road surfaces here, the overlying deposits being dumps of clean silt which were notably whitish and clayey in Area 1 and also in Area 6. The obscure origin and date of this deposit has been discussed. Although it could have been late Roman on the evidence obtained, the balance

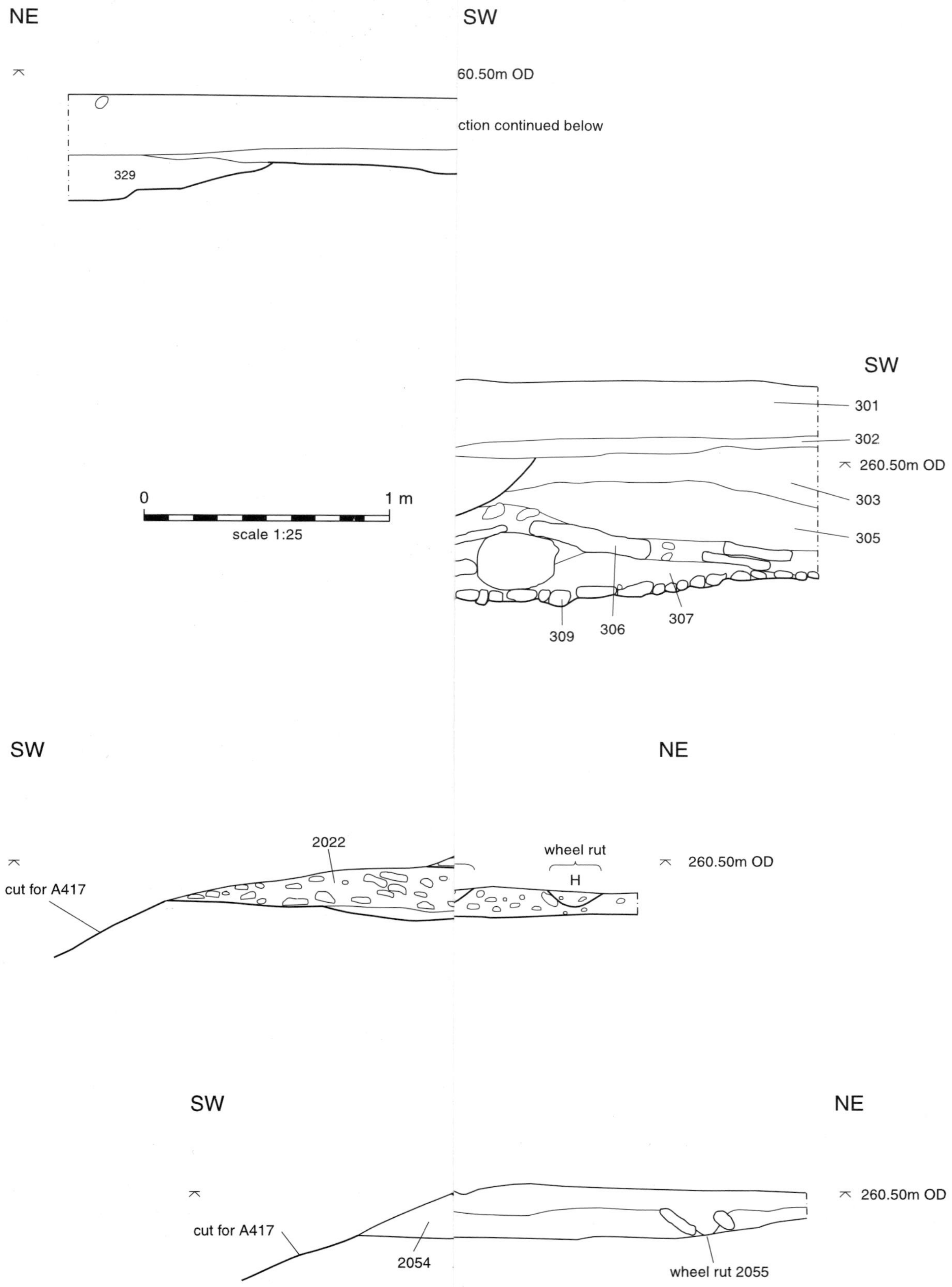

*Birdlip Quarry, Ermin Street Trench 3 and Area 5, sections.*

394869
213347
Trench 1
Trench 2
S318 figure 4.101
Trench 4
Trench 3
S313 figure 4.101
Post-medieval ditch
Ermin St. Trench 3
S302 figure 4.101
0
5
10m
scale 1:150
394838
213347

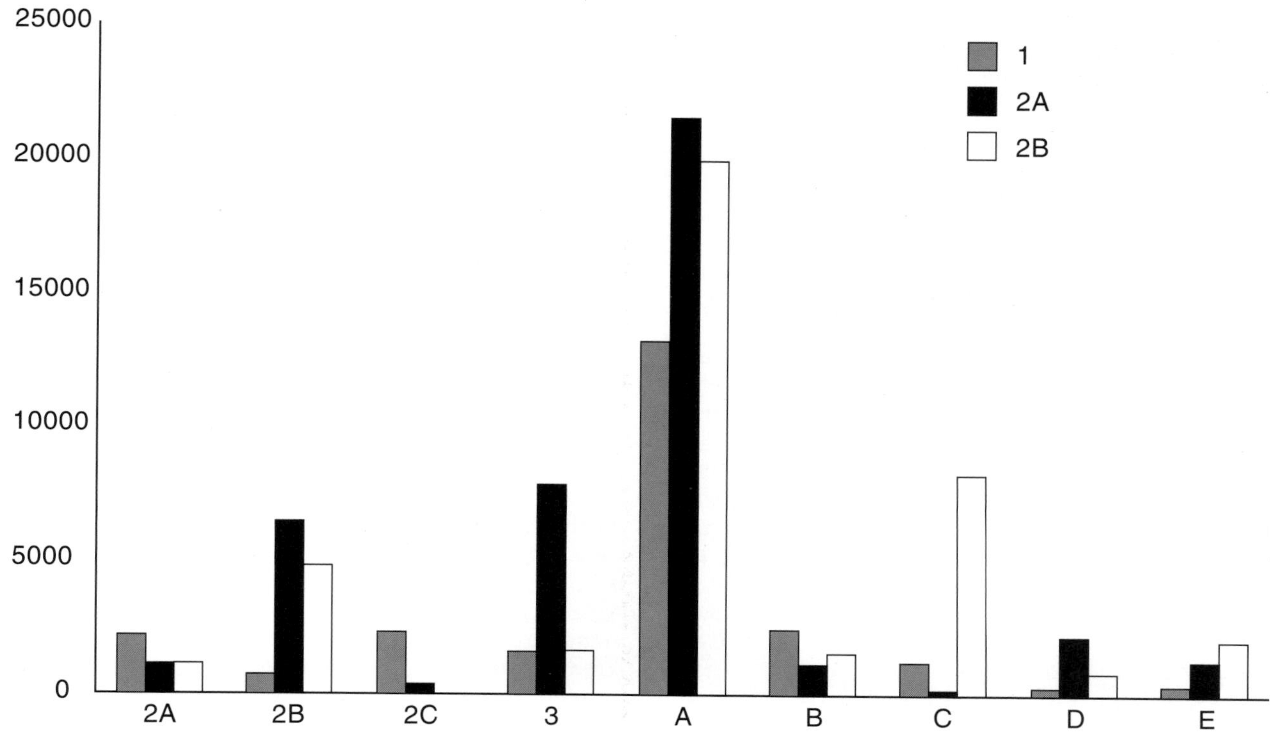


*Figure 4.103 Birdlip Quarry, pottery weight by Area and period.*

of probability indicates that it was part of an embankment of the turnpike era. A comparison with the other road sections would further suggest that the scale of this re-building is indicative of a 19th-century road improvement, rather than an earlier one. There is no evidence that such a scale of road-building was undertaken in the 4th century, nor at any subsequent time until the early 19th century. The fact that this embankment directly overlay the Roman surface, without any intervening deposits, must be taken to indicate that the Roman road was in continuous use until then. The lack of evidence for this, when contrasted for instance with the number of horseshoes from the south-eastern section of road, is somewhat surprising, although it may be accounted for by the limited area of road exposed in the north-west section. The further difficulty of the silt dump infilling part of the Roman ditch in Area 1 can only be resolved by pre-supposing the presence of an unrecorded ditch cut into the top of the Roman one. This is, in fact, not unlikely since this same situation was observed in Area 2A and the ditches in both areas were seen to align. The coincidence of Roman and later ditches was also recorded in Area 5 and possibly, but less clearly, in Area 6. This suggests the Roman road had a profound and abiding influence, not only in its obvious function as an artery of communication, but also in the way it acted as a template conditioning the arrangement of later boundaries and landuse.

## Discussion of the finds

### *Pottery quantification*

The quantity of pottery by site sub-division and Period was compared in order to assess the distribution of material over the duration of the occupation. The results of this enquiry, using pottery quantification by weight, are shown in Figure 4.103. The results based on sherd number were very similar. It is immediately apparent that pottery is far more prevalent in Period 2 than Period 1. It is also clear that pottery from Period 2B contexts represents a considerable proportion of the pottery from the site (about 38%). This appears surprising given that this is thought to be the shortest period of occupation. At face value, the data may reflect an increasing use of pottery over time, perhaps relating to an increasing ease of supply together with a relative increase in the purchasing ability of the inhabitants. This interpretation is considered to be dubious. A more likely explanation is that there was a considerable amount of redeposition, with Period 2A contexts containing material from Period 1, and Period 2B contexts containing pottery from both the earlier occupations.

### *Residuality*

Timby comments on the fragmentary and mixed nature of the pottery assemblage which was probably due to the shortage of large negative features for rubbish deposition and the use of surface middens instead. It can be shown that 206 sherds (51%) of Central Gaulish samian (ie. that manufactured before *c.* AD 200) came from Period 2 contexts. As the longevity of this ware is uncertain, it is unclear whether this can all be considered to be residual. However, 23% came from Period 2B contexts of the mid to later 4th century, so it seems likely that the degree of residuality is at least of this order. Other early wares in Period 2B contexts include Savernake Ware (17% of the total of this ware), particularly from Area A; Wiltshire Orange Sandy Ware 231 (51%), particularly from Area A; Wiltshire Grey Sandy Ware 232 (19%), particularly from Area 3; and Wiltshire White Slip/ no Slip Ware (16%), most commonly from Area C.

It is therefore probably safe to assume that at least 25–30% of pottery is residual in later contexts. A recalculation of the percentages displayed in Figure 4.103 indicates that, assuming 25–30% residuality, the amount of pottery discarded in Period 1 would be around 32–34% of the total; that in Period 2A would stay the same at around 39%; and that in Period 2B would be reduced to 26–28%.

These figures indicate a slight increase in pottery from Period 1 to 2A followed by a reduction in the deposition of pottery in Period 2B. However, taking into account the estimated durations of each Period (70 years for Period 1, 80 years for Period 2A and 50 years for Period 2B - giving a duration ratio of 35:40:25), the rate of pottery discard can be seen to be the same for each Period.

*Period 2B*

Figure 4.103 therefore appears to be misleading as an indication of the rate of pottery deposition, and the apparent dramatic increase in pottery in Period 2 can largely be accounted for by the incorporation of residual material. However, it is still significant that an appreciable occupation took place in the mid to late 4th century (Period 2B) for which the evidence consists largely of soil middens with few associated structural features.

The principal occupation at this time appears to continue in Area A associated with the rectilinear stone walls and structure 713. The distribution of pottery in this period indicates that rubbish was deposited in and around the structure(s) rather than mainly in adjacent middens. The significance of this is unclear. There also appears to be a relatively high proportion of residual material in the layers of this Period, with, for example 13 sherds (11%) of all the Savernake Ware, 30 sherds (7%) of the Central Gaulish Samian and 76 sherds (32 %) of the Wiltshire Orange Sandy Ware, from these contexts. It is possible that this is related to a redeposition of midden material from elsewhere. A similar situation was found at Kingscote (Timby 1998a, 71) where the late occupation deposits contained large quantities of midden material covering two centuries of occupation, suggesting that late buildings may have been used as rubbish tips. However, there may be other factors involved, one of which is likely to be the normal archaeological practice of being 'cautious' in assigning material of doubtful provenance to the latest of its possible contexts. This also applies to material from general site cleaning.

The nearby midden areas, 2A and 2B were also receiving material in this phase, while 2C was not. This may be surprising in view of the fact that there was a large amount of Phase 2B pottery nearby from Area C, but this figure can largely be accounted for by a great deal of redeposited material in layer 18. This layer contained 6% of all the Central Gaulish samian and Wiltshire White Slip/no-Slip ware on the site. Again it is unclear why there was so much mixing in this area, but it seems unlikely to be connected with later ploughing.

Occupation material was also present in Areas B, D, E and 3. In Area 3 this was associated with a definite posthole structure (structure 1648) In Area D there were suggestions of a structure (stone layer 182), but it is unclear what form this might have taken. As with Area A, midden material seems to have accumulated in and around the structure rather than adjacent to it. Area E showed no evidence of a structure. Area B appears to have been used for rubbish disposal in Period 2B. Perhaps surprisingly, the amount of pottery in this area was never high and it may be suggested that the area was used mainly for the disposal of organic matter.

### *Pottery distribution*

*Pottery in relation to structures*

Pottery and other artefacts were found in close association with the evidence for structures and also in middens, ditches, wells and in the limited range of other negative features. In order to emphasise areas of primary deposition, data on relative sherd sizes for different classes of pottery were plotted. Average sherd weights were calculated for each pottery fabric, and for each context the relative average weight of each fabric was calculated and expressed as a percentage of the site average. In this way above average and below average sherd weights could be plotted.

Along with Severn Valley ware, Dorset Black Burnished Ware (DORBB1) was the most common in each of the three Periods on the site and had a long chronological range. The distribution of this fabric is similar to that of Severn Valley Ware and can be taken as typical of the pottery as a whole, illustrating the general areas of deposition. The above average sized sherds can be taken to indicate the areas of primary deposition, while the small sherds are likely to indicate a more general dispersal of material. As well as indicating areas of rubbish disposal the location of large sherds may suggest the location of in situ vessels, although fragmentary *in situ* vessels obviously would not show up by using this technique.

In Period 1 most pottery comes from structures 1463 and 1464 and the midden area to the south. There are a great many sherds in and around the entrance and a few sherds also on the western side. Pottery also comes from around the ovens in Area C and there are a scatter of sherds associated with Area 3 (structure 1683), Area D (structure 1456 and well 891) and Area E (well 299). There also appears to be primary rubbish in pit 180 in the north-east corner of the site. The distribution of small sherds is more widespread. There is a continuing concentration in and around structures 1463 and 1464 but more sherds from the penannular ditches, particularly on the northern side. There are more sherds in Area B and the associated ditches, a greater concentration in Area 2C, and a wider scatter in other areas of the site.

In Period 2A the distribution of large sherds is slightly more widespread, reflecting the general distribution of primary rubbish in occupation areas, midden areas and nearby features. There are a few sherds from layers within structure 1452 in Area A although none are especially large. The main concentration is outside the entrance and on the southern side of the structure. The distribution of small sherds is even more widespread and can be taken as illustrating the general spread and density of site finds. The absence of 'primary rubbish' from Area B may support the suggestion that this was a store of primarily organic matter used for manuring the fields.

In Period 2B the distributions are not dissimilar to those of the preceding period although both large and small sherds are found principally within the purported stone structures in Area A. Single large sherds come from the other occupation areas.

*Distributions of specific ware types*

Samian

In Period 1 the distribution of large sherds clusters around and inside the structures in Area A, with occasional sherds in the other occupation areas. Three large sherds also came from pit 180. The small sherds came from the same areas but the distribution is wider.

In Period 2A there is a particular concentration of large sherds in the midden area outside structure 1452 in Area A. They are also present in Areas C, B and 3, and in well 891 and the corn dryer in the northern part of the site. The small sherds are in quite similar areas.

In Period 2B the samian is probably mostly, if not all, residual. The distribution of small sherds illustrates quite a wide dispersal which is similar to the distribution in Period 1 and would be unsurprising in a residual context. However, there is a limited but significant presence of large sherds in Area A. The reason for this is unclear, and adds to the general difficulty of characterising the late occupation in this area (see discussion of Phase 2B.)

Samian pottery was common on the site although the range of forms was limited. Dishes and bowls accounted for 90% of the material (see Dickinson, Chapter 7). The unimportance of cups reflects the low proportion of all pottery classified as 'drinking vessels' (less than 5% of the total assemblage, see Timby, Chapter 7) and probably relates to the use of bowls for this purpose. This aspect of cultural identity would not be surprising on a site of strongly 'native' character (Okun 1989, 47). It is probably also significant that there were only three examples of decorated vessels (form Drag. 37) and these were among the earliest datable vessels on the site (Dickinson, ibid.). They were probably important possessions which remained in use for a long time. The possible significance of the piece from layer 840 as an item of display and offering drink is mentioned below (see, Patterning of Activities within Roundhouses). One other decorated fragment came from towards the back of the roundhouse (layer 731), and another was unstratified.

Dressel 20 Amphorae

The distribution of sherds of this large olive oil amphora may be expected to closely relate to the vessel's point of use in either a primary or secondary role. In Period 1 large sherds are restricted to Area A, particularly around the entrance to the structures, with a single large sherd in Area B. Small sherds are more widely scattered as would be expected. The absence of sherds from Area C may be significant given the distribution of Gallic amphorae (below). In Period 2A large sherds are again present close to structure 1452 in Area A, but are also more widely dispersed in ditches. They do not seem to be closely connected with the structures in Areas D and E, and are again absent from Area C. The reason for this is unclear but it is possible that the amphorae were used to transport liquids around the settlement, rather than being entirely static storage vessels. They may also have been used for other purposes if damaged or broken. In Period 2B large sherds are virtually absent and small sherds have a similar distribution to other rubbish. It appears that all sherds from this period are residual which may imply that the amphorae were no longer available or required. The contrast with the quantity of large sherds of samian in Area A in this period is of note but not easily explained unless it is assumed that some samian continued in use into the 4th century.

Gallic Amphorae

The distribution of sherds of this wine amphora show an interesting comparison with those of Dressel 20. In Period 1 both large and small sherds are almost exclusively restricted to the vicinity of Area C. A group of 12 large sherds is also present in pit 174 in the northern part of the site. In Period 2A large sherds come from layer 840 and the rubble layer 743 in Area A, both close to the entrances of the structures here. The possible significance of this is elaborated on below. Again, a sherd is present in the vicinity of Area C. This distribution is reinforced in Period 2B with 12 more sherds in Area C, almost to the total exclusion of other areas. A sherd also comes from Area A layer 7. While they are all above average size, it is likely that they were residual since Gallic amphorae are unlikely to have been imported in the 4th century.

Overall, over half the Gallic Amphora comes from Area C and nearby in Area 2C (42 sherds representing 61% by sherd number and 53% by weight). The reason for this restricted distribution is unclear but may be related to the particular function or status of the structure here. The absence of Dressel 20 amphorae from the same area may have a similar significance. However, that the two types were not necessary mutually exclusive is shown by the presence of both amphorae in similar contexts in Area A.

Savernake ware

Savernake ware dates from the 1st/2nd centuries with the predominant forms being large storage jars. They are thought to have been curated for a long time (see Timby, Chapter 7), so their presence in 3rd-century contexts would not necessarily imply residuality. They comprised 3.5% of the pottery from the site by number of sherds (Table 7.14). The distribution of large sherds may be related to their position of use. In Period 1, large sherds are uncommon and restricted to the south side of the entrance to the Area A structures (five sherds in rubble layer 803), to Area B and to well 891. The small sherds are far more widely scattered but mostly in the vicinity of Area A both inside and outside the structures. These are likely to include smaller forms of vessel as well as small sherds of storage jar. Their absence from Areas C, D or E is of uncertain significance. In Period 2A large sherds are present in and around structure 1452 in Area A, but also from Area B again and well 891. An exceptionally large sherd comes from pit 2020 (fill 2007) in Area 5, and a group of nine sherds come from ditch 1501 in Area 3. In Period 2B all the pottery is likely to be residual. Large sherds are totally absent except a sherd in the upper fill of ditch 1252 (Area 2B). Small sherds are quite widespread.

Judging by the distribution of the large sherds, the use of this type of storage jar appears to be closely associated with the structures in Area A and Area 3 and not the other areas of occupation. However, their presence in peripheral, field edge locations may suggest that they were carried away from the house on occasion. The quantities of sherds are small (three sherds from Area B and well 891 and a single sherd from pit 2020) but given the small overall quantity of this ware the distribution may be significant.

Late grog-tempered ware

This ware comprised large, hand-made storage jars dated to the later 3rd and 4th century (Period 2). Only 32 sherds were recovered from the site. It is possible that they replaced Savernake Ware as a container. The distribution of large sherds is quite similar to those of Savernake Ware and almost entirely confined to Areas A, B and 3. In Area A the large sherds come from outside structure 1452 in Period 2A.

Late Roman shell-tempered ware

This ware, dated to the later 4th century, was found in small quantities. Its distribution may be taken to indicate the main areas of activity in the latest phase. Large sherds came from Areas A, C, D and E, while small sherds also came from Area B. Layer 14 (Area D) actually contained one of the largest concentrations of this ware (20 sherds, 77 g), while layer 7 (Area A) contained the greatest quantity altogether.

### *Coin Distribution*

*Issue Phase A (before AD 259)*

There is a relatively sparse collection of coins from this issue phase which corresponds to site Period 1. It is unclear whether this distribution is related to the distribution of activity in Period 1 since a number of the coins are redeposited. This includes all the coins in Area A (which are from Period 2B contexts), and those from Areas C, 2C, E and 3. However, a few coins may have been in situ losses. These include three coins from layer 1266 in Area 2B. There are also two coins from fill 270 in Area D.

*Issue Phase B (AD 260–296)*

The great proliferation of coins in this issue phase are distributed principally in and around structure 1452 in Area A and nearby midden areas. Many are redeposited in later contexts but they undoubtedly reflect a burst of activity in this part of the site. The large numbers of coins from the midden in Area B re-inforces the suggestion that there is little difference in the treatment of coins and 'rubbish' in the later 3rd century. The concentration of coins in Area D is noteworthy and presumably relates to increased activity in this area, although again most of the coins are from later contexts (seven out of 16 from layer 14 and five unstratified). Relatively few coins came from Area C.

*Issue Phase C (AD 297–330)*

There are fewer coins generally in this issue phase. There is still activity in Area A and apparently a clustering on the north-east side of structure 1452. The major concentration in Area B continues while the coin loss in Area D has ceased completely. A few coins from peripheral ditches towards the north of the site suggests that the ditches were becoming infilled.

*Issue Phase D (AD 331–402)*

Area A dominates the coin loss in this issue phase, with a large concentration also in Area 2A. This distribution supports the suggestion that loci of occupation and rubbish disposal were closely associated in the later 4th century. There is a thin scatter of coins from other parts of the site, except

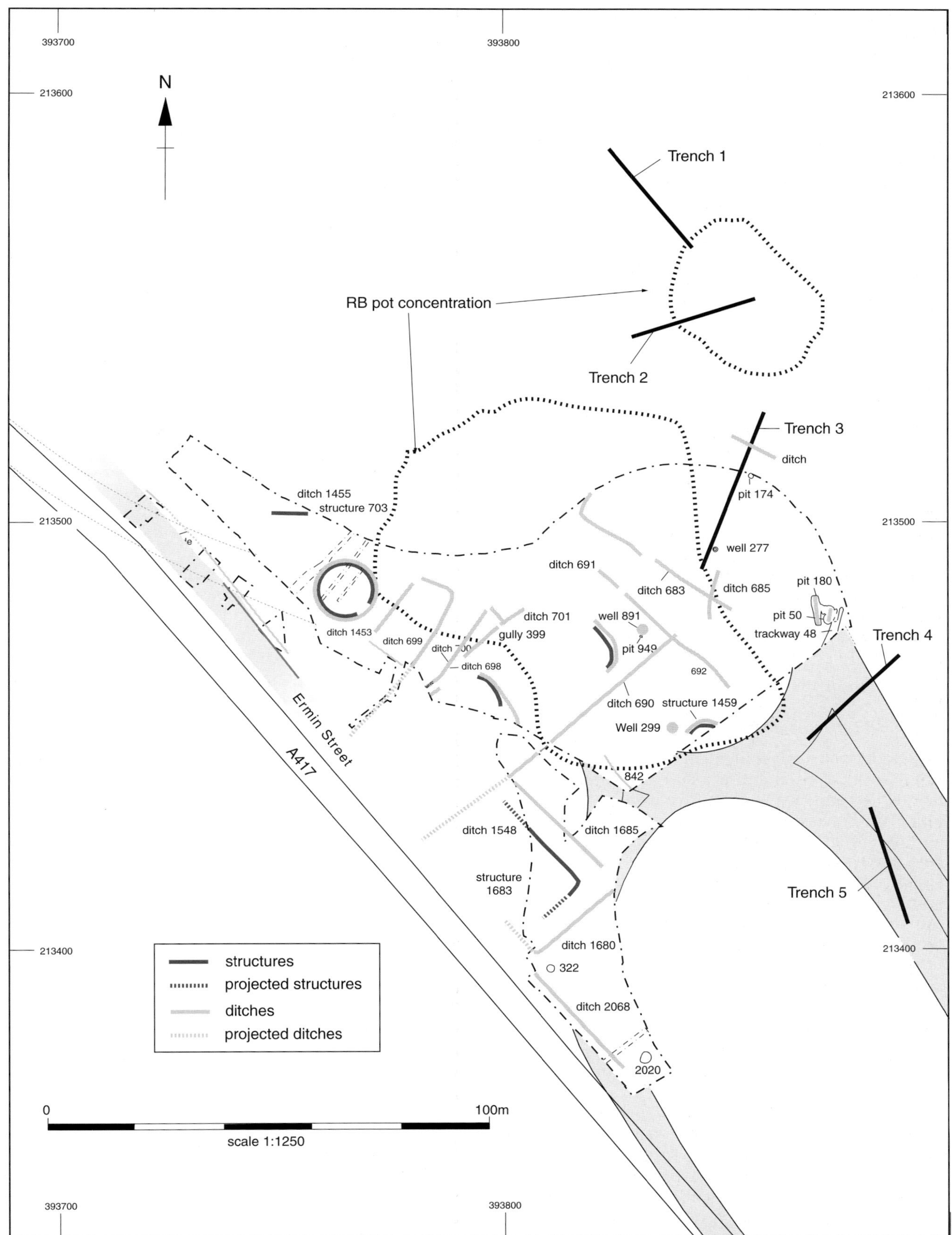


*Figure 4.104 Birdlip Quarry, summary site plan with locations of surface finds and evaluation trenches.*

Area D, even though the distribution of late Shelly Ware indicates that occupation continued here.

### *Distribution of horse gear*

The distribution of horse equipment is broken down into horseshoes (exclusively post-Roman), hipposandals, and cart fittings.

The horseshoes show a distribution closely associated with Ermin Street in Areas 2A, 5 and 3 and in Ermin Trench 3. Most came from silts overlying the road or nearby deposits. Although a few were found embedded in the Roman road surface, they are taken to indicate that the road surface was in use in the post-Roman period. The view that they may be later Roman artefacts is countered by their absence in any definitive Roman contexts on the site.

Hipposandals *(solae ferreae)* were probably used for protecting the feet of injured horses, rather than in the normal course of work (Dixon and Southern 1992, 229–31). A small number of fragments came from several areas of the site with a slight concentration in Area D, where three fragments came from Phase 2 contexts and one from Phase 1. In the latest phases of the site they have a thin but wide distribution. One was found embedded in the road surface in Ermin Street Trench 3.

Vehicle linch pins came from Area A phase 6, Area D Phase 2 and Area 3 Phase 1. This can be seen to re-inforce a suggestion of activity associated with horses or cattle in Area D in Phase 2 (Period 2A).

## Discussion of the site

### *Settlement origins and layout*

The Romano-British settlement at Birdlip Quarry was not examined in its entirety and any conclusions on its function and character must remain, to some extent, tentative. However, the excavations have provided a significant body of new evidence about a type of settlement which has never been examined to a significant extent in the Cotswold region, and at least some aspects of this site can help further our understanding of regional settlement and society in the Roman period.

The layout of the site consisted of a collection of roughly rectangular enclosures or partial enclosures containing a relatively widely dispersed group of structures which were sited on small terraces within a shallow dry valley and on the hillslope (Fig. 4.104). The site (for the area) is relatively well sheltered from adverse weather conditions which could be a factor in its location. The site appears to have been first settled with the construction of a roundhouse of native form in Area A (structure 1463) and other partly circular structures. The tentatively identified rectangular structure represented by ditch group 1455 in the north-west extension of the site may also have been one of the primary structures. The earlier boundary ditches and the wells were probably dug at this time. There were almost certainly other structures in the unexcavated part of the site and these may well have been founded concurrently with the identified structures, although there is no way of being sure of this. There is likely to have been a structure in the northern enclosure, just outside the excavated site, since a large number of finds came from the gullies here and there was evidence of occupation from the northern end of Trench 3 of the Stage 2 evaluation (GCC 1990, para. 4.5.4 and fig. 4).

The scatter of surface finds from fieldwalking covered a little under 1 hectare (Fig. 4.104) and, to judge from the excavated evidence, is likely to approximate to the overall size of the settlement. The surface scatter included what appears to be a discrete cluster higher up the slope perhaps indicating the site of another structure further north. However, two evaluation trenches targeted on this finds cluster failed to find any evidence of a building and the nature of this occupation remains unclear. This outlier was separated from the lower occupation by a 3m-wide clay-lined ditch running roughly east-west, found in Trench 3. This was the largest of the boundary ditches on the site, but, other than drawing attention to the possible significance of the feature, little can be added to this observation. There was no evidence of a continuation of the settlement east of the main excavation.

The excavated sequence indicates that the date of the initial settlement was around AD 160–180. Although the excavations yielded coins minted in the middle decades of the 2nd century and a few Hadrianic/early Antonine samian sherds, the presence of these finds can clearly be attributed to a long period of circulation and the date of the initial settlement is more likely to have been in the later 2nd century AD. A few finds stratified beneath the roundhouses may suggest some earlier activity of an undefined nature. The finds from fieldwalking and trial trenching in the other part of the site did not suggest occupation substantially earlier.

Despite the strongly 'native' character of the settlement, it is clear that it formed part of a distinctively Roman settlement pattern. The presence of Ermin Street must have been a determining factor in the settlement's location, but it does not appear to be a typical 'roadside settlement' and does not easily fit into any of the categories of such settlements with official or commercial functions discussed by Smith (1987). With certain qualifications, taking account of the possible destruction of archaeological evidence at the north-west end of the site and the unexcavated part of the street frontage, strip buildings with the short axis fronting the road seem never to have been built, and it does not appear that street frontage space was at a premium at any stage. With the exception of the possible sub-rectangular structure in Area 3 (structure 1683), there is nothing to suggest that Ermin Street was even of great importance in relation to the initial site layout. The other possible rectangular structure, represented by ditch group 1455, was 15 m or more from the projected line of Ermin Street, and furthermore, appears to have been set at an angle to the road. In the unexcavated part of the site, there is clearly room for further structures to have been located closer to Ermin Street, although it appears unlikely that anything substantial would have existed between Area 2B and Area 6. The gap south-east of Area 6 and in front of Area 2C must be a candidate for the location of another structure of some form, although a strip building would appear to have been unlikely given the potentially shallow depth of this plot (15 m or so) as against a width of 30 m. There is no evidence of occupation on the opposite side of Ermin Street, although since this area has not been explored archaeologically this absence cannot be regarded as definitive.

On current evidence, then, the primacy of Ermin Street to the original layout of the settlement is questionable, although the settlement can certainly be assumed to have had functions related to the road, as well as its obviously agricultural basis. It is worth noting that the 'hollow ways', which predated the structures in Area A and became defined by ditches in Area B, may indicate that there was also a route to higher ground up the dry valley. While it is suggested that these routes pre-dated the settlement, there is currently no evidence that they served an earlier Roman site from the road, and it seems possible that they formed a pre-Roman agricultural routeway up the dry valley. This may have been equally significant in the choice of settlement location, which can be seen to have been at a kind of crossroads, using both a traditional agricultural routeway while at the same time taking advantage of the Roman road. Emphasizing the agricultural basis of the settlement leads to the suggestion that its founding may have been as much related to land colonisation or agricultural intensification on the margins of expanding estates, as to the provision of services to road users. It can be noted that the site, at 250 m (820 ft) above sea level, while not marginal in terms of agricultural potential, occupies what one would assume to be a less than favourable site for settlement, and this in itself may explain a relatively late founding when the road itself had been established for a considerable time.

Regarding the origin of the settlers, there is firm evidence for late Iron Age/early Roman settlement about 2 km to the north-west near the Birdlip Bypass (Darvill 1984b, Parry 1998). The pottery from the excavations, which largely examined rubbish deposits, was limited to 1st century AD wares (Parry 1998). However, 2nd-century material was recovered in the fieldwalking survey (Darvill 1984b, 36) and purely in terms of chronology it is possible that the settlement here was abandoned at the time that at Birdlip Quarry commenced. An obvious motive for this change in location may have been the opportunities for trade or transport offered by Ermin Street. However, despite the relatively low status of the Birdlip Bypass site in the 1st century claimed on the basis of the pottery assemblage (Parry 1998), the presence of brick and tile in substantial quantities from the fieldwalking implies a site of rather different status and character to that at Birdlip Quarry (Darvill 1984b, fig. 26). This assessment must remain rather subjective, for it is by no means certain what a 'significant' volume of brick and tile is in terms of the type of structures which it may have represented. At Birdlip Quarry, the 13.65 kg of brick and tile recovered from the excavations can be judged to be insignificant in view of the evidence for the buildings. The pieces were probably collected casually and appear never to have been used for their original purpose, presumably serving for working surfaces and perhaps other ad hoc constructions. The concentrations recovered from the fieldwalking and trial trenching (Stage 2 Assessment) were judged to be low when compared with those interpreted as the direct residue of collapsed buildings, as at Birdlip Bypass (GCC 1990, para. 4.5.4). From the point of view of the buildings represented at the two sites, it therefore seems unlikely that the inhabitants at Birdlip Quarry were the people that moved from the settlement at Birdlip Bypass, although the evidence is certainly not conclusive. It is possible, for instance, that a change in roofing material may have had more to do with a decline in tile production than a radically different character of building (P. Booth, pers. comm.).

The enclosures at Birdlip Quarry were of somewhat irregular shape. The main ones on the eastern side of the site, which comprise the northern enclosure and those containing Areas D and E, may have been of a fairly standard size of a little over 30 m across. There is insufficient information to determine whether a modular unit of measurement was used. The dimensions of the enclosures mentioned appear to be under the standard actus of about 35 m (Dilke 1971, 82) for which there is evidence at Brockworth in the Severn Valley (Rawes 1981, fig. 1), and over the approximate 27 m standard claimed for Barnsley Park (McWhirr 1981, 101), the late 2nd-century layout at Roughground Farm, Gloucestershire, and other villa sites (Allen et al. 1993, 187). The distances between the major ditches running perpendicular to Ermin Street in Period 1 - ditch 699, a projection of ditch 688/690 and ditch 1680 - are approximately 30 m and 35 m (Fig. 4.104). This of itself does not indicate official involvement in the initial demarcation of the site, although, in view of the site's roadside location, such a suggestion would not be surprising since the acquisition of land here by settlers is likely to have been regulated by the authorities whether or not any closer control was exercised.

On the other hand, if the whole site belonged to one farming unit, one might not expect subdivisions of the land to reflect any official presence or be particularly precise. The apparently rudimentary nature of many of the structures has been taken to indicate a probable family farming unit with outlying workshops, but the spacing of the structures (each with its own well in Period 1) and the apparent lack of intercommunication between them does suggest that each area exercised a degree of independence and may have had separate land allotments, at least initially. From this point of view, it is possible that each of the enclosures was a household plot used for tethering animals, keeping pigs and perhaps for horticulture and other activities. The tenurial arrangements are, however, difficult to elucidate from the site plan or other archaeological evidence and this question must remain unresolved.

The smaller enclosure in front of the Period 1 structures in Area A, was probably closely associated with those houses and may have been within the same 'plot'. It can readily be seen as a small paddock for horses or cattle, although other interpretations are clearly possible. To the east of this enclosure a 5 m-wide trackway defined by ditches used the route of an apparently existing hollow way into the site. This may have been used to drive stock between grazing land in the valley and higher up the hill. Rough stone surfacing was laid where the trackway opened up (Area B) and also further up the slope. Another roughly metalled trackway (48) was present in the eastern corner of the site. Wheel ruts indicate that this was used by carts and it is possible that these were concerned with transporting the harvest from the fields. The presence of two large (storage?) pits in this area in both periods may be significant, as may the location of the corn dryer in this part of the settlement in the later period. The evidence would suggest that the arable fields lay on the higher ground to the north.

In Area B the trackway ditches silted up at the end of Period 1 and the hollow gradually filled after that. The area was probably used as a midden during the 4th century (Period 2 Phase 6). It is not known whether the silting of the ditches had implications for the organisation of the site or whether this area was still used as a routeway. It is possible that the midden was positioned to facilitate manuring the arable fields.

### *Site phasing and development*

The evidence for, and circumstances of, the founding of the settlement in the later 2nd century AD have been touched on in the previous section. It has been suggested that the site's location may have been determined by factors of landholding and agricultural expansion, as well as by economic opportunities presented by the road.

The nature and duration of the 'abandonment' of different areas of the site at the end of Period 1 (around the middle of the 3rd century) at Birdlip Quarry are difficult to assess. There is clear stratigraphic evidence that each area of the site was subject to a change of occupation during the 3rd century, although it is by no means clear that this change was synchronous, and a more piecemeal development might be envisaged. In Area A, the stake-walled roundhouse, structure 1464, went out of use at the end of Period 1 and a layer of soil developed over the area before the next phase of building. In Area D there is evidence that the eaves drainage gully associated with structure 1456 was allowed to fill (and hence was presumably not functioning) before the new structure was built. There is also a suggestion that the adjacent well (891) collapsed in the 3rd century, but that infilling to the ground surface did not take place until the later 3rd or 4th century. Similarly, in Area E well 299 may have gone out of use as early as the 2nd century, but appears to have been left to collapse and not filled in until the 4th century. This pattern is not evident from the structures themselves, however, where structure 1459 succeeded 1458 without any sign of a period of abandonment. In Area C the ovens and associated structure went out of use at the end of Period 1 when a ditch was dug through the area, although the nature of subsequent land-use remains unclear. In Area B the ditched-defined hollow way also went out of use at about this time and silts began to accumulate. It is also clear that many of the site boundary ditches had silted up by the end of Period 1.

Observations against an interpretation of widespread abandonment of the site include the fact that the positions of the structures of Period 2 were closely related to, even conditioned by, the earlier structures, and the fact that localised abandonments did not appear to coincide with a diminution in the deposition of finds. It therefore seems likely that there was always occupation in some part of the site. The fact that the boundary ditches silted up and the wells went out of use by the end of Period 1 may relate to a lack of maintenance of the ditches and a reorganisation of the site, rather than actual abandonment. On balance the middle part of the 3rd century may be seen as a period of gradual change, with areas of the site falling into temporary disuse, rather than a period of hiatus, although the possibility of more sudden and fundamental site-wide change cannot be ruled out.

The revival of occupation in the later 3rd century (Period 2A) appears to be part of a regional pattern. This has long been seen as a period of dramatic change in the west country with the establishment of a large number of villas, making the region unusual in national terms (McWhirr 1981). Branigan (1976) estimated that 40 villa sites in the south-west provide satisfactory evidence for foundation during this period, and about the same number with less rigorous evidence were probably also of this date. Villa building and expansion continued into the 4th century. This phenomenon has been linked to a decline in municipal government and a switch in patronage by the social elites to rural locations. Millett has seen this as a return to the late Iron Age pattern of political power emanating from elites based on rural estates (1990, 195). The relationship between the Birdlip Quarry settlement and the local rural centres of power is not known, but the evidence would suggest that Birdlip Quarry was affected by the dynamics of change in rural settlement in the same way that villas were, and may have had a quite significant position within the social and economic sphere of the elite.

A major re-organisation of Ermin Street and Area 3 took place in the early 4th century (Period 2B). This involved a widening of the road in Area 5 (Phase 3) and an infilling of boundary ditch 1681 in Area 3 (Phase 2) which, it has been argued coincided with the abandonment of structure 1684. The coin evidence indicates that this took place in AD 320–330 or very shortly after. This event appears to be traceable in Area 6 where a probable road surface sealed a coin of AD 324–8. Whether these changes reflected a more widespread reorganisation of the settlement is unclear, but the balance of evidence suggests that the later phases elsewhere (Phase 6 in Area A, and Phase 3 in Areas C, D and E) were slightly later, towards the middle of the 4th century. The sequence of deposits in Area 2A would suggest that the infilling of the roadside ditch and a presumed repositioning of the road, took place rather earlier, perhaps in the later 3rd century, but this may have been a local change related to developments in Area A. In the road sections to the north-west there was no dating evidence for the road surface and little reliable evidence for the date of the ditch fill. The road in Area 1 was of a different character to the late surfacing found in Area 5, and had been worn into a hollow way. This suggests that it was the original road rather than the 4th-century expansion, although all the erosion could have been caused in the post-Roman period if it were the later surface.

The layout of the site in the mid to late 4th century is enigmatic. With the exception of structure 1648 in Area 3 and the walls in Area A (which, it has been suggested, relate to a domestic structure), there is no evidence of buildings. It is considered likely, however, that wooden sill-beam or post-pad construction replaced the buildings in the other occupation areas and left no recognisable trace. The change in architectural form is similar to that found at the Alchester Road suburb, Towcester, where irregular D-shaped or circular buildings were replaced by rectangular structures around the middle of the 4th century, the evidence for which consisted mainly of post-pads and stylobates (Brown and Woodfield 1983, 134). Area B was probably occupied by a midden, although the lack of evidence of a structure may be misleading given the general paucity of such evidence in this period. There is no evidence of a late re-digging of the boundary ditches, and it appears that these were allowed to silt up or were deliberately filled in. These latest deposits appear to be a similar phenomenon to the 'dark earth' of urban sites and are equally enigmatic.

At Kingscote, Gloucestershire, major changes in the layout of the site can be dated to the earlier 4th century (Period 4) when the group of strip buildings on the site were replaced by a large residential villa building and a possible workhall and stables (Timby 1998a, 68). The change in site layout was obviously radical and may relate to the establishment of an estate centre. The next phase (Period 5) appears to have been equally dramatic with the burning and abandonment of the main residence shortly after the mid-4th century. It has been noted that fire has been cited as the cause of the demise of a number of villas in the wider region (Timby 1998a, 71), with a few on the periphery of this group in the Gloucester-Cirencester region (Branigan 1976, fig. 29), a phenomenon which has been linked to political events around AD 367 (Branigan 1976, 136). Timby is surely correct in doubting that the archaeological evidence can support such a unitary explanation, although the demise, or at least radical alteration of these villas in the later 4th century, which may be shown in their failure to recover from fire damage, accidental or otherwise, is a pattern which demands some sort of explanation at the regional scale. The abandonment of the settlement of Birdlip Quarry around this time may be assumed to reflect the wider changes and developments in settlement which affected the villas, but these issues require much more research.

### *The economy*

The animal bone and charred plant remains indicate that mixed farming was practised throughout the duration of the settlement. This was undoubtedly the basis of the economy. The cereal assemblage was dominated by spelt wheat, the principal crop in the Roman period, with small amounts of barley also present. A background scatter of grain, chaff and weeds of cultivation from a large number of samples form a pattern which suggests that cereal processing took place within the settlement. This is supported by a number of fragments of rotary quern. A T-shaped corn dryer provided evidence for crop processing in the later period. There is some evidence that malting spelt wheat took place in the earlier period for which ovens of a different form may have been used. There is no strong indication of a change in the cereal and weed composition over time and it is likely that cereal production remained consistently important during the life of the settlement. There was no evidence of granaries or four-post structures on the site and it is unclear where the harvest would normally have been normally stored. It is possible that it was stored in another part of the site, perhaps with the implication of a more centralised organisation of this aspect of the economy.

The range of grass and weed seeds in the charred assemblages indicate that a wide range of soils were cultivated. The soils include heavy calcareous clays as well as lighter and possibly sandy soils. There were some species of damp grassland present and some suggestion of the cultivation of rather marginal land close to water. It is unclear what this implies as regards the area of land farmed, or the sources of any imported material and foodstuffs. Hay, fuel and crops may have been brought in from quite a wide area with varied ecologies, or alternatively the flora may be representative of a mosaic of more local soils.

The animal bone assemblage was dominated by sheep and cattle, with cattle the more numerous by bone count (NISP), but sheep more numerous calculating the minimum number of individuals (MNI). Both species were undoubtedly important in the economy of the site. Horse was unusually common, while pigs were also kept and probably under-represented in the bone assemblage. Wild animal resources appear to have been insignificant. There is no indication of a significant change in species composition over time. Animal bones were far more frequent in Period 2 than Period 1, amounting to about 78% of the total site assemblage. This is similar to the frequency of pottery in Period 2 (75%), which can largely be accounted for by the longer duration of this period and the accumulation of residual material. It seems, therefore, that the increase in animal bone is not a reflection of changes in the economy of the site.

The age profile of the sheep bone assemblage indicates that sheep were husbanded on an unspecialised, subsistence basis, with meat the main product, but with some older animals probably kept for wool and milk. The absence of loomweights and the rarity of spindle whorls recovered from the excavation supports the suggestion from the bone assemblage that woollen textile production was not a significant aspect of the economy. It is possible that fleeces were used instead, or sold, although there is no supporting evidence for this.

The preponderance of mature cattle is notable suggesting that they were kept as draught animals. This is supported by the unusually common evidence for work-related stresses. An adult pattern of slaughter is characteristic of towns and military sites in the Roman period, and has been explained as reflecting marketing on the hoof, and the need for products such as horns and hides (King 1978, 55). The evidence from Birdlip Quarry suggests that the use of cattle for traction, perhaps mainly for ploughing, but also for long-distance transport, may have been significant on rural sites. High proportions of mature cattle have been recorded from other rural sites in the region, including Haymes and Portway as well as the Frocester and Barnsley Park villas. It is worth re-iterating King's view that a greater proportion of mature cattle in the Roman period compared with the Iron Age would have meant a greater emphasis on animal husbandry and a requirement for more pasture and hence more land. It has been suggested that this might have been linked to an increasing use of heavier soils (King 1978). The implications for this dynamic in the Cotwold region have yet to be analysed. Contrary to the opinion expressed by King, however, it must be doubted whether this development of animal husbandry necessarily reflected a more prosperous economy. It may in fact imply the opposite since a more pronounced consumption of old beef at Birdlip Quarry and other sites would appear not to be an aspect of diet arising from choice and could be taken to imply poverty.

Horses would also have been used as working animals at Birdlip Quarry, and pathological traits indicate that they, like the cattle, were probably overworked. They may have been used for farm duties, although the unusually high proportion of horses (16% in Period 1 and 13% in Period 2 by fragment count) may well indicate that they had a function relating to the settlement's location on Ermin Street. The proportion of horse bones is higher than the usual 4–5% from the larger rural bone assemblages in the region (Noddle 1987, tab. 6c) and is actually higher than that from the Iron Age site at Mingies Ditch, Oxfordshire, which, it has been argued, may have had a special concern with rearing horses (Wilson 1993, 133, tab. 13; Lambrick 1992b, 94). Robinson (1992b, 56) has also suggested that horses would normally have been more common than indicated by numbers of bones since they lived longer than cattle or sheep. The settlement at Birdlip Quarry. may well have taken advantage of its location and served as a minor waystation, used for the trading or changing of horses. The hipposandal fragments from the site may principally have been used by horses.

The range of industrial or craft activities carried out are not unusual and do not suggest any specialisation. Lead casting was carried out, apparently on a small scale and perhaps only in the later period. The same may be true of copper casting which was represented by only a few small fragments of waste. There is no indication where the focus of this activity was. Lead casting waste was also found at Weavers Bridge and the activity does not appear to have been unusual. Three lead steelyard weights from Birdlip Quarry provide evidence of commercial exchange, at least on a small scale. A fragment of iron stylus from pit 39 may suggest an occasional official presence. Large numbers of styli came from Kingscote and also from Barnsley Park and Catsgore. They have been linked to the presence of officials concerned with the collection of the annona or corn tax (Timby 1998a, 292). The small collection of items of military equipment (particularly sword and belt fittings) is of interest and may be connected with an occasional military presence (see Scott, Chapter 7). Military items of 2nd to 3rd-century date have been found on a number of sites of undoubtedly civilian character and may reflect some official concern in the settlements' functions. The presence of a posting-station or relay-station would be a possible context for this concern, but the precise significance of this metalwork is at present unclear and there may be alternative explanations. Small quantities of iron smithing slag indicate metalworking associated with structure 1452. This activity is so common on Romano-British sites that it must be considered a normal domestic practice. The lump of hearth-bottom or smelting slag from the fill of the corn dryer was the only other metal residue found and is anomalous, but may have derived from activity on the unexcavated part of the site. The number and range of iron tools is unremarkable and suggest no more than subsistence agricultural and craft activities.

### *Circular stake wall structures (1463 and 1464)*
*(Figs 4.45 and 4.49)*

#### *Structural technique*

The two successive stake-built roundhouses have clear Iron Age antecedents. Indeed, almost precisely similar examples, including the details and dimensions of the door, occur at Danebury (Cunliffe and Poole 1991, 43–45). The lack of evidence for internal roof supports at Danebury led the excavator to suggest that the whole structure could have been of woven wattle with an integral or separately constructed roof. Such a construction seems possible for the houses at Birdlip Quarry, although their diameter – 12 m – is larger than the largest stake-walled house at Danebury (9.5 m) and on the large side for roundhouses of any structural form. It is unclear whether this would have implications for the structures' feasibility. It seems unlikely that the thrust of an independently constructed roof, of whatever material, could have been borne by a stake wall without internal supports, but it is possible that an integrally woven structure may have been viable without them. In particular, the waterlogged remains of wicker-walled roundhouses from the rath at Deer Park Farms, Northern Ireland, suggests that an entirely woven structure would not have been out of the question, although the largest of the excavated examples was only 7 m in diameter (Lynne 1979). It appears that the particular constructional technique used a series of quite short uprights of a metre or less, with each successive ring of stakes being driven into the completed lower ring of stakes and woven horizontal rods. There was probably no distinction between the wall and roof. The wattle wall is described as being remarkably solid. There seems to be no reason why this principle of construction should not have been applied to larger houses, although the practical difficulties of completing the roof, which must have reached around 8 m high, would have been considerable. In terms of resources used it is worth noting that at Deer Park Farms an estimated five miles of hazel rods was used to build each house. It appears that the walls were of double thickness at least in part, but even to a single thickness the Birdlip Quarry houses would have needed half as much wattling again, indicating that this resource was available in considerable quantities. Regardless of the precise technique of construction the finished structure must have looked as impressive as many of its contemporary rural buildings.

*Iron Age tradition*

It was suggested that the Deer Park Farms roundhouses, dating to the 7th and 8th centuries, represented the end of a once widespread prehistoric tradition of house-building (Lynne 1979, 196). While comparable middle Iron Age structures from Danebury have been mentioned, and there were undoubtedly numerous closer, albeit less well preserved, examples in the Upper Thames Valley, the derivation of this particular form of structure in the Cotswold region is not clear. In the Upper Thames it has become fairly evident that the tradition of stake-walled roundhouses, or indeed roundhouses of any sort, became very uncommon from the late Iron Age onwards on all types of site (Allen *et al.* 1984, 100; Keevill and Booth 1997, 41), although the early Roman compound at Roughground Farm, Lechlade, probably contained a roundhouse (Allen *et al.* 1993, 51 and fig. 34). Roundhouses are more commonly found in the Roman period in Northamptonshire and Buckinghamshire (Keevill and Booth 1997, 42), and, although this distribution may partly reflect the survival of stone foundations, there is also enough evidence of wooden roundhouses (encompassing timber- and stake-built structures) to suggest that the tradition survived better in this region than it did in the Thames valley. In the Cotswolds there have been far fewer excavations of a sufficient scale on Iron Age or Roman sites to be able to establish such trends. At Crickley Hill the early Iron Age roundhouses were post-built with a circle of interior roof supports, of type known to be widespread and possibly constructed like the Pimperne house (Reynolds 1982) and at least as large (Dixon 1973b). The middle Iron Age roundhouses at Salmonsbury were almost certainly of the wall-post type with the entrance marked by larger postholes (Dunning 1976, 82 and fig. 2; 87 and fig. 8). The houses were small, their diameters being between 6 m and 8 m, but the position of the surrounding drainage gullies makes it clear that the posts formed wall-lines rather than interior supports and central roof supports may have been employed. Other middle Iron Age sites in the region have yielded conspicuously little evidence of buildings. This includes sites investigated on the current project (Chapter 3). This absence of evidence continues through until the 1st century AD at Middle Duntisbourne and Duntisbourne Grove where large areas within the enclosures were stripped and where the material from within the enclosure ditches makes it highly probable that structures were once present. It is possible that stake-wall structures were built as these would have left little trace on ploughed sites.

Records of roundhouses in the Roman period are becoming increasingly common in various parts of the country. In Gloucestershire, evidence for circular buildings, probably dating to the 2nd century, comes from Brockworth (Rawes 1981). There was insufficient evidence to determine the structural method as only the penannular drainage gullies of two structures remained. At Bourton-on-the-Water, on the Fosse Way, excavations have been patchy but there is evidence, so far, of five stone-based circular structures (Timby 1998a, 379–81). The suggestion that any of these are shrines has little basis and can be rejected. Some of the other somewhat tenuous identifications (the 'transport café' and 'posting-station') appear to be largely based on preconceptions about what ought to be present at this roadside settlement, and their interpretations are also questionable (ibid.). The circular structures, like the rectangular ones, are found both adjacent to and away from the Fosse Way (ibid., fig. 143), although their chronology and functions remain obscure.

Further afield at Whitton, Glamorgan, the round house tradition continued until the beginning of the 2nd century AD (Jarrett and Wrathmell 1981). The houses were constructed using the outer wall of contiguous wooden planks or split logs as the principal support for the rafters. These were deeply bedded and probably protruded only a metre or so above ground. A detailed consideration of how the roof would have been constructed suggested a massive conical form which could have been partly pre-fabricated (ibid., fig. 36). The evidence for stone-based round buildings in the south midlands region has recently been reviewed and the dating, function and status of many of these structures has been assessed (Keevill and Booth 1997). Stone-footed circular buildings have also been considered in relation to the structures at Bancroft villa, Buckinghamshire (Williams and Zeepvat 1994, 207). The evidence will not be re-iterated here. Circular buildings of various functions appear to have been constructed throughout the Roman period alongside rectangular stone and timber-framed buildings. There is perhaps a particular association of roundhouses with 'high status' rectangular buildings, as at Stanwick, Northamptonshire (ibidem., 39). While continuity of the Iron Age tradition underpins the explanations for their presence, comparisons using solely the circular form of the structure as the basis of similarity fail to distinguish between buildings which are truly a continuation of the Iron Age tradition, and those which may be circular for functional or other reasons. At Redlands Farm, Stanwick, Northamptonshire, for instance, a circular building replaced a rectangular stone barn in the mid-3rd century. In this instance, an explanation relating to the function or practical structural considerations may be more important than a continuation of (or reversion to) the Iron Age tradition. Furthermore, there is a tendency to link all circular structures into a common 'tradition' without taking account of methods of construction. The use of pitched stone foundations and mortared masonry on a number of sites indicates considerable Roman influence in the technique of construction, suggesting a different set of social circumstances to those operating when traditional techniques were used. This is not to deny that these stone-built circular structures may owe a great deal to Iron Age traditions. A number of sites, particularly in Northamptonshire (Keevill and Booth 1997, 31–34) appear to indicate a direct replacement of wooden with stone-founded buildings. These include Overstone, Thorplands and probably Clay Lane (Windell 1983), where the stone buildings occupied the same plot as the earlier ones. It is worth noting that the dating of the Overstone building to the late 3rd century, after one or two phases of timber circular building from the 2nd century onward, is very similar to the sequence at Birdlip Quarry. The dating and sequence at Thorplands, Northamptonshire, is also similar (Hunter and Mynard 1977). At Stanwick there may have been a complete replanning of the settlement/villa estate at the end of the 1st century AD with a concomitant change from wooden to stone-founded circular buildings (Neal 1989). However, these stone-based structures should be seen not merely as Iron Age survival but as a Romano-British development of the Iron Age vernacular tradition. What distinguishes structures 1463 and 1464 at Birdlip Quarry is that they appear to represent a distinctive form of construction which remained unchanged for several hundred years, despite inhabiting an environment of quite widespread and fundamental political, social and economic change.

From the perspective of constructional technique, it is also possible that the ring-post, wall-post and wall-slot structures at Crickley Hill (Dixon 1973b), Salmonsbury (Dunning 1976) and Whitton (Jarrett and Wrathwell 1981) respectively, should not be considered direct antecedents of the Birdlip Quarry stake-wall houses, but part of separate local traditions. The significance behind these variations in structural form is, however, far from clear. It is evident that different techniques could be used side by side, and it is furthermore possible that wattle roundhouses existed at other Iron Age sites in the region, together with ring-post and wall-trench constructions, but that evidence of them is simply lacking.

A more fundamental approach to an explanation for the continuity and development of circular structures into the Roman period is to consider what they represented and why they were considered important. A number of authors have considered the phenomenon of roundhouses from the perspective of their symbolic importance to their occupants. In their spatial organisation they may be seen as reflecting the symbolic universe of society and as ordering the cycle of social and agricultural activities (Hingley 1990; Parker Pearson 1996; Fitzpatrick 1997). While the nature of the archaeological evidence suggests that the link between spatial patterning within and among structures on the one hand, and social or symbolic activities and meanings on the other is never straightforward, there seems little doubt that, at a basic level, the persistence of this particular tradition is directly linked to a continuation of a social life to which the form of the house was integral. Some aspects of the spatial patterning within and around these structures will now be examined.

### *Orientation*

The predominantly easterly or south-easterly orientation of the doorways of roundhouses has long been recognised, but it is only relatively recently that serious consideration has been given to the idea that a symbolic code was involved in structuring the orientations of the buildings, along with other aspects of the archaeological record which had conventionally been treated as open to strictly pragmatic interpretations. A desire to shelter from the prevailing winds has normally been invoked as the reason for the direction in which the building faced, but, while this may have always been an influencing factor, the precise orientation of the entrance appears to be structured more tightly than can be accounted for by this explanation. Plotting the orientations of a large sample of Iron Age roundhouses Oswald (1997, fig. 10.4) has neatly demonstrated that the distribution in the south-eastern quarter is not random but that most buildings face approximately 90° (due east) or 130° (just north of south-east) – corresponding to the positions of sunrise on the equinoxes and mid-winter solstice respectively. These dates were apparently associated with seasonal festivals (Fitzpatrick 1997, fig. 9.1). The orientation of the Birdlip Quarry buildings is 135°. It is possible that the midwinter sunrise was significant in this instance although this is uncertain. Many factors determining this orientation could be taken into account, including the method by which the alignment was made, its intended precision and the effect of the foreshortened horizon in this direction. However it seems highly probable that the orientation, like the form of the roundhouse itself, was determined by structuring principles similar to those operating in the Iron Age.

That this structuring principle was dominant is emphasised by the fact that the buildings faced away from the road rather than towards it. The buildings actually faced a small enclosure. There is no evidence as to the purpose of this enclosure, but it is perhaps reasonable to see it as a corral for cattle or horses whose importance may be implied by the enclosure's location.

*Patterning of activities within the roundhouses*

Roundhouse 1463 and its successor 1464 were stratified beneath later deposits and were reasonably well preserved. It was, however, difficult and frequently impossible to distinguish features associated with one house from those associated with the other, and there is a certain amount of arbitrariness to Figures 4.45 and 4.49. The superimposition of the later stone-founded building 1452 on the same site resulted in the destruction of some of the earlier features and also created problems of interpretation. That said, the survival of floor surfaces and other features which are normally lost on ploughed sites makes some of the evidence uncovered here exceptional.

There is no way of being sure about the function of the roundhouses, but the quantity and range of domestic refuse in the middens outside the buildings, and to a certain extent within the buildings and their encircling ditches, suggests that they were the focus of domestic activity. The presence of at least one hearth may be taken as support for this interpretation, although there were a number of patches of burning which may suggest that non-domestic activities were also carried out. The flooring was rudimentary and patchy with an earthen floor apparently serving for most of the house. It is possible that stone flagging was originally more extensive and had been re-used in the later phases, but this is considered to be unlikely. Prepared flooring is predominantly absent at the back of the house, precisely the area of soil build-up after structure 1464 was abandoned. The patchy distribution of floor surfacing is typical of Iron Age houses, such as those at Danebury, where only those areas prone to most wear were surfaced. These are typically the approach to the house, and the area immediately inside the doorway, eg. Brigstock (Jackson 1983, fig. 4). There was also an area of 'mortar' flooring towards the back of the house on the left hand side (looking into the building), which may have been present in both phases. In other areas the earthen floor was deemed adequate. Hearth 756, was probably the main domestic hearth. It is shown as belonging with structure 1463, although it may have belonged with structure 1464, or both. It would have been located close to the wall of the building in either case and, unlike a central hearth, was probably not suitable for communal gathering. The area of burning, 1033, was possibly too extensive to have been a hearth and may either have been connected with craft activities, or be the remains of an accidental fire. It was close to a hollow which contained a jumble of stones interpreted in two phases, feature 1064 (Fig. 4.45) and feature 718 (Fig. 4.49). These are enigmatic but are considered likely to have related to craft or agricultural activities. The small areas of burnt stones suggest that fires were lit in the area inside the front door for some reason. The fire-pit (1035) towards the back of the house is somewhat isolated.

The distribution of selected categories of finds inside and immediately outside the houses is shown in Figures 4.105–4.106. This shows amphorae, mortaria, Savernake Ware and beakers, and identifiable forms of samian, Severn Valley Ware, and Dorset Black Burnished Ware. The last two wares are the most common and widespread. The forms shown are jars, dishes and bowls.

The clearest pattern to emerge is the concentration of pottery around the entrance and particularly on the left hand side (facing the building). This is particularly evident on Figure 4.106 and has been commented on in the discussion of the finds (Pottery distribution – above). This distribution undoubtedly occurred in both phases of building although it is impossible to identify the midden deposits specifically associated with structure 1463 (Fig. 4.105), and the recutting of the penannular ditch resulted in the removal of much of the earlier phase deposits at the front of the house. Finds from within the building and from the other sections of ditch were far more infrequent. The distribution of 'rubbish' in relation to houses appears rarely to have been considered in the Roman period. It may relate to purely practical considerations. At Birdlip Quarry, it may have been convenient to throw rubbish immediately outside the doorway, and down the slope on the left hand side. It seems possible, however, that this pattern of rubbish disposal arose from the same structuring principles which ordered the orientation and form of the house itself. That most material from Iron Age roundhouses comes from the terminals of the surrounding ditch is a common observation (Allen *et al.* 1984, 90). There is also some evidence that Iron Age roundhouses showed a left/right division of material with more finds coming from the left hand side, looking towards the building (Fitzpatrick 1994), an observation which is apparent in a published example of pottery distribution from Claydon Pike, Gloucestershire (Allen, Miles and Palmer 1984, fig. 6.3), and Cats Water subsite, Fengate (Pryor 1983, figs 4–5). It was also commented on at Mingies Ditch, Oxfordshire, although the picture was more confused by the multiple phasing of the structures (Allen and Robinson 1993, 90 and fig. 43). At the latter site it was suggested that rubbish disposal reflected the direction of the prevailing wind and that the door may have been hinged on the right hand side (viewed from the outside). At Dunston Park,

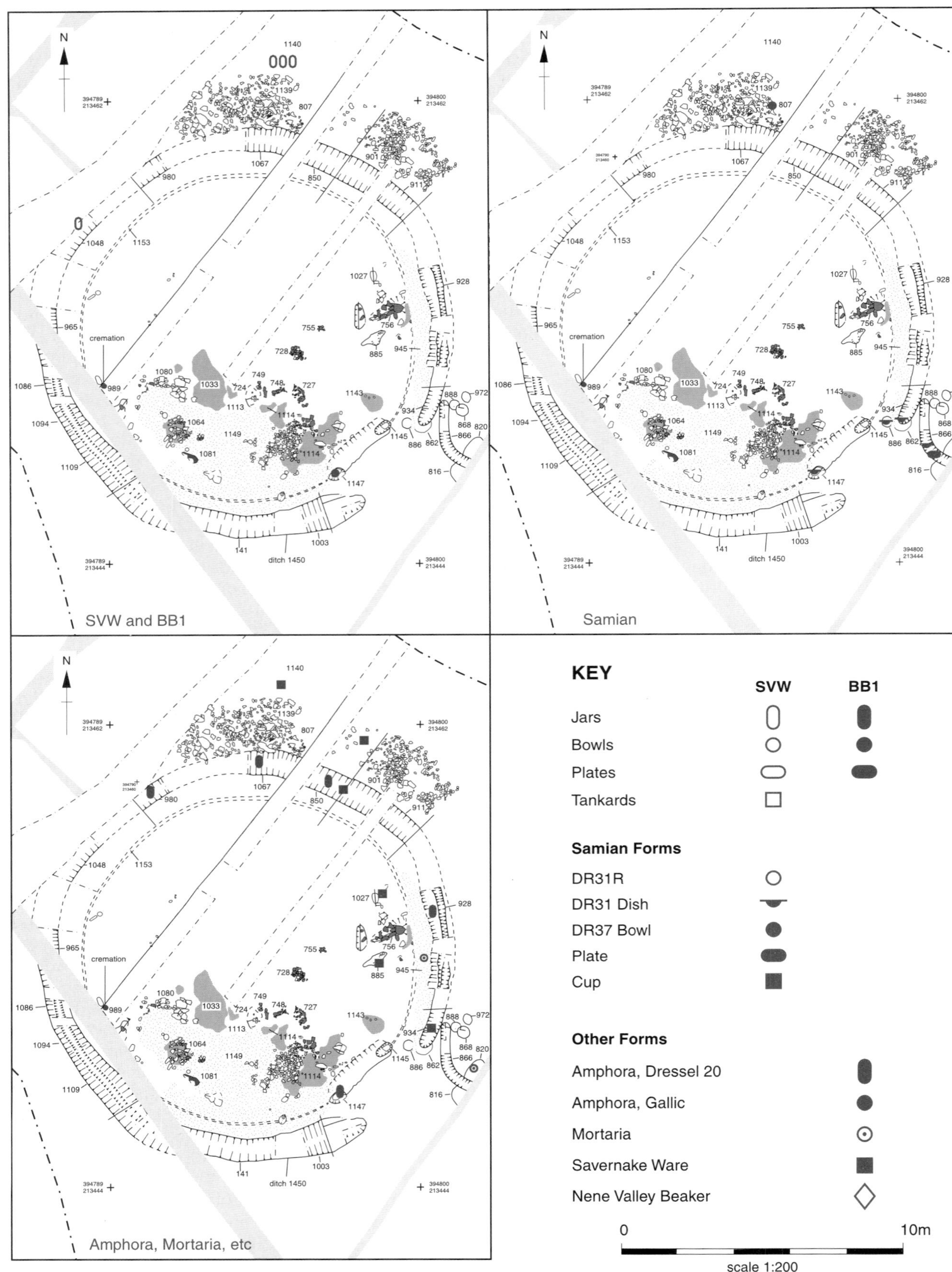


*Figure 4.105 Birdlip Quarry, structure 1463 (Area A), distribution of selected pottery forms.*

Thatcham, this distribution has been interpreted as reflecting a separation between a living area on the left side and a sleeping area on the right (Fitzpatrick 1994, 69–70). However, other interpretations at this site are clearly possible and since finds from the house analysed appear to have come almost exclusively from postholes, it seems possible that they derived from middens outside the house, at the front and to the left, rather than activity areas within it. More general statements about the front door location and possible symbolic significance of later prehistoric middens have also been made (Parker Pearson 1996). It is, furthermore, interesting to note that at the late Iron Age temple on Hayling Island, most of the votive offerings came from the area towards the outer boundary of the enclosure at the front and left hand side of the circular temple (King and Soffe 1994, 115). This is more convincingly a pattern arising from deliberate deposition than from more random disposal. From a small number of examples it is impossible to be sure whether the patterns relate to a fundamental and long-lived structuring principle within Iron Age and native Romano-British settle-ments, or whether the explanations are more mundane or the patterns more random. Exploration of this topic requires further spatial analyses of this kind on a large number of sites.

The pattern of finds within the roundhouses is difficult to interpret and does not readily suggest activity areas. However, it is probably significant that 22 large sherds (over 4.2 kg) of Dressel 20 amphora came from just inside the door on the left hand side. Although these were recorded as coming from the overlying Phase 3 layer (840), a large number of them were clearly found at the base of the layer and appeared to represent a vessel broken *in situ*. They would therefore have been associated with structure 1464 (Fig. 4.106). A large sherd (80 g) of Gallic amphora also came from this layer as did one of only three sherds of decorated samian from the site, and it is considered possible that these sherds are also significant. Pit 1100 contained a large number of sherds from a Dorset Black Burnished Ware jar, although this was associated with burnt deposits which appeared to represent backfill brought from elsewhere. The location of the Dressel 20 amphora in particular suggests that liquids were stored in this area. This part of the building is sometimes seen to be significant on Iron Age sites. At Danebury stake-built alcoves just inside the door were consistently present (Cunliffe and Poole 1991, 47). They occurred on either side of the door, but appear to be more common on the left side. This area of the Danebury buildings was not generally found to be associated with finds except in one case (CS56) where an anomalous concentration perhaps represented a single vessel (Cunliffe 1995, 185 and fig. 93). At Catsgore, in the 2nd-century polygonal structure, building 1.2, a line of pitched stone slabs may have demarcated a similar alcove just inside the door (Leech 1982, fig. 47).

At Ironmongers Piece, Marshfield, Gloucestershire, the late 2nd-/early 3rd-century circular masonry building had a pit containing two perinatal skeletons and a broken colour-coated flagon on the left side just inside the door (Blockley 1985, 25 and fig. 12). Although there are grounds for interpreting the building as a temple rather than a domestic dwelling this is by no means certain (see comments by Keevill and Booth 1997, 39). In more general discussions of the distinction between Iron Age temples and houses it is unclear what archaeological correlates should be applied. The emphasis in current research on the incorporation of what might be termed ritual practice into the domestic sphere, gives reason to doubt the maintenance of a strong distinction between the two categories of building. In either case the position of these votive or dedicatory deposits may, therefore, reflect some symbolic significance of this part of the building. It is also worth noting that the hearth in the first phase of the Marshfield building was on the right hand side (Blockley 1985, fig. 9) like that at Birdlip Quarry, and a similar structuring of activities might be implied.

The distribution of jars, bowls and dishes of Dorset Black Burnished Ware and Severn Valley Ware have also been plotted. There is no clear pattern to this distribution although the concentration of debris towards the front of the building is again evident. It does not seem to be possible to distinguish areas of food preparation/storage from areas of consumption by these distributions. There are a few jar sherds in the area of hearth 756 although it is possible that these belong to the Phase 4 structure. The location of the dedicatory vessel in pit 942 is also shown although this may also belong with the later structure. The distribution of Savernake Ware is more unusual since there are a relatively large number of sherds on the right hand side of the building and fewer in the middens, although the only exceptionally large sherd came from midden layer 803. Since the sherds mainly come from storage jars it is possible that this reflects the main area of storage, at least for some categories of materials. There were also small sherds from the area of stones 718. The distribution of mortaria is again towards the front of the building although there were a few sherds on the right side where the area of food preparation might be expected. Samian is more widely distributed. Only identifiable forms are shown. The pottery might be expected to relate to food consumption rather than preparation, although there is no obvious pattern to the distribution to support this. The largest sherds of dishes (DR31) came from posthole 1147, possible posthole 886 on the other side of the doorway (which yielded a rouletted dish), antenna gully 866 (which also yielded the only fragment of plate from this area) and the midden layer 780. There were also other small sherds from around the doorway. Fragments of deep bowl (DR37) also came from this area. The decorated sherd of DR37 from layer 840 has already been mentioned, and there was also a small sherd from the right side of the door (layer 1013). A small patch of burning towards the centre of the building (725) contained fragments of both DR37 and DR31R. The form DR31R appears to have a wider distribution. The largest sherd came from floor 1009

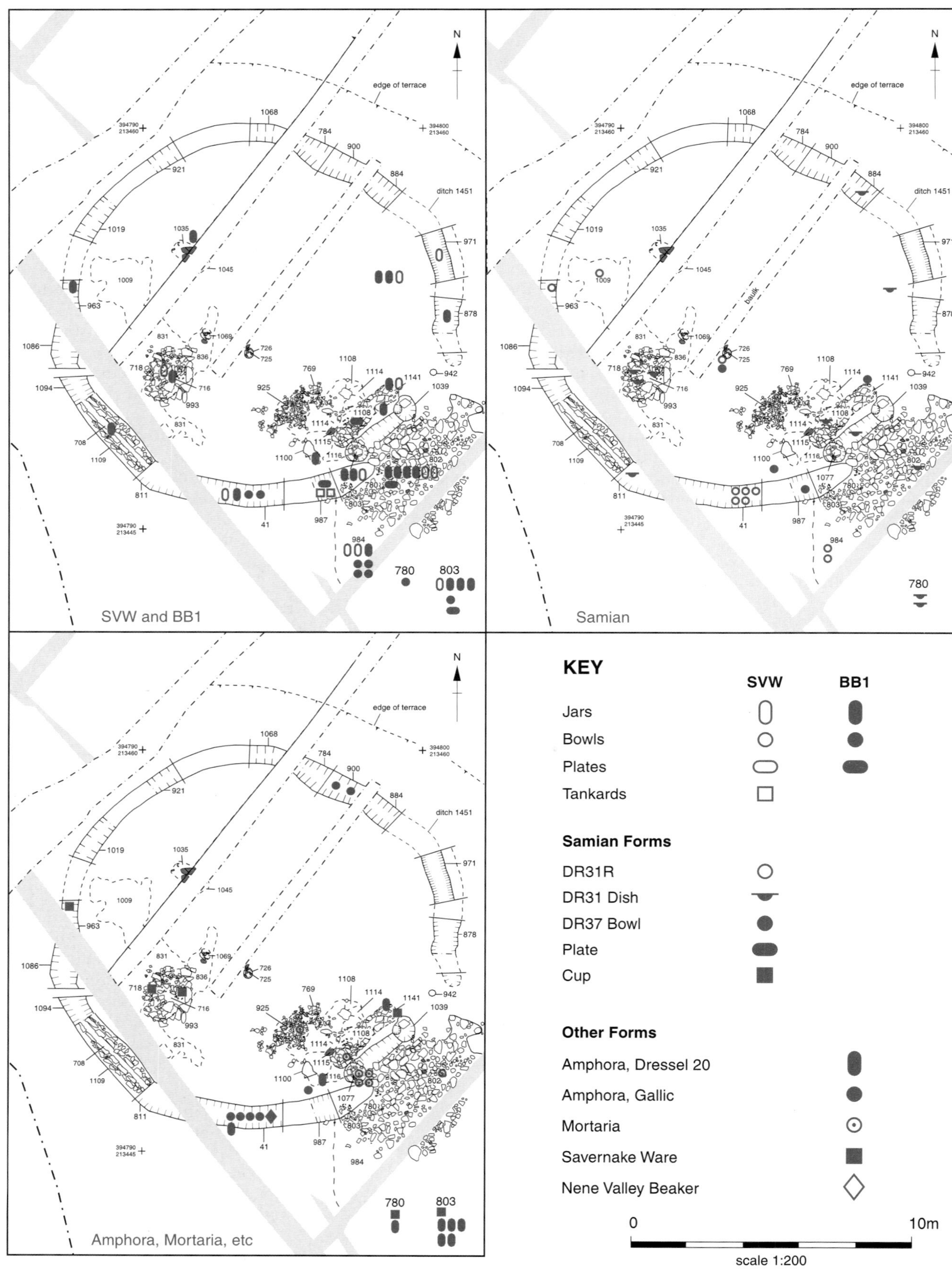


*Figure 4.106 Birdlip Quarry, structure 1464 (Area A), distribution of selected pottery forms.*

towards the back of the building. It joined with sherds from the later posthole in this area (1087) and also layer 704. Two large sherds of a similar vessel came from segment 963 of ditch 1451. It is possible that the vessels were used or stored in this area. Most of the other large sherds of DR31R came from the midden and ditch deposits at the front of the building (layer 984 and segment 141 of the penannular ditch).

The distribution of individual categories of finds, then, does not greatly aid the interpretation of activities carried out within the building possibly because there were no strong correlations between the types of vessels and the areas in which they were used, but perhaps more importantly because their place of final deposition does not necessarily coincide with their place of use. However, taken in conjunction with the internal features some suggestions about the organisation of domestic space can be made. Hingley (1990) has suggested that roundhouses can sometimes be divided into a central public area and a peripheral private area. This arrangement appears to be more convincing in houses with a central hearth where eating, drinking and socialising could have taken place. In structures 1463 and/or 1464 the main hearth, to the right, appears marginal and may not have formed a focus for socialising. It can be suggested that the public area of the house was in the front half where most of the flooring was, and it is possible that the various areas of burning towards the centre of the building were foci for guests, while to the right was a more domestic area. The stored liquids immediately to the left of the door, may then have been for offering to guests. It must be assumed (and is not unlikely) that the Dressel 20 amphora was reused for holding water or perhaps beer rather than its original contents of olive oil. The Gallic wine amphora may also have been re-used for a similar purpose although, as a more fragile vessel it was probably not so long-lived and may have primarily held wine. It is possible that the decorated samian bowl was part of a suite of vessels used in this public domain for display and offering drink. The 'working hollows' further towards the back of the building may represent a more private area of craft or agriculturally related activities, although perhaps partly in the public domain. The stone culvert inserted into the surrounding ditch suggests that there was a back entrance facing the road, although there was no other evidence of a doorway here. As Fitzpatrick (1994) has suggested, the roundhouse may be axially divided into a living/working area on the left and a sleeping area on the right. The additional front/back distinction between public and private space suggests that a fourfold division of the roundhouse is appropriate, so that on the right side the domestic cooking/storage area is more in the public space than the sleeping area behind. It is further possible that there was a conceptual link between the right/left division of the house and female/male activities carried out in them. This is to some extent compatible with Hingley's (1990, 132-133) suggestion that the organisation of space in Iron Age society may be reflected in a range of binary oppositions of which public:private, day:night and male:female may be seen in the evidence from structures 1463 and 1464.

### *Stone-based circular/polygonal building 1452*
*(Fig. 4.76)*

#### *Structural techniques*

The building which replaced the stake-wall structure 1464 in Period 2A represented a change to a different structural technique. Little remained of the stone walls but it is clear that, for the most part, the stones were laid directly on the ground without any form of foundation and without bonding. Pitched stone within the fill of the earlier penannular ditch appears to have been intended to consolidate the ground on the northern side. The form of the building was circular or polygonal and probably about 11 m in diameter internally. It seems likely that the wall was a footing, rather than the base of a wall which was carried to eaves height in stone. This interpretation must remain to a certain extent speculative since it is not impossible that the building was of mass stone construction. It is worth noting that the pitched stone was used in some areas of flooring in building 1452, which were consequently more solid constructions than the wall footings. The technique of wall construction can therefore be assumed to be deliberate and functional, rather than an ill-conceived imitation of Roman techniques. The surviving evidence is very similar to that relating to the early 2nd-century buildings at Catsgore, (Leech 1982, Buildings 1.1 and 1.2 – although building 1452 lacks door postholes) and the argument for their interpretation as 12-sided timber-framed buildings resting on stone sills is convincing. Mass walling in cob or turf is another possibility, although in this case there would appear to be no advantage in a polygonal over a circular shape as there would be with timber framing.

A number of buildings from several sites were interpreted by Leech as polygonal rather than circular in plan (Leech 1982, 27-31). There appears, however, to be no general correlation between this form in plan and the structure of the wall footings so few other precise parallels can be found. Building 1452 is similar in form and size to the stone building at Overstone, Northamptonshire (Williams 1976), re-interpreted, surely correctly, as polygonal rather than circular (Leech 1982, 28). This had pitched stone foundations of more solid construction than those of building 1452, but the interpretation of the superstructure remained unresolved by the excavator. At Thorplands (Hunter and Mynard 1977) the published plan and sections suggest that the stone wall footings were laid on the ground rather than in foundation trenches, although earth-filled foundation trenches are shown under the walls (ibidem., fig. 6 sections 1 and 7). A similar practice may also be identified at Alchester, building A (dating from the mid-3rd century), which was of very similar dimensions and shape (Keevill and Booth 1997, fig. 8), the buildings at both site being more oval than circular, and not obviously polygonal. At

Alchester a soil-filled trench under the drystone wall was interpreted as an abortive foundation trench (ibid., 29). Certainly neither of these 'foundation trenches' appear to have been particularly functional. It is unclear what this implies for the superstructure. It could perhaps be pointed out that a polygonal timber frame could be constructed to a less than precise shape, and, particularly with a large number of sides, may be supported on footings of quasi-circular plan. However, mass walling may be more likely in this instance (as preferred by the excavator) and stone, cob or turf are possibilities. Mass walling, employing cob or turf, has been suggested as being one of the principal techniques of house construction from the later Iron Age in Oxfordshire and Gloucestershire (Keevill and Booth 1997, 43), based largely on the lack of evidence for timber-built roundhouses in this period. It has been suggested that the appearance of stone-walled buildings in this region may therefore "represent a conversion of a mass wall building tradition into stone, from about the mid 2nd century onwards" (ibid.). From the perspective of the Birdlip Quarry stake-wall buildings, this view requires reconsideration, at least in its applicability to the Gloucestershire Cotswolds.

At Winterton, Lincolnshire, (Stead 1976) a group of three 'circular' buildings of the late 1st and 2nd centuries have been interpreted as polygonal by Leech (1982, 28). They may actually represent slightly different structural techniques which appear to have been in use concurrently and their disposition in relation to the later rectangular villa buildings suggests that they may have been the villa's direct precursors. Building H probably had most in common with structure 1452 at Birdlip Quarry and was in many ways the most curious of the structures. It was incomplete but probably over 16 m in diameter. The 4 m-wide entrance approached by a rutted ramp suggests that the building may have been a barn or store (Keevill and Booth 1997, 35), although it has also been argued that all these buildings were dwellings (Goodburn 1978, 94). The wall was narrow, and was without foundations or interior facing stones. There was evidence for a plaster face on the interior. A timber superstructure appears likely, as suggested by the excavator, and it is difficult to envisage mass walling on such a scale and on such narrow footings. Following the logic of timber construction, a polygonal shape is probable. However, the published plan (ibid. fig. 34) does not corroborate this or is at best inconclusive. To the south, building J had deep (0.6–0.7 m) pitched stone foundations and mortared walls or footings surviving to two courses, indicating not only Roman influence on the building technique, but that it is likely to have been built in stone to eaves height. Leech's claim for a polygonal shape cannot be supported by the published plan. Building E, on the other hand, appears to have been genuinely 12-sided. It was very large – about 17 m in diameter - and had four internal post-bases for roof supports. Its stone footings were deeper than those of building J and overlain by two surviving courses of mortared masonry. Such solid foundations would suggest a stone construction like building J, even though the polygonal form would not have been of any advantage with this method.

This consideration of a number of comparable buildings has been somewhat inconclusive, but shows that several different techniques of building existed in Roman Britain even within the relatively narrow category of 'circular' construction. It, furthermore, seems likely that the character of building foundations did not have an automatic corrollory in the form of the superstructure, so that a simple correspondence between timber-framing and shallow foundations or a polygonal form is not necessarily correct.

The course of the wall on the north-eastern side of structure 1452 appears to have been joined by an irregular abutment of larger stones, which included a rectangular block with grooves on the upper surface. The purpose of this abuttment is unclear, but it may have defined a particular area of activity. It can be noted that at Marshfield the right hand side of the door of the circular building was occupied by a bounded stone surface (330 - described as a path although it clearly does not lead anywhere), and a short section of contemporary wall (Blockley 1985, fig. 14). Both were of unknown significance.

The large worked stones which may have marked the entrance on the eastern side seem inexplicable in functional terms, but their inclusion in the wall (or perhaps adjacent to the wall in the case of the grooved stone in 840) can hardly have been accidental. The re-use of architectural masonry in buildings of lower status is not uncommon in the Roman period. Examples include stone stylobates supporting wooden uprights from 4th-century contexts at the Alchester Road Suburb, Towcester (Brown and Woodfield 1983). It is assumed that such pieces were collected casually and used because they were suited to a particular purpose. However, the stones in building 1452, while of unknown origin, are not obviously architectural and do not appear to have been chosen to fulfill a particular requirement. While their selection and use may have been entirely extemporary, a consideration of the use of stone on this site in other contexts suggests that they may have had some kind of comparable, possibly symbolic, significance. The insertion of the stone culvert associated with structure 1463 (Period 1) and the use of stone 'revetments' in the ditches associated with structure 1684 in Areas 3 and 5 (Period 2), do not appear to be purely functional. Indeed, it is difficult to see that the 'revetment' walls in the ditches served any ultimately useful purpose at all and it seems possible, although this is no more than an impression, that they may have had a more symbolic role connected with protection.

### *Spatial distributions of finds*

Structure 1452 had an extensive stone surface outside the building at what is assumed to be the front (layer 188) and a stone pathway running south-west. If the doorway faced east, it is possible that the flagging was

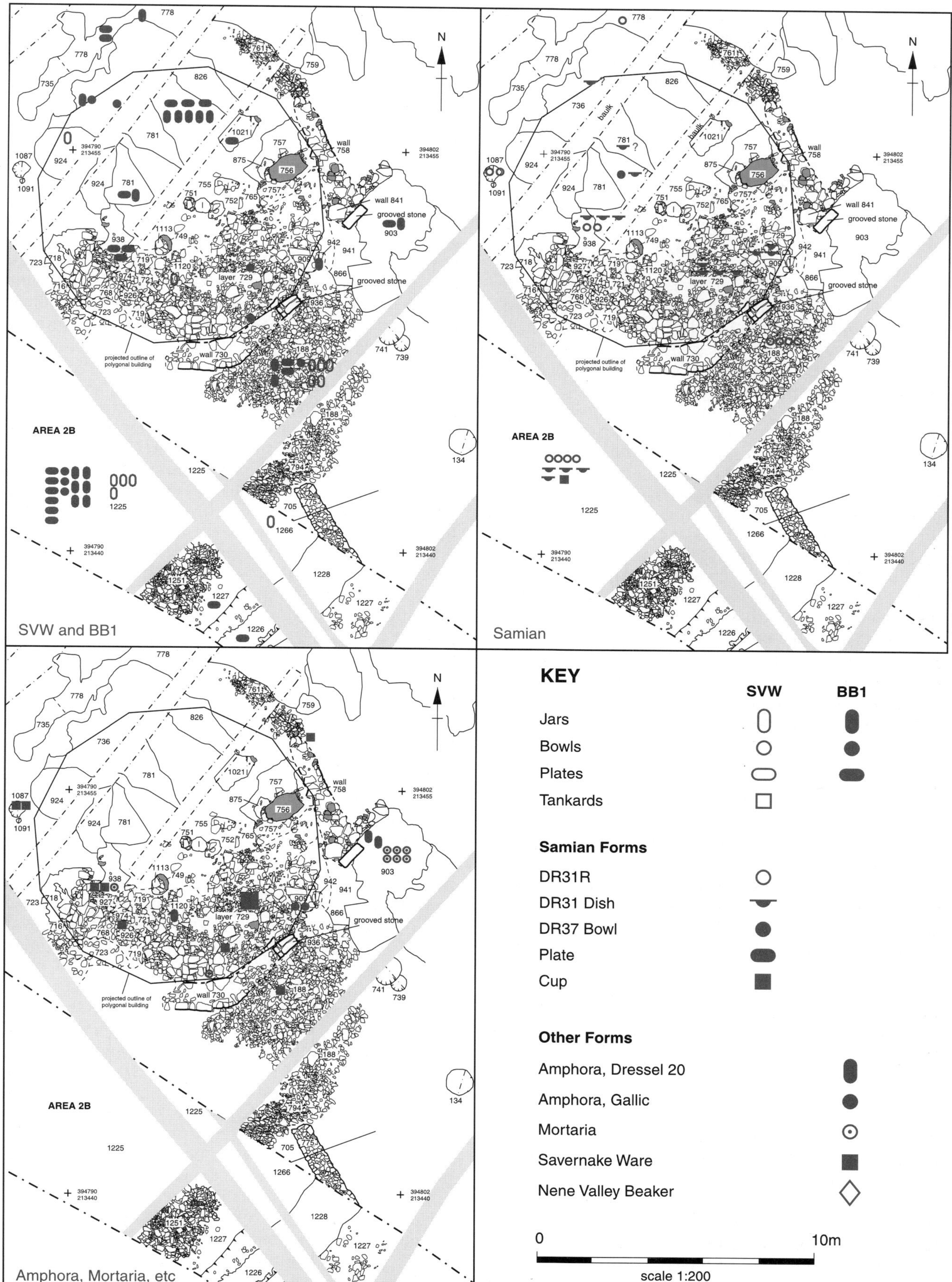


*Figure 4.107 Birdlip Quarry, structure 1452 (Area A), distribution of selected pottery forms.*

originally more extensive in this direction. The interior showed extensive flooring of both pitched and flat stone on the eastern and southern sides, which included episodes of patchy re-flooring. The northern and western areas of the building may have had an earthen floor (although it is possible that stone had been re-used) which was overlain by thin, grey, occupation layers.

The distribution of activities within the building is even less clear than in the previous phases. It is uncertain whether there was a hearth contemporary with this building. The hearth could have been re-used, but there was no indication that it had been reconstructed and the fact that it had been so completely destroyed by the end of the occupation suggests that it belonged exclusively with the earlier period. It is possible that one or more of the other burnt areas formed a hearth for this building, or that there was a raised hearth somewhere. Despite the absence of obvious traces of a hearth, the location of the structure and the large quantity of finds from this area, suggest that this was another domestic building. Most finds came from the midden areas to the south and there were relatively large quantities from the 'occupation' layers and among the stones within the building itself. There did not appear to be as many finds near the entrance (if this were on the eastern side), but this may be due to the greater truncation of deposits here. Overall the distribution of rubbish appears to have been similar to that in the previous period.

The distribution of finds within the building is not particularly revealing (Fig. 4.107). Severn Valley Ware and Dorset Black Burnished Ware were ubiquitous, with many sherds coming from the occupations layers (particularly 768) and under the re-flooring 729. There was no good indication that the distributions had any relation to function and a degree of reworking and redeposition may be suspected, particularly from the small size of most sherds. Tiny sherds of samian, probably from the same vessel came from layers 736, 798 and 781. The fact that other sherds of the same type came from underlying layers 848 and 849 means that there may be significant redeposition from the earlier occupation. Joining sherds of a samian dish came from floor layers 909 and 729; the second of these deposits also yielding one of the few fragments of a samian cup.

There were no large sherds of Dressel 20 amphora from the building, although three large sherds of Gallic amphora from 743 (directly over-lying the stone floor 909 at the possible entrance) may be significant since they were the only ones from this part of the site (Fig. 4.107). There were very few mortarium fragments definitely assignable to this phase and no indication of where food processing was undertaken. There were, however, a few large sherds of Savernake Ware storage jar which may indicate areas of storage (Fig. 4.107). Two came from pit 1087 and a further two sherds came from the 'occupation' layer 704, which may be significant despite the frequent presence of other wares, because most other sherds were tiny. Four large sherds (215 g) came from beneath floor 729. Small sherds had a widespread and unremarkable distribution. Metal finds were widespread but unremarkable, most being small miscellaneous fragments of iron wire, rod and plate.

### *Other circular, partly circular or irregular buildings*

#### *Area C: ovens and structure (Period 1) (Figs 4.53–7)*

The shallow terrace in Areas C and 2C was occupied by a series of ovens (643–647) bounded on the northern side by a shallow curving drainage gully and slot which probably indicates a rudimentary stake wall (Fig. 4.55). Two morticed stone blocks on the probable wall-line may have served as post-sockets, but these were the reasonably clear indications of post positions. That the deposits within this terrace were unploughed and therefore relatively well-preserved emphasises the genuinely slight nature of the archaeological evidence. From this it seems unlikely that the structure was roofed, and the evidence appears to represent simply some sort of windbreak on the northern side of the terrace. There was no prepared floor surface associated with the ovens, although the stone surface 302 to the west (Fig. 4.58) may have been partly contemporaneous. The ovens themselves, which were modifications and re-linings of a sub-rectangular pit, were not large but were of a different construction to most of the ground-level hearths on the site and presumably had a function other than as domestic hearths (Fig. 4.56).

The purpose of the structure here is likely to be related to the function of the ovens, but there was no clue from either their form or contents as to what this might have been. Partially open structures are not uncommon on Iron Age and Roman sites and there is evidence that they were often used as workshops (Drury 1982). The range of late Roman examples from Alchester Road, Towcester, included a structure (building 4/2a) defined solely by a curving gully, which was not a segment of a circle and bears a strong resemblance to the structure in Area C. The amount of hammer-scale from the gully strongly suggested that it was connected with smithing (Brown and Woodfield 1983, 57 and fig. 13). Another building, which was probably D-shaped (building 4/5) contained a sub-rectangular pit described as a furnace and clear evidence of lead working (ibid., 58).

The structure in Area C at Birdlip Quarry is unlikely to be associated with smithing, since in that case traces of hammer-scale at least should have been present in the soil samples taken from the oven. Lead-casting is a more probable activity, and the presence of lead-casting waste from a number of contexts indicates that it was practised on site (see Allen, chapter 8). However, none of these contexts need belong to Period 1 and the waste was widespread across the site with a casting sprue from 227 and a miscellaneous piece of waste from 31 the sole fragments from this area. There is certainly no evidence to link this activity to the ovens here. It is possible, then, that the ovens were related to another type of activity. The charred plant assemblage associated with ovens 643 and 647 suggests that weeds and chaff were used as fuel or kindling although mixed charcoal was also present. At Marshfield, a simple rectangular oven of the late 3rd century AD (oven 502 in room 3 of building 3) was thought to be for drying or malting corn, although without botanical evidence (Blockley 1985, fig. 22), and it seems possible that such structures were used alongside or were replaced by the well-known corn dryers of more elaborate form. It is worth noting that at Wavendon Gate, Buckinghamshire, a 3rd-century corn dryer (378) was located within a small curving enclosure and apparently associated with a cobbled surface which may have been used for processing wheat (Williams *et al.* 1996, 72–4, fig. 43).

Despite the impression that the structure in Area C was unlikely to have been roofed, there were a large number of finds from the deposits within the terrace and in the nearby middens to the south. Of particular note was the presence of Gallic amphora, which was almost exclusively confined to this area and appears to have been associated with the activities carried out here (Fig. 4.103). The reason for this is unclear. A probable *in situ* Dorset Black Burnished Ware jar within gully 697 is noteworthy although not necessarily contemporary with the ovens. Jars are not infrequently found set in pits within buildings and may have been functional or dedicatory. At Kingscote a Black Burnished Ware jar was placed in the 4th-century 'barn' (building VII) near a corn dryer (Timby 1998a, 44 and fig. 29). At Catsgore, Somerset, the base of a greyware jar was found in a small pit next to the hearth in building 1.2 (Leech 1982, 59).

*Structure 1456 (Period 1, Area D)*

This structure, like that in Area C, is likely to have been quite insubstantial and probably no more than a screen or fence along the lip of the drainage gully 269 (Fig. 4.62). It did not form part of a circle. The presence of a hearth (264), which was destroyed in the subsequent phase, also echoes the sequence in Area C, although it appears that this surface hearth would have had a different function to the ovens in Area C. It is probable that this structure was used as a workshop of some kind, although there is no evidence from the finds as to its precise purpose. It was contemporary with well 981 to the north-east which by reason of its location would appear to have been specifically related to the structure.

*Structure 1457 (Period 2A, Area D)*

Structure 1457 was a circular or partly circular building 9 m in diameter (Fig. 4.108). Its precise form and method of construction are not clear, but it is likely that gully 340 held a stake or wattle wall. There is no discernible pattern to the associated small postholes to indicate the position of supporting posts. The two large post-pits, 275 and 434 were probably associated with this structure and may have been roof supports. Even if there had been opposed posts removed by the lynchet, the arrangement of major support posts is unusual and without parallels known to the author. If they were the only posts of a semi-circular or partly circular building, the disposition of these supports is even more curious. Given this, it must been considered possible that the posts belonged with the subsequent structure (Phase 3) whose form of construction is even less clear. However, it can be noted that the post-pits do occupy a symmetrical position with respect to structure 1457. If a diametric line is taken through stake-hole 650 at the southern terminal of gully 340, the post-pits are bisected by a line 90° to it (Fig. 4.109). This suggests that there is some regularity to the structure and that, consequently, the post-pits may have been positioned as structural components to hold the roof. It is also considered possible that the wall gully was dug in a series of straight sections rather than a curve, adding further to the regularity of the structure, but this was not clear one way or the other. Figure 4.109, which is somewhat speculative, shows that the structure, whether circular or semi-circular, could have been based on a twelve-sided polygon.

There is no good evidence for the structure's function. Like its predecessor 1456, it was probably a workshop or outbuilding rather than a dwelling. There is no indication that it was used for metal-working, although the relatively high concentration of hipposandals (four out of the ten fragments from the site, including three out the four from Period 2A) may suggest that it was connected with maintaining horses or cattle. Other metal finds include a linch pin (cat. 587) and a bucket handle mount (cat. 570) (Fig. 4.109). Twenty-nine sherds from a Dorset Black Burnished Ware jar, set in the floor, appears to represent the remains of an *in situ* vessel and may well have belonged to this phase. It contained calcareous residue from holding hot water. The number of large sherds of Severn Valley Ware, from features on the northern side of the structure, may indicate an area of activity or storage.

The structure was probably contemporary with another area of occupation to the north (layer 58 and associated gullies) which was probably related to a small structure whose function is uncertain.

*Structure 1458 (Period 1, Area E)*

Although only part of this structure was excavated, it was probably partly circular or curving like structure 1456 (Area D). The evidence suggested that it was equally insubstantial and there was no clue as to its function (Fig. 4.64). Like 1456 it was also associated with a well (299) which probably went out of use when the structure was abandoned.

*Structure 1459 (Period 2A, Area E)*

This replacement for structure 1458 in Period 2A was of uncertain size and form, but may have been hexagonal or partly hexagonal, rather than circular

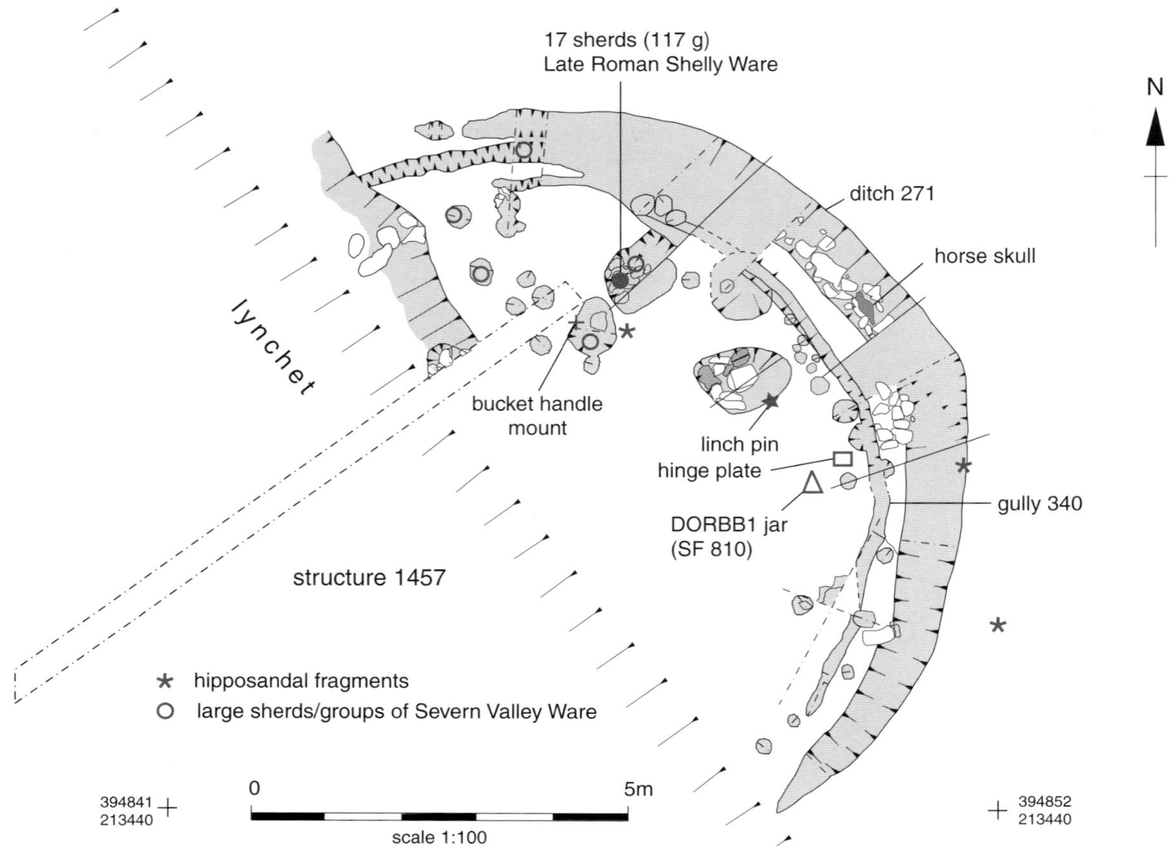


*Figure 4.108 Birdlip Quarry, structure 1457 (Area D), distribution of selected finds.*

(Fig. 4.80). There were no clues as to its specific function and little more can be said about it.

*Penannular structure 985 (Period 2B, Area A)*

Structure 985 was a penannular stake-walled structure with a 6 m wide opening facing south (Fig. 4.90). The nature of the structure is unclear and it is not certain that it would have been roofed. The curve of the wall gully is quite precise with the centre of the gully (the presumed wall line) lying on an arc 6.5 m in diameter which runs for *c.* 240°. This suggests some care in laying out the structure. The geometry of the structure suggests that 30° or 60° segments may have been significant, although it does not appear that the wall was constructed in a series of straight lengths.

*Partially circular structure 713 (Period 2B, Area A)*

Structure 713 (walls 122 and 714) was a later building in precisely the same location as structure 985 and built of stone (Fig. 4.91). It was substantially robbed and it is unclear how complete a circle it originally formed. The quite precise alignment on it of wall 1245 suggests that the wall 714 straightened and joined 1245. It may have formed an embayment at the end of the pitched stone path 1224, rather than a structure, or even a large apsidal building, but these possibilities are considered less likely than a small penannular structure like its predecessor.

There is a growing body of evidence for semi-circular structures and penannular structures with wide entrances in the Iron Age and Roman periods, despite the acknowledged difficulty of correctly distinguishing partially circular structures from circular structures which are partially complete (Lambrick and Robinson 1979; Drury 1982). In many cases they have been linked to agricultural or industrial activities requiring an open side for light, air or access, with smithing being one obvious function. Drury considered the Iron Age examples from Great Oakley, Northamptonshire, to have been roofed although the consequent structural implications are not fully understood (Drury 1982, 10). At Farmoor, Oxfordshire, a penannular slot (F5) of the 4th century AD, with a 5 m-wide opening, was interpreted as an animal pen. The structure, of upright timbers, was 10.5 m in diameter and was suggested to be for a limited number of animals such as prize bulls or stallions (Lambrick and Robinson 1979, 73–4 and fig. 6). A number of partially circular or D-shaped structures in the Alchester road suburb, Towcester, also of 4th-century date, appeared to be largely associated with metal-

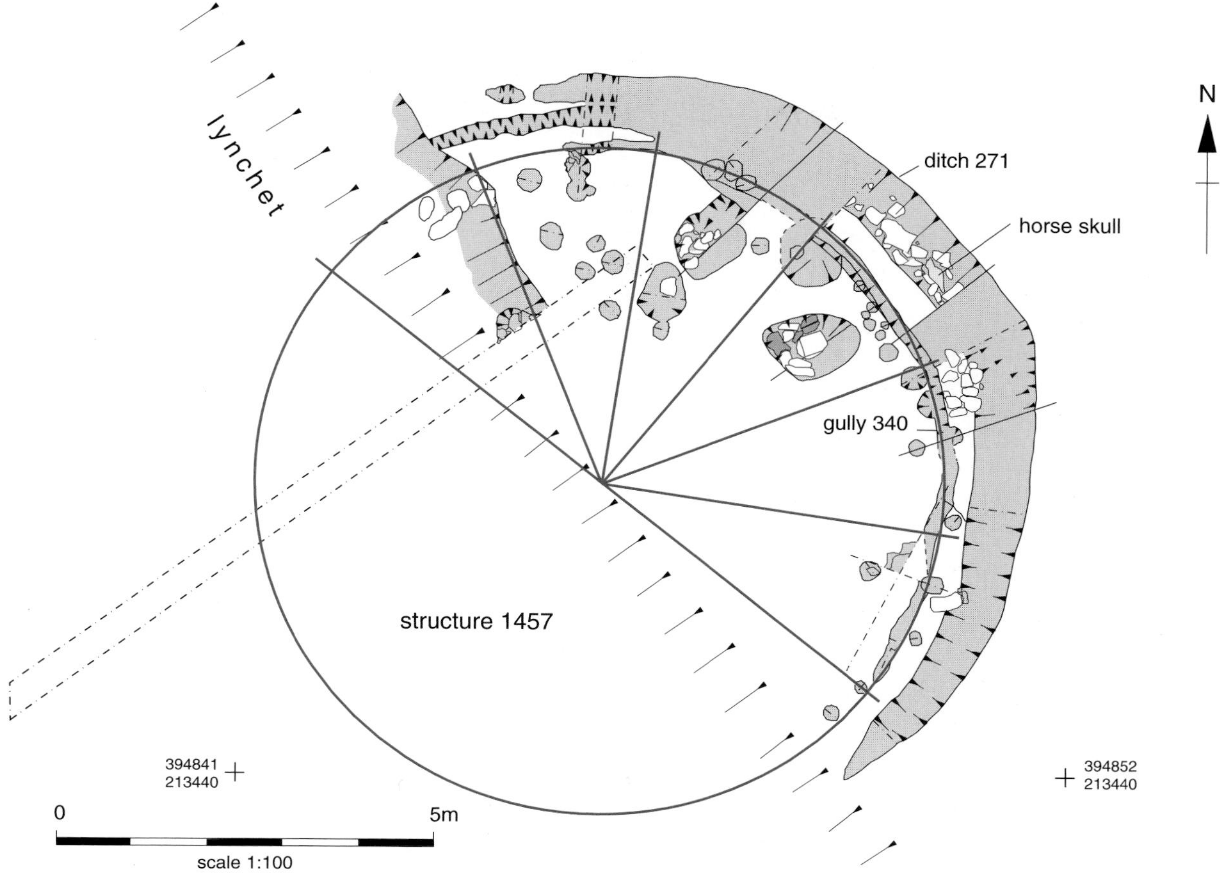


*Figure 4.109 Birdlip Quarry, Area D, possible interpretation of structure 1457.*

working (Brown and Woodfield 1983, buildings 4/2a, 4/5, 4/7 and possibly others). Like structure 985 and its successor 713, buildings 4/2a and 4/5 at Towcester were positioned close to the road and linked to it by stone causeways.

There were no features inside structures 985 and 713 and no evidence as to their function. It seems unlikely that they would have been used for smithing or metalworking without leaving some residue, although other craft activities may have been practised. The fact that the structures faced the road and were provided with a stone path to it suggests that street access was important. This may mean that they are unlikely to have housed animals, unless these were, for example, horses needed for the road. The building may alternatively have served as a store room or other small domestic structure.

### Wells

In Period 1 it appears that each structure was provided with a well nearby. This was certainly the case for the northern enclosure (well 277) and Area E (well 299), and highly probable for Area D (well 891) (Fig. 4.43). There was also a possible well in Area 2B (an unbottomed pit, 1263) (Fig. 4.44) and next to Area 3 (an unbottomed pit, 322) (Fig. 4.84). Digging the wells through solid limestone clearly involved a great deal of effort and it is unclear why so many were needed. The implication that each of the enclosures had a certain degree of independence has already been mentioned. Further to practical considerations of water supply, it is possible that the excavation of the wells had some kind of propitiatory or religious significance which may have been related to the founding of certain buildings. Wells, (together with springs, rivers and other features such as rocks and trees), also often had significance as boundary markers, whose laying out and observance had religious connotations for the Romans (Dilke 1971, 98–99). The location of well 277 may be significant in this regard, and it can be noted that pit (or well?) 332 and pit 2020 (Area 5) appear to have been dug in the corners of the roadside plot defined by stone-revetted ditches on two sides. In Period 2A, sometime in the 3rd century, the wells (together with pits 1263 and 332) went out of use and were filled in. They do not appear to have been replaced. This clearly must have had implications for the way the settlement was organised in Period 2, although springs are present in the vicinity of the site (Fig. 4.40) and there are unlikely to have been difficulties of water supply. It may mean that more widespread resources became available to the settlement from the later 3rd century. The wells may have been abandoned because they dried up, although again religious factors may have been involved. Timby (1998a, 388–89) remarks on the curious number of deliberately backfilled wells at Lower Slaughter and their possible ritual significance.

### *Corn dryer 42*

The T-shaped corn dryer was situated in a relatively isolated position in the northern part of the site (Fig. 4.73). Following the work of Van der Veen (1989) it now seems likely that 'corn dryers' were used for a variety of drying purposes, including the roasting of germinated grain for the production of malt and the drying or parching of grain as preparation for storage. They may also have been used for drying other crops and smoking meat and cheese (Morris 1979, 8). The botanical evidence from the lower fills of corn dryer 42 suggested that the activities taking place involved the processing of grain for consumption or storage, rather than for malting (see Pelling, Chapter 8), although clearly this may only have related to the most recent activity and would not preclude other activities having taken place.

Although there was no dating evidence for the construction of the corn dryer, it appears to have been in use in the later 3rd to 4th centuries. In both its T-shaped form and late Roman date the corn dryer at Birdlip Quarry is typical. Morris (1979, 20) has suggested that, while normally of 3rd and 4th century date, the T-shaped dryer appeared in the 2nd century. The earlier of the two T-shaped corn dryers at Wavendon Gate (corn dryer 505) was thought to be dated to the late 2nd to early 3rd centuries. Van der Veen claims 1st-century examples of 'corn dryers', although there is a danger of confusing the function of the 'corn dryer' or 'malting oven', which need not be of any particular form, with the more common definition which is based on the T- or other distinctive shape. The late 1st-/early 2nd-century malting oven from Bancroft villa, for example, does not appear to have been of typical 'corn dryer' form (Williams and Zeepvat 1994, fig. 77). Van der Veen (1989, 315) links the adoption of corn dryers generally to large-scale cereal processing, although there are doubts as to whether this would be either necessary or possible with this size of oven on rural Romano-British settlements. A domestic context appears to be more likely at Birdlip Quarry and other sites. Surely the size and number of corn dryers, rather than their mere presence, are of more relevance to the scale of processing carried out.

The location of corn dryer 42 at some distance from any contemporary structures is also not untypical and may be linked to a need for a reliable flow of air and/or the avoidance of a fire hazard. Morris (1979, 11–12) suggested that most dryers were in a structure of some sort, since experiments have show that otherwise dryers are too susceptible to changing winds. There was no indication of an enclosing structure at Birdlip Quarry. From the degree of preservation of the corn dryer and the pitch of the packing stones behind the walls, it is estimated that only about 0.10 m of the Roman ground surface had been lost, so had any enclosing structure existed it must have had very shallow foundations.

Generally, there does not seem to have been a preferred location or orientation for this type of oven and the presumed requirement of a strong air flow does not appear to have been a determining factor in many cases. At Catsgore, all four corn dryers were located within buildings or annexes which may have been barns. Adjacent storage areas for fuel or crops were identified in three instances. At Kingscote, Gloucestershire, a 4th-century corn dryer was located inside a subsidiary building convincingly interpreted as a barn (Timby 1998a, 44). Nearby millstones suggest that crop-processing was a major activity in this building. At Marshfield the elaborate late 3rd/4th-century corn dryer was located in an isolated position about 35 m north-east of the contemporary residential building, although other ovens of varying forms were within the building itself. At Gorhambury, Hertfordshire, a late 3rd-century corn dryer was located near the eastern entrance to the farm/villa enclosure, not far from a circular structure interpreted as an animal pen (Neal *et al.* 1990, fig. 96). At Roughground Farm, Gloucestershire, a late Roman corn dryer was located within an enclosure in an area of ovens at some distance from the villa itself, suggesting that it was part of the estate bakery (Allen *et al.* 1993, 189–191). It appears that, in some instances at least, the position of the corn dryer may have been influenced by access to the fields while at other times the location of storage and other processing facilities was more important.

At Wavendon Gate, Buckinghamshire, a corn dryer within a small semi-circular(?) enclosure in the south-eastern corner of the site was replaced by one in a similar position also within an enclosure (Williams *et al.* 1996, figs 31 and 37). The later corn dryer appeared to have been associated with a cobbled area, which it was suggested had been used for the processing of grain. The location of this corn dryer with respect to an associated enclosure ditch and cobbled area, recalls the layout of Area C (Period 1) at Birdlip Quarry (Fig. 4.55) where the sequence of ovens appeared to have been within a rudimentary structure of probable semi-circular form adjacent to an area of stone. While the ovens here were all of rectangular or oval shape, it is possible that they were also used for processing grain. The lack of burning within oven 644 has led to the suggestion that the fire was located outside the oven itself and that hot air may have been directed into the chamber. Later the oven was modified with evidence of intense burning inside the chamber and this may correspond to a change in use, or simply to a change in design, with the heated air passing into a higher chamber. If the 2nd-century date of pit 180 is accepted, the evidence in its base for malting grain at least suggests that there should be some form of corn dryer present in Period 1, and it seems unlikely that corn dryer 42 would have operated from the 2nd century. It is possible, then, that the ovens in Area C were associated with crop processing (including, perhaps, malting) in Period 1 - a function which was transferred to the corn dryer in the northern area in Period 2 when the ovens went out of use. It is interesting to note that at Bancroft villa, evidence for the malting of spelt came from a late 1st to late 2nd-century oven of non-corn dryer type (Williams and Zeepvat 1994, 148 and fig. 77) suggesting that the adoption of the 'corn dryer' form was not related to a specific innovation of crop processing, but rather the further refinement of practices already well developed.

Most of the fills of corn dryer 42 represented the collapse of the flue structure and subsequent deliberate infill. Despite the distance of the feature from occupation areas, there was a large amount of pottery from the backfill of the bowl (fills 190, 81 and 33), which appears to represent midden material. The finds included an almost complete conical flanged bowl from 190, and from the upper fill (33) the only large fragment of hearth bottom or (less likely) smelting slag cake from the site.

**Area 3: rectangular structures**

The wall and stone surfaces in Area 3 are interpreted as the remains of a rectangular building, of at least two and probably three phases, within an enclosure (Figs 4.66, 4.82 and 4.94). The rectangular form is unusual on this site, as is its roadside position with its long axis parallel to the road. The first phase (structure 1683 – Fig. 4.66) was probably a timber-framed construction within a shallow trench, although the evidence was extremely limited. This was replaced by structure 1684 in an identical position which was probably also timber-framed, but with a drystone wall footing which formed a revetment within a drainage gully, and a floor of pitched and flagged stone (Fig. 4.82). In the final phase, the gully was filled in and a line of postholes inserted through the wall. This is likely to represent a similar building of a slightly different construction (structure 1648 – Fig. 4.94). The bay widths would have been about 2.8 m. The overall size of these buildings remains unknown but they were clearly substantial – over 16 m long and over 7 m wide. Assuming that they were positioned symmetrically with regard to the main boundary ditches (ditches 1680/1681/1682 and the projection of ditches 690/688) they could have been 25 m long (Fig. 4.104).

The interpretation of this sequence of buildings is far from clear although it seems inherently likely that they served a similar range of functions. Their rectangular form and roadside position and orientation are also likely to be significant. The range of finds from this area of the site are not unusual and do not aid an interpretation of the buildings. They include a moderately large quantity of pottery and coins and also the only copper alloy spoon from the site (Fig. 7.23.536), suggesting that the buildings' functions cannot be covered by the term 'outbuilding'.

At Bancroft, building 9, which was a large rectangular building with its long axis fronting the road, was interpreted as animal stalling (Williams and Zeepvat 1994, 143-8). It contained a row of posts, 2.4 m apart along the side of the building opposite the road. At 26 m x 9.5 m in size it was one of the largest buildings on the site, only slightly smaller than the main residential building 30 m to the west.

Traces of a rectangular posthole building were found at Catsgore (building 3.16, complex 5) dating to the 4th century (Leech 1982, fig. 70). This was interpreted as a timber-framed building initially of three bays with an added two-bay extension. It was one of the few buildings identified with its long axis clearly fronting the road and appears to have replaced building 2.13, of similar dimensions and probably of timber-framed construction on stone footings. While the two buildings were interpreted as partly contemporary, this seems unlikely as building 3.16 would have partly blocked the entrance to 2.13 (ibid., fig. 17). It is therefore possible that 3.16 replaced 2.13 closer to the road and it may have had similar functions. A similar position and sequence of construction have been envisaged at Birdlip Quarry, and the buildings' functions may also have been similar. It can also be noted that Catsgore building 2.13 had an entrance about 3 m wide facing the road. A corresponding entrance to building 3.16 may be identified in the initial central bay which was 4 m wide. This compares with the other bay widths which were about 2.8 m and a wide entrance here seems a reasonable explanation for this difference. Although all the buildings in this complex were seen as houses, it seems likely that the buildings aligned parallel to the road could have had functions related to road access, such as stabling, accommodation for carts and storing produce for transport.

At Kingscote, Gloucestershire, the 4th-century complex included building IX which was aligned with the road and had a wide road-side entrance (Timby 1998a, fig. 37). This was a large and relatively narrow building (22.7 m long and 6.7 m wide) and with a timber trough running parallel to the roadside wall and a line of postholes close to the opposite wall. It was interpreted as stalling for animals, although the presence of ovens and an unusual range of finds including copper working debris suggested other activities which may have included furniture making (ibid., 291).

The limited evidence from Birdlip Quarry and the possible parallels from other sites suggests that the buildings may have had a number of uses for which road access was required, including stalling for animals. It may have been a building of a certain 'type' found in a number of road settlements, although this suggestion remains speculative. No evidence can be marshalled to support a specific function as a *mutatio* or relay station, although it is unclear what suite of features would identify such a building. *Mutationes* have not been recognised archaeologically (Black 1995, 89) and since they did not include a lodging, it has been suggested that they can only be identified through the provision of stables, features which have not been identified with any certainty in any roadside settlement (Smith 1987, 17) and in the absence of longitudinal drainage gullies may not be recognised as such (ibid.). The evidence from the structures in Area 3 therefore remains inconclusive on this question. However, there appears to be no reason why the buildings could not have served as some sort of waystation, perhaps of a more informal kind.

#### *4th-century structures in Area A, Period 2B*

*Structural sequence*

The rectilinear walls and small semi-circular structure in Phase 6 present a difficult arrangement to interpret (Fig. 4.91). To start with, the relationship between the curving wall (122) of structure 713 and wall 36 is not clear. Although it is possible that 36 butted 122, a consideration of the structure of wall 36 at this point, particularly the lack of facing stones, suggests that 122 was inserted into it. The jumbled stones here may have been used to bolster a pitched stone plinth (717) outside wall 122, paired with a similar platform of pitched stone (720) next to wall 714. The problem of the stratigraphic position of the penannular stake-wall structure (985) has been mentioned (see Areas A, 2B and 2C: Phase 6), but it seems that it must have directly preceded structure 713 and therefore could have been contemporary with wall 36. Accepting the primacy of wall 36 (with wall 205 to which it was bonded) means that no more than two episodes of construction need be envisaged in this area, with a first episode consisting of structures 985 and 36/205 and the second episode the addition of structure 713 and the wall abutments 35 and 54. Of course the real situation could have been far more complex. The partly circular structures have been discussed above.

*Linear walls*

It has been suggested that walls 36 and 205 formed two sides of a narrow rectangular structure, perhaps constructed with dry stone to eaves height if the pitched rubble, 127, came from wall 36. With this interpretation the building would have been about 9 m long and no more than 2.5 m wide. The later walls 54 and 35 may have formed extensions or annexes either side. They may also have served as revetment walls and as a boundary separating the structures from the land to the north.

There are a number of difficulties with this interpretation. Neither the building technique – dry stone without foundations – nor the final form of the building, have ready parallels. It is, of course, possible that the walls were bonded with clay or earth which has since weathered away, but there was no evidence of this. There were no definite roof-slates from the excavations and insufficient ceramic tile to make it likely that this, or any other structure on the site, was so roofed. A thatched roof is most probable. The narrowness of the structure has no counterparts known to the author although the corridor of the common rectangular farmhouse or 'cottage villa' may have been the model.

The impression from the structures in this area is that they were relatively unimportant outhouses or byres. However, the amount of pottery and other finds from this area of the site strongly indicate that there was a main domestic residence in this area. Figure 4.106 shows the distribution of large and small Dorset Black Burnished Ware sherds on the site in this period, which may be taken as an indication of the areas of primary rubbish disposal. The evidence from the finds is not clear-cut. Contemporaneous middens occur in the other main 'occupation areas' without good evidence for structures of any sort and it is possible that the areas of occupation were different from the areas of rubbish disposal at this time. On balance this seems unlikely because no evidence of structures was found elsewhere on the site and there is hardly any suitably level ground outside the occupation terraces on which they could be sited. There is also slight though unequivocal evidence for a late-phase rectangular post-built structure in Area 3 (structure 1648) sited on the earlier building. This type of evidence is normally difficult to see in the dark soils and is commonly lost or overlooked. Timber-framed buildings on ground level sill-beams or post-pads may have been the most common type of construction in the later 4th century. At the Alchester road suburb, Towcester, the replacement of partly circular buildings with rectangular timber buildings in the later 4th century appears to have been widespread (Brown and Woodfield 1983, 134–135). The evidence for these later structures was largely confined to the positions of stone stylobates or post-pads.

Another difficulty is the large number of re-deposited sherds in the Area A material of this period (see Discussion of Finds, Period 2B). This suggests that the midden material did not gradually build up, but was a dump brought in from elsewhere, a situation also noted at Kingscote (Timby 1998a, 71) where it was suggested that midden material may have been used as stalling for animals. This particular difficulty of interpretation cannot be resolved here though it can be noted, that the downgrading of domestic residences to outhouses, byres or workshops on late Roman sites (something which appears to be common in the literature) merely poses a further problem of where their former residents were to be found: the more this interpretation is invoked the less tenable it becomes. On balance, a continuation of occupation seems the most probable explanation, even though the nature of the houses and the pattern of rubbish disposal remain enigmatic.

*The development of the structures in Area A*

The development from circular stake-wall buildings in the late 2nd and early 3rd centuries, through a circular or polygonal stone-based building, to possible rectangular buildings in the mid 4th century represents a clear progression of vernacular building technique in the late Roman period. A possibly similar sequence of construction from the 2nd to the 4th century can be seen at Barnsley Park in the peripheral southern area associated with the villa (Webster 1981a). The structure of the site has been re-interpreted by Smith (1985) and his argument for a sequence of houses, rather than animal pens or barns, in this area is convincing and to some extent has influenced the interpretation of the evidence from Birdlip Quarry. A summary of Smith's interpretation of Barnsley Park and the possibly similar sequence at Birdlip Quarry is shown in Figure 4.110. The southern group of structures in Phase 1 at Barnsley Park (AD 140–275) are difficult to interpret but include a curving gully and a layer of ash as well as other gullies. Despite the suggestion of a rectangular, timber-framed building (building D), it seems possible on the basis of the plans presented, that the features here were associated with a round house (Webster 1981a, fig. 3). The remains are quite similar to the plan of building 42 and structure 43 at Gorhambury (Neal *et al.* 1990, fig. 90) which were interpreted as a circular building and adjacent animal pen (ibid., 67). At Barnsley Park in the late 3rd century (Phase 2) these traces were succeeded by a pair of two stone-founded circular or polygonal buildings G and F. It is unclear whether the larger building, F, succeeded G, or whether the latter was a semi-circular annexe. No detail of these structures is given. Although they are described as "circular pens" in the excavation report (Webster 1981a, 34), there seems to be no reason for this identification; despite the absence of evidence of a hearth, and a building for habitation and/or agricultural activities appears to be more likely. The larger building was about 9 m in diameter internally – not dissimilar to structure 1452 at Birdlip Quarry. In the earlier 4th century (Phase 3), this was replaced by a long rectangular building (M), about 15 m long and 4.5 m wide, of dry-stone construction which was built up against the boundary wall. This may have been a barn, although Smith (1985, 345) prefers to see it as another house, an interpretation which becomes more convincing in Phase 5/6 (*c.* AD 360) when it was replaced in mortared masonry and subdivided into rooms. Building M was associated with other rectangular buildings, one of which appears to have been replaced by another circular or polygonal building (R) in the mid 4th century (ibid., fig. 6). Like structure 713 this was small (c. 7 m in diameter) although it was provided with a hearth. The presence of a phase of timber construction for this building also has a curious counterpart at Birdlip Quarry (structure 985), although at Barnsley Park the posthole structure appears to have been inserted into the stonework rather than to have pre-dated it.

Smith interprets the site at Barnsley Park as being divided into three separate areas, representing three farming families forming part of a kin group which worked the land (1985, 342). The villa developed in the central area, but not until the mid-4th century. Before then there are indistinct traces of rectangular timber-framed buildings. At Birdlip Quarry, it is apparent that the sequence of houses in Area A were near areas of occupation to the north and west (in the unexcavated part of the site) which probably included other houses. Ditch group 1455 and structure 703 are thought to be the traces of a sequence of a rectangular, timber-framed buildings lying largely outside the excavation area. Without necessarily accepting the model of kinship, and without prejudice to their social status, it is possible to see the occupants in Area A as a distinct social (probably family) group

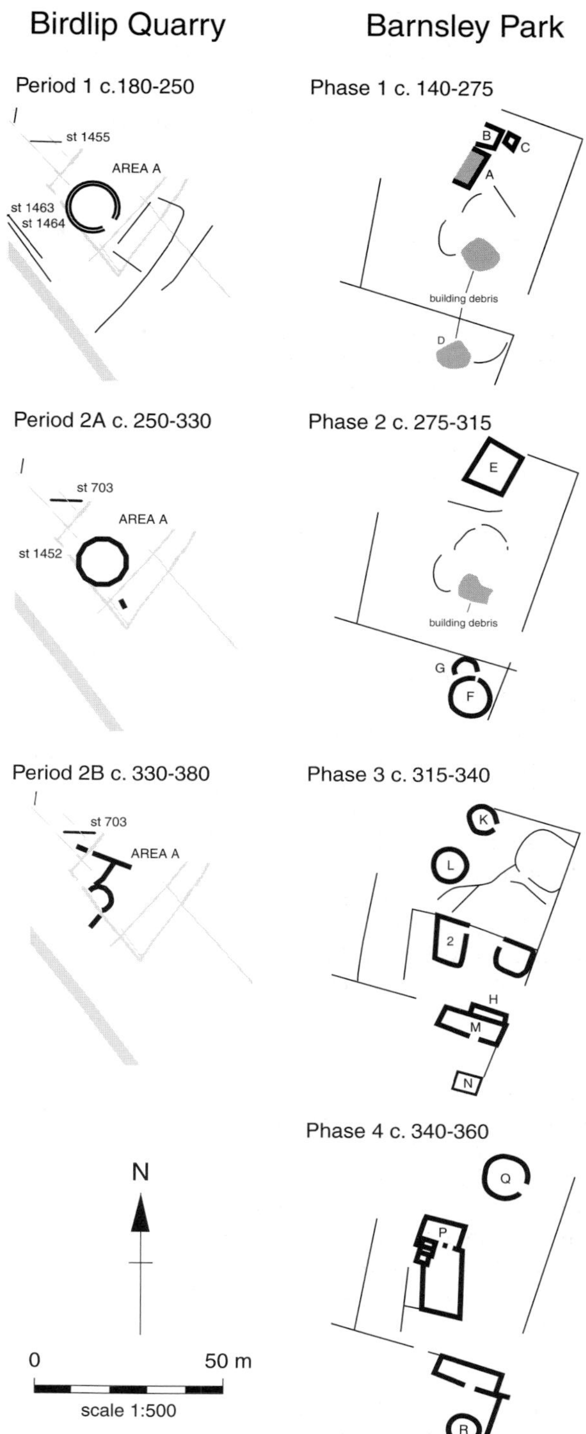


*Figure 4.110 Birdlip Quarry, Area A, comparison with Barnsley Park.*

functioning within the overall farming unit, in a similar fashion to that proposed by Smith at Barnsley Park (1985). In the later 4th century the occupation at Birdlip Quarry ceases, while at Barnsley Park the rectangular building (M) becomes orientated towards the developing villa to the north (Phases 5/6) and continues.

The significance of this re-interpretation is not only that the sequence of building types, and, as far as the evidence can be taken, the dating of the sequence, are similar at both sites; but that such a pattern of archaeological deposits may be identified with a group of farming people with a distinct identity. This hypothesis must remain tentative but it may be possible to see the development as a typical transformation for a particular kind of farming group in this region.

It is possible that similar groups may be recognised elsewhere. At Gorhambury, Hertfordshire, a small number of circular buildings were associated with the villa and its predecessor in what appear to have been subsidiary positions (Neal *et al.*, 1990). It is perhaps significant that, after the construction of the 'fully Romanised' villa in the 2nd century, the circular buildings were confined to the outer 'farmyard enclosure', at some distance from the villa itself (ibid., figs. 56, 73 and 96). Building 42 (Period 9, AD 175–250), which was mentioned above, is of particular interest since it was located close to the entrance of the enclosure facing an adjacent cobbled area (structure 43) interpreted as an animal pen. The building itself, estimated to have been 12 m in diameter perhaps with a clay wall, contained 21 small ovens of probable domestic nature. This association of a traditional domestic circular structure with a larger farm, but set apart from it, and apparently concerned with animal husbandry, may correspond to the situation at Birdlip Quarry.

# Chapter 5: Road Excavations

*by Andrew Mudd and Simon Mortimer*

## INTRODUCTION

The A417/A419 road improvement was the most recent engineering project directed toward the provision of a road across this 25 km stretch of landscape, a route which owes its origin to Roman military construction in the 1st century AD. While the archaeological importance of Ermin Street is self-evident, its incorporation into the modern highway network has generally allowed little opportunity for examining the Roman road or its successors. From the outset the investigation of the road was regarded as an important aspect of the archaeological programme on the current project.

Eleven trenches were specifically designed to examine Ermin Street north of Cirencester (Fig. 5.1), seven of these providing complete cross-sections through the modern A417. The other four were smaller. To the south of Cirencester the opportunities were more limited and the Roman road surface was exposed in only one trench. On the eastern side of the town the course of Fosse Way/Akeman Street was investigated with two long sections through the modern Burford Road. The post-Roman elements of all the major road trenches appear in this chapter. Also presented in this chapter is new and unexpected evidence from The Lynches Trackway of a Roman route running up the Churn Valley. The locations of these investigations are shown in Figure 5.1.

Roman trackways were also encountered at Field's Farm, Duntisbourne Leer, and Court Farm. These are described together with related features in Chapter 4 although included in the wider discussion of Roman roads in this chapter. Miscellaneous post-Roman road features are described in Chapter 6.

## ERMIN STREET TRENCHES NORTH OF CIRENCESTER

### Introduction

Ermin Street was examined by seven excavated sections across the carriageway and verge of the A417 between the Cowley and Itlay underbridges (Trenches 6, 7, 5, 11, 9, 8 and 10 - Fig. 5.1). Another section (Trench 12) was recorded in a watching brief immediately south of Dower's Lane Underbridge. In addition, four trenches between Birdlip Quarry and Highgate House were excavated on the verge of the modern road (Trenches 1 and 2 shown on Fig. 5.1). Those at Birdlip Quarry specifically investigated the Roman road margin adjacent to the later Roman settlement there (see Chapter 4).

The sections through the modern road (Trenches 5–11) were mechanically excavated to undisturbed geology. The exposed section was then cleaned, drawn and photographed. A strip *c.* 1.7 m wide from the exposed section edge was then excavated by hand and the section drawing amended as necessary. The other trenches (1–4) were hand-excavated after the removal of modern overburden by machine. Each road surface encountered was planned at 1:20.

Trench 3 at the Birdlip Quarry site and Trench 4 to the north-west of the site are described with the Romano-British settlement in Chapter 4. Trench 3 provided evidence of a 4th-century road surface. Trench 4 revealed a highly disturbed Roman road surface but provided little new information.

Trenches 1 and 2, located on higher ground between Cowley Underbridge and Gloucester Beeches, were unhelpful and it was not possible to establish whether there were any surviving Roman surfaces. Trench 11 at Five Mile Underpass was also badly disturbed and it was not possible to identify the Roman surface. It revealed a large undated quarry pit. No further description of these trenches is warranted here, and the following account will be restricted to the remaining more informative trenches.

### Description of archaeological contexts

The road sections were similar in general terms, but each was sufficiently different from the others to make the establishment of a concordance of road structures from the amalgamated sections impossible in any definitive sense. All the trenches suffered from similar problems of interpretation, the most acute of which was the lack of dating evidence. A total of only 198 sherds (590 g) of Roman, medieval and post-medieval pottery was recovered from 38 contexts – the average sherd weight being about 3 g. Some iron finds, particularly horseshoes, were also recovered although these are controversial as dating evidence (see Clark 1995, 79–81, for a summary of the evidence for Roman horseshoes, which can be dismissed under critical examination). As well as the problem of the chronological insensitivity of horseshoe types, it must be considered inherently likely that horseshoes were lost in ruts and pot-holes, particularly on poorly metalled surfaces, to be recovered as intrusive finds. The truncation of road surfaces presented further problems of cross-correlation, most obviously in the shallower sections where recent construction had resulted in the removal of upper deposits. However, there is a

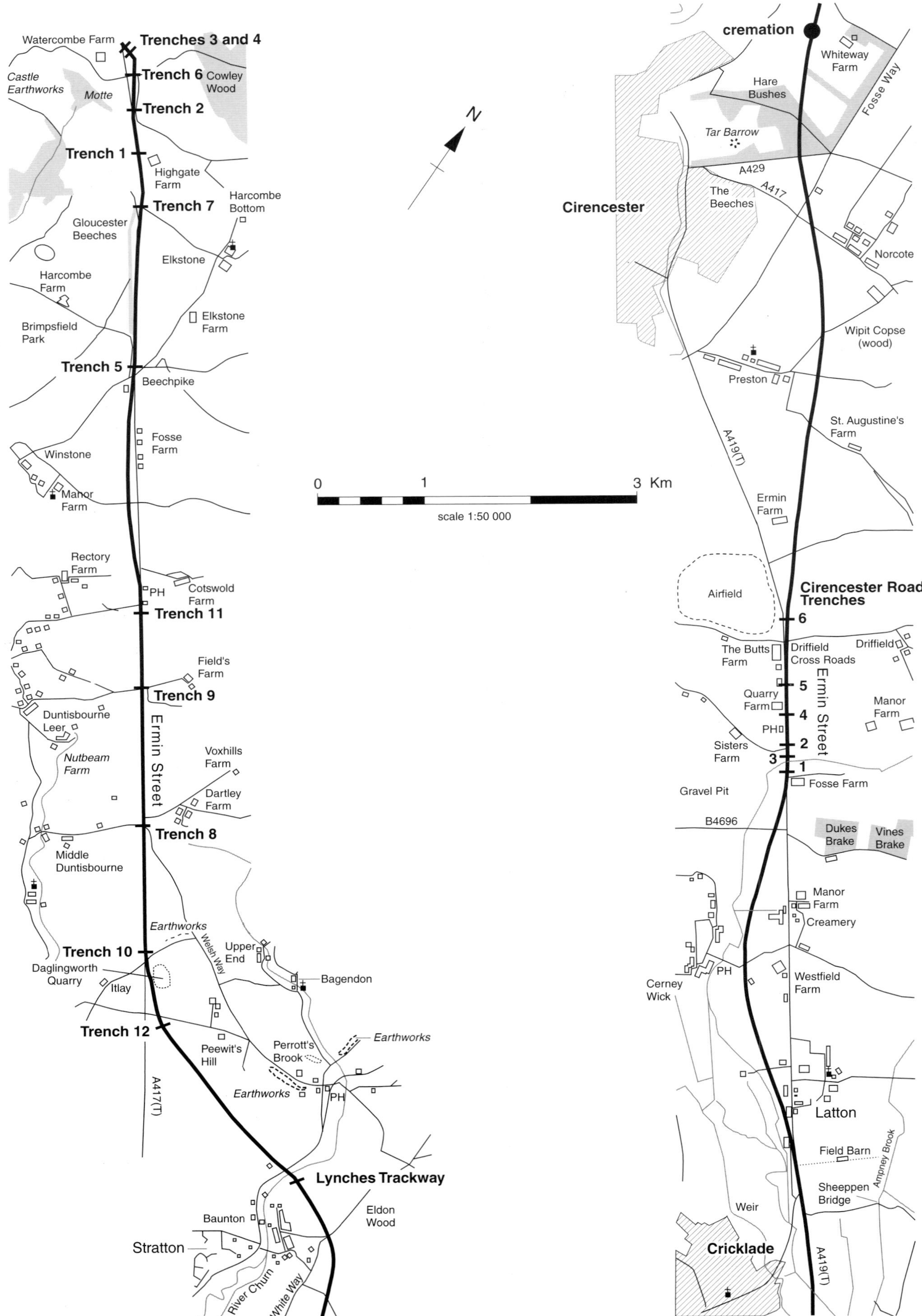


*Figure 5.1 Locations of Ermin Street sections.*

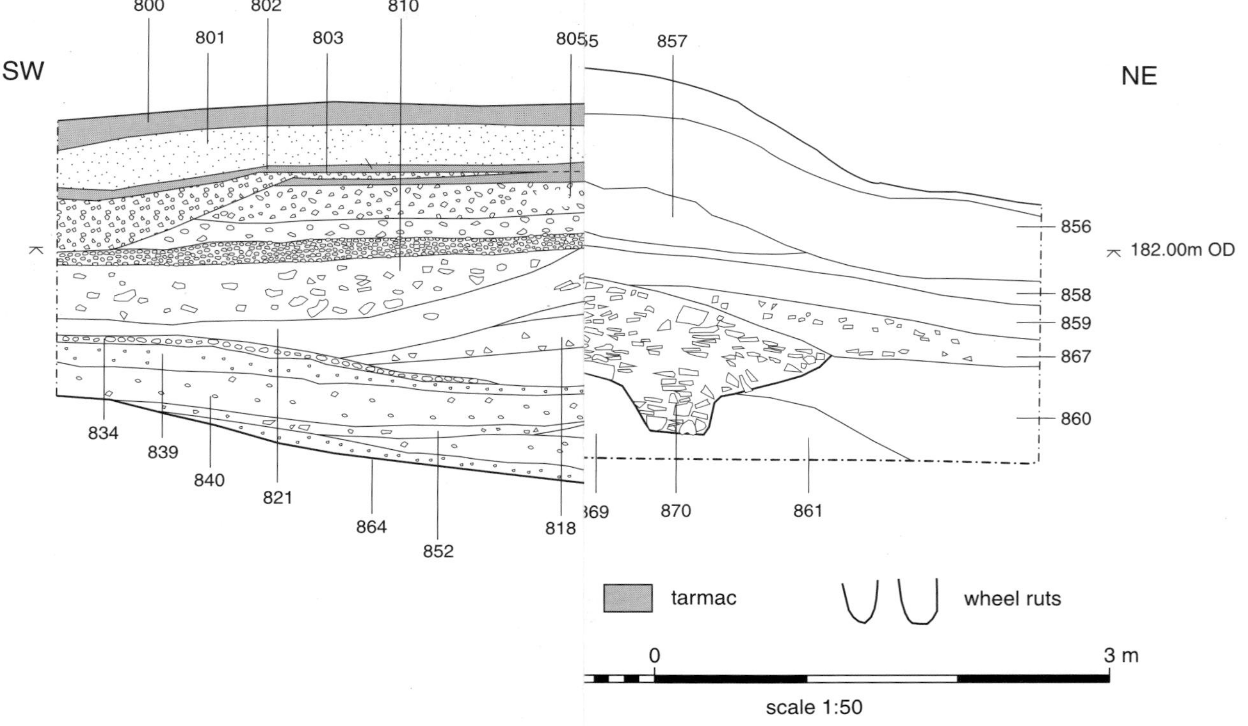


*Figure 5.2 Dartley Bottom, Trench 8, section.*

section

N
615
gravel make-up
13
616
617
618
613
622
619
619
639
641
638
613
626
627
644
643
658
676
250.50m OD
649
650
653
658
675
677
581
686
1
0
3 m
scale 1:50

d surfaces

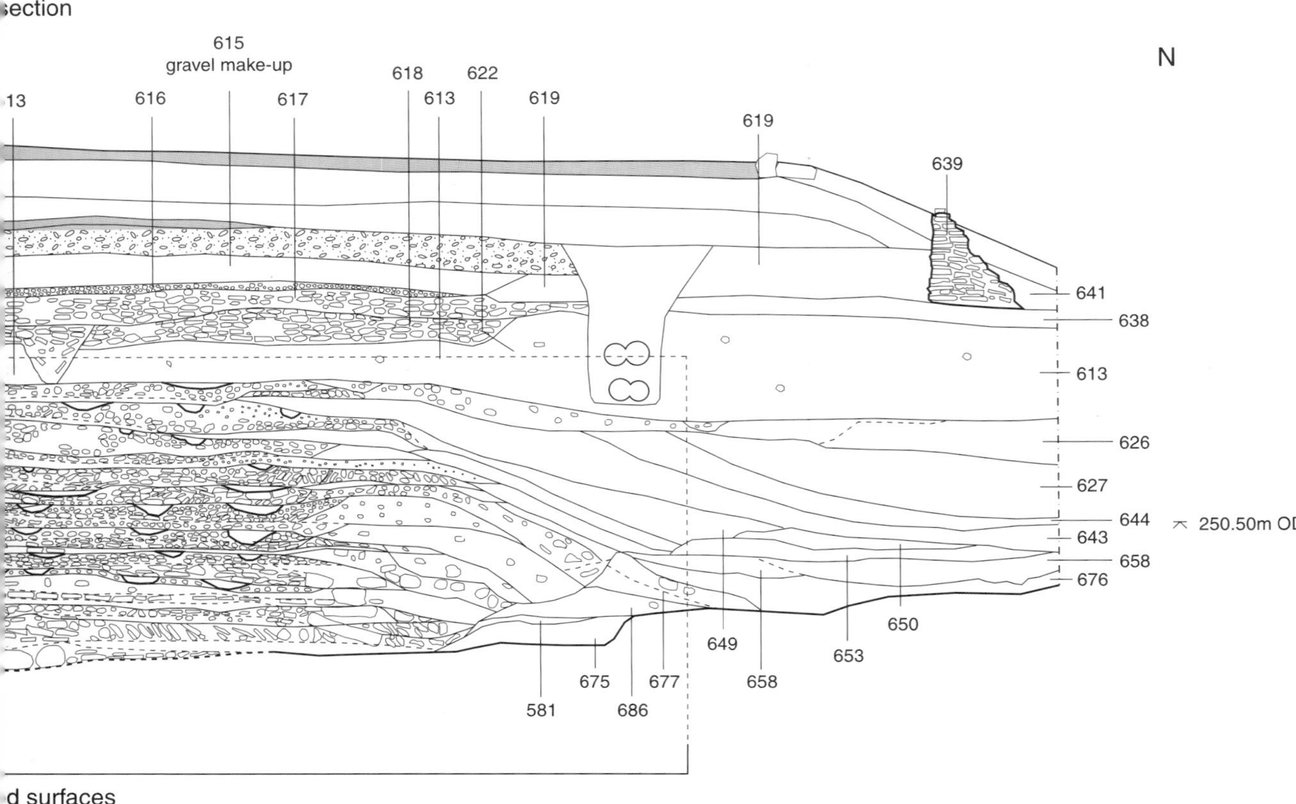

N
660
640
651
655
613
661
646
693
691
652
622
BT cable trench
644
643
649
250.50m OD
653
658
676
677
666
684
682
680
679
681
678
675
686
690
670
662
674
0
1 m
scale 1:25

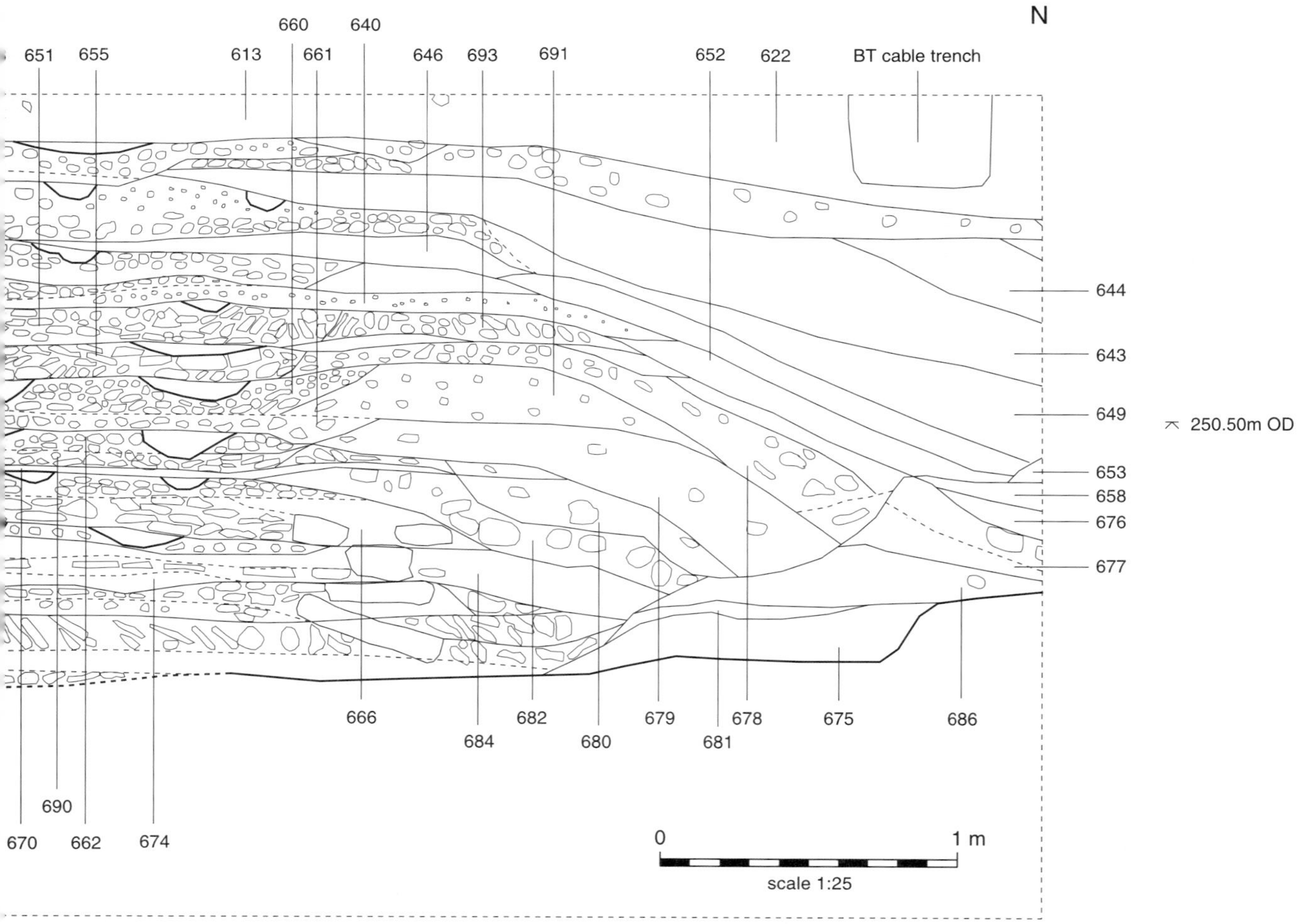

Plate 5.1 *Dartley Bottom, Trench 8. Roman road surface 871.*

potential problem with any sequence of roads where heavy use, and any reconstructions which involved digging down rather than building up, will result in the removal rather than the addition of stratigraphy.

To avoid excessive repetition a detailed description of each road section will not be presented here. The deeper sections at Dartley Bottom (Trench 8) and Cowley Underbridge (Trench 6) will be described in detail in order to establish the general sequence and characteristics of Roman and later road construction and use. The evidence from the other trenches will be brought in to augment and extrapolate these observations where possible.

### *Dartley Bottom (Trench 8)* (*Fig. 5.2, Plates 5.1–2*)

The sequence of road surfaces at Dartley Bottom was one of the most informative regarding the way in which variations in building technique can be shown to correspond to discontinuities in the sequence of roads (Fig. 5.2). There is, however, little evidence to aid the absolute dating of this sequence, which, furthermore remains singular enough to be unsuitable as a 'key' to the interpretation of the other sections.

The trench was situated south of the Burcombe Lane section (Trench 9). The Roman road here was constructed in the head of the valley which fell away towards the north. Snails from the buried colluvial soil, 877, indicate that woodland had existed in this area before the road was constructed (see Robinson, Chapter 8), although had the ground surface been truncated at all for road construction, it is possible that this reflects woodland which had been cleared some time earlier, rather than the immediate pre-road environment. The section does suggest some levelling of the ground, although this would seem unlikely to have been more than the minimum to provide a reasonably horizontal road base. It is therefore considered possible that the road was laid out through woodland. The initial road make-up layer, 881, was composed of limestone rubble bedded in clayey silt and capped with a surface of limestone gravel, 880. Later, a substantial amount of rubble and silt (875/879, 883) was imported to redress the slope at the northern edge of the road and raise the level of the surface (876). This may have been done to aid drainage since clayey lenses in the underlying layer, 882, suggest that the ground was occasionally subject to flooding.

The subsequent road was the most solidly constructed, with a base formed of tightly packed pitched stone, 874, capped with 'cobbled' surface 871. The two later surfaces, 851 and 842, were similar but laid on thin make-up layers, 866 and 865, which had the effect, intentional or otherwise, of increasing the camber of the road and narrowing its width.

The next phase of construction is the most difficult to understand. A substantial deposit of limestone rubble, 847, was used to raise and widen the road. This did not have a worn surface and it appears to have served as a make-up layer for surface 838 which was a single layer of worn 'cobbles'. Surface 838, however, extended for a considerable distance (over 3 m) to the north of 847 where it overlay a dark silt, 841. It seems that this extension to the surface, constructed on a fundamentally different base, could not be part of the road, unless it was simply not intended for the same sort of traffic as the 'main' part of the road. While the function of 838 cannot be resolved from this relatively small trench, it is unlikely that two techniques of construction for essentially the same road would have been employed. It is more probable that there are two separate constructions here, the first the rubble base 847 capped with 838 or an equivalent surface which had been worn away, and the second the extension of the road surface over layer 841. This can be assumed to be a deliberate surfacing rather than a spread of metalling from the main road, because of its width and because it extended up the slope. It is difficult to know whether this extension to the road was substantially later than the surfacing of the main road. Much depends on the interpretation of layer 841. This was a friable dark brown silt with only a small quantity of weathered limestone fragments. It was probably colluvial in origin, although it was interpreted in the field as a redeposited dump to support surface 838. It clearly butted 847, but if it were a deliberate deposition it need not considerably post-date that road make-up. If, however, it were interpreted as a natural colluvial accumulation, the dating could be substantially different. Three small sherds of medieval pottery from 841 suggest that surface 838 is medieval or later, but, given the equivocal nature of the evidence discussed, this need not imply a similar date for 847.

The next road surface in the sequence, 832, follows a substantial discontinuity. This is most noticeable in its position, a metre or more north of the earlier roads, but also in the intervening accumulation of silts (833 and 836) which put surface 838 out of use. The new road was only a little over 3 m wide, but was constructed on a substantial rubble base (835) up to 0.35 m thick, cut into the colluvium. The surface was heavily worn and deeply rutted. The succeeding three roads were constructed in a similar manner, with substantial dumps of rubble make-up, particularly on the southern side, which had the effect of widening the road in this direction. A sherd of pottery dating to between the 17th and 19th centuries from rubble layer 829 give some supporting indication that these roads are turnpike and later constructions.

Another road or track surface to the south (834), was contemporary with surfaces 832 or 830, but unlike them was without rutting. It was built upon a layer of clayey silt (839) which provided a slight camber but little solidity. A horseshoe from this layer suggests a post-medieval date for its construction. It appeared to be running approximately east-west and was probably a side-road, perhaps a surface of the drove road Welsh Way which crossed Ermin Street in this vicinity.

***Cowley Underbridge (Trench 6)*** *(Figs 5.3–4, Plates 5.3–4)*

The deepest sequence of road surfaces was found at Cowley Underbridge, where Ermin Street crossed the narrow valley 200 m south-east of Birdlip Quarry. The slightly oblique angle of the crossing meant that the road was constructed on a slope from north to south (Fig. 5.3). The ground within the valley was damp and the soil under the road (673) was found to contain waterlogged plant remains (see Pelling, Chapter 8). These indicated a predominantly open grassland environment, although with an arable and

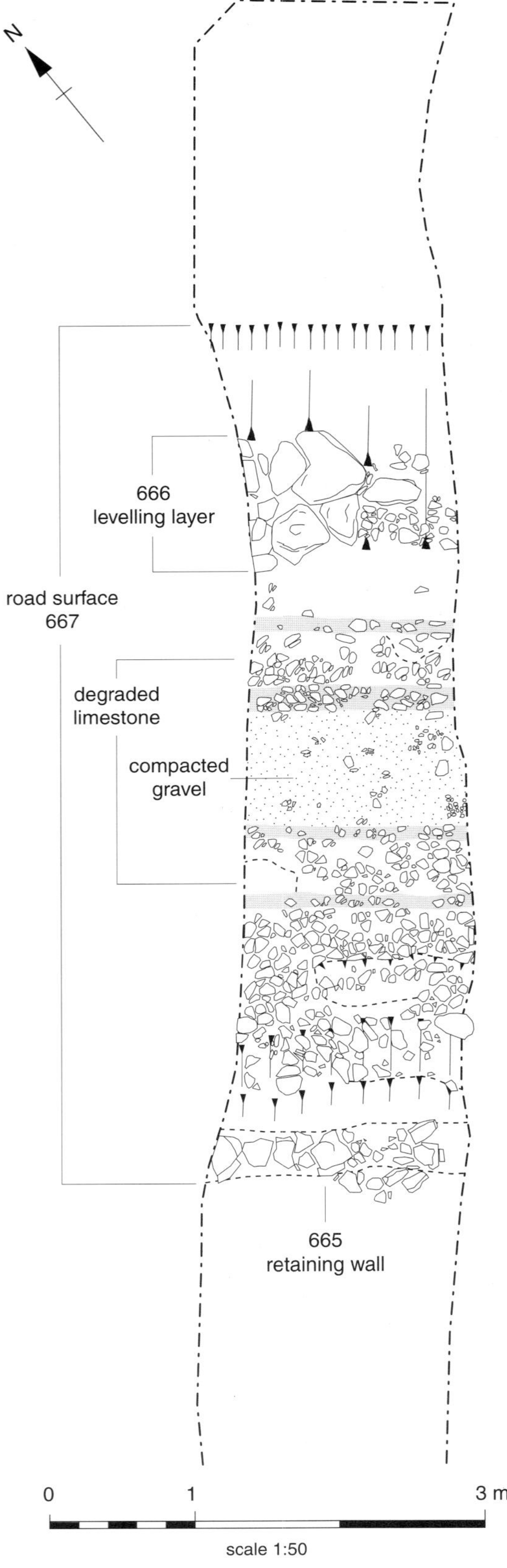


*Figure 5.4 Cowley Underbridge, Trench 6, plan.*

ruderal element to the flora. The preservation of these plants would suggest that the levelling of the ground for road building did not involve comprehensive de-turfing, and it is possible that the turf was removed from the top of the slope and used to raise the ground further down. Flecks of charcoal in the top of 673 may indicate that some of the vegetation in the road corridor was cleared by burning although this would not have been likely, or necessary, within the valley itself. It appears that the Roman road builders terraced the slope to the north in preparation for the construction. Deposits 675 and 686, interpreted as colluvium, appear to have been cut through and may have been deposited as a bank (deposits 650, 653) on the northern edge of the road to stop water running across its surface. There were no roadside ditches associated with this phase of construction. The first road make-up layer, 672, consisted of mixed limestone rubble in an orange-brown silty clay. This was capped by 671 which was composed of larger limestone slabs, many pitched at an angle, set in a light bluish grey clay. Slabs protruding from the surface of layer 671 were clearly incorporated into surface 669, which may have been a second phase of surfacing rather than the original one. This layer formed a central corridor, 3.6 m wide, of small rounded limestone 'cobbles' flanked by rather larger flat slabs. The Roman road was thus almost exactly 6 m wide at its base and up to 0.38 m deep. Wheel ruts in the surface of 669 were relatively broad and shallow.

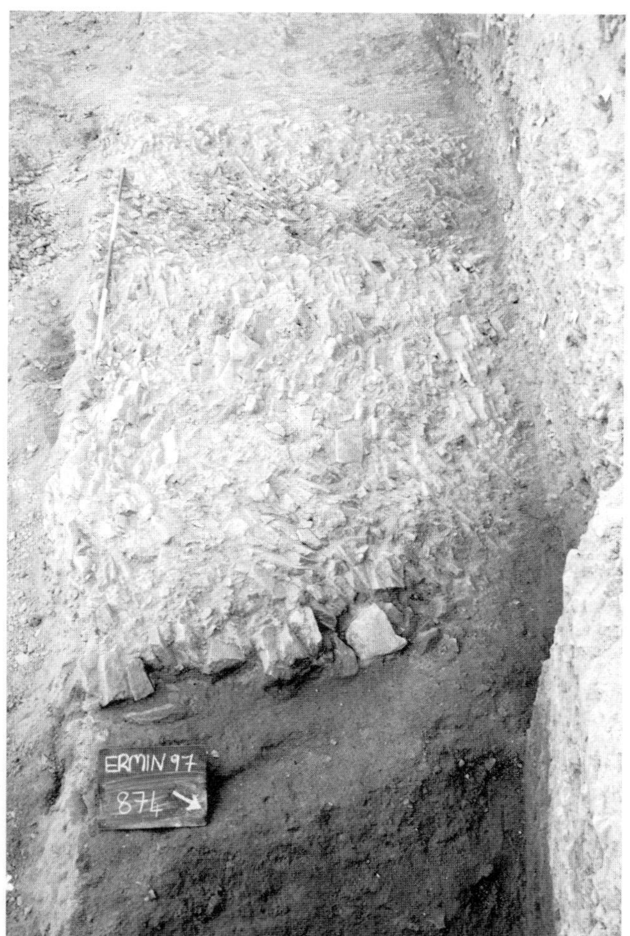


*Plate 5.2 Dartley Bottom, Trench 8. Pitched stone foundation (874) for road surface 871.*

The silt deposits 636, 637, 645 and 685, to the south of the road were mixtures of redeposited natural silt with some stone rubble and appear to have been deposited to consolidate the edge of the road and to prevent the road base from spreading laterally under the pressure of traffic. A total of ten sherds (76 g) from a single early Severn Valley Ware vessel dating to the later 1st century AD derived from deposit 636. This deposit was stratigraphically earlier than road surface 669, and provides the most conclusive evidence from any of the excavations for the presence of the original Ermin Street. The care taken over the construction of the road and the distinction between the road foundation and surface, appear to be typical of the early Roman road. In this instance it is clear that there were two make up layers resulting in an extremely solid graded stone *agger*, with a camber such that the centre of the road was *c.* 0.1 m higher than the edges.

The difficulty with understanding the Cowley Underbridge section lies in deciding where the highest Roman surface lies. The section shows a sequence of ten road surfaces directly above 669 before a layer of silt, 613, appears to indicate that the road in this location went out of use. The sequence of roads shows similarities of construction technique, although there are also some distinctive individual characteristics. In general, each road surface was composed of small limestone 'cobbles' on a base of larger stones, which in turn were bedded into a levelling layer of clayey silt laid on the earlier surface. Surface 664 was associated with a drystone retaining wall, 665, on the south side. On the north side the terrace cut into the colluvium acted to prevent the road spreading in this direction. Higher up, surface 655 was observed to have kerbs of larger stones, although it is possible that this was a fortuitous exposure of the larger foundation stones by erosion, rather than a deliberate technique (as with surface 667, Figure 5.4). A road wash deposit (634) associated with this surface yielded a number of sherds (40 g) of early Severn Valley Ware of the 1st to 2nd centuries. This is suggestive of a relatively early date for this surface, particularly as the sherds may have come from a single thin-walled vessel broken in antiquity and are, perhaps, unlikely to have been redeposited. However, this dating evidence cannot be regarded as conclusive.

The subsequent road surface (651) was again well-constructed and had a distinctive edging of pitched stone and smaller rubble (693). This had the effect of widening the road to about 4.5 m, although only the central 3.0 m over the more solid base was rutted. The road was also distinctive in having a relatively large quantity of burnt stone in the make-up. A Roman cart linch pin came from surface 651. The southern edge of the road may also have been reinforced at this time with a dump of brown clay (633), although this

*Plate 5.3 Roman road surface 669 at Cowley Underbridge (Trench 6).*

may have belonged to a later phase. It appears that the friable road wash silts 634 were cut back to an almost vertical face to receive this deposit.

Above surface 651 the road was constructed to a poorer standard. Surface 648 comprised a thin layer of cobbles on a sandy base. This was replaced by 647, consisting of a relatively thick rubble dump the surface of which had been worn smooth. There was no evidence of cobbling. Surfaces 625 and 623 again consisted of cobbling over a base of larger stones, but were poorly constructed and heavily worn.

After the deposition of silt, 613, the sequence again continues when road foundation 618 was dug into this deposit directly above the earlier road surfaces and to the same width. This became worn and was later repaired and slightly widened (617). This late road is clearly post-medieval and is distinguished from the Roman roads by the fact that the road foundation was dug into the underlying deposits. There was no dating evidence from 618 nor from the underlying silt 613. Below the silt, road surface 623 contained a horseshoe of probable late medieval or post-medieval date and a fragment of horn beaker (cat. 660) of 17th- to 19th- century date. This suggests that the latest Roman surface lay below 623, although it may have been a late Roman surface which had continued in use into the post-medieval period. There is nothing in the construction of 623 to indicate that it was not Roman.

**Discussion**

There can be little doubt that the earliest roads in Trenches 6 and 8 were Roman military constructions. They were built on solid rubble foundations up to 0.4 m thick and capped with limestone metalling. The road surface was about 4 m wide. Similar constructions were found in Trenches 10, 5 and 9 and in the Dower's Lane watching brief. Gloucester Beeches, Trench 7 (Fig. 5.5) was the exception in this, as in other respects, as the first *agger* (756) was relatively slight and composed of smaller stones. It is probable that the solidity of the road foundation was related as much to ground conditions as to the prescribed method of construction. It is known from excavations in other parts of the country that the size and composition of the *agger* could vary substantially without any apparent reason (Taylor 1979, 67–69). From the Burford Road sections (see below and Figs 5.9–5.10) it appears that metalling was sometimes laid directly on bedrock where this was considered solid enough.

It is apparent that Ermin Street was repaired or reconstructed on a number of occasions during the Roman period. The Dartley Bottom section (Fig. 5.2) indicates that there were at least five Roman constructions here, the third of which, with an *agger* of pitched stone, was perhaps the most solid. Of the eleven road surfaces at Cowley Underbridge (Fig. 5.3), the first seven (up to surface 651) are almost certainly

*Plate 5.4 The earliest Roman road surface (669) beneath Cowley Underbridge (Trench 6).*

Roman, with the pottery from layer 634 suggesting a date for the sixth surface (655) no later than the 2nd century. Surface 651 used pitched stone in its construction, but the technique was mainly used in the road edging. It is worth noting that the sixth road construction at Burcombe Lane (Trench 9), 1 m above natural subsoil, was also of pitched stone capped with metalling, as was the fifth construction identified in the watching brief at Dower's Lane Underbridge, 1.2 m above natural. There was also some pitched stone in the road foundation 1036 at Itlay Underpass (Trench 10) towards the top of the sequence (Fig. 5.6). There is no evidence that these are not Roman. It is possible that the use of pitched stone was a technique particularly prevalent in the later Roman period in this area. At the Birdlip Quarry settlement it was used from the later 3rd century (and probably not before), although the domestic context of this site may not be comparable with the road. Even in the later period Ermin Street seems likely to have been constructed either directly by military engineers or civil engineers trained in the military method (Taylor 1979, 52).

Pitched stone was used for the earliest road at The Highwayman (Fig. 5.7) where the *agger* (533) was carefully constructed and sealed with redeposited local clay (532). Elsewhere in this trench the use of pitched stone was not evident and it was absent from Gloucester Beeches (Trench 7). The number of Roman surfaces in Trenches 5, 7 and 10 is open to question. At Gloucester Beeches (Fig. 5.5) there are likely to have been no more than two (733 and 771/734) although the later wheel ruts makes this difficult to assess. A post-medieval horse shoe came from rut 770. Itlay Underpass (Fig. 5.6, Plates 5.5–6) and The Highwayman (Fig. 5.7) both show an uninterrupted sequence of road surfaces until they are truncated by the modern road. It is unclear how many are Roman but at Itlay Underpass the use of kerb stones as a revetment for surface 1051 (robbed on the south-west side) is similar to the technique used for surface 664 at Cowley Underbridge, and it seems reasonable to assume that this was also a Roman construction. If the later use of pitched stone in 1036 is equivalent to 651 it would indicate a similar long sequence of Roman construction at Itlay Underpass. The evidence, then, may suggest a systematic rebuilding of Ermin Street later in the Roman period, but it is not conclusive, particularly as pitched stone was used in a likely post-medieval context at Burford Road Trench 3 (layer 309, Fig. 5.9).

Despite these reservations, it is clear from the excavations at Birdlip Quarry with Trench 3 of the Ermin Street sections (Fig. 4.101–4.102) that road construction did continue into the 4th century, albeit in a more rudimentary fashion. At this site the lateral expansion of Ermin Street with the deposition of a layer of cobbles can be dated reasonably securely to *c.* AD 320–330. The context of this development is unclear, but the extent of the cobbling south from the roadside settlement, up to 10 m wide and parallel to Ermin Street proper, suggests that this was more than a local surfacing related to site access. At Field's Farm, 6 km to the south, a cobbled surface was found to have been laid over an infilled quarry pit (Fig. 4.3). The pit was probably connected with the construction of Ermin Street and the cobbling certainly appears to represent a later widening of the road. The intact surface was exposed for a width of 1.4 m. Since the original road was not encountered it is unclear how wide this surface was, but a projection of the road from Ermin Street Trench 9 indicates that this cobbling may have extended 8 m from the main alignment. An early 4th-century coin (cat. 217) from the surface of the cobbling suggests that it may have been laid around this time. The location of this road surface at some distance from a contemporaneous settlement supports the suggestion from Birdlip Quarry that the road surfacing was not associated with access to the settlement. It also appears to have been unrelated to the funerary monument at Field's Farm whose ditch had probably silted up by the 3rd century. In addition, a worn cobbled surface at the margin of Ermin Street was recorded in Trench 1 at Daglingworth. Its proximity to the post-medieval dewpond in this trench (Chapter 6) suggested that the two may have been associated but the surface was undated. It is worth noting that a 4th-century coin (cat. 219) came from the overlying layer. At Sly's Wall South remnants of peripheral cobbling could not

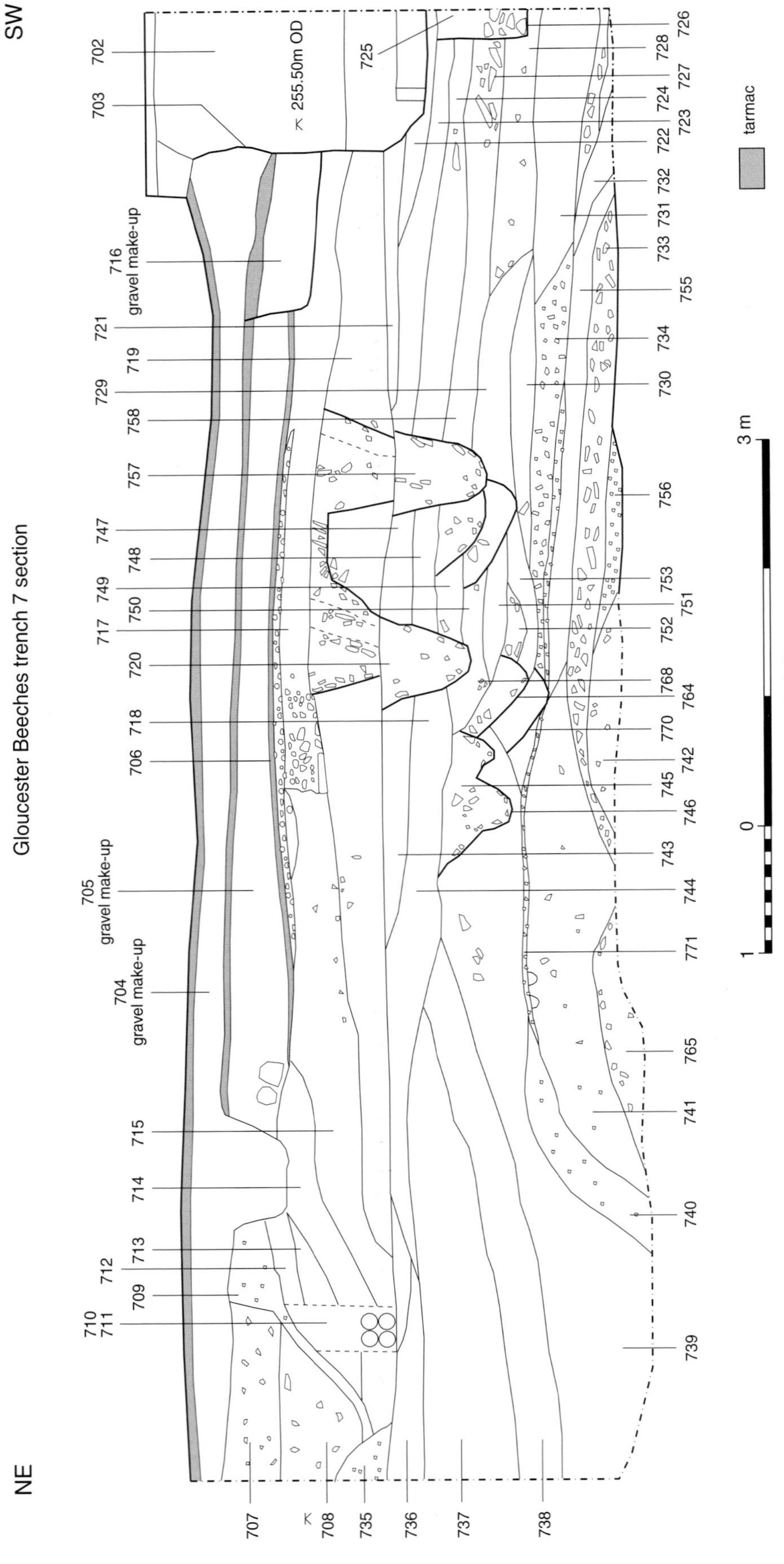

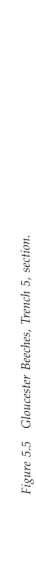

*Figure 5.5 Gloucester Beeches, Trench 5, section.*

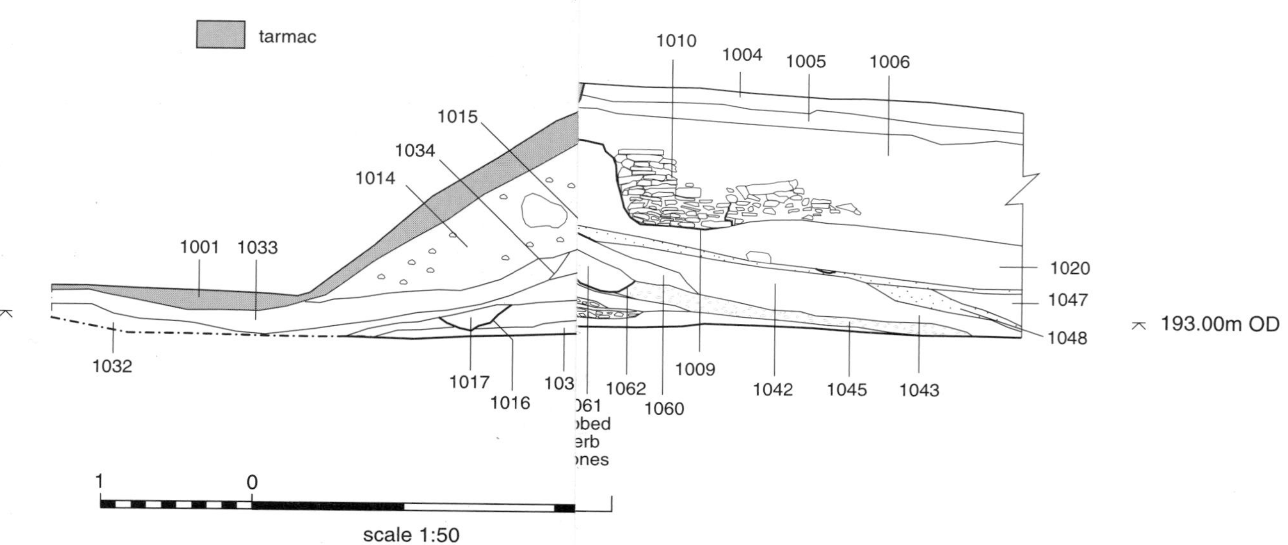


*Figure 5.6 Itlay Underpass, Trench 7, section.*

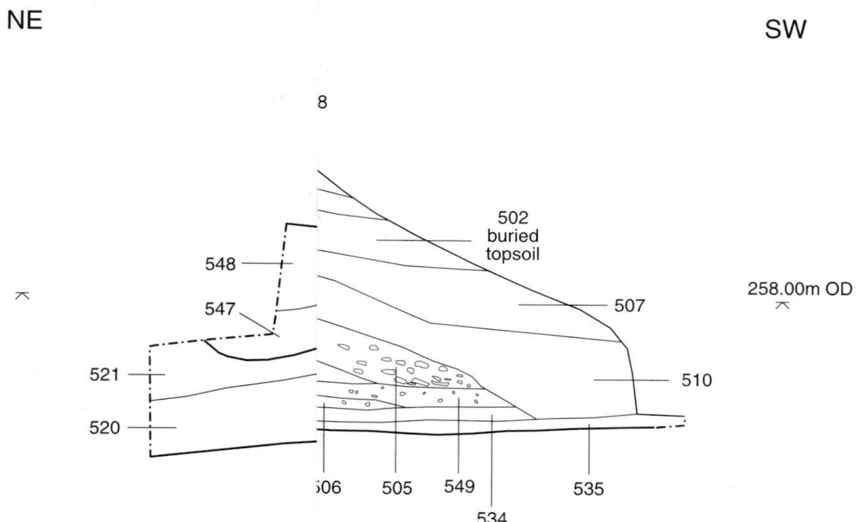


*Figure 5.7 The Highwayman, Trench 10, section.*

*Plate 5.5 The earliest Roman road surface (1066/1067) in Trench 10 at Italy Underpass.*

clearly be a late Roman road, although this does remain a possibility.

At Cowley Underbridge (Fig. 5.3), surface 648 (conceivably but not demonstrably 4th-century in date) was a poor quality cobbled surface, but it did not widen the road. The Gloucester Beeches section further south (Fig. 5.5) is difficult to interpret. There was a widening of the road with surface 771 and this was directly overlain by a thick deposit of silt 739, so the surface may have been late Roman. The trench at The Highwayman (Fig. 5.7) gave little clue as to the date of any of the road surfaces above the earliest one, although layer 505 appears to represent a widening of the road, albeit on the other (south-west) side. The Dartley Bottom trench provides the most intriguing evidence for late road widening in the form of cobbled surface 838, but the medieval dating evidence from 841, while contestable, could identify this as a post-medieval surface rather than a 4th-century one (Fig. 5.2). The other road sections, including the Burcombe Lane trench, just 120 m south-east of Field's Farm, yielded no useful evidence on this question, probably due to truncation. The main road sections therefore give no reliable support to the suggestion of a general road widening in the 4th century although the question still remains open. It may be argued that these sections, the points where the road crossed dry valleys, should be viewed as special cases where road widening would have been less practicable and therefore less likely even if it had been undertaken on the flatter ground. The question as to why widening the road should be considered necessary at all is a further enigma. It may have been an alternative to strengthening the main body of the road by allowing an alternative or more dispersed passage, although this would appear to be an unconventional, and perhaps, unlikely response to the problem. Another possibility is that it was a pavement to one side of the road for horses and pedestrians. Either intention carries the implication that the road was considered important at this time although its repair was to a lower standard and, as far as can be judged, not influenced by Roman engineering textbook practice.

The difficulty of understanding the middle sequence of roads at Dartley Bottom (Fig. 5.2) has been discussed. The clear discontinuity above the make-up/metalling 847/838 would suggest that this was the latest Roman construction and that it was followed by a period of soil accumulation. The translation of this sequence to the Cowley Underbridge section implies a sequence of eleven Roman road surfaces before a standstill in construction and soil accumulation. However, as well as medieval pottery from 841 at Dartley Bottom (which is unhelpful but can be accommodated in this interpretation) there are also two horseshoe nails from surface 842 which suggests that this was the road surface inherited in the medieval and post-medieval period, and that the overlying road (847) was almost certainly of turnpike date. With this alternative date, the re-alignment and narrowing of the turnpike road with the later construction of 835, then needs explaining.

If the implications of a turnpike road lying directly on a Roman road surface extended to the section at Cowley Underbridge (Fig. 5.3), similar difficulties of interpretation are introduced. Here, the turnpike road

*Plate 5.6 Italy Underpass, Trench 7, section.*

construction equivalent to 847 is likely to be 647. This is different from the underlying roads in that it consisted of a relatively thick layer of rubble with a smoothed and rutted surface, but without evidence of metalling. It also appears to have been associated with a consolidation of the southern road margin in the form of a dump of clay 633. It is similar to layer 530 at The Highwayman, although they are not necessarily equivalent and neither contained dating evidence. The later surface, 623, was almost certainly used in the post-medieval period, but if it were a turnpike repair rather than the surviving Roman surface, the layer of silt (613) before the presumably 19th-century reconstruction (618) again needs to be explained.

One key to interpreting these sections is to understand how the post-medieval roads were constructed and what evidence to look for. The course of Ermin Street from Cirencester was on the principal route between London and Gloucester in the 17th century (Albert 1972, 36), an importance which it had presumably held since the Roman period. It may therefore have been repaired at any time from then using the traditional parish-based system of labour which was formalised by statute in 1555 (Jackman 1962, 33–36). However, the lack of a significant volume of wheeled traffic before about 1600, coupled with the comparatively high quality of the original Roman construction in this section of the road, makes it unlikely that any substantial repairs were undertaken until the 17th century at the earliest. Even then, these are likely to have been *ad hoc*, intermittent and of variable quality, and may have involved merely patching the Roman road where it was considered necessary. The evidence for extensive wheel rutting in all the roadside excavations of the project, which included the erosion of a hollow way at Middle Duntisbourne, suggests that had any road repairs been undertaken before the turnpike era, they were entirely inadequate.

The importance of this route between London and Gloucester is reflected in the comparatively early date at which most of it was turnpiked. The section from Gloucester to the top of Birdlip Hill was one of the earliest turnpikes in the country (by an Act of 1696/7) and other sections of the route, via Lechlade and Henley, followed. The road from Cirencester to Lechlade was turnpiked in 1727. The road between Birdlip and Cirencester, turnpiked in 1747, completed the route. Whether the turnpiking led to any substantial reconstruction of the road is open to question. Road construction in the early stages of turnpiking was not necessarily based upon sound engineering principles, most of the effort of road maintenance being expended on measures to impose restrictions on road users (Albert 1972, 132). It was only in the later 18th century that a consensus on best practice began to emerge. This became more formalised in the early 19th century, particularly under the influence of J L McAdam and the pressure of official concerns, such as those of the Board of Agriculture and the Post Office. With regard to the operation of the Turnpike Trusts, Albert (1972, 138) states that:

'Although construction of foundations and attention to road form were an important part of the repair procedure of certain trusts, most trust repair was concerned primarily with placement of large quantities of materials upon the road. The majority of repair orders dealt with the acquisition of materials, and carting and material costs generally comprised the greatest proportion of repair expenditure. However there were but few directives made which stipulated how the materials were to be applied ... This suggests that on many roads the placement of materials may have been as haphazard as some critics have claimed.'

It is possible, then, that the earliest turnpike road consisted of dumps of rubble, such as layers 847 and 647 (Figs 5.2 and 5.3), upon the worn Roman surface. Only in the early 19th century were more fundamental road constructions undertaken, involving the more marked elevation of the road surface at Cowley Underbridge (618) and Dartley Bottom (832). The dump, 719, at Gloucester Beeches may also be identified with this phase, although the material was almost pure silt. All these constructions can be seen as following the methods of J L McAdam whose aim has been summarised by Albert as 'the construction of a smooth, elastic road surface formed upon a dry subsoil' (Albert 1972, 142). McAdam's main principles of construction were that the road should be raised above the level of the surrounding ground to aid drainage, with the addition of side ditches if necessary; and that the road surface should be made as impermeable as possible by rolling or ramming in a surface of metalling. He gave less importance than Telford did to building the foundation of solid stone which he considered both expensive and unnecessary, for he said that a properly consolidated road surface formed upon a well-drained subsoil could support any weight. In the interests of economy he also did not construct roads wider than necessary for the volume of traffic, and 14 to 16 feet (4.5–5.0 m) of metalled surface was normally considered sufficient (Jackman 1962, 276, footnote 1).

If these elevated road surfaces at Cowley Underbridge and Dartley Bottom mark an early 19th-century road improvement, silt deposits 613 and 833 would have to be seen as imported rather than accumulated material. There was no real indication that this was the case, although since the 'McAdam method' recommended the use of cleaned or sifted materials, it is possible that the resultant homogeneity of a road embankment would appear similar to a natural accumulation. Certainly, the clean dumps of silt on the Roman road surface at Birdlip Quarry (Area 1, context 1206; section 270 Area 6, context 1163, section 268 – Fig. 4.100; and possibly Ermin Street Trench 4, context 404) would suggest that this recommendation was put into practice on Ermin Street.

The successive rebuilding of the 19th-century road at Dartley Bottom is noteworthy. Five cobbled road surfaces can be identified before the first, relatively narrow, tarmac surface (806) which was probably laid shortly after 1900 (Trinder 1992, 632). Due to the truncation of the upper road surfaces in the other sections, it is unclear how typical this sequence might be, but it may be seen in the local context of the difficulties posed in negotiating this particular valley with a road of acceptable width and gradient.

The conclusion from these sections is that well-constructed Roman road surfaces continued to be laid on top of the original military road probably into the 2nd century or even into the 3rd century AD. This resulted in a stratified sequence up to 1 m thick in places. There may have been some late Roman surfacing of a more rudimentary nature, but the use of the Roman road throughout the next 1500 years with *ad hoc* repairs as required and when resources allowed makes it impossible to identify the latest Roman surface with any confidence. In the turnpike era more large-scale repairs were undertaken, but in the early years these were probably no more than deposits of rubble on the worn road surface. These are thought to have included layers 847 at Dartley Bottom and 647 at Cowley Underpass. The late 18th and early 19th centuries marked a more fundamental reconstruction of Ermin Street on banks of imported silt into which the road foundation was inserted. This had the effect of improving drainage and easing the gradient while appreciably widening the road corridor, although the metalled surface itself was still relatively narrow.

## ERMIN STREET TRENCHES SOUTH OF CIRENCESTER *(Fig. 5.8)*

### Introduction

Six trenches were excavated from the new Driffield Junction to Fosse Farm on Cirencester Road (Fig. 5.8), in order to investigate archaeological deposits associated with Ermin Street. The positioning of the trenches followed topsoil stripping which was monitored to establish areas of greatest archaeological potential, taking into account the depth of the engineering formation level which was not to be exceeded. All the trenches were outside the road corridor of the old A419. Only one trench (Trench 3) revealed a fairly well-constructed, rutted road surface, which was almost certainly Roman. The other trenches revealed little of archaeological interest.

In addition to these trenches the margin of Ermin Street was revealed at Street Farm, Latton. This is described below.

### Cirencester Road Trench 3

#### *Description*

The trench was 12 m long by 2.2 m wide excavated perpendicular to the modern road. A metalled road surface (3004) was encountered under overburden. Only the eastern edge of the road was revealed and indicated that the road was over 7 m wide. Wheel ruts indicated that the road ran at an angle to the modern

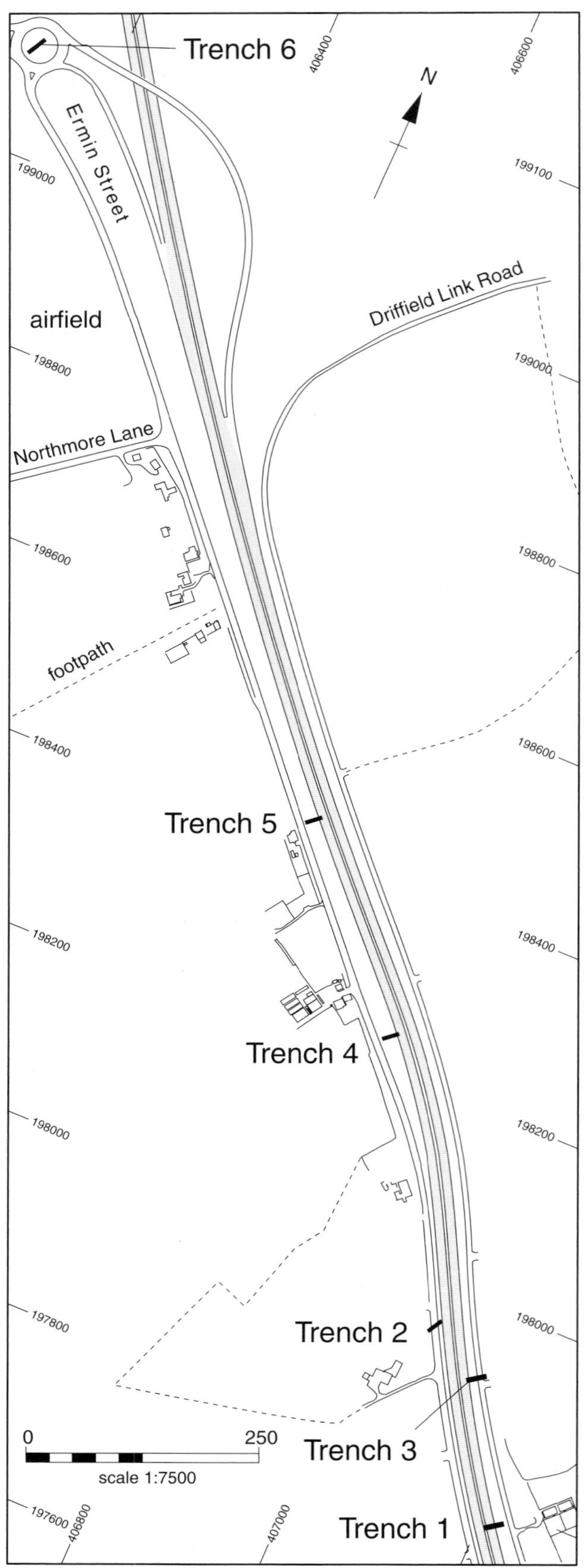


*Figure 5.8 Cirencester Road, Trench locations.*

one, in a more east-west direction. The road was built upon dumped deposits of clay and stone, up to 0.12 m thick, which rested upon natural alluvial clay. Above this was a foundation layer (3005) which was a dump of 60% small and medium stone supporting the metalling. The foundation and metalling reached a maximum thickness of about 0.25 m over the dumped deposits. The road was therefore a solid construction although the *agger* was relatively slight and there was no noticeable camber.

### *Discussion*

It is not surprising that five of the trenches failed to encounter Roman Ermin Street since it had been presumed to lie under the modern A419. From the results of the trenching it can perhaps be assumed that, for the most part, it does. In view of this, the road in Trench 3 was somewhat unexpected. There is no reason to suppose that it was not Ermin Street, although it lacked the depth of deposits and re-surfacings which were evident in the trenches excavated north of Cirencester. This may be due to its different topographic position or history of use. The construction was not substantially different from that found in the sections of the road excavated north of Cricklade (Wainwright 1959, fig. 4), where the road was about 8 m wide and 0.5 m high and apparently only of one phase. It was also similar to the section of road excavated at Weavers Bridge in Stage 2 Evaluation Trench 1 (CAT 1994) which was about 7 m wide with a very slight clay *agger.*

Another puzzle is the slightly different alignment of the road. This may be explained by the local topography since Trench 3 was positioned in a shallow valley where the road crosses a small stream (Muttleford Stream on the map of Andrews and Drury 1773) just north of Fosse Farm. The alluvial clay in this trench contrasted with the natural limestone geology in all the other trenches. It is possible that the road deviated in order to follow the most suitable ground in this, presumably rather boggy, area. It is further possible that this road represents one of an unknown number of alternative routes across this valley – one which later became abandoned as the road followed a new course just to the south. This is one possible explanation for the lack of evidence for re-surfacing.

A projection of the road eastwards would indicate that it increasingly parted company from the A419 for a short but unknown distance before being re-aligned in a more southerly direction, possibly closer to Fosse Farm than any of the current roads. The area excavations at Fosse Farm, on the other side of the A419, revealed no trace of the Roman road, although it would not have been expected this far south-west in any case. In a westerly direction a projected alignment follows the south course of the A419 Cirencester Road tolerably well. The absence of roadside ditches from all the trenches here suggests that they were never dug in this section of Ermin Street, although it does not prove it since the other five trenches, as well as the

Fosse Farm and Lower Street Furlong excavations, may have been positioned too far from the Roman road.

### Ermin Street at Street Farm

The edge of Roman Ermin Street was exposed in the excavations at Street Farm, Latton on the extreme south-east margin of the site. It was observed running for 33 m. Hand excavation in a 3 m-wide section (Transect 1) examined the gravel *agger* to a width of 2.2 m. The construction was found to be about 0.4 m thick with a slight camber. It overlay a buried soil.

The *agger* was constructed with a series of six compacted gravel layers. These were very clean and showed no signs of wear. Similar bands of natural gravel were seen in the sides of nearby quarry pits reinforcing the suggestion that the road here reflected a single phase of construction, with gravel laid down as it was excavated from nearby pits. The underlying soil was a reddish brown, almost stone-free clay loam. There was no evidence to date the construction of the road. In Transect 2 quarry pitting of probable Roman date was examined. This was much disturbed by later quarrying, but appeared to represent linear quarrying associated with the construction of the road.

Little of the Roman road was exposed. As it survived it appeared to represent a single phase of construction, but there was no evidence of a road surface and it appeared that the original surface or surfaces had been truncated. It therefore remains unclear what the sequence of construction and repair was on this section of road.

## BURFORD ROAD SECTIONS *(Figs. 5.9–10)*

### Introduction

The excavations at Burford Road, Cirencester, comprised two long transects, each measuring *c.* 50 m by 4 m, positioned to obtain cross-sections through the modern road in order to examine its precursors - in particular the Roman Fosse Way (Fig. 3.28). The work was conducted in two phases to allow for road closure and the diversion of traffic along a temporary road. Initial excavations were undertaken in Trenches 1 and 2 to the south of the A419 and in Trenches 3 and 4 to the north of the road. The central sections (Trenches 5 and 6) came in the second phase and completed two continuous transects through the road and its surrounds. The eastern transect thus comprised Trenches 1, 5 and 3 (Fig. 5.9) and the western one Trenches 2, 6 and 4 (Fig. 5.10).

The OAU trenches were located in the area of CAT evaluation trenches 512, 513, 514 and 515 (CAT 1991a). While these were unable to section Burford Road itself, some evidence was obtained to suggest the presence of the Roman road and roadside ditches/quarries as well as roads and quarries of the turnpike and later eras. It is not the intention to re-examine this evidence in detail, although some comments are warranted in the light of the OAU excavations, particularly as the evaluation results have been included in a recent synthesis of the archaeology of Cirencester (Darvill and Gerrard 1994, 53).

### General results

One of the main features common to both transects was the substantial loss of ground on the southern side of the road due to post-medieval quarrying. This impression is exaggerated by the depth of made ground under the modern road. Even so, in Trench 2/6/4 a projection of the surface of the bedrock from beneath the modern road suggests that up to 2.5 m of ground has been lost (Fig. 5.10). This may, in fact, be an underestimate since it is unclear whether the original surface of the bedrock is evident anywhere in Trench 2. In Trench 3 the depth of quarrying may have been shallower, but not a great deal. To the north of the A419, there had been less quarrying, although post-medieval quarry 415 (Trench 4) had truncated the earliest road surface in this transect (410) and removed the ground to the north for a distance of over 6 m. It may have been the same feature as the slightly narrower quarry found in Evaluation Trench 514, about 10 m to the west (Fig. 3.28), and was about the same width as the post-medieval quarry in Evaluation Trench 513 to the east which again cut the earliest road surfaces. There therefore appears to have been substantial linear quarrying on this side of the road in the post-medieval period, although not on the scale of that to the south. This has undoubtedly affected the survival of Roman features.

In Trench 3 the shallow quarry 319 was almost certainly Roman, but remains the only feature in the current excavations with convincing evidence for a date this early. The road surfaces themselves lacked any such evidence. In Trench 2, the potsherds from the quarries 204 and 213 on the southern side of the A429 were exclusively Roman, although, taking account of the more recent ground loss here, it is unclear whether quarries of this size are likely to be of Roman date. Evaluation Trench 512 yielded exclusively Roman pottery from a surprising depth (more than 3 m below the modern surface) and it is seems likely that there was a Roman quarry here, although the excavations were too limited to substantiate this and, since the depth to bedrock remained unrevealed, it was unclear how deep the original features might have been. A Roman roadside ditch was identified in Evaluation Trench 514, although there is a problem with post-medieval material which may have been intrusive. In Evaluation Trench 515 the presence of a Roman roadside ditch was also asserted on the grounds of morphology and alignment, although there were no finds. The evidence for Roman activity in this area therefore remains slight and there has been significant truncation by later features.

Only 99 sherds (696 g) of pottery, from 17 contexts, were recovered. They dated to the Roman and post-medieval periods. The Roman pottery dated predominantly to the 2nd to 4th centuries AD and the post-medieval material was mainly 18th-century or later. There were a number of other finds, including nails, horseshoes and miscellaneous iron objects, and some brick and tile. Most of this material was unhelpful for dating purposes.

### Trench descriptions

A similar sequence of road surfaces and associated deposits were encountered in both trenches. In Trench 1/3/5 the earliest definable road construction, 553, overlay silts 529 and 573 (Plate 5.7). This was heavily rutted, the ruts from this surface probably causing the apparent rutting in silt layer 529 which, however, is less likely to have been used as a road surface. It is unclear how well this road was originally constructed. The only evidence for road foundation was on the southern edge where surface 575 was laid on a base of small rubble and silt. It is possible that this was a better preserved remnant of 553 which had been intensively churned elsewhere. To the north, a thin layer of stones, 317, over 325 appears to have been at least partly contemporary with 553 but perhaps a later extension. It was possibly as much as 6 m wide. There were no finds from the road layers themselves but the overlying greyish silts 535 and 320 contained a fragment of bottle glass, two clay pipe stems and a horseshoe fragment. In Trench 2/6/4 the equivalent road construction, 661 and perhaps 673, were limited to the area overlying surface 410/663. The later road appears to have been laid after cutting into accumulated silts 409 and 620. The surviving evidence indicates that this road was only about 3 m wide, although it is possible that its extent to the south was removed when the make-up to the subsequent road, 621, was prepared. Two farthings of Charles II (1660–85) came from 620 (cat. 223–224). This is important dating evidence since the coins were found close together and are likely to have been associated, ruling out any question of residuality. At face value, this gives a quite precise *terminus post quem* for road surface 661.

Road 621 was a far more substantial construction. Preparatory works appear to have included levelling the ground to the south and dumping a bank of silt (405) on the northern side. The road was constructed of limestone rubble, up to 0.4 m thick, without any evidence of a separate surfacing. It is possible that quarry 415 to the north was dug to supply the stone.

In Trench 1/5/3 the equivalent construction 302/524 followed a phase of road which was constructed of pitched stone (309). This was offset north of the earlier main roads. It was not evident in either Trench 4 or Evaluation Trenches 513 and 514, probably because of the later quarrying. The technique of construction is unusual in the post-medieval period but there can be little doubt that it was of that date. A horseshoe of post-medieval type came from the stones themselves while a post-medieval sherd and a clay pipe stem came from the overlying silt 310.

The detail of the subsequent road 302/524 was better preserved in this trench. It can be seen to have been flanked by substantial deposits of imported silt 313/303/542/527 cut by a shallow ditch, 528, on the southern side. The road make-up consisted of limestone rubble in a matrix of redeposited natural silt, and may have had an integral surface of more tightly-packed stones (301/523). Despite the relatively massive construction of road 621/302/524, the road was still quite narrow (4-5 m).

In the next phase the road corridor was widened to the south with a considerable dump of silt, 602 and 529. This was retained by drystone walls 605 and 566 (later repaired with concrete blocks 536). It is likely that this coincided with the major period of quarrying to the south and it appears that the quarry to the north was filled in. To judge from section 6, the new road (627) did not fill this corridor. This was left to the later roads of the 19th and 20th centuries whose basal layers (610/545/509) became surfaced with tarmac to a width of 8 m or more.

The earliest deposit in Trench 2/6/4 was the fragmentary remains of road surface 410/663 which had been laid directly on limestone bedrock. To the south the surface was unrecognisable although the natural limestone which had been worn and eroded (629) appears to have been used as the road. The truncation of 410 to the north left an intact surface only about 3 m wide. This was probably the same as the earliest road surfaces in Evaluation Trenches 513 and 514 which were also laid directly on bedrock. In Trench 1/5/3 there seems to have been no corresponding surface, the earliest deposit being a stony silt, 574, which probably represented the eroded remains of one. This was overlain by an accumulation of less stony silt 579/325 and 573. A horseshoe from 573 suggests that this material was medieval or later in date. It is significant that the earliest deposits in both transects lay in slight hollows suggesting that the earliest road surfaces had been largely worn away. Layer 325 sealed a shallow quarry, 319, which was largely filled with a pale yellow silt (323) yielding 39 sherds of 2nd to 4th-century pottery and some Roman tile. A fragment of late medieval or post-medieval horseshoe (Type 4) and a horseshoe nail also came from this feature, but these are judged to be insufficient as dating evidence and these items were probably intrusive. A further seven sherds of later Roman pottery came from fill 318. It is probable that this quarry was Roman and may have marked the northern edge of the Fosse Way. In that case the Roman road would have been 5–6 m wide.

### Discussion

The Burford Road excavations failed to find any incontrovertible evidence for a Roman road under the modern one, although the earliest surface in Trench 2/6/4 (layer 410/663) is considered likely to have been one. This appears to have been completely worn away further south and also in Trench 3/5/1. The coins of Charles II from the overlying silt, 620, suggest that the Roman road was in continuous use, without repair, into the turnpike era, with the resulting formation of a slight hollow way in the limestone bedrock.

The Roman road does not, in any case, appear to

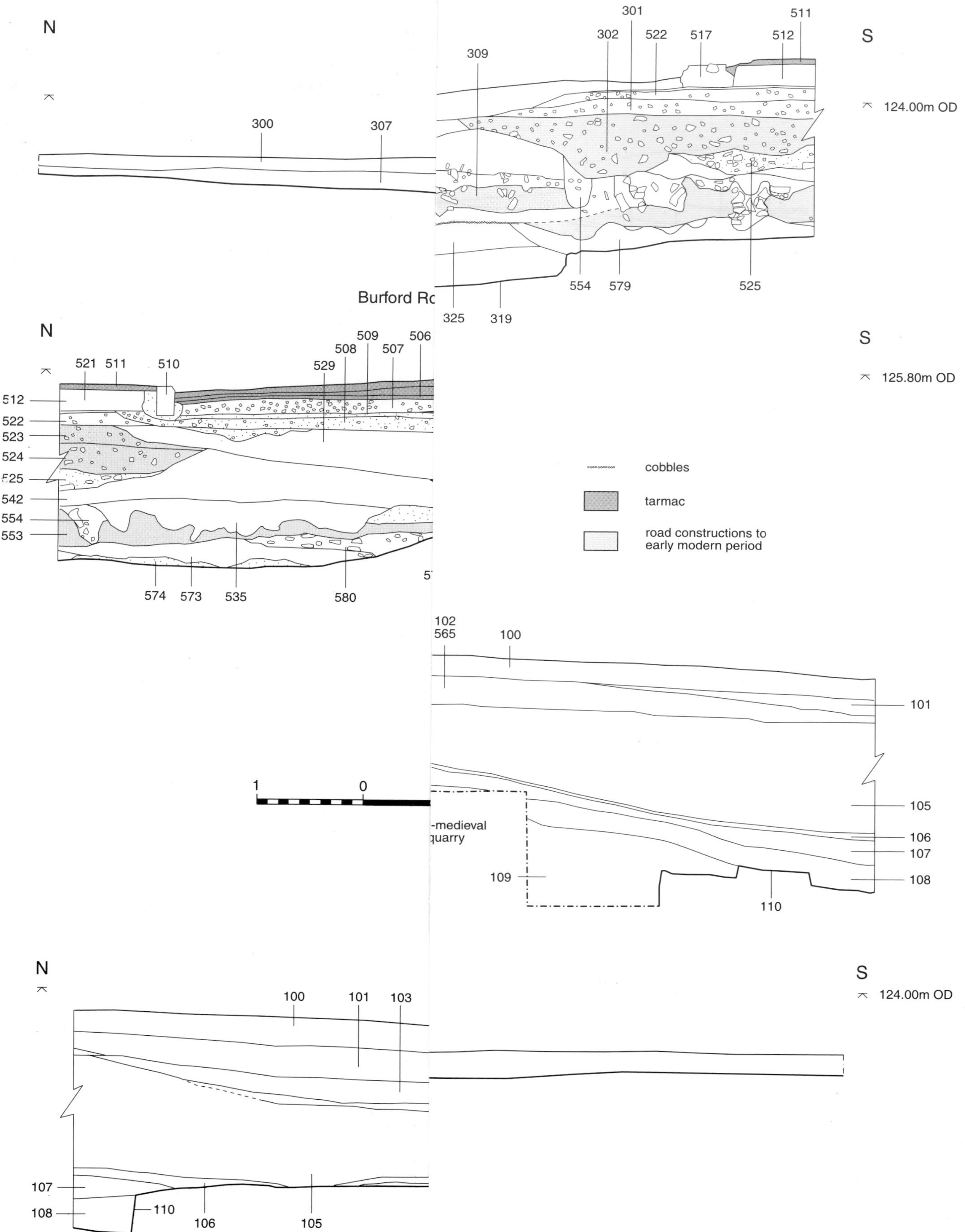


*Figure 5.9 Burford Road, section 3/5/1.*

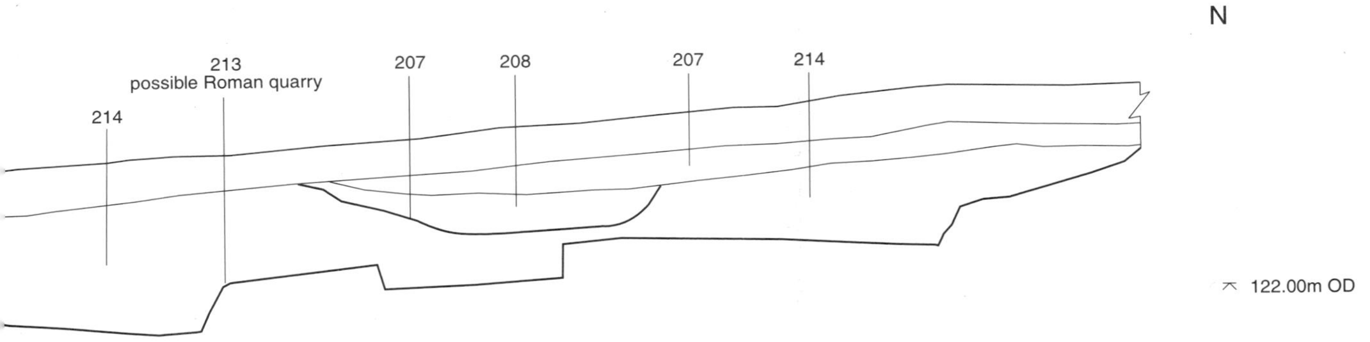

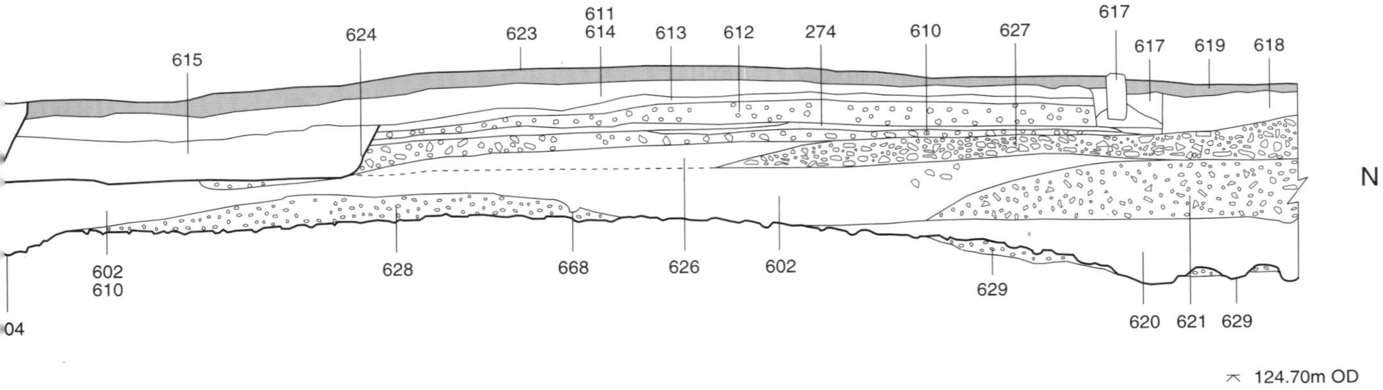

N
213
possible Roman quarry
207
208
207
214
214
122.00m OD

611
614
617
624
623
613
612
274
610
627
617
619
618
615
N
602
610
628
668
626
602
629
04
620
621
629
124.70m OD

tarmac

1
0
3 m

scale 1:50

N
400
414
415
417
415
Post-medieval quarry
124.70m OD

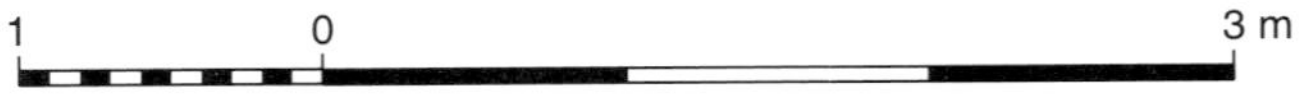

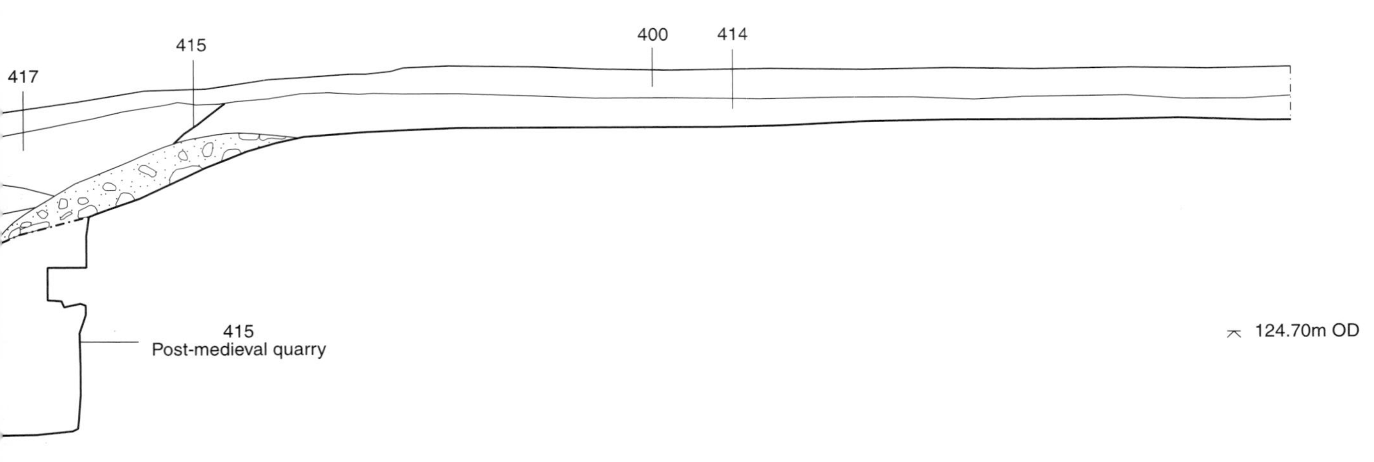

*Plate 5.7 Heavily rutted road surface (553) under the modern Burford Road (Trench 5 looking south-east).*

have been a substantial construction and was without evidence of an *agger* (although this may have been eroded away completely). It was probably considered that the bedrock provided sufficient foundation for the road surface. In common with the situation found in the Ermin Street sections, it does not seem to have been generally thought necessary to dig roadside ditches. Quarry 319, which may have been of linear form, presumably provided the metalling.

The dating evidence, such as it is, indicates that the subsequent road surfaces were probably post-medieval. This evidence should not necessarily be taken at face value, since the very nature of road use and repair before the modern era would suggest that finds may have come from deep ruts and pot-holes which became filled in with material of similar character to the original road. However, road surface 553 appears to be securely later than quarry 319 and must have been late Roman at the earliest even if the medieval *terminus post quem* provided by the horseshoe from 573 is ignored. The finds from the overlying greyish silt and the pitched stone surface 309 provide what, even in these circumstances, must be considered overwhelming evidence of a post-medieval date for these layers. A post-medieval horseshoe embedded in road surface 661 corroborates the numismatic evidence from Trench 6, and it would be difficult to advance any argument to support a Roman date for these layers.

These observations are at variance with the conclusions arrived at for Evaluation Trench 513 which indicated the survival of a number of intact Roman road surfaces (CAT 1991a, 59–62). The evidence for these, as presented, is sufficiently unique to make it incompatible with that from the current excavations. In particular, the sequence of 'mortared drains' were not found in either transect. From the section of Evaluation Trench 513 they appear not to be significantly earlier than the adjacent post-medieval quarry and their interpretation as Roman drains must be doubted. From the experience of the road sections in the current project they appear more likely to have been deep wheel ruts of post-medieval date, the impression of stone lining being given by stones being pitched and compacted against the sides of the ruts. A photograph of the surface of the Fosse Way uncovered to the west of Cirencester provides an indication of this (McWhirr 1982, plate 4). It is considered probable that only the lowest remnant of road surface in this evaluation trench is likely to be Roman as there is certainly no evidence for the survival of a substantial sequence of Roman road deposits in this area.

The context for these earliest post-medieval road surfaces was probably the turnpiking of the 18th century. The date of the turnpike construction along the Burford Road probably came after the Act of 1753 (Gerrard and Viner 1994, 135). The Fosse Way from Cirencester to Stow-on-the-Wold was turnpiked in 1755 and provides an alternative, albeit very similar date of construction. The pitched stone surface in Trench 3/5/1 is of uncertain context and may be relatively localised. The fact that these roads were not particularly well-made and became heavily rutted cannot be taken as evidence that they were of pre-turnpike date. Turnpiking was no more than a method of raising money for road repairs or construction and had no necessary implications for the method of construction itself. The quality of road construction continued to be highly variable at best, and even roads that were praised in the earlier part of the century had often deteriorated through use to a considerable degree a few decades later. The major change in road construction leading to lasting improvement came through engineering solutions in the later part of the 18th and the early 19th centuries. Road 302/524/621 is a clear example of a 'macadamised' road, the principles of which have been outlined above (see Ermin Street Sections). It may, in fact have been built by John McAdam himself, who is known to have constructed, or reconstructed, the Trunk road from Dorchester-on-Thames to Cirencester (via Faringdon and Lechlade) in the 1820s (Jackman 1962, 293) – the Cirencester section of which had been administered by the first Turnpike Trust in the area after the Act of 1723.

## THE LYNCHES TRACKWAY *(Figs. 5.11, Plates 5.8–9)*

### Introduction

The Lynches Trackway (Glos. SMR 2085) is a routeway of uncertain origin which runs from Cirencester up the Churn Valley (Fig. 8.23). It is on the line of the pre-turnpike road which runs on the opposite side of the valley to the present road (A435).

In the Stage 2 evaluation the Lynches Trackway was examined with a single trench (Tr 1991/506) which tentatively identified two phases of trackway construction thought to date to the medieval and post-medieval periods. Further examination of the trackway was required as part of the mitigation strategy, and accordingly a 4 x 15 m trench (Trench 1) was positioned immediately adjacent to the location of the evaluation trench. The site was stripped of topsoil and a 1 m wide central area was excavated by hand down to the natural limestone substrate.

### The Roman trackway

#### *Description*

The excavation revealed that the earliest trackway had been cut into the valley slope forming a *c.* 2.2 m wide hollow up to 1 m deep in the hillside with a *c.* 1.4 m wide, 0.4 m high, bank on the downslope side (Fig. 5.11). This natural bank appeared to have been enhanced by the addition of stony material (14) excavated from the hollow. Though no trace of wheel ruts were discovered on the cut natural surface, the limestone did show traces of wear.

Overlying this earliest surface was a layer of dark grey-brown silt (23) which contained over 80 sherds of 2nd-century Roman pottery. Re-examination of the sherds thought to be of medieval date from the equivalent layer in the evaluation trench indicated that they were in fact Roman. The associated tile and nails were also probably Roman. Otherwise, the sequence of deposits in both trenches was quite similar.

Above deposit 23 was a compact layer of stony material (22) which may have represented a re-surfacing of the trackway. The 28 sherds of pottery recovered from this deposit were all mid to late Roman in date, as were the majority of the 29 sherds from the succeeding stony deposit 21, which appears to have resulted from slumping of the upcast material 14. Sherds from the same vessel came from 21, 22 and 23. The non-Roman pottery consisted of a few residual Iron Age sherds.

These deposits were all subsequently buried beneath a *c.* 0.4 m thick band of silty clay colluvial soil (15), which was in turn overlain by another colluvial deposit (8) which was lighter in colour and less compact. Both deposits contained only small numbers of Iron Age and Roman sherds and it remains unclear when the colluvial accumulation started. However, it seems likely to have been caused by post-Roman ploughing. Downslope of the trackway was a further series of colluvial deposits which underlay the second phase of trackway construction. These were presumably of similar derivation to 8 and 15, but no finds were recovered and their date could not be established. A thin, dark sediment (3) lying on the slope above the trackway yielded a relatively high concentration of Iron Age pottery (11 sherds), including a notched rim of probable early Iron Age date. A small number of Roman sherds were also present.

The date for the demise of this earliest phase of trackway is uncertain but it seems unlikely to have lasted beyond the Roman period. However, the general route of The Lynches Trackway clearly survived as a terrace in the hillside and resurfacing in a slightly different location was undertaken in medieval or post-medieval times (below).

#### *Discussion*

The amount of Roman pottery recovered (together with 57 fragments – 339 g of animal bone) leave no doubt that the associated deposits are Roman rather than medieval. The surfaces of the road were also distinctively well-made to the degree that their Roman appearance was remarked upon in the evaluation report despite apparently contradictory dating evidence.

The fact that the road was cut into solid bedrock and carefully constructed implies that it was of some importance. However, the upcast material, 14, was only 0.1 m thick and not sufficient to have been derived from digging out all the hollow, so probably this was a pre-existing hollow way. However, in the evaluation trench the upcast material was 0.4 m thick, and taking into account subsequent erosion this may account for the excavated hollow. The upcast material did not seal a buried soil and this may mean that a corridor of land was stripped in preparation for road building.

The presence of substantial quantities of Roman pottery, much of which was not heavily abraded, indicates a 2nd-century site in the immediate vicinity. An early Iron Age site also appears to have been adjacent, presumably above the valley. However, no trace of settlement was found during the watching brief in this area.

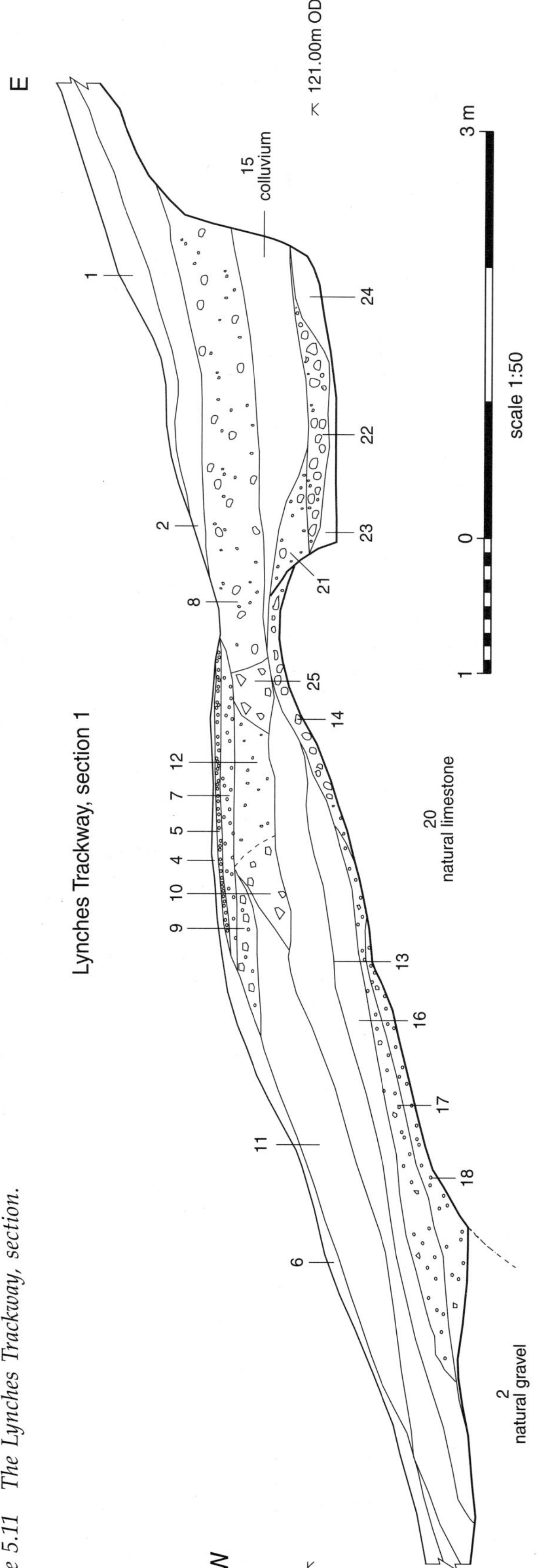


*Figure 5.11 The Lynches Trackway, section.*

### The post-medieval trackway

A second phase of trackway construction, post-dating the Roman route, was recognised at The Lynches Trackway. This later phase lay above and a few metres to the west of the original Roman construction on the edge of the present terrace (Fig. 5.11).

Two stony banks (10 and 25) were built on top of colluvial deposit 13. The stratigraphic link between the eastern bank 25 and colluvial deposit 8 was not firmly established, though both were stratified above the earlier bank material 14. Whether bank 25 was cut into deposit 8, or deposit 8 was built up against 25, remains unclear. The area between these two containing banks was filled with a silt deposit (12), presumably as a make-up layer for a relatively narrow surface which no longer survives.

Colluvial deposit 11 and stony deposit 9 were both built up at the edge of the terrace against the western bank 10. It is unclear whether 9 represents a deliberate consolidation of the terrace edge or the eroded material from the road. At a later date a *c.* 0.1 m thick stony band of material (7) was laid down over revetments 10 and 25, and deposits 9 and 12.

Deposit 7 most probably represents a make-up or bedding layer for the overlying cobbled surface (5), which was utilised until recently as a bridleway. Surface 5 showed traces of rutting and evidence of repair. Above 5 was a thin band of trampled silty clay (4), which was partially overlain by topsoil.

The only securely datable finds from this later phase of trackway construction were four sherds of residual prehistoric pottery from the silty deposit (12) between revetments 10 and 25, and four sherds of post-medieval pottery from the cobbled surface 5. The date of the initial reconstruction of the trackway with its associated banks is therefore unclear and could have been in the medieval period or slightly later.

## THE ROAD EXCAVATIONS: DISCUSSION AND CONCLUSIONS

### Ermin Street

The project afforded an opportunity of investigating Ermin Street more extensively than had hitherto been possible. The excavations through and adjacent to the road represent a considerable effort directed towards understanding the Roman military road and its subsequent development, and despite the inconclusive nature of some of the results, due mainly to a lack of dating evidence, the information is presented and discussed on its merits.

The road is conventionally thought to have been constructed in the late 40s AD, shortly after the Roman settlement of the region. While Darvill and Holbrook (1994, 52) draw attention to the normally scant evidence for the dating of the Roman road network, an early date for Ermin Street is implied in their discussion of the regional road alignments, since the Leaholme Fort at Cirencester (founded AD 45–50) appears to have been sited upon the line of Ermin

*Plate 5.8 Trench excavated through The Lynches Trackway on the side of the Churn Valley. looking north-east.*

Street, and for this reason the road may have been the primary feature. Unsurprisingly, the excavations of Ermin Street contributed nothing to the refinement of the dating. The later 1st-century sherds from layer 636 at Cowley Underbridge (Ermin Street Trench 6 – Fig. 5.3), may, on the face of it, suggest a later date for the initial road construction, but it is actually unclear whether the road surface which they underlay (669) was the first or second construction here, and it is perhaps more likely to have been the second.

Several authorities have commented upon the expertise of Roman surveyors in establishing the lines of roads which frequently represented an almost perfect compromise between minimising the distance and maximising the ease of road construction and travel between two, often extremely widely spaced, points (eg. Margary 1973, 17–18; Taylor 1979, 35–57). The knowledge of the regional topography and the exact relationship between places to be connected is made more remarkable by the fact that roads were frequently planned, surveyed and laid out in the middle of a military campaign (Taylor 1979, 54). The line of Ermin Street between Cirencester and Gloucester is one example which, while not a great distance in terms of the national road network, is notably direct in its negotiation of the terrain. Margary has described the 16 miles (25 km) stretch of this road. It leaves Cirencester to the north-west and runs in a virtually direct line to the highest part of the route (279 m) at Gloucester Beeches, with an almost imperceptible change of direction near Daglingworth. This is actually at the point where the road crosses the alignment of a cross-ridge boundary, or dyke, at Milestone Plantation (Glos. SMR 2045). The date and significance of this feature are unclear, as is its possible influence on the alignment of the road. An evaluation, as part of the Stage 2 mitigation, of a cropmark which continued the alignment of the earthwork on the western side of the road revealed nothing of archaeological significance (GCC 1990, 51). At face value this may suggest that the earthwork ran up to the road and therefore post-dated it. From Gloucester Beeches a slight adjustment of course allowed Ermin Street to avoid the steep head valleys of the river Frome to the west and follow another straight line as far as Nettleton. From here the most radical change in direction took the road to the Cotswold scarp at Birdlip, and thence, with another minor change in course, to the Kingsholme fort near Gloucester. The fact that the area around Dartley Bottom and the Duntisbourne sites was wooded in the immediate pre-conquest period, and may have been so at the time the road was surveyed, had no effect on the alignment of the road. Alternatively, the directness of the road may argue that the land had already been cleared by the time of the conquest.

South-east of Cirencester, Ermin Street changes direction just outside Leaholme fort at a point near the later Silchester Gate, alters course again west of Driffield Crossroads and then continues in a fairly straight course past Cricklade. The current project did

*Plate 5.9 The Lynches Trackway showing Roman surface (22) and stony bank to left. The central slot has been excavated to bedrock.*

not offer much opportunity to examine this section of road, although the trenches along the Cirencester Road between Driffield Junction and Fosse Farm provided some confirmation of the course of Ermin Street largely through negative evidence. A slight change in alignment near Fosse Farm was suggested by the presence of the road in Trench 3. This may have been due to the need to ford a small stream here at a suitable point. It is worth noting that the change in direction just outside Cirencester, which has been discussed recently by Darvill and Holbrook (1994, 52), may be explained by the need to cross the Churn here at a suitable fording point. The evidence indicates that Ermin Street crossed the Churn again somewhere near Weavers Bridge (Wainwright 1959; CAT 1991c), where again the road alignment changes slightly. The excavations there did not extend close enough to the present river to uncover the road, although it was identified at the evaluation stage in the expected position (CAT 1994). The complex and extensive post-Roman changes in the river course identified from the excavation area would suggest that the original river and crossing may be difficult to pinpoint even assuming the evidence survives.

There seems little doubt that a great deal of effort was expended in the construction and maintenance of Ermin Street in the 1st and 2nd centuries. The evidence for this really only comes from the sections north of Cirencester where, despite difficulties of interpretation, a number of superimposed road constructions were identified as almost certainly Roman. At Cowley Underbridge (Trench 6) it seems probable that the original military road was repaired on seven occasions, perhaps all before the 3rd century, which raised the road level by almost 1 m. At Dartley Bottom (Trench 8) there appear to have been four repairs and a similar number may be identified at Burcombe Lane (Trench 9) and the Dowers Lane Watching Brief section. If these interpretations are correct, it also appears that solid pitched stone *aggeres* were constructed relatively late in the sequence, although they were also evident in the original constructions at Cowley Underbridge and The Highwayman (Trench 5). It cannot be assumed that road repairs were continuous along this stretch of road and they may reflect the particular problems posed by crossing the valleys where the trenches were located. The absence of roadside ditches may also reflect these particular topographic positions although they may have been located further away. Ditches were certainly present where the road verge was exposed on the flatter ground north of Birdlip Quarry, but south of Birdlip Quarry and at Field's Farm it appears that the 'roadside' ditches may have been specifically related to the nearby settlements rather than the road itself.

The evidence for an early 4th-century road surface at the late Roman settlement at Birdlip Quarry is unequivocal. The surface here was poorly constructed, consisting merely of a single spread of limestone cobbles on unprepared ground which widened the road on the southern side of the site by up to 10 m. It remains unclear whether this was purely local or part of a more systematic attempt at improvement. On the whole the cobbling appears too extensive to be related to access to the settlement, and it is clearly possible that the remodelling was widespread. There was no firm evidence of this from any of the major sections although there were possibilities, and in any case, their topographic positions may have made them untypical of the road as a whole. There was, however, some suggestion of a late road extension at Field's Farm. Road construction at this date should not necessarily be unexpected since economic activity in the countryside was widespread. At the Alchester Road suburb, Towcester, a modification of the main road and the construction of a new branch road were dated to the late 3rd to 4th centuries (Phase 3. Brown and Woodfield 1983, 53). However, the logic behind the road widening at Birdlip Quarry is difficult to understand since the surface lacked a solid foundation. The construction would appear to owe little to Roman military engineering practice and it is unclear who would have undertaken road main-tenance at this time.

The evidence for road construction south-east of Cirencester is much more limited. The single exposure of the road in Trench 3 near Fosse Farm, and the record in Evaluation Trench 1 at Weavers Bridge yielded evidence not dissimilar to that already published from the Cricklade area (Wainwright 1959), indicating a comparatively slight *agger* with a single, eroded metalled surface. It is impossible to say whether this apparent contrast to the road constructions found north-west of Cirencester owes anything to policy in the Roman period, or whether it can be accounted for by local topographic circumstances and later use. It can be noted that Ermin Street, at all these locations south of Cirencester, was constructed on alluvial clay or silt, and road construction may have been at least as demanding in the Lower Churn/Upper Thames region as it was in the Cotswolds, despite the flatter ground. It cannot therefore be assumed that the road required less attention.

### The Fosse Way and other roads east of Cirencester

The puzzling alignments of the Fosse Way, Akeman Street and White Way east of Cirencester have attracted some attention and the problems have been usefully summarised by Darvill and Holbrook (1994, 51–53). The road sections excavated across Burford Road failed to conclusively identify, let alone date, the Roman road here (whether it be called Fosse Way or Akeman Street), but this was probably due to later erosion along the line of the road. There is no particular reason to doubt that it existed here, and the Roman quarries were probably associated with it. Margary (1973, 148–9) argued that the Fosse Way did not originally extend to Cirencester but was aligned south at Raggedhedge Covert and continued (along the line of Cherry Tree Lane/Kingshill Lane) so as to meet Ermin Street at Preston Bridge three quarters of a mile south of the Silchester Gate. A spur road (the later Burford Road) was than constructed extending west from Hare Bushes Lodge to the *Verulamium* Gate. Following this argument, the fact that Akeman Street was aligned upon Hare Bushes Lodge, rather than the *Verulamium* Gate is evidence that the spur road from the Fosse Way already existed. This would make Akeman Street a relatively late addition to the road system here, although it is not clear how late this need be. This hypothesis does not comfortably accord with the evidence from Oxfordshire that the road was of early military strategic origin and, from excavated evidence, at least pre-Flavian (Booth 1997, 150), and quite probably Claudian (Hands 1993, 11–12).

Another possibility, expressed by Kenyon and Wacher (cited in Darvill and Holbrook 1994, 53), is that the course of the Fosse Way south at Raggedhedge Covert was a diversion from an original alignment which took it straight to the eastern gate of the Leaholme fort where the *Verulamium* Gate was subsequently sited. It has been noted that the Tar Barrows may be early Roman monuments which, if this projected alignment is accepted, would have occupied a typical roadside position. An early Roman funerary monument adjacent to Ermin Street at Field's Farm was excavated as part of the current project. There may be another example near Smallbeech Copse visible on an aerial photograph (Glos. SMR 4783) located 20–30 m from the Roman road. The funerary enclosure outside the Bath Gate has been discussed (Chapter 4, Field's Farm). It is possible that such monuments were not uncommon in the Cirencester region. An isolated Roman cremation was found in the watching brief north-west of Whitelands Wood (NGR SP03220374). It was much disturbed but may have originally been in a wooden box. This may conceivably have been near a roadside. Although it was about 300 m away from the projected alignment of the Fosse Way just discussed, it was very close to a possible alignment of the Fosse Way from Raggedhedge Covert to the north gate of the town, which Margary has suggested is the main alignment of the road (Margary 1973, 148). This alignment would have some merit in accounting for the puzzling course of the Fosse Way on the south-western side of the town which was well to the north of the Bath Gate. Margary was inclined to dismiss the suggestion that the road was ever built on this alignment because of a complete lack of field evidence. The results of the present project have done nothing to contradict this although the cremation at Whitelands Wood remains intriguing.

The suggested alignments of the Fosse Way to the north or east gates of the Roman town do not appear to have been targeted in the Stage 2 evaluation while the watching brief during groundworks yielded only the Roman cremation discussed. The context of this burial therefore remains unclear. There was absolutely no suggestion of a contemporary settlement in the road corridor here and, unless there was one somewhere on either side, a roadside location for the burial must still be considered possible despite the absence of evidence for a road.

The question of the origin and possible original alignment of the White Way has received some attention although there is little direct archaeological evidence to contribute to the discussion (Margary 1973, 145–6; Darvill and Holbrook 1994, 53; CAT 1991a, 133). The anticipated alignment of the road south of Exhibition Barn was investigated with the excavation of a 250 m-long trench (Chapter 4, Fig. 4.33). This revealed a Roman ditch on approximately the alignment of the road, and another one was found in the watching brief 75 m to the east. There was no trace of a road and the ditches are more likely to be field boundaries than roadside ditches. Unless the original White Way lay rather further to the east of the excavations and was not evident under the conditions of the watching brief, it appears that there was no identifiable Roman road crossing the corridor of the present project.

### Minor roads and trackways

The east-west ditches at Norcote Farm are considered likely to have been Roman and may have defined a trackway linking the known Roman settlement at Witpit Copse (Glos. SMR 3176) with the Roman road at Kingshill Lane (Fig. 3.31). The nature and status of this settlement is unknown, although most of the dating evidence recovered so far appears to be of the 3rd and 4th centuries (information from SMR).

The excavation of The Lynches Trackway yielded a large amount of pottery from the earliest deposits above the natural limestone furnishing incontrovertible evidence that the trackway was in use in the Roman period. Whether it was a Roman creation, or inherited from the Iron Age, is not certain. The Iron Age pottery from the excavations was not found in primary contexts. The course of the track, which winds along the slope of the Churn valley, is not typically Roman, since it would have been easier to construct a new road on level ground. It therefore seems more likely to have been an older route which had become a hollow way and had been re-surfaced in the Roman period. It is possible that it was connected with the centre at Bagendon, whose precise nature is debatable but whose importance appears to span both periods. A Roman road surface is known to run up the hill towards the present village from the direction of the Welsh Way river crossing (Glos. SMR 9800 and 9317). Alternatively, The Lynches Trackway may have served the nearer Romano-British settlement on Baunton Downs (SP 025058) although this would not have been the obvious route to take. The status of this site is unclear although the cropmarks and surface scatters indicate that it was extensive and the finds include at least two uninscribed altars (RCHME 1976, 13). The quantity of pottery from The Lynches Trackway actually suggests a much nearer settlement although no further finds came from the watching brief between the trackway and White Way to the east, and the derivation of the pottery is unclear.

Another trackway, this time heading more directly towards Bagendon, was revealed at Trinity Farm. It followed the line of the modern public footpath which runs from the Cheltenham road (near the Cirencester Golf Club House) in a straight line as far as Welsh Way, where it changes direction towards the present village. This dog-leg may be accounted for by the need to avoid the earthwork along Welsh Way. While the trackway was clearly in use in the post-medieval period, the fact that it ignores all the modern field boundaries indicates that it pre-dates enclosure and had come into disuse before then. It may have been the one of the principal routes to Bagendon before the Cheltenham road was turnpiked in 1827, although, from Cirencester, the route up Ermin Street would surely have been easier. The origin of this trackway is unknown and it is a subject which is worth further investigation. The directness of its trajectory for over 1 km suggests that it may have been laid out in the Roman period, although this suggestion is extremely speculative on current evidence.

The excavated trackways joining Ermin Street near Field's Farm have been discussed. That to the north of the Roman funerary monument ran to an enclosure just south of Field's Farm itself (Fig. 4.2). The trackway was a relatively early feature since it predated the 'roadside' ditch, although it was blocked by a later ditch segment. It is possible that it was directly contemporary with the adjacent square barrow, which was also constructed before the 'roadside' ditch was dug and had probably silted up before the 3rd century. Thus both features appear to have been relatively short-lived. This may have implications for the date of the associated? settlement although corroboration is required. The trackway on the opposite side of the road (Duntisbourne Leer, Area 2) appears, in contrast, to have been long-lived. Although only a single recut was identified in each ditch, the presence of both 1st-century and early Saxon pottery suggests that the trackway was maintained over a long period. Unlike the trackway on the opposite side of the road it also appears to have had a cobbled surface. It led to a Romano-British settlement or building 400 m away (Glos. SMR 3644) about which little is know despite some archaeological attention. The trackway further north (Duntisbourne Leer, Area 1; Glos. SMR 11203) was poorly preserved and yielded little information. The settlement it served has not been identified. The possible trackway ditch (ditch 90) excavated at Sly's Wall South (Glos. SMR 9432) presents a number of problems of interpretation and was not confirmed as Roman.

Other ditched trackways in the vicinity of Ermin Street are known from aerial photographs. Most of these are likely to be Roman, although requiring confirmation. Just east of Stockwell, Cowley, a ditched trackway running north-west (NMR SO 94914/2) may have served the known Romano-British settlement on Shab Hill (Glos. SMR 3810 and 3811). South of Cowley Wood a possible ditched trackway runs past the eastern entrance of an undated sub-rectangular enclosure (Glos. SMR 4697; NMR SO 9513/8 and 16). Faint traces of a ditched trackway run from Ermin Street near Highgate House, and this may be the same feature (NMR SO 9512/2, 3 & 6). In the same area part of a large rectangular enclosure lies behind Highgate House and appears to be served by a hollow way from

Ermin Street. These are undated. In the parish of Duntisbourne Rouse there is a cropmark of a ditched trackway heading from Ermin Street towards Voxhills Copse (NMR SO 9807/5). There is also a small enclosure at Voxhills Farm (NMR SO 9908/1), although this may not be related.

There is good evidence for a Roman trackway at South View Farm, north of Stratton, where a ditched trackway aligned at right angles to Ermin Street runs to a Roman settlement (Glos. SMR 9692). This is represented by a group of enclosures and other features with surface finds indicating a date from the 1st to the 4th centuries. The trackway reaches a possible boundary ditch and then turns and heads towards Baunton (NMR SP 0104).

South of Cirencester, Roman trackway ditches (Wilts. SMR SU09NE615) associated with the multi-phase Scheduled Ancient Monument were examined at Court Farm, Latton. A narrow trackway 4.5–5.5 m wide (of two phases) may have been replaced by a wider one, 15.5 m wide. It was not possible to date the trackways closely. The area was considerably disturbed by Roman quarrying which was seen to largely respect the first phase of trackway. If the quarrying was related to the original construction of Ermin Street, a very early date for the primary trackway might be implied. However, it is impossible to be sure of the date of the quarrying which, while probably associated with the road, may have been mostly or entirely related to its maintenance rather than original construction. The pottery from the excavations was largely residual. The Roman pottery was confined to the 1st and early 2nd centuries AD and was present in sufficient quantities to suggest an early Roman site in the vicinity. It was unclear whether this was something which the quarrying had obliterated, or whether it lay close by outside the excavated area. There was certainly no possibility that structures had survived within the zone of quarrying. If the quarrying had destroyed an earlier Roman building or settlement of some kind, this in itself would indicate that most of the quarrying, at least, was unconnected with the construction of the original military road, although it remains possible that some of it was.

There is abundant evidence for Roman settlements on both sides of Ermin Street between Cirencester and Cricklade, although little of this was explored in the present project. These were undoubtedly connected by an extensive network of roads and tracks of which cropmark evidence provides some indication. A full treatment of this evidence is beyond the scope of this report, although the probable Roman element of the cropmarks between the settlements at Court Farm and Weavers Bridge, Latton are shown in Fig. 4.32.